MAGILL'S
SURVEY
OF
CINEMA

MAGILL'S SURVEY OF CINEMA

Silent Films

VOLUME 2
FLE-POT

Edited by

FRANK N. MAGILL

Associate Editors

PATRICIA KING HANSON

STEPHEN L. HANSON

SALEM PRESS
Englewood Cliffs, N.J.

LIBRARY OF CONGRESS CATALOG CARD NUMBER: 82-60577

Complete Set: ISBN 0-89356-239-4
Volume 2:   ISBN 0-89356-241-6

PRINTED IN THE UNITED STATES OF AMERICA

LIST OF TITLES IN VOLUME TWO

MAGILL'S
SURVEY
OF
CINEMA

FLESH AND THE DEVIL

Released: 1927
Production: Metro-Goldwyn-Mayer
Direction: Clarence Brown
Screenplay: Benjamin Glazer; based on the novel *The Undying Past* by Hermann Sudermann
Titles: Marian Ainslee
Cinematography: William Daniels
Editing: Lloyd Nosler
Art direction: Cedric Gibbons and Frederic Hope
Costume design: André-ani
Length: 9 reels/8,759 feet

Principal characters:
Leo von Sellenthin .... John Gilbert
Felicitas von Kletzingk .... Greta Garbo
Ulrich von Kletzingk .... Lars Hanson
Hertha Prochvitz .... Barbara Kent
Pastor Brenckenburg .... George Fawcett
Leo's mother .... Eugenie Besserer
Count von Rhaden .... Marc MacDermott

If there had ever been any doubt in the minds of studio executives at M-G-M that Swedish actress Greta Garbo, whom Louis B. Mayer had imported, was a great star, that misgiving vanished after the release of *Flesh and the Devil*, her third film for them. She did not get star billing in the film, having been featured after John Gilbert and Lars Hanson, but she was indubitably the film's central attraction. She did not get star billing, in fact, until her fifth feature for M-G-M, *The Divine Woman* (1927), a picture now lamentably "lost."

Flesh and the Devil was an immediate box-office success, just as were Garbo's first two films in the United States, which had been released in 1926 and which were based upon Vicente Blasco Ibáñez's stories *Torrent* and *The Temptress.*

Flesh and the Devil has the gloss of a fine German classic. It is the story of two upper-class boys, born Leo von Sellenthin and Ulrich von Kletzingk. One day when they are in the company of a little girl with whom they have both grown up, Hertha Prochvitz, they row over to the Island of Friendship, where the boys go through a serious ritual, swearing a blood bond of eternal friendship. The boys continue to be the closest of friends throughout military school, and as the years pass they grow to be everyone's idols. The adult Leo is played by John Gilbert, and Ulrich is played by Lars Hanson.

After graduation, with the young men and their families meeting at the railway station, Leo gets his first glimpse of the woman known as "Felicitas" (Greta Garbo). She smiles when he returns a glove she has dropped, but the carriage drives on, and he believes her to be one of those beautiful out-of-towners invited to the military ball that evening. Leo sees Felicitas again at the ball, and ignores Hertha (Barbara Kent) to go over to Felicitas and ask her for a dance. She dances with him, the camera following them seductively as they turn on the floor. He asks her to go outside with him for a breath of air, and after she assents, the pair is seen in matchlight and the glowing tips of their cigarettes, the first of several entrancing love scenes.

The next time they are seen, they are in her boudoir, and it is obvious that their relationship has become a more intimate one. Her husband, Count von Rhaden (Marc MacDermott), enters unexpectedly, and it is the first time that the audience and Leo know that Felicitas is married. The two men quarrel, and Leo is challenged to a duel publicly because they have quarreled at cards, but actually because Felicitas' husband has caught her in a compromising situation with Leo. The count is killed in the duel, and because he was a man of public importance, Leo is advised to seek five years of military service abroad. At the railway station he begs his friend Ulrich to seek out Felicitas, now a widow of course, and console her in his own absence.

Three years later, Leo is pardoned by the emperor and cannot wait to get home to Felicitas and marry her. On his first visit to her, however, he realizes that Felicitas is now the wife of Ulrich, his friend. Felicitas will not make a decision between the two men; she would be happy if they could go on as a threesome; thus, between the two of them, she would enjoy Ulrich for his wealth and Leo for his love.

When she broaches such a scheme to Leo, he is horrified and is about to strike her when Ulrich enters the room. There are bitter words between the men, and they agree to meet the following morning on their beloved island, now shrouded in snow and ice, to fight a duel with pistols.

Hertha learns of the forthcoming duel and goes to Felicitas to persuade her to intervene. Felicitas suddenly realizes that she might lose both men, and grabbing up a fur coat, she makes her way across the frozen river to the island. As the men take up their positions with pistols and turn to aim and fire, the veil lifts in Ulrich's mind and, aghast, he lets the pistol fall into the snow. At the same time, Leo drops his weapon unfired, and the two men make their way toward each other through the snow, embracing in forgiveness and remembering the vow they had made of eternal friendship.

Felicitas hurries, but the ice breaks, and she falls into the cold water and drowns. After this, there is a brief epilogue, showing that Hertha, now very much a young lady, gets Leo as a lover and husband.

It is a curious triangle because one is captivated at once by the Garbo mystique, and although she is playing a selfish woman of the world, she becomes and remains sympathetic. Leo and Ulrich are ony pawns in her game, and she plays them off, one against the other. The weekly *Variety* noted that in Garbo, M-G-M had everything and that "properly handled and given the right material, will be as great a money asset as Theda Bara was to Fox in years past." Garbo never made a film in America for any other studio but M-G-M. From 1926 to 1941, with twenty-five vehicles, she stood at the top, above and beyond all the other M-G-M stars; and she was such in spite of the fact that barely a half-dozen or so of her features were lustrous and worthy of her presence.

Garbo and Gilbert became an immediate "team." After *Flesh and the Devil*, they made three other pictures together: *Love* (1927), a silent version of *Anna Karenina*; *A Woman of Affairs* (1928), a sterilized version of *The Green Hat*; and eventually *Queen Christina* (1933), because Garbo realized that a youthful Laurence Oliver was wrong as a partner for her image and told M-G-M brusquely, "Get Gilbert." They got him, and in spite of Mayer, who loathed him, he had a chance to prove that not only was there nothing wrong with his vocal delivery, but that he also could still carry his part with a great female star. On the screen they were always ideally matched.

They had been lovers in reality too, however briefly. Clarence Brown, the director of *Flesh and the Devil*, once revealed that while making the picture, "they were in that blissful state of love which is so like a rosy cloud that they imagined themselves hidden behind it, as well as lost in it." "Sometimes," he added, "I felt I was intruding on the most private of emotions."

She called him "Yacky," and he called her "Flicka," but when she consented to marry him at a double ceremony, in which the other couple was Eleanor Boardman and King Vidor, Gilbert was on hand, but Garbo had changed her mind, and never showed up. It provoked a brutal physical fight between Mayer and Gilbert, when Mayer muttered a vulgar derogation of Garbo, and Gilbert sprang to her defense at once. Mayer threatened publicly to ruin Gilbert professionally, which he did. It was like a scene in an Adrian-dressed melodrama which M-G-M made so successfully, as written by Adela Rogers St. Johns, a scene about Garbo but without her.

Garbo lives every time one of her films is flashed upon the screen, even though in real life she has been retired since her final film, *Two-Faced Woman*, released in 1941. She was an international star, and when the world was in chaos, she withdrew. One hears of her now walking alone along the streets of Manhattan, sometimes visiting briefly in Hollywood, sometimes in her native Sweden, or taking the sun in some Mediterranean port, but she is usually contentedly alone, despite the intense interest of millions of fans who are still intrigued by her mystique.

She was age thirty-six when she left the screen, and now she has survived more than another thirty-six years as that one woman who lighted up the screens of the world with a living magic that has never shone again.

DeWitt Bodeen

THE FOLLIES GIRL

Released: 1919
Production: Triangle Film Corporation
Direction: John Francis Dillon
Screenplay: Charles M. Peck; based on an original screen story by W. C. Wonderly
Cinematography: Steve Norton
Length: 5 reels

Principal characters:

Doll	Olive Thomas
Ned	Wallace MacDonald
Edward Woodruff	William V. Mong
Nina	Claire McDowell
Swann	J. P. Wild
Basil	Lee Phelps
Fredric	Raymond Griffith

The Follies Girl is an aptly named film for Olive Thomas, because she was one of the Florenz Ziegfeld's most popular glorified beauties to go into films. Thomas became a cinema favorite, as did several other Follies girls such as Marion Davies, Billie Dove, Mary Nolan, Mae Murray, Martha Mansfield, Dorothy Mackaill, and Marilyn Miller. Her shocking death in 1920 was the first really big scandal of the film industry, and because of her youth and bright future, it seemed more tragic than the Fatty Arbuckle, William Desmond Taylor, or Wallace Reid sensations that followed.

Thomas was born in Charleroi, Pennsylvania, on October 16, 1898. By the time she was sixteen, she was married and had joined the Ziegfeld Follies. She soon became Ziegfeld's mistress, but by the time that Ziegfeld's wife Billie Burke found out about them, their affair was over, and Thomas was engaged to marry Jack Pickford, Mary Pickford's brother.

Her film career began at Paramount with the lead in *A Girl Like That* (1916). When Thomas Ince saw that picture, he immediately put her under contract to his company, Triangle, and for a year, she turned out a feature every two months. All her films were popular, and they alone kept Triangle from going under. Starting with *An Even Break* (1917), she became known to cinema audiences as the unsophisticated beauty who is introduced to the ways of the world. The titles of her films spelled glamour to her fans: *Frankly Chaste* (1917), *Limousine Life* (1918), *Indiscreet Corinne* (1918), *An Heiress for a Day* (1918), *Prudence on Broadway* (1919), and, of course, *The Follies Girl* (1919).

Triangle went bankrupt at the beginning of 1919, and Lewis J. Selznick signed her to star for his company, Select. Again, she was the saving grace of a film company, and her pictures kept Select in the major league. Selznick kept her so busy that when she married Pickford she was not able to go immediately on a honeymoon. Then, when she was ready, Pickford was not, for he had to finish work on one of his films for Associated First National; so Thomas sailed alone for Europe and waited in Paris for her husband to arrive. Shopping kept her busy, but stories began to circulate about her visiting sleazy apache dives in the company of crooks and gigolos. When Pickford finally arrived, the young couple began frequenting the chic nightclubs and carrying on very gaily.

One morning they got in particularly late, closed the drapes, and began to prepare to retire. Thomas was in the bathroom, while Pickford waited for her in their bed. He later testified that he heard her painful screams and ran into the bathroom to find her lying on the floor writhing in agony. She had taken a large dose of bichloride of mercury, a poison as burning as Drāno. Her death four days later was put down as accidental. Pickford said she had mistakenly picked the wrong bottle from their medicine cabinet. Rumors of suicide were prevalent, but denied. Some sources indicate that Thomas was alone when she died, and Pickford was not even in Paris at the time. Suicide or not, the reason for the presence of the bichloride of mercury in their medicine cabinet was not investigated and remains a mystery, as do the other circumstances of her death. In 1920, the drug had several uses, one of them being a treatment for syphilis.

Ziegfeld always blamed Pickford for Thomas' death. When, later in the 1920's, Pickford began seeing Ziegfeld's top star, Marilyn Miller, the producer became very angry. He pleaded with Miller not to continue seeing Pickford, but she would not listen and eventually married him. Ziegfeld had more than one confrontation with Pickford in various nightclubs and had to be restrained by waiters from causing a scene. Pickford and Miller divorced not long after their marriage, and Pickford died in the early 1930's, at the age of thirty-seven, looking sadly ravished.

The Follies Girl opens in the palatial mansion of old Edward Woodruff (William V. Mong), who is lying in his bed, dying. Around his deathbed sit three distant relatives: Nina (Claire McDowell); her brother, Fredric (Raymond Griffith); and Basil (Lee Phelps), her fiancé, who are concerned about the delirious pleas of the old man to see his long lost granddaughter. The granddaughter has not been seen for more than a decade because Woodruff's daughter had left home after an argument, taking her own daughter with her. Woodruff particularly wants now to see his granddaughter before he dies, because he has recently disowned his other grandchild, Ned (Wallace MacDonald), his son's child, because the young man married a Follies girl.

Nina, Fredric, and Basil go downstairs to the drawing room to discuss the old man's ravings and their own predicament in front of the ornate marble fireplace. Woodruff has left almost all his money to the granddaughter, with

Nina as the executor; but if the granddaughter does not claim the money, it must all go to charity. Nina looks up at the full-length portrait of the estranged daughter and muses, "I wonder where your little girl is now?"

Her brother, Fredric, tries to cheer her up by suggesting that they all drive into town and dine at the restaurant on the top of the New Amsterdam Theater and take in the new Follies show. From their ringside table, Nina detachedly watches the lavish show, while lost in her own thoughts. Fredric, who has been having a delightful time, calls Nina from her trance by saying "Isn't that girl a beauty, Nina, and doesn't she look like the old man's daughter in the painting?" With an indulgent, faint smile at Fredric, Nina looks over at that particular Follies girl and suddenly sits up in her chair. A scheme has entered her mind, and she intently watches the girl for the rest of the performance. After the show, Nina asks the two men to wait for her, and she makes her way backstage, paving her way with tips.

Doll (Olive Thomas) the girl onstage, is now removing her costume, when Nina walks up behind her. Nina asks if she can talk to Doll in private, and Doll leads the way to a quiet corner. Nina asks the girl if she would like to make a lot of money and help make peaceful an old man's last days. Doll is interested but frightened until Nina mentions the old man's name, and then she quickly joins Nina's plan.

When Doll is taken into Woodruff's bedroom and presented to him as his granddaughter, his sudden joy almost brings on a fatal attack. The next day, however, when Doll visits him, he is much better and sitting up in bed. They spend much time talking and as Nina listens outside the door, she is happy that her deception is working.

The old man gets stronger and more cheerful each day in the anticipation of seeing Doll, however much to Nina's dismay. One day the disowned grandson Ned shows up, insisting that he see his grandfather. Nina tries to keep him away from his grandfather, but he forces his way in. The grandfather even seems happy to see Ned again, which makes Nina furious.

As the days pass, Nina notices that Ned and Doll seem to be falling in love; then one night she spies on them kissing in a cottage on the estate and hurries back to tell the old man. He follows Nina, ready to chastise the adulterous lovers, and breaks in on them. The young couple is sitting together watching a baby play on the floor.

The old man and Nina demand an explanation, and Doll tells them that she has been Ned's wife for two years and that the baby is their son. Furthermore, she tells the flabbergasted Nina that she really *is* the "long lost" granddaughter.

Larry Lee Holland

A FOOL THERE WAS

Released: 1915
Production: William Fox for Box Office Attractions
Direction: Frank Powell
Screenplay: Roy L. McCardell; based on the play of the same name by Porter Emerson Browne and the poem "The Vampire" by Rudyard Kipling
Cinematography: Lucien Andriot
Length: 6 reels

Principal characters:
The Vampire	Theda Bara
The Fool	Edward Jose
The Fool's wife	Mabel Fremyear
The wife's sister	May Allison
The child	Runa Hodges
The man	Victor Benoit

To the seemingly innocent America of the years immediately prior to World War I, Theda Bara epitomized sin. She was the screen's first and foremost vamp, a totally artificial creation even down to her name, an anagram of "arab death." Bara (1890-1955) was born Theodosia Goodman and worked on the stage before *A Fool There Was* made her a household name—and not a particularly polite one. As the teens progressed, Bara's style of acting, or vamping, went out of style; what was once considered sinful became ludicrous, and what once passed in certain circles for art became kitsch. By the 1920's Bara was reduced to playing parodies of herself on the screen, and she retired in the mid-1920's, happily married to her one-time director Charles Brabin.

The film that, literally, created the legend that was Bara was *A Fool There Was*, and it would be easy to dismiss it as the filmic equivalent of the formula romance novel that was so popular at the same time. *A Fool There Was*, despite its lurid plot line, is a surprisingly well-made film, and, unlike many of the features from the teens, is still remarkably entertaining today.

Frank Powell, who had learned his craft with D. W. Griffith, had been assigned by producer William Fox to direct *A Fool There Was*, to be released by Box Office Attractions, a company which distributed other Fox films of the period. The film was based on a popular play of the time by Porter Emerson Browne, which, in turn, had been adapted from the poem, "The Vampire," by Rudyard Kipling. The stage version of *A Fool There Was* had originally opened at New York's Liberty Theater on March 24, 1909, and ran for ninety-three performances. Katherine Kaelred had been the original vamp, and Robert Hilliard played the poor, unfortunate husband. For the film version, Powell considered a number of would-be or had-been stage vamps, including Virginia Pearson and Valeska Suratt. The latter was a popular vaudeville performer who was later to enjoy a modest film career as a vamp. One day, however, he met the future Bara, an out-of-work stage actress, and after what today would be described as a screen test, he decided to offer her the role. Fox agreed with Powell's decision, and the two men, with the aid of a few press agents, christened their new star Theda Bara.

The Fool (played by stage actor Edward Jose) is happily married and living with his wife (Mabel Fremyear) and daughter (Runa Hodges) in Larchmont. He is a fine, virile man—although as portrayed by Jose somewhat advanced in years—and living a clean and wholesome existence, until he meets the Vampire (Theda Bara). At first he tries to resist her advances, but he becomes more and more fascinated by her. In turn, the Vampire is willing to bide her time, knowing from past experiences that the Fool will eventually become her plaything. She has already disposed of her current victim (Victor Benoit).

When the Fool receives a telegram from the president requesting that he leave immediately for a delicate mission in England, he expects his wife and child to accompany him, but the wife's sister (May Allison, who was later to star in a series of romantic films with Harold Lockwood) meets with an accident, and wife and child must stay behind to nurse her. When the Vampire reads in the newspaper of the Fool's mission, she decides to travel to Europe on the same ship. At the dockside, she encounters one of her past victims, an elderly derelict, who crys, "See what you have made of me—and still you prosper, you hellcat." Also on board ship is the most recent victim, who shoots himself after a final rejection by the Vampire. The new Fool soon falls completely under the spell of the Vampire. Relaxing with her on the Italian Riviera, he forgets his diplomatic mission, his wife, child, and career. Meanwhile, back in Larchmont, the wife has learned of her husband's indiscretions. When her daughter asks her, "Mama, is a cross a sign of love," the wife responds, "Yes, and love often means a cross."

In London, the Fool is dismissed from his diplomatic mission by a terse telegram stating, "On account of your disgraceful conduct, you are hereby dismissed." He attempts to rid himself of the Vampire and of the drugs and alcohol with which she has been plying him. He returns to the United States, but the Vampire follows her Fool. "The 'rag and a bone and a hank of hair' to whom he has 'made his prayer' toys with him like a tigress with her prey." She humiliates the Fool by having him take her to the opera where they will be seen together by the Fool's family and friends. Even the entreaties of his small daughter are ignored.

In a final, drunken and drugged fling, the Fool throws a huge party, at the height of which wife, child, sister-in-law, and brother-in-law appear to beg the Fool to return with them to the respectability of Larchmont. The Fool, however, can only grovel at the feet of the Vampire, who orders him, "Kiss me, my fool." As he crawls to her side, he collapses, and the Vampire, with an inscrutable smile on her face, scatters rose petals over his body. A final title comments—possibly erroneously, because the Fool certainly appears to be dead—"So some of him lived, but the soul of him died."

A Fool There Was is a fascinating piece of harmless mediocrity, enthusiastically acted by a cast which obviously should have known better. It is totally outrageous, wildly improbable, and great fun. When all is said and done, the film's preachment can hardly be ignored, as humorist S. J. Perelman noted in a 1952 reappraisal of the production in *The New Yorker*, "For all its bathos and musty histrionics, *A Fool There Was* still retains some mysterious moral sachet."

Contemporary audiences loved the film, and so did the critics. Peter Milne, in *Motion Picture News* (January 23, 1915), praised the acting, directing, and photography; he wrote, "Aside from the fact that it will do the very young little good, and perhaps harm, to witness the film, it is exceedingly excellent." An early feminist critic, Margaret I. MacDonald, commented in *The Moving Picture World* (January 30, 1915), "The production is a successful artistic effort in every respect. True, there has been made no attempt to get under cover; moral truths have been given in all their nudity, and 'sin' has been presented in its most revolting aspect." The anonymous critic of *The New York Dramatic Mirror* (January 20, 1915) noted, "It is bold and relentless; it is filled with passion and tragedy; it is right in harmony with the poem."

The Vampire continued on her career and so did the screen's best-known Vamp, Theda Bara. Few of the actress' films have survived; fortunately, *A Fool There Was* is among those that have. It provides a unique and engrossing glimpse at a very unique and engrossing screen phenomenon, Theda Bara.

Anthony Slide

FOOLISH WIVES

Released: 1922
Production: Carl Laemmle for Universal
Direction: Erich Von Stroheim
Screenplay: Erich Von Stroheim
Titles: Erich Von Stroheim and Marian Ainslee
Cinematography: Ben Reynolds and William Daniels
Art direction: Richard Day and Erich Von Stroheim
Lighting: Harry J. Brown
Music: Sigmund Romberg
Length: 14 reels/14,120 feet

Principal characters:
Count Sergius Karamzin	Erich Von Stroheim
"Princess" Olga Petschnikoff	Maude George
"Princess" Vera Petschnikoff	Mae Busch
Maruschka, their maid	Dale Fuller
Andrew J. Hughes	Rudolph Christians
	(later, Robert Edeson assumed the role)
Mrs. Helen Hughes	Miss DuPont
Cesare Ventucci	Cesare Gravina
Marietta, his daughter	Malvina Polo
Prince Albert	C. J. Allen

In attempting to define "genius," Friedrich von Schiller declared that genius was always true to itself but never, never decent. "Corruption alone is decent," he remarked. To Schiller, genius could be counted on to oppose the superficial decency that forms the essence of bourgeois respectability. It was bound to conflict with the habits and expectations of a comfortable society because its role is "to enlarge the circle of nature." That definition of genius fits director Erich Von Stroheim. Acknowledged as the supreme filmmaker by such other master filmmakers of diverse styles and interests as Sergei Eisenstein and Jean Renoir, Von Stroheim's works influenced countless other filmmakers and regularly appear on lists of the greatest films of all time.

Foolish Wives was Von Stroheim's third film as a director and is a masterpiece typical of Von Stroheim. Brilliant yet controversial, *Foolish Wives* was both praised and condemned with equal vigor. With this film, Von Stroheim surpassed the artistic promise of *Blind Husbands* (1919) and *The Devil's Passkey* (1920, and now lost). He also surpassed all previous records set for expenditures on one film. According to his own calculations, he spent $735,000 on the production; the studio first said one million dollars and then later $1,103,000. The rumors flew that director Von Stroheim was a profligate, arrogant man whose inexplicable obsession with the smallest details left Universal with the biggest bill in history for one film. Von Stroheim had begun *Foolish Wives* as the darling of Universal, but by the time of the film's completion, he was a prodigal to be watched and worried over by ambitious studio executives such as young Irving Thalberg. The latter offered up Von Stroheim's expenditures on *Foolish Wives* as the horrible results of letting directors, even prestige directors with five-year contracts, have too much autonomy.

Foolish Wives marked the beginning of Von Stroheim's maturity as a creative artist and the beginning of the end of his career in Hollywood. The film signaled the deterioration of his relationship with the Hollywood studio system and set the disheartening pattern of how his films would be handled by that system and the popular reception they would receive. Censors by the score and "civic-minded" groups too numerous to count regarded *Foolish Wives* as decadent and morally objectionable. *Photoplay*, then a respected representative of Hollywood opinion, rather than a fan magazine as it later became, called the film "an insult to every American," and much of middle America noticed the film's lack of "decency." Assailed in the newspapers, banned in cities and states, and shredded by the censors, *Foolish Wives*'s reception foreshadowed the response to Von Stroheim's greatest masterpiece, *Greed*, made one year later.

Foolish Wives was what was popularly referred to as "a continental story." Set in post-World War I Monte Carlo, with its gambling casinos and splendid villas, the film seemed to promise the appeal of exotic locales which would tempt Americans with sights they had never seen. Von Stroheim, however, dared to show more than the beautiful haunts of the rich. He also reveals the back alleyways and crumbling tenements that are the haunts of the poor. He sets his story of the conflict between Old World and New World manners and mores in a Monte Carlo of both glamour and wretched poverty.

Rubbing elbows with both rich and poor are Count Sergius Karamzin (Erich Von Stroheim) and his two female "cousins," Olga and Vera Petschnikoff (Maude George and Mae Busch). They live a life of ease in their rented villa, appropriately named Villa Amoroso. A *ménage à trois* of self-proclaimed Russian aristocracy, they live on their gambling winnings, counterfeit currency, and the money Karamzin wheedles out of his female acquaintances, including his maid, Maruschka (Dale Fuller). The three decide that they need some real money, however, and the Count reads about a potential mark in the newspaper. A new American envoy and his wife are arriving in Monte Carlo. Karamzin is particularly fond of American women because they provide such an irreproachable cover for illegal activities. Mrs. Helen Hughes (Miss DuPont) becomes the object of Karamzin's "amorous" attentions. While her husband, Andrew (Rudolph Christians; Robert Edeson assumed the role when Christians died during production), is busy with diplomatic duties, Mrs. Hughes idly sits in the sun and attempts to read a new book, *Foolish Wives*.

Karamzin introduces himself and begins showering her with flowers and flattery. His smooth manners contrast sharply with the awkwardness of Mr. Hughes, who bungles his own introduction to Monaco's Prince Albert (C. J. Allen). American customs are further satirized in the depiction of the peculiar rituals of American bedtime preparation. Mrs. Hughes, complete with cold cream and curlers, is the archetypal American housewife. Mr. Hughes is relaxed and diffident. Von Stroheim shows precisely enough to make the final revelation—separate beds—seem the greatest oddity of all.

The next day Karamzin and Mrs. Hughes go on a little rural excursion that ends with their being caught in a rainstorm. The Count takes Mrs. Hughes to the hut of an old woman who is obviously familiar with this routine. Here, as in previous scenes, character is revealed through marvelous details of behavior. Karamzin pretends to turn his back discreetly while Mrs. Hughes sheds her wet clothing, but he surreptitiously watches her in a small mirror. His seduction of her is averted only by the unexpected arrival of a monk, and in a moment of typical Von Stroheim humor, Karamzin is forced to sleep in a corner with only the company of the goats.

In the morning, Princess Olga tells Mr. Hughes that his wife was with her and the Count. Later, at the gaming tables, however, Mr. Hughes begins to realize the Princess is not to be trusted. While he is at the casino, Mrs. Hughes receives a desperate message from Karamzin begging her to come visit him at the villa; and she goes to meet him. He tells her that he will be forced to kill himself if he cannot repay his debts, so Mrs. Hughes willingly gives him ninety thousand francs of her gambling winnings. Maruschka eavesdrops on their conversation and realizes the Count's promises to marry her have only been a ploy to get her savings; so, she locks Karamzin and Mrs. Hughes in the room and sets fire to the villa. In a scene of incredible visual beauty and dramatic pathos, the distraught Maruschka commits suicide by jumping into the sea. Karamzin and Mrs. Hughes try to escape the flames, but are trapped on a high balcony. When firemen provide a safety net, the Count's impeccable manners are suddenly forgotten when his life is threatened. He ignores Mrs. Hughes and leaps into the net. Later, he justifies his cowardly behavior by proclaiming that Mrs. Hughes was afraid to jump and he was forced to show her how.

Mr. Hughes finds the letter from Karamzin to his wife. He confronts the Count, insults him, and orders him to leave Monte Carlo. (In this scene Mr. Hughes' actions very much resemble those of a frontier lawman telling the local "varmint" to get out of town.) Olga and Vera decide that they too must make their escape, and they deride Karamzin for botching all their lovely plans.

The Count decides the night is too young to waste arguing, so he goes to the house of the counterfeiter Cesare Ventucci (Cesare Gravina). He has plans of raping Ventucci's lovely, but half-witted, daughter Marietta (Malvina

Polo). Karamzin manages to climb into her window, but he upsets a flower pot, and Ventucci is awakened by the noise. In the next shot, Ventucci is seen dragging Karamzin's lifeless body to the sewer, where he unceremoniously stuffs the body down a manhole. Karamzin's end is almost Biblical in the appropriateness of the judgment. It echoes Ecclesiastes' warning that "He that digs a pit shall fall into it." Ironically, the morally minded people who protested the film never seemed to recognize this strain of Christian fatalism in Von Stroheim's work.

Von Stroheim's films are much more "moral" in the traditional sense of evil receiving its just punishment, than the sex comedies of Cecil B. De Mille or numerous other post-World War I directors. Others tacked on endings that allowed silly sinners to repent in the last reel. Von Stroheim often kidded sex, and he was especially adept at kidding the censors' view of sex in film (as in *The Wedding March*, 1928), but he was never exploitative of sex, and he concerned himself with more important issues than deciding who was naughty and who was nice. He records human frailty, human desire, human vulnerability to small vices and enormous evil. Von Stroheim very often shows his audience the grotesque, and occasionally he allows a glimpse of the sublime. The sublime in Von Stroheim's films is usually to be found in the tenuous existence of young, true love. In *Foolish Wives*, Von Stroheim offers some hope in Mr. Hughes's reaffirmation of his relationship with his wife.

In the last scene (as it now exists), Mr. Hughes comforts his wife. (Before the film was cut by censors, Mrs. Hughes gives premature birth to her husband's child immediately before this scene, but audiences were confused, apparently, into thinking that Karamzin was the father.) Mr. Hughes quotes from the very book his wife had earlier been reading, *Foolish Wives*, and reads, ". . . disillusionment came finally to a foolish wife who found in her husband the nobility she had sought in 'a counterfeit.'" Perhaps Mrs. Hughes has learned her lesson and cast off her naïveté. There is no reassurance that the couple will now lead a blissfully enlightened life together or that they have changed substantially. As Von Stroheim envisioned the film's ending, the last scene would show Karamzin's body floating out to sea with the rest of Monte Carlo's sewage. Von Stroheim never flinched at showing the physical or emotional ugliness of life; in no way can *Foolish Wives* be interpreted as presenting a comforting view of life.

Upon completion of filming after eleven months, Von Stroheim had shot 320,000 feet of original negative, during a period when most films were less than ten thousand feet in length. He wanted to cut the film so that it might be screened in two parts on two different nights at theaters, but Universal regarded this idea as untenable. The film was trimmed to a three-and-a-half-hour version that had its premiere in New York especially for critics, invited guests, and twenty-two wary censors (invited by Carl Laemmle, head of Universal). This version was praised by the critics, but many thought it too long. Laemmle used this as an excuse to go back on his promise to support exhibition of this version if it were a critical success. A film of such length meant fewer shows per day and therefore less profit. The film was cut from fourteen thousand to ten thousand feet for general release, and Laemmle trumpeted the fact that the public was now seeing less than three percent of the original filmed footage to the world's first million-dollar film.

Trimmed or not, *Foolish Wives* still outraged the censors and the proponents of censorship. The DAR, the American Federation of Women's Clubs, the Women's Vigilante Committee, and others vociferously protested. They were joined by more than a few voices in the press. The *New York Morning Telegraph* passionately declared that the film "should be prohibited. It's a case of high treason to Americans and an insult to women in general. I'd kill anyone who took my children to see this film." Laemmle's million-dollar film was viewed by many to be a million-dollar attack on American moral fiber and Americans in general.

Ironically, the American characters in the film are seen in a more flattering light than the Europeans (if there is such a thing as "flattering light" in Von Stroheim's films. It cannot be denied, however, that *Foolish Wives* did attack American superficiality, blustering affability, and seeming pride in ignorance flattering itself to be innocence. In the figure of Mrs. Hughes, Von Stroheim was blasting satisfied matrons who were comfortable with moneyed purposelessness. French critic Lo Duca observed that *Foolish Wives* "shook the habitual American thinking of the time as it had never been shaken before." Von Stroheim questioned American values and life-styles. Many regarded that questioning as nothing less than an unforgivable insult delivered by an impertinent foreigner.

Von Stroheim's aristocratic bearing, his seeming relish at playing villains, and his artistic inflexibility as a director, combined with American postwar distrust of anyone or anything remotely Teutonic, served to increase public opinion against him. The actor who was "the man you love to hate" on screen became the director many hated for what he dared put on screen. Hollywood has always tolerated a limited amount of eccentricity, especially when it makes a product or personality more profitable. Clara Bow's chow dogs dyed to match her hair were an example of the acceptable kind of eccentricity. Von Stroheim and his refusal to conform to Hollywood standards of what a respectable, talented director should be was definitely not.

Laemmle even tried to exploit the confusion between Von Stroheim the villain in films and Von Stroheim the director. In publicity material for *Foolish Wives*, the studio declared that Von Stroheim was "so consummate an actor that many people think the renegade Russian Count is Erich Von Stroheim. . . . So artful in his villainy that even the critics hated him." (The last sentence is a stroke of publicity "genius.") In Laemmle's foreword to the original program for the film, he was quick to point to the thorough Americanness of the film, as if the public should be reassured that if they felt insulted by the film, they might take heart in the fact that other Americans were important participants in the insult. American architects, American engineers, American specialists, American costumers, American artists are all cited by Laemmle as forming the backbone of the film's production at that conclave of American filmmaking—Universal. "With the exception of Erich Von Stroheim," Laemmle continues, "nearly all of the characters are American born." Laemmle's comments are a disturbing commentary on American prejudice.

Foolish Wives, in spite of the controversy surrounding it at the time of release, is now regarded as a master work that reveals the completeness of Von Stroheim's talent. He could coax marvelous individual performances from both amateurs such as Miss DuPont (Patsy Hannen) and professionals such as Maude George and elicit ensemble acting of subtle timing and finesse. His ability to tell a story visually was matched by a talent for words that produced, in *Foolish Wives*, some of the loveliest, impressionistically poetic titles in the history of silent film. His camera technique was never ostentatious, but he could create moments of unforgettable visual effect, such as the first shot of the Monte Carlo plaza. Through the same visual control, he was also capable of showing intimate moments of emotion, as when Karamzin eyes Ventucci's daughter within the confines of a shuttered room lit only by shafts of dust-laden light.

Von Stroheim understood the particulars of human behavior and could record his impression of them in all their minute detail. Here resides the uniqueness of his talent. One modern historian-critic has commented that artists now attempt to base their work in generalities—on theories—in an attempt to express the universal. They fail because they do not realize that only in the particular can one come to understand the true nature of universal "truths." Von Stroheim was able to show the particulars of human existence. His tragedy was that he was a great observer of life and a great artist, but he never compromised himself to the idea that the artist who chooses film as his palette must also be an astute businessman. He was doomed to fail in a system that seems always to prefer the latter to the former. Perhaps true genius can never be comfortable in that system and can expect ruin if it refuses to mix artistic giving with corporate taking. Jim Tully, a literary crony of H. L. Mencken, eloquently summed up Von Stroheim's and his own situation when he once speculated: "For in that day when those who follow us will be able to set a perspective on film history, Stroheim is likely to be considered the first man of genius and original talent to break his heart against the stone wall of cinema imbecility."

Gaylyn Studlar

FOREVER
(PETER IBBETSON)

Released: 1921
Production: Famous Players-Lasky for Paramount
Direction: George Fitzmaurice
Screenplay: Ouida Bergère; based on the novel *Peter Ibbetson* by George du Maurier and the play of the same name by John Nathan Raphael and Constance Collier
Cinematography: Arthur Miller
Length: 7 reels/7,236 feet

> *Principal characters:*
> Peter Ibbetson .... Wallace Reid
> Mary "Mimsey,"
> Duchess of Towers .... Elsie Ferguson
> Colonel Ibbetson .... Montagu Love
> Major Duquesne .... George Fawcett
> Dolores .... Dolores Cassinelli
> Monsieur Seraskier .... Paul McAllister
> Monsieur Pasquier .... Elliott Dexter
> Duke of Towers .... Jerome Patrick

The career of George Louis Palmella Busson du Maurier is unique. He had been a successful illustrator and cartoonist for the British humor magazine *Punch* for more than thirty years when he wrote *Peter Ibbetson*, a romantic novel about two lovers who spend their entire relationship literally in a dream world. He was fifty-seven years old when he wrote the novel, and was amazed when it became a great literary success. The novel was eventually dramatized, subsequently turned into a grand opera, and has continued to enjoy popularity to this day.

Three years after writing *Peter Ibbetson*, and considerably heartened, he published another romantic novel, *Trilby*, and its success surpassed even that of *Peter Ibbetson*. He had never before written anything except letters and captions for his cartoons, but suddenly he found himself a lion in the literary world. His son, Gerald du Maurier, an actor-manager, became the most illustrious of all drawing-room comedians in the theater; and his granddaughter, Daphne du Maurier, is a contemporary writer of best-selling novels, such as *Rebecca* and *My Cousin Rachel*. Without any doubt, he became the progenitor of a family that has enjoyed extraordinary fame through three generations for their contributions to fiction and the theater.

Both *Peter Ibbetson* and *Trilby* were not only dramatized for the stage (John Barrymore, Lionel Barrymore, and Constance Collier played in du Maurier works on Broadway), but both also have found popularity in films. A beautiful version of *Peter Ibbetson* was made for silent films, directed by

George Fitzmaurice and co-starring Wallace Reid and Elsie Ferguson, and retitled in the United States as *Forever*. Reid was especially pleased when he was cast in the title role of *Peter Ibbetson*. "Wally *became* a good actor," Mrs. Reid has said. "In the beginning, his popularity was based on his good looks and engaging personality, but when he was offered a challenge, as he was with *Forever*, he rose to the occasion."

Elsie Ferguson was at her loveliest as Mary, Duchess of Towers, always exquisitely gowned, and she and Reid made a handsome couple on screen. Fitzmaurice was much admired for his sensitive direction, as was George Fawcett for his performance of Major Duquesne, who had once fought with Napoleon. Montagu Love also was impressive with his work as the dastardly villain, Colonel Ibbetson.

In 1935, a handsome talking version of *Peter Ibbetson* was made by Paramount, co-starring Gary Cooper and Ann Harding. Anybody knowing the original saw at once that Peter's slaying of his cruel uncle had been changed to his killing the Duke of Towers who had lashed out at him with an accusation of adulterous behavior with his wife. This alteration of the original plot confused and weakened the intended mysticism of the play.

Oddly enough, the story line of *Peter Ibbetson* parallels the personal story of du Maurier. Like Peter, du Maurier was born in Paris, the son of a French father and an English mother. He was taken very soon after birth to London, and later returned to live in France, at Passy. He came back to England when he had reached his maturity and attended University College as a chemical student. Du Maurier, when his father died, gave up chemistry, returned to France, and entered Gleyre's *atelier*, which forms a good part of the background for the early Bohemian part of *Trilby*.

Peter Ibbetson first appeared as a serial in *Harper's Monthly*, and then immediately was issued as a book, illustrated by du Maurier himself. Thus, the Duchess of Towers is pictured as he describes her, tall, long-legged, a beautiful giantess of a woman.

In the story, young Peter, also known as "Gogo," is living in Passy with his mother and father. They all befriend Madame Seraskier and her daughter, who is a semi-invalid called "Mimsey." As a friend, Peter often reads to Mimsey, and when he does, both are transported to another world. When Mimsey begins to recover from her wasting illness, the families go for walks; but Mimsey tires easily, and Peter must carry her home on his back. Apart from time together, they also share many tastes, such as music, Byron's poetry, roast chestnuts, domestic pets, and autumn weather when the leaves turn.

Young Peter never forgets the days he shares with Mimsey, and he loves the days of their youth, spent in Paris. With the years, however, changes come. Peter's father is killed in an accident, and a relative of his mother, a Colonel Ibbetson, comes to Passy and takes Peter off to London, while soon afterward Mimsey goes to live in Russia with her father.

Peter comes to loathe Colonel Ibbetson, who is a liar, a womanizer, and a brute, and he avoids him as much as possible, spending a year in the service of the grenadiers. He rarely goes out socially, but at a musicale some years later he meets an extraordinarily beautiful woman, tall, with laughing eyes, whose name is the Duchess of Towers.

There commence from this point a series of incidents, or nightmares, from which he is always rescued by the Duchess. She chides him once with "You are not dreaming true." She knows who he is, and he now learns, as he has always suspected, that she is Mimsey, his childhood sweetheart grown up. She explains what "dreaming true" is, which was taught to her by her father:

> You must always sleep on your back, with your arms above your head, your hands clasped and your feet crossed, the right one over the left . . . and you must never for a moment cease thinking of where you want to be in your dream till you are asleep and get there; and you must never forget in your dream where and what you were when you awake. You must join the dream on to reality.

From this point on, they "dream true" many times. She is a martyr to a husband who abuses her; she comes to his aid financially only when he faces bankruptcy, and in so doing, secures her legal separation; thus, removing any Victorian qualms she has about sharing a dream romance with Peter.

Colonel Ibbetson is revealed to be the worst kind of a blackguard and liar. Peter learns that Ibbetson has told people that Peter is his bastard son, which enrages Peter and prompts him to seek out his uncle. When Ibbetson returns to his home on St. James Street after a drinking session, Peter faces him with the truths he has learned. Ibbetson, infuriated and drunk, attacks him with a Malay creese, while Peter defends himself with a walking stick. The servants try to break down the door, but succeed only after Ibbetson is killed; his head crushed by a blow from Peter's walking stick.

Peter is tried, found guilty, and condemned to death. In his death cell, the Duchess comes to him, telling him that she knows he was provoked to kill. Through her influence, his sentence is commuted to life imprisonment, and he is moved to a more tolerant prison. Now begins a love story that will last for twenty-five years. In their dreams, they go to the theater together, to operas, they walk in gardens, and go to museums. They even travel in their dreams, going to such places as Naples, and even Yosemite Valley. They live a magical life, but their only children are the children they themselves were, Mimsey and Gogo.

Peter knows instinctively one day that Mary, Duchess of Towers, has been killed, because she does not come to him, although he "dreams true." He learns that she is indeed dead; she was killed at a Metropolitan Railway Station while rescuing a child who had fallen onto the rails. She was not run over and made it safely inside the carriage, but she was dead before the train reached its next station. She died, as the captain proclaimed, at the age of fifty-three.

Peter loses all reason and tries to commit suicide, but he fails. Mary, however, comes to him again when he is at wit's end. She is now a ghost without a body and tells Peter that he must not hasten the moment of death. Time now means nothing to her. She is even beginning to believe that there is no such thing; there is so little difference between a year and a day, she explains to him. Finally, one morning, the time comes when his spirit is freed. He dies, and they are joined forever.

DeWitt Bodeen

THE FOUR HORSEMEN OF THE APOCALYPSE

Released: 1921
Production: Metro
Direction: Rex Ingram
Screenplay: June Mathis; based on the novel of the same name by Vicente Blasco Ibáñez
Cinematography: John F. Seitz
Editing: Grant Whytock
Length: 11 reels/9,000 feet

Principal characters:
Julio Desnoyers .... Rudolph Valentino
Marguerite Lurier .... Alice Terry
Madariaga .... Pomeroy Cannon
Marcelo Desnoyers .... Josef Swickard
Karl von Hartrott .... Alan Hale
Tchernoff .... Nigel De Brulier
Laurier .... John Sainpolis
Captain von Hartrott .... Stuart Holmes

Vicente Blasco Ibáñez's novel *The Four Horsemen of the Apocalypse* is a long, at times tedious, book, and the same can be said of Rex Ingram's screen adaptation. It should be a great film: contemporary critics would have one believe it was a great film, but it is far from flawless. Too much time—the first three reels of the film—is devoted to the life of the Madariaga family in the Argentine. Similarly, the war at times seems endless. Finally, and this is a major problem with almost all of Ingram's films, each scene has the pictorial quality of a great painting. Films are not still life, and life is what always seems to be lacking from an Ingram production. A valid similarity may be drawn between the films of Ingram and those of a more recent vintage directed by Vincente Minnelli. Both directors seem unable to produce anything but static, unemotional features. It is interesting to note that Minnelli was chosen to direct the 1961 remake of *The Four Horsemen of the Apocalypse*, which updates the story to World War II, and compared to which, the Ingram version is a masterpiece.

Ingram (1893-1950) was, his faults notwithstanding, a major figure in the history of the American silent screen. After several years as an actor, he began directing in 1916 with the Universal production of *The Great Problem*. He had already directed fourteen features before commencing work on *The Four Horsemen of the Apocalypse*, which is his best-known achievement. It was followed by a number of major films for Metro, including *The Conquering Power* (1921), *The Prisoner of Zenda* (1922), *Scaramouche* (1923), *Mare Nostrum* (1926), and *The Garden of Allah* (1927). He directed his last film, *Baroud* (in which he also starred) in 1932, and then retired to a life of painting, sculpture, and writing, keeping himself divorced from Hollywood and all it represented.

The Four Horsemen of the Apocalypse may be Ingram's best-known work, but the reason for that does not rest on his skills as a director, but rather in his selection (with the screenwriter June Mathis) of Rudolph Valentino to play the central character of Julio Desnoyers. Valentino had been acting in films for several years and, during 1919 and 1920, had been given featured roles in a number of productions, but it was *The Four Horsemen of the Apocalypse* which made him a star, and Ingram's next film, *The Conquering Power*, which consolidated that status.

Ingram began shooting *The Four Horsemen of the Apocalypse* on July 20, 1920, and was to spend six months on the production. The Desnoyers castle and adjoining village were built in the hills of Griffith Park in Los Angeles. The Gilmore Ranch, which is now part of Los Angeles' Farmers Market, was utilized for the South American scenes. Contemporary publicity indicates that 125,000 tons of masonry were used to build the sets (more than had been needed to construct the Woolworth Building in New York), 12,500 personnel were involved in the production, more than 500,000 feet of raw film stock was exposed, and fourteen cameramen were used to film the battle scenes from the various angles, supervised by fourteen assistant directors.

The Four Horsemen of the Apocalypse opens in Argentina, where Madariaga (Pomeroy Cannon), known as the Centaur, is a wealthy ranch owner, with two daughters, one of whom is married to a Frenchman and the other to a German with strong Prussian traits. The Centaur's favorite is Julio Desnoyers (Rudolph Valentino), the son of the French side of the family, who is a fun-loving individual. With a sensuality that overcomes the silliness of so many of his later screen roles, Valentino dances the tango, employing grace and style.

When Madariaga dies, his family divides the estate, and they leave Argentina for France and Germany. Marcelo Desnoyers (Josef Swickard), Julio's father, has a passion for collecting works of art, and he purchases a castle to house his treasures at Villeblanche. Julio becomes an artist and, along the way, seduces Marguerite Laurier (Alice Terry), the wife of a French senator (John Sainpolis). Their affair begins at a fashionable tango palace, but continues at Julio's apartment. In the apartment above lives a mysterious bearded philosopher of Russian origin, named Tchernoff (Nigel De Brulier). It is he who summons forth the Four Horsemen of the Apocalypse, representing Conquest, War, Famine, and Death, and who in turn herald World War I— "The brand that will set the world ablaze."

It is not long before Marguerite's husband learns of her extramarital activities, announces his intention to divorce her, and challenges Julio to a duel. Fortunately for the latter, the war intervenes. The senator joins his regiment and, in an effort to atone, Marguerite becomes a nurse. Because of his Argentine nationality, Julio is not required to enlist. The Germans capture Marcelo Desnoyers' castle, and he is ill-treated until the arrival of Captain von Hartrott (Stuart Holmes), who it transpires is Desnoyers' nephew from the German side of the family. Meanwhile, Julio again meets Marguerite, this time at Lourdes, where she has taken her blinded husband. Julio realizes that he is unworthy of Marguerite's love and decides to enlist, while Marguerite, despite her continuing love for Julio, decides to stay with her husband, who does not even know that it is she who is nursing him.

On the battlefield, Julio meets his death after an encounter with his German cousin, von Hartrott. His death comes in the nick of time, for Marguerite was again considering leaving her husband. Julio's father, who has escaped from his castle prison, meets the mysterious Russian Tchernoff in a cemetery, where his son's grave is but one of thousands. Asked if he knew Julio, Tchernoff replies, "I knew them all."

The film is tedious, but it has many good points. The allegory of the Four Horsemen, together with their visualization, is surprisingly effective. The photography of John F. Seitz is excellent, and most of the acting is free of unnecessary melodramatics. Particularly memorable is the performance of Alice Terry as Marguerite Laurier. Wearing a blond wig, she was one of the silent screen's most beautiful stars, dignified and quiet in her playing at all times. Terry and Ingram were married in November of 1921, and the actress played leading roles in all but one of the director's films during the 1920's. In *The Conquering Power*, she is billed above Valentino, but her best work was undoubtedly in Ingram's 1926 production of *Mare Nostrum*, again based on a novel by Blasco Ibáñez.

Contemporary critics were impressed by the film, but a number of them pointed out that it suffered from the defects of the novel. By 1921, also, critics were able to look back on World War I somewhat dispassionately, and a number complained that the film was too one-sided in its placing the blame for the atrocities of the conflict entirely on the Germans. *Exceptional Photoplays* (March, 1921) commented, "The picture achieves distinction through its sheer bulk and its linking up of widely separated places and events." *The New York Times* (March 7, 1921) wrote, "it is as a work in kinetic photography the screened *Four Horsemen* should first be considered, because its standing as a photoplay depends upon its pictorial properties and not upon its relation to a widely read novel."

Two major critics praised the film. In *Life* (March 24, 1921), Robert E. Sherwood wrote, "*The Four Horsemen of the Apocalypse* is a living, breathing answer to those who still refuse to take motion pictures seriously. Its production lifts the silent drama to an artistic plane that it has never touched before." Burns Mantle, writing in *Photoplay* (May, 1921), commented, "*The Four Horsemen of the Apocalypse* is interesting, and sufficiently away from the conventional story of the screen to give it a distinctive value of its own."

Perhaps most important of all, at least to the director and his company, Blasco Ibáñez said of the film,

> It is such a masterful realisation of my novel that I feel I owe a grand debt of gratitude to Mr. Ingram for the artistry of his direction. . . . I am particularly indebted to Alice Terry and to Rudolph Valentino for their realisation of my characters of Marguerite and Julio.

Anthony Slide

FOUR SONS

Released: 1928
Production: Fox Film Corporation
Direction: John Ford
Screenplay: Philip Klein; based on the short story "Grandma Bernle Learns Her Letters" by Ida Alexa Ross Wylie
Cinematography: George Schneiderman and Charles G. Clarke
Editing: Margaret C. Clancey
Music: S. L. Rothafel
Song: Erno Rapee and Lee Pollack, "Little Mother"
Length: 9-10 reels/8,962-9,412 feet

> *Principal characters:*
> Mother Bernle .... Margaret Mann
> Joseph Bernle .... James Hall
> Franz Bernle .... Francis X. Bushman, Jr.
> Johann Bernle .... Charles Morton
> Andreas Bernle .... George Meeker
> Annabelle .... June Collyer
> Major Von Stomm .... Earle Foxe
> The Postman .... Albert Gran
> The Burgomeister .... August Tollaire
> The Iceman .... Jack Pennick
> Innkeeper .... Hughie Mack
> Joseph's son .... Robert Parrish

John Ford's *Four Sons* is most advantageously discussed in terms of what it refers to rather than what it is. What it is is a three handkerchief soap opera about a brave mother, her staunch sons, the death of three of them in World War I, the survival of one in the United States, and her arrival at his home in freedom-loving America. It refers, through themes and visuals, to the films of D. W. Griffith and F. W. Murnau. Griffith is invoked through the film's strong regard for country and family and the sentimental glorification of the mother. To Griffith, mothers were sacrosanct, and film after film deified them practically beyond recognition. For his own reasons, Ford was only too happy to follow this tradition. *Four Sons*, however, looks like a Murnau film, and indeed, some of its sets had been used for *Sunrise*, released the year before and starring one of Ford's favorite actors, George O'Brien. Herman Bing, who had worked with Murnau, wrote the first draft of the script, although Philip Klein received credit for the screenplay.

In *Sunrise*, Murnau took material equally as trite as that in *Four Sons* and transcended it, making the film magical, mysterious, and compelling, as well as striking to the eye. In 1928, however, even with a script he wanted to direct, as opposed to one assigned to him by Fox, Ford cannot breathe much life into *Four Sons*. By the time Ford made *Stagecoach* (1939), with its heroine/ whore, Dallas, redeemed by love and surrogate motherhood, he was in command of his material. In the 1920's, Ford needed a strong story and a great deal of action, *The Iron Horse* (1924) being the paramount example, and like *Four Sons*, one of the few silent Ford films to survive to the present.

The film is the tale of a widow, Mother Bernle (Margaret Mann), living in a Bavarian garrison town before World War I with her sons: Franz (Francis X. Bushman, Jr.), a soldier; Johann (Charles Morton), a blacksmith; Andreas (George Meeker), a shepherd; and Joseph (James Hall), a farmer. Joseph has a friend in America who invites him to come over, and soon Joseph is managing a delicatessen in New York. Then, the streets being paved with the proverbial gold, he owns the deli. He marries, and his wife, Annabelle (June Collyer), has a son (Robert Parrish, who became a director in the 1950's and 1960's). Meanwhile, war has broken out and the remaining three sons go off to fight and are all killed. Ironically, Andreas dies in Joseph's arms, without any explanation of how they found each other in battle. Joseph returns to his adopted country and arranges his mother's passage to the new world. Mother Bernle arives at Ellis Island, and, when Joseph arrives after hours to pick her up, she is told that she will have to stay until the morning. She, however, disappears into Manhattan but eventually finds her way to the family apartment. Joseph and his wife come home to find Mother Bernle asleep by the fire, her grandson dozing in her lap.

Four Sons is ponderous; Ford lingers lovingly, but interminably over each scene; for example, Ford introduces the sons to the audience through a device of showing Mother Bernle putting their laundry in drawers labeled with their names. As each drawer is opened by her gnarled, work-worn fingers, the scene fades to a shot of the son at work, then back to the drawers. Mother Bernle is apotheosized through her humble, but dignified labor, such as making honey cake, pounding the laundry on a rock by the village stream, and fidgeting around her immaculate home waiting for the boys to come home. She is frequently lighted from behind, the lighting conferring sainthood on her with an implied halo over her white hair.

Pictorially, *Four Sons* is extremely beautiful; unfortunately its loveliness never obscures the inanities of the script, and the men are never able to overcome the impression that they are merely handsome ciphers.

Ford employs several interesting artifices in the course of telling his lengthy story. A black cat crosses the path of the troops leaving the village, and he shows the men departing for war by shooting past a graveyard toward the marchers. When the fat, mustachioed postman (modeled on Emil Jannings' proud, uniformed doorman in *The Last Laugh*, 1925), brings Mother Bernle the letter telling of her sons' deaths, his shadow, holding the black-bordered envelope is seen first, and the villagers are clearly relieved to learn that the letter is not for them. Mother Bernle watches her third son, Andreas, get his army haircut through the barracks window the night he leaves for the front: she stands in the rain, her head covered by her ubiquitous shawl, a basket over her arm. She walks along with Andreas to the station and is separated from him by the rest of the men brushing past her to climb aboard the train. When Andreas dies, Ford shows Joseph in his trench with his friend the iceman (Jack Pennick) listening to the cries of the wounded Germans across no-man's land. One yells "Mutterchen" ("little mother") and the iceman remarks, "I guess those fellows have mothers, too." The scene is covered with a thick white mist which obscures all but the figures in the foreground. Joseph finds Andreas, gives him water, and cries as his brother dies in his arms. Smoke and fog swirl around Andreas, turning him into a ghost and conveying the ambiguity of Joseph's emotions: Andreas is his brother, but he fights for the enemy.

The end of the war is symbolized in two ways: by the ringing of the village bells and the suicide of the cruel German major (Earle Foxe) at the instigation of his men, and by Joseph and the iceman returning to find that Annabelle has turned the deli into a large, swank tea shop in their absence. Ford demonstrates his own love for his country and his respect for its values, not by emphasizing Germany's defeat, but by displaying the triumph of the American impulse toward mercantilism. In *Four Sons*, as in many of his best films, Ford celebrates the virtues of small-town life, the worth of bucolic endeavor, and the support that each member of a small community can give the other residents. It glorifies honest toil, loyalty to the fatherland, and the warmth and sustenance of family life. For all the positive values they impart, these qualities cannot mask the fundamental silliness of the film. *Four Sons*, however, was very popular in its time, and Ford remembered it with fondness.

Four Sons is a transitional film. The viewer can see the film straining to talk. The second half of the picture is filled with talking heads, and the dialogue panels are interruptions in what should be a seamless narrative. The synchronized music and effects track only stresses the fact that motion pictures would soon be talking, and in fact, the following year, Ford's first talkie, *The Black Watch*, was released. From then on, the spoken word was as important to his films as Ford's imposing visual style.

Four Sons was remade by Archie Mayo in 1934. It starred Don Ameche and marked the screen debut of Eugenie Leontovich as Frau Bernle.

Judith M. Kass

THE FRESHMAN

Released: 1925
Production: Harold Lloyd for Pathé Exchange
Direction: Fred Newmeyer and Sam Taylor
Screenplay: Sam Taylor, John Grey, Ted Wilde, and Tim Whelan
Cinematography: Walter Lundin and Henry Kohler
Length: 7 reels/6,883 feet

Principal characters:
Harold "Speedy" Lamb .... Harold Lloyd
Peggy .... Jobyna Ralston
College cad .... Brooks Benedict
College hero .... James Anderson
College belle .... Hazel Keener
College tailor .... Joseph Harrington
College coach .... Pat Harmon

The Harold Lloyd screen *persona* is a spirited, self-confident, fresh-faced lad, a comic combination of Douglas Fairbanks' all-American hero and Charles Ray's small-town boy. Lloyd played the friendly, aggressive, enterprising, eternally optimistic young Horatio Alger type; he was a little guy in horn-rimmed glasses whose ideas failed because his naïveté would eventually obliterate his self-assurance. He would constantly take advice from those who saw no need for honesty. To his audience's delight, he would play the fool; yet, by the finale, his basic goodness would allow him to triumph.

Lloyd was no zany Zorro or ribtickling Robin Hood—at least, perhaps, until the final reel. While Charlie Chaplin, Buster Keaton, and Harry Langdon were funny because their characters were unique, Lloyd relied almost exclusively on his scripts, which could have been successfully filmed with another comedian as star. Lloyd could not simply enter the scene and bring guffaws; it was his acting and his reactions to the situations that he created for his films which made him so successful. Although critically overshadowed by Chaplin and Keaton, he ranks with them among the greatest of silent clowns.

The Freshman and *Safety Last* (1923) are Lloyd's two most famous and well-remembered features. In *The Freshman*, he stars as Harold "Speedy" Lamb (his characters in his features are always named Harold) commencing his initial semester at Tate College. The naïve, anxious young man fantasizes that he will rapidly become a campus superhero. His bedroom at home is adorned with a Tate banner, and he practices the school cheers. On the train to Tate, he meets Peggy (Jobyna Ralston), who works in the checkroom of a hotel near the school. Harold may not know it yet, but he is in love.

Harold's goal of being "Big Man on Campus" is not attained easily or quickly; and, while he suffers, the audience laughs. First, some upperclassmen mischievously inform him that a car has arrived to transport him to campus. The auto, however, is really the dean's. He ends up on stage, in front of his fellow students, where he stutters, then blurts out, "I'm just a regular fellow— step right up and call me 'Speedy'" and then dances a jig, two "acts" that he is sure will make him "Number One" on campus. Instead, he is suckered into buying ice cream for practically the entire student body. He is now nearly broke, but he thinks that he has made a hit and is unaware that he is really a chump.

Harold conveniently finds less expensive accommodations in a boarding-house operated by Peggy's mother. He believes that his best chance for success at Tate will be on the gridiron, so he tries out for the football team. Unfortunately, he is used as a tackling dummy. When he makes the squad, or so he thinks, he is actually the water boy.

In the film's funniest sequence, Harold hosts the "Fall Frolic," a party that will open the Tate social season. Unfortunately, his tailor has constant dizzy spells that can only be cured by alcohol. The man is a bit too tipsy even to thread a needle, and Harold's tuxedo is not sewn but merely basted. He is accompanied to the dance by the tailor, who continuously faints. Harold's jacket and pants promptly fall apart creating the ultimate embarrassment— he has lost his clothes in public. The laughter now turns to pathos. A rival who has been making passes at Peggy finally tells Harold the truth, that his schoolmates have been kidding him. His "regular fellow" line and his jig, in short his "act," have made him a laughingstock.

Harold, with the support of the comforting Peggy, ultimately realizes his dream of becoming a "regular fellow." He is sent into the big football game against Union State to which Tate is losing, 3-0. Harold's teammates are all battered, and there is no one else left on the bench. Harold begs the coach to allow him to play, and the coach relents only when the referee rules that the game will be forfeited if there are no more Tate replacements. Harold may be enthusiastic, but he is also uncoordinated. He is knocked unconscious but quickly reenters the game.

Eventually, he fields a punt. With the assistance of an unlaced ball, he eludes Union State's defense and galavants across the field. He hears a whistle—but not the referee's—and stops several yards before the goal line. He does, of course, finally score the winning touchdown. The jeers for Harold Lamb now turn to cheers; but, in keeping with the spirit of the film, the hero is accidently drenched in the shower in the finale.

Despite the football sequences and Harold's redemption—after all, he never rejects the values of college life or his desire to conform and "make the team"—*The Freshman* is still a biting satire on the so-called jazz age of the 1920's, the popularity of football, and the shallow veneer of college heroics. The Tate student population is collectively depicted as cruel and unfeeling. They hustle the poor, deluded Harold, and are selfishly immersed in their superficial fads and games. Harold wins them over not by kindness or friendship but by scoring a touchdown in a game. He still remains a clown: the film ends not with him winning a Heisman Trophy but with him as the brunt of a gag. Despite his exploits, Harold Lamb remains "all wet."

Still, Harold is all too human, a reminder of the imperfection in us all and the struggles we all must endure to get ourselves through difficult situations. He does not succeed effortlessly, as he is led on and then laughed at by his fellow students. He is humiliated, and he is hurt, but he keeps on trying until he wins. Harold is a dreamer, an outsider looking in. When he arrives at Tate, a group of students are waving school pennants and cheering the arrival of the school hero (James Anderson); Harold stands off to the side in dreamy admiration. When he understands the reality that people are laughing at, not with, him, he matures. He does what he must, getting in the big game and winning it, to reach his goal. The viewer can easily identify with him and can effortlessly root for him to win the fair Peggy and succeed on the gridiron.

Jobyna Ralston, Lloyd's leading lady in *The Freshman*, was his most prolific co-star after 1921, when he restricted himself to making only features. She also appeared with him in *Why Worry?* (1923), *Girl Shy* (1924), *Hot Water* (1924), *For Heaven's Sake* (1926), and *The Kid Brother* (1927), which comprised all of Lloyd's films between 1923 and 1927.

The Freshman was codirected by Fred Newmeyer and Sam Taylor. Newmeyer directed three of Lloyd's features by himself, and Taylor did two. As a team, they made five others. Both are remembered more for their association with Lloyd than for anything accomplished separately. Taylor's fame is actually more attributable to a credit line in *The Taming of the Shrew* (1929), with Douglas Fairbanks and Mary Pickford which read: "By William Shakespeare, with additional dialogue by Sam Taylor," which caused considerable laughter then and since. In fact, Lloyd claimed to have practically done all his own direction: "The directors were entirely dependent on me. I had these boys there because I felt they knew comedy, they knew what I wanted, they knew me—and they could handle the details."

Critics were disappointed with *The Freshman*, comparing it unfavorably to Lloyd's earlier credits; but it was a box-office bonanza and helped to make its star one of the richest men in Hollywood. Lloyd re-released the film in 1953 with less success and included it in its entirety in the compilation film *Harold Lloyd's Funny Side of Life* (1966) along with excerpts from *For Heaven's Sake*, *Girl Shy*, and *The Kid Brother*. A large part of the film's climactic football sequence may also be found at the beginning of Lloyd's final cinematic venture, *The Sin of Harold Diddlebock* (1947), also known as *Mad Wednesday*, directed by Preston Sturges. These scenes were shot during the winter of 1924-1925 at the Berkeley Bowl, during halftime of either the East-West game or a contest between California and Stanford.

The premise of *The Freshman* is dated today; certainly, Harold Lamb's desire to be a "regular guy" is irrelevant to all but the most insecure of contemporary collegians. The film, however, remains a perfect vehicle for its star; the audiences of any generation can relate to Harold Lamb's personal struggle for self-respect, success, friendship, and love.

Rob Edelman

FROM THE MANGER TO THE CROSS

Released: 1912
Production: Kalem Company
Direction: Sidney Olcott
Screenplay: Gene Gauntier
Cinematography: George K. Hollister
Length: 5 reels

Principal characters:

The Christ	R. Henderson Bland
The Virgin Mary	Gene Gauntier
The Boy Christ	Percy Dyer
Mary Magdalene	Alice Hollister
Martha	Helen Lindroth
John	Jack J. Clark
Andrew	J. P. McGowan
Judas	Robert Vignola
Lazarus	Sidney Baber

Films of the Passion Play had been a staple part of cinema since the late 1890's. The birth of the Savior had been the subject of a number of early one-reelers, and the figure of Christ has been represented sometimes by an actor and sometimes simply by a shadowy figure or a lighting effect in such films as *The Kiss of Judas* (1909), *Though Your Sins Be as Scarlet* (1911), *The Illumination* (1912), and *Satan or the Drama of Humanity* (1912). The most important production detailing the life of Christ of the silent-film era, however, was the 1912 release of *From the Manger to the Cross*, produced by the New York-based Kalem Company.

The Kalem Company had already made filmmaking excursions to Ireland and to Germany when a group of its personnel, led by director Sidney Olcott and screenwriter-actress Gene Gauntier, arrived in Palestine in the final days of 1911 with the intention of filming a number of one-reelers, including *The Fighting Dervishes of the Desert*, *The Prisoner of the Harem*, *An Arabian Tragedy*, and *Captured by Bedouins*. At what point it was decided to film a life of Christ is not certain. According to Gauntier:

And it's an odd fact, that it was a film we had not started out to make. It was terribly hot in the Holy Land, and because we worked steadily day after day in a heat that was more awful than I had ever known, I suffered a sun-stroke. It was when I was recovering from it, that I wrote the scenario *From the Manger to the Cross*. . . . We worked late into the night every night preparing for our work of the next day—and then the next day would be spent under the burning sun on the burning sands. . . . And so *From the Manger to the Cross* was filmed. One hot day succeeded another hot day, and one sticky night was just like the preceding sticky night. But we felt repaid, for we knew the results were good.

Legend has it that the owners of the Kalem Company were unaware that Olcott and associates were filming a life of Christ and that, as a result of their actions, everyone involved was fired. This seems highly unlikely. First of all, it would be difficult for a group of filmmakers to keep secret their activities from their bosses, particularly with several film papers publishing stories on such activities. Furthermore, in an interview published in *The Bioscope* of May 9, 1912, Frank Marion (president of the Kalem Company) discusses the proposed film, noting that one sequence, the flight into Egypt, had already been shot.

In fact, there appears to be as much mythology associated with *From the Manger to the Cross* as is to be found in the Book of Genesis. The Jerusalem studio of the Kalem Company was located between a monastery and a nunnery. Forty-two actors and actresses were dispatched from England to Palestine to participate in the production. The film cost $35,000 to produce, and its profits equaled almost a million dollars. Legend has it that the Church expressed grave concern that the Virgin Mary was portrayed by Gauntier, a divorced woman, but there is absolutely no evidence of such an expression. During the filming of the procession to the Cross, the Reverend Mother from the convent of St. Veronica was so overcome that she came to bring wine to the actor-Christ just as 1900 years previous St. Veronica had ministered to the real Christ.

Five persons portrayed the Christ in *From the Manger to the Cross*. The first was a newborn baby borrowed from its Australian parents, who were living in Cairo. The second was a youngster of two, the third a boy of eight, while the youthful Christ was portrayed by the thirteen-year-old Percy Dyer. To play Christ as a man, Olcott hired R. Henderson Bland. According to Bland, Olcott telephoned him on April 26, 1912, and asked him if he would be willing to play the part. After consultation with his wife, Bland agreed. There is little question that Bland, an Englishman, was somewhat an unusual character. Obviously, he believed that during the production he had become Christ. He authored two books on the subject, *From the Manger to the Cross* (1922) and *Actor-Soldier-Poet* (1939). In each, he writes as if he had been Christ, heading chapters with titles such as "The Call" and "The Preparation" and noting, "I felt as if I was being enveloped by some strange power and being led gently on." Later Bland commented, "I feel that I shall never be able to pick up my life where I dropped it on the Hill of the World's Redemption." He did, however, and the strength he gained from his portrayal of Christ enabled him to fight courageously and kill a number of enemy Germans during World War I.

From the Manger to the Cross, as its title suggests, is a straightforward retelling of many of the events of the life of Christ, including his birth, his flight into Egypt, the calling of the disciples, the turning of water into wine, the raising of Lazarus, the forgiveness of Mary Magdalene, the Last Supper,

Gethsemane, the trial, and the crucifixion. The film does not deal with the resurrection, preferring to end with Christ on the cross. The production contains few surprises in terms of film technique, although there is one excellent shot of the boy Christ carrying a plank of wood from his father's carpentry shop, with the camera panning down to the shadow which appears to be of Christ on the cross.

The film received its world premiere at the Queen's Hall, London, on October 3, 1912, before an audience which included one thousand clergymen. Dr. William Inge, the Dean of St. Paul's, commented, "I thought the exhibition reverent and beautiful. I shall certainly recommend others to see it." A screening at London's Albert Hall followed, and the critic for the *Daily Express* wrote,

> So great, it seems to me, are the possible results of a general presentation of this film that I left the Albert Hall yesterday longing for its exhibition in all the cathedrals, the churches and the chapels in the land, placed, that is, in the atmosphere of reverence and worship to which it absolutely belongs, and used to quicken the imaginative life which is becoming so woefully stunted in an age of triumphant mechanics.

Perhaps in answer to this desire, Pope Pius X issued a decree that no film, however religious, might be shown in churches, "in order that the sacred character of the buildings should be safeguarded."

The New York premiere of *From the Manger to the Cross* took place at Wanamaker's Auditorium on October 14, 1912. W. Stephen Bush in *The Moving Picture World* (October 26, 1912) wrote,

> The titles of this production to be classed as the greatest achievement in cinematography are many, but chief among them is the realism of it all. It is not a Passion Play; it is the very story of the Passion and of many incidents recorded by the evangelists. It is indeed a cinematographic gospel. Because of its sublime work it will be easier than it was before to "go forth and teach all nations."

The critic in *Photography* (March 15, 1913) commented, "*From the Manger to the Cross* is splendid. It is the kind of production that will interest a clientele that does not come under the classification of film fan." He goes on to say that "it is this tremendous clientele that must be reached and every effort to do it should be encouraged."

From the Manger to the Cross was first reissued by Vitagraph in 1917. Its most important reissue came in 1938, when it was completely revised, by the addition of fake close-ups, by the Reverend Brian Hesson and released with a musical score and narration.

Anthony Slide

THE GAUCHO

Released: 1927
Production: Douglas Fairbanks for the Elton Corporation; released by United
    Artists
Direction: F. Richard Jones
Screenplay: Lotta Woods; based on a story by Elton Thomas (Douglas Fair-
    banks)
Cinematography: Tony Gaudio
Editing: William Nolan
Length: 10 reels/9,256 feet

> *Principal characters:*
> The Gaucho .... Douglas Fairbanks
> The Mountain Girl .... Lupe Velez
> Girl of the Shrine .... Eve Southern
> Ruiz .... Gustav von Seyffertitz
> The Gaucho's first lieutenant .... Charles Stevens
> The Padre .... Nigel De Brulier
> Victim of the "black doom" .... Albert MacQuarrie
> Our Lady of the Shrine .... Mary Pickford

Aside from *The Iron Mask* (1928), *The Gaucho* is the last of Douglas
Fairbanks' swashbuckling silent features. It carries on the tradition established
in *The Mark of Zorro* (1920), *The Three Musketeers* (1921), *Robin Hood*
(1922), and *The Black Pirate* (1926), but it lacks the fervor and the excitement
of the earlier films. The spectacle is there, and Fairbanks displays all his old
athletic tricks, but the spirit seems weak. One of the problems is undoubtedly
the religious theme of the film. It was acceptable to have a priest in *The Mark
of Zorro*, but the religious motif of *The Gaucho* bears heavily on the production and its star. Religious miracles are believable in religious productions,
but they seem strangely out of place in a Fairbanks swashbuckler.

The Gaucho opens with the miracle—shot in Technicolor—in which a young
girl sees the Virgin Mary after falling down a cliff. Appropriately enough,
Fairbanks selected for the role of the Virgin Mary his own Mary—Mary
Pickford, who is quite clearly recognizable as the Madonna. (This was not
the first time that Pickford had made a cameo appearance in one of her
husband's films; previously she had replaced Billie Dove for the final romantic
clinch in *The Black Pirate*.) On the spot where the Virgin Mary appeared,
a city is built, known as the City of the Miracle. The shrine continues to be
cared for by the young girl, aided by a kindly padre (Nigel De Brulier), but
the city is taken over by Ruiz the Usurper (Gustav von Seyffertitz), who
becomes wealthy through the gold that the pilgrims bring to the shrine.

The Gaucho (Douglas Fairbanks) is a bandit living in the mountains above the city, and he has given his heart to a wild singing and dancing gypsy known as the Mountain Girl (Lupe Velez), who provocatively teases the bandit. The Fairbanks character here is initially a villainous one, who rides at the head of his own army, looting and terrorizing the towns of the Andes, and, eventually, arrives at the City of the Miracle. Single-handedly the Gaucho takes the city, and after a drunken orgy, he attempts to seduce the virginal Girl of the Shrine (Eve Southern). The Mountain Girl comes upon the two, however, and manages to wound the Gaucho with a knife. Earlier, the Gaucho had offended a victim of the "black doom" (Albert MacQuarrie) by telling him that anyone suffering from such a disease should go forth and put an end to themselves. The victim of the "black doom" now seeks his revenge, touching the Gaucho's wound and inflicting him with the dread disease. The Gaucho sees his hand go black and is about to kill himself when the Girl of the Shrine leads him to its healing waters.

The Gaucho, however, is thrown in jail by Ruiz, who has again retaken the city. He escapes, thanks to some help from a clump of trees—swinging from branch to branch—and uses a herd of longhorn cattle (imported from Mexico for the occasion) to storm and retake the city. The Gaucho becomes a changed man, marries the Mountain Girl, and the shrine and its protectors are assured of, presumably, permanent security.

The change in the Gaucho's character is rather difficult to understand, for even if viewer's accept the fact that he was healed miraculously, there is no reason, given his earlier behavior, for him not to become his old, villainous self. Similarly, the Mountain Girl's change in character at the end of the film, when she settles down to a life of domesticity with her gaucho is hard to accept.

Throughout the film Fairbanks gives a mannered performance as the Gaucho. He swaggers as he tells the padre, "I get what I want—without the help of God and his Holy Book." He always lights a cigarette from the butt of an old one, which he then puts on the toe of his shoes and kicks away. Fairbanks also introduces a new novelty in his use of the South American bola, a T-shaped rope made of plaited leather with weights fastened at each end used to entangle animals. Supposedly, Fairbanks brought two champion bola throwers from the Argentine, Nick Milanesio and Andres Rodrigues, to teach him the finer points in the use of the weapon, and he even gave a demonstration at the World's Championship Rodeo held in Los Angeles in the summer of 1927.

Contemporary critics all liked *The Gaucho*. Mordaunt Hall in *The New York Times* praised the settings—the shimmering pure white City of the Miracle is particularly impressive—Fairbanks' agility, and the work of the supporting players, although he did express concern over the two extremes of gaiety and dark tragedy which at times seemed to meet and clash. *Variety* (November 9, 1927) announced, "Doug Fairbanks is at it again. He still knows how to do those acrobatics."

Variety also went on to note that Fairbanks did not "hog" the picture, "but permits a little Mexican girl, new to films, in on the racket, and this baby is over. She scored 100 per cent plus and is established as a feminine Fairbanks." The girl in question was Lupe Velez, and *Photoplay* (January, 1928) was quick to note, "Doug's leading lady actually overshadows him as far as their respective performances are concerned."

Lupe Velez (1908-1944) began her career in films approximately a year earlier in Hal Roach comedy shorts. *The Gaucho* was her first feature-length production and established the actress as a beautiful, fiery Mexican star. With her role in *Lady of the Pavements* (1929), under D. W. Griffith's guidance, Velez proved herself to be a capable actress, but unfortunately her later films—particularly the series in which she was billed as the "Mexican spitfire"—do not do her justice. Her personal life was apparently as stormy as the lives of many of the characters she portrayed on the screen, and Velez ended her life with a highly theatrical, highly publicized suicide.

The Gaucho's other leading lady, Eve Southern, is a well-matched counterpart to Velez. The two women admirably represent the good and evil sides of the character of the Gaucho. The contrast between the two leading ladies is as pointed as the contrast between the behavior of the Gaucho at the film's beginning and the film's close.

Although *The Iron Mask* was still to come, *The Gaucho* represents Fairbanks' farewell to the silent cinema. He is still the lithe acrobat of old, but age is beginning to take its toll, a fact of which both the audience and Fairbanks himself must have been aware.

Lennox Sanderson, Jr.

THE GENERAL

Released: 1926
Production: Joseph M. Schenck for Buster Keaton Productions
Direction: Buster Keaton and Clyde Bruckman
Screenplay: Buster Keaton and Clyde Bruckman; based on Al Boasberg's and
   Charles Smith's adaptation of the *The Great Locomotive Chase* by William
   Pittenger
Cinematography: Dev Jennings and Bert Haines
Editing: Buster Keaton (uncredited)
Length: 8 reels/7,500 feet

Principal characters:
Johnnie Gray	Buster Keaton
Annabelle Lee	Marion Mack
Her father	Charles Smith
Her brother	Frank Barnes
Confederate general	Frederick Vroom
Captain Anderson	Glen Cavender
General Thatcher	Jim Farley

Buster Keaton is considered by virtually all cinema critics and historians as one of the two greatest silent-film comedians and most rate him as one of the best filmmakers of all time—silent or sound, comic or otherwise. Keaton's reputation is based principally upon nine or ten feature films he made between 1923 and 1928, and of this group, *The General* is almost universally regarded as the best. It has taken several decades, however, for Keaton and *The General* to reach this lofty position. When the film was first released, its reception at the box-office was unexceptional, and the critical reaction was distinctly unfavorable. Some of Keaton's lesser works were much better received by both public and the critics in the 1920's. Then, in 1928, Keaton came under the control of the Metro-Goldwyn-Mayer studio and—whether coincidentally or not—the quality of his films soon plummeted. It was not until the late 1940's that his films made in the 1920's finally began to be recognized as classics, and not until the 1960's that he received full appreciation of his talent and artistry. Before his death in 1966, he was, therefore, able to enjoy a few moments of glory after suffering decades of neglect.

The source of *The General* is a true story of a Civil War adventure in which a group of Northern spies stole a Confederate train and tried to take it back to the Union Army while destroying the railroad and communication lines behind them. An account of this event entitled *The Great Locomotive Chase* was found by one of Keaton's writers, Clyde Bruckman, who brought it to Keaton. Keaton also recognized the possibilities of the book, and the two planned a film in which the story would be told from the viewpoint of the

Southern engineer whose train is stolen. As was usual for Keaton's films, they did not write a complete script but left most of the details to be developed during the shooting of the film.

The film begins by introducing engineer Johnnie Gray (Buster Keaton) and showing that there are two loves in his life—his engine, which is named The General, and Annabelle Lee (Marion Mack). He soon loses both and spends the rest of the film trying to regain them. In essence, there are five parts to the film. In the first, he loses Annabelle; in the second, he loses The General and chases it; in the third, he rescues both Annabelle and the engine; in the fourth, he, Annabelle, and the engine are pursued; and, in the last, he and the Southern troops are victorious.

Keaton's heroes are frequently inept and bumbling in the first part of the film and then become proficient later, but in *The General* Johnnie is skillful at most things throughout the film. Indeed, it is through no lack of his skill or effort that Annabelle rejects him in the first part. He is visiting her when her brother (Frank Barnes) brings the news that Fort Sumter has been fired upon, and he and his father (Charles Smith) immediately leave to enlist in the Army. Johnnie leaves after they do, but by taking a shortcut is the very first in the enlistment line. He is rejected for the Army because he will be more valuable as an engineer, but the officials do not explain this to him; they merely say, "We can't use you." Undaunted, he tries twice more to be accepted, but when he is finally rudely booted out of the recruiting station he says, "If you lose this war, don't blame me." Annabelle does not believe his story and tells him that she does not want to see him again until he is in uniform. A dejected Johnnie sits down on the large connecting rod between the two biggest wheels of his engine and does not even notice at first when the engine begins to move, lifting him up and setting him down again. (This seemingly simple shot involved quite some risk to Keaton, for if the engine's wheels had slipped, he could have been severely injured or killed.)

A title then states that a year has passed, and a Union spy, Captain Anderson (Glen Cavender), explains his plan to steal the train and burn the bridges behind it as it goes north. Next, the train is seen leaving, and viewers learn that it is headed by The General, driven by Johnnie, and that Annabelle, who still shuns Johnnie, is a passenger who is going to see her wounded father. When the train is stopped at Big Shanty for dinner, and all of the passengers, except Annabelle, who has gone to the baggage car to get something from her trunk, are off the train, the disguised Northerners quickly jump aboard and start the engine. Johnnie looks up from washing his hands just in time to see his train leaving and calls for the other men to help him catch it. They follow only briefly, but Johnnie continues his pursuit, employing a handcar, then a bicycle, and when he reaches another station, another engine—The Texas. Unfortunately, the car full of Confederate soldiers who are to help him is not coupled to The Texas; so he goes off alone.

Johnnie pursues The General as the men on that train try to stop him by throwing railroad ties on the track, detaching a boxcar from their train, and switching The Texas onto an alternate track. Johnnie overcomes these obstacles and more, but as he is absorbed in the task of chopping wood in the tender, he does not notice that he is passing through the retreating Southern forces and the advancing Northern ones. This sequence is one of the memorable images of the film: Johnnie intently chopping wood on the moving train as the troops pass behind him. Finally, he notices that he is in Union territory, and the men he is pursuing notice that he is alone in his engine. He is forced to abandon The Texas as night and rain begin to fall.

The tone of the film changes once Johnnie is away from the engine. He seeks food and shelter in a house but discovers that is is a Union headquarters. He hides under a table just in time and soon learns that the Union soldiers are planning a surprise attack in the morning and that Annabelle is their prisoner. With daring and ingenuity, he rescues Annabelle and the two escape into the rainy forest.

The next day, Johnnie, disguised as a Northern soldier, puts Annabelle in a huge sack, loads her onto the Northern supply train, which is headed by his stolen engine, and steals The General back. Johnnie is now in The General, which is pulling only the tender and the boxcar in which he put Annabelle, who previously had disconnected the rest of the train. Thus the pursuit of the second part of the film is now reversed, with Johnnie and The General being chased by the Northerners, who are in two trains.

Johnnie is more successful in hindering the pursuit than the Northerners had been. Also, he soon goes to the baggage car and frees Annabelle, and she helps him. Her "help" is at first inexpert and infuriating to Johnnie, but she rapidly learns to handle the engine. In an early sequence, however, Johnnie asks her to put wood in the engine's firebox. As she does so, she first throws away one sizeable piece of wood because it has a knothole in it, then she takes a broom and begins sweeping the engine floor. Next, as Johnnie watches incredulously, she puts a quite small stick of wood into the fire. Johnnie then sarcastically hands her an even smaller bit of wood, which she nonchalantly adds to the fire. In exasperation he grabs her neck to choke her, but he quickly regains control of himself and kisses her instead. Later, her attempts to assist sometimes cause comic problems, but they are not her fault. For example, one time the engine starts moving while she is on it, but Johnnie is on the ground. Johnnie realizes that the train is going around a hairpin curve; so he takes a shortcut and scrambles down a hill to catch it. Meanwhile, however, Annabelle has stopped and reversed the engine to return to the spot she left Johnnie, who arrives at the bottom of the hill only to see the engine backing away from him. Eventually, however, they get to the Rock River bridge, where the North plans to attack. Johnnie builds a fire on the bridge, and after a few more mishaps, he, Annabelle, and The General arrive at a Confederate division headquarters and warn them of the coming attack. Annabelle is also reunited with her wounded father.

When the Union train reaches the burning bridge, General Parker (Frederick Vroom), who is on horseback, orders the train to continue because the bridge is not burned enough to stop it. When the train reaches the middle of the bridge, however, it collapses and the train falls into the river amidst clouds of smoke and steam. The Southern troops then overwhelm the Northern ones, both in spite of and because of Johnnie's comic attempts to be a sword-wielding soldier. After the victory, Johnnie returns to the engine and finds General Thatcher (Jim Farley), the Union general he had knocked unconscious when he took the train, just coming to. He marches him to the Confederate headquarters as a prisoner and is rewarded with a lieutenant's commission and uniform. Now finally a proud soldier, he starts to kiss Annabelle. As is usual in a Keaton film, however, there is one last obstacle to his final embrace with the girl. As each soldier walks by, he must stop and salute. Finally, he rearranges the two of them, and the final image of the film is Johnnie and Annabelle kissing as they sit on the connecting rod of The General while Johnnie mechanically salutes the passing troops with his right hand.

The General was shot in Oregon, where the scenery seemed appropriate and the logging companies still had narrow-gauge railway, and at the studio in Hollywood. According to Marion Mack, who made a personal appearance with the film in 1972, many of the details were developed or improvised on the spot, although the precision timing of a gag might require five or six takes. She and Keaton improvised much of the sequence with the bits of wood while the cameras were turning, for example. In many of Keaton's films, the heroine had little to do in the film except to be an inspiration to the hero, but in *The General*, Mack has a significant part, and her natural style of acting contributes to the success of the film. Keaton's acting, of course, is central to the effect of the film. He was often called The Great Stone Face because he never smiled on screen, but many fail to recognize how expressive his face could be. As Clyde Bruckman, co-author and co-director of *The General*, remarked, "He could tell his story by lifting an eyebrow. He could tell it by *not* lifting an eyebrow." Also, Keaton's talent as an actor and a director was to allow improvisation without ever losing control or artistry. By simply looking at the film, a viewer cannot tell which parts were devised well in advance and rehearsed and which were created on the spur of the moment. The finished film is certainly a carefully crafted masterwork. The Disney studio used the same source material to make a "serious" film in 1956 entitled *The Great Locomotive Chase*. According to Keaton, the "first mistake" Disney made was to film the adventure from the Union soldier's viewpoint.

Today, *The General* receives almost universal high praise. In a 1972 international poll of film critics, it was chosen as one of the best ten films ever made; it also is the subject of two complete books and many articles as well as the recipient of extensive treatment in virtually all histories of cinema as well as in the many books written specifically about Keaton.

Timothy W. Johnson

A GENTLEMAN OF PARIS

Released: 1927
Production: Famous Players-Lasky/Paramount
Direction: Harry d'Abbadie d'Arrast
Screenplay: Chandler Sprague; based on Benjamin Glazer's adaptation of the story *Bellamy, the Magnificent* by Roy Horniman
Titles: Herman Mankiewicz
Cinematography: Harold Rosson
Length: 6 reels/5,927 feet

> *Principal characters:*
> Edward, Marquis de Marignan ...... Adolphe Menjou
> Joseph Talineau (the valet) .... Nicholas Soussanin
> Jacqueline .... Shirley O'Hara
> Yvonne Dufour .... Arlette Marchal
> Henri Dufour .... William B. Davidson
> Cloakroom girl .... Lorraine Eddy
> Henriette .... Ivy Harris
> General Baron de Latour .... Lawrence Grant

After appearing in *A Woman of Paris*, directed by Charles Chaplin in 1923, Adolphe Menjou quickly rose to become a star at Paramount with prominent billing. Until talkies supplanted silent films, he turned out a fast stream of sophisticated comedies of consistent quality. Although he was actually born in Pennsylvania, most filmgoers thought that he was a Parisian since almost all of his starring features were set in Paris. The suave actor also had the reputation of being the best-dressed man in films; in fact, the title of his autobiography is *It Took Nine Tailors*.

In *A Gentleman of Paris*, Menjou portrays Edward, the Marquis de Marignan. As the film opens, Edward has been out all night at one of Paris' night clubs and has totally forgotten that his fiancée, Jacqueline (Shirley O'Hara), and her father, the General Baron de Latour (Lawrence Grant), are coming to his house that morning to discuss the upcoming marriage. Edward's very efficient valet, Joseph (Nicholas Soussanin), has not forgotten, however, and has frantically been going through his master's little black address book all morning, calling lady friends. Unfortunately, a telephone call to Yvonne Dufour (Arlette Marchal) is answered by her husband. When Joseph asks if the Marquis de Marignan is there, the husband, Henri Dufour (William B. Davidson), asks why in the world would he be there at eight in the morning.

Jacqueline and her father arrive moments before Edward appears in his tuxedo. The valet quickly warns him so that he uses the back door. The valet then tells Jacqueline that he will tell his master that she is waiting and hurries to help Edward dress. With Edward's head protruding from the shower curtain, Joseph shaves his master's face with a straight razor with frighteningly rapid strokes. Edward is dried and dressed in a gray flannel morning suit in record time and is soon greeting the General and kissing his fiancée's hand. He has not fooled the old General, however, and is given a little lecture in the library. Edward promises to change his flamboyant life-style.

The next day, Edward sets about telling his lady friends that he will be seeing them no more. He calls Yvonne Dufour, but she says that she cannot talk, and that they should meet at their favorite café that afternoon. He arrives a little late, however, and the pretty blonde cloakroom girl (Lorraine Eddy) tells him that Madame Dufour is in a private dining room upstairs. When he enters, Yvonne is upset and tells him that she thinks her husband suspects them because of the phone call Edward's valet made one recent morning. Edward says that they have nothing to fear because they will not be seeing each other anymore. At this point, there is a knock at the door, and the cloakroom girl enters breathlessly to announce that Yvonne's husband is downstairs; another knock sends the two women scurrying into a draped alcove. Henri Dufour bursts in, demanding to see his wife. Edward tells him that there is no one present as he can well see, and asks him to leave. Henri is about to go when he sees one of the curtains rustle. He starts to pull them aside, but Edward jumps in front and admits that there is a lady present. Although she is not Henri's wife, he states, she is entitled to her privacy all the same. Henri asks how he will know it is not his wife if he cannot see the lady.

"Would you know your wife's foot?" Edward inquires. "Of course," answers Henri. Edward asks for the lady's foot to be put through the drapes. The cloakroom girl, of course, places her own foot through. Henri, however, is not convinced, much to Edward's irritation, because, as he explains, a foot is a foot.

"Well, then," snaps Edward, "are you sufficiently acquainted with your domestic affairs to know your wife's hair?" Henri assures Edward that that would certainly convince him one way or the other, so the cloakroom girl puts one of her long blonde tresses through the curtain. Henri can thus do nothing but apologize, since his wife is a brunette, and he finally leaves the room, looking puzzled.

Edward must next visit another of his lady loves, Henriette (Ivy Harris) the modiste, at her little salon. He is announced and led to her office in the back. She acts nervous, and each time that he attempts to broach the subject of their past relationship, she moves her eyes toward a corner of the room. Not understanding her intent, Edward tells her that they must end their affair; he then suddenly notices a man's shoes under the curtain. Edward rips open the drapes and is startled to see Joseph, his valet. Joseph acts like the wounded husband, which Edward cannot account for until he learns that Henriette and Joseph are actually married.

Edward assures his valet that he would never have done it, had he known, and is terribly sorry. Joseph is too wounded and states that he shall, of course, quit working for the Marquis. Edward appeals to him not to leave and finally gets Joseph to agree to give him eight days' notice.

The next morning, however, Edward's shave by his valet becomes an experiment in terror. Joseph strops the straight razor until it is exceedingly sharp, and the shave that follows is an ordeal for Edward and for the viewer as well. The Marquis finally breaks the tension by saying, "You'd probably like to slit my throat, Joseph?" The valet answers, "No, sir, there is more than one way to slit a marquis' throat."

Edward and Jacqueline are married the next day, and are quite happy. She does, however, knit him a horrible-looking tie, which he is obliged to wear instead of his usual silk tie, but outside of that, she proves to be a charming wife. Soon, her father invites them to his country estate for a house party. While the men play cards, the women spend the day embroidering and gossiping. Edward has particularly good luck, and his winnings are the subject of much amazement and envy. Joseph now sees his chance to ruin Edward, and proceeds to hide an ace in the Marquis' cuff. He dresses him with his usual efficiency, but at the door Edward stops and turns to him saying lightly, "Joseph, I don't know what I'll do without you."

That evening Edward's luck holds as usual, and he wins a particularly large amount from Henri Dufour. During a break in the game, Joseph catches Henri alone and tells him that the Marquis has been known to pull a few aces out of his sleeve. At the game table Henri loses more and more money to Edward, and to the shock of all present, accuses him of cheating.

Edward finds the accusation amusing, and when Henri asks for him to be searched, he good-naturedly agrees. The ace is found in his cuff, Edward is bewildered, Jacqueline is crushed, and the General is disgusted.

When he goes to his room in disgrace, Edward finds that the General has left a pistol on the desk top—a subtle hint to him to take the honorable way out. Edward picks up the gun and holds it limply, as the scene fades out.

Downstairs, the party has taken a somber turn. Then the crack of a pistol shot makes Jacqueline cringe, and Joseph noticeably pales. When Henri tells the party that the Marquis did what cheaters must do, Joseph breaks down, crying. He confesses to the gathering that he framed the Marquis. Edward then appears at the foot of the stairs with a smoking revolver. He smiles kindly. "I knew you'd confess when you heard the shot, Joseph. I don't know what I'd do without you."

Larry Lee Holland

THE GIRL I LOVED

Released: 1923
Production: Charles Ray Productions; released by United Artists
Direction: Joseph De Grasse
Screenplay: Albert Ray and Harry L. Decker (continuity); based on the poem
   of the same name by James Whitcomb Riley
Titles: Edward Withes
Cinematography: George Rizard
Art direction: Robert Ellis
Length: 8 reels/7,100 feet

> *Principal characters:*
> John Middleton .... Charles Ray
> Mary .... Patsy Ruth Miller
> Willie Brown .... Ramsey Wallace
> Mother Middleton .... Edythe Chapman
> Minister (circuit rider) .... Lon Poff
> The Judge .... George F. Marion

When Ernst Lubitsch came to the United States to work in 1923, he was asked whom he considered the best actor then appearing in American films. Without hesitation he replied, "Charles Ray." If Lubitsch had just seen Ray in his production of *The Girl I Loved*, which is possible because it was released in 1923, Lubitsch's remark about the high rating he would give Ray is very much to the point. *The Girl I Loved* and *The Tailor-Made Man* (1922), which preceded it, were both released by United Artists, and owners Mary Pickford, Douglas Fairbanks, Charles Chaplin, and D. W. Griffith were thinking seriously of allowing Ray to become one of their company's partners.

Unfortunately, the very next release by Ray was the ambitious but awful *The Courtship of Myles Standish* (1923), which bankrupted Ray. Any chance of his becoming one of the United Artists was gone. The old Hollywood adage, "You are only as good as your last picture," was, in this case, too true. For a while, it looked as if Ray might go back to Thomas H. Ince's producership, because he did two more films for Ince, but around that time Ince died, leaving Ray free to battle the producer/distributor field again. Ray did two bucolic comedies for Chadwick release, and then luck shone on him, and he had a year's M-G-M contract, followed by one at Producers Distributing Corporation. During these years, he was treated with respect again, and he had little difficulty getting lucrative assignments as a leading man. He was never again, however, to do anything of the quality of *The Girl I Loved*, which was a perfect idyll of young love. It would not even be possible today to find a re-creation of such a pastoral scene, even in the American Middle West.

Ray's interpretation of a simple-hearted country boy was a classic, far more solid and moving than *The Old Swimmin' Hole* (1921), which had been so simple and plotless that it had no subtitles whatsoever, and its scenes simply flowed ideally from one to another. It could be typed with some of the better farmboy Ince comedies such as *His Own Home Town* (1918) and *Hay Foot, Straw Foot* (1919), but certainly he had attempted nothing as dramatic as this since the early Triangle days when Ince released his film, *The Coward* (1915).

In *The Girl I Loved*, Ray plays John Middleton, the only son of a widow (Edythe Chapman). He lives a carefree, healthy, sun-filled, barefoot existence during the summer and goes to the local little red schoolhouse during the winter. He lives to go fishing, to eat his mother's cooking, and to dream of days to come.

At first, he resents Mary (Patsy Ruth Miller), the girl his mother adopts, but as time passes, he looks upon her with different, lovesick eyes, for she has become the only girl in the world to him. He dresses up, stays clean, and even wears shoes because he wants to impress Mary. He also does things the other boys resist doing because they are regarded as "sissy": he learns to dance, and he loves to read. He begins to grow up—and all because of Mary.

Too shy to tell her of his affection, he is astonished when Mary announces with shining eyes that she is engaged to wed Willie Brown (Ramsey Wallace). It has never occurred to him that Mary would do so awful a thing, nor can he conceive of life without Mary.

John is almost speechless when Willie Brown comes to him and asks him if he will be best man at the wedding. John nods that he will, but Willie is abhorrent to him. He begins to think of things that might put off the wedding, and in his imagination he takes a gun, a big revolver, and points it at his own forehead. He does not pull the trigger, however, for it is only a daydream. Another time he plots to kill Willie Brown, for he wonders why Willie should steal the girl he loves and still go on living. There is a scene at the wedding, and John is not in attendance. As the preacher speaks the words of the ceremony, John appears on the scene and fires the gun at Willie, who drops dead as Mary looks on, horrified. This, too, takes place only in John's imagination, for he does not even own a gun, nor would he know how to fire it.

The wedding day arrives, and the ceremony proceeds on schedule. John gives the ring to Willie and watches him put it on the finger of Mary, who is radiant with complete happiness. Then everybody is kissing the bride, but when Mary comes to him for his kiss, he holds back. She kisses him anyway, causing his eyes to fill with tears. He cannot stay and let everybody see him weeping, so he slips out of the room and hides under the house.

When the wedding party comes out of the house, Mary and Willie get into a carriage. Mary looks around and suddenly notices John's absence. "I wanted to tell him goodbye," she says, and John's mother reassures her that she will tell him that Mary was looking for him. The carriage drives off; and John, choked with tears, bites his knuckles to hold them back.

The *Motion Picture News* reviewer noted that "A number of the scenes by Ray are truly works of art and will go a long way toward placing him back in the top-notch position he once held among film stars." This was ironic because, in retrospect, *The Girl I Loved* marks the very peak of his acting career. After his downfall, Ray did everything to gain a reprieve for his dying career, even accepting bit parts. After he had been divorced from his first wife, she went to Detroit to become the personal designer and dressmaker to Mrs. Henry Ford. Ray married a second time, but that wife died shortly thereafter. He himself died on November 23, 1943, of an impacted infected tooth. "That is the official diagnosis," wrote Louella O. Parsons, "but I think Charles Ray died of a heartache that began many years ago, when, broke and discouraged, he realized his bright, particular star had set, and there was no comeback."

DeWitt Bodeen

THE GLORIOUS ADVENTURE

Released: 1921
Production: J. Stuart Blackton
Direction: J. Stuart Blackton
Screenplay: J. Stuart Blackton
Cinematography: William T. Crespinel
Art direction: Felix Orman
Length: 7 reels/6,600 feet

Principal characters:
Lady Beatrice Fair	Diana Manners
Hugh Argyle	Gerald Lawrence
Cecil Humphreys	Walter Roderick
King Charles II	William Luff
Bulfinch	Victor McLaglen

The primary significance of *The Glorious Adventure* in film history is its development and use of Prizmacolor, a two-color additive process introduced in 1918. As employed by the director, J. Stuart Blackton, Prizmacolor represented a major step in the filmmaker's art by improving upon all other color systems in use at the time and paving the way for further refinements in film color. The employment of color had long been a feature in photography before it was made adaptable to cinematic use. The representational requirements of cinema have always been substantially more stringent than those of photography, and it is not surprising that accurate and successful color usage would take decades to evolve. In the years before 1918, screen color was usually achieved by tinted film, where a given scene would take on an associated color, such as blue for night or yellow for day. The obvious drawback, however, was that only one color would appear on the screen at a time. There was also a tedious method wherein the individual film frames were colored by hand-cut stencils. This system allowed for the use of more than one color at a time; but the process greatly extended the time necessary to make such a film.

After these processes, and other unsatisfactory experiments to project color in cinema, came the so-called additive techniques. The first was Kinemacolor in 1906, followed by Chronochrome in 1912. These two color methods were tried but were only partially successful in representing natural colors and, therefore, were rapidly abandoned. Prizmacolor, which first appeared in 1918, was a technique that originated in the United States. The earliest versions of it involved the photography of every other frame through various colors of filters on black-and-white film. The camera, meanwhile, was required to operate at double the usual speed. The use of this technique before *The Glorious Adventure* was confined to the much shorter one- and two-reel films and was perceived as not being practical or consistent enough in quality for a feature-length film to be visually accurate. Blackton had the requisite boldness to make the attempt at a longer film, and while *The Glorious Adventure* has never earned significant critical acclaim, it is, nevertheless, a distinctly important milestone in filmmaking.

The choice of *The Glorious Adventure* for Blackton's experiment was a wise one. It is a period costume drama whose action takes place in and around the seventeenth century English court of Charles II. The characters were attired in multihued costumes which challenged the camera to record, color by color, all the swashbuckling action. *The Glorious Adventure* is, unfortunately, heavily melodramatic. Also, there are probably too many characters involved who, once introduced, reappear throughout the seven reels in an overly complicated plot. Audiences certainly must have had difficulty understanding the plot maneuvers and character motivations, even without the dynamically new and mentally distracting brilliant screen colors.

The film itself is a mélange of romantic involvement, adventure, and clandestine activity. During the period of the cavaliers, there was supposedly a custom whereby the accrued gambling debts of a noble lady were assumed by a condemned criminal when she married the criminal. His execution wiped away the debt. *The Glorious Adventure* was centered around such a notion, and Blackton used the setting and story for background to much swordplay and a fire that consumed the city of London.

In the story, Lady Beatrice Fair (Diana Manners) loses a great deal of money at the gambling table, having been cheated by Walter Roderick (Cecil Humphreys) and Bulfinch (Victor McLaglen), who are involved in an extravagant plot to steal the estate and title of Hugh Argyle (Gerald Lawrence). Because of the large debt, Lady Beatrice is obliged to pay it or expunge it by marrying a condemned criminal. After several complications, it is revealed that the condemned criminal is Bulfinch, and he escapes from prison and takes Lady Beatrice with him, against her will. While he and Beatrice are in hiding, the Great Fire of London breaks out and ravages the city. Argyle then arrives and heroically rescues Lady Beatrice to bring the film to an end.

It is during the Great Fire sequence that Blackton triumphs in his use of color. The vividness of the fire is a spectacle with few equals, even by modern standards. In fact, the fire alone may have been evidence enough to other filmmakers that producing color feature films was not only possible but also desirable, if future large audiences were to be attracted.

Obvious weaknesses in Prizmacolor were the facts that not all of the colors appeared to be natural or even consistent in shade from one scene to another; and, in scenes where the characters are in motion, the details of their faces cannot be discerned. It is because of such flaws that Prizmacolor and the other additive color processes were relatively short lived. In time, they were replaced by the subtractive methods, and others, that would lead to the technically advanced state of color cinema in modern times.

Nevertheless, Blackton's *The Glorious Adventure*, with its seven reels of vivid action and bright costuming, was undoubtedly a crucial contribution to the transitional phase between the earlier black-and-white era and the later color era. Blackton's willingness to gamble, in making a feature-length color film, permanently altered the course of motion-picture history.

Thomas A. Hanson

GO WEST

Released: 1925
Production: Joseph M. Schenck for Buster Keaton Productions; released by
  Metro-Goldwyn-Mayer
Direction: Buster Keaton
Screenplay: Raymond Cannon; based on an idea by Buster Keaton
Cinematography: Elgin Lessley and Bert Haines
Editing: Buster Keaton (uncredited)
Length: 7 reels/6,293 feet

Principal characters:
Friendless .... Buster Keaton
Ranch owner .... Howard Truesdale
His daughter .... Kathleen Myers

Making a film that parodies other films or film conventions entails at least
three large risks. One is that the humor of the parody will be exhausted long
before the film is over. Many truly funny ideas leave the filmmaker with
nothing to develop after a few scenes. Another risk is that the audience will
resent the ridiculing of films it likes and will be actively hostile to the parody.
A third risk is that the film will be of interest only for its parody and will fail
to involve its audience in the plot or characters. This latter risk is not important
for short films, but in a feature-length film, the audience usually needs to care
about the characters. Buster Keaton succeeded in avoiding or overcoming
these risks to produce a fully realized film with a premise that seems to be
more ridiculous than humorous: *Go West* is a Western in which the heroine
is not a woman but a cow.

Although parody and the cow-as-heroine premise are essential elements
of *Go West*, the overall tone of the film is by no means dictated by these
elements. Indeed, the film is characterized by a strong element of pathos that
is decidedly unusual for Keaton. The film begins with a shot of a statue of
newspaper man Horace Greeley, with his famous saying "Go West, Young
Man, Go West" inscribed upon it. Then it introduces the "hero," Friendless
(Buster Keaton) with the title "Some people travel through life making friends
wherever they go, while others—Just travel through life." Keaton then uses
precisely the right semihumorous tone to show the pitiful state of Friendless
so that viewers can laugh occasionally at his condition without ever losing
sympathy for him. He first takes all his worldly possessions—including a bed,
a small dresser, and a stove—to a general store, where he receives only $1.65
for everything. When he then takes a few personal items—including a picture
of his mother—from one of the drawers, the store manager charges him for
them. After he uses all but a nickel of the money he has left to buy some

bread and sausage, a young woman collecting for charity comes in the store and takes the nickel. This sequence is concluded with a final indignity: Friendless pats a dog in front of the store, and the dog immediately walks away.

Friendless does not heed Greeley's injunction yet, however, but instead boards a boxcar headed for New York. It is partially filled with boxes, and when Friendless sits on one while holding his long loaf of bread, the image ironically resembles that of a king sitting on a throne. The adventures of Friendless in the big city are, however, decidedly less than royal. He is overwhelmed by the throng of people on the sidewalk and struck by a huge automobile when he ventures into the street. A superimposition of the figure of Greeley over that of Friendless then lets viewers know that he has remembered Greeley's advice, and he climbs into a boxcar bound for Arizona. He arrives there unceremoniously when the empty barrel in which he has crawled rolls out the door of the boxcar and shatters in the desert.

Friendless is finally in the West, but his prospects for success, or even survival, do not seem promising. He is frightened even by jackrabbits. It is at this point that the heroine of the drama is introduced; she is a cow called Brown Eyes and is as friendless and inept as the hero. The men at the ranch reject her because she does not give milk, and the rest of the cattle also ostracize her. Thus is set up the coming "romance," but before Friendless meets Brown Eyes, he first gets a job as a ranchhand. He puts on some discarded cowboy paraphernalia (although he retains Keaton's trademark porkpie hat) and gets a job from the ranch owner (Howard Truesdale), even though he falls down when he tries to walk with a Western swagger. He then meets the rancher's daughter (Kathleen Myers), but she dismisses him with a sarcastic remark, and he proceeds to his assigned task of milking a cow. He places the empty milk pail under the cow's udder and simply waits for her to produce the milk.

The scene is a minor gem in which Friendless tries everything he can think of to encourage the cow, but none of his methods produce results. He tries waiting patiently; he tries showing the cow the empty bucket; he even moves the milking stool to several different locations, but he is, of course, unsuccessful. Up to this point, the film is fairly typical of Keaton in that the hero has proven his ineptness and a young woman has been introduced, but she has rejected him. Knowing the frequent pattern of Keaton films, the audience expects the hero to become skillful at something and win the woman. The only strange note so far is pathos. A Keaton hero often is unsuccessful or inept at the beginning of the film, but in no other film is he devoid of family, friends, money, or employment. In fact, in such films as *The Navigator* (1924) and *Battling Butler* (1926) he is rich and spoiled. Many critics attribute the pathos in *Go West* to the influence of the films of Charlie Chaplin, in which the effects usually depend to some degree upon pathos. Some critics see the sentimental elements of *Go West* as an imitation of Chaplin, others as an affectionate *hommage*, and others see these elements as a pointed parody of Chaplin.

Go West begins to take an unexpected turn when Friendless sees Brown Eyes and notices that she has a stone in her hoof. Friendless removes the stone and tips his hat to her. Soon she returns the favor by saving him from an angry longhorn when his foot is caught in a gopher hole. Friendless again tips his hat to Brown Eyes. Then Brown Eyes follows him, and when he extends his hand, she licks it. This act is astounding to this man who has experienced nothing but rejection. From this moment on, the two become virtually inseparable. Friendless misses meals and sacrifices sleep to care for or protect Brown Eyes, and the scenes are well played and directed so that the emotion rather than the absurdity of the situation is conveyed. (Keaton was, as usual, directing himself.) In one instance, he saves Brown Eyes from a painful branding by lathering her flank and then *shaving* a brand on it.

The plot then takes another twist when the rancher announces that he is shipping his cattle to market; he will be ruined financially if he does not sell them immediately. A neighboring rancher, however, warns that he will stop the shipment because he thinks they all should keep their cattle off the market until the price is higher. For Friendless, however, the main problem is that Brown Eyes is to be shipped along with the others. He tries several tactics to prevent this, but all are in vain. He therefore boards the car with Brown Eyes as it leaves for the stockyards in Los Angeles. As the rancher's daughter watches in surprise, a cattle car passes by with Friendless and Brown Eyes placidly looking out.

The other rancher and his men attack the train, and during the battle, the engineer is forced to start the train and then jump off. Friendless gets back on the train and rejoins Brown Eyes, unaware that he is the only human aboard and that the train is out of control. Finally, he does realize this and, in a marvelous acrobatic feat, walks along the tops of the cars as the train speeds around curves, finally racing to the engine just in time to stop the train at a siding in Los Angeles. Remembering that the cattle must be delivered to the stockyard to prevent the rancher's ruin, he lets the cattle out of the cars and begins taking them through the streets of the city.

The march of the cattle through the streets is, as might be expected, both funny and chaotic. By now, however, Friendless has become skillful, and he manages the cattle drive as well as possible. Indeed, this sequence is a counterbalance to his early misadventures in New York City. The cattle, of course, scare most of the people who see them, particularly when they invade such places as a department store and a barber shop. (One of the customers in the barber shop, incidentally, is played by Joe Keaton, Buster's father.) The comic chaos intensifies when Friendless, who has been told that cattle will follow something red, puts on a devil's costume. At the climax, the rancher and his daughter have arrived at the stockyards and are in despair because the cattle are not there when Friendless, dressed in the devil's costume and riding Brown Eyes, arrives with the cattle. The rancher offers him any reward he wants, and Friendless answers, "I want her." For a moment it seems that he is referring to the daughter, but it is Brown Eyes instead. In the last shot, the four drive off in an open automobile, the rancher and his daughter in the front seat, with Friendless and Brown Eyes in the back seat. As the film ends, however, Friendless does lean forward to talk with the daughter.

In addition to the possible parody of Chaplin, Keaton is also poking some fun at the Western film with the comic role reversal that makes a heroine out of a cow. Even more specifically, *Go West* is also having some fun with the films of D. W. Griffith. In Griffith's *Intolerance* (1916) two of the characters are Brown Eyes and The Friendless One. Also a scene in *Go West* shows Friendless playing poker (to win enough money to buy Brown Eyes) when he notices that one of the other players is cheating. He complains, and the other player pulls a gun and says, "When you say that—SMILE." Friendless uses his fingers to force his face into something resembling a smile. This scene echoes one in Griffith's *Broken Blossoms* (1919), in which the character played by Lillian Gish is brutalized by her foster father. When he then complains that she never smiles, she forces a smile in the same manner. This scene also has an additional overtone, since Keaton was famous for never smiling in his films. The parodic aspects of *Go West* merely add an extra element to the film, though; they do not overwhelm or distort it. A viewer could completely enjoy and understand the film without any knowledge of Chaplin or Griffith.

Go West thus artfully combines subtle comedy, acrobatic feats, parody, and absurdity with a moving pathos that is impossible to convey on the printed page. It certainly displays what critic James Agee called Keaton's "curious and original spirit."

Timothy W. Johnson

THE GOLD RUSH

Released: 1925
Production: Charles Chaplin for United Artists
Direction: Charles Chaplin
Screenplay: Charles Chaplin
Cinematography: Rollie Totheroh
Length: 9 reels/8,555 feet

Principal characters:

The Lone Prospector	Charles Chaplin
Big Jim McKay	Mack Swain
Black Larson	Tom Murray
Georgia	Georgia Hale
Georgia's friend	Betty Morrissey
Jack Cameron	Malcolm Waite
Hank Curtis	Henry Bergman

Of the vast array of unforgettable images that films have given the world, few are as widely recognized or as well loved as that of the Little Tramp, Charlie Chaplin's inspired comic creation. Chaplin's popularity dominated the realm of screen comedy during the years of silent films, and never was his particular blend of humor and pathos put to more effective use than in *The Gold Rush*. Made in 1925, *The Gold Rush* has appeared repeatedly on critics' lists of favorite films and is considered by many to be Chaplin's finest comedy.

The film's story is set in Alaska during the Gold Rush. Chaplin's Tramp, described here as the Lone Prospector, goes North to search for gold. Forced by a blizzard to take refuge in an isolated cabin, Charlie discovers that it is owned by an outlaw, Black Larson (Tom Murray). Big Jim McKay (Mack Swain), another prospector seeking shelter, soon joins them. Black Larson tries to force both men to leave, and he battles Big Jim for possession of his shotgun, while Charlie scrambles frantically to avoid the swerving gunbarrel. Finally, Big Jim triumphs and Black Larson is forced to go off in search of help. When he fails to return, Charlie and Big Jim find that they are trapped with no food, and starvation soon becomes a very real possibility. Ever resourceful, Charlie prepares a meal of boiled boot and, in the film's most famous sequence, proceeds to eat the unpalatable meal as if he were dining on the finest of foods. Big Jim, however, becomes desperate for real food and begins to imagine that Charlie is a giant chicken. Charlie is saved from Big Jim's axe when he spots a wandering bear and shoots it. The blizzard stops, and Charlie and Big Jim, fortified by a feast of bear meat, leave the tiny cabin. Charlie heads for a nearby town, while Big Jim sets off to find the claim he had discovered before the storm. There he finds Black Larson, who knocks him unconscious with a shovel, but is then killed in an avalanche.

Charlie, meanwhile, has reached the town where he enters a saloon and falls immediately in love with a dance-hall girl named Georgia (Georgia Hale). She, however, has no interest in the ragged little tramp, who soon leaves and persuades one of the townsmen to take him in. While the man is away and Charlie is staying alone in the cabin, Georgia and her friends come to call. When a hidden photograph reveals Charlie's devotion to Georgia, she and her friends accept his invitation to New Year's Eve dinner, hoping to amuse themselves at his expense. Charlie works hard shoveling snow to earn money for the dinner, then sits alone in the cabin as the hours pass and Georgia fails to appear. Falling asleep, Charlie dreams that the girls have arrived and he is entertaining them by performing a clever skit using two rolls stuck on forks as dancing legs. He awakens to the realization that Georgia is not coming, and he leaves the town in despair. Georgia remembers the dinner and comes to the cabin only to find Charlie gone and the decorations for the party still in place. She realizes too late how much her thoughtlessness has hurt him.

Charlie soon encounters Big Jim again, but finds that he is suffering from amnesia, caused by Black Larson's blow with the shovel, and is unable to remember the location of his claim. Charlie agrees to help him and the two proceed to the mountains, where they are once again trapped in Black Larson's cabin by a storm. During the night, the cabin slides to the edge of a cliff, and when Charlie steps outside in the morning, he narrowly avoids plummetting to his death. He and Big Jim then engage in a hilarious struggle to get out of the cabin before it slips over the edge of the precipice. Succeeding at last, they discover that the cabin has left them on the site of Big Jim's claim.

Wealthy now, and elegantly dressed, Charlie and Big Jim are on board a ship preparing to sail from Alaska. Having changed back into his old clothes for the benefit of photographers, Charlie falls down a flight of stairs to the lower deck and discovers that Georgia is also on board. Believing Charlie to be a stowaway, she tries to hide him and is amazed to discover that he is a millionaire. Declaring his love for her, Charlie proposes to Georgia, and the two set sail for a new and happier life.

The Gold Rush contains scene after scene in which Chaplin demonstrates his comic virtuosity. Chaplin's inspiration for the film was the notorious Donner party, a group of nineteenth century settlers who were trapped in the Sierra Nevada mountains by winter blizzards and were forced to resort to cannibalism before help reached them. Chaplin was able to draw on this grim event and turn it to his own comic devices. The sequence of the film in which a hunger-crazed Big Jim chases Charlie with an axe is both horrifying in its implications and exceedingly funny in its execution.

This mixture of emotions lies at the heart of all of Chaplin's best work, giving it a richness and depth that are rare in silent comedy. Charlie's efforts to charm Georgia in the dance hall take on humorous dimensions when he unwittingly uses a dog's leash to tie up his pants—with the dog still attached. Audiences laugh at his predicament, but they are also saddened by his humiliation in front of the woman he loves. The famous "Oceana Rolls" scene, in which Charlie dreams he is entertaining Georgia and her friends, is a delight to watch; yet viewers know that he will soon wake up to discover he is alone.

The Tramp's vulnerability is offset, however, by his resourcefulness and determination. When he must think of a way to earn money for his New Year's Eve party, he shovels a huge pile of snow from one doorstep to the next, charging each occupant for its subsequent removal. He proceeds from house to house in this manner, collecting a fee at each door. The best embodiment of this quality of resourcefulness is the legendary shoe-eating scene. In Charlie's agile hands, the shoelaces become spaghetti and the nails are delicately nibbled like bones. With its combination of humor, cleverness, and the underlying seriousness of Charlie's situation, this scene stands among the finest moments of screen comedy.

A third aspect of Chaplin's artistry is also evident in *The Gold Rush*, that of his astonishing physical agility. Although he is frequently stumbling, struggling with inanimate objects, or leaping about to escape imminent danger, his actions are as graceful and as carefully choreographed as a dancer's. From his first appearance, teetering on one foot around corners on the icy mountain paths, to his final shipboard tumble down the stairs to Georgia, Chaplin's moments of slapstick are pure poetry.

Finally, *The Gold Rush* serves to demonstrate the universality of Chaplin's appeal. The Little Tramp, at first appearance, seems to be a hopeless bumbler. Upon closer examination, however, viewers see that his problems stem from the fact that he is at odds with society and is trying haplessly to fit in. The more he struggles to observe social conventions and proprieties, the more absurd and isolated he becomes. His actions are a reminder, albeit on a much less catastrophic level, of the universal frustration of trying to reconcile individuality with society's demands.

Janet E. Lorenz

THE GOLEM

Released: 1920
Production: Ufa
Direction: Paul Wegener and Carl Boese
Screenplay: Paul Wegener and Henrik Galeen
Cinematography: Karl Freund
Art direction: Hans Poelzig
Length: 6 reels/5,200 feet

Principal characters:

The Golem	Paul Wegener
Rabbi Loew	Albert Steinrück
Rabbi's daughter	Lyda Salmonova
Rudolph Hapsburg	Hans Strum
Assistant	Ernest Deutsch
Jester	Fritz Feld
The Knight	Lathar Menthel

The inspiration for a film based on the ancient Jewish cabalistic legend of the Golem enveloped actor-director Paul Wegener in 1913, while he was on location filming his first version of *The Student of Prague*. Wegener, regarded by most historians as the first significant German filmmaker to understand the medium fully, was an avid student of Germanic myths and legends, particularly those interpreted by the great writers of German Romanticism. While in Prague, the Prussian actor encountered and became fascinated with the popular Jewish myth of an avenging giant fashioned from clay by a sixteenth-century Talmadic scholar, the Rabbi Juda Low Ben Bezalel. This figure "without a soul" became a defender of the city's Hebrew community against the wrath of an emperor enraged by false charges of ceremonial murders of children by adherents of the Jewish faith.

Wegener, however, updated the story to the present in his 1915 treatment of the legend, *The Golem*. In his version, the clay figure is unearthed by modern workmen digging on the site of an old synagogue. They sell their "find" to a knowledgeable collector of archaeological curios who uses some of the old cabalistic scriptures to return it to life. Once breathing again, the Golem becomes a servant to the old man, who does not yet realize that the figure was originally created for more exalted purposes. According to the old scriptures, anything less than the noblest of motives will cause the creature's strength and power to become increasingly ungovernable. When the clay figure falls in love with the old man's daughter, who understandably rejects his attentions, the legend is borne out, and the Golem rampages through the city until he is finally killed in a fall from a tower.

Wegener's fascination with the creature, which he himself portrayed, did not wane with the film's completion, and he brought it back to life in 1917 for *Der Golem und die Tanzerin* (*The Golem and the Dancing Girl*). Between the first and second versions, however, another director, Otto Rippert, made a six-part serial, *Homunculus* (1916), with a theme that was markedly similar to that of Wegener's film.

Homunculus is a man created in a laboratory test tube who demonstrates great powers, particularly those of intellect; yet, he is driven by a feeling of rejection because of his unique origin to use these powers to become a dictator and to foment a world war. In the end, he is cut down by a thunderbolt. The most significant aspect of Rippert's film is that it strongly anticipates the expressionistic style of filmmaking that would become a German obsession following the debut of Robert Wiene's *The Cabinet of Dr. Caligari* in 1920. *Homunculus* made an interesting use of *chiaroscuro* lighting and exaggerated acting which effected a certain amount of external representation of each character's psychological states—both of which would become hallmarks of expressionism.

Expressionism took solid hold on German filmmakers in 1920 after Wiene's film, with its abstract sets and unusual costumes, created a stir in European critical circles (France, in fact, was even moved to lift its postwar ban on German films). To an art form which measured its accomplishment according to the extent to which it succeeded in a photographic reproduction of reality, *The Cabinet of Dr. Caligari* constituted a major upheaval with its obviously hand painted backgrounds and (power failure induced) subdued lighting. This distortion of settings was justified, however, in the early expressionist films as constituting an artistic manifestation of the filmmakers' concern with the duality of man's nature and of the role of fate in human life, not to mention a somewhat morbid fascination with assorted types of nonhuman creatures arising out of the German Romantic literary tradition.

Although the variety of abstractionist distortion embodied in the settings of *The Cabinet of Dr. Caligari* proved to be an artistic dead end, the more subtle aspects inspired by the literary tradition, with its emphasis on natural settings, came to dominate German films of the 1920's. It was this mode of expressionism that permeated Paul Wegener's third adaptation of the Golem legend in 1920.

This time, however, Wegener adhered more faithfully to the original Jewish legend, although he changed the story's emphasis somewhat to coincide with his own thematic concerns. Accordingly, he instructed a noted architect, Hans Poelzig, to reconstruct the ancient quarter of Prague on the lot of the Ufa studio in Germany. Poelzig had recently designed the Grosses Schauspielhaus for Wegener's theatrical mentor, Max Reinhardt, so he was highly qualified for the filmmaker's assignment. Poelzig constructed the Jewish quarter with the lights and camera in mind, incorporating psychological moods and tones into the architecture itself. This style was carried over into the interiors, particularly the womb-like vaulted room (the Rabbi's cabinet) where the Golem is constructed from clay. Other rooms reflect other moods ranging from the light and airy to some that are heavy and somber, as in the case of the emperor's throne room.

In a sense, then, the primary interest of *The Golem* lies in Poelzig's architectural constructions and in the manner in which they emphasize the film's thematic tones. In this way, the expressionistic motifs were conscientiously translated into the unique language of the film rather than being dropped in indiscriminately as in the manner of *The Cabinet of Dr. Caligari*. The settings of *The Golem* were thus natural in appearance and added to the film in a complementary way. One cannot ignore, however, the considerable contributions of Wegener himself. The actor-director, like Poelzig, had also obtained considerable experience with Reinhardt's theater and was equally familiar with the Expressionistic style. Yet, as many critics have noted, Wegener was a highly individualistic filmmaker and could not simply translate Reinhardt's technical ideas to the screen without putting his own stamp on them, making them forever unique to his concepts of cinema. Although *The Golem* was made in a studio, a situation that would normally invite the use of rigidly traditional theatrical lighting, Wegener creatively employed the same kind of environmentally variable lighting that he had used successfully in the natural settings of his early films such as *The Student of Prague*. Consequently, the moods and tones of *The Golem* range from a breezy radiance, illustrated by a scene of children playing at the entrance of the ghetto, to warmer hearth and torch illuminated interiors with their *chiaroscuro* lighting effects. The shifts in tones of lighting are subtly, almost effortlessly, managed in a manner that would seemingly support Wegener's later denials of making an intentionally expressionistic film if it were not for the sets designed by Poelzig under his direction. The resulting film is, intentionally or not, a prime example of the use of an underplayed mode of expressionism, and consequently, it provides a counterpoint to the less subtle manifestation of the genre in *The Cabinet of Dr. Caligari*.

As Siegfried Kracauer notes in *From Caligari to Hitler: A Psychological History of the German Film*, Wegener had a passion for drawing screen effects from fantastic themes. The legend of *The Golem*, like that of the earlier *The Student of Prague*, possesses a theme of mortal man experimenting with supernatural forces that he cannot fully control and which eventually destroy him. In the beginning, however, it is the Jews of Prague who are facing destruction and expulsion from their ghetto on the orders of the Hapsburg Emperor, who mistakenly believes them to be guilty of murdering innocent children as part of their religious rituals.

The Rabbi Loew (Albert Steinrück) is determined to prevent the expulsion of his people from the Prague ghetto by resurrecting the legendary Golem, a life-size figure of a man that he has constructed entirely of clay. In his laboratory, the Rabbi and his assistant (Ernest Deutsch) trace a magic circle of about twelve feet in diameter and then step into its center. Admonishing his helper not to leave the circle's confines, he then invokes Astaratt and other spirits of the dead and induces them to reveal the mystical word that will bring the figure to life. As he states the names, the ground around the circle splits and flames arise while lightning flashes in the distance. Ghosts and horrifying specters fill the air with some of them hovering close enough to snatch at the fluttering mantle worn by the Rabbi's terrified assistant, which finally bursts into flames and floats away.

Out of the mouth of a large demoniac head emerge the fragments of the ancient Hebrew word that will bring the Golem to life. The word is "Shem" which, when encased in a clay star that is, in turn, affixed to a socket in the Golem's breast, will result in bringing the monster to life. Additionally, the star, when twisted in certain ways, endows the creature with the attributes of indestructibility and power. The creature can only be rendered lifeless again by the removal of the star from his breast.

The Rabbi takes his resurrected Golem (Paul Wegener) to the palace, where he demands an audience with the emperor Rudolph Hapsburg (Hans Sturm). The Rabbi magically projects a scene of Moses leading the Jews out of Egypt as part of his argument to convince the Emperor not to initiate a pogrom. When the boorish members of the court, led by the jester (Fritz Feld, who later became a popular character actor in American films for more than fifty years), erupt in laughter, the Rabbi angrily orders the Golem to destroy the palace, which the brute effortlessly proceeds to do. The Emperor is terror-stricken and quickly accedes to the Rabbi's requests to cancel his campaign against the Jews of Prague. With his conditions granted, the Rabbi directs the Golem to prevent the palace roof from falling and to save the members of the court.

The declaration of expulsion is rescinded by the Emperor. While the Rabbi has been busy negotiating at court, however, his daughter (Lyda Salmonova) has been flirting with one of Ludwig's most foppish knights (Lathar Menthel). This does not sit well with the Rabbi or, in fact, with the Golem—who is taking on increasingly human characteristics. The creature desires to be more than a water carrier, woodchopper, and instrument of war. He wants to be loved. He too develops human feelings for the Rabbi's daughter. He is thus suddenly a liability to the Rabbi, particularly now that there are no lofty missions to accomplish; hence, he must be destroyed.

The Golem, having tasted life, does not want to return to mud. He rebels and embarks on a reign of terror to destroy the ghetto and get revenge upon the people who created him. In scenes presaging the climax of James Whales' *Frankenstein* (1931) more than a decade later, the Golem attempts to carry off the Rabbi's daughter and is pursued by villagers carrying torches. Yet in the end, it is a little girl who finally destroys him. Escaping from the ghetto, the creature pauses near a group of little girls who are playing outside. His presence scares the children and all run off except one—the smallest. The creature lifts the child gently, and she becomes innocently fascinated by the star. She pulls it off to look at it and the creature crumbles back into clay.

The Golem is a symbolic work that is sufficiently ambiguous to verge on being all things to all viewers. Essentially, the film contains a multiplicity of symbols without taking on imposing allegorical postures. Ideas are presented but they do not hinder the narration of the tale nor its exciting impact on the audience. Kevin Thomas, in a 1969 review of the film in the *Los Angeles Times*, illustrated various approaches to the film's allegorical structure. "On the most obvious level," he stated, "it is an inspirational tale, a projection of the dreams of an oppressed people." He concedes, however, that the very wizardry which makes Rabbi Loew a hero in the ghetto could be a justification to gentiles for their prejudice and repression revolving around the issue of mystical rites. Yet it is also possible to see the twisted distorted sets of the ghetto two ways. One, Thomas has noted, is as a symbol of necromancy, and the other is as a manifestation of an atmosphere of simple oppression.

Other critics, notably Kracauer in *From Caligari to Hitler*, view the overall theme as concerning the interaction of reason with brute force. The powers of intellect, embodied in the Rabbi, exercise control over their physical complement, the brute strength of the Golem. Yet, to accept this interpretation which has admittedly become the standard one, one must somewhat loosely define the powers of the mind to include mystical or occult characteristics. Pure reason or cognition has very little to do with conjuring an avenging monster or, for that matter, in controlling him once he has come to life. The Golem is earth. He does not ask for life. He, in fact, struggles against it and is only resurrected through a fiery invocation of supernatural powers. Once his mission is completed, he must commute his existence through no choice of his own. As long as he carries water or cuts the Rabbi's wood, he can exist as a subhuman slave embodying brute force. Yet, let him aspire to the dignity and characteristics of a human being and his existence must be terminated by the same magic that brought him into the world. At the end, however, the act of termination is effected by an Aryan girl in an ironic act that makes a martyr of the earthen being. He has saved the people of the ghetto from the persecution by the gentiles, but in the end, in a bizarre re-creation of the New Testament, the "son of the earth," like the Christian "Son of God," is driven by his own people into the hands of the gentile executioner.

Wegener displayed his greatest artistry as a director in maintaining a consistent production and walking a tightrope between the various levels of meaning. In retrospect, it is tempting to use it as a vehicle for various speculations concerning the nature of the Aryan mind and its evolution over the centuries as well as a consideration of the Christian epic. It is also a simple matter to note the distinct parallels between this film and the later *King Kong*

(1933, particularly in the scene where the enraged Golem carries the Rabbi's daughter to the top of a tower) and Whale's *Frankenstein*. Yet, monster or Messiah, *The Golem*, in the depth of its significance and richness of its symbolism, transcends other film versions based on the legend. Even its method of unfolding the story, without the commonly accepted directness and coherence of modern narrative forms, makes it seem completely a part of the age which it treats.

The film's power flows from a combination of expressive settings and exceptional acting, particularly on the part of Paul Wegener. The backgrounds and settings convey a realistic feeling of an unearthly time and place that could not be expressed in any other way. Poelzig's constructions are as much characters in the story as are any of the actors.

It is Wegener, though, who brings the Golem to life. As Boris Karloff later made Frankenstein's monster his own, Wegener places his own imprint on the clay Golem. The figure is primarily defined by Wegener's face, which was described by contemporaries as possessing "timeless tartar features." It conveys extremes of feeling ranging from naïve brute strength to raging anger to a frightful sincerity that has survived the ages. Although the other actors indulged in the inevitable pantomimic action characteristic of the period, Albert Steinrück and Lydia Salmonova also defined their characters clearly and created personages capable of supporting all of the allegorical levels of the narrative.

In the end, however, it is the collaboration of Wegener and Poelzig which translated the naturalistic settings and events of Prague into an expressionistic vehicle that transcends its time. Its subtle interaction of character and setting, more than that of *The Cabinet of Dr. Caligari*, has influenced a succession of films that reach to this day. Without *The Golem*, there would not have been a *Frankenstein* or other films of that genre. Yet, more importantly, modern films that attempt to express the interplay of the human soul and its surroundings would be sadly lacking without the developments of Wegener and Poelzig.

Stephen L. Hanson

THE GOOSE WOMAN

Released: 1925
Production: Universal
Direction: Clarence Brown
Screenplay: Melville Brown; based on the short story of the same name by Rex Beach
Cinematography: Milton Moore
Editing: Ray Curtiss
Art direction: E. E. Sheeley and William R. Schmidt
Length: 8 reels/7,500 feet

> *Principal characters:*
> Mary Holmes/Marie de Nardi .... Louise Dresser
> Gerald Holmes .... Jack Pickford
> Hazel Woods .... Constance Bennett
> Jacob Riggs .... Spottiswoode Aitken
> Reporter .... George Cooper
> Mr. Vogel .... Gustav von Seyffertitz
> Detective Lopez .... George Nichols
> Amos Ethridge .... Marc MacDermott

Rex Beach, one of the best popular-fiction writers during the first half of the twentieth century, wrote novels, short stories, a play, and an autobiography. Everything he wrote reveals a professionalism that is enviable, and his first novel, *The Spoilers* (1906), is still exciting and very readable; it has been adapted to the screen five times. It, and everything else he wrote, were natural choices for adaption to the screen, and nearly every year he published a new novel. He had more than thirty to his credit when he committed suicide in 1949, because he was suffering from cancer of the throat.

"The Goose Woman" was a short story he published in 1925, and it was immediately bought and made into a feature film that same year. It had its premise in fact, for there had been a murder in the early 1920's known as the Hall-Mills case, where the principal witness was a woman known as the "pig woman," because she kept pigs. Mary Holmes, the central character of *The Goose Woman*, keeps geese. She lives in a shack in the marshes of New Jersey, and no one knows who she was, or is, because she has no visitors and, seemingly, no friends. No one would want to know Mary Holmes, a filthy, dirty, slovenly drunkard, not fit even to tend geese. The only thing interesting about her is that an occasional passerby sometimes hears a phonograph being played in her hut, and although the records are worn and scratchy, the singer is obviously an operatic soprano of great talent.

The film begins on a dark, dank night. The headlights of a car cut through the river fog, as the car comes to a stop. There is the sound of gunfire, and then silence. Mary Holmes (Louise Dresser) has heard the shot, and opens the door of her wretched dwelling. All she can see is a taillight of a car disappearing into the fog. She is drinking and has nearly had her fill for the night. The geese had been aroused by the sound of the gunfire, but now there is only the usual silence of the night, broken only by crickets chirping and the occasional call of a night bird. There is a record being played on the phonograph, and it comes to an end. Mary closes the door, turns the record over, and sits down to listen.

The next day the murdered body is discovered, and Mary is besieged by reporters wanting to know if she had heard anything unusual the preceding night. At first she is noncommittal, but then she learns that the murdered man was Amos Ethridge, a millionaire who backed the local stock company. The papers are full of stories about the murder, and she takes a freakish delight in reading them. One of the reporters (George Cooper) suspects an unusual angle in her own personality, and he digs deep into the newspaper files, uncovering the fact that Mary Holmes was really a famous soprano named Marie de Nardi, who had been the toast of the operatic world.

He tells his editor about Mary's past, and the editor has a marvelous idea. They bring Mary to town, register her at a deluxe hotel, and start cleaning her. She is given the full treatment, and when she appears again, she is a lovely, middle-aged woman, wearing a tea-gown and pearls and with beautifully coiffured hair. She grants an audience to the press and makes the front pages. Mary revels in the stories they want, and she fabricates new ones of her glamorous past, how she lost her voice and sought seclusion.

What she does not realize is that the more she talks, the closer she weaves a net that implicates her own illegitimate son Gerald (Jack Pickford). The truth is that the birth of her son robbed her of her glorious voice, and she has sought anonymity because she wants no one to know the truth. She had raised her son with neither love nor affection, and on the night of the murder, Gerald had come early to see her, and she laughingly had told him of his illegitimacy.

The police detect tire tracks near the scene of the murder, and they match them to the tread of the tires on Gerald's car. Most damning of all, however, is that Gerald is in love with a girl, Hazel Woods (Constance Bennett), who is an actress in the local stock company. Amos Ethridge (Marc MacDermott) has already tried to seduce Hazel, as he has many other actresses in the company, but she has resisted him. Gerald has had bitter words with Ethridge and has warned him to keep away from Hazel.

With the stories she has invented, Mary has become the key witness in the case and is glorying in her publicity. While the police question Gerald, Hazel goes to Mary and tells her how the stories she has invented only implicate her own son, who is entirely innocent. Mary, in a burst of compassion for the boy she has nearly put on trial for his life, calls in the press and retracts her testimony. The real murderer, it develops, is the stage doorman, who confesses that he had shot Amos Ethridge to protect Hazel. Mary blesses her son and the girl he is to marry. She has had her hour in the headlines, and it has nearly brought havoc upon her head and those whom she really loves now.

The Goose Woman was the last film director Clarence Brown made for Universal, and its beautiful professionalism gave him the attention he needed for the final push. The next year he signed with M-G-M, where he began his career by directing *The Flesh and the Devil* (1927), and he stayed at the studio throughout the rest of his long and successful career as a director.

The Goose Woman was remade by RKO as *The Past of Mary Holmes* (1933), but it is not particularly notable; although it had Helen Mackellar and a young Jean Arthur in its cast, it did not have Brown or any other good director behind it.

Louise Dresser was one of the best actresses in the history of cinema. Her years as a singer on stage, and the fact that she was the wife of Paul Dresser (brother of novelist Theodore Dreiser) and an exceptional musician, led her to theatrical stardom. Pauline Frederick, one of her best friends, introduced her to the screen in *The Glory of Clementina* (1922), and from then on, Dresser's work was always outstanding. No one who saw her in *The Goose Woman* could forget her. She played Catherine the Great and co-starred with Rudolph Valentino in another Clarence Brown film, *The Eagle* (1925) and she was nominated the first year of the Academy Awards for her work in *A Ship Comes In* (1928). She made her talking-picture debut in *Mother Knows Best* (1928); she played as the Empress Elizabeth to Marlene Dietrich's Catherine the Great in *The Scarlet Empress* (1934); and she co-starred with Will Rogers in everything from *State Fair* (1933) to *David Harum* (1934). She died in 1965 at age eighty-six, but had retired much earlier, because of increasing deafness.

Jack Pickford was excellent as her son in this film, and Constance Bennett gave another good performance in a career that was only beginning in these last years of the silents. Pictures as good as *The Goose Woman* are rare, and credits for its excellence are to be divided between Rex Beach the writer, Clarence Brown the director, and Louise Dresser the actress.

DeWitt Bodeen

THE GRAND DUCHESS AND THE WAITER

Released: 1926
Production: Adolph Zukor and Jesse L. Lasky for Famous Players-Lasky; released by Paramount
Direction: Malcolm St. Clair
Screenplay: Pierre Collings; based on John Lynch's adaptation of *La Grand-duchesse et le garçon d'étage* by Alfred Savoir
Cinematography: Lee Garmes
Length: 7 reels/6,314 feet

Principal characters:
Albert Belfort .... Adolphe Menjou
The Grand Duchess Zenia .... Florence Vidor
The Grand Duke Peter .... André Beranger
The Grand Duke Paul .... Lawrence Grant
The Countess Prascovia Avaloff .... Dot Farley

In the mid-1920's, American filmgoers delighted in viewing a genre of comedy which depicted marital unrest with a lighthearted, continental flair. It is understandable that the post-World War I, "jazz-mad" generation would flock to films portraying love and marriage in a worldly manner. The genre might not have developed, however, had it not been for the initial success of Ernst Lubitsch's comedy of manners, *The Marriage Circle*, in 1924. On the heels of this witty tale, Famous Players-Lasky/Paramount and Warner Bros. generated a succession of films satirizing life among the wealthy, principally directed by Lubitsch, Malcolm St. Clair, Paul Bern, and Harry d'Abbadie d'Arrast.

The Grand Duchess and the Waiter, one of the finest examples of this genre, was selected as one of *The New York Times'* ten best films for 1926, and is possibly the best conceived project of St. Clair's prolific career. One of the few silent-film directors born in Los Angeles, St. Clair entered the industry as a bit player and gag writer for Mack Sennett in 1915, while still in his teens. He directed comedy shorts for a few years, followed by a brief fling with action pictures. Then came *Are Parents People?* in 1925; with this film, he proved he could direct society comedy. With the subsequent release of *The Grand Duchess and the Waiter* in February, 1926, he established himself as a leading director of sophisticated comedy films.

To characterize the genre, one need only examine the components of *The Grand Duchess and the Waiter*. A romance of society folk is unraveled through an enjoyable series of unorthodox adventures of the naughty-but-fun ilk. Adolphe Menjou plays a rich society playboy, and it is interesting to note that this Pittsburgh-born performer acts the debonair lead role in almost every major film of the genre, starting with *The Marriage Circle*. The story is set in Paris, a city so magical to American audiences that all disbelief is suspended whenever the events occur there. To intensify the excitement, this particular screenplay is based on a play actually written by a Frenchman and performed in Paris in 1924.

The Grand Duchess and the Waiter opens on "a June night in Paris—an ancient city with delightfully young ideas." A group of *bons vivants* at the ballet are awaiting the arrival of their friend Albert Belfort (Adolphe Menjou), who has been detained by "business affairs." The scene cuts to Albert kissing the hand of a woman with whom he definitely had not attended a business conference.

Inside the theater, the Grand Duchess Zenia (Florence Vidor) watches the ballet. She has "sought shelter in France from the storms of revolution in her native Russia." Her arms are strewn with jewels. Having joined his friends inside the theater, Albert spies Zenia through opera glasses, is smitten by her beauty, and sends her his card requesting an introduction. Had this film intended merely to tell a tale, she would simply have torn up the card, but *The Grand Duchess and the Waiter* is a stylized comedy of manners. In that tradition, the card is first handed to one of her male companions, then to her second male companion who is about to tear it up. Zenia then takes the card, reads it, and tears it up. She and her entourage leave the ballet without acknowledging Albert.

In the belief that their exile may be nearly over, the group returns to the Hotel St. Antoine. Albert follows and learns from the hotel manager Zenia's identity and the fact that she and her entourage are in the royal suite. "Her country is a republic now but she refuses to know it," says the manager. Albert engages the rooms directly below the royal suite. From this point in the film, the drama revolves on action within these suites and interaction of the two suites caused by a chandelier in Albert's room which sways whenever someone paces upstairs.

In the royal suite, a telegram arrives from Ivan of Odessa. "The revolution continues disastrously. We hold no hope for your return to power. Send money immediately. We are destitute." Zenia paces the floor, the chandelier in the room below sways, and Albert blows a kiss upward.

Albert telephones Zenia, but the Grand Duke Peter (Andŕe Beranger) speaks to him; then the Grand Duke Paul (Lawrence Grant) speaks to him; finally, her companion the Countess Prascovia Avaloff (Dot Farley) speaks to him, then they hang up the telephone. Standing up to the challenge, Albert telephones his valet Charles and orders his belongings moved to the Hotel St. Antoine. Arriving the next morning, Charles asks, "What brings us here, sir?" to which Albert responds, "Love, Charles, love! But it's *real* love this time, Charles."

The inhabitants of the royal suite are not as elated as Albert. The hotel bill for the suite which occupies the entire third floor is unpaid. The champagne

Peter consumes has skyrocketed to a sum of 4,453 francs, and Paul's cigars cost 259 francs. The bill totals 275,420.90 francs, and the royal family has no money. Peter explains that he tried to earn money by buying automobiles on credit and selling them cheaper for cash, but the police objected. Paul paces the room, and the chandelier sways in the room below. Albert, seated directly under the chandelier, looks up from his breakfast to throw a kiss. The hotel waiter says, "It's the Duchess," because he has the honor of waiting on her daily, a job Albert says he would relish.

That afternoon Albert dresses in the uniform of a hotel waiter to serve tea to the royal suite. Inside the suite, however, trouble is brewing. The hotel manager has come to collect the bill, and Zenia must sell Catherine the Great's necklace to meet expenses. Albert serves tea in a most conspicuous manner, and, when Zenia announces that "the tea is vile," Albert agrees. Albert is so clumsy that the royal family assures him that if he were in Russia he would be flogged. As Albert cleans the mess he has made of afternoon tea, Zenia smiles. Albert must ask Prascovia if he can continue to serve the Grand Duchess, and she says no. Zenia intervenes, however, saying, "We are touched by this man's expression of loyalty. We will give him another chance." At that moment, Albert almost drops the samovar and succeeds in breaking several plates.

Prascovia warns Zenia that it is a mistake to keep Albert in their service, that possibly he is in love with her. Laughing, Zenia replies, "Ridiculous, a waiter in love with a grand duchess!" Peter, too, laughs and then summons Albert to Zenia, at her request. Zenia pretends to be asleep, and Albert descends to one knee and kisses her foot. She jumps up and roars, "To the salt mines of Siberia!" Albert runs from the room and is stopped by Prascovia who asks him where he is going. "To Siberia for some salt," he says. Zenia calls him back for punishment: she will have him perform all her services personally.

Back in his rooms after a hard day as a waiter, he sleeps in his own bed, attended by Charles. In the morning, four waiters serve a luxurious breakfast to Albert who also wears a waiter's uniform. The manager pleads with Albert to give up the charade, fearing for the reputation of the hotel, but Albert assures him it will be only a few more days. He tips the waiters and goes to work.

Albert draws a bath for Peter but refuses to polish Paul's shoes. Then, he refuses to walk the dogs, explaining that he is the personal servant to the Grand Duchess. He is ordered to Zenia's bedroom, where she orders him to walk the dogs; so, Albert summons Charles to bring his car. From the back seat of his convertible, Albert "walks" the four Russian wolfhounds, a Pomeranian, and a poodle through the park. Seeing Zenia and Peter on horseback in the park, Albert quickly gets out of the car and begins to walk the dogs properly. She orders him to return to the hotel to wash the dogs, and when next seen, Albert is shampooing a poodle in Peter's wash basin.

If Albert is having difficulty winning the affection of Zenia, he certainly is not without female companionship in the royal suite. Maxine, Zenia's maid, flirts with Albert and chides him for not paying attention to her. Albert sews Zenia's clothing while the Grand Duchess bathes in the next room, and upon noticing that it is the royal lingerie which he is mending, he kisses the delicate garment. Zenia then summons Albert to the bathroom, but she must call him three times before he can believe that he is being summoned to so private a place. He enters with both eyes shut, then he opens his eyes to see that she is standing to the side of the tub, wearing a dressing gown. He must fish her book from the tub.

Shortly after his departure from the bathroom, Maxine dries his coat sleeve as Albert complains that such tasks will drive him mad. Maxine explains that "a servant is not supposed to be a real man." "I understand," Albert answers. "Sexless like the angels." Maxine flirts with Albert once more, but the scene is interrupted by the entrance of Zenia. She administers more punishment for Albert by ordering him to sleep on the mat in front of her bedroom door. Albert laughs as he leaves the room for this punishment appeals to him.

That night, Zenia discovers that her money has doubled. She summons Albert to his sleeping place, and he arrives wearing a silk dressing gown. "I thought you'd like it," he says, as he primps before bed. She turns to him just as he is blowing a kiss in her direction. She leads him to his mat, and, as she enters the bedroom, she tells him she is nervous and sleeps with a loaded revolver. "If by accident this door should open during the night, you would be greeted by six bullets—not one of which would miss its mark." She sends him for a drink while she returns to counting her money. Albert brings a bottle of champagne with two glasses. She asks why there are two glasses, and he tells her they cannot both drink from one glass. She smashes his glass and says she could not imagine drinking with a waiter. Then she questions him about the money. Albert admits giving it to her, and she accuses him of being a blackmailer, spy, or thief and threatens to telephone the police. He calls the police for her, but she fails to report him. They kiss passionately: "With me it was love at first sight." "And I've loved you ever since you spilled the cream over me. It was fate."

The Grand Dukes enter and are shocked to see a Grand Duchess kissing a waiter, and such a bad waiter at that. Zenia quickly explains she was not serious and sends Albert from the room, then begins to cry. Peter rushes into the room with a newspaper and shows them a photograph of Albert with a horse. The caption reads that he is a millionaire turfman named Albert Belfort.

The next morning, impassioned by the kiss, Albert buys back Catherine the Great's necklace and reports to the royal suite without his uniform. He spots the newspaper and an envelope addressed to Albert Belfort. A note reads, "Albert—I am leaving Paris to start life anew. Thank you for trying to help us all. Can you forgive me? Zenia Pavlovna."

In the room below, Charles watches the chandelier swaying, but it is only the rumble of Albert exiting. Albert searches France for Zenia. Months pass, and it is the day of the races. The royal Russians are running an inn in the countryside. Paul says he would not be scrambling eggs if she had married Albert, but Zenia insists they have found their level and must make the best of the situation. Peter waits tables and brings a glass of wine to Albert at his car. They recognize each other, and Albert enters the inn. Zenia races out the back door to the garden, and Albert follows. There, they embrace, while the rest of the royal entourage dances with joy for all their good fortune.

The film is not technically innovative but produced with care and a substantial budget. Relating a romance of fashionable people in a witty manner, it is a prime example of the society comedy film of the mid-1920's. The story is lighthearted, not surprising or instructive, but it is told with expert pacing and style.

Audrey E. Kupferberg

GRASS: A NATION'S BATTLE FOR LIFE

Released: 1925
Production: Ernest B. Schoedsack, Merian C. Cooper, and Marguerite Harrison; released by Famous Players-Lasky
Direction: Ernest B. Schoedsack, Merian C. Cooper, and Marguerite Harrison
Screenplay: documentary
Cinematography: Ernest B. Schoedsack and Merian C. Cooper
Length: 7 reels/3,800 feet

> *Principal personages:*
> Merian C. Cooper and Ernest B. Schoedsack, originators and photographers of the documentary
> Marguerite Harrison, principal financial backer
> Haidar Khan, chief of the Bakhtiari tribe
> Lufta, his son

Even today, nearly sixty years after its first release, *Grass: A Nation's Battle for Life* evokes wonder at the bravery, fortitude, and inventiveness of both its subject, thousands of migrating Persian tribespeople, and its filmmakers. The film was conceived and photographed by Ernest B. Schoedsack and Merian C. Cooper. After this documentary account of rather exciting events in an exotic setting, the two went on to do other films together, the most notable being *King Kong* (1933), a fictional presentation of exciting events and an exotic setting.

Grass is one of two major documentaries of the silent era; the other is Robert Flaherty's *Nanook of the North* (1922). Indeed, *Grass* was apparently to some degree inspired by *Nanook of the North*. In 1922, having heard of Flaherty's film but not having seen it, Schoedsack and Cooper decided to make a documentary with the same theme—man's struggle against nature. Unfortunately, they were unable to obtain sufficient financial backing to do any significant research or preliminary investigation on the subject. Essentially, however, they assembled what supplies and equipment they could afford and went looking for a nomadic Asian tribe, even though they had no precise or definite information about where they would find one. They also added another member to their party, Marguerite Harrison, an adventurous woman who had helped Cooper survive earlier when he had been a prisoner in Russia. She invested $5,000, nearly half of the money raised for the production, and was part of the expedition from start to finish, but she did none of the filming.

The party encountered numerous problems in finding a suitable tribe, but at last they reached the Bakhtiari in what is now western Iran. The tribe was soon to make its annual migration to its summer pasturing grounds in the highlands. Some fifty thousand people and half a million animals were involved. Schoedsack and Cooper, unfortunately, did not know exactly what the migration would include; so, they had to allocate their limited supply of film by guesswork, never knowing whether the next day or the next week would present them with a spectacular view or event for which they should have saved more film. As it turned out, they reportedly had only a few minutes of film left at the end of the trek, but they had thoroughly covered all the essential elements of the journey, or at least all that took place during daylight.

Because each day's journey usually began before daybreak, the two had to wait until there was enough light before they could begin filming. If one looks at the film a second time, one can see that some of the early material might have been left out if the filmmakers had been able to show more footage of some of the later events. One also recognizes, however, that the entire film was artfully edited to present a gradual progression from the interesting to the amazing—from a puppy carried in a cloth bag, near the beginning of the film, to a girl climbing a rocky mountain face while carrying a live calf on her back, near the end of the film.

The mere fact that this large group, including children and young animals, made such a long trek is impressive, but what makes the journey—and the film—truly amazing are the monumental obstacles that are overcome. The first of these is the Karun River. It is about one-half mile wide with a swift current, and there are no bridges or boats. When he first saw it, Cooper wrote in his diary that it "would have given any army commander heart failure." He had no idea how the tribe would get across it. He soon found out, and he recorded well with his camera the age-old method, in which goat skins are inflated and used to construct primitive rafts. On these rafts are transported the supplies, women, children, and young animals, while most of the men and the fully grown animals swim through the dangerous current. In this crossing at least two men and many animals were drowned in a whirlpool that Cooper and Schoedsack filmed. The animals were herded across by men who swam back and forth using pairs of inflated goat skins as water wings, creating an unforgettable sight.

After the six days and nights it takes for all the people and animals to cross the river, they are faced with a stretch of 150 miles of rugged mountainous terrain. After weeks of struggling through this, they reach a sheer rock wall that seemingly would stop anyone but the most experienced and well-equipped modern climber; however, the entire group scales it. The scenes presented are nearly unbelievable, but Cooper has written that because of darkness they were unable to film some even more astonishing scenes of people lifting the animals up the rock.

Beyond the rock cliff is snow, and to break a trail through the deep drifts, the men must remove their light footgear that would disintegrate in the snow and walk barefoot to pack it down for the others. Finally, the group makes it through the snow and over the mountain called Zardeh Kuh "with frozen, bleeding feet and pain-wracked bodies." Then they go down the other side to the grazing land, and a title informs us "They have reached the Promised Land . . . the land of GRASS." The film ends with shots of tents, of animals grazing, and of the chief of the tribe and his son.

Appended after the last shot is a shot of a document attesting to the fact that the three are the first foreigners to cross the pass and make the migration with the tribe. It is a forgivable moment of self-congratulation for the film-makers, since they not only made the difficult and dangerous journey, but they also occasionally had to take extra risks in order to get their cameras in the proper position.

Schoedsack and Cooper are also to be congratulated for their adherence to fact. They were working at a time when no standards of the documentary had been established and when hundreds of "newsreels" had been made in which events were simply re-created with actors and sets. Apparently, the two simply filmed the actions that they saw and put the results into a film. They have said that their only "instruction" to the people they were filming was to avoid looking at the camera. For this they may be forgiven the occasional excesses in the wording of the titles. For example, the puppy in the cloth sack is made to say, "Gosh, it's another day."

Once they reached the summer grazing lands, the filmmakers realized that they would have an even better film if they could film the return journey at the end of the season, but they were unable to raise the money to do so. At first, *Grass* was used as part of a lecture tour by Cooper, but then the studio, now known as Paramount, acquired the rights in January of 1925 and released the film theatrically. Today it remains an astonishing film, but it is seldom seen despite its quality and its reputation as one of the two early classic examples of the documentary.

Timothy W. Johnson

THE GREAT K AND A TRAIN ROBBERY

Released: 1926
Production: William Fox
Direction: Lewis Seiler
Screenplay: John Stone; based on the novel of the same name by Paul Leicester Ford
Cinematography: Dan Clark
Length: 5 reels/4,800 feet

Principal characters:

Tom Gordon	Tom Mix
Madge Cullen	Dorothy Dwan
Eugene Cullen	Will Walling
DeLuxe Harry	Harry Grippe
Burton	Carl Miller
Bandit leader	Edward Piel

In the entire history of the motion picture, there are no other Western stars who have had the lasting appeal of Tom Mix. He made his film debut in 1910, and by the early 1920's, he had no rival as a cowboy star. In 1927, it was claimed that Mix was Hollywood's highest salaried player, and his parties and life-style became legendary. He had no problems starring in vaudeville, and he made an easy transition to talkies. In the 1930's, Mix toured with his Wild Animal Circus. From 1933 through 1950, *The Tom Mix Ralston Straightshooters* was a popular radio series, exploiting Mix, despite the cowboy star's having nothing whatsoever to do with the program. Even in the 1950's, more than ten years after the cowboy's death, Tom Mix gloves were still a popular item in department stores.

Born in 1880 in Clearfield County, Pennsylvania, Mix had a colorful early life if the reports of his publicists and biographers are to be believed. He may have been one of Teddy Roosevelt's Rough Riders, and also may have served in the Spanish-American War and fought in Peking during the Boxer Rebellion. The truth is probably that he never did any of those things, however, except in the imagination of his press agent and his adoring fans. More certainly, Mix did serve time as a real-life cowboy and, at one time, was sheriff of Dewey, Oklahoma, which now boasts a museum in his honor.

Mix made his screen debut in a short entitled *Ranch Life in the Great Southwest*, produced by the pioneering Selig Polyscope Company, and released on August 9, 1910. Shortly thereafter, Mix was put under contract with the Selig forces and remained with them through 1917, starring in dozens of fairly mediocre Western subjects, which are thankfully often relieved by a rough-and-ready humor aimed at the star himself. The Selig films were popular—they had to have been for Mix to remain so long with the company—

but they did little to build a screen image for Mix, and certainly during this period, his importance was overshadowed by that of William S. Hart, whose screen *persona* had become very recognizable and pronounced.

In 1917, Mix joined the William Fox Company, and, at last, began to develop into a screen legend. The features boasted action-packed adventure, with touches of ingenious humor, and, in all of them, Mix was partnered by his horse, Tony. Many of the Selig cowboy films had been shot on location in Prescott, Arizona, and because of this experience, Mix preferred to shoot his Fox Westerns away from the confines of the studio, utilizing many of the National Parks of the Western United States.

Of his screen character, a 1927 writer noted,

> In no picture does Tom do the slightest thing to which the most exacting mother could object if copied by her own child. In no picture has he ever been known to take a drink; in no picture has he ever been seen to smoke; in no picture has he ever played a scene showing him gambling with cards or in any way taking unfair advantage of an adversary. In no Mix picture has he ever gained a monetary award. At no time has Mix even been pictured as a rich man in the final scenes. Usually his reward comes in the shape of a promotion to the foremanship of a ranch, a good job, or the hand of some nice girl.

Mix was starred in more than fifty Fox features, of which the most important are *Just Tony* (1922), *Sky High* (1922), *Dick Turpin* (1925), *The Rainbow Trail* (1925), *Riders of the Purple Sage* (1925), and *The Great K and A Train Robbery*. The last, apart from being a vastly entertaining film, is one of a handful of Tom Mix Westerns which has survived, and it has been preserved by the Museum of Modern Art.

In the film, Mix portrays a detective named Tom Gordon, who has been hired to investigate a series of robberies on the K and A Railroad. He boards the train disguised as a bandit, a disguise which does not totally fool Madge Cullen (Dorothy Dwan), the daughter of Eugene Cullen (Will Walling), the president of the railroad, who falls in love with Tom. Madge is loved by her father's secretary, Burton (Carl Miller), but it does not take Tom long to discover that Burton is one of the bandits, and it takes Tom even less time— in this surprisingly short feature—to round up the remainder of the bandits and win Madge's hand. Like so many of the Mix features, *The Great K and A Train Robbery* mixes a variety of elements: Western drama and a railroad mystery. It opens with a magnificent stunt in which Mix is discovered by the train robbers and slides down a rope from the top of a tall gorge right into Tony's saddle. It is as awe inspiring as Douglas Fairbanks' slide down the ship's sail in *The Black Pirate* and several times more daring.

The Great K and A Train Robbery was shot on location in Royal Gorge, Colorado, near the town of Glenwood Springs. As befitted his image, Mix arrived in fine style, in two special luxury Pullman coaches. While there, Mix staged a rodeo, including Roman chariot races and parachute jumps. He also staged a variety show with Dorothy Dwan, often his leading lady, although she is perhaps better known as Larry Semon's wife and leading lady.

It would be wrong to describe *The Great K and A Train Robbery* as a major production, for it most certainly was not. It was simply a typical Mix program picture, which was not even reviewed by *The New York Times*. Those reviewers, however, who did bother to catch it were more than enthusiastic. Sime Silverman, editor and founder of *Variety*, wrote in the October 27, 1926, edition of his paper,

> This picture is perfect as a western. . . . Tom Mix, always the great looking guy in a picture, has set a high mark for the "western boys" in this one. They will have to go a lot to approach it ˇn action; and, in fact, Tom will have to do the same to keep up with his record here. *The Great K and A Train Robbery* could safely be billed as the fastest-moving picture ever put on the screen.

Photoplay (December, 1926) commented,

> Tom Mix shoots, rides, lassos and loves in a breezier manner than ever before in this ripping Western. Of course Tony helps Tom do all these things—a Mix picture wouldn't be complete without Tony. The scenery alone in this picture is worth seeing. . . . There's a good evening's entertainment here.

Along with Mary Pickford and one or two others, Mix typified the film star living in high style. His Beverly Hills mansion was the scene of boisterous parties, many of which were perhaps a little rowdier than his screen image would suggest. He was probably the first cowboy star to dress exuberantly, adopting a style later to be copied by Will Rogers, and Mix was particularly proud of his silver saddle and his title "America's Champion Cowboy."

As sound came to films, Mix left Fox, moving over to FBO (Film Booking Office) for a series of talkies. He briefly retired from the screen in 1929, but returned to the film industry in 1932 to star for Universal. Mix's screen career ended in 1935 with the Mascot serial *The Miracle Rider*, but the cowboy continued to entertain his fans in person with his circus and rodeo. Mix was killed in an automobile accident near Florence, Arizona, on October 12, 1940.

Of Mix and his contribution to the cinema, film historian William K. Everson has written,

> If William S. Hart brought stature, poetry, and realism to the Western, Tom Mix unquestionably introduced showmanship, as well as the slick, polished format that was to serve Ken Maynard and Hoot Gibson in the Twenties and Gene Autry and Roy Rogers in the Thirties. His influence as such outlived that of Hart in the long run.

Lennox Sanderson, Jr.

THE GREAT MOMENT

Released: 1921
Production: Famous Players-Lasky; released by Paramount
Direction: Sam Wood
Screenplay: Monte M. Katterjohn; based on the novel of the same name by Elinor Glyn
Cinematography: Alfred Gilks
Length: 7 reels/6,372 feet

> *Principal characters:*
> Nadine Pelham/
> Nada Pelham, her mother .... Gloria Swanson
> Bayard Delaval .... Milton Sills
> Sir Edward Pelham .... Alec B. Francis
> Eustace .... F. R. Butler
> Howard Hopper .... Arthur Hull
> Sadi Bronson .... Julia Faye

After Gloria Swanson had played leads in six Cecil B. De Mille productions, it seemed only natural for Paramount to decide that she was ready for a career as one of their major stars. In order to provide Swanson with the proper vehicle, Paramount asked novelist Elinor Glyn, one of Swanson's greatest supporters, to write a story that would be the basis for the actress' starring debut with that studio. Glyn, whose novels had provided suitable material for many films, was very willing to accept the offer and was promised a handsome sum for the screenrights to her story. The story had to be sexy, it had to have at least one sequence that everybody would be talking about, and it also had to pass the censors. Glyn provided Paramount with exactly the story they wanted.

In the film, Nadine Pelham (Gloria Swanson), an English heiress, is visiting Nevada when she meets the hero, Bayard Delaval (Milton Sills), who is the chief engineer for the Great Gold Stamp Mining properties. Even after only a few days, they seem to sense that destiny means them to be together; his mind is filled with her beauty and charm, and she is about to forget that she is engaged to the rich young man her father has selected to be her husband. While they are out in the desert, Nadine drops a glove and bends down to pick it up. There is an ominous warning sound and then Nadine cries out in sudden pain as a rattlesnake bites her on the breast. Bayard turns to her quickly and rips the soft cloth away from her wound, then sucks the venom from the snakebite on her breast. She collapses in his arms, and he carries her to a nearby cabin, where he lays her down on a cot and takes care of the wound, pouring whiskey on it, forcing it to bleed, and sucking the last vestige of poison from the bite. Thus, film audiences were provided with the sequence that "everybody would be talking about" very early in the film.

While Nadine is in a state of delirium, she dreams about her mother, Nada (also played by Gloria Swanson), a gypsy who had died at her daughter's birth. She also thinks back on her education which was carefully supervised by her noble father Sir Edward Pelham (Alec B. Francis). Even though her mother was a gypsy, Nadine had only heard rumors about them. It almost seemed as if her father had wanted to stamp out any record or memory of Nadine's inheritance. Despite her father's efforts, however, Nadine had read about the Tartar gypsies and knew about how they lived, loved, and died. She also knew that she was one of them.

With daylight, Nadine regains consciousness. She has spent the night in a cabin in the company of a tall, handsome man who is concerned for her welfare, but when her father arrives at the cabin with her fiancé, Eustace (F. R. Butler), he feels that she has been compromised. Nadine now will have to forget the fine marriage which he had planned for her. The only solution to avoid further scandal will be marriage to Bayard, a man who is almost a stranger to her.

Bayard comes to her, smiling grimly, and says "I hope that this is not too unpleasant for you. We shall have to go through with it. Please see it sensibly." She somewhat reluctantly agrees, and so they are duly and solemnly married, after which they immediately part so that they will be able to be divorced. Such was the dilemma of *The Great Moment*. The audience is left to wonder whether fate will ever allow "The Great Moment" for Bayard to speak of his love for Nadine. The problem, as Glyn saw it, was that their backgrounds had kept them apart. The couple separate because of Nadine's reserve from years of restrained living, not allowing her gypsy heritage to surface, and Bayard's gallantry; he is too much of a gentleman to force the issue.

In a week, the divorce is granted by the Nevada courts, but Nadine still dreams that Bayard will come back into her life. When he does not, she plunges into a round of social gaiety and meeting new people. A wealthy pork packer, Howard Hopper (Arthur Hull), proposes and gives her a huge diamond ring, but her father commands that she return to her English home. Nadine obeys for the duration of the social season, and she is followed everywhere by Hopper. At the last ball of the season, Hopper tells her "Your former husband is here tonight."

Unable to get Nadine out of his system, Bayard meets her and takes her into his arms for a passionate kiss. Then he goes to get a special license so that they can be remarried at once. Alone, she is almost thwarted when Hopper, who has overheard the plan, tries to divert it, but Bayard returns and frustrates the fractious Hopper. Finally, Nadine and Bayard are now free and together.

This is the kind of story that Glyn had wanted, and she made it work. Swanson now became the reigning idol of the screen. Her leading man, Milton

Sills, was also firmly on the road to stardom in his own right after this film. Director Sam Wood, who had been an assistant once to De Mille, knew the kind of extravagance that creates a star, and, through his help, Swanson was quickly the top female box-office star at Paramount. There were nine other program features that Wood directed after *The Great Moment*, one of which was *Beyond the Rocks* (1922), in which Rudolph Valentino was Swanson's leading man. This also was a story concocted by Glyn and showed the lovers in several previous romantic periods of history.

Then Swanson broke free from Hollywood and traveled to New York to become the queen of Paramount's Astoria Studios on Long Island, while Pola Negri seemed to supplant her in Hollywood as the reigning star. Starting in 1924, Swanson began to prove that she was indeed the absolute top star at Paramount when she came under the directorship of Allan Dwan. With Dwan, she achieved even greater stardom with such box-office successes as *A Society Scandal* (1924), *Manhandled* (1924), and *The Coast of Folly* (1925). She then went to Paris and, according to her own admission in later years, nearly died after an abortion, but she emerged as the star of *Madame Sans-Gene* (1925). When this film opened in Hollywood at Grauman's Chinese Theater, Swanson received what was possibly the greatest outpouring of public affection and enthusiasm of any star to date. Later, in *Sadie Thompson* (1928), her acting abilities were recognized by the Motion Picture Academy with an Oscar nomination for best actress of the year.

Swanson has remained active to the present day and has made sporadic appearances on film and in television. She received her third Academy Award nomination as Best Actress for *Sunset Boulevard* (1950) after an absence of several years from the screen, in a role that parodied herself to a certain extent. She recently wrote a best-selling "tell-all" autobiography, *Swanson on Swanson*, and has appeared frequently to promote the book. There are certain stars whom adversity and bad luck cannot defeat, and Swanson has remained a star above all stars.

DeWitt Bodeen

THE GREAT TRAIN ROBBERY

Released: 1903
Production: Edison Manufacturing Company
Direction: Edwin S. Porter
Screenplay: no listing
Cinematography: no listing
Length: 1 reel/302 feet

> *Principal characters:*
> None named or credited, but G. M. (Bronco Billy) Anderson played several parts, and one source says that Marie Murray, George Barnes, and Frank Hanaway also appeared.

In order to understand the significance of Edwin S. Porter's *The Great Train Robbery*, one must appreciate the rudimentary state of filmmaking in the year in which it was made. It was 1903 and filmmaking was still less than a decade old. There were few, if any, theaters in existence that were designed or used solely for the exhibition of films, and motion pictures were usually seen in penny arcades or in vaudeville theaters along with the regular vaudeville acts. Some of the films then exhibited were less than one minute long and simply showed one simple scene in one shot, such as a part of a parade. Others were longer and often portrayed some sort of a story, but they usually did so as if each individual shot were a scene on a stage. Probably the most impressive of these were the films of the French showman George Méliès. In such films as *A Trip to the Moon* (1902), he presented fanciful stories and used cinematic tricks, such as double exposures and instantaneous disappearance or transformation of actors and objects. The editing of Méliès, however, was pedestrian. One scene followed another just as it would in a stage presentation.

The contribution of Porter in *The Great Train Robbery* was that he made the first influential narrative film in which the editing was imaginative and contributed to the development of the plot. Porter had not, however, gone into the film business with the idea of breaking artistic ground. His chief interest apparently was in machinery. He began his employment for the Edison Company in the mechanical department and then began photographing and directing films. Most of the films he made were unexceptional, but inspired by Méliès, he occasionally used trick photography. Then in 1903, he decided to imitate the storytelling of Méliès. In his first such effort, *The Life of an American Fireman* (1903), he combined several existing shots of firemen in action with a few new scenes to tell a simple story of a fireman dreaming of a woman and child in danger and then going to the fire and rescuing the two.

Then, later that year, Porter made *The Great Train Robbery*. It lasts less than twelve minutes and is made up of only fourteen shots, but its popularity and its influence were enormous. It begins in a railroad telegraph office. Two masked men enter and force the operator to signal an approaching train to stop and then give a false order to the engineer. The robbers then bind and gag the telegraph operator and sneak aboard the train as it stops to take water. Some of the bandits enter the express car, kill the man there and blow open the strongbox containing valuables. Others force the engineer to stop the train, and then they make the passengers leave the coaches and take from them all their valuables. The bandits then escape and ride off on their waiting horses. The film returns to the telegraph office where the operator is freed by his daughter who has come to bring him his dinner pail. The operator then goes to a dance hall and tells his story; the men form a posse and pursue and kill all the robbers.

The primary originality of *The Great Train Robbery* was in its editing and construction. Rather than following only one story thread in chronological order it presents two separate and (presumably) simultaneous actions in the last part: the actions of the robbers and the actions of the operator and the posse. Its cut from the robbers riding off on their horses back to the telegraph office was a startling innovation at the time. The film also gained much of its effect from its exciting story and outdoor shots, including one shot on a moving train. For extra excitement, a shot of one of the robbers firing directly at the audience was placed at the end of the film (although the Edison catalogue stated that the shot could also be used to open the film).

Many of the prints had hand-painted color added to some scenes, the most effective, perhaps, being the multicolored smoke resulting from the explosion of the strongbox in the express car.

In such a short film, there was almost no time for acting, the young girl playing the telegraph operator's daughter being the only player called upon to express emotion, but *The Great Train Robbery* did feature one actor who later became famous. His name was Max Aronson, but he did not achieve fame until he changed his name to G. M. Anderson and played the character of Bronco Billy in hundreds of short films between 1907 and 1914. He received a special Oscar in 1957.

Porter did not build on the success or the artistic techniques of *The Great Train Robbery*. He did make some social justice dramas, such as *The Kleptomaniac* (1905), and an intensely inventive film full of camera trickery in the manner of Méliès, *The Drama of a Rarebit Fiend* (1906), but by 1915, he was no longer making films. Instead, he had returned to his interest in machines and experimented with film techniques and equipment. It was not until the films of D. W. Griffith that film technique and film artistry were to take their next big step.

Seen today, *The Great Train Robbery* remains an interesting if unpolished short film, especially in the hand-tinted prints, that is well worth watching even for the viewer who is unaware of its importance in the history of cinema. For any viewer with a knowledge of its background, it is doubly fascinating. One can realize why the first audience that ever saw it demanded that it be immediately reshown.

Timothy W. Johnson

GREED

Released: 1925
Production: Erich Von Stroheim for Metro-Goldwyn-Mayer; released by Metro-Goldwyn Distributing Corporation
Direction: Erich Von Stroheim
Screenplay: Erich Von Stroheim and June Mathis; based on the novel *McTeague* by Frank Norris
Titles: Joseph W. Farnham (uncredited)
Cinematography: Ben F. Reynolds, William Daniels, and Ernest Schoedsack (uncredited)
Editing: Joseph W. Farnham, and Erich Von Stroheim (uncredited), Rex Ingram (uncredited), and June Mathis (uncredited)
Length: 10 reels/10,212 feet

Principal characters:
McTeague ("Mac") .... Gibson Gowland
Trina .... ZaSu Pitts
Marcus Schouler .... Jean Hersholt
Maria Macapa .... Dale Fuller
Mr. Sieppe .... Chester Conklin
Mrs. Sieppe .... Sylvia Ashton
McTeague's mother .... Tempe Piggot

Critical consideration of Erich Von Stroheim's *Greed* must invariably acknowledge two films, even though one no longer exists and was never exhibited to the public. The *Greed* known today is a concrete object—ten reels in length (approximately two and one-half hours), released by the Metro-Goldwyn Distributing Corporation in December, 1924, one of the great works of the American cinema. The other *Greed*, assembled in forty-two reels (approximately ten hours) by its creator, is a legend—perhaps the cinema's most intriguing. The tragic story of the film's production and subsequent mutilation is a staple of every history of film, and the reverence with which the "complete" or "uncut" *Greed* has been regarded traditionally has assumed unmistakably religious overtones. One chronicler has likened the uncut version of *Greed* to a "Holy Grail" of the cinema, its discovery in some unlikely corner of the globe is an archivist's dream, and the constant recounting of the film's torturous reduction from forty-two reels, to twenty-four to eighteen and finally to ten reels, has become a kind of film historians' litany. Any meaningful analysis of the film cannot ignore the legend and the circumstances of its birth.

To further compound the critical problem, *Greed*'s creator is himself one of the cinema's most legendary and controversial figures. The popular image of Von Stroheim is a curious amalgam of fact and fiction, and estimates of his importance as a filmmaker tend to fall along two basic lines of thought. The first, propagated largely by the director's more romantically inclined advocates (several of whom also happen to have been his personal friends), holds that he was one of the cinema's greatest artists, an embattled genius who waged a noble but futile war against the narrow-minded moguls of the American film industry, who butchered his films for commercial motives. Those on the opposite side of the argument, while often conceding his artistry, regard Von Stroheim as impossibly intransigent in his dealings with his employers, and extravagantly wasteful in his obsessive pursuit of the minutest details. As one of his greatest enemies, Louis B. Mayer, remarked years after their conflict, he "was the greatest director in the world. . . . But he was impossible, a crazy artist. If he had only been ten percent less himself and ten percent more reasonable, we would still be making pictures together." Neither view is completely acceptable, but neither is without some truth. Most unfortunate, however, is the fact that the Von Stroheim legend has tended to overwhelm the films themselves, which are often cited in film histories but seldom revived. This is particularly ironic, for when fact is separated from fiction (as nearly as possible at this date), Von Stroheim's films are his best defense. Even though seven of his nine features were released in versions severely altered from his own, Von Stroheim's artistry shines through. Although the circumstances of his life may thus be placed in something resembling their proper perspective, they should not—and cannot—be disregarded. Von Stroheim's life and his art are inseparable.

According to his most reliable biographer, Von Stroheim was born in Vienna in 1885 and emigrated to the United States in 1909. He began his film career in 1914, as an extra in D. W. Griffith's *The Birth of a Nation* (1915), later serving as an assistant to Griffith (on *Intolerance*, 1916 and *Hearts of the World*, 1918) and other directors at the Triangle-Fine Arts studio. He gained his first notoriety as an actor during World War I, when his vivid portrayals of the stereotypical German "Hun" in war films earned him the press-agent's label "the man you love to hate," which was to dog him for the rest of his life. His ambition, however, was to be a director, and in 1919 he persuaded Carl Laemmle, founder and head of Universal, to give him a chance to make a film based on his own original story, "The Pinnacle." Its title was changed to the more commercial *Blind Husbands*, and the film became a critical and box-office success, as was *The Devil's Passkey* (1920), his second effort. Laemmle, gratified by the success of his "discovery," made plans for Von Stroheim to direct Universal's most lavish production to date. Inspired by a trip Laemmle had taken to Reno, Nevada—with the setting changed to Monte Carlo at Von Stroheim's suggestion—the film was to be called *Foolish Wives*. In addition to writing the scenario and directing, Von Stroheim was also to play the leading role, as he had done in *Blind Husbands*.

The seeds of the *Greed* tragedy were sown during the production of *Foolish*

Wives (1922). Laemmle, although committed to an expensive undertaking, unwittingly got in over his head. He authorized the building of several elaborate sets on the Universal lot—including a full-scale replica of the central plaza of Monte Carlo—and generally acquiesced to Von Stroheim's wishes, including his insistence on numerous excursions to various locations along the California coast. The shooting of *Foolish Wives* consumed nearly a year, not only because of the scale and complexity of the film, but also because of Von Stroheim's extraordinary attention to detail, and his willingness to expend as much time, money, and film as necessary to obtain the precise effects he wanted.

Laemmle, although he extracted full publicity value out of the situation (exaggerating both the film's cost and its director's "extravagance" for maximum effect), became more and more nervous as expenses mounted. His concern brought him increasingly under the influence of his young production executive, Irving Thalberg. Thalberg, who despite his tender age (he was only twenty-one when production began on *Foolish Wives*) was in charge of Universal's day-to-day operations and regarded Von Stroheim's perfectionist methods as wasteful. During the latter stages of shooting, the two clashed frequently, and it was Thalberg who ultimately terminated the production, although not until most of the shooting had been completed. More difficulties lay ahead, however; Von Stroheim's first cut of the film was approximately seven hours long, which was unacceptable to Laemmle and Thalberg. At their insistence, he was able to reduce it to about five hours; still dissatisfied, Thalberg authorized further cutting despite Von Stroheim's objections. *Foolish Wives* had its premiere in New York in January, 1922, at a length of fourteen reels (about three and one-half hours); the critical notices were excellent, but cries for censorship arose from various quarters in reaction to the film's preponderance of unsavory elements. (The main characters were high-class swindlers who reveled in sundry decadent and perverse activities.) For its national release, *Foolish Wives* was cut to ten reels, and additional trimming by state and local authorities—for the film had become quite notorious—ultimately resulted in versions of seven or eight reels, the length of most surviving prints.

Estranged from Laemmle and at odds with Thalberg over the handling of *Foolish Wives*—which even at the relatively generous length of fourteen reels he referred to as "the skeleton of my dead child"—Von Stroheim nevertheless undertook another large-budget film for Universal, *Merry-Go-Round* (1923). During the first weeks of shooting, rumors of the director's megalomania and his increasing obsession with minor details began to circulate, each more outrageous than the last. The wary Thalberg kept a close eye on the situation, and after five weeks of production, he fired Von Stroheim, replacing him with Rupert Julian, who finished the film. Although this action severed Von Stroheim's association with Universal, he was hardly an outcast, for the artistic and financial success of his first three films had made him one of the most talked-about and sought-after directors in Hollywood. He soon signed a contract with the Goldwyn Company, and it was announced that his first production would be an adaptation of Frank Norris's classic naturalist novel *McTeague*, published in 1899.

Von Stroheim had long dreamed of adapting *McTeague* to the screen. Most historians claim that he first encountered the novel during his days as a Griffith extra, although Von Stroheim himself once related a colorful story of his discovery of the book in a seedy New York hotel in 1913, the year before he came to California. On the basis of surviving stills, it has also been suggested that a long-forgotten 1915 film version of the book, called *Life's Whirlpool*, may have had some influence. Whatever the circumstances, *McTeague* had, by 1922, become an obsession with Von Stroheim. He envisioned something far beyond a standard novel-to-film adaptation—he was determined to bring the book to the screen in its entirety, omitting no detail, and to film the story in the actual California locations described by Norris.

The extraordinary circumstances of *Greed's* production have been well documented, and a brief summary will suffice. Von Stroheim achieved his goal of filming in authentic locations, even to the extent of taking his cast and crew into the forbidding wasteland of Death Valley for the re-creation of Norris's brutal and graphic climax. The shooting consumed approximately 200,000 feet of film and nine months, and the editing took even longer. During the latter period, Von Stroheim's problems in assembling the film were exacerbated by corporate forces that were beyond his control. He had joined the Goldwyn Company (with which Samuel Goldwyn himself was no longer associated) at a time when negotiations were under way for a merger with Metro Pictures Corporation. They were not yet completed when Von Stroheim assembled his first version of *Greed*, at a length of forty-five reels; this he reduced to forty-two reels, running approximately ten hours, which he showed to a small audience of friends and associates at the studio in January, 1924. This was the film that has entered the annals of legend as the "complete, uncut" *Greed*.

Von Stroheim was at work on a version that would ultimately comprise twenty-four reels (whether on his own initiative or at the behest of the Goldwyn executives is not clear) when the Metro-Goldwyn merger was finalized in April, 1924. The merger radically altered the situation under which Von Stroheim was working. In place of the relatively liberal Goldwyn management, which had approved and financed the project, he now found himself confronted with Louis B. Mayer, whose independent company had also been included in the merger, and who was named Metro-Goldwyn's head of production. Mayer, whose name would soon be added to the corporate banner, had also recently acquired a new assistant—Irving Thalberg, lured away from Universal by a salary increase and the promise of increased power.

Mayer and Thalberg inherited *Greed* in twenty-four reels, and they were not pleased. Mayer's reaction was largely personal: he disliked Von Stroheim and felt that the film itself was a vile insult to everything he believed in. Both men, however, felt that it was a potential box-office disaster, lacking as it did both major stars and "entertainment" values. They scoffed at Von Stroheim's suggestion that the film be released in two parts, demanding instead that he cut it to ten reels. Unable personally to comply, Von Stroheim secretly shipped a print to his friend, director Rex Ingram, in New York. Ingram, one of the few who had seen the longer version, managed to reduce the film to eighteen reels, but Mayer and Thalberg were unshakable.

The film was finally taken away from Von Stroheim and cut to the prescribed ten reels by Joseph W. Farnham, a studio editor. Farnham probably worked under the supervision of the studio's scenario chief, June Mathis, who had been at least marginally involved with the *Greed* project since its inception and who ultimately received co-writing credit. This was the form in which *Greed* was given its premiere in December, 1924, and the form in which it has survived. The remainder of the original negative was probably burned to extract its silver content, although rumors of the existence of a complete print continue to surface to this day. Although his filmmaking career was not ended, nor his creative spirit completely broken, Von Stroheim was understandably embittered by this experience. "I consider that I have made only one real picture in my life and nobody ever saw that," he once said. "The poor, mangled, mutilated remains were shown as *Greed*."

The released version of *Greed* begins with a brief "prologue," set in Placer County, California, in 1908, in which McTeague "Mac" (Gibson Gowland) is introduced. A worker in the Big Dipper Gold Mine, McTeague is a large, simple-minded fellow whose temperament encompasses both compassion and brutality. His mother (Tempe Piggot), hoping for a better life for her son, arranges for his apprenticeship to a traveling dentist.

The story proper begins in San Francisco years later, McTeague having established a dental practice on Polk Street. Mac's best friend is Marcus Schouler (Jean Hersholt), who one day brings his cousin and sweetheart, Trina Sieppe (ZaSu Pitts), to the office for some dental work. While waiting, Trina buys a lottery ticket from the scrubwoman Maria Macapa (Dale Fuller). Over the course of Trina's several visits, McTeague falls in love with her. Because of his great affection for McTeague, Marcus agrees to "give her up," so McTeague proceeds with a courtship. Trina, although at first fearful of McTeague, finally accepts his proposal, and their engagement is celebrated by a theater party, attended by Trina's entire family.

Returning to Mac's quarters after the show, the group discovers that Trina has won five thousand dollars on her lottery ticket. This situation awakens a covetous resentment within Marcus, who feels that the money could have been his. Mac and Trina are married, but the wedding night is a traumatic experience for Trina. Always thrifty, Trina gradually becomes miserly. She refuses to touch her five thousand dollars, and the couple lives frugally, Trina even lying to McTeague in order to ferret away as much money as possible. Marcus's resentment continues to build, and his friendship with Mac is broken off after a saloon argument during which he throws a knife at McTeague, narrowly missing. McTeague becomes more and more irritated with Trina's stinginess, but his anger is kept in check by her carefully applied affection.

One day, Marcus drops around to announce that he is going away—to go into cattle ranching—and never coming back. Mac and Trina are happy to see him go, but they soon receive a letter representing his farewell gesture— a notice to Mac from the Board of Dental Examiners to cease practicing dentistry because of his lack of proper credentials. Faced with this disaster, Trina still refuses to part with her money, and the two are forced to sell their property and move into cheaper lodgings. McTeague, unable to hold a job, begins drinking heavily, and his baser instincts come to the fore. He starts abusing Trina, even biting her fingers to force her to give him money. He finally deserts her, and she takes up employment as a scrubwoman in a kindergarten—still hoarding her lottery winnings, to which she has by this time developed a pathological attachment. McTeague finds her, but she refuses to have anything to do with him. One night, as she is working alone, he enters the school, murders her, and steals her money. Wanted for the murder, McTeague flees the city.

Meanwhile, Marcus, at a remote outpost in the desert, sees the wanted poster. Still hoping to recover the lottery winnings for himself, he offers his services to the sheriff's posse. They pursue McTeague to the edge of Death Valley. The sheriff refuses to lead the posse into the valley, but Marcus goes on alone. After a long and grueling pursuit in the extreme heat of the valley, Marcus finds McTeague. They realize they are doomed, because they have no water, but they nevertheless engage in one last struggle over the money. McTeague kills Marcus, but as his last act, Marcus succeeds in handcuffing McTeague's wrist to his own. Manacled to the corpse, McTeague sits to await his own death.

This summary synopsizes *Greed* as it is known, but in fairness to its creator, the film must be evaluated as nearly as possible as a reflection of its larger, lost version. Somewhat paradoxically, but fortunately for such a critical purpose, the "complete" *Greed* is not entirely inaccessible. In fact, for a film that existed for only a brief time, completely out of public view, the uncut *Greed* is remarkably well preserved. The separate publication of Von Stroheim's original script (annotated to indicate cut scenes), and of a book composed of hundreds of stills representing much of the lost material, make possible a sort of ersatz "reconstruction" of the vanished film. Given Von Stroheim's professed fidelity to both the letter and the spirit of *McTeague*, comparison with the Norris book can also prove illuminating. Such a comparison can also help to dispel the misconception, perpetuated by the more common film histories, that Von Stroheim "simply" filmed the book, page by page, scene by scene. This is an unfair simplification, for Von Stroheim's was a true adaptation, retaining the novel's themes and narrative incidents, but also adding original material, and always recognizing the stylistic differences between fiction and film.

The published resources make possible an exhaustive catalog of the various scenes which did not survive the editing, but such a list is beyond the scope of this essay. Von Stroheim's major addition to the raw material of the novel was a lengthy "prologue" (of which only a few minutes remain), dealing primarily with McTeague's parents—in particular his alcoholic father, the source of the "foul stream of hereditary evil" which ultimately helps to bring about McTeague's downfall—and on his period of apprenticeship to the itinerant dentist. Most of the remainder of the film was derived directly from *McTeague*. The excised material consists of three basic types: subplots involving characters other than McTeague himself, various details of Mac and Trina's evolving relationship, and most of the film's more fantastic or symbolic elements.

The major subplots eliminated included two parallel love stories, each intended to reflect and comment upon certain aspects of the Mac-Trina relationship. The more important of the two involved Maria Macapa and a junkman named Zerkow (Cesare Gravina), whose perverse relationship is based on an unadulterated lust for impossible wealth. The insane Maria tantalizes Zerkow with tales of the golden table service that her family allegedly once possessed. Driven mad by his lust, he ultimately murders her when she cannot produce the treasure, then commits suicide by throwing himself into San Francisco Bay. The other love story took place between Old Grannis (Frank Hayes) and Miss Baker (Fannie Midgley), an elderly couple who live in McTeague's boarding house, and who carry on a chaste romance that was meant to provide an idealistic counterpoint to the sordidness of the other relationships.

Of these four characters, only Maria survives to any extent in the ten-reel film and only to serve her function in the main narrative, the sale of the fateful lottery ticket to Trina. Old Grannis (who also owns the dog hospital where Marcus works, although this is not mentioned) serves as best man at McTeague's wedding, but is not identified; Miss Baker is glimpsed briefly in several scenes; and Zerkow, since he existed only in relation to Maria, was removed without a trace. The loss of the Maria-Zerkow story is especially unfortunate, for it was designed both to recall the life of McTeague's parents and to presage the depths to which McTeague and Trina would eventually sink.

One salient point lost in the editing was the fact that Mac and Trina, after the loss of the dental practice, move into the hovel once occupied by Maria and Zerkow. Judging by surviving stills, this story was also the source of several visually fascinating scenes; particularly intriguing was a sequence in which Zerkow dreams of unearthing Maria's golden treasure in a surreal graveyard. In addition to the love stories, one other sequence accounts for a great deal of lost footage: all the scenes of the Sieppe family, including the relationship between Trina and Marcus, which took place before the meeting of Mac and Trina.

It is problematic whether or not, as some have suggested, the elimination of these subplots may have prevented the film from sinking under its own weight. The effect of the second major group of cuts, however, involving many of the details of the McTeague-Trina relationship, is somewhat easier to gauge. As the film stands, the characters' transformation seems excessively precipitous. The high points of the dissolution of their marriage are rather neatly covered, but the ultimate effect, while undeniably powerful, is too one-dimensional to be truly involving. Von Stroheim's careful attention to motivation and behavioral detail—not to mention the finer nuances of Gibson Gowland's and ZaSu Pitts's excellent performances—has largely been sacrificed in the interests of keeping the narrative in high gear (or perhaps, given the "distasteful" nature of some of the excised material, to avoid dwelling unnecessarily on the unpleasant or the grotesque). Related to this problem is the loss of an extensive sequence covering McTeague's wanderings around San Francisco and Placer County, between the murder of Trina and his arrival at Death Valley—resulting in one of the film's most bothersome continuity gaps.

The third major type of excision involved the film's more bizarre or fantastic elements. Much of the overtly symbolic material—such as inserts of skeletal hands fondling gold coins and objects (a few of which remain), and the visual motif of the giant gilded tooth that is Mac's prized possession—was removed, as well as several more extended scenes. Chief among the latter were Zerkow's nightmare of unearthing Maria's family treasure, and Trina's hallucinations of the smiling corpse of Maria, entreating her to buy a lottery ticket. Also lost today is the hand-coloring which was originally applied to all gold-colored objects in the film. The almost-total loss of these elements has contributed to the film's somewhat inappropriate reputation as a masterpiece of "realism." Von Stroheim, however, was not striving for realism *per se*, but for a cinematic equivalent of the literary "naturalism" of novelists such as Norris and Émile Zola. This fact also tends to be obscured by the "actuality" of the film's physical locations.

Although most of the film's symbolism was eliminated in the editing, one major visual motif remains, that of linking the major characters with various animals, which once again reveals Von Stroheim's alliance to the Griffith tradition. McTeague's character is established by his kindness to a crippled bird—he picks it up and kisses it—and his brutal treatment of a fellow worker who knocks the bird to the ground. His wedding gift to Trina is a pair of lovebirds, and they are depicted cooing, or quarreling, in direct reflection of Mac and Trina; they are also threatened at several points by a cat—the symbolic representation of Marcus Schouler. When Mac leaves Trina, he takes the birds along, and during his final flight into Death Valley, keeps the remaining bird in its cage strapped to his mule. (One of the lovebirds dies after Mac's murder of Trina, although this was eliminated from the released version.) McTeague's last act of the film is an echo of his first—he takes the bird from its cage, kisses it, and releases it, only to see it fall dead on his empty canteen. Perhaps this obvious symbolism suffers somewhat from the focus brought to bear on it by the exclusion of most of the similar elements, but it nevertheless tends to date the film for modern audiences.

The annotation of the published script indicates that much of the cutting involved the elimination of entire sequences, rather than a great deal of careful trimming within scenes, and the composition of new titles to bridge the resulting gaps in continuity. One fortunate side effect of this cosmeticized butchery is that many of the individual scenes remain substantially as Von Stroheim conceived and edited them. Any attempt to "reconstruct" the complete *Greed*, therefore, can be solidly grounded in a stylistic analysis of the extant film.

Greed is a full-blooded example of Von Stroheim's remarkable control of the film language. While not an innovator in the same sense as Griffith, Von Stroheim stretches the conventions of the silent cinema to their limits. Usually beginning a scene with a "master shot," he frequently abandons it to engage in a counterpoint of close-ups which expressively illustrate the psychological struggles of his protagonists. His use of emotion-signifying close-ups—of hands, feet, clenching fists, mouths, eyes, and other parts—marks him as a disciple of Griffith. It also, however, anticipates a later stylistic use of the close-up which is more forceful and less simply illustrative. Several of the film's most effective moments are abrupt cuts to extreme close-ups, unusual in the silent American cinema, and Von Stroheim occasionally uses the device of McTeague leaning or advancing toward the camera, sometimes even going out of focus as he looms up threateningly in the frame.

When Von Stroheim employs a medium or long shot, his use of backgrounds or background action is equally expressive. Examples are numerous: the passersby glimpsed through the windows near the corner table, as Marcus relinquishes his claim to Trina; Mac and Trina sitting on the sewer cover, the very unpicturesque San Francisco Bay in the background as he plays "Nearer My God To Thee" on his concertina; the rushing, Freudian locomotives during his aggressive proposal to Trina; the trackless wastes of Death Valley, which provide a silent and foreboding backdrop to the mortal struggle of McTeague and Marcus; and perhaps the film's most celebrated shot, as the camera assumes a high angle during the wedding to show, through the window, a funeral procession on the street below, as the wedding continues in the foreground. Von Stroheim insisted that the focus be maintained for both foreground and background wherever possible, and the results clearly anticipate the deep-focus techniques exemplified by the later work of cinematographer Gregg Toland and director Orson Welles. The photographic quality of the film seems all the more remarkable when one considers the extensive and virtually unprecedented use of natural interiors, rather than studio sets.

Von Stroheim's understanding of camera placement is nowhere more evident than in the scenes between Trina and McTeague, where the compositions are devoted to visually defining the shifting dominance in their relationship. From their first scene together, throughout the early stages of the film, the force of McTeague's desires overwhelms the shy and gentle Trina. As she sits in Mac's dental chair, he leans over her, and the camera alternately represents the point of view of each: looking up at McTeague, down at Trina. Reinforced by the camera, McTeague's initial dominance culminates with the wedding night sequence. In this sequence, following a scene between Trina and her mother on the staircase (where a high-angle shot presents Trina in the most visually subordinate position thus far in the film), the camera takes her point of view during the couple's preparation for bed. Terrified at the pending consummation of their marriage, Trina looks frantically around the room— at Mac, at the bed, at the lovebirds (the wedding gift from Mac) trapped in their cage as surely as she feels herself trapped with McTeague. The sequence ends with one of the most expressive camera movements in the silent cinema: as Trina, resigned to her fate, sits on the bed, the camera tracks backward, out of the room; Mac comes forward to draw the curtains closed, ending the scene and beginning the marriage on a somber note indeed. This shot is particularly notable because of the camera's deliberate, nonnatural movement—it is not moving unobtrusively, to follow or contain action, but independently, to make a purely visual statement.

As the marriage progresses, and Trina's hoarding becomes more and more obsessive, her psychological manipulation of the slow-witted McTeague gradually makes her the dominant force in the relationship, and the camera is used to reflect this change. For example, as a title states that Trina's "outbursts of affection" serve to ameliorate Mac's growing discontent, she is seen sitting on his lap, sweet-talking him; the effect is similar to that of the earlier dental-chair scenes, with the roles reversed. This visual reversal continues through the loss of Mac's dental practice and reaches an opposite extreme with another staircase scene. Trina, having browbeat Mac into going out immediately to look for another job to replace the one from which he has just been fired, looks down at him from the top of the stairs and refuses him a nickel for carfare. This scene (which echoes the earlier moment between Trina and her mother and is strikingly similar to a shot in Welles' *Citizen Kane*, 1941) marks the furthest degree to which Trina is to oppress Mac. Immediately afterward, he takes refuge from a sudden downpour in a saloon, where he gets drunk for the first time. The whiskey unleashes his baser instincts, and he begins a pattern of abuse that makes him once again the dominant figure, but this time with a new, sadistic edge. When Trina refuses him money, he bites the ends of her fingers, and when she pleads "Don't you love me?" he pushes her violently away.

It is significant that Von Stroheim, having established this visual pattern—the actual effect of which is far more subtle than a printed description makes it sound—abandons it during the murder scene, Mac and Trina's final moments "together." Most of the scene is visually intense—tight close-ups, stark lighting—but for the murder itself the camera abruptly shifts to a neutral point of view, carefully framing a lighted doorway over which Christmas bunting is decoratively strung. Immobile, it watches as McTeague pursues Trina through the door into the hallway, then bursts through yet another door into a room beyond, where a struggle ensues; they emerge once again into the hallway, grappling for a time, then disappearing off to the left. It is during this time that the actual murder takes place, with the camera merely waiting until McTeague reappears. In contrast to the charged, dynamic nature of the earlier part of the scene, the camera's sudden placidity is horrifying. It is also, however, compassionate; Von Stroheim realizes the inappropriateness of taking sides visually in this final conflict, for both parties are to be pitied. His sudden distancing of the viewer is an invitation to reflect on the forces that have conspired to bring the characters to the depths they have reached. His manipulation of the depth of the shot via the use of three distinct planes of action, and of offscreen space, attest to a mastery of the medium that was certainly ahead of its time.

"Poor, mangled, mutilated" as the existing *Greed* may be, it is nevertheless a masterpiece, albeit a fragmentary one. Nearly sixty years after its release, its power is largely undiminished, not only because of Von Stroheim's direction but also because of the excellent performances by Gowland, Pitts, and Hersholt. Occasionally mannered, and certainly robbed of much of their depth by the editing, the three characters are remarkably well controlled by silent-film standards. Regarding the editing, Von Stroheim once declared that the man who prepared the final version had "on his mind . . . nothing but his hat"; the evidence, however inconclusive, belies this harsh judgment. Given his charge to deliver a film of acceptable length to Mayer and Thalberg, Farnham was really exercising his only option by shaping the film as he did. Although he admittedly was working with superior material, it is only fair to acknowledge that the final result is a compelling and reasonably coherent film. The rewritten titles (probably also by Farnham) reduced the loose ends to a minimum, and in fact the editing may have even heightened the film's impact by focusing so intently on the McTeague-Trina relationship and its dissolution.

Yet, when all is said and done, the nagging question remains: what was the "complete" *Greed* actually like? Some critics have declared it, on faith, the greatest of all films, but this is hardly an objective response to the evidence at hand. Unfortunately, this evidence is—like the extant film—fragmentary and inconclusive. In addition, as noted at the beginning of this piece, "objectivity" is itself highly problematic in this context—usually falling victim to one's attitudes toward Von Stroheim and toward the conflict between creativity and commerce. Only one eyewitness account of the January 24, 1924, screening of the forty-two reel version is available, that of Idwal Jones, a friend of Von Stroheim and the drama critic for the San Francisco *Daily News*. The small audience, according to Jones, was appreciative, and he himself thought highly of the film, although he expressed some misgivings about its length. The reaction of the studio executives is unrecorded. It seems a distinct possibility, however, that the uncut version, venerated by film historians, was a "rough cut," perhaps never seriously considered for exhibition by Von Stroheim. He himself once wrote that he had

set out with the idea of making the film in two parts, ten or 12 reels each. . . . When I was through making the film as written and passed by Goldwyn, I found myself with forty-two reels. Even if I wanted the film to be shown in two parts, it was necessary to cut half of it. This I accomplished myself.

One could conclude from this testimony that Von Stroheim suffered no undue agony in reducing the film to twenty-four reels, and that the "complete" (forty-two-reel) *Greed* is thus something of an illusion—given the strength of the *Greed* legend, an almost heretical notion.

Perhaps it is the twenty-four-reel *Greed* whose loss should truly be lamented; it was certainly a film with which Von Stroheim would have been satisfied, and, if the studio had not been so inflexible, might have represented an excellent compromise. At six hours, it could have included much of Von Stroheim's complex adaptation, yet not so much that the film would be turgid and unwieldy—as the ten-hour version may well have been. A few critics have suggested that *Greed* is so intense and unrelenting that anything more would be too much; this rather myopic point of view ignores the fact that the telescoping of material represented by the final version necessarily rendered the film more forceful by stripping it of its additional dimensions. *Greed* in ten reels may seem like too much to some, but the evidence supports the belief that it is not nearly enough.

Greed, like its creator, carries great symbolic weight in the history of the American cinema. Emerging from World War I with a clear dominance of the world market, the American film industry took several years to develop the highly structured "studio system" that was to characterize Hollywood filmmaking until the 1950's. Ironically, this adaptation of the assembly-line principle was substantially perfected during the 1920's—the same period when the cinema was beginning to be acknowledged as an art form. In the studio system, the most powerful figure was not the director but the producer— exemplified by Irving Thalberg; Metro-Goldwyn-Mayer, the studio he helped to build, was to become the premier example of that system in action. In this milieu, an intransigent artist such as Von Stroheim was indeed "the man you love to hate."

Producers acknowledged Von Stroheim's brilliance and knew that his cre- ative energies were the life-blood of their industry; yet, they had to be har- nessed and channeled for the good of that industry. The producer was the King of Hollywood, and his rule was often less than benevolent. Today, although the director's star has risen again, the power and function of the producer remain much the same, having survived the radical changes of the system in which it had developed and flourished. The conflict between art and economics (the latter abetted by the spectre of "popular taste") is still at the core of the motion-picture industry, and the case of *Greed*—extreme but hardly unique—remains as significant as in its own time.

Howard H. Prouty

HANDS UP!

Released: 1926
Production: Adolph Zukor for Paramount
Direction: Clarence Badger
Screenplay: Monty Brice; based on an original screen story by Reginald Morris
Cinematography: H. Kinley Martin
Length: 6 reels/5,883 feet

> *Principal characters:*
> Jack .... Raymond Griffith
> Mae Woodstock .... Marion Nixon
> Alice Woodstock .... Virginia Lee Corbin
> Silas Woodstock .... Mack Swain
> Captain Logan .... Montagu Love
> Abraham Lincoln .... George Billings
> Sitting Bull .... Noble Johnson
> Brigham Young .... Charles K. French

Although he was popular from 1924 to 1929, Raymond Griffith is a forgotten silent-film comedian today. There are several reasons for this: his period of stardom was brief, only a handful of his films survive, and he could not make the transition to sound because a vocal dysfunction prevented him from speaking above a hoarse whisper.

A fourth reason for his obscurity was advanced by Walter Kerr in his book *The Silent Clowns*.

> [Griffith] is no memorable grotesque, made instantly indelible by his outline. Rather, he is slight, trim, neatly mustached, most often equipped with opera cape and top hat. At a glance he belongs to the Max Linder tradition, too much the habitue of drawing rooms and boudoirs ever to escape the polite formulas of boulevard farce.

Griffith, however, did escape. After serving an apprenticeship with a number of studios in the teens and early 1920's—including Vitaphone, Kalem, Sennett, Goldwyn, and Universal—he became a star in films such as *Paths to Paradise* (1925), *A Regular Fellow* (1925), and *You'd Be Surprised* (1927), all made for Paramount. The film that clinched his reputation more than any other, however, was *Hands Up!*, a Civil War comedy released at the same time as Buster Keaton's *The General*. Although *Hands Up!* is nowhere near as ambitious or masterful as *The General*, it is a comic gem, a joyous escapist film deserving of greater recognition than it has achieved.

The story is a simple one. Abraham Lincoln (George Billings) learns of a gold mine in Nevada that can replace the Union's depleted gold reserve. General Robert E. Lee learns of it, too, and assigns a soldier named Jack

(Raymond Griffith) to steal it for the Confederacy. The next six reels show Jack's various misadventures en route to carrying out his mission, with a wry sexual twist in the final reel.

With a premise such as this, one might expect a film full of running gags, pratfalls, and chase scenes, with a happy ending. In *Hands Up!*, however, Griffith blithely reverses all such expectations with the clipped precision of a master choreographer, playing against his good looks to comic effect in the process. An analysis of the film's contents reveals that it is not so much a story, as a series of precisely engineered vignettes; the premise is not actually a plot, but a plot device, prefiguring the tradition of Alfred Hitchcock's "maguffin." This is evidenced by the fact that it takes Jack ten months to complete the simple mission of stealing a gold shipment (the film begins on June 10, 1864, and ends on April 9, 1865). As the opening title card explains, the film is "An historical incident with variations."

The tongue-in-cheek incidents begin after the somber opening scene with Abraham Lincoln, when Jack volunteers as a spy in order to steal gold from the new mine. As Lee asks Jack if he is ready to face death, the roof of the shed they are in with a third soldier almost caves in from a nearby cannon blast, leaving Jack with a round box on his head, shaken silly. Then, just as Lee is proclaiming "This is just between the three of us" and shaking Jack's hand, a cannon ball rolls under the shed, blowing it to pieces. When the smoke clears, Lee is still pumping Jack's hand. The third soldier suddenly drops dead, and Jack amends, "The two of us, sir." It is this wry twist on reality that makes the scene funny and prepares the audience for the comedy to come.

The real fun begins with the next scene, which takes place several months later in a Nevada mining town. It opens with a crowd pummeling someone with rocks until a firing squad suddenly takes aim. The crowd scatters at once, revealing Jack dressed as a dandy in a tuxedo, tie, and top hat, about to be executed for some unexplained reason; presumably the charge is spying. Again, the film reverses expectation because the audience would not expect a spy to be formally dressed, since he would be far too conspicuous.

This, however, is only the beginning. So many things get in the way of the firing squad doing its duty that the sequence looks like a live-action Bugs Bunny cartoon, with the squad commander doubling for Bugs's nemesis, Yosemite Sam. First, two gravediggers measure Jack for his grave with a shovel, then a pretty young girl walks right in front of the firing line carrying a basket. "Pardon me," Jack brittlely informs her, "this is strictly a private execution." She flees, leaving her basket behind. Jack seizes his opportunity and as the soldiers take aim, he takes a dish from the basket and tosses it in the air. The soldiers shoot the dish instead of Jack, so he repeats the maneuver, to the annoyance of the Union captain in charge of executing him. He tries to shoot Jack himself but is foiled as well by the throwing-the-dish-in-the-air ploy. Jack then reverses the situation by having the captain hold tea cups for target practice.

The humor in this reversal is that Griffith, like Bugs Bunny, executes it with such utter, matter-of-fact aplomb. One does not expect a spy to turn his own execution into a skeet shoot. Jack is not through yet, though. The captain has Jack tied up to make sure he cannot move, with a dish in back to mark the spot. Suddenly, Captain Logan (Montagu Love) shows up with orders from Lincoln, and the execution is momentarily forgotten. When it is resumed, the firing squad discovers Jack has fled, leaving a suit of clothes painted on the wall and a picture of a plate in the middle inscribed "Till we meet again." This reversal is funny simply because it is impossible. The audience knows that Jack could never get buckets of paint on such short notice and could not possibly paint his facsimile so quickly, especially with the townspeople watching his every move. The key word for this entire sequence is speed, because everything happens so quickly that the audience has to laugh at the sheer surprise of it all and has no time to question its plausibility.

The longest and most cleverly sustained vignette takes place in a stagecoach. Mine owner Silas Woodstock (Mack Swain) and Captain Logan are sitting on top with the driver, while Jack is inside with Woodstock's pretty, bubble-headed daughters, Mae (Marion Nixon) and Alice (Virginia Lee Corbin). At first, he stands out of courtesy, newspaper in hand. Finally, he sits, eyeing the girls back and forth, then takes out a pair of dice, acts as though he wants to engage the girls in a game of craps, then changes his mind. He leans backward and falls, instantly breaking the ice and gaining the sympathy of the girls. He then reads their palms: "You're each going to marry a dark man," he tells them. He pulls out a deck of cards, plays with them momentarily, then quickly snatches them away in embarrassment. All the while, he is thinking up various ways to flirt with the girls, who are acting coy and demure.

This scene is both hilarious and incredible (it runs four and a half minutes but seems shorter because of the deft pacing and nimble editing) because Griffith is constantly in playful motion, like a seasoned magician thinking up new tricks to amuse his audience every few seconds. He quickly goes from one gag to another, leaving viewers laughing and in awe of his inventiveness, physical dexterity, and expressively puckish eyes.

In the following scene, everyone in the stagecoach is captured by a band of Indians. This does not perturb Jack, though. He simply rolls with the punches and ends up teaching Sitting Bull (Noble Johnson) to play craps, taking him for his shirt and headdress.

The best scene, and arguably one of the funniest scenes in film, is when Jack and his fellow captives are treated to a tribal war dance. Jack is not frightened of the significance of the dance; instead, he proceeds to teach the Indians the Charleston even though the dance was not invented until the

1920's. It is anachronistic, but hilarious for precisely that reason: the audience does not expect to see Indians doing a jazz dance. This was the secret of Griffith's success: taking an audience by surprise with zany, mischievous, upside-down jokes and all with an intent to charm in the middle of a belly laugh. He does not take himself seriously, so neither does the audience, as he continually turns potential calamity into side-splitting farce.

The film concludes with the end of the Civil War, the gold going nowhere, and Jack in despair. The sudden appearance of Brigham Young (Charles K. French) and his wives in a stagecoach, however, gives him an idea. Instead of trying to decide which of Woodstock's daughters he will marry, he absconds with both of them to Utah to become a Mormon. Thus, Griffith has it both ways: the star gets both girls and gets the idea of bigamy past the censors because of its Mormon—and therefore obliquely moral—implication. Unfortunately, most prints of *Hands Up!* today are without this ending, showing only that Jack is left hanging over a failed mission and the end of the war. It is a curiously depressing note for a comedy.

Griffith's career ended sadly. At the peak of his fame in 1929, talking films cut him short. Although he appeared in a couple of talky shorts (still extant), his screen career was over. His last appearance was a mute one as the French soldier killed by the Lew Ayres character in *All Quiet on the Western Front* (1930). Thereafter, he became an associate producer for Warner Bros. for a few years, working on *Golddiggers of 1933* and *Voltaire* (1933), among other projects. He joined Twentieth Century Pictures in 1934 at the behest of Darryl Zanuck and stayed with the company when it became Twentieth Century-Fox in 1935. He spent five fruitful years with Fox as an associate producer on a variety of films, retiring in 1940 at the relatively young age of forty-six.

When Griffith died in Hollywood of a heart attack on November 9, 1957, at the age of sixty-three, his onscreen work was long forgotten by the public because silents were a thing of the past, and because he had not been able to be successful in talkies. Had he had a voice and been able to make the transition, he would perhaps be better known today. As it is, Griffith's surviving films are waiting to be rediscovered and laughed at and appreciated for their wit, whimsy, and dapper wackiness.

Sam Frank

HE WHO GETS SLAPPED

Released: 1924
Production: Metro-Goldwyn
Direction: Victor Seastrom
Screenplay: Carey Wilson and Victor Seastrom; based on the play of the same name by Leonid Nikolaevich Andreyev
Cinematography: Milton Moore
Editing: Hugh Wynn
Art direction: Cedric Gibbons
Costume design: Sophie Wachner
Length: 7 reels/6,953 feet

> *Principal characters:*
> He Who Gets Slapped .... Lon Chaney
> Consuelo .... Norma Shearer
> Bezano .... John Gilbert
> Count Mancini .... Tully Marshall
> Baron Regnard .... Marc MacDermott
> Tricaud .... Ford Sterling
> He's wife .... Ruth King

Lon Chaney is so well known for playing ugly cripples and psychopaths that his more restrained work is often overlooked. A striking example of one of his less flamboyant roles is *He Who Gets Slapped*, a surprise commercial success in 1924, that was shot in less than a month for only $140,000. The director was the Swedish master Victor Seastrom (née Sjostrom), who had recently arrived in Hollywood and whose first two American films, including *The Master of Man* (1923), had been critical and financial failures.

Those poor showings notwithstanding, Metro-Goldwyn allowed Seastrom to adapt a vehicle for Chaney that would make full use of the actor's penchant for suffering and pathos, but without the physical deformities that previously characterized his screen *persona*. In *He Who Gets Slapped*, Chaney plays a French research scientist whose thesis on the origin of the species is stolen by his supposed benefactor, Baron Regnard (Marc MacDermott), and delivered by the Baron before the Academy of Scientists. When it comes time for He (Chaney's only name in the film) to address the Academy, he is laughed off the podium. Not only does he lose his life's work and his reputation, but he also loses his wife (Ruth King) to Regnard.

The scornful derision of his peers destroys He's will to continue as a scientist, but does inspire him to a new line of work: as a clown whose specialty is being slapped and humiliated in front of paying audiences. He feels that if he is going to be mocked, why not do it on a grand scale? Thus, he arrives at his new identity, "He Who Gets Slapped," the star attraction of a prestigious

Parisian circus. What appeals to the crowds about He's masochism is what has always appealed about tragic figures, that it reflects and shoulders their own fears of pain, rejection, and setback. He therefore is a clownish martyr for the masses.

A bareback rider named Consuelo (Norma Shearer) joins the circus and falls in love with her handsome partner, Bezano (John Gilbert), not knowing that He is in love with her. Compounding the triangle is the irony that Consuelo's father, Count Mancini (Tully Marshall), is an impoverished Italian count who plans to marry her to Regnard, who has long since dumped He's wife. He discovers this marriage plot and foils it by having a lion attack and kill Regnard. He, in turn, is fatally stabbed by the Count and stumbles back into the arena one last time to be slapped and die for the audience.

At first glance, the plot sounds contrived and corny. It is difficult to believe that a noted scientist would abandon his career to become a clown, however much he has been publicly degraded. Yet, the wonder of *He Who Gets Slapped* is that the audience does believe it and for several reasons: Seastrom's controlled writing and direction, and his use of naturalistic lighting; Milton Moore's deep-focus cinematography; and Chaney's charismatic acting. For an early Metro film, *He Who Gets Slapped* is daring in its use of high contrast photography, suffusing the frame, especially in the circus scenes, with stark highlights and deep shadows. The audience is placed in a world of exaggerated reality, where dedication is rewarded with suffering, and pain is greeted with laughter. Fortunately, Seastrom was able to convince Metro executives of the merits of this type of lighting as opposed to the diffused lighting which gave a glossy look to their usual films.

With any other leading actor, the film's premise might not have worked, but it does work for Chaney because of his expertise as a mime and his skill as an actor. As He, Chaney is part Weary Willy, the melancholy hobo, and part Pagliacci, the noble clown who suffers for love.

He Who Gets Slapped is filled with scenes and images that reverberate long after the final shot. For example, the scene of He's humiliation before the Academy of Scientists is enhanced by kaleidoscopic collages of the laughing scientists with Regnard and He's wife, thereby exaggerating what is really taking place so that the sequence, as a whole, takes on an air of nightmarish, sinking unreality. One can understand why He would flee one vocation and begin another.

The first scene in the circus where He is introduced and slapped by a chorus of clowns has just the right pathetic ring to it, both because of the stark photography and Seastrom's staging. Viewers cringe with every blow, horrified that the circus crowd is enjoying this, but realizing as well that the crowd is an extension of the general public, symbolizing man's insatiable appetite for inflicting cruelty, however indirectly.

The most poignant and piercing scene is the last one, when He takes his final bow, bleeding to death before a laughing audience. He stands alone in a spotlight in the circus arena, his life trickling away. The light goes out, leaving only He's white greasepainted face visible. This haunting image, in turn, slowly fades to black, bringing to an end He's suffering but not the viewer's own. Herein lies the main point of the film: one cannot suffer forever through surrogates but must assume life's risks whatever the cost if one is to grow and mature as a human being.

Yet, for all its visceral impact, *He Who Gets Slapped* is undercut as a potential masterpiece by holes in the plot, miscasting, and misguided direction. First, Marc MacDermott plays Regnard with such transparent comic menace that viewers have to wonder why He trusts him with a copy of his thesis, why He's wife is attracted to the Baron, and why, once Regnard has addressed the scientists, He does not simply denounce his former benefactor as a thieving fraud. Unlike He, the Baron has never had scientific work published, to the viewer's knowledge, and one would assume that the Academy of Scientists would support He's position.

Second, the romantic subplot is a weak one, partly because Shearer and Gilbert make a bland love team, but mainly because, for all her radiance, Shearer was not a good actress. All she could project was her impersonal beauty, making it hard to believe that Chaney or Gilbert would fall for her past the initial physical attraction.

Finally, the scene where Regnard is killed is unintentionally funny, especially a shot where a lion is seen smacking his lips. Surely, Seastrom and Carey Wilson could have devised a better revenge for He than siccing a lion on the Baron. That or the scene could have been staged less comically. The following, climactic scene mitigates some of the previous one's corniness, but not entirely.

Even so, for most of its running time, *He Who Gets Slapped* has visual and dramatic eloquence because Seastrom, through Chaney, has stylized a potentially laughable story into a richly symbolic tragedy. Some excellent 35 mm prints of the film are available today, so it can be seen as its first audiences saw it: as a compelling though flawed saga of one man's struggle with adversity and how he uses his misfortune to make the world laugh with him, even as it also cries.

Sam Frank

THE HEART OF HUMANITY

Released: 1919
Production: Universal-Jewel
Direction: Allen Holubar
Screenplay: Allen Holubar and Olga Scholl
Cinematography: King D. Gray and A. McClain
Technical adviser: Erich Von Stroheim
Length: 9 reels

Principal characters:
Nanette .... Dorothy Phillips
John Patricia .... William Stowell
Jules Patricia .... Lloyd Hughes
Louis Patricia .... George Hackathorne
Paul Patricia .... Robert Anderson
Maurice Patricia .... Frank Braidwood
Widow Patricia .... Margaret Mann
Father Michael .... Walt Whitman
Clancy, an Irish-American .... Pat O'Malley
Lieutenant von Eberhard .... Erich Von Stroheim

When World War I ended on November 11, 1918, many film producers had war films still in production. It was, however, predicted at the time that any picture with a war theme would probably repel patrons, and, in fact, several of the "hate" pictures failed miserably at the box office. Universal had a very expensive war film, *The Heart of Humanity*, ready for release at the time of the Armistice. Although they knew that it was a good picture, they released it, expecting the worst. Reviewers, fortunately, praised it; audiences were thrilled by it; and exhibitors made large profits with it at the box office. As a result of its success, the director, Allen Holubar, was given *carte blanche* at the studio. Holubar's wife, Dorothy Phillips, became Universal's most important star, and action-technical adviser, Erich Von Stroheim, got his big break to direct and star in *Blind Husbands* (1919).

Director Holubar took his inspiration for *The Heart of Humanity* from D. W. Griffith's *Hearts of the World* (1918). In fact, many of the best moments in Holubar's picture had their origins in some other film, but audiences loved his interpretation of the material and forgave him if it did not all seem original.

The film opens in a rural village in Quebec, Canada. Nanette (Dorothy Phillips), a pretty French orphan, lives in the care of her uncle, Father Michael (Walt Whitman). Some neighbors—the Widow Patricia (Margaret Mann) and her five sons—also care for her as if she were a member of the family. All five of the boys, however, soon grow to love her as more than a sister, prompting some good-natured rivalry among them. Of all the sons, however,

John Patricia (William Stowell), the oldest, is the one whom Nanette actually loves.

The boys work as lumberjacks in the forests that surround their world. One day, a stranger comes to the little town, a German named von Eberhard (Erich Von Stroheim). He is invited to dine at the Patricia home and sees Nanette for the first time there. The five sons find his manners very strange, because he clicks his heels and is stiff and formal in his manner. He is also overly polite to Nanette. When the dinner conversation slips briefly to politics, von Eberhard reveals his deep beliefs in the superiority of the German system of government.

Several days later, Nanette accidentally encounters von Eberhard at the lake. After a few pleasantries, he tries to kiss her but she repulses him, telling him that she intends to marry John Patricia. This admission wounds the German's pride, and he leaves town.

On a lovely day in August, 1914, John and Nanette are married. The festivities, however, are clouded by news of Germany's invasion of Belgium. Within a week, John and three of his brothers have joined the army, and they are soon shipped overseas where John applies for aviator training. His brothers become foot soldiers, however, and two of them soon are killed in the first German offensive.

Nanette has a baby on the same day that a letter arrives informing the Widow Patricia of the loss of her two sons. Louis (George Hackathorne), the youngest son, now becomes determined to become a soldier and avenge his brothers. He cannot be deterred from volunteering by his mother's pleas. For the next two years, Nanette rears her baby alone, with only John's letters for comfort. Louis' letters, however, fill her with anger since he chronicles the miserable conditions of the war orphans, children left homeless by the indiscriminate bombings of both sides. His letters prompt Nanette to become a Red Cross nurse.

She leaves her child in the keeping of its grandmother and is assigned to a convent that the Red Cross has occupied in Flanders. There, she begins to care for the homeless children. The German line is dangerously near the children's refuge, and, by coincidence, John bombs the Germans to keep them back. His plane crashes, however, on the wrong side of the lines, and he is taken prisoner. The Germans then make a push and capture the town and the Red Cross center. Von Eberhard now appears again in the uniform of a German lieutenant. He uses his newly acquired power to force again his attentions on Nanette. She snatches up an infant, runs upstairs, and locks herself in her room.

To get at the nurse, Lieutenant von Eberhard breaks down the door. Nanette valiantly places herself between him and the baby. The German begins to rape her, but the baby's cries annoy him, so in the film's most shocking scene, he stops pawing the girl, and crosses the room to the infant.

He grabs the child and pitches it out the window. Seeing this, Nanette faints in terror and her captor has his way with her.

John, meanwhile, escapes from his German guards and makes his way to the convent. Nanette, however, has barred her door. Thinking that John is another German coming to rape her, she stabs herself. Fortunately, she does not die and is reunited with her husband. After the war, she and John return to Canada and their son.

Phillips started her film career in 1910 with Essanay. After she moved to Universal, she became a star in 1917, with a drama set in San Francisco's Barbary Coast, *Hell Morgan's Girl*, co-starring William Stowell and Lon Chaney. She then married Holubar, who was a Universal director, and they began making a popular series of films that peaked with *The Heart of Humanity*.

As a result of that success, Universal allowed them bigger budgets, and they made *The Right to Happiness* (1919) and *Once to Every Woman* (1920). Leaving Universal, they got a contract at Associated First National, where they made the very lavish *Man-Woman-Marriage* (1921). In it, Phillips played the wife of a United States senator who becomes shocked by her husband's political corruption and runs against him in an election, and wins. Using a device popular with Cecil B. De Mille, the film showed flashbacks from the Stone Age to the present. This production brought them a big contract at Metro-Goldwyn, but Holubar was suddenly taken ill and died. The studio cast Phillips in a supporting role in Norma Shearer's *Upstage* (1926), and then canceled her contract, so she moved to Fox. She played in several roles there, and then became a bit player until well into the period of talking films, when she retired and left the industry. She moved North to live with an older sister, and nobody knew where she was, until a one-liner was printed in a newspaper about her death in 1980; she was then in her nineties.

William Stowell started in films in 1909 with producer William Selig in Chicago and played several roles in Selig's expensive three-reel feature, *The Coming of Christopher Columbus* (1912). He often appeared with Phillips at Universal before *The Heart of Humanity*. Late in 1919, Stowell was sent to Africa by Universal to star in a big-budget adventure epic, but while he was traveling by train over mountains to the Congo, a runaway boxcar, going one hundred miles per hour, crashed into the last coach where Stowell sat, killing him instantly.

Larry Lee Holland

HEARTS OF THE WORLD

Released: 1918
Production: D. W. Griffith for D. W. Griffith, Inc.; released by Paramount-Artcraft
Direction: D. W. Griffith
Screenplay: Gaston de Tolignac (D. W. Griffith) and Captain Victor Marier (D. W. Griffith)
Cinematography: G. W. Bitzer
Editing: James Smith and Rose Smith
Technical supervision: Erich Von Stroheim
Music: Carli Elinor and D. W. Griffith (arrangement)
Length: 12 reels/7,056 feet

Principal characters:

The Mother	Josephine Crowell
The Girl, Marie Stephenson	Lillian Gish
The Boy, Douglas Gordon Hamilton	Robert Harron
The Father of the Boy	Jack Cosgrave
The Mother of the Boy	Kate Bruce
The littlest brother	Ben Alexander
The Boy's other brothers	Marion Emmons
	Francis Marion
The Little Disturber	Dorothy Gish
Von Strohm	George Siegmann

Hearts of the World was D. W. Griffith's third feature film and the second of four dealing with the effects of war or revolution on ordinary people. The others were *The Birth of a Nation* (1915), *Orphans of the Storm* (1922), and *America* (1924), all of which had varying degrees of success, both critically and commercially. *Hearts of the World* was made at the invitation of the British government, which was anxious for a propaganda film that would encourage American involvement in World War I. By the time the film was released in April, 1918, however, America had been in the war for several months, but that only served to enhance its commercial value. What the Allies got for their money was a prowar film that transcended its genre to become an epic of innocence altered and uplifted by war and its holocaust.

Indeed, *Hearts of the World* has such visual and dramatic sweep and fervor that it has the unsettling effect of making war seem both brutal and romantic, a necessary evil to do away with evil, which, in this case, is the irredeemably barbaric Germans. They are portrayed as being so utterly ruthless and blood-thirsty that the audience is moved to cheer for their annihilation.

Hearts of the World does not begin with the war, however, but with the inhabitants of an unnamed French village whose lives will be devastated by it. Here, as so often, Griffith establishes a rural idyll (the time is 1912) in which sweetly innocent love flourishes. The romance that is central to the story is not between French lovers, however, but transplanted Americans: Douglas Gordon Hamilton (Robert Harron), called the Boy, and Marie Stephenson (Lillian Gish), known as the Girl. They meet when a wandering gosling catches the Girl's eye and leads her to the Boy. Within the span of a few masterfully conceived and edited closeups, Griffith establishes their immediate mutual attraction, as though they were made for each other.

Complicating their courtship is a tomboyish street imp called the Little Disturber (Dorothy Gish). She is smitten with the Boy and embraces him in a village street in full view of the Girl. Just as the audience begins to get involved in this romantic triangle and in the lives of the villagers in general, war breaks out. The Germans attack the village, laying it waste and killing the Girl's mother (Josephine Crowell) in the process. As viewers witness scene after scene of appalling devastation, they cannot help but root for the Boy, now a soldier, to help defeat the enemy and restore peace and order to his adopted homeland.

What Griffith lacks in subtlety in terms of the political complexities of the war, he makes up for in broad dramatic strokes that intensify and inform viewers of the human complexities, if only from the Allied point of view. Nevertheless, Griffith shifts between scenes of explosive power and scenes of tender, aching reflection so that the war comes to have personal meaning for the audience.

In one scene, for example, the Girl goes into shock after seeing her mother die at the hands of a German. Not knowing what to do or to whom she can turn, she wanders, zombie-like, past the village into the battlezone where she receives another shock: the Boy lying wounded. Thinking him dead, she spends the night tightly embracing him, as though to comfort his soul. When he is taken away for medical treatment in the morning, the still disoriented Girl returns to the village, only semiconscious of where she has been and what she has experienced.

In another scene, when the Boy's mother (Kate Bruce) is killed, his younger brothers (Marion Emmons, Francis Marion, and Ben Alexander), mere boys, bury her, symbolically holding the family together in the face of death. Throughout, the acting is understated rather than overdrawn, as was the norm for prowar films of that time. The effect is to draw the audience into supporting the resolve of the survivors to destroy the heartless enemy at any cost.

This dramatic strength is also the film's failing because it paints a moralistically black-and-white picture of the war. The German general Von Strohm (George Siegmann), for example, is a lecherous beast who is simply the foreign version of the mulatto opportunist Silas Lynch, whom Siegmann played in *The Birth of a Nation*. He is a stock villain with no human traits, and such is the power of Griffith's direction and editing that viewers are roused to anger by Von Strohm and relieved when he is shot to death by the Boy.

Similarly, Griffith evokes pity when it seems as though the Girl and the Boy have no way out of the war except through suicide—death before dishonor, a familiar Griffith theme—saving them at the last possible moment (the famous crosscutting technique) by having the proverbial cavalry come to the rescue, in this case the Allied armies. Griffith shamelessly manipulates the audience, who, in turn, just as shamelessly respond because of his skill as a director and the humanity of his leading actors.

The finale of *Hearts of the World* is baldly patriotic and a bit much to swallow for modern audiences because of the way it glamorizes "The war to end all wars." The lovers are safely reunited, overseen by a smiling portrait of Woodrow Wilson. This is followed by victorious Allied troops marching under the flags of France and the United States, with a final montage ethereally depicting the Girl and the Boy under a halo of light. They are not only survivors, they are innocents reborn into a world of hope, peace, and justice.

Griffith here is repeating himself because his endings for *The Birth of a Nation* and *Intolerance* (1916) are remarkably similar; and they are just as distasteful. In the former, Henry B. Walthall and Lillian Gish are overseen by a visage of Christ, seemingly bestowing his blessings on them and the Ku Klux Klan for which they stand. In the latter, as intolerance and injustice come to an end, heaven is viewed as a lily-white utopia where all join hands. Griffith obviously had a predilection not only for epic-length films—*Hearts of the World* in its full length runs more than two-and-a-half hours—but also for unrealistic notions of a great, perfect society. This is to be expected considering his background as a Southern gentleman who was reared on romantic tales of the Confederacy. Such sentimental prejudice, however, somewhat undercuts his greatness as a director and his power as a man of ideas. *Hearts of the World* is an uplifting experience by sheer virtue of technique and acting, but its potential as a masterwork is severely mitigated by its narrow view of war and the effect it has on all sides, German included. *All Quiet on the Western Front* (1930) and the Japanese film *Fire on the Plains* (1963) are superior films in that respect, because they depict war from the point of view of the so-called enemy. "War's peace" as Griffith eloquently calls it in *The Birth of a Nation* has a debilitating effect on all who take part in it; savagery is not and never has been bounded by nationality.

Thematic considerations aside, Griffith owed much of the success of *Hearts of the World* to his loyal repertory company, especially Harron and the Gish sisters. Harron in particular is a fine actor with a boyish screen presence. He would surely have become one of the major stars of the silent screen if, in 1920, he had not been killed accidentally at age twenty-six while on a hunting trip.

Lillian Gish was and remains an actress of beauty and strength, at once fragile and tough. Her love scenes with Harron, particularly the dazed one on the battlefield, are sensitive and moving because of their underplayed intimacy. Griffith reteamed them as lovers for *True Heart Susie* (1919), although not as effectively because of that film's saccharine, manipulative plot and coy, puritanical sexuality.

For all the charisma of the Gish-Harron pairing in *Hearts of the World*, it is Dorothy Gish as the perky, puckish Little Disturber who steals the film, making viewers wish there was more of her. Griffith was never at ease with comedy, but Dorothy Gish brought a manic sort of whimsy to her role that leavened the surrounding somber melodrama, taking the edge off it. When the film was first released, Gish's Little Disturber was singled out for special praise by the critics and remains the film's running highlight. Having delighted in this sexually spunky performance, one wishes that the younger Gish sister had made more films and played many more such roles, although she is also outstanding in *Orphans of the Storm* playing Lillian's estranged sister.

Today, *Hearts of the World* is rarely revived. It has played on public television and at museum screenings in recent years, but its prowar, anti-German stance makes it a difficult sell for any but dedicated Griffith fans. Even so, it is well worth seeing, both for its overall style and impact, and for Dorothy Gish in one of her most memorable roles.

Sam Frank

HELL'S HINGES

Released: 1916
Production: Thomas H. Ince for Triangle Film Corporation
Direction: William S. Hart and Charles Swickard
Screenplay: C. Gardner Sullivan
Titles: Mon Randall
Cinematography: Joseph H. August
Length: 5 reels

Principal characters:
Blaze Tracy .... William S. Hart
Faith Henley .... Clara Williams
Reverend Robert Henley .... Jack Standing
Dolly .... Louise Glaum
Silk Miller .... Alfred Hollingsworth
A clergyman .... Robert McKim
Zeb Taylor .... J. Frank Burke

Hell's Hinges is a classic William S. Hart Western, and this credit alone qualifies it as a classic of the entire genre. Hart, a former stage actor and unbending advocate for presenting the "true West" in films, made Westerns from 1914 through 1925. In those few years, he not only popularized the genre as a blend of realism and romantic melodrama, but he was also instrumental in shaping the screen Western into a structured formula. Hart surpassed his predecessors, such as G. M. (Bronco Billy) Anderson, in dramatic sense and thematic maturity. Although others, such as ex-outlaw Al Jennings, actually brought great realism to their films, what Hart sacrificed in realism was compensated for by the sincerity of his presentation and the force of his own personality.

Hart's Westerns were not escapist entertainment for children, but adult melodramas in which the interior turmoil of the characters was as important as defeating the villain. In Hart's films, the moral and emotional growth of the hero usually took precedence over the display of his athletic grace on a horse or skill as a quick-draw gunslinger. He not only was called upon to confront the villain but was also forced to come to terms with his own conscience and, on more than one occasion, with God.

Hart's films combined Victorian melodrama and morality with realism. It was inevitable that the realism in Hart's work would conflict with the former characteristics, and this conflict was a source of the aesthetic tension in his films. Victorian sentimentality, black-and-white characterization, and poetic preachiness were blended with a sense of realism and an appreciation of the complexity of human nature. Hart's heroes, mostly outlaws, but sometimes virtuous men drawn to revenge, could be cowed by the mere glimpse of a good woman. The real villains were bested, and sin, even the hero's, had to be atoned for. During World War I, the country wanted entertainment with a clear definition of right and wrong (to parallel its own involvement in a "righteous" war), and Americans looked to entertainment to reinforce their national pride. After the war, a changing social and moral climate led to a precipitous decline in Hart's enormous popularity, because while the times had changed, Hart had not.

Even as early as 1916, the release of *Hell's Hinges* prompted both praise from critics and warnings that Hart was letting himself be trapped by his own inflexibility. The films' strict sense of right and wrong and their emphasis on character and psychology, combined with Hart's dependence on melodrama and his insistence upon presenting the West as hard, drab, and dangerous, became liabilities rather than assets. Hart's position as the preeminent cowboy hero was challenged by more youthful-looking rivals such as Tom Mix, who offered implausible action, flashy costumes, and the appeal of entertainment unburdened by introspection.

Hart had offered the Western as melodramatic and often excessively sentimental fare, and also as a form with emotional complexity, visual interest, and a sense of spiritual values. In the Westerns that followed, these qualities would be in short supply. Reflection was out, good reflexes were in. The West of films became a haven for adventure-loving supercowboys with the sensibilities of overgrown adolescents. Hart's films had been a startling advance for the genre, but his refusal to revise his moral and dramatic tenets eventually condemned his films to be regarded as quaintly archaic. Mix supplanted Hart in popularity, and the Westerns of the 1920's and 1930's tended to inherit Mix's disregard for both Western authenticity and emotional authenticity.

Hart's commitment to bringing the real West to the screen was as uncompromising as his Victorian sensibility. That commitment was forged from his own childhood experiences, although the exact nature of his early life was clouded by Hart's own melodramatic enhancement of changing versions of his stories. His love for the West, however, was unchanging. Born in New York in 1870, Hart was the son of a ne'er-do-well miller who roamed the Midwest in search of a financial success that never came. With limited education and financial resources restricting his career options, Hart fell into acting and carved out a career on the stage for himself, largely in character roles, such as Messala in *Ben-Hur* and Cash Hawkins in *The Squaw Man*. He came to Hollywood in 1913 with the specific purpose of making good Westerns that would not desecrate his own ideas of what frontier life had been. With the help of screenwriter C. Gardner Sullivan, Hart molded himself into the screen's archetypal Westerner. This screen *persona* of the Good-Bad Man, with crouched shooting pose and two guns blazing, became as well known to millions of filmgoers as Charlie Chaplin's Little Tramp or Mary Pickford's Little Mary.

Hell's Hinges' Good-Bad Man, Blaze Tracy, is a typical Hart protagonist. Like the heroes of James Fenimore Cooper's *Leatherstocking Tales* and nineteenth century dime novels, Hart's heroes are resolutely individualistic loners who live on the edge of society and outside the boundaries of the law. They are capable of violence, brutality, and even lust, but retain a vulnerability brought to the surface when they are introduced to "The Pure Female."

Hart's Good-Bad Man *persona* was the first outlaw Western hero to be popularized in film. He served as the prototype for the standard Western character still found today, particularly in the films of Clint Eastwood. Unlike Eastwood and other current antiheroes, however, Hart's hero retained his capacity for redemption. He adhered to his own code of behavior that distinguished him from the villain and possessed an almost Puritanical sense of good and evil. In the end, his own judgment against himself was inevitably harsher than any society would render. Although he did not feel the need to justify his own lawlessness, his sense of right and wrong was usually already developed and only lying dormant, ready to be unleashed by his contact with the forces of good as personified by the heroine.

Hart's own austerely beautiful face and dignified bearing do much to express the latent goodness in the character. In *Hell's Hinges*, Blaze Tracy is introduced with a title that informs viewers of his ambivalent nature. He is, the screen states, "the embodiment of the best and worst of the early West." Tracy is hired to meet the town's new preacher and send him on his way before he can do any harm to the interests of saloon owner Silk Miller (Alfred Hollingsworth). Silk and his wild friends have kept the town of Placer Center saddled with a reputation as "a good place to 'ride wide of'" and worthy of the nickname of "Hell's Hinges."

The new minister, the Reverend Robert Henley (Jack Standing) is a failure from the East. Accompanied by his sister Faith (Clara Williams), he has come West not for any highminded purpose, but because his own church superiors had decided he was too weak in character to withstand the temptations of the big city. Unknowingly, they have sent him to a little town where temptations are already firmly entrenched. The minister daydreams of his new assignment in the West as an opportunity to comfort "spiritually" bevies of willing señoritas. The reality he confronts upon his arrival at Hell's Hinges is nothing like his daydreams.

Treeless, dusty, and totally graceless, Hell's Hinges reflects the inhospitable nature of the surrounding frontier. The town's inhabitants are as rough as their environment. As the poetic titles declare, the good folk in town are but "a drop of water in a barrel of rum." When the new minister and his sister step off the stagecoach, Tracy is ready to tell the minister to "git." He makes his way through the crowd that surrounds the new arrivals, but is stopped in his tracks by the sight of Faith Henley innocently offering her hand to him in a gesture of friendship. The titles remark, "one who is evil, looking for the first time on that which is good." The crowd is appropriately astonished by Tracy's behavior and Tracy himself is later dumbfounded by his own actions.

This scene is characteristic of Hart's films and is one which helps account for the opinion that Hart was already out of date in 1916. The heroine's purity is her most powerful weapon. It is strong enough to change the life of the outlaw hero. Clara Williams is less attractive than many Hart leading ladies, but no matter their degree of prettiness, Hart heroines tend to wear drab frocks and often (as in *The Toll Gate*, 1920) have the worn look that undoubtedly was part of the unfortunate reality for women who faced the hardships of frontier life. Whatever the difficulties (and sometimes Hart heroines were very roughly treated by the hero until his reformation), these women still have the strength to turn the hero to the cause of the good. In many Westerns, the female mediates between the hero and civilization, but in Hart films, she is also called upon to mediate between the hero and his conscience and the hero and God.

Instead of running the preacher out of town, Tracy becomes the protector of Faith, her brother, and "the preacher's herd." He comes to the church, hears Faith talk about God, and knows he "has been riding the wrong trail." He stops a raid on the church services by some of Silk's hooligans and takes to reading the Bible. While Tracy is in the process of getting religion, however, Reverend Henley proceeds to lose his. Silk Miller, realizing the minister's weakness, changes tactics and uses Dolly (Louise Glaum), a dance-hall girl, to seduce the not unwilling man of the cloth.

On Sunday morning, Faith, Tracy, and the congregation wait for the minister to dedicate officially the new church building, but they find him in bed with Dolly, sleeping off a drunken night. Tracy and Faith take the minister home. Tracy rides to fetch a doctor for the Reverend, but upon waking, the Reverend has other plans. He decides to join his new friends, who are infinitely more fun than his old congregation. Silk uses liquor to convince Henley to burn down his own church. The best efforts of Faith and the congregation cannot stop the Reverend, Silk, and the mob.

When Tracy returns, he finds the church ablaze and Faith collapsed over the body of her dead brother who has been shot in the assault on the church. In this scene, Tracy's compassion for Faith is matched by his growing anger at the destruction of the town's spiritual hope. After making sure that Faith is all right, he decides to send all of Hell's Hinges back to hell. In a scene that could be the model for the finale of Clint Eastwood's *High Plains Drifter* (1973), Tracy brings the evil town to justice. He outwits the mob and corners them in the saloon. Hart's intensity at this moment is particularly effective, as it often is when he finally unleashes pent-up emotions. He shoots down the lanterns to set the saloon on fire, and in a magnificently apocalyptic scene, the town of Hell's Hinges goes up in flames. The direction of the crowds, the use of long shots, and the silhouetting effects in this scene are impressive, and Hart seizes on this very dramatic situation to bring his film to its climax.

The talents of Hart as a director have been championed by film historian William K. Everson, and it is fair to say that despite the limitations of Hart's Victorian world view, his films are often directorially impressive. Although some sources indicate that Thomas H. Ince directed the fire scene in *Hell's Hinges*, others maintain that Ince never personally directed Hart, and that this masterful climax is Hart's alone.

The denouement is a disquieting one. Faith mourns at her brother's grave in an expression of the brother-sister love often present in Hart's films and which apprently had its emotional basis in Hart's own close, lifelong relationship with his sister Mary Ellen, "Mamie." Tracy shows great tenderness with the distraught Faith, but she is inconsolable. He comforts her and persuades her that they can face the future together. Surrounded by beautiful mountain terrain, they turn their backs on the memory of Hell's Hinges and set off to build a new life. The audience is given a version of a "happy ending," but as in many of Hart's films, there is a sense of loss and the recognition that life is tragic.

Hart lived until 1946 and thus saw the West he adored pushed off the screen by Hollywood's disregard for authenticity. Perhaps the sense of loss communicated in his films related to his recognition that not only was the West he knew and loved gone, but the appreciation for what it represented was also endangered. Hart presented a West that was romanticized and melodramatic, but he cannot be accused of being emotionally glib or exploitative. His sincerity of purpose is obvious. In the 1950's, the birth of the "adult Western" would be heralded, yet the real beginning of the mature Western had come thirty-five years earlier, with the films of William S. Hart.

Gaylyn Studlar

HER SISTER FROM PARIS

Released: 1925
Production: Joseph M. Schenck for Associated First National
Direction: Sidney Franklin
Screenplay: Hans Kraly; based on the play *Maskerade* by Ludwig Fulda
Titles: George Marion, Jr.
Cinematography: Arthur Edeson
Art direction: William Cameron Menzies
Costume design: Adrian
Length: 8 reels/7,255 feet

Principal characters:
Helen Weyringer/Lola .... Constance Talmadge
Joseph Weyringer .... Ronald Colman
Robert Well .... George K. Arthur
Bertha .... Margaret Mann

Her Sister from Paris is one of those sophisticated, frothy, domestic comedy-dramas that are frequently described as French farces. In this case, however, the setting is romantic Vienna, and in fact, the screenplay was written by Hans Kraly, Ernst Lubitsch's long-time collaborator.

The film is based on a play by German playwright Ludwig Fulda (1862-1939), whose most famous work to be presented on film was *The Pirate*, which he wrote in 1911 and which S. N. Behrman adapted in 1942 for the Theatre Guild production, starring Alfred Lunt and Lynn Fontanne. *The Pirate* was later turned into a screenplay by Albert Hackett and Frances Goodrich as a 1948 Arthur Freed-M-G-M production with Cole Porter music, starring Judy Garland and Gene Kelly.

Her Sister from Paris was especially tailored to the considerable talents of its star Constance Talmadge, one of the screen's first and loveliest natural comediennes. The vehicle provided a dual role for the charming Talmadge, and while the story was hardly new, it was a popular summer diversion when it opened at New York's Capitol Theater on August 23, 1925.

The story opens in the well-appointed Viennese home of Joseph Weyringer (Ronald Colman), a temperamental young novelist. He and his dull, but equally temperamental wife Helen (Constance Talmadge) are having a domestic quarrel which climaxes with Joseph smashing dishes against the walls. Helen announces that she has had enough of his indifference toward her and that she is leaving him to return home to her mother. The apathetic Joseph makes no effort to stop his demure wife as she leaves.

At the train station, the distraught Helen runs into her irrepressible sister Lola (also played by Constance Talmadge), an alluring and famous dancer known as La Perry, a brazen and boisterous *femme fatale* who has had many men, and even kings, at her feet.

Lola is starring in Vienna that evening and invites her timid sister to join her backstage. Coincidentally, Joseph and his friend Robert Well (George K. Arthur) also attend the theater that evening. Well is the "keeper of the monocles and marmalade" at the British Embassy, and from their box in the theater, both men flirt with the lovely dancer on stage.

Backstage, Lola diagnoses Helen's marital problems as too much domesticity and not enough kisses and suggests Helen disguise herself as La Parry and have some fun with both her husband and Well. Helen cuts her hair, acquires a glamorous wardrobe, which includes diamond bracelets on her ankles, and sets out to captivate her two unknowing suitors. Of course, her keenest attentions are directed at her husband, who completely falls under her captivating spell.

She entices Joseph to run away with her, and in preparation for the departure, she takes Joseph to the Viennese hotel suite in which he and she (as Helen) had spent their honeymoon. The memories of his honeymoon in these very rooms awakens his conscience and Joseph realizes that he still loves his wife Helen. At this point, Lola reveals her masquerade and the couple reconcile in a happy ending.

Her Sister from Paris opened at the Capitol Theater in New York accompanied by the usual opulent stage show—the eighty-piece Capitol Grand Orchestra under conductor David Mendoza, the Ballet Corps, and a vocal ensemble of twenty-five, plus two shorts: a United States Navy aviation film entitled *Wings of the Fleet* and a Bruce Overture Scenic called *The Lace Surf*, and the Capitol News. The advertisements for the film contained a now-amusing addenda: "It's always cool at the Capitol. Complete changes of air every 5 minutes."

The film was welcomed by both the critics and the public as a familiar but delightfully naughty comedy. All were impressed with the vivacious Talmadge, and one critic called it all around entertainment but not for children because of its "almost" risqué plot. Donald Burney of *The New York Review* had particular praise for the subtitles by George Marion, Jr.: "[They] are clever in the extreme and carry out the genuine comedy view of this outrageously amusing piece."

Her Sister from Paris was remade in 1941 in an updated adaptation by S. N. Behrman, Salka Viertel, and George Oppenheimer entitled *Two-Faced Woman*. George Cukor directed the remake, and it starred Greta Garbo. The results were disastrous, and it turned out to be Garbo's last film.

The dual role impersonation theme has been a plot twist in many films. Very similar to *Her Sister from Paris* was *Moulin Rouge* (1934), based on the play by Lyon de Bri and starring Constance Bennett. Ferenc Molnar reversed the masquerade in *The Guardsman* (1931), with the dual role being played by the male star, the eminent Alfred Lunt, and the part of the wife was played by Lynn Fontanne.

Talmadge was the middle of three sisters from Brooklyn (who also included Norma and Natalie) all of whom were bright lights during the silent era, but whose Brooklynese accents reportedly prevented their transistion into talking pictures. In fact, Constance retired in 1929, never having appeared in a talkie.

Constance was one of the screen's most popular comediennes, and in 1921, she and Norma tied as the number two box-office stars of the year. Constance became a star by playing The Mountain Girl in D. W. Griffith's *Intolerance* (1916) and when her sister Norma married Joseph M. Schenck in 1917, Schenck set up production companies for all three sisters as well as Natalie's husband, Buster Keaton.

Constance's popularity peaked in the early 1920's, during which time she made six films directed by the able Sidney Franklin: *The Primitive Lover* (1922); *East Is West* (1922); the popular *Dulcy* (1923); *Her Night of Romance* (1924), also starring Ronald Colman; *Learning to Love* (1925); and *Her Sister from Paris* (1925).

Her Sister from Paris helped solidify Ronald Colman's reputation as a purveyor of sophisticated comedy, and this film was his second feature opposite Constance, the first being *Her Night of Romance*, also directed by Franklin and written by Kraly. Colman had been chosen by Lillian Gish as her co-star in *The White Sister* (1923) and would achieve major stardom with *Beau Geste* in 1926.

The Scottish born George K. Arthur also received positive reviews for his comic portrayal of Robert Well. Critics all noted his versatility, as this film marked a change of pace from the part which first brought him acclaim—that of the derelict in Josef von Sternberg's dreary and depressing *The Salvation Hunters* (1925).

Franklin was regarded as a meticulous craftsman and a superb woman's director. Although he was usually called a "respectable"—meaning "dull"—director, his Hollywood career is nevertheless quite remarkable. A native San Franciscan, he began as an actor and assistant director and graduated to directing with his brother Cester M. Franklin. *Her Sister from Paris* was one of six Constance Talmadge films he directed, and in 1928, Irving Thalberg hired him at M-G-M, where he earned his reputation as a woman's director, with such films as *The Actress* (1928), starring Norma Shearer; *Wild Orchids* (1929) with Greta Garbo; *Private Lives* (1931) and *The Barretts of Wimpole Street* (1934) both with Shearer again; and *The Good Earth* (1937) with Luise Rainer, which brought him his only Academy Award nomination for directing. He abandoned directing in 1937 for producing and his credits include *Waterloo Bridge* (1940), *Mrs. Miniver* (1942, Best Picture), *Random Harvest* (1942), *Madame Curie* (1943), and *Command Decision* (1949). His only return to directing was in 1957 with the remake of his own *The Barretts of Wimpole*

Street, this time starring Jennifer Jones.

Reviews of *Her Sister from Paris* praised Franklin's smooth continuity and especially pointed out the "startling convincingness" of his handling the double exposure scenes in which Talmadge plays both the wife and her sister, and in which one can be seen talking with the other and even embracing the other.

Much of the sophisticated wit of this film should be credited to screenwriter Hans Kraly. The German-born writer was the long-time collaborator of Ernst Lubitsch and went on to work on nine films directed by Franklin, including *Quality Street* (1927),*Wild Orchids*, and *Private Lives*.

Critics also commented on the film's "gorgeous" costumes; the film is one of the first screen credits for Gilbert Adrian, known simply as Adrian, who, after designing Rudolph Valentino's costumes for *The Eagle* (1925) and Cecil B. De Mille's productions of *The Volga Boatman* (1926) and *The King of Kings* (1927), went on to become M-G-M's renowned costume designer.

Her Sister from Paris is a typical entertainment of the period—no award-winner but popular with audiences and critics alike. It is also an example of the collaborative cohesiveness of early Hollywood, a cohesiveness which almost no longer exists. Joseph M. Schenck produced the majority of Constance Talmadge's best films, most of which were released through Associated First National; Talmadge and Colman proved to be a popular screen team in two films: this and *Her Night of Romance* (1924). Sidney Franklin directed six of Talmadge's films, Kraly wrote nine Franklin-directed films, and Adrian was costume designer for nearly all of Franklin's M-G-M films. The confidence and familiarity created by this collaborative "system" in early Hollywood was responsible for each studio's being able to produce some fifty films per year.

Ronald Bowers

HIS MAJESTY, THE AMERICAN

Released: 1919
Production: Douglas Fairbanks Pictures; released by United Artists
Direction: Joseph Henabery
Screenplay: Joseph Henabery
Cinematography: Victor Fleming and Glen MacWilliams
Art direction: Max Parker
Length: 8 reels

> *Principal characters:*
> William Brooks .... Douglas Fairbanks
> Marguerita .... Lillian Langdon
> Felicè, Countess of Montenac ....Marjorie Daw
> Émile Metz .... Jay Dwiggins
> Phillipe the Fourth ....Sam Southern
> Grand Duke Sarzeau .... Frank Campeau

His Majesty, the American was produced in 1919, the first year that United Artists was in business. The company was founded by Douglas Fairbanks, Charles Chaplin, D. W. Griffith, and Mary Pickford, whom Fairbanks would marry the following year. Fairbanks was a canny producer who had the sense to capitalize on what the United States, just emerging from World War I, wanted to see on the screen. People wanted escapism, and whether they got it from *His Majesty, the American*, with its combination of Western hijinks and Ruritanian romance, or from the later *Robin Hood* (1922) or *The Thief of Bagdad* (1924), they did not much care.

In 1918, Fairbanks had been a tremendous success selling war bonds with Chaplin and Pickford—he had fallen in love with Pickford, "America's Sweetheart," on that cross-country trip—and it was clear he could sell America on anything. Virtually until 1929, when he, with Pickford, made his first talking picture, *The Taming of the Shrew*, which was not a success, he was Hollywood's golden boy. His career went rapidly downhill after that, as age and expanding girth took over his athletic physique. He died in 1939 at the age of fifty-six.

Fairbanks' screen personality was essentially forged by writer Anita Loos, who thought that "Doug was just a big kid, and films a big romp." In films like *His Picture in the Papers* (1916), and *In Again Our Again* (1917), written by Loos, he sails through comedy, acrobatics, and romance with panache and grace. *His Majesty, the American* could have used some of Loos' breezy style. Director Joseph Henabery (perhaps most famous for playing Abraham Lincoln in *The Birth of a Nation* 1915), certainly shows little sense of comic timing, or even of knowing what to make of his star's formidable spirit.

Nevertheless, in *His Majesty, the American* Fairbanks embodies what Americans like to think are their best qualities: youth, a zest for adventure, and boundless optimism. However much time Fairbanks spends out of doors, he is basically a creation of urban culture, a man of the gym, not the jungle, like Tarzan. He was cinema's first urbane leading man, paving the way for later stars such as William Powell, Fred Astaire, and Cary Grant.

William Brooks (Douglas Fairbanks) is one of those suave heroes. The film begins in New York City where playboy Bill chases fire trucks and police cars. He rescues a family from a blazing tenement, swinging from building to building on a fireman's rope, then finds a missing girl in a den of iniquity which looks like the set from any Lon Chaney/Tod Browning melodrama. When a crusading district attorney cleans up the city and puts Bill out of business, he embarks for Murdero, Mexico, where amid Francisco (Pancho) Villa's bandits and the harsh countryside, he hopes to find adventure again. He teams up with Pete, one of Villa's favorite enemies, and accompanies him home to see Pete's mother. Bill is jealous of the fact that Pete *has* a mother: the only companion he has had is money. At this point, *His Majesty, the American* joins two parallel story lines. Up to this point, Bill's escapades have been interwoven with the story of strife and spies in a mythical European country called Alaine. Now Bill receives a telegram inviting him to go to Alaine incognito, so he quickly cleans up Murdero and sets off for Europe. When Bill arrives at the train station, there is a great deal of skullduggery involving the traitorous war minister, his agents, and the agents of King Phillipe (Sam Southern), all in identical tailcoats and top hats. There is also much ado over an agreement between the plotters and the neighboring enemy state with whom they are in cahoots. Eventually, the schemers are unmasked, and Bill is proclaimed heir apparent to the throne and reunited with his mother. He and Felicè, the Countess of Montenac (Marjorie Daw), become engaged and the film ends with the happy couple beaming down on a ballroom full of cheering Alainian nobles.

The plot of *His Majesty, the American* is schematic and silly, but no more idiotic than any other Ruritanian fable such as *The Merry Widow* or *The Student Prince*. *The Prisoner of Zenda*, with its interestingly flawed aristocrats, and equally flimsy premise, is not really of the same ilk. (The 1937 film version of the story starred Douglas Fairbanks, Jr., and showed definitively that the son was a "chip off the old block," and a better actor.) The protagonists here are solid cardboard with nothing more than the outlines of their characters to give them individuality. The denizens of the Western Hemisphere, both in New York and Murdero, are more sharply defined in temperament and appearance than any of the Alainians, and in light of subsequent developments, the viewer leaves them behind with regret. Out West, Bill's exploits are limited to leaping on and off horses, and in and out of gullies, but the rogues and peasant slaves he meets make up for his lack of derring-do. In Alaine, he vaults around his hotel and over balustrades, frequently puffing nonchalantly on a cigarette; he leads a charge on horseback and walks across the shoulders of a mob to rescue the king. He is a laughing cavalier who tosses quips and bodies with equal aplomb. Bill's most daring feat of physical prowess occurs when he jumps from his hotel to a nearby building and bounds around the roofs making his getaway. It is in this last sequence that Fairbanks gives his public what it had paid to see—the superb athlete carrying off heroic deeds with wit and élan.

The most entertaining moments in the film, however, have nothing to do with Fairbanks' obvious gifts. The first takes place in Murdero. When Bill is about to leave for Alaine, he tells Pete to dispose of Villa, whom he has captured. "Here, Pete, turn this fellow over to Carranza (one of Villa's foes) or put him in the movies." It is a reference to director Raoul Walsh's exploits in Mexico trying to make a film for Mutual about the Mexican revolutionary, and a bright bit of film self-consciousness. The second transpires before two easily beguiled chambermaids in the hotel room. Fairbanks mugs into a mirror, then puts a one hundred franc note on the dresser, saying, "It's a high note, but I'll try to reach it." He then mimes playing a piano on top of an open drawer to their wholehearted enjoyment. These vignettes and the shots of Manhattan, circa 1918, with its blazing tenements and the empty spaces around the Plaza Hotel and its fountain, are the most entertaining aspects of *His Majesty, the American*. The film cannot compare to those which are constructed around Fairbanks' amazing gymnastics and the story is too silly to be taken seriously on its own.

An unexplored subtheme of the film is the search for the mother. Bill has apparently grown up knowing nothing of his parents, and the most rewarding feature of his homecoming—if it can be called that—is not his victory over the villains or his engagement to Felicè, but finding his real mother. Unfortunately, the film does nothing with this notion except to have Bill express envy over Pete having one and to have him cuddle up to his own mother at the end. It is as though writer Joseph Henabery did not know what to do with the idea and director Henabery could not find a way to help him out, so the thought merely hangs around waiting for a development that never materializes.

Fairbanks always made the audience an *accomplice* in his films, and he initiates this relationship in *His Majesty, the American* before it even begins, by bounding through the title and winking at the viewers. Not infrequently, Fairbanks will halt the action momentarily to wink at the audience as if to say, "Aren't you having a good time? I am!" or "Watch this; it's fun!"

Fairbanks was more than a film actor; he was a personality, a little boy in grown-ups' clothing whose sheer moral force convinced people that whatever he did was right. Alistair Cooke once said, "At a difficult period in American history, Douglas Fairbanks appeared to know all the answers." Fairbanks, Jr., added, "Behind the . . . optimism and good cheer which were part of his philosophy, was the thought that if you had enough confidence in yourself, and were quickwitted enough, everything would come out all right." It is significant that, while actors like Jason Robards and Lon Chaney, also the sons of famous actors, dropped the "Junior" from their names, Douglas Fairbanks, Jr., has not, proving that there really is only one Douglas Fairbanks.

Judith M. Kass

HOLLYWOOD

Released: 1923
Production: Famous Players-Lasky for Paramount
Direction: James Cruze
Screenplay: Tom Geraghty; based on an original story by Frank Condon
Cinematography: Karl Brown
Length: 8 reels/8,100 feet

Principal characters:
Angela Whitaker .... Hope Drown
Joel Whitaker .... Luke Cosgrave
Lem Lefferts .... George K. Arthur
Grandmother Whitaker .... Ruby Lafayette
Dr. Luke Morrison .... Harris Gordon
Hortense Towers .... Bess Flowers
Margaret Whitaker .... Eleanor Lawson
Horace Pringle .... King Zany
Fat man in casting
director's office .... Roscoe "Fatty" Arbuckle
Guest Appearances .... Gertrude Astor,
Mary Astor. Agnes Ayres, Noah Beery, William
Boyd, Betty Compson, Ricardo Cortez, Viola Dana,
Cecil B. De Mille, William deMille, Douglas
Fairbanks, Sid Grauman, Alan Hale, Lloyd
Hamilton, William S. Hart, Jack Holt, Leatrice Joy,
J. Warren Kerrigan, Lila Lee, May McAvoy, Thomas
Meighan, Owen Moore, Nita Naldi, Pola Negri,
Anna Q. Nilsson, Jack Pickford, Mary Pickford, Will
Rogers, Ford Sterling, Anita Stewart, Gloria
Swanson, Ben Turpin, Lois Wilson, and others

    Hollywood recounts the familiar tale of a young girl who heads for California hoping to be the next Mary Pickford. Along with *The Extra Girl* (1923), *Merton of the Movies* (1924), *Ella Cinders* (1926), and the appropriately titled *Broken Hearts of Hollywood* (1926), *Hollywood* presents the reality that very few film hopefuls can close their eyes, snap their fingers, and find their names splashed across motion-picture marquees from Maine to New Mexico. The film was, in fact, produced as part of a propaganda effort to reduce the annual pilgrimage to Hollywood of thousands of young girls blinded with visions of film stardom. It is as much a product of the events of its day, however, as it is of a desire on the part of its makers to allow the public a voyeuristic peek at life in Hollywood once the cameras stop rolling.

    Angela Whitaker (Hope Drown), a poor young girl from the boondocks, dreams of film stardom. Her elderly grandfather, Joel (Luke Cosgrave), is ill and the pair travel West ostensibly for his health, but Angela feels that this will be her chance to crash the pictures. She drags herself from studio to studio, meeting but not recognizing many celebrities. Ironically, a director spies Joel, and decides that the old man would be perfect for his next film, so it is Joel who becomes a star.

He enjoys his sudden fame, learning how to play golf and personalizing his cigarettes by having his name and phone number embossed on them. Flustered by her grandfather's good fortune and by her continuing failure, Angela writes to her family for help. The old man's wife, daughter, and a cousin, Lem Lefferts (George K. Arthur)—who is also Angela's boyfriend—hurry to the coast to rescue Joel. They too, however, all become film actors. Cecil B. De Mille hires the women to act opposite Joel, and William S. Hart sees in Lem the potential for stardom as a screen hero. Lem plays in Hart's next picture, and does become a star.

After all this, Angela is still jobless. She and Lem marry, and the pair produce twins. Even the babies, who are named Doug and Mary, after Douglas Fairbanks and Mary Pickford, and the family parrot get to play in a film. Angela finally realizes that screen stardom is not meant to be, and settles into a life of wife-and-motherhood.

While none of the actors playing roles in *Hollywood* were then, or ever were, "names" (with the possible exception of George K. Arthur, who starred in Josef von Sternberg's *The Salvation Hunters*, 1925, and acted in films into the 1930's), the stars still do shine in the film. More than seventy-five stars, supporting players, directors, and other celebrities, however, appear throughout. The film is one of the first to feature the gimmick of casting dozens of Hollywood luminaries in cameo, bit parts, and nearly everybody then under contract to Paramount (and some who were not) are featured. Charlie Chaplin smiles proudly as a fan tells him she enjoyed his most recent film; she then addresses him as "Warren Kerrigan." Fairbanks and Pickford are shown in front of their estate Pickfair, with Doug sporting long hair grown for his role in *The Thief of Bagdad* (1924). Some actors perform in character: Will Rogers throws a lasso, Ben Turpin rolls his eyes, and Nita Naldi vamps. Others, from Gertrude Astor to Lois Wilson, Ford Sterling to Gloria Swanson, appear and smile, smile, smile.

On one level, *Hollywood* is an entertaining travelogue of the film capital. Yet, it is also an eight-reel public relations effort by Jesse Lasky and Paramount to convince the American public that Hollywood is not Sodom, that it is just a regular old place and film stars are just regular old people. In 1923, the year in which *Hollywood* was released, the film capital was still reeling from recent scandals such as the Fatty Arbuckle-Virginia Rappe affair: in 1921, the rotund funnyman, at the height of his popularity, was ruined when Rappe, a starlet, died of a ruptured bladder after allegedly being sexually assaulted by Arbuckle at a San Francisco party. Although Arbuckle was eventually acquitted, he never shook the stigma of the scandal. In 1922, William Desmond Taylor, a director at Famous Players-Lasky and president of the Screen Directors Guild, was murdered in his apartment. Actresses Mary Miles Minter and Mabel Normand had visited him on the night he was killed. He was allegedly having affairs with both, as well as with Minter's mother, Charlotte Shelby. The crime remains unsolved. Also in 1922, Wallace Reid, a popular leading man at Paramount, was committed to a sanatorium because he was addicted to morphine. He died there early the following year. (James Cruze, the director of *Hollywood*, often worked with both Arbuckle and Reid; his best-known film is the groundbreaking Western, *The Covered Wagon*, released in the same year as *Hollywood*.)

"Don't believe all the bad publicity you read in the tabloids," Lasky and company seem to be saying. They wanted the public to think that if they came to Hollywood, they would see that everyone was nice and innocent and moral. They also wanted the message to come across that if a young girl craved stardom in film, she would feel at home in Hollywood even if, like Angela Whitaker, she did not realize her dream. She could even remain in Hollywood, marry her sweetheart, and become a mother.

While Lem Lefferts is traveling by train to rescue Joel from the clutches of filmland, he has a surreal nightmare depicting evil, secretive men and women which culminates in an attempt on his life. When he arrives, he sees the reality—according to the filmmakers—and has no qualms about taking the role in Hart's picture. The spirit of Hollywood, according to *Hollywood*, is best represented by a sequence in which Thomas Meighan treats youngsters to candy and toys. "Lem" was a popular name for characters who travel to Hollywood on such missions. In the seductively titled short, *Uncensored Movies* (1923), Will Rogers plays another Lem, a representative of the "Cleaner Screen League" who visits filmland and reports to his provincial colleagues on its "evils." Hilariously, Rogers imitates William S. Hart, Tom Mix, Rudolph Valentino, and a D. W. Griffith hero.

All of the young hopefuls who fail in Hollywood do not end up like the unfortunate Virginia Rappe. In *Hollywood*, Angela Whitaker does not become a fallen woman; she has her babies *after* she marries Lem. In fact, Arbuckle, Rappe's "murderer," appears briefly in the film, in a sequence that could easily be edited out of the final print. He is billed as Roscoe Arbuckle, the "fat man in casting director's office"; a window is slammed shut on him, and he joins a crowd of actors who have also been unsuccessful at finding work. The message to the audience is clear: "We have cleaned up our act. We will police ourselves." Will H. Hays, former postmaster-general in Warren G. Harding's cabinet, became president of the newly formed Motion Picture Producers and Distributors of America in 1922, and it was his job to purify, cleanse, and sanitize Hollywood.

On April 12, 1922, Arbuckle was officially acquitted of any crime against

Rappe. The jury that freed him issued the following statement: "Acquittal is not enough for Roscoe Arbuckle. We feel a grave injustice has been done him and there was not the slightest proof to connect him in any way with the commission of any crime." Paramount still cancelled his three-million-dollar contract. His unreleased films remained so. He died on June 28, 1933, penniless and a broken man, which is perhaps the true story of *Hollywood*.

The film may be a likable comedy-drama, and it is always fascinating to see film stars "out of character." A more realistic picture of Hollywood can be seen in such films as *Sunset Boulevard* (1950), *The Bad and the Beautiful* (1952), and more recently *S.O.B.* and *True Confessions*, both released in 1981. These films beautifully illustrate the fact that for every glamorous star there is a faded starlet and for every successful director or writer there is a down-on-their-luck has-been.

Rob Edelman

HOTEL IMPERIAL

Released: 1927
Production: Famous Players-Lasky and Erich Pommer for Paramount
Direction: Mauritz Stiller
Screenplay: Jules Furthman; based on the novel *Színmü négy felvonásban* by
    Lajos Biró
Cinematography: Bert Glennon
Length: 8 reels/7,091 feet

> *Principal characters:*
> Anna Sedlak .... Pola Negri
> Lieutenant Paul Almasy .... James Hall
> General Juschkiewitsch .... George Siegmann
> Elias Butterman .... Max Davidson
> Tabakowitsch .... Michael Vavitch
> Anton Klinak .... Otto Fries

Hotel Imperial, although made in Hollywood by Paramount, is really an international production. Its director, Mauritz Stiller, who was born in Finland, had made his reputation in Sweden and had discovered Greta Garbo. Its production supervisor, Erich Pommer, was German and had been associated with the German classics *The Cabinet of Dr. Caligari* (1920), *Dr. Mabuse the Gambler* (1922), *Variety* (1926), *Metropolis* (1927), and later *The Blue Angel* (1930), and various films made in England. Its featured performer, Pola Negri, was Polish and had been a star in German films before embarking on her Hollywood career. Most indicative of the internationality of the film, though, is that it is stylistically closer to the more innovative European films of the period than to anything American.

Negri stars as a Hungarian Mata Hari named Anna Sedlak. The year is 1917, and the action takes place during World War I. Six Hungarian hussars, tired of battle, gallop into a frontier town somewhere in Galicia and find it taken over by Russians. Lieutenant Paul Almasy (James Hall) implores his men to fight, but his horse topples down. Delirious, he drags himself to the porter's lodging in the Hotel Imperial, where he passes out. Anna, a chambermaid, carries him to a bedroom and hides him. She is helped by Elias Butterman (Max Davidson) and Anton Klinak (Otto Fries), her fellow servants.

If he is discovered, Paul will surely be shot, so the following day, Anna persuades him to act as a waiter. The weary soldier is suddenly transformed into a well-groomed attendant. The Russian General Juschkiewitsch (George Siegmann), a drunkard, throws alcoholic orgies in the hotel and lusts after the reluctant Anna, who accepts the General's advances, only to protect Paul.

Tabakowitsch (Michael Vavitch), a Russian spy, returns to the hotel and demands that Paul prepare a bath. Paul learns that Tabakowitsch has information regarding the movement of the Hungarian troops that could result in a great military victory for the Russians, so he murders the spy, and Anna makes the death appear to be a suicide.

General Juschkiewitsch senses that Tabakowitsch's demise is the result of foul play and has Paul investigated. Anna defends the "waiter," which further enhances the Russian's suspicions. In the film's dramatic highlight, he realizes Anna loves Paul. "You were a servant once—you shall be a servant again," he pronounces, and then orders Anna, whom he has liberated from the drudgery of servant life and dressed in the finest clothes, to clean the floor in front of the startled guests and soldiers in the hotel. The ending is happy, however, as the Hungarians recapture their town. Paul and Anna survive and are united.

Stiller's direction of *Hotel Imperial* is visually impressive, particularly at the opening: as dawn approaches, the streets of the village are quiet and deserted, when the serenity is broken by the arrival of the soldiers. The orgy and revelry sequences are also quite memorable, with George Siegmann's alcoholic general a particularly dastardly villain. Actually, *Hotel Imperial* is as much Pommer's film as Stiller's; he supervised the production and director closely during the shooting, and even may have cowritten the screenplay.

The film is also noteworthy as the first to be made utilizing a "composite set." The stage on which the hotel was constructed was one of the biggest in Hollywood. Eight rooms were built, complete to the most minute detail, with four leading off each side of the lobby which ran the length of the building. Suspended above were rails from which the cameras, attached to a small carriage, "traveled" at the director's command. Shots could be made from above and from every possible angle. Actors could move from room to room with the cameras capturing all the action. Stiller did not need to yell "cut" when an actor exited a room. The result was an added intimacy and sense of drama, as the film could be shot as much as possible in sequence and with a minimum of continuity loss. The director was able to fill *Hotel Imperial* with striking camera angles and compositions, with an emphasis on atmosphere.

The film received mixed reviews. The direction, performances, and production values were generally praised; the plot, however, was regarded as a trivial, stale spy tale. This analysis is fair: *Hotel Imperial* has an entertaining but predictable and melodramatic scenario. Still, the film is one of the better of the silent era, and one of Paramount's biggest money-makers. It was remade in 1939 by Robert Florey, with Isa Miranda as Anna, Ray Milland as the lieutenant, Reginald Owen as the general, and J. Carroll Naish as the spy. It is only an average melodrama.

Negri most decidedly gives the best performance of her American career as Anna. Allegedly the daughter of a gypsy violinist who died while in exile in Siberia, Negri studied ballet in Russia, appeared in Polish films beginning in 1914, and German films in 1917. Her work in Germany, particularly with Ernst Lubitsch, won her offers to go to Hollywood. She came to America in 1923 and immediately became a sensation. She had a love affair with Rudolph Valentino—he died when she was completing her final scenes in *Hotel Imperial*—and then married a count and a prince, in succession.

Negri was no more than an adequate actress, but her natural style and charisma endeared her to audiences. Her screen roles were generally earthy, exotic, and erotic; she specialized in playing cynical, shopworn women who were "experienced." Because of the European flavor of her films, she appealed to both sophisticates and the masses, who had grown tired of the "innocent" characterizations popularized by Mary Pickford and Charles Ray. Critically, though, her work never justified her European reputation. Her most typical credits are self-explanatory: *A Woman of the World* (1925), *The Woman on Trial* (1927), *The Woman from Moscow* (1928), *The Woman He Scorned* (1930), and *A Woman Commands* (1932).

Negri is given fine support by James Hall and Siegmann. Hall, a leading man during the latter part of the silent era and early talkie period, is best known for his work in Howard Hughes' *Hell's Angels* (1930), with Jean Harlow and Ben Lyon. Siegmann, one of the better and busiest character actors and villains of the silent screen, appeared in dozens of films, from D. W. Griffith's *The Birth of a Nation* (1915, as Silas Lynch, the mulatto Lieutenant Governor) and *Intolerance* (1916, as Cyrus the Persian) to *The Three Musketeers* (1921), *Anna Christie* (1923), *The Cat and the Canary* (1927), and *The King of Kings* (1927).

Stiller entered the Swedish film industry in 1912 and, with Victor Seastrom, became one of the top directors of the Golden Age of the silent Swedish cinema. After directing Garbo in *The Atonement of Gosta Berling* (1924), the pair came to Hollywood at the invitation of Louis B. Mayer. The mogul wanted Stiller with Garbo only as a secondary thought. Once in California, however, the positions became reversed. Garbo was groomed for stardom while Stiller, who deplored Mayer, remained idle. He was merely an assistant director and interpreter on Garbo's first American feature, *The Torrent* (1926), directed by Monta Bell. At the actress' insistence, Stiller was assigned to direct her in *The Temptress* (1926), her next project, but after several clashes with M-G-M executives, Stiller was replaced by Fred Niblo.

Stiller then went over to Paramount, where he made *Hotel Imperial* and *The Woman on Trial*, also with Negri. He again battled with studio executives and was replaced by Josef von Sternberg in midproduction of his third American feature, *The Street of Sin* (1928), starring Emil Jannings. Stiller was broken, so he left Hollywood to return home, and while his protégée was embarking on her career as one of Hollywood's great legends, he died of a respiratory ailment in 1928. Despite Pommer's contribution to *Hotel Imperial*,

Stiller displays enough style in the film to have become perhaps one of Hollywood's pantheon directors.

Rob Edelman

HUMOROUS PHASES OF FUNNY FACES

Released: 1906
Production: J. Stuart Blackton
Direction: J. Stuart Blackton
Screenplay: J. Stuart Blackton
Cinematography: no listing
Animation: J. Stuart Blackton
Length: 1 reel/150 feet

Principal character:
Cartoonist .... J. Stuart Blackton

Sometime during the late 1890's, a young English-born newspaper cartoonist and vaudeville sketch artist named J. Stuart Blackton arrived at Thomas Edison's Black Maria film studio in West Orange, New Jersey, to interview the famous inventor for the *New York World*. While there, Blackton partook of the then unique opportunity to observe the process of motion-picture production and even had his own vaudeville "chalk talk" act photographed by the Edison camera. The resulting film, a short piece entitled *The Enchanted Drawing* or *Blackton, The Evening World Cartoonist* (1896), was one of the first—if not the very first—attempts at cinematic animation and, as such, has become recognized as an important pioneering step in the development of the animated cartoon.

Blackton emerged from his sessions with Edison fascinated by films and determined to crash the growing and already competitive motion-picture business. He entered into partnership with William T. "Pop" Rock (owner of one of America's first motion-picture houses, Vitascope Hall in New Orleans) and an exnightclub entertainer named Alfred E. Smith, a man who furthered the technology of the cinema by his invention of an improved shutter and reframing device for projectors. The three men named their new company Vitagraph (the firm incorporated in 1900) and quickly went about the business of producing motion pictures.

They set up a studio on the roof of the Morse Building at 140 Nassau Street in New York City and built an outdoor stage that could revolve to follow the sun's light. Their first film was *The Burglar on the Roof* (1896), a crude affair photographed by Smith, written and designed by Blackton, who also did the acting chores. Two years later, they capitalized on the public hysteria over the Spanish-American War with *The Battle of Santiago, or, Tearing Down the Spanish Flag*, in which they ingeniously used models of warships photographed in a bathtub to simulate real events.

Other early Vitagraph efforts included *Happy Hooligan* (1903), a film based on a popular newspaper comic strip in which Blackton played the lead role, and *The Humpty Dumpty Circus* (1903), in which the stop-motion technique was employed. In 1904, they persuaded Mark Twain to let them make a film based on his story, "A Curious Dream," the results of which Twain himself described as "frightfully and deliciously humorous." Also released during this period were filmed parts of two successful Broadway plays, *A Gentleman of France* (1903) and *Raffles, the Amateur Cracksman* (1905).

In 1906, Vitagraph produced what has been recognized by film historians as the first film to utilize animated drawings photographed with the single frame method, *Humorous Phases of Funny Faces*. To audiences of the period, the film must have been a pure delight and even today its simple humor remains fresh and clear.

It opens with title letters forming out of small white lines which appear individually out of thin air. What follows are seven separate segments, each quite short and unique. In the first segment, a hand (Blackton's) is seen drawing two cartoon faces on a chalkboard; a bald man with long sideburns and a pretty, young, bareshouldered woman. As the animation begins, the man's eyes roam toward the woman, and he smiles. She returns his smile and winks provocatively. Then the man begins to grow hair, a jauntily angled top hat pops onto his head, and a smoking cigar appears in his mouth. Quickly, however, the cigar smoke obscures the woman entirely, and the cartoonist's hand returns to wipe the images away.

The next segment follows immediately, but this time no hand is seen drawing the figure of a portly man wearing a bowler hat and brandishing an umbrella. The appearance of the artist is now unnecessary, for the first segment has revealed the animation process, and the audience has now learned exactly how the drawings are made to appear and move. After the portly man throws his umbrella around a few times, he simply disappears and the next segment begins.

Now that the audience knows the mechanics of animation, Blackton begins to play around with different ideas, for he realizes that viewers will be able to follow all of his tricks. The third segment is shown in reverse time; that is, the action progresses from its real ending backward to its initiation. Thus, the first image is that of an erased board. Then the clouds of rubbed chalk gradually disappear to reveal beneath them the faces of a man and woman talking to each other. After this scene continues for a few moments, the two figures disappear line by line and the segment closes with a clean chalkboard.

Next comes the animated antics of a circus clown who doffs his pointed hat several times and then performs some tricks with a poodle that jumps up and down and through a hoop. The section ends with the artist's hand returning to wipe away first one half of the drawing and then the rest of it.

The fifth section is the most disturbing one to modern audiences, for its humor relies on racial stereotyping and caricature. Blackton begins by drawing the word "coon" on a large sheet of white paper, and then, by using the two "o's" as eyes, he draws a grinning black face, bug-eyed and thick-lipped; the archetypal portrait of racial caricature. Next, he writes the name "Cohen" and draws the stereotyped Jewish face around it. The "C" becomes the Jew's large nose and a dark, black beard rounds out the figure. Obviously, this was a high point of Blackton's vaudeville "chalk talks," and contemporary audiences surely loved these caricatures, although seen today, they seem hateful and ugly. They do serve, however, to illustrate the pervasiveness of American racial and ethnic prejudice.

The final two segments are reeled off rather quickly. First, Blackton draws a side-view portrait of a friend and after both men leave the frame, the drawn figure comes to life, smiling profusely and smoking a large cigar. The last section involves, for the first time, the drawn use of inanimate objects: a wine bottle, seltzer bottle, and wine glass. The wine bottle's cork pops and the bottles pour liquid into the glass. Then Blackton appears, tears the paper and leaves, after which the rest of the paper tears itself into little bits and *Humorous Phases of Funny Faces* comes to an end.

After 1906, Blackton and Vitagraph continued to break cinematic ground. In 1908, they released *The Haunted Hotel*, which used the single frame technique of *Humorous Phases of Funny Faces* with real objects rather than animated figures. One year later, Blackton produced and directed what could be considered the first feature-length film, a five-reeler entitled *The Life of Moses*. Because of resistance on the part of the Motion Picture Patents Company (the infamous "Trust") and its distributing arm, General Film, however, *The Life of Moses* was sent to theaters one reel at a time for five weeks. By 1914, however, the Trust's influence was on the wane and Vitagraph was able to release *The Christian* as an eight-reel feature.

In 1918, Blackton withdrew from running Vitagraph and control of the company passed to the Guarantee Trust Company where it remained until its sale to Warner Bros. in 1925. Blackton formed his own production company and continued to make films in New Jersey through the 1920's, producing and directing such films as *The Glorious Adventure* (1922), photographed in Prizmacolor; *The Redeeming Sin* (1925), starring Nazimova and Lou Tellegen; and *Bride of the Storm* (1926), with popular star Dolores Costello. Blackton died in 1941.

Blackton and his Vitagraph Company were very important pioneers of the American cinema in its formative years, and one of their most lasting efforts, *Humorous Phases of Funny Faces*, marked the true beginning of American animation, a small but unique step forward which explored the wondrous capabilities of the new medium of motion pictures and provided inspiration for those which were to follow.

Daniel Einstein

THE HUNCHBACK OF NOTRE DAME

Released: 1923
Production: Universal Super Jewel
Direction: Wallace Warsley
Screenplay: Perlez Poore Sheehan; based on the novel *Notre-Dame de Paris* by Victor Hugo
Cinematography: Tony Karuman and Robert Newhard
Length: 12 reels/12,000 feet

Principal characters:
Quasimodo .... Lon Chaney
Esmeralda .... Patsy Ruth Miller
Phoebus .... Norman Kerry
Clopin .... Ernest Torrence
Gringoire .... Raymond Hatton
Dom Claude .... Nigel De Brulier
Justice of the Court .... John Cossar

Victor Hugo's famous novel *Notre-Dame de Paris* (*The Hunchback of Notre Dame*, 1831) has proven to be a durable subject for filmmakers, forming the basis for a variety of films. The best-known adaptations, however, are the three films bearing the title *The Hunchback of Notre Dame*. Of the three, the 1956 version with Anthony Quinn is perhaps the weakest. The 1939 version starring Charles Laughton and directed by William Dieterle, a master of pictorial composition and an adept hand at managing crowd scenes, was a triumph of studio technique. Yet, the most interesting version was the 1923 vehicle that made Lon Chaney a star.

In theory, the sheer magnificence of the spectacle with its meticulously re-created settings (notably the cathedral itself) should have (as it did to some degree, in the 1939 version) dwarfed the individual performances. That did not happen, though. The character of Quasimodo the bell ringer towered above his settings and in some way affected the lives of all of the other characters. That this happened is no little testament to the acting abilities of Chaney. Whereas the 1939 remake emerged as a superior work of horror, the 1923 version had less ambitious pretensions and became, through Chaney's individual effort, a historical spectacle as well as a commentary on man and his society. Quasimodo became the focal point and the representative of the forces of the city and of the church. The inherent danger in portraying a character with the physical deformities of the hunchback is the tendency to rely too heavily on the physical aspects, hence creating a one-dimensional portrait. The resulting lumbering brute would thus become little more than a foil for the other characters.

Chaney's depiction establishes Quasimodo as an instigator who moves the action forward as a result of well-defined and inherently logical motives. For example, at the beginning of the film, he is a loyal and devoted servant to the priest Dom Claude (Nigel De Brulier) until forced to make a decision between him and the gypsy Esmeralda (Patsy Ruth Miller) whom the priest is attempting to victimize. Esmeralda is gentle to the hunchback where Dom Claude had been stern. Thus, the misshapen creature's devotion for her increases to such a point that when she is threatened by the mob, his love for her transforms itself into an intense hatred for those who would do her harm. The depth of the emotion manifests itself in his throwing rocks, timbers, and hot metal from the ramparts of the cathedral down upon the rabble. His pantomimic art in expressing these emotions and thought processes deepens the characterization beyond the superficial, physical effects of makeup and costume.

The film is set in fifteenth century Paris where a crowd has gathered to celebrate a double feast day—Epiphany Sunday and the Feast of Fools. Thus, there is more than the usual amount of high spirits and frivolity as dancing girls, street vendors, clowns, and wandering entertainers fill the streets. Among the motley celebrants, though, is a young dancing girl, Esmeralda, a gypsy, who, despite a prohibition against her people, has secretly entered the city to intercede with King Louis XI on behalf of the gypsies. While trying to find a way to arrange an audience with the King, she bides her time by dancing and performing magic tricks with a trained goat. Several feet away from her, Gringoire (Raymond Hatton), a poet-playwright, is attempting to act out an allegorical play with little success. The jeering crowd pays scant attention to his efforts as, instead, they try to stage their own pageant—a contest to select a "Pope of Fools" who would be the ugliest man in Paris.

The crowd gasps in horror, however, as the hideous face of Quasimodo, the bell ringer at Notre Dame appears through the paper rose screen on the outdoor stage. He is instantly acclaimed the Pope of Fools and a jester's cap with bells is placed on his head. For his part, Quasimodo is delighted. Normally he has been regarded as a monster to be shunned by the townspeople, but now he is for one brief moment the center of attention, even if it is only as a king of fools. He is a foundling with a legion of deformities, including an immense hunchback, a misshapen face with one eye that droops almost halfway down his cheek. The other eye is not much better. The cheek that holds it twists upward, forcing the eye to turn outward above a shapeless nose. His mouth is full of jagged teeth and his legs are twisted. (Film historians have recently speculated that Quasimodo suffered from the same disease as John Merrick, the nineteenth century "Elephant Man.") His days of glory are few, so he is enjoying himself when the festivities are suddenly ended by Dom Claude who, in a rage, forces the hunchback to return to the cathedral. Quasimodo is heartbroken but follows his guardian back to the church.

The priest, although occupied with his charge, also notices Esmeralda.

Despite his vows of chastity, he becomes overcome with lust for the gypsy girl and, that night, sends Quasimodo to bring her to him. Esmeralda is terrified by the hunchback's appearance and runs away. The misshapen creature, though, is possessed of wonderful strength and agility and seizes her and carries her off. The abduction is witnessed by Phoebus (Norman Kerry), a captain of the guards who, with his men, rescues her and subdues Quasimodo.

While this is taking place, Gringoire, wandering through the streets in search of a place to spend the night, accidentally stumbles into a Parisian slum inhabited by crooks, cutthroats, and beggars. He is captured by some of the denizens of this underworld and taken before Clopin (Ernest Torrence), the reputed king of beggars. Although intruders are normally put to death, he is given a chance to live if he can survive a ritual test. He must successfully pick the pocket of a trick mannequin that has been rigged with bells for use as a practice dummy for the ghetto's light-fingered pickpockets. Gringoire fails miserably and is about to be put to death when the recently rescued Esmeralda enters the scene. Taking pity on him, she saves him from execution by agreeing to marry him in a mock ceremony, although she has actually fallen in love with her handsome savior—Captain Phoebus.

Phoebus has meanwhile taken Quasimodo before a deaf judge (John Cossar) who does not notice that Notre Dame's bell ringer's hearing is likewise impaired. The hunchback does not understand the judge's questions and is consequently sentenced to a punishment by flogging because the other man thinks that his own deformity is being mocked by Quasimodo's wild gestures in trying to make his own condition known. He is flogged before the doors of Notre Dame and then left in chains to be humiliated by the mob. Dom Claude will not come to his rescue, but, ironically, Esmeralda happens by and gives him some water, although only a few hours before he had tried to abduct her. Through this act of charity, she wins his unceasing devotion.

Although his plan for abducting the gypsy girl has failed so ignominiously, Dom Claude continues to plot the conquest of the object of his lust. When he subsequently sees her embracing Phoebus, he stabs the soldier in a fit of jealousy. Yet, again he lets someone else take the punishment for his act. This time it is Esmeralda who is arrested—for murder. Because of her magic tricks, she is sentenced to be hanged as a witch in the cathedral square. Quasimodo, however, comprehends the situation and while her "husband" Gringoire watches helplessly, the misshapen creature swings down from the cathedral and snatches Esmeralda from the hangman just as she is about to be executed. He quickly swings back into the cathedral with his prize.

Although Esmeralda is temporarily safe, Clopin, fearful that some of the nobles might attempt to violate the sanctuary of the cathedral to recapture their victim, gathers his band of criminals and rushes to her rescue. Unable to dissuade him, Gringoire writes an appeal to the King. Clopin's idea is to extricate the girl from Notre Dame and move her to a place of concealment, but Quasimodo, seeing the mob of beggars and thieves converging on the church imagines the worst. Fearful that the group will harm Esmeralda, he protects her by throwing stones and timbers from the cathedral's reconstruction down upon the heads of her would-be rescuers. Just as Clopin's ragged troops are about to break through the doors, the hunchback seizes caldrons of molten lead intended for repairs to the roof and pours the burning liquid into the rain gutters. The fluid drains through the mouths of gargoyles which act as rain spouts pouring the melted lead on the crowd and killing Clopin.

At this point, the King's troops arrive, and Quasimodo realizes that he has made a mistake. Gringoire's plea has been granted by the King, and Esmeralda's safety is guaranteed. At this moment, however, she is still very much in danger. Dom Claude, realizing that the tide has turned against him, pursues Esmeralda to the bell tower where she rings the bells for help. Quasimodo, dimly hearing the clamor, rushes to her rescue and, turning against his master, hurls him to his death. Esmeralda then learns that Phoebus had only been wounded and is still very much alive. She marries him and leaves the creature whose devotion more than any other had sustained her through her persecution.

Chaney's interpretation of the role of the hunchback has become a classic and, viewed today, it is difficult to realize in a number of instances, that it was merely an actor playing a role. In many scenes, he resembles a gargoyle that has come to life as he scrambles about his domain in the rafters of the cathedral roof. Yet, from under the weight of the layers of makeup which took hours to apply, there emanated emotions of hurt, tenderness, devotion, and also of hatred. This was a flesh-and-blood man. If viewers responded to the hunchback with feelings of sympathy and respect, it was Chaney and not the makeup or the story that elicited them.

The makeup worn by Chaney and the pain it caused him has become something of a legend, however, and bears repeating. The humps were created through the use of a harness that held molded rubber mounds in front and back to simulate the hunchback. It also restricted the actor's body so that he could not stand erect. A rubbery substance resembling skin with tufts of hair on the shoulders, arms, and chest was placed over the harness. The entire outfit weighed slightly more than seventy pounds and was capped by the actor's face which had been transformed. The eyes, nose, and cheekbones were built up with mortician's wax and jagged false teeth were fitted with wire to force Chaney's mouth to gape. Finally, the entire face was covered with greasepaint, and a dirty wig and bushy eyebrows completed the effect. Seldom has an actor suffered so much to create a character.

The Hunchback of Notre Dame is today the best remembered of all of Chaney's films. It provided an opportunity for the actor to reveal, in depth, the many sides of his art within a single characterization. Although one might be tempted to draw comparisons between it and Laughton's 1939 treatment of the role, and even Quinn's 1956 attempt, it would be unfair. All are different and pursue different goals. Whereas the 1939 version is remembered for many different values, the 1923 original will always be linked to Chaney's performance. It is his picture and will always stand as a tribute to his art.

Linda Edgington

INTOLERANCE

Released: 1916
Production: D. W. Griffith for Wark Producing Corporation
Direction: D. W. Griffith
Screenplay: D. W. Griffith
Titles: Anita Loos and Rabbi L. Myers
Cinematography: G. W. Bitzer
Editing: James Smith and Rose Smith
Art direction: Frank Wortman
Length: 14 reels/11,811 feet

Principal characters:
Of All Ages
The Woman Who Rocks the Cradle .... Lillian Gish
The Modern Story
The Dear One .... Mae Marsh
Her Father .... Fred Turner
The Boy .... Robert Harron
Arthur Jenkins .... Sam De Grasse
Mary T. Jenkins .... Vera Lewis
The Friendless One .... Miriam Cooper
The Musketeer of the Slums .... Walter Long
The Kindly Policeman .... Tom Wilson
The Judaean Story
The Christ .... Howard Gaye
The French Story
Brown Eyes .... Margery Wilson
Prosper Latour .... Eugene Pallette
Catherine de Médicis .... Josephine Crowell
Marguerite de Valois .... Constance Talmadge
The Babylonian Story
The Mountain Girl .... Constance Talmadge
The Rhapsode .... Elmer Clifton
Prince Belshazzar .... Alfred Paget
Attarea .... Seena Owen

The sheer creative genius of D. W. Griffith was such that within weeks of completing his first master work, *The Birth of a Nation* (1915), he had commenced preparations for his second great achievement—one which was possibly more important than its predecessor: *Intolerance*. From the drama of America's Civil War and its aftermath, Griffith turned to not one historical episode, but to four—a modern story, France in the sixteenth century, ancient Babylon, and the life of Christ—linked by a common theme, intolerance. A massive subject, Griffith treated it with all the spectacle that it deserved, at the same time not allowing the gigantic proportions of his theme to dwarf the intimacy of the human dramas being played out. Contrary to some critical opinion, Griffith was not seeking to atone for any supposed wrong caused by *The Birth of a Nation*. He had nothing for which to atone, and *Intolerance*, under its working title of *The Mother and the Law*, was already planned when the storm of racial protest broke over *The Birth of a Nation*. *Intolerance* was "A Drama of Comparisons," depicting "Love's Struggle throughout the Ages." It was, as *Photoplay*'s Julian Johnson succinctly put it, "a collective story of the penalities paid through the centuries to those 'who do not believe as we believe.'"

Griffith saw intolerance as a danger to artistic freedom. He expanded the original production of *The Mother and the Law* into the film subsequently released as *Intolerance*; and in conjunction with the feature, he published a pamphlet entitled *The Rise and Fall of Free Speech in America*. The director continually spoke out against film censorship, and he spoke not from purely personal motives; he objected vehemently to the many local ordinances proposed across America to regulate motion pictures.

The stories comprising *Intolerance* were carefully researched by the director, who utilized many sources. The Bible, of course, provided background, as did a Federal Industrial Commission report, which detailed the profits of various large companies as well as the wages paid the workers of those companies. One episode on which Griffith did not base the Modern Story of *Intolerance* was the Stielow Case, an incident which involved a last-minute reprieve from hanging similar to the one in *Intolerance*. Griffith had already filmed his last-minute rescue of the boy at the gallows before the Stielow Case came to its climax. Here was one example of life imitating art, and not art imitating life. To link his various tales of intolerance, Griffith chose some lines from Walt Whitman's *Leaves of Grass*: ". . . endlessly rocks the cradle, Uniter of Here and Hereafter." His choice was no casual one, but a quotation remembered from a conversation with actor Wilfred Lucas when the two men were in the same road company at the turn of the century. The evidence seems to indicate that Griffith did indeed carry the scenario for *Intolerance* in his head, only trusting his thoughts for the next day's shooting to paper at the end of each day's production, dictating it to his associate Frank E. Woods. Although Anita Loos has taken credit for the writing of the subtitles in *Intolerance*, it appears that she contributed only a few comic titles to the production, with the bulk of the film clearly being the sole work of Griffith.

Intolerance was shot at the Fine Arts studio at 4500 Sunset Boulevard in Los Angeles. The gigantic Babylonian sets, which towered over the small community of Hollywood, were constructed under the supervision of Frank (Huck) Wortman. For the scenes of the siege of Babylon, filmed in March, 1916, some three thousand extras participated, and according to a report in *Photoplay*, only one person was killed—not an actor but a workman dismantling part of the set. 300,000 feet of film were supposedly exposed during the production, and, in fact, the finished feature gives hints of scenes that Griffith must have been ruthlessly forced to excise from *Intolerance*. One whole episode involving St. Veronica is gone as is a sequence involving a mother whose dead child Christ resurrects on his way to Gethsemane, which is an obvious parallel to the child taken from its mother in the Modern Story.

Griffith did have to contend with one form of censorship during the production. When the B'nai Brith learned that the director was planning to depict the Jews crucifying Christ, it registered a strong objection, pointing out that censorship boards, state governors, and even the President would be called upon to ban the objectionable scenes. Griffith had no alternative but to burn the negative of the offending sequences and reshoot the episode showing Roman soldiers nailing Christ to the cross.

Employing the entire Griffith stock company, *Intolerance* used several performers in more than one role. Constance Talmadge "starred" as the Mountain Girl in the Babylonian Story, but also had a minor part as Marguerite de Valois in the French Story. Major stars to be, such as Bessie Love, George Walsh, and Wallace Reid, played relatively unimportant roles, while appearing in the ranks of the extras were the likes of Sir Herbert Beerbohm Tree, Douglas Fairbanks, and Owen Moore. Ruth St. Denis choreographed the dances in the Babylonian sequence, but does not seem to have participated in the actual scenes. She is about the only person who did not. Margery Wilson became a star thanks to her role as Brown Eyes. Mae Marsh, Robert Harron, Miriam Cooper, and others from *The Birth of a Nation* proved that their performances in the latter film were no flukes. Lillian Gish who had "starred"—although Griffith never starred his actors in the current sense of the word—in *The Birth of a Nation*, appears here in the minor, but crucial role of the woman who rocks the cradle which links the various stories of *Intolerance*.

As has already been stated, *Intolerance* is composed of four distinct stories, linked by a common theme. The film moves backward and forward in time as it brings the four stories to their climaxes, of which all but one are tragic. The least important of the stories are those concerned with the life of Christ and the St. Bartholomew's Day Massacre of 1572. The Judaean Story treats only three episodes in the life of Christ: the miracle at Cana in which Christ (Howard Gaye) turns water into wine, Christ's sympathy toward the woman taken in adultery, and his Crucifixion. All of these have obvious parallels with present-day "do-gooders," such as prohibitionists, those who would set themselves up to judge the sexual behavior of others, and similar individuals. The French Story, for example, has Catherine de Médicis (Josephine Crowell) persuade her son, King Charles IX of France, to sign the order for the massacre of the Protestants (or Huguenots), who are opposed to her power. On the eve of their wedding, two young people, the Protestant Brown Eyes (Margery Wilson) and the Catholic Prosper Latour (Eugene Pallette), are victims of the massacre. For pageantry, the French Story is almost as impressive as the Babylonian sequence. The portrayals are a curious mixture of malevolent melodrama (as represented by Josephine Crowell in the role of Catherine de Médicis) and the pure Griffith-inspired innocence of Brown Eyes, whose fiancé Latour is portrayed by a relatively slim version of well-known 1930's character actor Eugene Pallette. One brief moment which always moves an audience has a Catholic priest hiding a Protestant child under his gown, to save it from slaughter. Yet the nagging suspicion remains that Griffith included this sequence chiefly to appease any potential criticism from the Catholic Church.

The most visually impressive of the four stories is the Babylonian one. Nabonidas is King of Babylon, a city of happy and contented people, where live and let live is the order of the day, and where Nabonidas' son Prince Belshazzar (Alfred Paget) is loved by the Princess Beloved and also unknown to him, by one of his lowly subjects, the Mountain Girl (Constance Talmadge). She, in turn, is loved by the Rhapsode (Elmer Clifton), a servant of the High Priest of Bel, who is against the introduction of the worship of Ishtar into Babylon. The High Priest conspires with Cyrus the Persian to capture the city. The first attack on Babylon is repulsed, but the Mountain Girl learns of a plot by the High Priest to have the city gates opened to the invaders. She races in her chariot back to Babylon to warn her adored Belshazzar, but it is too late, and both Belshazzar and the Princess Beloved commit suicide rather than be captured by Cyrus.

The Babylonian episode, aside from its splendor, has some genuine comic moments such as when the Mountain Girl is offered in a marriage auction, or as she swooningly thinks of the Prince Belshazzar while milking a goat. Constance Talmadge never again attained the brilliance which her performance in this role displayed. Also deserving of praise is Elmer Clifton as the Rhapsode, an effete-looking character far removed from the reassuring masculinity of his Phil Stoneman in *The Birth of a Nation*.

The Modern Story is concerned with the Dear One (Mae Marsh) and the Boy (Robert Harron), both of whom suffer as a result of the actions of wealthy mill owner Arthur Jenkins (Sam De Grasse), who lowers the wages of his workers in order to pour more money into his sister's charitable activities. In the city, the Boy marries the Dear One and decides to sever his connections with the criminal element, led by the Musketeer of the Slums (Walter Long). The Musketeer, however, has had one of his henchmen plant stolen goods on the youth, and the Boy is sent to jail. The Dear One is comforted by her new-born child, but it is taken away from her by the Jenkins Foundation, which declares her to be an unfit mother: in addition to the fact that the father is in prison, the Dear One has been spotted drinking a glass of beer. When the Boy is released from jail, his troubles are far from over, for he is again arrested. He is convicted for the murder of the Musketeer, who was actually killed by a jealous girl friend, the Friendless One (Miriam Cooper). After the Boy is sentenced to death, the Dear One attempts in vain to gain a reprieve. Just as all seems lost, the Friendless One confesses to the Dear One and to a friendly neighborhood policeman (Tom Wilson), and the Boy is saved at the last second after a race by car and train to get to the governor and then to reach the prison.

The acting in the Modern Story is of a style against which all silent-film acting must be measured. Mae Marsh's performance is unsurpassed and is climaxed by the much-discussed courtroom scene in which her hands and face demonstrate the anguish she feels as her husband is sentenced to death. Yet, that scene is insignificant when compared to an earlier sequence in which Marsh as the Dear One realizes that her baby (thanks to the lack of care by the Jenkins Foundation) is dead.

The response to *Intolerance* was mixed. Griffith in *Motion Picture News* (September 16, 1916) explained his motives behind the structure of the film,

> I have endeavored to make the incidents which I have shown on the screen of such a nature that the audience on viewing the picture conceives and elaborates the story in his mind. In other words, the greatest value of the picture will be in its suggestive value to the audience, in the manner in which it will force it to create and work out the idea that I am trying to get over. I have made little or no attempt to tell a story, but I have made an attempt to suggest a story, and to my mind, it is a mighty big story. Whether or not it will succeed in its object remains to be seen.

Unfortunately, as far as the contemporary audiences were concerned, *Intolerance* did not succeed. For despite the fact that it is relatively simple for an audience to follow the interweaving stories today, audiences and critics in 1916 could not; or, perhaps more accurately, would not do so. Typical of the critical response is Alexander Woollcott's comments in *The New York Times* (September 10, 1916), "Unprecedented and indescribable splendor of pageantry is combined with grotesque incoherence of design and utter fatuity of thought to make the long-awaited new Griffith picture at the Liberty an extraordinary mixture of good and bad—of wonderful and bad.

Intolerance cost, according to its director, five times as much as *The Birth of a Nation* to produce, which would make its budget anywhere between one and two million dollars. It never regained its cost, and ran into further troubles as America geared up for entry into World War I, and the film's apparent pacifist undertones became unacceptable. In 1919, Griffith tried releasing two of the stories as separate features, *The Fall of Babylon* and *The Mother and the Law*, but they aroused only minor interest.

Anthony Slide

THE IRON HORSE

Released: 1924
Production: Fox Film Corporation
Direction: John Ford
Screenplay: Charles Kenyon; based on an original screen story by Charles Kenyon and John Russell
Titles: Charles Darnton
Cinematography: George Schneiderman
Length: 11 reels/10,424 feet

Principal characters:
Davy Brandon	George O'Brien
Miriam Marsh	Madge Bellamy
Peter Jesson	Cyril Chadwick
Deroux	Fred Kohler
Ruby	Gladys Hulette
Judge Haller	James Marcus
Thomas Marsh	Will Walling
Sergeant Slattery	Francis Powers
Corporal Casey	J. Farrell MacDonald
Private Schultz	James Welch
Dinny	Jack O'Brien
Tony	Colin Chase
Abraham Lincoln	Charles Edward Bull
General Dodge	Walter Rogers
Colonel William F. Cody ("Buffalo Bill")	George Waggner
Wild Bill Hickok	Jack Padjan
David Brandon, Sr.	James Gordon
Cheyenne Chief	Chief Big Tree
Sioux Chief	Chief White Spear
Davy (younger)	Winston Miller
Miriam (younger)	Peggy Cartwright

The Western has been a staple of screen entertainment since the cinema's earliest days. The revolutionary impact on film exhibition of *The Great Train Robbery* (1903) is generally credited as giving the genre its initial impetus, although there had been earlier films with "Western" settings (usually filmed in the wilds of New Jersey). Westerns had great audience appeal and could be made cheaply on outdoor locations, and, by 1910, most companies included them as part of their regular output. The genre's popularity took a big stride as the focus of film production shifted from New York to Los Angeles, beginning around 1907, since the rugged and varied scenery of Southern California made the Eastern locations look pale by comparison, and the new employment opportunities represented by the films attracted an abundance of real cowboys, who had been thrown out of work by the closing of the frontier. The presence of these men gave many Westerns of the period a truly authentic flavor. As a result of the introduction of G. M. Anderson's "Bronco Billy" character (which first appeared in 1908), the Western was at the forefront of the rapidly developing "star system." In the next decade, the genre became very personality oriented, as William S. Hart, Tom Mix, Harry Carey, and other cowboy stars rose to prominence.

During this same period, as the wild and woolly days of the "Old West" began to recede into the past, the mythologizing of the frontier experience accelerated. It was inevitable that motion pictures, which in their brief existence had established themselves as a powerful medium for shaping cultural awareness, would contribute to this process. Although most of the early Westerns were little more than "pulp" entertainments, one can discern the dawning of a historical consciousness. For example, there was a film about Custer's Last Stand in 1912, and Buffalo Bill Cody (in a logical extension of his Wild West Show) enacted a semifictional film version of his own life the following year. The conception of such films, however, usually stressed melodrama over any consideration of larger historical processes.

The breakthrough film, *The Covered Wagon*, did not appear until 1923. Directed by James Cruze for Famous Players-Lasky/Paramount, the film was set against the background of the pioneers' trek along the Oregon Trail—the first concentrated national thrust westward, and thus, a fitting subject for what is usually acknowledged as the first "epic Western." More significantly, *The Covered Wagon* was a major box-office success, thus clearly indicating a profitable new direction for the genre. Among the first to seek ways in which to capitalize on the new trend was producer William Fox, who set about planning a film about the building of the first transcontinental railroad, to be called *The Iron Horse*. To direct his epic, he chose a young director under contract to his studio, twenty-eight-year-old John Ford.

Ford, born Sean O'Feeney in Maine in 1895, had come to Hollywood in 1913 and had worked as an assistant to his older brother, serial star and director Francis Ford, at Universal for several years. He graduated to directing in 1917 and, in seven years, had made a total of forty-nine films, most of which were Westerns. He became a contract director at Fox in 1921 and, two years later, directed his biggest production to date, *Cameo Kirby*, starring John Gilbert. Released in October, 1923, to excellent notices, the film had the fortuitous result of bringing Ford to the attention of Fox as he was looking for a director for *The Iron Horse*. Ford's extensive experience with Westerns, coupled with a maturity and authority that belied his relative youth, made him the logical choice for the job.

Reportedly budgeted at the then-enormous sum of $450,000 (although one Ford biographer puts the cost at $280,000), *The Iron Horse* was the Fox Film

Corporation's most expensive production to date. The cast list includes "a complete regiment of U.S. Cavalry, three thousand railroad workers, one thousand Chinese laborers, eight hundred Pawnee, Sioux and Cheyenne Indians, two thousand horses, thirteen hundred buffalos and ten thousand head of cattle." These figures were probably inflated by Fox's publicity department, but the logistics of the production were still impressive. The studio was fully prepared to commit the funds necessary to surpass the scale of *The Covered Wagon*, but decided to save some money on salaries by casting an unknown in the lead, instead of an established star. At Ford's suggestion, George O'Brien, a young assistant of cinematographer George Schneiderman, was given a test; impressed by his good looks, excellent physique, and athletic ability, the studio awarded him the part.

Wadsworth, Nevada (about forty miles east of Reno), was selected as the primary location for the filming. *The Covered Wagon* had been made in the same vicinity, and the area was fairly remote, making it necessary to transport everything to the site. In fact, the two towns constructed for the filming also doubled as housing for the cast and crew. Production began in January, 1924, with the cold winter weather and makeshift accommodations causing enough difficulties, but to make matters worse, the region was hit by a major blizzard only a few days after shooting commenced. After a month on location, the film was far enough behind schedule to prompt Fox to dispatch his production chief, Sol Wurtzel, to survey the situation in person. Wurtzel's report helped to allay Fox's fears, for he observed not only the working conditions but also the exceptional quality of the film that had been shot. Production continued with Fox's full support, and in mid-March, the company returned to Hollywood, where Ford went to work editing the film. The studio, in the meantime, devised a huge publicity campaign to increase the probability that *The Iron Horse* would earn back its sizable investment. Fox need not have worried, for the film more than justified his gamble. *The Iron Horse* had its premiere on August 24, 1924, at Sid Grauman's new Chinese Theater in Hollywood, and went on to enjoy a huge popular success.

The Iron Horse begins sometime before the Civil War in Springfield, Illinois ("in the days when a transcontinental railroad was still a dream") where the audience is introduced to Davy Brandon (Winston Miller) and Miriam Marsh (Peggy Cartwright) as childhood sweethearts. Davy's father (James Gordon) dreams of crossing the western wilderness, but Miriam's father, Thomas Marsh (Will Walling) scoffs at Brandon's ambitions. Yet, his pioneer vision is endorsed by a young Abraham Lincoln (Charles Edward Bull). "Impelled westward by the strong urge of progress," Brandon and his son set off for the West. They soon discover an important pass through the mountains, but their joy is short lived as the elder Brandon is killed in cold blood by a two-fingered white man leading a band of Indians. Davy, who takes cover, witnesses the murder from hiding and is later found by a scouting party.

At this point, the film jumps forward in time to 1862, as President Lincoln signs a bill authorizing the construction of the transcontinental railroad. Thomas Marsh is to be the contractor, and his daughter Miriam (now played by Madge Bellamy) is betrothed to Peter Jesson (Cyril Chadwick), her father's engineer. The early stages of the railroad work are depicted briefly, before another ellipsis advances the narrative to 1865. A title informs viewers that although Lincoln has been assassinated, the important work goes on, with many ex-soldiers from both North and South joining in the task. Among these workers are four Irishmen, Sergeant Slattery (Francis Powers), Corporal Casey (J. Farrell MacDonald), Private Schultz (James Welch), and Dinny (Jack O'Brien), and an Italian, Tony (Colin Chase). The work is hazardous and the weather harsh, but one problem stands out above all—the necessity of finding a shortcut through the Black Hills. (This, incidentally, is a geographical misrepresentation, despite the film's claim to be "accurate and faithful in every particular.") The longer route that they would otherwise have to take runs through the fictional "Smoky River" region, thereby representing a huge profit to the man who controls the property—Deroux (Fred Kohler), the richest landowner in the Cheyenne country. Meanwhile, a large number of the foreign laborers, led by Tony, threaten to quit because of the adverse conditions and inadequate food supply. They are restrained, however, by a patriotic appeal from Miriam.

In the interest of accurate film history and criticism, one must note here that for the British release of *The Iron Horse*, Deroux was renamed "Bauman" and Private Schultz became "Private Mackay." This, added to the fact that four characters—Slattery, Casey, Schultz, and Dinny—are usually depicted in two variant groups of three, with Schultz and Dinny alternating as the third member, has been the source of some confusion in many discussions of the film. The character of Dinny is omitted from most cast lists, but his prominence in the byplay of this group has often caused actor Jack O'Brien (George's brother) to be mistakenly identified as James Welch, who plays Schultz. The American character names are used here, even though the print under review is of the British version; apparently there are no significant differences between the two versions, but all direct quotations in the text should be regarded with this in mind. In addition, Schultz has been identified as an Irishman, for the sake of simplicity; this may not be technically correct, but the camaraderie among the four men subverts the issue of nationality.

As the story continues, Deroux, with the help of Ruby (Gladys Hulette), a dance-hall girl, enlists Jesson as an ally in his efforts to prevent a new pass from being discovered. The next day, a Pony Express rider is saved from pursuing Indians by jumping aboard the train; he turns out to be the adult Davy Brandon (George O'Brien). He is immediately attracted to Miriam, even before either recalls their long-ago acquaintance. His ardor quickly cools, however, when he meets Jesson. When Marsh explains the railroad's dilemma, Davy tells him about the pass that he and his father had discovered years before. His claim is disputed by Deroux, but Marsh commissions Davy to go with Jesson to locate it. They find the pass, but Jesson, under Deroux's influence, cuts through a rope on which Davy is descending into a ravine. Leaving Davy for dead, he fails to notice that his victim's fall has been broken by a tree. Jesson returns to railroad headquarters, where he reports that no pass was found and that Davy was killed accidentally. Davy soon returns on foot, however, and a fight between the two seems inevitable. Miriam hears of the impending conflict and makes Davy promise not to fight Jesson— revealing in the process that it is Davy whom she really loves. Jesson tries to shoot Davy in the back, however, and in order to defend himself, Davy is provoked into a fight despite his promise. The fight is interrupted by Miriam, who refuses to listen to Davy's explanation, and so the two part.

Meanwhile, Deroux visits the Cheyenne Indians and incites them to make war in a last-ditch attempt to influence the railroad's direction. At this point, viewers are given further evidence of what has been fairly obvious from Deroux's first appearance—that he is, in fact, the man who, disguised as an Indian, murdered Davy's father years before. The Cheyennes attack the railroad workers at the end of track, but Davy and Casey escape with the locomotive and return to town for help. At first, the foreign workers refuse to fight, because the promised food, beef, has not arrived; just then, however, the cattle drive which had begun weeks before concludes, flooding the streets with thousands of head of cattle. Loaded with both men and women, the train rushes to the aid of the besieged group, and a terrific battle ensues.

During the action, Deroux, garbed once again as an Indian and directing the attack, moves in close to act as a sniper. When he shoots Ruby, Davy goes after him. In hand-to-hand combat, he discovers Deroux's two-fingered right hand, realizes that his opponent is his father's murderer, and kills him. The Indians are routed, but one wounded brave gets off a last shot, fatally wounding Sergeant Slattery. Davy and Miriam remain unreconciled, and Davy departs with Corporal Casey for the Central Pacific Railroad, working from the opposite direction. A heated track-laying race culminates in the joining of the two lines at Promontory Point, Utah, on May 10, 1869. At the ceremony, as the transcontinental railroad is symbolically completed by the driving of the golden spike, so too are Davy and Miriam finally united.

The Iron Horse, often praised for its historical verisimilitude and its exciting action sequences, is just as often criticized for its narrative shortcomings, particularly its failure to integrate the penny-dreadful "revenge" plot with the film's larger thematic concerns. Admittedly, the plot device of the two-fingered white man disguised as an Indian seems hackneyed today, but it hardly dominates the film to the extent to which some detractors have alleged. This criticism is also somewhat unfair, for *The Iron Horse* is an ambitious film, both thematically and narratively. If any criticism can be justly leveled, it is that the scenarists were trying to juggle too many plot threads. Ford, for his part, had never worked on such a large scale and could hardly have been expected to pull the disparate elements together with complete success. Ford was assigned to deliver an "epic," and he certainly did, although in general, the demands of the theme are sacrificed to the necessity of keeping the story moving. Perhaps the most serious problem, however, is that the film's central relationship, between Davy and Miriam, is neither very interesting nor particularly well developed.

The film opens promisingly, economically establishing not only the Davy-Miriam connection, but also the basic theme of westward expansion—embodied in the person of the elder Brandon, "the dreamer," and given symbolic blessing by the presence of Abraham Lincoln. With the murder of Brandon, however, and the introduction of the unnecessarily mysterious aspect of the two-fingered renegade, the narrative is splintered, and the film's symbolic force begins to dissipate. The subsequent attempts to relate the character's personal destinies directly to the historical processes often seem forced and artificial.

The fragmented nature of the film is further exacerbated by the semi-detached manner in which various events—such as the buffalo hunt and the cattle drive—are presented. The ultimate effect is to make the spectacular set-pieces appear somewhat one-dimensional, despite their impressive staging. The last reel of the film clearly illustrates this narrative dichotomy. Following the resolution of the revenge plot, Davy goes off to join the Central Pacific, on the basis of a rather trivial misunderstanding with Miriam. By the time the two lines are joined, however, their quarrel has apparently simply been forgotten, and they engage in a coy cat-and-mouse game with Davy refusing to come over to Miriam's side until the connecting spike has been driven. The track-laying race and the actual ceremony at Promontory Point are exciting and authentic-looking historical recreations; yet, they have no particular resonance with other elements of the film, existing primarily to provide a temporary separation of Davy and Miriam. The couple's ultimate reunion seems as arbitrary and unmotivated as their parting; whatever tension exists in the latter part of the film is that which grows out of the dynamic staging of the track-laying race.

Such dislocation of narrative and thematic elements is a problem throughout the film, but despite its structural unevenness, *The Iron Horse* is still an exciting and entertaining film. As Ford's first major assignment, it marks an important milestone in his career and provides a convenient critical bridge between his early Westerns and his prestigious later work. Ford may not have yet been equipped to deliver a masterpiece, but the film contains many individual flashes of brilliance—not only in the superb action sequences, but in the more intimate moments as well. *The Iron Horse* may be somewhat misshapen, but the theme of westward expansion obviously appealed strongly to the director, and the film is clearly the work of a man who had the makings of a major film artist.

In *The Iron Horse*, as in many of his later works, Ford reveals an affinity for the human details of history. Without slighting the epic or melodramatic aspects of railroad building, he also devotes considerable attention to the everyday existence of men and women in the midst of that process. Typically, Ford focuses on the community of railroad workers and camp followers as it moves westward and on the contributions of various individuals and institutions to its vitality. Through the vivid depiction of such institutions as "Judge" Haller's "Hell on Wheels," a combination traveling saloon and courtroom, or as a title puts it, "a bar of justice and likker," presided over by a Judge Roy Bean-like character, Ford stresses the itinerant nature of frontier life.

Several critics have observed that every death in a Ford film is meaningful, an axiom which holds true for *The Iron Horse*. This is expected with the deaths of such sympathetic characters as Slattery and Brandon, Sr., but the emotional weight which Ford gives to the demise of anonymous figures is truly remarkable. On two occasions—once after an Indian attack, again as the community abandons one site to follow the railroad—Ford lingers in the wake of an event to depict the burial of casualties. Particularly striking, partly because it is unexpected, is the latter scene, a beautifully composed shot of a makeshift graveyard by the side of the tracks with the gravediggers going brusquely about their work in the presence of a few solitary mourners, while, in the background, the loaded train pulls away, bound for the next stop. "The price of the town's last night of orgy," reads a title. This treatment of death in the face of history approaches the abstract, but Ford, as usual, is even better when dealing with individuals. One of the film's best moments occurs near the beginning of the first major Indian attack. A brief throwaway scene, it begins when one of a group of four men descends from a handcar and climbs a telegraph pole in order to wire a warning to headquarters. As another man watches with a worried expression, a simple title—"His brother"— reveals their relationship. A moment later, the climber is shot down by an Indian with a rifle, and one of the other men sets the handcar in motion to escape. As the car picks up speed, the brother of the stricken man stands helpless, watching his brother topple to the ground, mortally wounded.

There is a tragic beauty to this scene, and it is a measure of both the film's strengths and its weaknesses that the suddenly interjected drama of these two anonymous men (neither is seen before this incident and the survivor is not seen again) is more genuinely affecting than the tribulations of the main characters. The film's various contemplations of mortality are visually eloquent and not in the least heavy-handed. Although surprisingly melancholy for the work of such a young man, they are typically Fordian, reminiscent of the elegiac feeling of such later films as *The Man Who Shot Liberty Valance*

(1962) and *Cheyenne Autumn* (1964).

Another aspect of the film common to Ford's work is the roughhouse humor. Some of this low comedy takes place in Judge Haller's courtroom/ saloon, but it primarily features the "comrades," Slattery, Casey, Schultz, and Dinny. The antics of these four Irish working-class types, for whom Ford had a special fondness, are certainly broad, but no less so than the comic happenings in such Ford films as *The Quiet Man* (1952) and *Donovan's Reef* (1963). The comedy, unlike some of the historical set-pieces, is an integral part of the film; the handful of extended routines, such as Casey's visit to the dentist, are far outnumbered by the liberal sprinkling of comic moments throughout.

Ford uses the humor both as "comic relief" in its purest sense, and to further reflect on the film's themes. An example of the latter comes when the graveyard scene (noted above) is followed immediately by Judge Haller's impromptu marriage of an unlikely elderly couple—who request a divorce when the train reaches its destination a few hours later. At one point, Ford uses the humor as an effective counterpoint to what otherwise might have been an oppressively suspenseful scene, the buildup to the fight between Davy and Jesson. First, the large mirror behind the bar is lowered for its own protection; then, with Deroux's henchmen poised to ambush Davy, all attention is focused on the door of the saloon. Yet, the tension is hilariously defused when the four Irishmen saunter in nonchalantly. The "Irish" humor is so infectious that even the "Eye-talian," Tony, eventually announces that he too has become an Irishman—"I marry Nora Hogan!" The pop-eyed J. Farrell MacDonald is excellent as Corporal Casey, particularly as he turns blue in the face trying to avoid the impropriety of spitting tobacco on the floor—in front of a general, no less. The most delightful Fordian bit comes at the very end of the film, when Casey expresses shock and outrage at Dinny's thoughtless christening of a locomotive—a flagrant waste of a perfectly good bottle of liquor.

Thematic elements aside, perhaps the film's most interesting aspect is its visual style. *The Iron Horse* is filled with shots that are recognizably Fordian, even at this relatively early stage of his career. In addition to the funeral shots already mentioned, these include riders on the horizon, hordes of mounted Indians plunging down a sandy hillside, dynamic tracking shots of horsemen (for which Ford had a distinctive style), and one shot of a curving line of cavalry that is virtually identical to a shot in Ford's *Stagecoach* (1939). The shots of Indians are often strikingly composed, in the "noble savage" manner that characterized most of Ford's Westerns. Occasionally, he gets a bit artsy— Indians' shadows on the side of a train as they ride up to the attack, or the fight between Davy and Jesson, excitingly staged in semidarkness, illuminated by a swinging lantern—but for the most part, he exhibits the visual understatement which makes his best work so eloquent and unpretentious.

Although his control of the narrative may not be completely satisfactory, he already shows a solid command of the techniques of cinematic expression. One illustration of this is his judicious and always appropriate use of the moving camera. Ford often takes the opportunity to mount his camera on the moving train, which not only enhances the visual dynamism but also subtly underscores the theme of national movement. One scene which did not utilize the moving camera for maximum effect was that with the two brothers— although the scene was still effective enough that at least one latter-day critic has attributed to it a few nonexistent camera moves.

The critical consensus today favors Ford's *Three Bad Men* (1926) over *The Iron Horse*. Unfortunately, most of his silent work (which comprises almost half his total output) has vanished, and historians must base their interpretations of the formative period of his career on a relatively small handful of films. Nevertheless, *The Iron Horse* will always be ranked high among Ford's early films, for it unmistakably points the way toward his later achievements as the premiere epic poet of the American cinema.

Howard H. Prouty

ISN'T LIFE WONDERFUL

Released: 1924
Production: D. W. Griffith; released by United Artists
Direction: D. W. Griffith
Screenplay: D. W. Griffith; based on the short story "Isn't Life Wonderful!"
  by Geoffrey Moss
Cinematography: Hendrik Sartov and Hal Sintzenich
Music: Cesare Sodero and Louis Silvers
Length: 9 reels/8,600 feet

Principal characters:
Inga	Carol Dempster
Hans, son of the professor	Neil Hamilton
Grandmother	Helen Lowell
The professor	Erville Anderson
The brother, Theodor	Frank Puglia
The aunt	Marcia Harris
Rudolph	Lupino Lane

D. W. Griffith probably never dreamed that *Isn't Life Wonderful* would be his last important film. Some of the others he did subsequently, such as *Sally of the Sawdust* (1925), *The Sorrows of Satan* (1927), *Lady of the Pavements* (1929), and his first talking film, *Abraham Lincoln* (1930), had moments of cinematic beauty and wonder, but there was not one of them that was not hopelessly flawed. *Isn't Life Wonderful*, however, is a great picture, a perfect testimonial to Griffith's belief in the strength of the human spirit. It is honest, believable, and moving, and it is absolutely wonderful.

It is not without a certain touch of the documentary, dealing, as it does, with the deprivations suffered by the German people defeated in World War I. Aware of prevalent anti-German propaganda that was still alive, Griffith made his chief protagonists Polish refugees who are living outside of Berlin, scraping together what food they can buy or grow, and there is little doubt that Griffith himself, troubled by the inhumane way he had presented the Germans in *Hearts of the World* (1918) deliberately made them sympathetic here. Even the villains of this story have been made evil by the hunger visited upon them. They steal and appear to be criminal beasts, but essentially they are hungry men trying to exist in an unbearable poverty forced upon them.

That he should deal with such a story about treating aliens in this predicament had been suggested to him by a friend, his financial adviser, J. C. "Little" Epping, who was a German citizen and had relatives in Germany. Epping had made a trip to his homeland in 1922 and had reported to Griffith the suffering his people were enduring; similarly, Major Geoffrey Moss, author of the short story "Isn't Life Wonderful!," had witnessed those conditions and deplored them. Griffith signed a releasing contract with Adolf Zukor and set sail for Germany with a small cast of American actors, headed by Carol Dempster and Neil Hamilton. The entire picture was shot in Germany as it existed in 1924, with such locations as the streets in old Berlin, the forests of Crampnitz and Sacrow, the shipyard at Copenick, and the potato patch at Grunaw providing backgrounds.

In the story, the little group of alien Poles sit at their table, forcing themselves to eat their dull repast of turnips. They are all old people, old before their time, except for an adopted orphan named Inga (Carol Dempster) and Hans (Neil Hamilton), the son of the professor (Erville Anderson). These two are in love and hope to marry, although they are discouraged from doing so because of the times.

One of the most dramatic moments in the film occurs when some meat is offered for sale at the butcher's, and a little line of women forms, with each woman clutching her few coins to buy. Inga watches the signboard outside the butcher's, and as they move closer, the price of meat rises and is noted accordingly on the blackboard. Inga, watching the rising prices, recounts the little hoard she has brought with her; and then, just as she nears the door, the price is again hoisted. There is not enough money, and even as she ponders, the door of the butcher's shop is locked for the day. Griffith creates a moment of hopeful suspense which ultimately turns to despair.

Hans procures a piece of communal land, builds a cottage, and secretly grows potatoes. He brings some home and, with sausage provided by Rudolph (Lupino Lane), the family celebrates the forthcoming wedding of Hans and Inga, who have decided to marry in spite of their poverty. Grandmother (Helen Lowell) brings out the wedding dress she has secretly made for Inga, and the scene is very gay. Inga has been working on refinishing furniture and has built up a small dowry. Grandmother keeps saying, however, that their marriage must wait until the potato crop has been harvested.

The potatoes are soon ready to be harvested, and Hans and Inga go to the little piece of land they have been alloted and gather the potatoes into their cart. Then, tired but contented, and looking forward to Grandmother's consent to their marriage, they begin hauling their crop from the field. On the edge of the forest, a handful of hungry workers has gathered, and now they advance upon the cart. Inga and Hans pull at it, running faster and faster, knowing that their future happiness lies in the safety of the crop they have harvested. The workers reach the fleeing couple, however, and detain them forcibly. They hold back the protesting Inga, and several men attack Hans, knocking him to the ground, unconscious. Quickly, they transfer the potatoes to sacks and abandon Inga and Hans. Inga crawls to Hans, caressing his face. When his eyes open, and she realizes that he lives, she hugs him to her, crying, "I have you, and you have me, and oh! isn't life wonderful!"

It is at this ecstatic point that Griffith had intended fading out his story, but he was forced to tack on a happy ending. One year later the little family has come into an unexpected windfall from America. Now they do not lack for food, and Hans and Inga have been able to marry. The scene fades out on them gathered around the table, with joy reigning as they celebrate their good fortune. The ending is totally out of place, but Griffith plays it for comedy, thanks to Lupino Lane's clowning, and the picture ends with laughter.

The marvel of the film is Dempster's performance of Inga. Previous to *Isn't Life Wonderful*, her presence as one of the Griffith girls had been noted in his films, only as an "also ran." About the same time, another girl, Clarine Seymour, was appearing in parts for Griffith, and she was so fascinating, with her bubbly personality, that Dempster seemed to fade out of focus. Seymour had been scheduled to play the role of Kate Brewster in *Way Down East*, but early in 1920 she suddenly became ill and was rushed to the hospital, where she died of pneumonia, and the part she was to have played went to Mary Hay. After Seymour's death, Dempster was promoted to more important roles, but she was undistinguished in such features as *Dream Street* (1921), *One Exciting Night* (1922), *The White Rose* (1923), and *America* (1924). No one who followed Griffith films ever expected a great performance from her, but in *Isn't Life Wonderful*, without the benefit of any fancy wardrobe, and with her straight hair pulled back into an unbecoming knot, she gave a luminous, extraordinary performance. It made the audience see what Griffith must have seen in her and caused him to stick by her and give her so many chances to shine on her own.

As Hans, her lover, Hamilton was always effective in the picture. A handsome young man, he appeared in three Griffith-directed features and was under contract to Griffith, who lent him out to other studios, mostly Paramount, before he signed exclusively with that studio. His career as a leading man went on profitably in talking pictures, radio, television, and the theater. Although retired, he is the only major Griffith leading man still living.

The odd circumstance about the distribution of *Isn't Life Wonderful* was that it was not distributed by Zukor for Paramount after Zukor had put up the money for making the picture. Griffith was obliged to turn over releasing rights to both *Isn't Life Wonderful* and *Sally of the Sawdust* to United Artists before he could fulfill obligations made to Zukor.

It was small wonder that Griffith yearned for the time to come when he could be his own boss. Yet when that time came, he had lost faith in himself, the one thing his characters had almost never done. He slipped into the nonactive last years he lived after *The Struggle* (1931), his second and last talking feature, and he died on July 23, 1948, after collapsing at the Hollywood Knickerbocker Hotel. It was a sad and lonely end for a penniless man who had once virtually created the town that was Hollywood.

DeWitt Bodeen

THE ITALIAN

Released: 1915
Production: Thomas H. Ince for the New York Motion Picture Company and
Paramount
Direction: Reginald Barker
Screenplay: C. Gardner Sullivan and Thomas H. Ince
Cinematography: no listing
Length: 5 reels/2,157 feet

> *Principal characters:*
> Beppo Donnetti .... George Beban
> Annette Ancello .... Clara Williams
> Her father .... J. Frank Burke

The Italian is an unusual social drama from cinema's infancy. It is rich in
detail and contrasts and superbly acted by George Beban and Clara Williams.
Beban had been on the stage since the age of eight, when he was billed as
"The Boy Baritone of California." He worked in minstrel shows, musical
comedies, and in the revues of Weber and Fields. Beban was noted for his
portrayal of Italian stereotypes, particularly in the play *The Sign of the Rose*,
which he filmed in 1915 under the title of *The Alien*, and later remade in 1922
under its original title. The actor's popularity endured on stage and screen
through the 1920's until his death in Los Angeles on October 5, 1928.

It was Thomas H. Ince who signed Beban for his screen debut in the late
summer of 1914, for a film initially entitled *The Dago* and released as *The
Italian*. Contemporary publicity maintained that Beban and a cameraman
were to go to Italy (Naples and Venice) to shoot "fifty odd scenes" for the
film; but, in reality, the Italian scenes were all shot in the Los Angeles area,
chiefly at the seaside resort of Venice, whose canals are as well-known to
Californians as those of the town's Italian namesake. The ghetto scenes were
filmed both in Los Angeles and San Francisco.

The Italian opens with Beban, the actor, reading a book entitled *The Italian*
by C. Gardner Sullivan and Ince. (Ince generally insisted on credit for himself
in his films as either director, writer, or both, and *The Italian* is no exception.
Authorship of the film should presumably be attributed to Sullivan, although
it also seems highly probable that Beban contributed something to the story.)
Beban is next seen in somewhat romanticized Italian attire as Beppo Donnetti,
a handsome young gondolier, who is in love with Annette Ancello (played
by Ince contract star Clara Williams). Annette is also loved by Roberto, a
wealthy merchant. Her father (J. Frank Burke, another Ince contract player)
decides that Donnetti may have a year to make good and furnish a home for
his daughter, and if, at the end of that time, he is still penniless, Annette
must marry Roberto. The far-from-youthful Roberto decides to get rid of

Donnetti by telling him of the wealth and opportunity to be found in America, to where the gondolier decides to emigrate.

A subtitle, "Youth, heated by the fires of love and ambition, rushes on to meet the future," introduces a scene of Donnetti and Annette as they walk happily along the crest of a hill. The next title, "While old age, ever shrinking back, stops to warm itself by the dying embers of the past," introduces a shot of Annette's father sitting by the fire. The sequence ends with a shot of Donnetti and Annette silhouetted on a cliff-top, looking out to sea, while the sun sets in the distance, and, presumably, they consider the new life ahead in the United States. The Italian scenes in the film glitter with happiness; the festival spirit abounds in Venice and this is carried forward in the scenes of the grape harvest.

In strict contrast with the gaiety of Italy are the scenes of the steerage passengers as they disembark from the ocean liner, to join the seething mass of humanity on New York's lower East Side. Here Donnetti sets up a boot-black stand, and before the year is out he has sufficient money to pay for Annette's passage to the New Land. Her entry into America is not particularly auspicious; because she is unable to make the immigration officials understand that she has someone to take care of her, she is sent to Ellis Island, where Donnetti eventually finds her, and the two are immediately married.

In time, a baby is born to the couple, and Donnetti takes an instant liking to the child when it displays a gesture with its hand, similar to one of his own. An intense heat wave grips the city, and there are scenes of slum urchins following the ice-wagon in the hope of obtaining chips of ice and soaking in the water from the street-cleaning truck. These are scenes that have the same human, carefree feeling that was apparent in the earlier shots in Venice. Then Donnetti and Annette's child is taken seriously ill during the heat wave, and the doctor tells them that the baby must have pasteurized milk, or it will die. With what little money he has, Donnetti sets out to purchase the all-important milk; but on the way, he is set upon by a couple of gangsters and robbed. When he is arrested after putting up a fight, he appeals to the ward boss, Corrigan, for help, but is repulsed and sent to prison for five days. When he is released from jail, Donnetti discovers that his baby has died, and over its empty coffin he swears vengeance upon Corrigan, whom he holds responsible.

It is not long before fate provides Donnetti with his chance. Corrigan's child is taken seriously ill with "brain fever," and absolute quiet is decreed in an effort to save the child's life. Silence pervades not only the Corrigan house but the street outside as well. Disguised as a peddler, Donnetti enters the Corrigan home and sneaks into the child's room. Just as he is about to throw a lampshade down upon the baby, the child puts its arm under its chin in a gesture similar to that of Donnetti's own baby. A chastened Donnetti leaves the room, putting aside his desire for revenge at the memory of his own infant. Donnetti goes to the grave of his baby boy, spreads flowers on the ground and softly murmurs, "My leel boy, my leela boy." The final shot is of Beban, the actor, putting down the book of *The Italian*. The curtains, which opened as the film commenced, close and the play ends.

The Italian is an extraordinarily gripping drama, which seems to have aroused little critical interest on its initial release. *The New York Dramatic Mirror* (December 30, 1914) did note, however, that "The production is notable. More than that, one might safely name it as unique among pictures scheduled on the Paramount programme—a programme confessedly aimed at a more cultivated public than has been reached by that useful trinity, bathos, sentimentality and melodrama." To be sure, *The Italian* is sentimental and melodramatic, but it has an earthy, raw quality to it, thanks to its use of authentic ghetto settings and its capturing of the essence of life for poor Italian immigrants in turn-of-the century America. The early scenes of Italian life remain in the mind of the viewer, placing him in much the same situation as Donnetti—transported from a warm, carefree environment to a harsh, brutal one, where law and order is represented by the criminal element.

One major critic who did realize the unique quality of *The Italian* was Vachel Lindsay, who discusses it in his 1915 volume, *The Art of the Moving Picture*. Lindsay noted that the strength of the film lay to a large extent in the performances of Beban and Williams.

> They owe the force of their acting to the fact that they express each mass of humanity in turn. . . . The hero represents in a fashion the adventures of the whole Italian race coming to America: its natural southern gayety set in contrast to the drab East Side. The gondolier becomes a boot-black. The grape-gathering peasant girl becomes the suffering slum mother. . . . *The Italian* is a strong piece of work.

The Italian's director was Reginald Barker (1886-1937), who began his career under Ince and made most of his best films for that producer. Aside from *The Italian*, Barker's credits with Ince include *The Bargain* (1914), *The Coward* (1915), and *Civilization* (1916). His career lasted through the mid-1930's.

Curiously, *The Italian* does have more recent film counterparts; they are not American-produced films, but rather the early works of Italian directors Roberto Rossellini and Vittorio De Sica. *The Italian* was, without question, ahead of its time, and one can be thankful that unlike most features of its time period, it has survived to take its rightful place among the classics in the history of motion pictures.

Anthony Slide

AN ITALIAN STRAW HAT

Released: 1927
Production: Albatross/Sequana
Direction: René Clair
Screenplay: René Clair; based on the play *Un Chapeau de Paille d'Italie* by Eugène Labiche and Marc Michel
Cinematography: Maurice Defassiaux and Nicolas Roudakoff
Art direction: Lazare Meerson
Length: 3 reels/2,757 feet

Principal characters:
Fadinand, the bridegroom .... Albert Préjean
A cousin .... Alice Tissot
Tavernier .... Vital Gaymon
Hélène ....Marise Maïa
Anaïs .... Olga Tschechowa
Nonancourt .... Yvonneck
Uncle Vézinet .... Paul Olivier
Bobin, a cousin .... Pré fils
Beauperthuis .... Jim Gérald

An Italian Straw Hat was René Clair's sixth film. Starting with the experimental comedy *The Crazy Ray* (*Paris Qui Dort*, 1923) and the outrageous Dadaist film *Entr'acte* (1924), his aim had been to prove that cinema was, or at any rate ought to be, something other than filmed theater. Theatrically based films were a tradition which remained particularly strong in France in the wake of the prestigious productions of Film d'Art which, a decade or so earlier, had allowed film audiences to see some of the major stage stars of the day in the new and still somewhat unrespectable medium. For Clair, this was a definite step in the wrong direction, because he felt that cinema could not be "recounted verbally." His theory was that people "have been spoiled by thirty-odd centuries of chatter: poetry, theatre, the novel, and so on. Audiences have to get back to seeing things through primitive eyes." Given his feelings about filmed theater, it is surprising that his first indisputable masterpiece should have been based on a rather tired turn-of-the-century stage comedy—more properly, a vaudeville—by Eugène Labiche and Marc Michel, one of the period's most prolific playwriting teams. Clair himself was aware of the contradiction and spoke at the time of wanting to remain faithful to the "spirit of the work, not to its form, which was conceived for the stage." He wrote the screenplay for the film himself, trying to make it as close as possible to what Labiche and Michel might have written if they had done it themselves.

Clair's film remains closely based on the plot of the play, but he makes a number of fairly crucial changes, the most important of which is to update the story from 1851 to 1895—the year during which the play was written. This has the effect of introducing into the film an element of self-parody: in addition to being a lightweight satire of social mores, *An Italian Straw Hat* is also a parody of an outmoded theatrical form, the vaudeville, and, through it, a satire of the society which had produced and consumed the vaudeville. Aided by Lazare Meerson's lavish but slightly exaggerated recreation of the period, Clair was among the first to realize the comic potential of what was only beginning to be referred to as "la Belle Epoque." The original play tells, in a fairly pedestrian but quite successful farcical structure, the story of a bridegroom's efforts to find an identical replacement for an Italian straw hat eaten by his horse on the way to the wedding ceremony. The quest is made all the more urgent by the fact that the hat was on the head of a married lady sporting behind a bush with a belligerent army officer. The gist of the story is one of the mainsprings of French farce, and Clair certainly exploits the farcical potential of the plot. Indeed, he frequently improves on Labiche and Michel by adding a whole series of visually conceived comic details which would have been impossible in any other medium. His film is above all, however, a hilarious satire of the attitudes of the turn-of-the-century French bourgeoisie and its obsession with social ritual and correctness, particularly of dress.

The film opens with a lengthy dressing scene as the families of the bride and groom (Albert Préjean) prepare for the wedding. Each member is completely taken up with ensuring that his or her appearance is perfect and that no crack should appear in the family's façade of respectability. In addition, the best man's enjoyment of the day is ruined by losing one of his gloves, and he spends the rest of the film attempting to hide his indecently naked hand behind his hat, his back, or anything until, in the last seconds—long after it has ceased to matter—he rediscovers the lost glove in his breast pocket. The incident of the straw hat is something which threatens to destroy the day's proprieties entirely. The bridegroom's discreet efforts to sort out the crises are constantly interrupted by an at first apologetic but gradually more insistent valet attempting to make sure that his master does not take a step without the sartorially essential top hat and white gloves.

As the wedding day progresses, every sacrosanct ritual of that most sacrosanct of all bourgeois institutions is gradually reduced to absurdity by the bridegroom's ridiculous but desperately urgent quest for a replacement hat (the officer has promised to destroy his apartment if he does not come straight back with one). He arrives late at the Town Hall (his absence being signaled by the now ludicrous hat and white gloves solemnly awaiting him on an empty chair); then, when the Mayor's pompous speech seems to be going on too long, the groom breaks it off with rapturous applause and rushes from the room, followed by the bemused guests. At times, it appears Clair may have gone too far for the more conservative among his audience. A riotous sequence in which a wife tries to tell her husband that his tie has come adrift and succeeds in getting every man *except* her husband to check his tie seems to have caused a fair amount of offence in 1927: marriage was not something to be laughed at.

The enduring value of *An Italian Straw Hat* comes not so much from the subject matter of Clair's film as from his treatment of it. What makes a comedy comic is not usually easy to define, any more than it is easy (or wise) to attempt to explain a joke. It is worth noting, however, two recurrent techniques in Clair's film, both indicative of his attempts to evolve new forms of expression and a new cinematic language. The first is the way in which he quietly emphasizes the absurdity of the self-obsessed bourgeois world he is satirizing by means of ironic camera angles: the overhead shot of the bride's family gathering for departure which makes the whole business of handshaking look like some grotesque ritual in a chicken coop; the mock-heroic low-angle of the mayor declaiming from beneath a solemn official statue; and (particularly) the ridiculous caperings of the guests at the reception seen from behind a chair in which a little girl sits demurely—a child's eye view of adult behavior echoed some fifty years later in the early wedding sequence of *Cousin, Cousine* (1976).

The second technique is the series of running jokes Clair maintains throughout the film, all of them neatly tied up in the closing sequence: the image of the bridegroom's deaf father with his ill-fitting shoes, his ear trumpet, and his incongruous pot of myrtle; the lost glove; the luckless valet attempting to interpret his master's concerns and instructions; the junk man who is passing more or less every time the officer throws a piece of furniture from the bridegroom's window, and who loads it onto his cart as though such things were always happening to him. Indeed, it is Clair's control of this aspect of the narrative which is the most impressive element in *An Italian Straw Hat*. The structure and rhythms of the Labiche-Michel vaudeville could not have been transferred directly to the silent screen, even if Clair had wanted to do so. For them, he substitutes a carefully paced series of visual gags and a structure which neatly dovetails the two chief elements of the plot: the wedding and the search for the straw hat. With a brilliant use of parallel editing— scarcely innovative in 1927 but nonetheless remarkably assured—he keeps both strains in constant focus, never allowing one to fade from the viewers' attention and never holding onto it for too long and thus losing their interest.

After a somewhat slow start, Clair manages to convey the complex plot developments which are the backbone of farce with impressive economy, and above all visually: the film contains comparatively few titles. The best sequences from this point of view are the scene in which the groom tells the whole story of the hat to its owner's husband without for a moment guessing whom he is talking to; and the one in which, while trying to behave normally at the reception, he imagines the officer destroying his apartment and decides that it is time to resume the quest. What makes *An Italian Straw Hat* one of the masterpieces of French silent cinema and almost certainly its best comedy is Clair's ability to restructure and rescore the original vaudeville in a way which is predominantly cinematic; a way which comes as close as any silent comedy to enabling the audience to "get back to seeing things through primitive eyes." Clair's only real rivals in this respect were comedians Charles Chaplin and Buster Keaton.

Nick Roddick

J'ACCUSE!

Released: 1919
Production: Pathé
Direction: Abel Gance
Screenplay: Abel Gance; based on the play *Miracle at Verdun* by Hans Chlumberg
Cinematography: Léonce-Henry Burel, Bujard, and Forster
Length: 11 reels

Principal characters:
François Laurin .... Severin-Mars
Jean Diaz .... Romuald Joube
Edith .... Marise Dauvray

Napoleon (1927), Abel Gance's lavish, majestic ode to the French emperor, was restored by film historian Kevin Brownlow more than fifty years after its initial release. In 1981, it played to capacity crowds at New York's Radio City Music Hall and other theaters throughout the country, creating a popular sensation. The finale is the film's highlight: triptychs presented in Polyvision, a three-screen process that anticipated Cinerama by more than three decades. *Napoleon* was perhaps the most compelling film to be seen on American film screens in 1981, and its success enabled its maker to be officially "rediscovered." The film, however, is not Gance's only silent epic. *J'Accuse!* (*I Accuse*, released in 1919) is the director's first masterpiece.

In *J'Accuse!*, Gance simply and stirringly evokes the waste and horror of war. He begins by celebrating life, with a sequence of a *farandole* in a small French village. François Laurin (Severin-Mars) is then introduced, his face being superimposed with that of a dog. He is sitting at a table with his hunting dog; they have just killed a fawn, and the animal's blood drips down into a puddle at Laurin's feet. His wife, Edith (Marise Dauvray), is horrified by his behavior; she is also alienated from her father, a bitter veteran, and her surroundings. She is loved by Jean Diaz (Romuald Joube), a pacifist poet who resides nearby with his mother. Diaz reads his compositions to pastoral drawings, most memorably a sun rising over a body of water.

Laurin is jealous of Jean, and when he finds the poet and his wife together in the woods, he takes out his gun, and shoots. He kills neither Edith nor the poet, however, only a bird. War is declared, skeletons dance about, and the scythe of the Grim Reaper is superimposed over pages of Jean's writings. Soldiers depart for war (and certain death) as Gance gives close-ups of hands clasping, praying, and lifting up wine glasses. Laurin joins the army, but because he is afraid that his wife will continue seeing Jean, who is a pacifist, he sends her away to his father in the Ardennes.

Elderly men, garbed in their old military uniforms, plot the war's strategy on a map. Edith's father receives a telegram informing him that his daughter has been captured and deported by the Germans, then Jean, angered, forgets his pacifism. He imagines the deportees, mutters the phrase "J'accuse," and enlists. He is assigned to Laurin's regiment as its officer, and when he receives papers ordering Laurin to undertake a dangerous mission, Jean goes in his place. When he returns unharmed, he and Laurin begin a friendship. They both love Edith and reminisce about her.

Jean returns home to care for his mother, who is ill. He is seen first on an idyllic countryside; then, as he reads his work to her, accompanied by the drawings shown earlier, she dies. Edith now comes back with a little girl: she had been raped by the Germans and subsequently gave birth to the child. Laurin is then sent home. He does not believe a story his wife invents to explain the child's presence, and, in fact, he is convinced Jean is the father.

Laurin tells Edith that the girl has been drowned, but when the hysterical mother runs to a pond, she only finds her daughter playing with Jean. Laurin grabs Jean by the throat, then Edith tells her husband the truth, and he almost kills the child. Laurin feels he must leave, but cannot bear to allow Jean to remain, so they both return to the front.

Jean contracts a fever before a battle and hallucinates. Laurin is killed, but before dying grabs Jean's hand. Battle sequences are then followed by shots of corpses in a church. Jean escapes from a hospital, returns home, and announces that the villagers are to meet at Edith's house for news of the war. He then evokes the ghosts of his fallen comrades in an allegorical sequence, showing the dead returning to see if their sacrifices have served any purpose. By now, Jean is irrevocably insane. He tears up his poetry, accuses the sun of having uncomplainingly observed the death and destruction, and drops dead.

J'Accuse!, one of the first films ever made about the futility of war, is a milestone in the history of French cinema. It is the first film to incorporate montage and superimposed images. It is a beautifully composed work with several breathtaking traveling shots, most impressively a slow one of the church after Laurin's death. Particularly outstanding are the "hands" sequence as the soldiers go off to war, the shots of Edith running to the pond, and the final sequence, a powerful, visually stunning climax to an already compelling film. Ironically, many actual soldiers used by Gance as extras during the filming died soon after: *J'Accuse!* was shot during World War I and released soon after it ended. The three leading roles are all solidly played; Severin-Mars, a star of the Comédie-Française, is particularly fine as François Laurin, effectively underplaying his role. The cinematography is also excellent. Corpses in battle scenes are tinted red; fire is colored orange; and water is used to illustrate Jean's poetry as blue. There are few titles in the film. Indeed, they are not necessary.

Gance originally planned to make *J'Accuse!* in 1917, when French privates on the front line had mutinied, but it was filmed soon after, when the war was winding down. Predictably, it was denounced immediately upon its release as "antimilitaristic." The director hoped it would be the first of a trilogy, but the other two films, "Les Cicatrices" (The Scars) and "La Société des Nations" (The League of Nations) were never made. In 1929, he made *La Fin du Monde* (*The End of the World*); its hero, Jean Novalic (played by Gance), is remarkably similar to Jean Diaz. Earlier, in 1922, the director reedited *J'Accuse!*, revising the plot and titles and contrasting the Return of the Dead sequence to a victory parade.

J'Accuse! was budgeted at 525,000 francs, a hefty sum for its time. Despite the climate in which it was made, it eventually turned a profit: by 1923, it had earned three-and-one-half million francs in France alone and enjoyed considerable success in England and the United States. Gance remade the film with sound in 1937, in an effort to denounce the oncoming world war. That effort was far less powerful cinematically than the original, with the possible exception of the Return of the Dead sequence. In 1956, Gance incorporated scenes from *J'Accuse!* and other films into *Magirama*, a demonstration of the triple-screen technique he had employed so superbly in *Napoleon*.

Rob Edelman

JANICE MEREDITH

Released: 1924
Production: Cosmopolitan for Metro-Goldwyn-Mayer
Direction: E. Mason Hopper
Screenplay: Lillie Hayward; based on the story "Janice Meredith, a Story of the American Revolution" by Paul Leicester Ford
Cinematography: Ira Morgan and George Barnes
Editing: Walter Futter
Set decoration: Joseph Urban
Length: 11 reels/10,655 feet

Principal characters:
Janice Meredith	Marion Davies
Lord Clowes	Holbrook Blinn
Charles Fownes	Harrison Ford
Squire Meredith	Maclyn Arbuckle
Mrs. Meredith	Hattie Delaro
George Washington	Joseph Kilgour
Martha Washington	Mrs. Maclyn Arbuckle
A British Sergeant	W. C. Fields
Paul Revere	Ken Maynard
Philemon Hennion	Olin Howland
Thomas Jefferson	Lionel Adams
The Marquis de Lafayette	Nicolai Koesberg
Louis XVI	Edwin Argus
Lord Cornwallis	Tyrone Power, Sr.
Benjamin Franklin	Lee Beggs

For almost sixty years, William Randolph Hearst was one of the dominant figures in American journalism. His journalistic methods were often "yellow" (through sensationalism, for example, he instigated the Spanish-American War), but he built a vast publishing empire, including daily newspapers in seventeen cities from New York to San Francisco.

Hearst did not only "create" a newspaper chain and a war, but he was also the mentor of Marion Davies, a pretty Brooklyn girl who was not without talent as a comedienne. Davies, thirty-four-years Hearst's junior, was the publisher's mistress. He starred her in film after film, mostly misusing her skills. Yet, Hearst publications heralded the arrival of each Davies vehicle, one of the most ambitious of which was *Janice Meredith*, a melodrama-romance of the Revolutionary War.

The plot of *Janice Meredith* is somewhat convoluted. Lord Brereton (Harrison Ford) is hurt by a lady friend, and, calling himself Charles Fownes, he sails to America and finds employment as the bondservant of Squire Meredith (Maclyn Arbuckle), a rich New Jersey landowner with an estate near New

Brunswick. It is 1774, and the tea-drinking habits of Meredith and those of his ilk are being protested against by the rebels. Janice (Marion Davies), the Squire's stubborn, flirtatious daughter, and Brereton/Fownes fall in love. The Squire is unaware of Fownes' identity and sends his child off to Boston to live with an aunt.

Janice meets Lord Clowes (Holbrook Blinn), discovers that the British are organizing a massive movement of troops to the Lexington, Massachusetts, arsenal, and sounds the warning that results in the midnight ride of Paul Revere (Ken Maynard). She then returns to New Jersey. Meanwhile, Fownes reveals his true identity and becomes an assistant and trusted friend to General George Washington (Joseph Kilgour). Janice and Fownes rendezvous, and he appropriates his favorite horse from the Squire's stable. When he returns, he is met by Lord Clowes, the Squire, and some British troops. He is captured and thinks Janice has betrayed him, but she helps him escape.

For her effort, Janice is sent to Trenton by Clowes. Fownes appears, disguised as a Hessian, and he is given papers which reveal the disposition of British troops. He is unmasked and ordered shot, but slips the papers to Janice who delivers them to Washington, who then makes his heroic crossing of the Delaware. As he is about to be executed, Fownes is saved by an explosion. Colonial forces seize Clowes as he is about to kill Fownes, who then tells Janice she must give up all Tory associations—including contact with her father.

Janice departs in anger and returns to Squire Meredith. She reluctantly agrees to wed the aristocratic Philemon Hennion (Olin Howland), her father's choice for her husband. Fownes, assisted by Continental soldiers, disrupts the wedding and seizes the Squire's property. Janice and her family, followed by Fownes, flee to Philadelphia. Meanwhile, as the British live in luxury, Washington and his troops are suffering at Valley Forge. Fownes penetrates the British lines just to see Janice. He is arrested; however, General Howe recognizes him as his old friend from England, Lord Brereton, and he is freed.

Janice and her father now travel with the British to Yorktown. While Washington and his troops attack, Clowes ties Janice up and takes her away in his coach. Predictably, she is rescued by Fownes after a furious chase. Finally, they are reunited at Mount Vernon, where they marry, with George Washington acting as their best man.

Unlike D. W. Griffith's *America* (1924), released only a few months earlier, *Janice Meredith* was made not out of a desire to recreate the highlights of the Revolutionary War accurately. The film, shot on location mostly in Plattsburg and Lake Placid, New York, was mounted as a showcase for its star. Hearst felt that Paul Leicester Ford's "Janice Meredith, a Story of the American Revolution" would be a perfect vehicle for Davies—even though Griffith was already in production with his film, and Hearst could not be persuaded to abandon the project.

Among the historical personages depicted in *Janice Meredith* are George and Martha Washington (the latter played by Mrs. Maclyn Arbuckle), Thomas Jefferson (Lionel Adams), the Marquis de Lafayette (Nicolai Koesberg), Louis XVI (Edwin Argus), Lord Cornwallis (Tyrone Power, Sr.), and Benjamin Franklin (Lee Beggs, who played Samuel Adams for Griffith). The major events of the era are included, such as the Boston Tea Party, Benjamin Franklin in France, Paul Revere's ride, and Washington crossing the Delaware. The last event is not found in *America*; allegedly, Hearst asked Griffith not to include such a sequence in his own film, in exchange for positive reviews by Hearst writers. The film was budgeted at almost one million dollars, an astronomical sum for 1924. The only sequence that really works is Valley Forge, which lasts fifteen minutes, and is easily the highlight of *Janice Meredith*. While little more than a recreation of a pastoral painting, it is still thrilling and visually exciting.

The film's other asset is Davies, who exhibits a spirited, racy charm as the devilish Janice. She wears twenty costumes through the eleven reels of the film, yet her character is no idle Betsy Ross who sits around sewing flags while the menfolk risk their lives. While she does have to be rescued by Fownes at the end, she is actively involved in numerous adventures and escapes for most of the scenario. The slightly built Harrison Ford had costarred previously with Davies in *Little Old New York* (1923); unfortunately, he is lifeless as Fownes. Holbrook Blinn is unexceptional as the heavy, Clowes. The director, E. Mason Hopper, had previously handled slapstick farces and dramas; *Janice Meredith* is easily the most prestigious film of his career. He later made programmers for Cecil B. De Mille and then "D"-grade talkies.

Janice Meredith received mixed reviews, including some positive notices from critics not in Hearst's employment. It was a box-office failure, however, everywhere but in New York City, where it was a first-run attraction for several months. It did not recoup its budget. Generally, it is inferior to Griffith's *America*, which surrounded a trite love story with marvelously accurate re-creations of Revolutionary War highlights. Yet, Davies outacts any performer in the Griffith film. Because of her relationship with Hearst, she was unfairly overlooked by the critics. She uplifts *Janice Meredith*, however, and also gave peppy performances in the silents *Little Old New York*, *When Knighthood Was in Flower* (1922), *The Fair Co-Ed* (1927), *The Patsy* (1928), and the best of her pretalkies, *Show People* (1928), where she deftly caricatured a film queen. Even without Hearst's sponsorship, Davies could still have become a star.

Today, *Janice Meredith* is of interest mostly for trivia buffs. At the bottom of the credits are two actors then virtually unknown to filmgoers: Ken Maynard, prior to his stardom as one of Hollywood's top Western heroes, appears briefly as Paul Revere; a mustachioed W. C. Fields has the role of "a British Sergeant" in his first feature-film appearance. He is garbed in a powdered wig, red coat, and three-cornered hat, and acts quite drunk as he jokes with Davies. This fact perhaps more than any other is what distinguishes *Janice Meredith* for film historians.

Rob Edelman

JOAN THE WOMAN

Released: 1917
Production: Cecil B. De Mille for Paramount
Direction: Cecil B. De Mille
Screenplay: Jeanie Macpherson
Cinematography: Alvin Wyckoff
Editing: Cecil B. De Mille
Art direction: Wilfred Buckland
Length: 12 reels

Principal characters:
Joan of Arc .... Geraldine Farrar
Charles VIII .... Raymond Hatton
General La Hire .... Hobart Bosworth
Cauchon .... Theodore Roberts
Eric Trent .... Wallace Reid
La Tremouille .... Charles Clary
Jacques d'Arc .... Horace B. Carpenter

Cecil B. De Mille was called the "master of spectacle," and he certainly lived up to that title. He was fascinated by history and by characters that made history, but his films were more than mere battle scenes with thousands of extras flailing about upon a field, as is often charged by critics. If there is a formula that defines the De Mille type of spectacle, it is, in his own words, "A very simple one: To tell an absorbing personal story against a background of great historical events." *Joan the Woman*, De Mille's first historical film, fits his own definition and also succeeds on its own terms.

De Mille's Joan of Arc is no spiritual, wild-eyed idealist. Instead, she is a meat and potatoes, flesh and blood French farm girl capable of feeling emotion and more politically motivated to save France from the English than driven by religious forces. De Mille's Joan is a strange combination of George Bernard Shaw's commonsense peasant in *Saint Joan* and Jean Anouilh's gamine, humorous lark who was not above acting as a coquette to attain her ends in *The Lark*. De Mille skillfully retells the familiar story of the French heroine who so bravely risked all to save her nation, but in this version, he comes as close to making a love story as one can when dealing with a saint. The title, *Joan the Woman*, meant that she was familiar and a new woman.

To play this very comtemporary Joan, De Mille cast Geraldine Farrar, the popular opera singer whom he had used in *Carmen* (1915). The role was a challenge for Farrar, for in *Carmen*, audiences at least had the memory of George Bizet's opera and Farrar's rendering of the famous songs. In *Joan the*

Woman, however, she had a challenge: to create a full-blooded character, albeit a familiar one who was known to every school child. De Mille's screenwriter Jeanie Macpherson wrote the script according to De Mille's vision of Joan as a strong peasant girl with a sense of humor, faithful to her voices, but also afraid at times, and tempted by earthly pleasures. This concept, set against some magnificent battle scenes and camerawork, is what makes the film shine as a forerunner of such costume epics as *Gone with the Wind* (1939) and *The Ten Commandments* (1956).

The film opens with a prologue set among the trenches of France during World War I. Eric Trent, an English soldier played by one of De Mille's stars, Wallace Reid, discovers the fragment of a sword he believes to be that of Joan of Arc. He feels connected in some way with Saint Joan and her mission, and in a flashback which hints at the idea of reincarnation, the film goes back to fifteenth century France, where Joan (Geraldine Farrar) is seen as a farm girl who is very much in command of herself. She is well liked by her family and friends, she is uncomplicated and self-confident. When she hears voices, she does believe them and sets out to do their bidding with a determination that is neither fanatic nor dreamlike. As the well-known story unfolds, Joan convinces King Charles VIII of France (Raymond Hatton) to raise an army for her against the English, and it soon becomes apparent that what causes kings and ministers to listen to *this* Joan is her innate good sense rather than her religious calling. Captured finally by an English soldier, the very same Eric Trent from the prologue, the story takes a strange turn. Trent becomes obsessed with the young woman and falls passionately in love with her, although he will ultimately cause her death. Once Joan is put on trial, there is nothing Trent can do to help her, for of course she will not relent. In a touching moment before Joan is tried, she virtually admits to Trent that if things were different, she could return his affections. When she is finally burned at the stake, Trent feels that his life is over. In the ironic epilogue which goes forward once again to World War I, the modern Eric Trent falls to his death in battle.

The filming of *Joan the Woman* was costly for its time and demanded strenuous work for all involved. The armor worn by Farrar was so heavy that she had to be lifted onto her horse. For the scene of Joan's burning, a real stake was constructed, and it was surrounded with fire that was also real. Farrar stood amidst the smoke and flames almost until the very last shot when a dummy was substituted for the actual burning of her body. The scene is vivid and tragic, for this all too human Joan is hard to lose. The film did not do well at the box office. For its day, it was extremely expensive, costing more than $300,000; it grossed only $600,000. It fascinated critics, however, and stands as a reminder that De Mille was one of the finest silent directors in motion pictures, and one of the few to continue and be just as successful in talkies. This was to be the first in a long line of De Mille epics, films that bore the personal stamp of the director and set the standard for big costume dramas everywhere.

Joan L. Cohen

THE JOYLESS STREET
(DIE FREUDLOSE GASSE)

Released: 1925
Production: M. Salkind and R. Pines for Sofar-Film
Direction: G. W. Pabst
Screenplay: Willy Haas; based on the novel of the same name by Hugo
  Bettauer
Cinematography: Guido Seeber, Kurt Oertel, and Robert Lach
Length: 10 reels/12,300 feet

Principal characters:

Councillor Franz Rumfort	Jaro Furth
Butcher of Melchior Street	Werner Krauss
Maria Lechner	Asta Nielsen
Greta Rumfort	Greta Garbo
Frau Greifer	Valeska Gert
Lieutenant Davis (Davy)	Einar Hanson
Max Rosenow	Karl Etlinger
Regina Rosenow	Countess Agnes Esterhazy
Rosa Rumfort	Loni Nest
Lia Leid	Tamara Tolstoi
Don Alfonso Cañez	Robert Garrison
Egon Stirner	Henry Stuart
Extra	Marlene Dietrich

After World War I, Germany was in economic and moral turmoil. This, coupled with the effects of industrialization on the masses, altered the consciousness and creative output of some of the nation's artists. German painters, for example, began depicting in their work the individual in relation to a society in crisis. Filmmakers, however, still kept churning out escapist dramas and fantasies in the 1920's, with no connection to the present reality.

G. W. Pabst was one exception. Although romantic and melodramatic, *The Joyless Street* (*Die Freudlose Gasse*) graphically and effectively delineates the physical and psychological effects of the war on a middle class in decline. The mood is somber and pessimistic as he focuses his narrative on a small, dimly lit street in postwar Vienna and how the lives of its residents are affected by inflation, prostitution, and corruption.

Pabst opens the film with a quote from Dante's *Inferno*: "Abandon hope all ye who enter here." The setting is Melchior Street, Vienna, the winter of 1923. Maria Lechner (Asta Nielsen), daughter of a poor cripple, and Greta Rumfort (Greta Garbo), an office clerk and the child of an impoverished civil servant, Councillor Franz Rumfort (Jaro Furth), wait patiently in a line outside a butcher shop. They are hoping for a bit of meat, but both are turned away. Maria returns to her dreary apartment where her father, who cannot work and must depend on his wife's washing for financial support, harangues her for her failure. She finds her way into her makeshift bedroom and day-dreams of the handsome Egon Stirner (Henry Stuart), secretary of General Director Max Rosenow (Karl Etlinger), a wealthy businessman.

Compared to Maria, Greta lives almost like a princess: her flat, where she resides with her father and younger sister, is at least homey. Still, there is little money. Meanwhile, Frau Greifer (Valeska Gert), a madame, is wel-comed into the butcher shop by its owner (Werner Krauss). The squalor of Melchior Street is contrasted to the bourgeoisie, living on the leftovers of the past. Don Alfonso Cañez (Robert Garrison), a rich international speculator—complete with villain's curled mustache—is introduced to Rosenow, Stirner, Rosenow's daughter Regina (Countess Agnes Esterhazy), Leid, a lawyer, and his wife Lia (Tamara Tolstoi). Cañez persuades Rosenow to participate with him in a stock swindle, while Egon pursues the beautiful Regina, who will only consider as a suitor a man with riches. Lia Leid flirts with Egon, who agrees to meet her later.

Near the Melchior Street butcher shop is a dress store, which serves as a front for Frau Greifer's brothel. Greta, waiting again in the meat line, passes out from exhaustion, while the butcher flirts with a streetwalker passing by his window. Maria learns from Stirner of his desire for finances and agrees to help him. Meanwhile, Councillor Rumfort is forced to resign his job; he is given some money as an inducement to leave, but invests most of it in the stock fraud. He insists that Greta purchase a coat with what remains. She enters Frau Greifer's shop and is ecstatic when trying on a luxurious fur coat.

Maria, desperate for money, is seduced by Don Alfonso, and becomes his mistress. Egon and Lia rendezvous in a hotel. Later, however, Regina, in the company of her society friends, learns that Lia has been murdered and robbed. She had overheard Egon and Lia planning to meet and is convinced that he committed the crime. Greta is now fired for resisting her boss' advances, while her father learns that he has lost his investment. Frau Greifer refuses to buy back Greta's coat, but instead offers to set up a meeting between her and a "respectable" man. The kindly Lieutenant Davis (Einar Hanson), an American, has become a boarder in the Rumfort home and appears to be a potential romance for Greta, but she still meets Frau Greifer's gentleman—who turns out to be the butcher. She fends off his advances, and he is instead satisfied with a full-course meal. He also agrees to attend a party given by the madame.

Maria, now garbed in a white gown with a glimmering crown atop her head, confesses to Don Alfonso that she had witnessed Lia's death. She, however, is the real culprit, murdering the woman out of jealousy. Maria learns that Egon is on trial for the crime and confesses her guilt to the police. Greta, stripped practically naked by one of Frau Greifer's attendants, makes an appearance at the party—where she finds Davis. Both are astonished. Then,

Herr Rumfort arrives. He has traced his daughter there and understands why Greta accepted Frau Greifer's invitation. The "entertainment" is contrasted to the ever-present line in front of the butcher shop. A young woman denied meat for her child murders the butcher. There is a commotion at the soiree, and after a series of shots—a drum and cymbal, burning cigarettes, and beer glasses—Greta and Davis are pictured before an open window. Perhaps the future will be happier than the present.

The Joyless Street is Pabst's third film, after *The Treasure* (*Der Schatz*, 1923) and *Countess Donelli* (*Grafin Donelli*, 1924). He cast some of the top screen actors on the Continent: German star Werner Krauss, who appeared in more than one hundred silents, Valeska Gert, internationally respected for playing villainesses, and Asta Nielsen, the leading tragedienne of the European cinema. The still unknown Marlene Dietrich also may be seen ever so briefly in the butcher-shop line. The director was having difficulty finding the right actress to play Greta Rumfort. He had liked Greta Garbo's performance in *The Atonement of Gosta Berling* (1923), directed by her mentor, Mauritz Stiller, but Garbo would not take the role without Stiller's approval. The Swedish director demanded script alterations; a salary of four thousand dollars in American currency; Garbo's living expenses during shooting; the most expensive film stock available for her photography (which was Kodak—most films were shot with Agfa); and the employment of actor Einar Hanson and cinematographer Julius Jaenzon. As Pabst wanted Garbo, he agreed to all except the last: he had already hired Guido Seeber, one of the top cinematographers in Europe, and would not replace him.

Garbo was at first frightened when shooting commenced. She was only nineteen years old and was little more than a puppet manipulated by her mentor. Her nervousness was visible in the early rushes, particularly an uncontrollable twitch in her cheek. Seeber reshot Garbo's scenes at an increased camera speed, and the blinking could no longer be detected. Pabst, who had been exhibiting patience and care with Garbo while banning Stiller from the set, then complimented the actress. Slowly, she became more confident, and her performance improved. She worked hard, often being the first person on the set each morning; Pabst worked the cast and crew for sixteen-hour stretches every day, while Stiller continued coaching his discovery from the sidelines. Her performance received mixed reviews, as she was still basically unformed as an actress and uncertain before the camera, but Garbo's sensuality is visible for the first time ever on film—particularly when she tries on the lush fur coat, with Frau Greifer tempting her.

The Joyless Street had its premiere in Berlin as *Die Freudlose Gasse*. The film received poor reviews, with critics agreeing that it was overlong and lifeless. It later opened in England, as *The Joyless Street*, and had censorship problems in France, Austria, and Russia: in France, every shot of the street was excised; in Austria, the butcher was eliminated; and in Russia, Davis became a physician and the butcher became Lia's killer. A cut version, entitled *The Street of Sorrow*, was shown in the United States in 1927, literally closing as quickly as it opened. Audiences everywhere found the film too dreary and depressing, and it was a box-office failure.

Still, M-G-M head Louis B. Mayer was impressed with Garbo's work in the film, and she and Stiller soon went to Hollywood. *The Joyless Street* is now regarded as a classic of the silent screen with Pabst presenting "real life," contrasting poverty and deprivation with luxury and corruption. Historically, it established the director as a major talent who went on to make, among other films, *Secrets of a Soul* (1926), *The Love of Jeanne Ney* (1927), *Pandora's Box* (1928), *Westfront 1918* (1930), *Kameradschaft* (1931), *The Threepenny Opera* (1931), and *L'Atlantide* (1932). By 1932, Pabst was respected as one of the top directors in the world.

Rob Edelman

JUDITH OF BETHULIA

Released: 1914
Production: Biograph Company
Direction: D. W. Griffith
Screenplay: D. W. Griffith; based on the narrative poem "Judith and Holofernes" and the subsequent play *Judith of Bethulia* by Thomas Bailey Aldrich, which were based on the Book of Judith in the Old Testament Apocrypha
Titles: Frank Woods
Cinematography: G. W. Bitzer
Length: 4 reels/1,647 feet

Principal characters:
Judith .... Blanche Sweet
Holofernes .... Henry B. Walthall
Naomi .... Mae Marsh
Nathan .... Robert Harron
The young mother .... Lillian Gish
The crippled beggar .... Dorothy Gish
Judith's maid .... Kate Bruce

The nearly five hundred films made by D. W. Griffith in his first years as a director, from 1908 through 1913, comprise the most important body of work in the early cinema. Employed by the American Mutoscope & Biograph Company (which became the Biograph Company in 1909), he was responsible for almost one-half of that firm's prolific output during this period. Fortunately, all but a handful of these films have survived the ravages of time, enabling historians to scrutinize closely Griffith's gradual evolution of the film language. Concurrent with that development was his struggle against various limits imposed by the Biograph heads, president Jeremiah J. Kennedy and vice-president/general manager Henry N. Marvin. By far the most bothersome of these restrictions—and most relevant to any discussion of Griffith's final Biograph production, *Judith of Bethulia* (made in 1913 but not released until 1914)—was that placed on the length of the company's films.

One reel (which equals approximately 1,000 feet and has a running time of approximately twelve to fifteen minutes) was the standard maximum length of a motion picture at the time Griffith began directing. This limit which was observed by all manufacturers, was most stringently enforced by the member companies of the infamous Motion Picture Patents Company (M.P.P.C., often referred to as "the Trust"). The goal of the M.P.P.C., formed in 1908 by the most prominent film producing and distributing firms, was to bring economic order to the lucrative but chaotic film business. Their methods included a distribution system that supplied their films only to theaters which were "licensed" under their terms, and the physical discouragement of outside, or "independent," competition. The United States Government eventually declared the M.P.P.C. to be in restraint of trade and ordered it to disband, but throughout the period of Griffith's employment by Biograph, the combine was the dominant force in the industry—and the Biograph Company was among its most influential members. The philosophy behind the one-reel policy held that motion pictures were industrial products and, as such, were most efficiently manufactured and marketed in a standardized format. Multi-reel films on prestigious subjects were occasionally produced (such as Vitagraph's five-reel *The Life of Moses* in 1909-1910), but these were aberrations and were invariably released serially, one reel at a time over a period ranging from several days to several months.

At first, Griffith experienced no difficulty in adhering to the prescribed one-reel format. Still feeling his way in the new medium, he was preoccupied with turning out his contribution to Biograph's busy (three films a week) release schedule. Still located on the East Coast, Biograph and other firms found it difficult to meet the ever-increasing demand for film product, because of the lack of adequate sunlight for exterior filming during the long Eastern winters. To circumvent this period of forced inactivity, Griffith convinced Biograph, in January, 1910, to follow what was becoming a common practice by dispatching a production unit to Southern California for the winter. As the company's most prolific and versatile director, it was only natural that he should lead this expedition—which was to be repeated annually thereafter. Ostensibly made to take advantage of the varied scenery and favorable climate of the Los Angeles area, these trips in future years assumed a more personal dimension, providing Griffith with a yearly excuse to remove his operations from close contact with the increasingly bothersome head office at Biograph.

During his first two years as a director, Griffith had made nearly 250 films; as his technical proficiency grew, so did his ambitions, and he soon felt a need to go beyond the bounds of the restrictive one-reel format. In late 1910, he filmed a Civil War drama in two reels and asked the company to release them as a single film. Not surprisingly, this request was refused; Biograph released the first reel under the title *His Trust* on January 16, 1911, following it three days later with the second reel, which was called *His Trust Fulfilled*. Biograph's advertisements acknowledged that the second reel was a "continuation" of the first, but also emphasized that each reel was "a complete story in itself." This actually was true; because Griffith, anticipating the company's decision, had designed the story with this eventuality in mind.

By the time *His Trust* and *His Trust Fulfilled* were released, Griffith was again in Los Angeles. This second winter trip lasted six weeks longer than the first, and it seems likely that the weather may not have been the only reason—Griffith was beginning to resent the company's tight control over his productions, and he probably welcomed the three-thousand-mile separation.

During the 1911 western trip, his output included a two-reel version of *Enoch Arden*, based on the Alfred Tennyson poem. His most ambitious project to date, it resulted in a minor breakthrough—although Biograph again insisted on releasing the film one reel at a time (on June 12 and June 15), they compromised slightly by designating them as "Part One" and "Part Two," and many exhibitors found themselves obliged by audience demand to combine them into a single feature. This was not completely unprecedented (in March, 1911, for example, Vitagraph's three-reel *A Tale of Two Cities* had been released and sporadically exhibited in a similar fashion), but its implications were seemingly lost on the conservative Biograph management. Griffith was instructed to stick to single-reel productions.

Prior to Griffith's 1911 California trip, his films (with the exception of *His Trust/His Trust Fulfilled*) had never exceeded the prescribed measurement of one reel or one thousand feet. From that time on, however, most were slightly longer than one thousand feet. The difference may seem inconsequential— it was rarely more than fifty feet, or about one minute—but if one regards the one-thousand-foot mark as a sort of line over which Griffith was forbidden to step, then the few extra feet take on a greater significance. Griffith's persistent assault on the one-reel barrier was a clear indication of his growing frustration. It was not until the following year that Griffith finally scored a small victory—*A Pueblo Legend*, filmed in New Mexico during the annual winter trip, became the first two-reel film to be released as such by the Biograph Company (although it was significantly unaccompanied by even the slightest fanfare).

Between the production of *A Pueblo Legend* in May, 1912, and its release in August, an event occurred that was to have a great effect on the movement toward longer films. This was the New York premiere, on July 12, of a four-reel French film, the Film d'Art production of *Queen Elizabeth*, starring Sarah Bernhardt. Although one's definition of the term is important, *Queen Elizabeth* is usually acknowledged as the first "feature film" shown in America. Essentially a photographed stage play, it contained only twelve individual shots in the course of its four reels. Despite its even then-antiquated techniques, however, it was an immediate success. Ironically, the Biograph heads, Kennedy and Marvin, had been instrumental in helping its importers to obtain a license for its exhibition. They were not, however, immediately influenced by its success, and they maintained their belief that Biograph's one-reel policy was a proven success and should not be altered.

Their attitude may have softened a bit, however, for in the latter part of 1912, Griffith was finally allowed to make a handful of longer films—*Oil and Water* (one and one-half reels), and *Brutality* and *The Massacre* (two reels each). Moreover, by the time he embarked for Los Angeles in late December, he apparently had been given verbal authorization to make additional two-reelers, as he thought appropriate. His decisions, however, were still subject to the approval of the home office; this was to be arranged through Biograph's secretary, R. H. Hammer, who accompanied the Griffith troupe and acted as a manager and financial overseer. Griffith was undoubtedly frustrated by this administrative hold, but he had no choice but to play by the company's rules. During his six-month stay in California, he managed to produce thirty-two films, seven of which were longer than one reel. The most productive of his winter excursions, it was also to be his last.

The success of *Queen Elizabeth* accelerated the demand for feature-length films and while Griffith was in California, there were several additional developments, one of which involved the Biograph Company directly. In the spring of 1913, Marvin and Kennedy negotiated an agreement with the prominent theatrical producers Marc Klaw and Abraham Erlanger to film their stage plays in five-reel versions, to be used for summer showings in the legitimate theaters controlled by Klaw & Erlanger. Griffith had been unaware of this impending development, and it did not really affect him until he returned to New York in July. Another event, however, had a more immediate, if long-distance, effect on his plans; this was the April 1 premiere in New York of the imported Italian epic *Quo Vadis?* (1912), in the unheard-of length of eight reels. Although Griffith could not have seen the film until after his return from California, he was undoubtedly aware of the stir it caused, and it is generally credited with turning his thoughts toward an epic of his own.

Ten days after the premiere of *Quo Vadis?* (in what scarcely seems like a coincidence), Griffith's assistant, Lee Dougherty, purchased a scenario entitled "Judith and Holofernes" from Grace A. Pierce of Santa Monica. Griffith's familiarity with Thomas Bailey Aldrich's play *Judith of Bethulia*, based on the same Biblical material, suggests that he may have already had the story in mind, and that the Pierce scenario may have been intended to refute possible charges of plagiarism (even though the basic material was in the public domain). It has been related that Griffith referred to the Aldrich play throughout the filming, and the film's main titles acknowledge it as the source (although these titles may date from the 1917 re-release of the film).

During the month of June, while Griffith was shooting several other films in the San Fernando Valley, he was also supervising the construction of a set representing the walled city of Bethulia, several miles to the west in Chatsworth Park. He managed to secure the company's approval of an eighteen-thousand-dollar budget, while concealing his intention to make a film of more than two reels. The actual shooting was apparently accomplished fairly quickly, for the unit returned to New York during the first week in July, with only a few interior scenes remaining to do (which Griffith planned to complete at Biograph's newly constructed studios in the Bronx).

Griffith's homecoming was less than pleasant. His employment of hundreds of extras, plus expenditures for costumes, horses, sets, and more, had escalated the cost of *Judith of Bethulia* to thirty-six thousand dollars, making it probably the most expensive American film to date. Kennedy and Marvin were, to put it mildly, displeased; not only did they refuse to renegotiate the terms of Griffith's contract (which had remained unchanged since late 1911), but he was also informed that he was not to begin any new films. After he had completed the shooting and editing of *Judith of Bethulia*, he was to assume a supervisory position at the studio. They subsequently informed him that he was not to be involved in the filming of the Klaw & Erlanger plays, but was welcome to continue with the production of one-reel subjects. This final blow to Griffith's ego and ambitions (both of which had grown considerably) convinced him that he should part company with Biograph. He did so auspiciously, trumpeting his departure with a full-page advertisement in *The New York Dramatic Mirror* on December 3, 1913.

This notice, concocted by Griffith's new "personal representative," Albert Banzhaf, listed 151 of his films (about a third of his total to that time), and stated that he had been responsible for "revolutionizing Motion Picture drama and founding the modern technique of the art"; included was a list of filmic techniques, including the close-up, the "switchback" (parallel editing), and "restraint in expression," alleged to have been his innovations. A few of these claims were overstated or simply untrue, but the underlying basis was solid: Griffith was unquestionably the most vital figure in the development of the cinema, and after years of anonymous toil, he was claiming his due. Griffith had been highly regarded for a long time within the film business, but in adherence to M.P.P.C. policy, his name had never appeared on the screen or in any of Biograph's promotional material. This public declaration of his accomplishments was also, in a sense, his debut.

Griffith's departure from Biograph was a logical and important move. He soon entered into a partnership with distributor Harry E. Aitken, and within a few years, with *The Birth of a Nation* (1915) and *Intolerance* (1916), he had achieved a level of personal recognition commensurate with his artistic status. For the Biograph Company, however, the loss of Griffith was a disastrous blow from which it would never recover. Griffith took with him virtually all the company's important acting talent—including Blanche Sweet, Henry B. Walthall, Mae Marsh, Lillian and Dorothy Gish, Robert Herron, Donald Crisp, and others, all of whom had developed a strong loyalty to the director— and when the Klaw & Erlanger deal failed to produce the anticipated financial bonanza, Biograph had few resources on which to fall back. They even failed to reap the full benefit from *Judith of Bethulia*, delaying its release until March, 1914, by which time feature films were rapidly becoming commonplace, and the film's potential impact had been considerably blunted. Biograph lingered until 1917 before folding; ironically, one of its last releases was a reissue of *Judith of Bethulia*, expanded to six reels by the inclusion of footage originally eliminated by Griffith, under the title *Her Condoned Sin*.

This eleventh-hour reissue of *Judith of Bethulia* is the source of some difficulty for present-day evaluators, since extant prints appear to be descended in part from that reedited version. The titles that appear in the film, for example, are not the simple white-on-black titles that characterized earlier Biograph releases, but are superimposed over "dark atmospheric backgrounds, selected from the negative," as described in a contemporary review of the later version. Although the print under consideration is four reels in length, it cannot be confidently determined precisely how closely it approximates the film as originally assembled by Griffith. Any close analysis, therefore—particularly of the editing—should be regarded as provisional.

The story centers around Judith (Blanche Sweet), the widow of Manasses, who leads a solitary life of prayer within the walled city of Bethulia, which guards the approaches to Jerusalem. Judith occasionally goes among the people of the city, by whom she is "held in great reverence," to distribute alms. The city comes under attack by the army of Assur, dispatched by King Nebuchodonosor (Nebuchadnezzar) to lay waste to the West. In their initial assault, the Assyrians, under the command of Prince Holofernes (Henry B. Walthall), capture the wells from which the city takes its water; they also take a number of prisoners, including the water-carrier Naomi (Mae Marsh), the beloved of Nathan (Robert Harron).

When an extended siege fails to breach the walls, Holofernes decides to starve the city. Judith, distressed at the suffering of her people, has a vision from the Lord which impels her to dress in all her finery and offer herself to Holofernes, with the intent of slaying him. The dreaded "Bull of Assur," however, proves to be charismatic and hospitable, and Judith weakens in her resolve. Ensconced in a tent provided by Holofernes, she wrestles with her passion; meanwhile, having nearly reached their breaking point, the Bethulians launch an ill-fated attempt to recapture the wells. That night, left alone with Holofernes, Judith seductively tantalizes the infatuated Prince, all the while pressing strong drink upon him, until he loses consciousness. Despite a last-minute hesitation, she then follows through with her plan by decapitating him. She returns to the city with his head, and the Bethulian forces rout the horrified Assyrians and burn their camp; in the nick of time, Nathan rescues Naomi from the flames. For her heroic deed, Judith is honored by the people of Bethulia.

The extensive attention paid here to the background of the film's production suggests that *Judith of Bethulia* is best appreciated in the context of Griffith's career. He was obviously attempting to expand the expressive and narrative possibilities of his editing techniques, and the film's somewhat archaic appearance today should not be allowed to obscure his accomplishments. Most interesting, in the light of his later work, is his attempt at weaving together several different interrelationships by means of parallel editing. His handling of the character of Judith, both in relationship to the Bethulian community and to Holofernes, is particularly good. Judith's spiritual bond with her people is succinctly embodied in her encounters with a young mother (played by Lillian Gish); the acting in these two brief scenes is as fine as any in the cinema of that period.

Equally impressive is Griffith's use of editing to establish an invisible bond (unencumbered by any overt statement) between Judith and Holofernes, long before they meet face to face. This is done by consistently placing Holofernes to the left of the frame and Judith to the right, often with empty space opposite. The subtle effect of this simple device is to make each seem incomplete without the other—a feeling confirmed by the intensity of their scenes together, which are among the best in the film. Although rudimentary, this is a far more psychologically advanced use of editing than was the "last-minute rescue" for which Griffith is most renowned.

The love story between Nathan and Naomi, on the other hand, gets almost completely lost in the shuffle and is redeemed only slightly by the charm of Mae Marsh and Robert Harron (although Harron's performance is considerably overdone). Nathan is glimpsed several times in the midst of the action, but his last-minute rescue of Naomi from the burning tent seems arbitrary and does not measure up to the standards set by Griffith himself. Again, this may be due to the vagaries of prints available today. It has been suggested that *Judith of Bethulia* employs a four-part structure that anticipates the complex narrative of *Intolerance*, but this seems to be stretching a point—the film is of great value to a study of Griffith's work despite the relative modesty of its cinematic accomplishments.

One immodest aspect of the film, by contemporary standards, was its spectacular staging. This was the largest scale on which Griffith had ever worked, and it clearly presages his later films. He shows a flair for background movement—during the early scenes at the wells, and on both sides of the wall during the siege of Bethulia—even though the battle scenes themselves are not wholly convincing. The movement of his crowds is certainly energetic, and the screen is often overwhelmed with frantic motion, but on close examination, the action looks fairly ludicrous, with much pointless sword and arm waving and little actual combat. Portions of the battle scenes in *The Birth of a Nation* can be criticized on the same grounds, but by that time, Griffith had become more adept at integrating personal drama and spectacle. Compare, for example, the rather insignificant presence of Nathan in the fighting with the stirring combat actions of the "Little Colonel" in *The Birth of a Nation*. In *Judith of Bethulia*, the crowds are almost completely anonymous, and the level of interest is primarily technical.

Griffith achieves his finest effects, however, in the film's more intimate moments: Judith's empathetic suffering at the plight of the Bethulians; the poignancy of her personal encounters with the people, in particular the scenes with the Gish character; and the vividly expressed struggle with her "sinful passion" as she hesitates in her resolve to kill Holofernes. The scenes between Judith and Holofernes are well handled, as is the depiction of the encroaching famine within the walls of the besieged city. The naturalistic acting style encouraged by Griffith is certainly in evidence in *Judith of Bethulia*, but it shares the spotlight with the more stilted attitudes which were even then deemed appropriate for Biblical subjects. All the various tendencies of film acting of the period—delicate expression, overwrought theatrical histrionics, stodgy piety—are crystallized in the full-blooded performance of Blanche Sweet as Judith. The character of Holofernes has fewer dimensions, but even rendered unrecognizable beneath a huge fake beard, Henry B. Walthall provides an impressive portrayal of the Assyrian commander.

Many of Griffith's Biograph films were more aesthetically satisfying than *Judith of Bethulia*, but none was ultimately as important. Whatever its relative merits, the film was a watershed in the director's career. The circumstances surrounding its production were instrumental in freeing him from the restrictive bonds of his Biograph employment and propelling him into a period of more adventurous activity. Only four months after the eventual release of *Judith of Bethulia*, Griffith began production on *The Birth of a Nation*.

Howard H. Prouty

THE KAISER, BEAST OF BERLIN

Released: 1918
Production: Jewel Productions
Direction: Rupert Julian
Screenplay: Elliott Clawson
Cinematography: no listing
Length: no listing

Principal characters:
Kaiser Wilhelm	Rupert Julian
Captain von Wohlbold	Allen Sears
Captain von Neigle	Nigel De Brulier
Marcas the Blacksmith	Elmo Lincoln
Ambassador Gerard	Joseph W. Girard
Admiral von Tirpitz	Lon Chaney
King Albert of Belgium	Alfred Allen

For good reason or bad, film has always proven to be a fertile medium for the creation and spread of various kinds of propaganda. Since motion pictures display illusions of reality, a director can make fanciful events upon the screen appear believable in order to produce some desired emotional or aesthetic reaction on the part of the viewer. When the intent of a film is propaganda, its effectiveness depends almost completely upon its successful operation on an emotional level. The message is generally one of immediacy, and the entreaty is highly spirited. Propaganda in films may be manifested in a variety of ways, and since the early years of the medium, audiences have been urged to rally to the cause of almost every political, sociological, and religious philosophy in existence. Some eras have been witness to a greater production of these films than others, however; the World War I period, in particular, saw a proliferation of numerous anti-German, or "Hate-the-Hun," films. In these films, Germans were characterized as evil, vicious, and forever bent upon villainy, and many included at least one scene of rape, or attempted rape, of an innocent girl, who was usually French. Understandably, such scenes were of a violent nature, and their intent was to incite race hatred among the Allied audiences. There were also numerous thematic sequences where some ordinary citizen decided to support the war effort by enlisting in the armed forces to help eradicate the detested "Huns."

In many cases, the propaganda films were hastily put together in a crude fashion and were blatantly obvious in theme. Others, such as *The Battle Cry of Peace* (1915), were substantially more artistic and subtle. Somewhere in between the extremes is a film entitled *The Kaiser, Beast of Berlin*.

This profoundly anti-German 1918 film from Jewel Productions is one of the elusive "lost" films. The American Film Institute has called *The Kaiser,*

Beast of Berlin one of its ten most wanted films because it is "historically and artistically significant." The film featured Rupert Julian as the dreaded Kaiser Wilhelm II, who pompously swaggered from scene to scene throughout the seven reels. The film attempted to pull together a number of events in the life of the Kaiser and present them as a loose biographical narrative. There was no real plot, however, since most audiences were well aware of recent events in Europe, and almost any account of the Kaiser's career would produce the desired volatile effect.

There are many vivid scenes in *The Kaiser, Beast of Berlin* which contributed to its success, one of which is the sinking of the Lusitania by German submarines. The submarine commander, Captain von Neigle (Nigel de Brulier) is decorated by a proud Kaiser (Rupert Julian), but he descends into insanity later in the film. Contemporary audiences must have thought it a fitting end for one who carried out so heinous a crime. Another important sequence concerns a proud, young German named Captain von Wohlbold (Allen Sears). The officer is deeply offended when the Kaiser reviews his troops and criticizes their less than perfect appearance. The captain becomes so overwhelmed with anger that he strikes the Kaiser, knocking him to the ground. When Captain von Wohlbold realizes the tremendous gravity of his disloyal act, he takes his own life. The obvious despair inherent in such an act was surely not lost on an audience hungering for the obliteration of the Hohenzollern empire. These two scenes were potent attempts at portraying the German military men, and probably all Germans, as unstable and mentally fragile.

Most of the film is set in Louvain, and the exterior scenes of the Belgian countryside, which open the film, are strongly idyllic and serve to contrast the strife, madness, and bloodshed which follow. In Louvain, there is a blacksmith by the name of Marcas (Elmo Lincoln). Marcas, a powerful but peace-loving man, witnesses, with his family, the destruction of Louvain by the Germans. In the chaos and terror, a wounded Marcas bravely defends his daughter from the attack of a German soldier bent upon rape. Whether Lincoln—best known as the silent Tarzan—performed superbly as contemporary critics stated, or whether he was playing to the sympathies of an audience which could easily be prodded to detest the Germans is uncertain. In any case, there was strong audience identification with the story of Marcas, even though this incident had little to do with the very loose plot.

Throughout *The Kaiser, Beast of Berlin*, Wilhelm displays his madness and his perverse desire to conquer the world. These characteristics, along with what *The Moving Picture World* called "his utter lack of human sentiment," were skillfully played by Julian, according to the few existing reviews. Julian apparently incited audiences to seething anger when he warned the Americans to stay out of his way and not attempt to stop the Kaiser on his inexorable march to destiny. The only suitable conclusion for such a dastardly career was a defeat at the hands of the Americans. The final scenes reveal the Kaiser sodden with guilt and, now captured, being consigned to King Albert of Belgium (Alfred Allen). In an ironic touch, and for immeasurable propagandistic value, the Kaiser's jailer was the noble blacksmith, Marcas. This last segment was, of course, not historical fact and merely gave a hopeful suggestion for the future.

Thomas A. Hanson

THE KERRY GOW

Released: 1912
Production: Kalem Company; released by the General Film Company
Direction: Sidney Olcott
Screenplay: Gene Gauntier (uncredited); based on the play by Joseph Murphy
Cinematography: George K. Hollister
Length: 3 reels

Principal characters:
Major Gruff/Kiernan, the drunkard .... Sidney Olcott
Patrick Drew .... E. O'Sullivan
Dan O'Hara .... Jack J. Clark
Nora Drew .... Alice Hollister

The Kerry Gow, released by the General Film Company in the fall of 1912, represents a unique experiment in early filmmaking, when the American Kalem Company filmed, on a regular basis, a considerable number of major productions on location in Ireland.

The Kalem Company first came to film in Ireland in the summer of 1910. As far as can be ascertained, it was the first American film company to shoot films on foreign locations, in the countries in which the stories were set. The man behind the decision to go to Ireland was the company's sole director Sidney Olcott, who was later to be responsible for such features as *Timothy's Quest* (1922), *Little Old New York* (1923), and *Monsieur Beaucaire* (1924), and who had codirected the most famous of early Kalem productions, the 1907 one-reel version of *Ben-Hur*. Olcott's mother was Irish and when asked by Kalem president, Frank Marion, where the company should shoot films, it was natural that Olcott should choose the land of his ancestors.

In company with his leading lady Gene Gauntier (who also supplied the scripts), actor (and later director) Robert Vignola, and cameraman George Hollister, Olcott arrived in Ireland in August of 1910 and immediately began looking for a picturesque spot to set up operations. His choice was the small village of Beaufort, a few miles outside of Killarney, which offered old-fashioned cottages, unspoiled countryside, and easy access to the lakes of Killarney. The company shot two Irish one-reelers in 1910, *The Lad From Old Ireland* and *The Irish Honeymoon*, and then went to Germany, where they filmed *The Little Spreewald Maiden*. This was no haphazard experiment, for the Kalem Company realized that films with Irish settings or films with German settings would appeal to immigrants from those countries now resident in the United States, and the company also knew that it was working-class immigrants, such as the Irish, which comprised the majority of early filmgoers.

The O'Kalems, as they laughingly came to be known, returned to Ireland, and to Beaufort, in July of the following year. They established a home with the O'Sullivan family and built a makeshift stage behind the family house. For the first time, the filmmakers turned their attention to the Irish-British political troubles and filmed a one-reeler titled *Rory O'More*, based on the life of the eighteenth century Irish revolutionary hero. In addition, the company filmed two major productions based on plays by Dion Boucicault, *The Colleen Bawn* and *Arrah-na-Pogue*. Each starred Gauntier and her husband, Jack J. Clark, and each was three reels in length. *The Moving Picture World*, the leading film trade paper of the period, hailed *The Colleen Bawn* as "the chef d'oeuvre of American motion picture production." The O'Kalems, led by Olcott and Gauntier, left Ireland in October of 1911 and, after a brief stay in America, moved on to the Holy Land, where they filmed *From the Manger to the Cross* that winter.

While the company was in Palestine, president Frank Marion acquired the rights to several well-known Irish plays, including Dion Boucicault's *The Shaughraun* and two plays by Joseph Murphy, *The Kerry Gow* and *Shaun Rhue*. Murphy had been touring the United States in these two productions for more than thirty years and, along the way, had made himself one of the wealthiest actors in the country. In addition to selling the film rights to his plays, Murphy "furnished many details of 'business' which made his plays so successful" (according to *The Moving Picture World*).

In July of 1912, the O'Kalems returned for what was to be their last visit to Beaufort as members of the Kalem Company. They filmed a number of one-reelers, including *The Mayor from Ireland, Conway, the Kerry Dancer, Ireland the Oppressed*, and *Lady Peggy's Escape*, together with two three-reelers, *The Shaughraun* and *The Kerry Gow*.

The Kerry Gow was typical of the American-Irish view of their homeland, a rosy-eyed vision of a country where good and evil are easily defined. It is a familiar old story of the villain who seeks to steal the beautiful daughter from the young hero/lover because he holds the mortgage on the father's cottage. The suspense in *The Kerry Gow* is created by a horse race, which will bring either the money to pay off the mortgage or villainous triumph. As the father is unable to attend the race in person, an elaborate system of carrier pigeons has been set up to inform him of its progress. The first carrier pigeon arrives with a message that the opening heat has been won by the right horse. The second bird brings news that the horse was defeated in the second heat. After an interminable wait, the third pigeon arrives, but it has lost the message. The tension mounts, and when the suspense has become almost unbearable, the hero himself rides up, happy but exhausted, to report that yes, indeed, their horse came first in the final heat. The mortgage can be repaid, and the villain is unmasked as having "planted" forbidden pikes in the hero's blacksmith shop. The villain is arrested and love and truth have triumphed once again in the best tradition of Victorian melodrama.

The hero was portrayed by handsome Jack J. Clark, with Alice Hollister, the wife of the Kalem cameraman, playing the heroine. The villain was unidentified in contemporary published credits, but appears to have been portrayed by Robert Vignola. A member of the O'Sullivan family was listed as an actor to play the part of the poor father, Patrick Drew. One thing that reviewers at the time noted about this and other Kalem Irish productions was the authenticity of the setting and sets. The hero was a blacksmith and so a real blacksmith's shop was utilized. Father and daughter lived in a poor cottage, and so a poor cottage was borrowed from one of the Beaufort villagers. As W. Stephen Bush wrote in *The Moving Picture World* (November 9, 1912),

> The charm and power of this version of the old play comes from the romantic little by-plays so dear to the Irish heart, the displays of Irish humor veering from the subtle to the rollicking and back again and always close to the fountain of tears, from the singular idyllic charm of the Irish landscape, from the excellent acting and the unmistakable air of realism with which this company has invested all its Irish plays.

In the fall of 1912, Olcott, Gauntier, and others left the Kalem Company, and Gauntier created the Gene Gauntier Feature Players Company, with Olcott as its director. The group returned to Beaufort in August of 1913 and shot several films there, *For Ireland's Sake* and *Come Back to Erin*. During the summer of 1914, there was a final filmmaking pilgrimage to Beaufort, this time by Olcott's own company, titled, appropriately enough, Sid Films, with Valentine Grant as the director's new leading lady. The films shot that year were *The Irish in America* and *Bold Emmett, Ireland's Martyr*. Then World War I broke out and filmmaking abroad was effectively halted.

The Kalem Company was not the only American film producer to shoot films outside of the United States in the early days of the cinema. Vitagraph sent a troupe of filmmakers, led by actor Maurice Costello, around the world, for example; but Kalem was the first to utilize non-American backgrounds on a regular basis and to appreciate the need for realism and naturalism in motion pictures. Sadly, the majority of the Kalem Irish films, including *The Kerry Gow*, are no longer known to exist. If they did, it is certain they would back up Olcott's claim to the title "The [David] Belasco of the Open Air."

Anthony Slide

THE KID

Released: 1921
Production: Charles Chaplin for Associated First National
Direction: Charles Chaplin
Screenplay: Charles Chaplin
Cinematography: Rollie Totheroh
Length: 6 reels/5,300 feet

Principal characters:

The Kid	Jackie Coogan
The Woman	Edna Purviance
The Man	Carl Miller
The Tramp	Charles Chaplin
The Policeman	Tom Wilson
The Bully	Chuck Reisner
A Crook	Albert Austin
Slum Woman	Nelly Bly Baker
Lodging House Proprietor	Henry Bergman
The Flirting Angel	Lita Grey

Charles Chaplin began the decade of the 1920's with *The Kid*, the first feature-length production to be both written and directed by the comedian. Although the earlier *A Dog's Life* (1918), *Shoulder Arms* (1918), *Sunnyside* (1919), and *A Day's Pleasure* (1919) had heralded a new era in Chaplin's career, they were more sophisticated than his previous films and were totally the comedian's creations. *The Kid* marked a turning point in Chaplin's work. Aside from two minor shorts, he was to devote the rest of his working life to feature-length comedies, for which a considerable amount of time was to be spent in preparation. The comedian devoted more than a year to *The Kid*, and it showed. The critic for *Variety* (January 21, 1921) noted, "*The Kid* . . . has all the earmarks of having been carefully thought out and painstakingly directed, photographed and assembled. The cutting, in some places, amounts almost to genius." The Chaplin stamp was to be firmly embedded in all of these later films, and, not always to the films' benefit, Chaplin was completely the *auteur*. Aside from producing, directing, writing, composing the score, and starring in these later comedies, one has the distinct feeling that Chaplin would have been happier had no one else, actors or cameramen, been associated with the productions.

The Kid is introduced by the title, "A picture with a smile and perhaps a tear," summarizing the new Chaplin approach to filmmaking: comedy with precisely the right blend of pathos. At times, unfortunately, *The Kid* has perhaps a little too much pathos, with its comments on "the woman whose sin was motherhood" and the symbolism in the cut to a shot of Christ bearing his cross. It is heavy-handed and illustrates the need (unaccepted by the comedian) for an outside control of his excesses.

The first scenes are of an unmarried woman (Edna Purviance) leaving a hospital with her illegitimate child. As she passes a church, the woman witnesses a wedding, and a flower from the young bride's bouquet falls, symbolically, to the ground. Unable to rear the child herself, the woman leaves it inside a waiting limousine, with a note asking that the baby be taken care of, and then rushes away. Unfortunately, the car is stolen, and when the thieves find the baby in the back, they dump it in an alley.

Halfway into the first reel, Chaplin as the Little Tramp appears, only to find the crying baby. Not knowing what to do with it, he attempts, without success, to leave it in an unattended baby carriage, but he reads the pitiful note and decides to rear the child himself. In the meantime, the mother has regretted her decision and searches in vain for the limousine, which she learns has been stolen.

Five years pass and the child has grown into an able accomplice to Chaplin. The former breaks windows and the comedian then appears to mend them, and both are pursued by a policeman (Tom Wilson, who had portrayed the friendly policeman five years earlier in D. W. Griffith's *Intolerance*). Playing "the Kid" was Jackie Coogan, a major find, whose performance at times almost steals the thunder from that of Chaplin. He is the archetypal cute, naughty boy—a fascinating mixture of charm and guile. The critics were quick to note that Coogan's performance was on a par with that of Chaplin. *Variety* commented that "It is almost impossible to refrain from superlatives in referring to this child . . . whose character work probably never has been equalled by a child artist." *The New York Times* (February 7, 1921) wrote, "Without the Coogan boy it couldn't be done. It is dreadful to think of such a perfection as this child pushing out of his treble exquisiteness into something perhaps theatrical and over-stimulated and unstable."

Coogan (born 1914) had already worked in vaudeville and on the screen prior to *The Kid*. As a result of his role in that film, however, his career took off, with a million-dollar contract, and starring roles in *Peck's Bad Boy* (1921) and *Oliver Twist* (1922), among others. In the 1930's, the lawsuit with his mother and stepfather over their squandering of his childhood earnings led to a Child Actors Law being passed, commonly known as the Coogan Act. The Act states that earnings of juvenile actors must be held in trust until they reach maturity. Coogan has continued to act sporadically in character parts through the present, and he became known to a new generation of children as one of the stars of the television series *The Addams Family*.

The plot of *The Kid* takes an unexpected turn at this point, the mother becoming a famous actress and reuniting with the child's father, who is now a successful fashion designer. The memory of her lost child has caused the mother to become a Lady Bountiful to the slum children, and in this capacity, she meets Chaplin and the Kid when stopping a street fight. Seeing that the child has been hurt, she has Chaplin call a doctor. The doctor, realizing that the Kid is not Chaplin's son, announces that arrangements must be made to put the child in an orphanage. When the truck from that institution arrives, the Kid is not seized without a struggle, but just as the vehicle is approaching the orphanage, Chaplin is able to grab the boy back.

The two cannot return to the home, which the Kid has been running so meticulously. The mother visits their former home to inquire into the child's well-being, and she finds the scribbled note she had left with her baby. The head of the orphanage learns of the reward that the mother is offering for the return of her child, and again has the boy snatched away from Chaplin.

A sad and despairing Chaplin walks the city streets, searching for his child until, exhausted, he falls asleep and dreams of his version of Heaven, labelled "Fairyland," in which he encounters the policeman (with wings) and a seductive angel (Lita Grey, whom Chaplin was to marry in 1924). The Chaplin slums are transformed into paradise with angels in white and festoons of paper decorations, but Chaplin is still pursued by the policeman and by the local bully. The policeman enforces brotherly love with a gun. As *Exceptional Photoplays* (January-February, 1921) commented, "What an ingenious travesty on our easy beatitudes."

In his dream, Chaplin is shot down by the policeman, and when he wakes up the same policeman is there to tell him that the mother knows the Kid needs his adopted father. So the Little Tramp drives (not walks) off, not into an uneasy future, but to a happy reunion with the Kid.

The Kid was received with universal acclamation. *The New York Times* wrote, "*The Kid* is not only the longest comedy in which Chaplin has appeared since becoming the best-known figure of the film world, but it is a real comedy." In *The New Republic*, Francis Hackett commented that *The Kid* "should go some way to revolutionize motion picture production in this country. From an industry *The Kid* raises production to an art." *Exceptional Photoplays* hailed *The Kid* as "An astonishing picture, true to the common stuff of human attributes."

The film paved the way for the later, and sometimes greater Chaplin features of *The Gold Rush* (1925), *The Circus* (1928), *City Lights* (1931), and *Modern Times* (1936). It also heralded a new era in screen comedy, as other comedians, such as Buster Keaton and Harold Lloyd, embraced the feature-length film farce and built on the ideas expounded by Chaplin.

Anthony Slide

THE KID BROTHER

Released: 1927
Production: Harold Lloyd for Paramount
Direction: Ted Wilde
Screenplay: John Grey, Lex Neal, and Howard J. Green; based on a story
   by John Grey, Tom Crizer, and Ted Wilde
Cinematography: Walter Lundin
Length: 8 reels/7,654 feet

Principal characters:
Harold Hickory .... Harold Lloyd
Mary Powers .... Jobyna Ralston
Jim Hickory .... Walter James
Leo Hickory ....Leo Willis
Olin Hickory .... Olin Francis
Sandoni .... Constantine Romanoff
"Flash" Farrell .... Eddie Boland
Sam Hooper ....Frank Lanning
Hank Hooper .... Ralph Yearsley

The amazing thing about the films of Harold Lloyd is not their quantity or
the years that they span—1913 to 1946—but rather that one is continually
surprised by the excellence of a newly rediscovered feature. Such is the case
with *The Kid Brother*, long unseen until fairly recent years, but a Lloyd vehicle
which must be considered one of the comedian's finest works, possibly superior
even to *Safety Last* (1923) or *The Freshman* (1925).

When it was first released, there was little question as to its popularity.
Mordaunt Hall of *The New York Times* saw it when it opened at New York's
Rialto Theater on January 23, 1927, and reported in the following day's issue
of his newspaper, "Mr. Lloyd displays no little ingenuity, none of his gags
being inspired by any other comedian." He goes on to comment that audiences
of all ages "simply let themselves roar to their heart's content." Laurence
Reid in *Motion Picture News* (February 4, 1927) called it simply, "A Great
Picture"; "Lloyd never mixed a pleasanter blend of laughter and pathos,"
reported *Photoplay* (March, 1927).

Laughter and pathos were the two elements present in many of Lloyd's best
films, such as *Grandma's Boy* (1922), *The Freshman*, *For Heaven's Sake*
(1926), and *Girl Shy* (1924), but not *Safety Last*. Lloyd seemed to have a way
with pathos that few of his contemporaries could match. Buster Keaton, of
course, seldom used pathos. Harry Langdon usually did, but not always with
perfect results. Charlie Chaplin is generally conceded to be the master when
it came to mixing pathos and comedy, but in too many cases there is a forced
artificiality to the Chaplin pathos. This is not true with Lloyd, to whom pathos

is genuine and a necessary part of plot construction. As with Lloyd's best films, the pathos in *The Kid Brother* is provided by the thwarted love affair between the comedian and his greatest leading lady, Jobyna Ralston, here making her final appearance with Lloyd.

The Kid Brother is set in a small mountain community, where Harold is the youngest, much maligned son of the county sheriff, Jim Hickory (Walter James). While Hickory and his two older boys, Olin (Olin Francis) and Leo (Leo Willis), handle the traditionally male chores, Harold takes care of the household tasks. He does the laundry: washing the clothes in the milk churn, feeding them through a wringer, and finally hanging them out on a line attached to a pack. He washes the dishes inside a fishing net, and when the plates are ready to dry, places them on a shelf over the stove. Harold Hickory is very much a comic version of the Richard Barthelmess character in *Tol'able David* (1921).

While his father and brothers are attending a town meeting, at which the father persuades the townspeople to hand over to him the money that they have collected for a new dam, Harold puts on his father's badge and gun just at the precise moment that a medicine show happens to be passing by. The show is operated by Mary (Jobyna Ralston), aided by two villainous characters. Mary easily persuades Harold, whom she assumes to be the sheriff, to give her a permit to play the town, although neither really sees the other. After the show is set up, Mary goes for a walk in the woods, pursued by one of her associates, the terrifying Sandoni (Constantine Romanoff). Mary and Harold meet, but just as they are getting acquainted Sandoni appears on the scene. Harold grabs a stick and, in horror, Sandoni runs off—the stick has a snake attached to it.

Mary has to leave Harold and return to her medicine show and there follows one of the most hauntingly beautiful farewell scenes ever filmed for a comedy or a drama. As Mary leaves, Harold climbs higher and higher up a tree so that he can still see her, calling out, asking for her name and where she lives. When he reaches the top of the tree, he shouts good-bye and from Mary, now only a speck in the distance, comes a tiny good-bye on the title card. In his happiness, Harold begins to sway backward and forward in the tree and, of course, eventually comes crashing down to the ground.

When his father learns of the permit for the medicine show, he sends Harold into town to close the show down. At the show, Harold is humiliated. At one point he is even suspended in air from a trapeze. When the show catches on fire, Harold saves Mary and takes her back home with him. Comical complications ensue when the brothers mistake Harold for Mary, who has promptly been removed to a neighbor's home. As the plot thickens, the money for the dam is stolen and, naturally, the sheriff is suspected. When Harold is accidentally set adrift in a small boat on the river, he floats down to an abandoned ship called *The Black Ghost*, on which he sees the monkey from the medicine show with the stolen money, taken by the two showmen. Harold witnesses a fight between the two men, during which one is killed; and then he must try to escape from the maniacal Sandoni. The sense of comic timing and the use of sight gags is perfectly coordinated as, for example, Harold places his boots on the monkey's feet to lead Sandoni astray. Just as the townspeople are about to lynch the sheriff for the crime he did not commit, Harold returns with the money, and his father greets him as "a real Hickory."

Obviously Lloyd's gag men deserve much of the credit for the film's comedic success, in particular writer-turned-director Ted Wilde, who, according to Adam Reilly in his book, *Harold Lloyd: The King of Daredevil Comedy*, took over from the original director, Lewis Milestone. As a result of his success with *The Kid Brother*, Wilde was asked to direct Lloyd's next film, *Speedy* (1928). Many of the critics were rather amused by the number of writers credited on the film. Louella Parsons commented, "I never saw so many names. Mr. Lloyd certainly believes in safety in numbers, for there are at least three men to every job."

It would be grossly unfair, however, to assume that the film's success lies solely on its sight gags. Without question, *The Kid Brother* appeals and delights thanks to Lloyd's acting. Here he demonstrates his ability not only to play comedy, but also to hold his own with a basically melancholy role. If one were to take away the comedy and play *The Kid Brother* as a straight, dramatic feature it would still have tremendous impact.

Anthony Slide

THE KING OF KINGS

Released: 1927
Production: Cecil B. De Mille for De Mille Pictures; released by Paramount
Direction: Cecil B. De Mille
Screenplay: Jeanie Macpherson; based on the Gospels from the New Testament
Cinematography: Peverell Marley
Editing: Anne Bauchens and Harold McLernon
Art direction: Mitchell Leisen
Length: 14 reels/13,500 feet

Principal characters:
Jesus, the Christ ....H. B. Warner
Mary, the Mother .... Dorothy Cumming
Peter ....Ernest Torrence
Judas .... Joseph Schildkraut
James ....James Neill
Mary Magdalene .... Jacqueline Logan

Cecil B. De Mille often remarked that *The King of Kings* was his favorite film, and he frequently showed it in his home. Aside from the enjoyment of the film as a work of art, however, De Mille, who certainly appreciated the commercial aspects of motion-picture production, probably was equally elevated by the fact that *The King of Kings* was one of his highest grossing films, second only to *The Ten Commandments* (1956). Additionally, until the recent annual revival of *The Ten Commandments* on television, *The King of Kings* has undoubtedly been seen by more people than any of his other films.

In the mid-1920's, De Mille began to make the type of film for which he is now best known, the epic, costume drama. Previous to this time, he had made a variety of films of diverse styles, including *The Squaw Man* (1914), *The Cheat* (1915), *Male and Female* (1919), and *Manslaughter* (1922). Although these films handled different types of stories and were set in different eras, the one underlying theme in all of De Mille's work was redemption. The recognition of sin and the application of solid Victorian principles was not only morally didactic, but good box office as well, because De Mille could pepper his morality stories with liberal amounts of sex, always a popular film topic.

Some critics have noted that the change in De Mille's films from sexy but moral stories to extravagant religious epics was due in large part to the power of the Hays Office in the mid-1920's, but this is not entirely true. De Mille always had the strands of Christian ethics in his films, and the new type of film merely expanded them. As an illustration of this point, one could look at the character Fannie Ward played in *The Cheat* and adequately compare it to Mary Magdalene in *The King of Kings*. Thus, the change in De Mille's films are more of scope and degree than complete turnabout.

In the film, which lasts for more than two hours, De Mille recounts the story of Christ's life approximately from the time that he assembles the twelve apostles through his crucifixion and resurrection. As the film begins, Mary Magdalene (Jacqueline Logan) is angry that one of her admirers, Judas Iscariot (Joseph Schildkraut) has left her to join Jesus of Nazareth (H. B. Warner), whom she and her friends think is a religious fanatic.

When one of her friends bets that Mary cannot lure Judas away from Jesus, Mary accepts the bet, saying that she has blinded more men than Jesus has supposedly cured. In one of the typically opulent scenes, Mary drives her chariot to the place where Jesus is staying in haughty defiance. When she sees Jesus, however, she is awed. In a very effective scene, Jesus casts out seven devils from Mary, representing the seven deadly sins. As Mary covers her scantily attired body with her robes, the devils beckon her not to abandon them in a photographic technique which is still impressive today.

After this dramatic opening sequence, the day-to-day life of Christ as he approached his crucifixion is portrayed. Most of the action, like that of the four Gospels, takes place in a series of vignettes, but there is a subplot about Judas's doubts throughout the film.

De Mille, who was known as a master showman, rather than an *auteur*, made considerable use of the various miracle's associated with Christ, including healing the sick, multiplying the loaves and fishes, and other well-known incidents. He did have a few small touches in the film which, although corny, brought life to the film. For example, after a particularly triumphant scene, Christ is approached quietly by a little girl with a doll. The title card explains that the girl wants him to fix her broken doll because people say he can cure the sick. H. B. Warner, who as Christ, looks rather serious and remote throughout most of the film, blushes slightly, then attempts to fix the doll— by human means. For all of the "humanization" of Christ in more recent films such as *The Gospel According to St. Matthew* (1966) and *Jesus Christ Superstar* (1973), this scene in *The King of Kings* seems much more expressive of Christ's human personality.

Following the Gospels fairly closely, primarily because audiences were so familiar with the material that not much could be changed, the film dramatizes Christ's life through the Last Supper—in which he and the Twelve Apostles are situated according to Leonardo da Vinci's famous painting of that name— his passion, and his crucifixion on Calvary. The death of Christ causes a number of catastrophic occurrences in Jerusalem which De Mille vividly illustrates, including what seems to be a simultaneous solar eclipse and an earthquake. In the middle of these calamities, Judas hangs himself and his body is seen falling as the tree he uses topples over in the quake. The film ends with the resurrection of Christ, in scenes which De Mille reportedly found so uplifting that they repeatedly brought him to tears.

For all of what modern critics think about De Mille, he did entertain and seemed to have a knack for knowing exactly what the public wanted. The acting in *The King of Kings* is too flamboyant (except for the stolid Warner), and the spectacle is a bit too much at times, but the film is good. De Mille knew what type of a film he wanted to make and the public loved it. It was a tremendous success in 1927 and is one of the few silent films to have been revived repeatedly during the sound era. It was a staple of Catholic entertainment for decades and was a frequent choice to be shown at schools and churches.

Today, critics do not like De Mille very much, but when *The King of Kings* had its premiere in April, 1927, such critics as Mordaunt Hall and Welford Beaton greatly admired it. As Beaton said in his review for *The Film Spectator*, "It was a great thing that Cecil DeMille [sic] conceived and executed—something that will live for a long, long time." Mordaunt Hall called it ". . . the most impressive of all motion pictures," and *Variety* said, "*The King of Kings* will live forever, on the screen and in memory." Most people predicted that it would be the highest grossing film of all time, and although inflation and a new type of supergrossing "blockbuster" has recently changed the list of the highest moneymaking films, in terms of 1927 dollars, *The King of Kings* was definitely a spectacular success.

Most assuredly because of the success of the 1927 film, the 1961 Nicholas Ray remake was not well received by the critics. It finally made money, but the unfair criticism of Jeffrey Hunter's performance (one wag called the film "I Was a Teenage Jesus") and the overall cold reviews hurt the film considerably. It was not a bad film, but people still remembered the *effect* of De Mille's version, even if they did not actually recall the film, and Ray's work could not come close to it.

Although Warner was a well-known actor throughout his lengthy career, *The King of Kings* provided him with his most famous role. In the 1930's and 1940's Warner played frequently in character parts, most notably in *Lost Horizon* (1937) and *It's a Wonderful Life* (1946), both for Frank Capra, and *Sunset Boulevard* (1950) in which he portrayed himself. He worked again for De Mille in what was to be the last film for both, the remake of *The Ten Commandments*. He died in 1958 at age eighty-two.

Carolyn McIntosh

KINO-EYE
(KINO-GLAZ)

Released: 1924
Production: Goskino
Direction: Dziga Vertov
Screenplay: documentary
Cinematography: Mikhail Kaufman
Editing: Yelizaveta Svilova
Length: 6 reels/5,338 feet

"The history of Kino-Eye has been a relentless struggle to modify the course of world cinema," declared Dziga Vertov, the Russian documentary filmmaker and cinema theoretician, in 1929. Kino-Eye was an attempt "to place in cinema production a new emphasis of the 'unplayed' film over the play-film, to substitute the document for *mise-en-scène*, to break out of the proscenium of the theater and to enter the arena of life itself." By definition, the term "Kino-Eye" refers to capturing life on celluloid as it is lived: the subject must be photographed so that he or she is unaware of the presence of the camera and does not become self-conscious.

Immediately following the Russian Revolution, a heated argument raged among Soviet intellectuals as to the role of the filmmaker and how art could best serve the state. Vertov, who had originally studied music and neurology and served in the Red Army, had organized the Kino-Eye group in 1918 and instigated the large-scale shooting of newsreel footage. Vertov hated the theater and the narrative film. To him, the occurrences in everyday life were far more interesting. He believed that they obtained a heightened value once they were filmed, edited, and screened.

In 1919, Vertov published the Kinoks-Revolution manifesto, the first of several papers in which he chastized the futility of fiction films. Three years later, he formally introduced his theory in a magazine article. "I am eye," he wrote:

> I am a mechanical eye. I, a machine, am showing you a world the likes of which only I can see. I free myself from today and forever from human immobility. . . . My road is towards the creation of a fresh perception of the world. Thus I decipher in a new way the world unknown to you.

That year, he started *Kino-Pravda*, a "cinema magazine." Each edition ran approximately one reel, consisting of a few episodes. In three years, he made twenty-three editions.

Specifically, Vertov wanted to document the lives of the Soviet people, ultimately propagandizing the proletariat revolution. This goal was accomplished by utilizing the camera and the facilities of the director, cinematographer, and editor, who do not "invent" as do the creators of narrative films but instead "record." A criticism of Kino-Eye is that, while the images are preserved, there is no attempt to explore feeling, to examine anything internal. Kino-Eye films are really composed of snapshots, as opposed to photographs.

Yet, Vertov did not demonstrate his theory in any meaningful manner until 1924, when he made a documentary entitled, appropriately, *Kino-Eye*. The sequences in *Kino-Pravda* were essentially newsreels, as were his other efforts: for example, *The Battle of Tsaritsyn* (1919), a chronicle of the conflict between Red and White armies; and *Kalinin—The Elder Statesman of All Russians* (1920), a filmed record of a propaganda trip Soviet Chairman Mikhail Kalinin made by train throughout the country. In *Kino-Eye*, shot with a single camera, Vertov set out to capture on film various subjects: things old and new; children and adults; the cooperative and the marketplace; urban and rural life; the importance and value of meat and bread; and "bad," such as disease, crime, insanity, lying, alcoholism, and drug addiction, compared with "good," courage, honesty, and health.

With his brother and cameraman, Mikhail Kaufman (Vertov was born Denis Kaufman and changed his name: "Dziga" is Ukrainian for "spinning top"; "Vertov" is Russian for the act of turning), the filmmaker shot footage in every section of Moscow and its outlying areas. Vertov and Kaufman immersed themselves in the project. They lived in a Pioneer camp, rode in ambulances, observed life among the criminal element and in the collective farm, and visited marketplaces, restaurants, and bars. They used every camera device or bit of technology known at the time: ultra-high speed, micro-cinematography, reverse motion, animation, and multiple exposure. They also shot at the most unusual camera angles they could devise. Reality—life as it is actually lived—was the goal. In fact, Vertov had come to believe that the camera was an even more perfect device for perceiving reality than the human eye. His wife, Yelizaveta Svilova, finally edited the footage into the complete film.

Kino-Eye opens with an uncomplimentary depiction of "old" Russia as drunken peasant women dance frenetically at a church holiday celebration. Vertov then cuts away to a popular symbol of the "new" nation—the young Pioneers. Typical sequences include a woman who backtracks after seeing a sign that reads "Don't Let the Merchants Profit. Buy at the Cooperative" and a slab of beef and loaf of bread that become "reversed" into a bull grazing in a herd and rye being harvested. The most famous scene of all chronicles the construction and opening of a Pioneer camp. Stunningly edited, it comprises most of Vertov's major themes, specifically new and old, children and adults, health and vitality, the union of the proletarian and the peasant. The film ends with the death of a watchman and the futile attempts to revive him using first aid. Here is the ultimate contrast—life and death.

Vertov intended *Kino-Eye* to be the first of a six-part series. The second and third films were to utilize four or five cameras and contrast the role of the Soviet and American worker. The fourth would focus on the "new society" developing in Russia; the fifth, divided into three sections, would center on other governments and social structures in the world; and the sixth would summarize the previous five, showing how the workers had rejected the bourgeoisie.

There was never a follow-up, however, as Vertov decided instead to apply his technique to specific themes. For example, *Lenin Kino-Pravda* (1925), a shorter film, centers around Lenin's funeral. Shots of grieving Russians are followed by a sequence highlighting the accomplishments of Lenin's programs in industry, agriculture, culture, and social life. Perhaps the director's best-known and most brilliant work is *The Man with a Movie Camera* (1929, also known as *Moscow Today* and *Living Russia or the Man with a Movie Camera*), a chronicle of life in the big city from daybreak to dusk, beginning and ending in a theater, and with the cameraman also shown laboring at his craft. *Lenin Kino-Pravda* is far more subjective than *Kino-Eye* in that its focus is solely on Lenin; *The Man with a Movie Camera* is more concerned with chronicling the relationship between cinema and reality than with pure Kino-Eye.

Although certain critics dismissed *Kino-Eye* and the Kino-Eye theory, the film was a great success; more notably, it was awarded a prize at the 1926 Paris Exhibition. In 1934, Vertov made *Three Songs of Lenin*, a fifty-six-minute documentary composed of stock footage and newly shot material which glorified Lenin. While not a pure Kino-Eye film, it is closer in feeling and technique to *Kino-Eye* than any of the shorts or features Vertov made between 1925 and 1934.

Rob Edelman

A KISS FOR CINDERELLA

Released: 1926
Production: Famous Players-Lasky; released by Paramount
Direction: Herbert Brenon
Screenplay: Willis Goldbeck and Townsend Martin; based on the play of the
    same name by James M. Barrie
Cinematography: J. Roy Hunt
Art direction: Julian Boone Fleming
Length: 10 reels/9,686 feet

> *Principal characters:*
> Cinderella (Jane) .... Betty Bronson
> Policeman (David) .... Tom Moore
> Fairy Godmother .... Esther Ralston
> Richard Bodie .... Henry Vibart
> Queen .... Dorothy Cumming
> Mr. Cutaway .... Ivan Simpson

Betty Bronson made her film debut at Paramount as the star of James M.
Barrie's *Peter Pan* (1924). Seven other features intervened between it and her
appearance as the star of another Barrie play brought to films, *A Kiss for
Cinderella*. The screen critic for the London *Picture Show* wrote: "*Peter Pan*,
on the screen, was wonderful. *A Kiss for Cinderella* is even more so."

Barrie had written them and other plays for Maude Adams to perform in
the theater. After she finished touring in *A Kiss for Cinderella*, Adams retired
from the stage for thirteen years, returning then only to play Portia in a revival
of William Shakespeare's *The Merchant of Venice*, a role very different from
that of Cinderella. Obviously, she, too, felt that so perfect a vehicle as *A Kiss
for Cinderella* could not be surpassed. In time, Bronson also knew that she
would never again get a role so becoming to her. She *was* Cinderella, or
"Cindy," or "Miss Thing," and she was also simply "Jane," which was her
real name in the story.

The film fades in the same way that the play opened. One night during an
air raid scare in London during World War I, a policeman named David (Tom
Moore), making a routine tour of inspection, knocks at the studio door of
Mr. Richard Bodie (Henry Vibart), a London artist, to tell him that light is
escaping from his skylight window. Bodie explains that the skylight had been
boarded up carefully and completely, but now some of the boards seem to
be missing. He concludes that they must have been taken by his little slavey,
"Cinderella" (Betty Bronson), who cleans the studio daily. David's suspicions
are aroused, and he says that he will hunt down the little slavey, who lives
in a poor part of the city.

With the boards she has taken from Bodie and others collected from alleyways where they had been discarded, she has built a very crude structure and is housing four waifs—a little Belgian girl, and English child, a French child, and a little German. They are all devoted to the little German and are apologetic about the child's nationality. David leaves Bodie's studio to clear up this mystery, but only gets as far as the pantry, from which he can see Cinderella as she bolts into the room.

It develops that Cinderella, besides making a home for the waifs, is running a "Penny Friend Shop," where, for a penny or two, she makes clothes for the poor, presses shirtwaists, and performs other menial tasks. She is only doing her bit, as she tells David when he makes himself known to her. He is satisfied that she is not an enemy or is giving shelter to potential enemies; but his curiosity has been aroused, and until it is allayed, he must follow her home when she leaves.

He does so and finds that everything she has told him is true. The orphans are Delphine, Marie-Therese, Gladys, and the little Gretchen. Cinderella invites him to share their dinner and presses the invitation when she finds that he has already eaten, or so he says; he has seen that there are only five baked potatoes. Nevertheless, Cinderella persuades him to share a snack with her, and they drink a toast in milk to the King, the Prince of Wales, "and father."

Cinderella is convinced that tonight is the night of a great ball, although she admits that she has not yet received her "invite." When the children fall asleep, David says that he must make his rounds. She follows him outside, confident that her fairy godmother will be coming and conduct her personally to the ball. She sits on the doorstep, and he leaves his lantern with the guard light turned down. He wraps his muffler around her and then leaves, after which she takes off the muffler and wraps it around her feet. Darkness comes, and with it, snow, and Cinderella falls asleep.

She dreams that her godmother (Esther Ralston) emerges from the dark and tells her that she shall have what she wishes for—her grand ball, and she will be loved by the man of her choice. The godmother says, "Now let this be my down-trodden godchild's ball, not as balls are, but as they are conceived to be in a little chamber in Cinderella's head."

In Cinderella's dream, the ball is precisely as it appears in the fairy tale, with Cinderella in white silks and furs. The mice she has brought in a cage grow just a bit, then a bit more, until they are four snow-white steeds, and the carriage, which had been a pumpkin, turns into a gorgeous equipage, and Cinderella finds herself seated next to the royal equerry, Mr. Cutaway (Ivan Simpson). The carriage is lifted up and travels into the sky above Buckingham Palace until it comes to a stop at just such a palace in the sky as Cinderella might have imagined, bursting through the high, Gothic arches, and stopping at a platform polished like glass. Mr. Cutaway helps her out of the carriage. The King wears a costume with "Clubs" as his emblem; the Queen (Dorothy

Cumming) rocks beside him, and when they stand to address their subjects, they hang onto underground straps to support themselves. The Queen eats a banana with great relish, and it is all as it might have been in the mind of Cinderella, the slavey.

The ballroom is thronged by policemen in dress uniforms. Opposite the King's throne is a gas meter, and when the flame goes low, Prince Hard-to-Please puts in a shilling. When Cinderella passes the test of being perfect by making ninety-nine on a clinical thermometer because of her dainty, extremely small feet, the prince is ecstatic. The clock strikes midnight, as Cinderella dances with her prince, and before the frantic exit that takes place in the fairy story can begin, the scene dissolves into Cinderella asleep on the doorstep, covered with snow.

Her prince, David, returns, carries her inside, and tries to revive her. She has pneumonia, however, and is taken to a hospital. When she is able to leave the hospital, Bodie sends her to a sister who has a cottage near the seaside. Bodie also has a brother who is a doctor, and he tends Cinderella in her illness. One day David comes to the cottage and speaks to Bodie before going to Cinderella. She is happy when she sees David at the cottage, and he wastes no time in proposing. David says, "I don't set up to be a prince, Jane, but I love you in a princely way, and if you would marry me, you wonder, I'll be a true man to you till death us do part."

Cinderella admits that she is interested, but she wants the satisfaction of having refused him once. He promises to ask her a second time, so she turns his proposal down loftily, and then says excitedly, "Quick, David!" He proposes a second time, and on this occasion, she accepts him poetically, and then asks wistfully, "David, do you think I could have an engagement ring?" He has brought a package with him, a rather large one, too big to hold an ordinary engagement ring. "It's a policeman's idea of an engagement ring," he explains, and opening the parcel, he discloses a pair of glass slippers, which he puts on her little feet. "They're like two kisses," she says, as they fit with ease.

They embrace, but there is a sad expression on his face, and the best way to account for it lies in Barrie's own final stage direction in the printed play: "He presses her face to him for a moment so that he may not see its transparency. Dr. Bodie has told him something."

This may not be evident to everybody in the audience, but it is there—the foreknowledge that Cinderella will slip from life, even if she lives long enough to marry her prince. It is Barrie's way of making a fantasy real, and Bronson and Tom Moore played it with great subtlety. Like many other film versions of Barrie's plays, *A Kiss for Cinderella* was very successful with audiences.

DeWitt Bodeen

LADY OF THE PAVEMENTS

Released: 1929
Production: Art Cinema Corporation; released by United Artists
Direction: D. W. Griffith
Screenplay: Sam Taylor; based on the story "La Paiva" by Karl Volmoeller
Titles: Garrett Lloyd
Cinematography: Karl Struss and G. W. Bitzer
Editing: James Smith
Art direction: William Cameron Menzies
Costume design: Alice O'Neill
Music synchronization: Hugo Riesenfeld
Song: Irving Berlin, "Where Is the Song of Songs for Me?"
Length: 9 reels/8,329 feet

> *Principal characters:*
> Nanon del Rayon .... Lupe Velez
> Count Karl von Arnim .... William Boyd
> Countess Diane des Granges .... Jetta Goudal
> Baron Finot .... Albert Conti
> M'sieu Dubrey,
> the Dancing Master ....Franklin Pangborn

The alleged decline of D. W. Griffith is one of the most unfortunate and unwarranted myths in conventional histories of the cinema. In recent years, renewed attention to some of his later films has revealed that in the final phase of his career, Griffith remained a creative and evolving artist who was not content to offer pale copies of his earlier triumphs. Griffith's last film, *The Struggle* (1931), has more recently been considered a landmark early talkie. Film historians now recognize its lasting artistry based on the film's "considerable dramatic and emotional power." *Lady of the Pavements* has been neglected even more than *The Struggle*, perhaps because it is an extremely rare film of which no more than a few prints survive. The relative unavailability of this film is very unfortunate because it is one of Griffith's most beautiful and perfect films, ranking with the more famous *True Heart Susie* and *Broken Blossoms* (both 1919). Lacking the scale and ambition of Griffith's most celebrated films, *The Birth of a Nation* (1915) and *Intolerance* (1916), these films are more intimate and subtle, possessing an extraordinary delicacy of emotional texture. *Lady of the Pavements* is especially notable in this respect because, on the surface, it is nothing more than an unoriginal romantic comedy in the manner of Ernst Lubitsch's films.

The story concerns a deception and the resulting romantic complications. Count Karl von Arnim (William Boyd), a member of the Prussian Embassy in Paris, discovers that his fiancée, Countess Diane des Granges (Jetta

Goudal), has been unfaithful. Angered by her cavalier treatment, he tells her that he would prefer to marry "a woman of the streets" and breaks off with her. The scorned Countess conspires with Baron Finot (Albert Conti) to obtain an elaborate form of revenge. They find a soubrette named Nanon del Rayon (Lupe Velez) singing at the Smoking Dog cabaret and groom her to pass as a lady. As planned, Count von Arnim falls in love with her. Nanon and the Count become engaged, then Countess des Granges reveals the deception. Nanon feels hurt and guilty and flees, but Count von Arnim's reaction is unexpected. Although he has been tricked into falling in love with Nanon, he recognizes that, essentially, she is innocent and that his callous former lover has manipulated them both. Indifferent to his rank and social position, he finds Nanon at the Smoking Dog and the two are reconciled.

Stories like this were very popular at the time *Lady of the Pavements* was made and remained so into the 1930's when sound demonstrated their adaptability to the musical genre. Allegiance to any real time and place was incidental, and the romantic intrigues of the upper classes could be treated with a light hand, resulting in elegant escapism of wide popular appeal. Lubitsch was the master of this type of film. He possessed wit and sophistication and undercut the superficial lightness of his films with his genuine affection for the characters and his insightful treatment of the relationships. It was not easy to imitate Lubitsch's sensibility without seeming graceless and awkward. *Lady of the Pavements* compares favorably with Lubitsch's films because Griffith projects his own personality into it. It was not a project he initiated or developed. He simply stepped in and directed it when the assignment was offered. The material might have seemed out of his range, but the warm mood with which he imbues the film shows that his response was profound. Unlike Griffith's earlier virginal heroines, Nanon del Rayon is an experienced "woman of the streets," but he treats her with the same respect. He appreciates her beauty, her sweetness, and her sincerity. He demonstrates that his lovers do not need to be innocent to be appealingly guileless.

The assumption that Griffith was ill-suited to anything other than Victorian melodrama and pastoral romance had always been a false one. In his Biograph shorts, he had treated a wide variety of stories, many of which were notably modern and free of sentiment. He is best appreciated as an artist bridging two worlds, the Victorian world into which he had been born and the twentieth century which questioned the values of that earlier world. His characters reflect this. Anna Moore (Lillian Gish) in *Way Down East* (1920) suffers from the same puritanism as those who persecute her, but both she and the film ultimately reject that puritanism. The one character in that film who is consistently admirable is the hero (Richard Barthelmess) whose values are far more flexible than those of his family and the community in which he lives.

There is a trace of irony to the moral codes evoked in many Griffith films. The punishments the characters suffer for transgressing, particularly in the case of the women, always seem ludicrously extreme. In this context, the lighter tone required in *Lady of the Pavements* permits Griffith to express a mature attitude to the realities of love. The heroine's virtue is never a cause of concern to the hero. Once the deception has been exposed, he does not hesitate for a moment to reconcile with her. The amusing irony of the film is that the Countess des Granges, who seeks to deceive and hurt the hero, is the one who gives him what he really wants by bringing the heroine into his life.

Lady of the Pavements was made partly to show off young Mexican actress Lupe Velez. As a result of Griffith's careful direction, the somewhat limited Velez displays a charm and sensitivity worthy of better actresses, such as Lillian Gish, Mae Marsh, and Miriam Cooper, with whom Griffith had been associated earlier. She is beautifully photographed and costumed throughout the film and makes a credible transformation from soubrette to refined lady. Jetta Goudal and William Boyd also give skilled performances, the latter in a role far removed from the Hopalong Cassidy characterization with which he came to be identified in later years. The distinctive tone of romantic comedy in this period is enhanced by the presence of Franklin Pangborn as a prissy etiquette professor whose fights with Velez are hilarious. Pangborn made a career out of playing this type in many famous films of the sound era.

The romantic aura which surrounds Velez is imparted to the entire production. It is one of the loveliest films of its type, with sets by the prodigious William Cameron Menzies, who later made immense contributions to the overall design of *Gone with the Wind* (1939) and *Kings Row* (1942), among many other films. Griffith does not stress cinematic virtuosity in any obvious sense. The camera moves with great fluidity at times, as in the subjective shot when the Count runs to the window and looks down at the street after Nanon has run away, but on the whole, the direction is distinguished by superb pacing, a fairy-tale visual atmosphere, and nuances which make the tender feelings of the characters vivid and affecting. The film demonstrates Griffith's versatility and undiminished mastery, but it is most memorable for the pure pleasure it affords.

In 1929, many silent films were to an extent made over as sound films, and this is marginally true of *Lady of the Pavements*. Irving Berlin wrote a haunting song, "Where Is the Song of Songs for Me?" which Velez sings to Boyd during a romantic sequence. A trade review indicates that this song and a synchronized music score constituted the extent of the film's use of sound, but another, very favorable, review which appeared when the film opened at the California Theater indicated there was also some spoken dialogue by Velez as well as additional songs. The film survives in a strictly silent version and is completely satisfying in that form. Fortunately, a recording of Velez singing "Where Is the Song of Songs for Me?" also still exists. At a rare showing of the film during a Griffith retrospective in 1969, the recording was played just prior to the actual screening of the film. The melody was utilized by the organist in his subsequent accompaniment and the song was able, once again, to become an integral part of the film. This unusual presentation is worth recalling because of the magical effect the song had before a single image had been projected and the way this effect informed the experience of watching *Lady of the Pavements*. Although the image of Velez actually singing the song in the film can no longer be experienced as it was in 1929, it may be evoked as an uncommonly touching souvenir of cinema.

Blake Lucas

LADY WINDERMERE'S FAN

Released: 1925
Production: Warner Bros.
Direction: Ernst Lubitsch
Screenplay: Julien Josephson; based on the play of the same name by Oscar Wilde
Cinematography: Charles Van Enger
Editing: Ernst Lubitsch
Art direction: Harold Grieve
Length: 8 reels/7,815 feet

Principal characters:
Lord Darlington	Ronald Colman
Mrs. Erlynne	Irene Rich
Lady Windermere	May McAvoy
Lord Windermere	Bert Lytell
Lord Augustus Lorton	Edward Martindel

Lady Windermere's Fan is an interesting film for several reasons: it is directed by the master of film wit, Ernst Lubitsch; it is taken from a play by one of the great wits of the English language, Oscar Wilde; and it has a fine performance by one of the cinema's cleverest actors, Ronald Coleman.

Wilde's wordy play seems totally unsuitable for almost any adaptation to the silent screen, yet it was very adroitly done by Lubitsch. The 1892 play had very little action and much witty dialogue, such as Lord Darlington's famous line, "I couldn't help it. I can resist everything except temptation." None of Wilde's delightful lines, however, found their way into the film's subtitles. Lubitsch took as bold a step when he dropped Wilde's epigrams as Sam Taylor did when he added dialogue to the talking version of William Shakespeare's *The Taming of the Shrew* (1929). The difference is that Lubitsch was successful.

To appreciate Lubitsch's delicate handling of the seemingly impossible task of translating spoken drama to the silent screen, one must first know the structure of Wilde's play. It is in four acts which occur within a twenty-four hour period, and the plot of which the film accurately follows. The first act takes place in Lady Windermere's morning room. Lord Darlington (Ronald Coleman), a bachelor, has come calling to wish Lady Windermere (May McAvoy) a happy twenty-first birthday and to be near her. She tells him he must stop paying her extravagant compliments since she loves her husband and is happy. Lord Darlington then implies that she is a fool because her husband (Bert Lytell) has been seeing a great deal of a woman named Mrs. Erlynne (Irene Rich) and is paying her bills. Lady Windermere is indignant, and she asks him to leave, which he does. She then opens her husband's desk and finds receipts made out to Mrs. Erlynne. Her husband catches her spying and asks her to trust him, and he reminds her that things are not always as they appear. Furthermore, he wants her to invite Mrs. Erlynne to her birthday ball that night. Lady Windermere refuses and threatens to strike Mrs. Erlynne with the fan her husband has given her as a birthday present.

Act Two is at the birthday ball. Mrs. Erlynne arrives, and Lady Windermere loses her nerve and does not insult or strike the woman. Lord Darlington asks Lady Windermere to leave her husband and run away with him to the Continent. She refuses, and he leaves her to think about the proposition. When Lady Windermere sees her husband introducing Mrs. Erlynne to their friends, she writes him a note stating that she is leaving him for Lord Darlington. Mrs. Erlynne intercepts the letter and tells Lord Windermere that Lady Windermere has a headache and has asked not to be disturbed, as she has gone to bed. Mrs. Erlynne then asks Lord Augustus Lorton (Edward Martindel), a wealthy suitor she has almost landed, to please get Lord Windermere out of the house and over to the gentlemen's club.

Act Three finds Lady Windermere being let into Lord Darlington's bachelor quarters by his butler. When informed that he is out, she says she will wait. Mrs. Erlynne then arrives and tries to argue some sense into Lady Windermere.

The butler lets in Lord Darlington with two of his friends. The two women hide behind some drapes and are horrified to see that the two guests are Lord Windermere and Lord Lorton. Even worse, Lord Windermere sees his wife's fan on a table and picks it up, looking quizzically at Lord Darlington. Lady Windermere accidentally moves the curtain slightly, and in a heroic gesture, Mrs. Erlynne steps out into the room. Lord Lorton assumes the worst of her, and the scene ends with her compromised and ruined.

Act Four takes place again in the Windermeres' morning room. Lady Windermere is feeling very depressed when her husband enters and apologizes for coming in so late the night before. He tells her that Mrs. Erlynne has turned out to be a perfectly horrible woman, after all. Lady Windermere defends the woman, to her husband's surprise.

Mrs. Erlynne is announced and says that she has come to return Lady Windermere's fan, which she had picked up by mistake last night. Mrs. Erlynne further announces that she is leaving London and would like a photograph of Lady Windermere. When Lady Windermere leaves the room to get the photograph, Lord Windermere denounces Mrs. Erlynne. He tells her,

> I supplied you with money to pay bill after bill, rather than my wife should know that her mother, whom she has taught to consider as dead is living, a divorced woman going about under an assumed name, a bad woman preying upon life.

Lady Windermere returns with her photograph and gives it to Mrs. Erlynne.

The sorrowful parting of the two women is interrupted by the entrance of Lord Lorton, who coldly greets Mrs. Erlynne. She asks him to accompany her to her carriage, and he acquiesces. Soon he comes back into the Windermeres' morning room and happily announces that he had misjudged Mrs. Erlynne. She only went to Lord Darlington's, he explains, to find him. She wanted to tell him that she had decided to accept his proposal. The curtain falls without Lady Windermere every knowing that Mrs. Erlynne is her mother.

The film does not leave out any of the play's plot, but Lubitsch "opened up" the play for his film, showing incidents that were only talked about in the play. One example of this comes at the end of the film: Mrs. Erlynne is shown leaving the Windermeres' home when she meets Lord Lorton coming up the walk. On seeing her, he drops his eyes, and she is shaken for a second. She quickly takes control of the moment by scolding him: "Your conduct last night was unforgivable. I have decided not to marry you, after all." With the tables thus turned, Lorton desires her once again and follows her into her taxi like a puppy, as "The End" is flashed upon the screen.

Lubitsch also updated the play with modern dress and automobiles (something he was fond of doing). In his *Forbidden Paradise* (1924), for example, a story of Catherine the Great, he has Catherine put down a revolution with her checkbook and travel in an automobile.

Another instance of Lubitsch's "opening up" the play occurs at Lady Windermere's birthday party. Mrs. Erlynne is spied by Lady Windermere out in the garden getting her hand kissed. Lady Windermere assumes that it is her husband and hates Mrs. Erlynne, even though the man's face is hidden by a hedge. The man is, in fact, Lord Lorton.

Lubitsch also created a wonderful scene set at the Ascot racetrack. Mrs. Erlynne makes her entrance at the stands, seen through the glasses of all the gossips present, most of whom are men. In fact, more glasses are trained on her than on the horses. A lady near Lord Windermere says something derogatory about Mrs. Erlynne, and he defends the woman, whom he, and later the audience, knows is his wife's mother. The defense leads to gossip, which later reaches his wife, who is sitting on the other side of him. When Lord Lorton first sees Mrs. Erlynne, it is at the races, and he follows her in a long tracking shot as she leaves the grounds. When he tips his hat to her, and the scene fades, it is obvious that she has made a conquest. Lubitsch filmed the racetrack scene in Montreal, Canada, to the displeasure of his boss, Jack Warner. Demanding to know why the added expense of traveling to Canada was necessary when Southern California had several tracks, Lubitsch informed Warner that although the English speak the same language, they race their horses clockwise, whereas it is the opposite in America. That attention to detail is part of what has come to be known as the "Lubitsch Touch."

Larry Lee Holland

THE LAST COMMAND

Released: 1928
Production: Famous Players-Lasky/Paramount
Direction: Josef von Sternberg
Screenplay: John F. Goodrich; based on an original story by Lajos Biró
Titles: Herman J. Mankiewicz
Cinematography: Bert Glennon
Editing: William Shea
Art direction: Hans Dreier
Length: 9 reels/8,154 feet

> *Principal characters:*
> General Dolgorucki/
> Grand Duke Sergius Alexander ....Emil Jannings
> Natascha Dobrowa ....Evelyn Brent
> Leo Andreyev/Director .... William Powell
> Adjutant .... Nicholas Soussanin
> Serge, the valet .... Michael Visaroff
> Assistant director ....Jack Raymond

Emil Jannings won the Academy Award as Best Actor in the first year they were given, a split year, 1927-1928, and he won for the two performances he gave during that time, *The Way of All Flesh* (1927) and *The Last Command* (1928). In both films, he gave virtuoso performances, but *The Last Command* is the more interesting motion picture.

The character he played, General Dolgorucki, was based on a real Russian who had become a Hollywood extra, General Lodijenski, who played bit roles and also ran a Russian restaurant in the late 1920's. The film begins as a Russian background film is being made, and the Russian-born director is riffling through some photographs. The director remembers back to a time when this man whose picture is in the files had been in command of the Czar's armies. "Have him report at 6:30 tomorrow morning," he tells his assistant (Jack Raymond), "and put him into a general's uniform."

Although Dolgorucki (Emil Jannings) is now a $7.50-a-day extra waiting in a rooming house for a call, he was once the cousin of the Czar. Now he suffers from a terrible affliction: his head and his hands shake constantly, and he looks older than his years. He is an imperious officer, beaten by circumstances, but too proud to admit it.

There is a flashback to the more glorious time when he was Grand Duke Sergius Alexander, the Czar's cousin. Two revolutionary suspects are brought before him; they are actors who have been entertaining the troops. One is Leo Andreyev (William Powell), director of the Kiev Imperial Theater; the other is an actress, Natascha Dobrowa (Evelyn Brent). Sergius Alexander gets rid of Andreyev, but he is attracted to Natascha, who lets him believe that she is a prisoner to his charms, although in reality she has a mission to kill him. She does not avail herself of that opportunity when it presents itself, however, and when he asks her point blank why she did not kill him, she answers truthfully, "I suppose it was because I could not kill anyone who loves Russia as much as you do."

He takes her with him in his train, but he is stopped and overrun by Bolsheviks. The mob, now taking over the train, would like to tear him apart, and Natascha seemingly joins their cause. "Make him sweat as we have sweated," she cries. "Make him stoke the train to Petrograd!" He is shocked by her treachery, but in the locomotive, she manages to explain confidentially, "Don't you understand? It was the only way I could save your life. I love you." She manages to give him her pearls so that he can pay his way out of Russia, and he waits for his chance to drop from the locomotive minutes before it crashes through a bridge and falls into the frozen river, killing everyone who was on the train.

Sergius Alexander develops a nervous affliction from the shock of that moment. He manages to buy his way out of Russia and ends up in Hollywood as a bit player. Now comes the final humiliation: he is brought before Leo Andreyev, the director, who reminds him of how he had once been slashed by the General's whip. Now the General is wearing that same uniform, but it is Leo Andreyev who is in command. "I have waited ten years for this moment, Your Highness," he says, looking at him with a supercilious smile. "The same coat, the same uniform, the same man—only the times have changed."

The scene that is to be played before the cameras is in spirit very much like the one the General had played once long ago in real life. He is reliving his past and is confused until the set musicians are called on to play. The studio orchestra—a piano, a cello, and a fiddle—begin to play the old Russian National Anthem, and the militant hymn brings new life to the General. He grabs up the standard and leads the charge, exultant. Then he chokes and crumples up on the imitation snow and barbed wire hillock. Andreyev, realizing that the old man is dying, tries to let him believe that the Russia he loved has come to power again. In his unbalanced mental condition, Dolgorucki believes him and smiles, as his facial muscles relax and set in death.

Andreyev then rises as the assistant director says, "Tough luck. That guy was a great actor." "He was more than a great actor," says Andreyev, "He was a great man."

Jannings made six features under his Paramount contract, and two of them today are recognized classics—*The Last Command* and the Ernst Lubitsch-directed *The Patriot* (1928), sadly a "lost" film. He returned to Germany, simply because he could not speak English well enough to warrant the studio's continuing with him as a star. In silent features, he was undeniably a star of great consequence; but he spoke what little English he knew with a most unpleasant German accent. He had been born in Switzerland, but his entire way of life was Germanic, and so it continued when he went back to Germany to work. His first talking feature in Germany was Josef von Sternberg's *The Blue Angel* (1930), which catapulted his co-star, Marlene Dietrich, to stardom. Her accent, however, was soft and pleasant. She became an international star, while Jannings was forced to remain a German-speaking one. It is no wonder he did not care for Dietrich very much. She not only stole the acting honors of *The Blue Angel*, but she also took over the international fame he had been forced to relinquish.

Jannings became a German cultural figurehead, and when World War II began, he was made a director of Ufa. He was hailed in Germany for his work in *Ohm Kruger* (1941), a prejudiced and often laughable film, particularly in its presentation of Queen Victoria as a villainess. After Germany's defeat, he made no more films and retired to Austria, where he died in 1950 of cancer at the age of sixty-three.

The Last Command was a giant step forward for William Powell, although, according to Sternberg, who directed the film, when Powell signed a new contract at Paramount, he specified that he would never again work in a Sternberg film. He did star, however, without protesting, in *The Drag Net*, released later that same year, 1928. Obviously, however Powell had previously felt, he changed his mind. Perhaps this was because he knew that films were on the threshold of being taken over by sound, and he, having been an accomplished stage actor, had nothing to fear from the dreaded "mike." He retired conclusively in 1955 after playing the doctor in *Mr. Roberts*.

Evelyn Brent's screen career survived the advent of sound, for she proved in *Interference* (1928) that she could do very well in the talking film. Her last film on her Paramount contract was *Paramount on Parade* (1930), in which she did a sketch with Maurice Chevalier, directed by Lubitsch. It was rumored that she broke her contract because she had had differences with Jesse L. Lasky, who had apparently called her "temperamental," although she referred to herself as a woman with a "mind of my own." She continued on in pictures, even at Paramount after Lasky had left the lot. She died of a heart attack in 1975 at the age of seventy-five, still remembered at least for two of the superb dramas she did for Sternberg at Paramount—*Underworld* (1927) and *The Last Command*.

DeWitt Bodeen

THE LAST LAUGH
(DER LETZTE MANN)

Released: 1925
Production: Ufa
Direction: F. W. Murnau
Screenplay: Carl Mayer
Cinematography: Karl Freund
Length: 8 reels/6,500 feet

> *Principal characters:*
> The doorman ....Emil Jannings
> Hotel manager ....Hans Unterkirchen
> The doorman's aunt .... Emilie Kurz
> The night watchman ....Georg John

An undisputed masterpiece of the silent cinema, *The Last Laugh* brought together four of the premier talents of the Golden Age of German film: director F. W. Murnau, screenwriter Carl Mayer, cinematographer Karl Freund, and actor Emil Jannings. Indeed, all four men collaborated on the final shooting script of this simple but eloquently told story. Murnau told the others that he wanted to use the moving camera extensively, and they prepared their contributions with this in mind. Together, the four produced a fluid study of pride and degradation conveyed through the account of a few days in the life of a hotel doorman, who becomes an almost allegorical figure.

Mayer had already written (with Hans Janowitz) the screenplay for the classic of German expressionism, *The Cabinet of Dr. Caligari* (1920), and was establishing himself as the most important writer of the flowering of German cinema after World War I. Jannings, too, had firmly established his reputation and was regarded as the most illustrious of German screen actors. Freund, however, was still at the beginning of his distinguished career that would see him photograph several German classics and then go to Hollywood, where he earned an Oscar in 1937 for *The Good Earth*. It was an ideal time for him to work with Murnau, for each could inspire artistic innovation in the other.

The simple and evocative plot of *The Last Laugh* is presented in such effective visual terms that it requires only one caption. The doorman (Emil Jannings) of a grand hotel glories in his position and particularly in the impressive uniform that he wears. The uniform inspires awe in the residents of the apartment building in which he lives, and the old man's pompous pride is seen as he walks by the respectful tenants. Yet an event of tragic proportions occurs. The hotel manager (Hans Unterkirchen) notices that the doorman is no longer able to handle large pieces of luggage and demotes him to the lowly position of lavatory attendant. The demotion is double degrading to the man because he no longer has a uniform with which to impress his neighbors. In desperation, he steals his old uniform from the hotel so that he can wear it home.

One day, however, his plot is revealed when his aunt (Emilie Kurz) takes some food to him at the hotel and finds him not at the door but in the lavatory. The humiliated man cringes when he sees her, but she quickly takes the news back to his friends and neighbors, who now belittle him just as enthusiastically as they revered him before. Finally, viewers see the weary old man in the dark lavatory covered gently with a warm blanket or coat by the hotel's friendly night watchman (Georg John). It seems to be the end, but then the single title states that the author, having taken pity upon the old man, will give him a better finish than he would have in real life. The man is then seen with a fortune left him by an American millionaire, and he is able to enjoy the hotel as a guest.

Throughout the film the camera is used daringly and creatively. It is continually moving, from the very first shot in which the lobby of the hotel is revealed by a shot from a descending elevator. Rather than following the standard practice of beginning a scene with a long shot and then cutting to a closer shot, Murnau preferred to have the camera move toward the subject to avoid the interruption of the cut. As several critics have noted, the camera becomes one of the characters in the film, and a rather lively one at that. The camera movement is, however, used to further the impact of the film rather than as an end in itself. The movements always reinforce the other elements of the film, but they do not distract the viewer's attention. Inventive camera angles are also used. The most notable are the low angle shots in which the camera looks up at the proud doorman in his uniform, with that angle emphasizing the feeling of importance that his own ego and the awe of his neighbors have given him. In contrast, after he loses his uniform, the camera frequently looks down upon him, emphasizing his humiliation. Also, when the old man gets drunk, the camera spins about to represent his subjective view.

The happy ending of the film has evoked much comment. Some see it as simply a surrender to popular taste, that the filmmakers wanted to have a happy ending to improve their chances at the box office. Others have the opinion that the ending was aimed solely at the American market, since many popular and esteemed German films had unhappy endings. The distinguished film historian Siegfried Kracauer, on the other hand, calls the ending "ingenious . . . a nice farce jeering at the happy ending typical of the American film." The English language title has also been criticized. It was not chosen by Murnau, and it is not merely a translation of the original. The German title is *Der letzte Mann*, which literally translated is, the last man. The English title overemphasizes the controversial ending.

Although the emphasis upon the uniform may be indicative of a characteristic of German culture, the film's deeper theme of the sources of individual self-worth and vanity is universal. Viewers can understand and feel the old man's humiliation even if they dislike his initial pomposity.

Jannings began his career on the stage and never completely adapted his theatrical acting style to the more subtle one required by the screen. His great talent and strong screen presence, however, made him a great film actor nevertheless, and when given the proper script and direction, he gave classic performances. *The Last Laugh* is arguably the first of those, and *Variety* (1926) and *The Blue Angel* (1930) are equally good. In *The Last Laugh*, incidentally, Jannings is convincing as the old man even though he was only thirty-nine at the time the film was made.

Much has been written through the years about who should be given credit for the overall quality of a film. Although it is usually admitted that film is the most collaborative of art forms and cannot be created entirely by one person as a novel can, most critics tend to give primary credit to the director. In the case of *The Last Laugh*, however, it can be seen, both from the evidence of the finished film and from what is known of its creation, that it is a prime example of the best kind of collaboration. Four remarkably talented men were able to see the project in the same manner so that each man's individual contribution meshed with that of the others to produce a work that is truly distinctive. (The same cannot be said, however, of the 1955 German remake of the film.)

The distinction of *The Last Laugh* has been recognized by audiences and critics from the time it was released until the present day, although—as is regrettably true of nearly all silent films—it is seldom shown today. It was largely on the basis of *The Last Laugh* that Fox Film Corporation gave Murnau a contract to work in Hollywood, a contract that resulted in another classic of the silent film, *Sunrise* (1927). Also, in 1958 a survey of film historians from twenty-six countries put *The Last Laugh* in the top eleven films of all time. Murnau was unfortunately not around to enjoy that selection; he had died in an automobile accident in 1931 at the age of only forty-two.

Marilynn Wilson

THE LAST OF THE MOHICANS

Released: 1920
Production: Maurice Tourneur for Associated Producers
Direction: Maurice Tourneur
Associate direction: Clarence Brown
Screenplay: Robert A. Dillon; based on the novel of the same name by James
  Fenimore Cooper
Cinematography: Philip R. Du Bois and Charles Van Enger
Length: 6 reels

> *Principal characters:*
> Magua .... Wallace Beery
> Cora Munro .... Barbara Bedford
> Uncas .... Albert Roscoe
> Alice Munro .... Lillian Hall
> Major Heyward .... Henry Woodward
> Colonel Munro .... James Gordon
> Captain Randolph .... George Hackathorne
> David Gamut .... Nelson McDowell
> Hawkeye .... Harry Lorraine
> Chingachgook .... Theodore Lerch
> Tamenund .... Jack F. McDonald
> General Webb .... Sydney Deane

James Fenimore Cooper's classic novel *The Last of the Mohicans* has been filmed at least three times: in 1936 by Edward Small Productions, with Randolph Scott and Binnie Barnes appearing under the direction of George B. Seitz; in 1963 by a Mexican production company; and, more importantly, in 1920 by Maurice Tourneur.

Maurice Tourneur (1876-1961) is generally recognized as one of the American silent cinema's great directors. He was a man noted for the pictorial qualities of his productions and a director of impeccable taste whose films were both subtle and restrained. *The Last of the Mohicans* was Tourneur's first film for a new producing consortium called Associated Producers, whose other members were Thomas H. Ince, Mack Sennett, Marshall Neilan, Allan Dwan, George Loane Tucker, and J. Parker Read, Jr. The film was shot largely on location at Big Bear Lake and Yosemite Valley in California, but, because of an accident during shooting, much of the direction was taken over by Clarence Brown, who had been Tourneur's assistant. Brown did a superb job—arguably better than Tourneur could have accomplished—and *The Last of the Mohicans* embarked him on a directorial career which was to include *Smouldering Fires* (1925), *Flesh and the Devil* (1927), *Anna Christie* (1930), *Anna Karenina* (1935), *Of Human Hearts* (1938), *National Velvet* (1945), and *The Yearling* (1947).

For Tourneur, *The Last of the Mohicans* also marked a changing point in his career. It can well be considered as the director's last major production and his last American film of any real consequence (despite Tourneur's continuing to direct in the United States through 1926). In view of its importance in Tourneur's career, it is unfortunate that the direction of *The Last of the Mohicans* may just as well be credited to Brown as Tourneur.

For his principal players in *The Last of the Mohicans*, Tourneur chose Wallace Beery to portray Magua (and a less likely and more melodramatic Indian it is hard to imagine), Albert Roscoe for Uncas, because he was supposedly part Osage Indian, and Barbara Bedford, who gives a sympathetic and restrained performance as Cora Munro and who is known to most film buffs only for her performance as William S. Hart's leading lady in *Tumbleweeds* (1925).

In an interview with film historian Kevin Brownlow, Brown remembered much of the production and acknowledged his considerable debt to Tourneur:

In *The Last of the Mohicans* we made much use of lighting effects and weather atmosphere. We used smokepots to create the suggestion of sunrays striking through woodland mist. The rainstorm in the forest was simply a fire engine and a hose. We got clouds because we waited for them, and used filters. Clouds normally did not register on the old ortho film. When the girls are escaping from the Indian ambush, I put the camera on a perambulator. We built it from a Ford axle, with Ford wheels, a platform, and a handle to pull it down the road. We follow the girls running away; suddenly, two Indians block their path. The camera stops—the perambulator stops—and this accentuates the girls' surprise. Tourneur saw all the rushes. He could be very blunt. The first raspberry I ever heard came from Maurice Tourneur—and when I heard it, I knew it meant a retake.

The film is fairly faithful to the novel. Cora (Barbara Bedford) and her younger sister Alice (Lillian Hall) are on their way to Fort Henry, not knowing that the Fort, under the command of their father (James Gordon), is besieged by Indians in league with the French. Magua (Wallace Beery), a crafty, untrustworthy Indian, who is an outcast from his own tribe, the Hurons, leads the girls, along with Major Heyward (Henry Woodward), who is in love with Alice. En route, the group is joined by David Gamut (Nelson McDowell), a religious fanatic. Magua pretends to be lost, but the group comes upon the camp of Uncas (Albert Roscoe), Chingachgook (Theodore Lerch), and the scout, Hawkeye (Harry Lorraine). When the latter realizes who Magua is, he tries unsuccessfully to capture him, but Magua escapes. Hawkeye then leads the group safely to a secret cave, where Cora finds Uncas' presence inspiring.

The next morning, the group is captured, but Uncas, Chingachgook, and Hawkeye escape. Magua tells Cora that if she will become his squaw, he will let Alice and Major Heyward go, but those two protest such a bargain. Eventually Uncas, Chingachgook, and Hawkeye rescue the party, but Magua again escapes. They reach Fort Henry, where Cora is wooed by the cowardly Captain Randolph (George Hackathorne). At this point, Colonel Munro is forced to surrender to the French, on the understanding that the women and children will be safe from the Indians. The Hurons, however, incited by Magua, attack, and there is a terrible massacre. Magua then takes Cora and Alice to the camp of the Delaware Indians, where he asks for sanctuary.

Here the group is found by Uncas and Major Heyward, and the former reveals himself as the last of the Mohicans, and, therefore, a member of the royal family of the Delawares. The Indian chief of the Delawares welcomes Uncas, but refuses to break Indian law by taking Magua's prisoners from him. Eventually, a compromise is reached whereby Cora agrees to go with Magua and Alice is freed. Uncas follows the pair and finds them on a high crag, from which Cora threatens to jump if Magua comes near her. She is murdered by Magua, who also kills Uncas after a violent struggle. Then Magua is killed by a gunshot from Hawkeye. The film closes with the Delaware Indians paying tribute to Uncas; the chief of the tribe wails, "In the morning of my race I have seen a winged ship arrive, bearing the white men who are to become the masters of our land, and before the sunset I have seen the passing of The Last of the Mohicans."

Viewing *The Last of the Mohicans* today, one is impressed not by the acting and certainly not by the story, but by the composition of the film, the handling of the massacre, and above all the scenes of Cora's murder and the fight to the death between Uncas and Magua. The men struggle in one of the most realistic fight sequences ever transferred to film, their bodies silhouetted against the skyline, with nature dwarfing but never overpowering the drama of the two Indians' fight to the death.

Critics were unanimous in their praise of the film. Laurence Reid in *Motion Picture News* (December 4, 1920) hailed Tourneur and commented, "It cannot be disputed that it is his greatest achievement, a picture which will be talked about as a masterpiece of its kind. . . . It's the greatest Indian picture ever shown." *The New York Times* (January 3, 1921) wrote, "Mr. Tourneur has made an extraordinary picture." In *Motion Picture Magazine* (April, 1921), Adele Whitely Fletcher commented,

> Everything taken into consideration, we are grateful to Mr. Tourneur for his sympathetic handling of this famous tale—he has remained faithful to the man in whose mind it was born, even to retaining the original title—if a similar treatment was assured, it would be pleasant to have other beloved works pictured for posterity.

Perhaps the finest tribute of all came from Burns Mantle, writing in *Photoplay* (April, 1921):

> If we had a National Cinematographic library, as we should have, into the archives of

which each year were placed the best pictures and finest examples of the cinematographic art achieved during that year, and I were on the board that voted upon the admission or rejection of submitted films, I certainly should include *The Last of the Mohicans* in my list of eligible exhibits. There is, to me, an impressive effort made in this fine picture of Maurice Tourneur's to treat a big subject with dignity and a certain reverence to which its traditions entitle it, and yet to do so without losing sight for an instant of its picture possibilities.

The Last of the Mohicans has been preserved at the International Museum of Photography at George Eastman House, Rochester, New York.

Anthony Slide

THE LIFE OF MOSES

Released: 1909-1910
Production: J. Stuart Blackton for Vitagraph
Direction: Charles Kent
Screenplay: Dr. Madison C. Peters
Cinematography: no listing
Length: 5 reels

Principal characters:
no listing

By 1909, Vitagraph had rapidly established itself as the foremost dramatic producer in the film industry. It had already commenced the establishment of a stock company of players, who would be featured in such major dramatic releases as *Uncle Tom's Cabin* (1903), *Francesca Da Rimini* (1907), and *Vanity Fair* (1911). The Vitagraph releases at this time were all one-reelers, running approximately ten minutes, which was the established length for the films from all the early studios. They utilized painted backdrops (indicating the theatrical origins of the motion picture and its creators), and when exterior scenes were needed, the company would take its players to the immediate vicinity of the Vitagraph Studios on Flatbush Avenue in Brooklyn, New York. Occasionally, there might be a trip to New Jersey or Staten Island, but in 1909, Brooklyn generally had everything to offer in the way of scenery for a motion-picture production.

When *The Life of Moses* went into production in the early fall of 1909, there was no problem in depicting the Red Sea, with the Atlantic Ocean only a few blocks away. With the use of double exposure, the company could even show Moses and the Israelites apparently walking through the water. The actors portraying the Israelites did not need to get their feet wet, but those playing the poor pursuing Egyptians did not fare as well; they were required to be seen plunging through the waves, and by the time their scenes were shot, the Atlantic Ocean had become somewhat chilly. As *Film Index* (February 5, 1910) explained, "A dozen ways were tried to do it—mechanical, scenic and otherwise, until it was decided nothing but a real sea of water would suffice and get it across to the audience."

J. Stuart Blackton, cofounder of Vitagraph, was in charge of production there, but the physical direction of *The Life of Moses* was handled by Charles Kent. A distinguished stage actor from 1875 onward, Kent had joined Vitagraph in 1906, after the loss of his voice. He was chiefly known as a character actor, specializing in kindly, white-haired old gentlemen, but he also directed a number of Vitagraph releases from 1909 through 1913. His screen career as an actor lasted until 1923.

As was the custom with all companies at that time, Vitagraph did not identify the players in its films, either on the films themselves or in printed publicity. Thus, none of the actors in *The Life of Moses* has been identified, with possible identification further hindered by Vitagraph's idea of Egyptian attire, utilizing false beards and hair pieces.

The Reverend Madison C. Peters was hired by Vitagraph to advise on the religious aspects of the film. The intention was to follow *The Life of Moses* with a series of Biblical productions, including *The Life of Joseph* and *King David*, but, for reasons unknown, this plan of action was never followed through. The company proudly announced that the scenes in *The Life of Moses* were based on paintings by Gustave Doré, Edwin Austin Abbey, Jean Léon Gérôme, and James Joseph Jacques Tissot, among others. Dr. Peters commented,

> Those taking part in the making of the picture could be seen through the weeks in the study of the bible in order that they might, in spirit, enter into what I had outlined in my manuscript story, and it is safe to say that few, if any, pictures which have been put on the market, have been more carefully wrought out and more reverently presented, an old yet ever new and thrilling story. . . . It is safe to say that churches looking for a unique entertainment will be looking this way; while I venture the prophesy that the Sunday schools of the future will be using the motion picture to set forth the story of the bible.

There were two remarkable things about *The Life of Moses*. The first was that Vitagraph produced five separate one-reel shorts, released at approximately two-week intervals. In fact, when the first short was released on December 4, 1909, the company had not completed filming of the final reels in the series. This was almost certainly the first time that a company had chosen to tell a story in five episodes. What happened next was not so much Vitagraph's doing, but that of the exhibitors, who discovered that their audience was equally happy to see all five reels in one sitting rather than spaced out over a two-month period. In choosing to screen these reels together, as a five-reel film, the exhibitors "invented" the feature-length production. The company quickly came around to the exhibitors' way of thinking, and, in the January 8, 1910, issue of *The Film Index* announced, "In large houses the entire five reels may be run in one day, preferably Sunday, or they can be run on successive days, one each day." Thus was the American feature-length production born, and most film historians agree that *The Life of Moses* may well be hailed as America's first feature-length film.

The following is a brief description of each reel of *The Life of Moses*, in which the events depicted were presented almost in tableau form, rather like a series of stage presentations. Reel One commences with the persecution of the children of Israel by the Egyptians. The Pharaoh orders that every male child born to the Israelites be killed. The child Moses is hidden by the river. The Pharaoh's daughter comes to the river to bathe and discovers the child, then she appoints Moses' mother and sister to care for the child on her behalf. Reviewing this first reel, *The Moving Picture World* hailed the production as "the most noteworthy film of the year," but, at the same time, suggested that it was imperative that exhibitors hire a lecturer to explain the film to an audience.

In Reel Two, released on January 4, 1910, Moses has grown to manhood and is outraged at the abuse of his people by the Egyptians. As a result of killing an Egyptian taskmaster, he is forced to flee into exile to the land of Midian, where he marries the daughter of Jethro. Forty years later, God speaks to Moses out of a burning bush and commands him to return to Egypt. Reel Two ends with Moses demanding that the Pharaoh release his people. Reel Three deals with the plagues of Egypt and the deliverance of the Hebrews and ends with Moses and Aaron leading the Israelites at the beginning of their exodus from Egypt. "The strength of the picture is so apparent and its richness and beauty is so pronounced that one can scarcely overpraise it," reported *The Moving Picture World* (February 5, 1910).

Part Four opens with the Israelites discovering that the Pharaoh and his men are pursuing them. Moses leads his people through the Red Sea. In the final scene—number nineteen—Moses erects an altar to commemorate Israel's victory. Part Five, released on February 19, 1910, is entitled "The Promised Land." Moses is given the ten commandments, but the people, believing he has forsaken them make and worship a golden calf. In anger, Moses smashes the tablets of the ten commandments, thus necessitating a second journey up Mount Sinai. When he returns with a new set of tablets, Moses finds the children of Israel reverently awaiting the words of God; and Moses prepares to dedicate the tabernacle of Israel to the worship and glory of God. The children of Israel refuse to enter the promised land and begin their forty years of wandering in the wilderness. Moses recommends Joshua as leader of his people. Under Joshua, the children of Israel move into Canaan, the promised land. In the Vale of Moab, where Moses is supposedly buried, stand the angels who carried him there, "for no man knoweth his place of burial unto this day." *The Moving Picture World* (March 5, 1910), reviewing this final reel, commented, "To follow the children of Israel in this graphic way from bondage through to the promised land is an education in biblical history which could be obtained in no other way."

Long considered a "lost" film, *The Life of Moses* was uncovered in an Eastern European film archives a few years ago and is now preserved at both the Museum of Modern Art in New York and the Library of Congress.

Lennox Sanderson, Jr.

LILAC TIME

Released: 1928
Production: John McCormick for First National Pictures
Direction: George Fitzmaurice
Screenplay: Carey Wilson; based on Willis Goldbeck's adaptation of the play
   of the same name by Jane Cowl and Jane Murfie
Titles: George Marion
Cinematography: Sid Hickox and Alvin Knected
Editing: Al Hall
Art direction: Horace Jackson
Music: Nathaniel Shilkret
Song: L. Wolfe Gilbert
Length: 11 reels/9,108 feet

> *Principal characters:*
> Jeannine (Jeannie) Berthelot .... Colleen Moore
> Captain Philip Blythe .... Gary Cooper
> Captain Russell (flight commander) ..... Cleve Moore
> The Kid .... Jack Stone
> Madame Berthelot .... Eugenie Besserer
> The Unlucky One .... Arthur Lake
> General Blythe .... Burr McIntosh
> Mike, a mechanic .... Edward Dillion
> The Enemy Ace .... Edward Clayton
> The Aviators .... Dan Dowling
>   Jack Ponder
>   Stuart Knox
>   Harlan Hilton

Lilac Time, generally forgotten in contemporary film histories, was a renowned film in its own time. In a year that included films such as *The Wedding March*, *Street Angel*, *The Patriot*, and *Show People*, *Lilac Time* attained the number eleven position in *Film Daily Yearbook*'s "Roll of Honor." The film was a respectable critical success, but at the box office, *Lilac Time* was an unreserved hit. Its female lead, Colleen Moore, recalled later that the film had an eight-month run at the Astor Theater in New York. Other sources, however, indicate that *Lilac Time* ran eight weeks at the Central Theater in New York and ten weeks at its premiere theater, Beverly Hills's prestigious Carthay Circle.

Coming during the transition period between silent and talking films, *Lilac Time* was one of those hybrids that did not have dialogue, but which successfully bridged the gap with a synchronized sound track made up of music and sound effects. The Vitaphone process, first used in *Don Juan* (1926), enhanced *Lilac Time*'s box-office power with a romantic musical score by

Nathaniel Shilkret and a love song that became a popular favorite. The sheet music for "Jeannine, I Dream of Lilac Time," with Moore's smiling face on the cover, ended up on many a parlor piano. Hollywood would learn to exploit this kind of publicity tie-in campaign with increasing cleverness, if not finesse.

Lilac Time also bridged the gap between the kind of films that were possible in the silent era, and new types of film that were more appropriately matched with the new, realistic device of sound. Sentimental romantic melodramas abounded in the silent era. They were the bread and butter offerings of both female stars such as Marguerite Clark and Norma Talmadge, and matinee idols such as Rudolph Valentino and John Gilbert. These films would be replaced by new offerings, in new genres keyed to sound, such as the musical and the gangster film. Gilbert's career would be effectively over with the advent of sound, not only because his voice tended to record high and thin, but also because his voice was now employed in uttering the flowery lines that seemed very romantic in silent-film titles, but were simply terrible as spoken dialogue.

Lilac Time is squarely within the silent-film aesthetic that permitted a kind of romantic fantasy which would later be lost in sound features. Without dialogue, film romance was capable of involving the audience in a fantasy world of love untouched by the necessity of anything so potentially deadening to emotional intensity as mundane speech. Only in silent films such as *Lilac Time* could a judge's son from Montana be unequivocally transformed into a Royal Air Force pilot who courts an innocent French peasant girl played by an Irish-American girl. As with opera and ballet, silent film was a medium a step removed from ordinary experience, and it engaged its audience's emotion and imagination through a combination of music, visual poetry, and titles. The latter, in particular, required the active cooperation of each individual in the audience to create a sense of intimacy unrivaled by the sound-film experience.

If *Lilac Time* was able to exploit silent film's capacity for presenting film romance, it was also successful in capitalizing on a popular trend at the time: the war story, and in particular, the aviation film. *Lilac Time* was one of several aviation films to come out in the late 1920's and early 1930's. These films included Howard Hughes' *Hell's Angels* (1930) and William Wellman's *Wings* (1927). By the late 1920's, a public removed from World War I by ten years could accept seeing the war dramatically and realistically reenacted. King Vidor's *The Big Parade* (1925) is considered a milestone by film historians because it depicted both American soldiers' ignorance of what the war was about and the actual horrors of warfare, yet contemporary audiences seemed to remember the gumchewing romance between Gilbert and René Adorée more than the film's graphic portrayal of the horrors of warfare.

Aviation pictures, with their emphasis on breathtaking stuntflying and spectacular crashes, were exciting and even more safely distanced from wartime trauma than were the films about dogfaced infantrymen. The romanticization of World War I was inevitable, and to make the aviator the focus of the screen's romanticization of the war was logical. Aviators symbolized the gallantry, skill, individuality, and excitement missing from ground combat where success was measured in yards of earth, not miles gained and casualties were numbered, not in single lives, but in thousands and hundreds of thousands. The aviator, unlike the foot soldier, was an individual who controlled some part of his destiny through his own skill as a flier. He was far removed from the miserably dirty, anonymous life and death of those in the trenches.

Lilac Time acknowledges loss of life: the entire company is killed except for Philip, but that loss is used more to bring tears to the eyes of the audience than it is to make the audience aware of the futile carnage of the war. The aviator is allowed moments of glory. He does not face mustard gas or tanks, but the enemy as a human individual. Philip and the German Ace shoot each other down, and when Jeannine comes upon the dying Ace, he shows her the picture of his beloved. Jeannine is overcome by this reminder of the universality of love and the brotherhood of all men. Although many films concerning World War I make the same point, *Lilac Time* seems to use such incidents to increase the poignancy of the central romance. World War I destroyed an entire European generation, but in this film, a bigoted father presents a greater threat to the future of young love than does the war.

Produced by John McCormick for Moore, who was his wife, *Lilac Time* served mainly as a vehicle for displaying Moore's piquant talents. Primarily a comedienne, she was regarded as a prototype flapper as the result of her performance in *Flaming Youth* (1923). Her outing in *Lilac Time* was called her first "dramatic role," but the film contains considerably less drama than sentimental melodrama, and it does not ignore opportunities to enliven the proceedings with comedy. Studio publicity called the Jeannine Berthelot character, "a perky pranky maid of France," and Moore lives up to the epithet. She evidences the same kind of spirited adolescent determination, alternated with innocent softness, that was also characteristic of Mary Pickford's screen *persona*. Jeannine Berthelot became Moore's most famous role, but it was her last big success. The film made her a top First National box-office star, but her stay at the top was short-lived. Although Moore would star in other films and give a moving portrayal in *The Power and the Glory* (1933), sound and the end of the flapper era would spell her box-office demise.

In contrast to the place *Lilac Time* held in the career of Moore, the film was an important stepping-stone in the advancement of Gary Cooper to stardom. Loaned out for the film by Paramount, Cooper had already been seen in secondary roles in some important films such as *Wings*, and *The Winning of Barbara Worth* (1926), and as leading man in a few moderate successes such as *The Children of Divorce* (1927), but he had also been in some very mediocre entries such as *Arizona Bound* (1927) and *Nevada* (1927).

Lilac Time was his first great success. Although he was criticized for his stiff acting in the film, he demonstrates, in his portrayal of Philip Blythe, the quiet strength and sensitivity that would become Cooper trademarks for thirty-five years. *Lilac Time* also marks one of his numerous roles as a World War I soldier. Just as John Wayne became the screen's archetypal World War II soldier, Cooper embodied the popular conception of the World War I dough-boy in such films as *A Man from Wyoming* (1930), *A Farewell to Arms* (1932), and *Sergeant York* (1941).

The melodramatic nature of *Lilac Time* is at once obvious in a recounting of the film's plot. Captain Philip Blythe (Gary Cooper) is a replacement flier for the Royal Air Force company billeted at the Normandy farm of Madame Berthelot (Eugenie Besserer). He makes his introduction to her daughter, Jeannine (Colleen Moore), by almost crashing his plane into her as he attempts to land. After a courtship that begins with the two as mocking antagonists, they fall in love, but Philip can only manage to tell her of his feelings immediately before he must leave on a dangerous mission. During an air battle in which he downs the German Ace (Edward Clayton), Philip is also shot down, but in a stroke of melodramatic coincidence, his plane crashes near the Berthelot farm. Jeannine has promised to wait for him, and she rushes to the plane to help the medics take his apparently lifeless body from the wreckage. Philip is taken to a hospital, but Jeannine does not know where he is, and she frantically searches for him. Instead of finding Philip, however, she encounters his father, the stern General Blythe (Burr McIntosh), who tells her his son is dead. The General says this to put an end to his son's relationship with a peasant girl whom the General regards as unworthy of Philip. Jeannine performs a farewell gesture to her supposedly dead love by sending lilacs, their symbol of love, to his hospital room. Upon receiving the flowers, Philip immediately realizes that they can only be from Jeannine, and he struggles to the window to signal her. Jeannine sees him, and the lovers are joyfully reunited.

With *Lilac Time*, George Fitzmaurice, who directed Valentino's last picture, the enormously successful *The Son of the Sheik* (1926), met the challenge of making a rather cloying romance entertaining. He manages to enhance the melodramatic material with some sense of restraint in the enactment, although Moore sometimes acts more like a smitten child than a young woman in love. Also, as one critic rightfully complained, the art director, Horace Jackson, ran amuck with lilacs. In spite of this, the film often does have a lovely fairy-tale version of France look.

If one accepts the romantic sensibility of the film and acknowledges the aesthetic framework of the silent era, then *Lilac Time* can still be enjoyable to watch. To understand its enormous success, one has to realize how the film fit into a popular genre of the time, how it exploited the new technical advances in synchronized sound, and what audiences of the time were willing to accept in the way of melodrama. *Lilac Time*, if viewed this way, provides some insight into popular tastes of the late 1920's. The film may not be art, but it is artfully made popular entertainment perfectly suited to its time.

Gaylyn Studlar

THE LODGER

Released: 1926
Production: Michael Balcon for Gainsborough
Direction: Alfred Hitchcock
Screenplay: Eliot Stannard and Alfred Hitchcock; based on the novel of the
    same name by Marie Belloc-Lowndes
Titles: Ivor Montagu
Cinematography: Baron Ventimiglia
Editing: Ivor Montagu
Length: 8 reels/7,500 feet

Principal characters:
The Lodger .... Ivor Novello
Daisy Bunting .... June, Lady Inverclyde
Mrs. Bunting .... Marie Ault
Mr. Bunting .... Arthur Chesny
Joe Betts .... Malcolm Keen

The Lodger was considered by Alfred Hitchcock to be his first "real" film.
Although Hitchcock had worked as an art director, title designer and writer,
and part-time assistant director for almost six years before production began
on *The Lodger*, it was the first film to display many of the characteristics
which scholars today point to as representative of the Hitchcockian style. The
director, who was born in London in 1899, began his career in films after a
few years of training and working in various aspects of engineering. Always
interested in films, however, Hitchcock decided to change professions and,
in 1920, he began working for a short-lived London branch of the Famous
Players-Lasky Corporation.

After a few years of doing various jobs on a number of productions, Hitchcock was given his first directorial assignment with *The Pleasure Garden*
(1925), an Anglo-German production which was actually filmed in Germany,
as was his next feature, *The Mountain Eagle* (1925). Thus, *The Lodger* was
Hitchcock's first *true* British film.

The Lodger, which was released in the United States as *The Case Against
Jonathan Drew* (a title which was quickly forgotten, virtually all criticism on
the film uses the British title), was subtitled "A Story of the London Fog."
Based on the novel of the same name by Marie Belloc-Lowndes, *The Lodger*
is a variation on the Jack-the-Ripper story. In the film, the central character,
called simply "The Lodger" (Ivor Novello), is an innocent man caught in the
trap of other peoples' suspicions. Because this lodger, who is renting a room
in the home of Mr. and Mrs. Bunting (Arthur Chesny and Marie Ault), seems
mysterious, he is suspected of being the notorious "Avenger," a killer who
has been stalking women in London and strangling them. Although the

Avenger's methods may vary from those of Jack the Ripper, the mood of terror which he causes in London has the same effect.

When the Lodger begins a friendship with the Buntings' daughter Daisy (June, Lady Inverclyde), her boyfriend, Joe Betts (Malcolm Keen), becomes unreasonably jealous and suspicious of him. Joe is a detective, and he mistakenly deducts that the Lodger is the Avenger. Hard evidence is, of course, nonexistent, but Joe's shortsightedness will not allow him to accept that reality, and thus he attempts to convince other people that his suspicions are correct.

As in many other films of this ilk, particularly Hitchcock's own *Suspicion* (1941), the audience is drawn into the self-deception as well. Suspicious actions, symbols, and a general tone of mystery make the audience accept, along with Joe, the probability that the Lodger is the Avenger. In the end, however, viewers learn that the suspect is, in fact, pursuing the Avenger himself, because the Avenger had killed the Lodger's own sister. In a tense climactic scene, the Lodger is chased by a mob that is convinced of his guilt, but at the last moment, the real killer (who is never actually seen on the screen) is revealed, and the innocent man goes free. The final impression left by the film is that the Lodger will now be able to marry Daisy not only because Joe has proven himself unworthy of her but also because the Lodger's revenge against the killer has finally been realized through the culprit's apprehension.

The Lodger is not a great film, but it contains so many points seminal to the study of Hitchcock's work, that it is often discussed. The first and most obvious theme in the film which fits into the Hitchcockian canon is the "wrong man" theme. The Lodger was the first of the Hitchcock protagonists to be either an innocent man falsely accused of a crime, or unfortunately involved with a crime about which he initially knows nothing. In *The Lodger*, as critic Donald Spoto has pointed out in his book *The Art of Alfred Hitchcock*, the protagonist is not really innocent because he plots the death of the Avenger himself, but he is, at least, innocent of actually being the Avenger.

A second major point about the film which runs through the entire range of Hitchcock's work is the staircase symbol. Perhaps because of his work in Germany in the mid-1920's when German expressionism was at its peak, or perhaps because of his own work as an art director, Hitchcock's films make significant use of concrete symbols. In *The Lodger*, as in *Suspicion*, *Rebecca* (1940), *Psycho* (1960), and others, a staircase plays a role as important as that of an actor. The staircase is used symbolically to delineate relationships and to "inspire" transitions. In *Suspicion*, for example, most of the major changes in Lina's (Joan Fontaine) thoughts about her husband Johnny (Cary Grant) happen on the long Georgian staircase in their house. In *The Lodger*, the staircase most significantly places a physical and, in essence, an emotional barrier between Mrs. Bunting who, like Joe, suspects the Lodger and her daughter Daisy.

The Christian iconography evident in this film was also a major aspect of Hitchcock's work. Hitchcock, who was a Roman Catholic and had a Jesuit education, often displayed religious motifs in his films, even though religion *per se* seldom entered into the plots. There are obvious instances where these religious symbols cannot be denied, such as the scene when the Lodger is manacled, thus making him a Christ-figure. Some film historians tend to dwell on these symbols to excess, however, often making the plots, actors, and settings of the story seem subservient to the overall religious design. It should be noted, though, that the last scene of *The Lodger*, like the last scene of *I Confess* (1953) in which the innocent man is pursued through the city streets by a vengeful mob, are blatant, albeit cinematically enjoyable, re-creations of Christ's walk to Calvary.

The irony of the Christ-figure motif is, however, that Hitchcock, by his own admission, wanted both *The Lodger* and *Suspicion* to end with the protagonist actually being guilty. The reason why neither film ended this way is that Ivor Novello and later Cary Grant were popular box-office stars, and the films' respective producers felt that a handsome matinee idol could not be a murderer in a successful commercial film. The evidence in *The Lodger* seems to be stronger throughout the film for the man's innocence than in *Suspicion*, where Johnny's guilt or innocence could have been satisfactorily proven to the audience with the alteration of only about two minutes of the last scene.

The Lodger was a very successful film and it proved to be a worthy beginning (or near beginning) for one of the screen's most significant and enduring directors. Although Hitchcock's next two or three films were not of the caliber of *The Lodger*, his mark on British, and later American, films had been unalterably established. He went on to make the first British all-talking film, *Blackmail* (1929), followed by some highly successful films in the 1930's such as *The 39 Steps* (1935) and *The Lady Vanishes* (1938). After moving to the United States in 1939, Hitchcock began making American films with *Rebecca* and continued making very commercially and (usually at a later date) artistically successful films, ending with *The Family Plot* (1976). He died in 1980 less than a year after receiving the American Film Institute's Life Achievement Award.

The Lodger was remade in 1944 in the United States starring Laird Cregar and Merle Oberon as the lead characters. Although the film was very successful, it had a different ending with the Lodger dying after his guilt had been proven. Instead of the detective (George Sanders) being a bumbling neurotic as in Hitchcock's version, he actually saves the heroine and becomes a sympathetic character.

Patricia King Hanson

LOMBARDI, LTD.

Released: 1919
Production: Metro
Direction: Jack Conway
Screenplay: June Mathis; based on the play of the same name by Frederic Hatton and Fanny Hatton
Cinematography: no listing
Length: 7 reels

Principal characters:

Tito Lombardi	Bert Lytell
Norah	Alice Lake
Phyllis	Juanita Hansen
Daisy	Jean Acker
Ricky Toselli	George McDaniel
Lida	Ann May

In 1920, Metro had six stars whose names preceded the titles of their films: Viola Dana, May Allison, Nazimova, Buster Keaton, Bert Lytell, and Alice Lake. *Lombardi, Ltd.* (1919) was a Bert Lytell feature, but it also made Alice Lake, his leading lady, a star. Lake was instantly moved to star status by Metro officials after her success in the film, and throughout the early 1920's, her films were very popular.

Lombardi, Ltd. was a popular stage play which Metro assigned to the actor who was then their only star leading man, Bert Lytell. He was a prestige star for the studio, having moved to films after a distinguished stage career. His first film was *The Lone Wolf* (1917) for Herbert Brenon. Metro put him under exclusive contract on the strength of that picture, and he began a long string of features. He played Boston Blackie twice in 1918 and made that character a screen favorite. Many of his features were crime dramas, one of the most popular being *Alias Jimmy Valentine* (1920).

After he left Metro, Lytell made several famous motion pictures: *To Have and to Hold* (1922), *Rupert of Hentzau* (1923), *The Eternal City* (1924), and *Lady Windermere's Fan* (1925).

In the film, Lytell plays Tito Lombardi, a dress designer and owner of the most exclusive salon in New York, Lombardi, Ltd. He is in love with his prettiest model, Phyllis (Juanita Hansen), and is trying to comprehend her seriousness. When she wonders out loud why he has never kissed her, he replies, "Me, I am a queer fellow. I wait for the 'one' woman." His eyes tell her that "the one woman" is herself, but she has set her sights on a rich broker. When she leaves Tito alone, he silently stays in the dressing room, unaware of the entrance of his devoted assistant, Norah (Alice Lake). She is a beautiful woman, although her looks do not have the blatant flash of

Phyllis'. She tells him that a customer wants something "different," and Tito leaves, murmuring the loathing he has for the dowager he must see. Norah, meanwhile, goes to the back room to see an old friend who is in trouble.

There, she consoles Lida (Ann May) who is crying. Norah does not understand her friend's tears, since she is kept by a rich man who has given her a beautiful apartment, jewels, clothes, and a car. The explanation comes when Lida sobs, "He has left me for a younger girl. Robert Terrant, the only man I have every loved, is gone!" Norah is startled because Robert Terrant is the name of the man whom Phyllis has been seeing. She says nothing to Lida, however, and only tries to soothe her.

There are other romances in the House of Lombardi. One of them involves a wealthy young man, Ricky Toselli (George McDaniel), who is masquerading as a chauffeur for a pretty model, Daisy (Jean Acker), and is trying to see if he can win her love as a poor man.

Lombardi, Ltd. is also having financial difficulties, for Tito is an artist, not a businessman. When Phyllis discovers the state of affairs at Lombardi's, she asks Tito to come to her dressing room and she tells him that she is quitting. Tito asks if it is because of a man, but Phyllis says no. Sitting unnoticed in a dark corner is Lida, who accuses Phyllis of having an affair with Robert Terrant. Tito is crushed, and his business is almost ruined. Norah offers him her life's savings, but that will not buy even one of Lombardi's gowns.

It is the wealthy young Ricky who saves the day. When Daisy agrees to be his wife, thinking him a poor man, Ricky is so happy that he offers Tito the money to save the company. Tito's pride at first makes him refuse Ricky's offer, but Daisy and Norah break down his pride. Tito learns something else from these events; he discovers Norah is his "one" woman.

Alice Lake was born in the East in 1896. As a child, she haunted the Flatbush Theater in Brooklyn; then, around 1913, she began to get some small roles at Vitagraph and appeared there regularly for the next two years.

Early in 1916, Roscoe "Fatty" Arbuckle was in the East looking for talent, and Lake was introduced to him. He liked her immediately and nicknamed her "Nut." He brought her back to California with him and used her as his leading lady; when he left Mack Sennett and formed his own company, "Comique," she went with him. By the end of 1918, she had left Arbuckle to try to work in features. She was in two other Lytell features before *Lombardi, Ltd.* Eventually, she was given her own unit at Metro, where she kept very busy. Among her credits at Metro is *Uncharted Seas* (1921) in which she starred with Rudolph Valentino. She had begun drinking, however, while working with Arbuckle's company, and eventually Metro grew alarmed at her conduct, and she was released in 1922. *Hate* was her last film there.

Moving back East, Lake made films for independent companies until the early talkies. She then returned to California but looked older than her thirty-five years, and she was forced to take on extra jobs when she could get them.

In 1953, from the room in which she lived, she told a reporter, "All gone. Fame, money, and false friends. I guess they went in that order."

Offered residence in the Motion Picture Country House at the end of the 1950's, she spent her days in her room looking over stills from her films. Residents of the Country House received a monthly allowance of twenty dollars then. On payday, Lake would get dressed up, leave the grounds, and head for her favorite bar. When she had spent her last dime, the bartender would call the Country House to send someone to take her home. She died at the Country House in 1967.

Larry Lee Holland

LONESOME

Released: 1928
Production: Carl Laemmle, Jr., for Universal
Direction: Paul Fejos
Screenplay: Edward T. Lowe, Jr., and Tom Reed; based on an original story
   by Mann Page
Cinematography: Gilbert Warrenton
Length: 7 reels/6,761 feet

   Principal characters:
   Jim .... Glenn Tryon
   Mary .... Barbara Kent
   Overdressed woman .... Fay Holderness
   Romantic gentleman .... Gustav Partos
   The Sport .... Eddie Phillips

   Paul Fejos is remembered mostly for the films he directed in Hungary
during the 1930's and for his groundbreaking efforts as a maker of scientific
documentaries. He did, however, work on a handful of films in the United
States. He had originally studied medicine and directed films in his native
country before coming to the United States to work as a bacteriologist for
the Rockefeller Institute. He could not avoid involvement in theater and film,
however, and in 1927, he directed *The Last Moment*, an experimental five-
reel feature about suicide with Georgie Hale, Charles Chaplin's co-star in *The
Gold Rush* (1925), and on an incredibly low (five thousand dollars) budget.
On the basis of *The Last Moment*, he was hired by Universal. His initial film
was *Lonesome* (1928), a charming, eloquent indictment of the dehumanization
of life in the big city, a story of how the individual can easily lose his identity
in the crowd and how he can survive, and perhaps thrive, with companionship
and love.
   Lonesome is essentially a two-character film, with a slice-of-life plot that
is simple if a bit gimmicky. Jim (Glenn Tryon), a drill press operator, and
Mary (Barbara Kent), a telephone operator, both live in New York City.
They are average, everyday, anonymous members of the working class who
are alone—and lonely. The film opens with a shot of skyscrapers and the sky.
Jim and Mary are in their respective rooms and are awakened to the sound
of their alarm clocks. Mary groans, as she would prefer a bit more sleep; Jim
dresses quickly, gobbles down a doughnut, and swallows his coffee. They
each work at their jobs in the morning, but it is Saturday, and they each have
the afternoon off.
   Separately, Mary and Jim follow a crowd to Luna Park at Coney Island,
New York, where most of the film is set. They become acquainted on the
beach, fall immediately in love, and spend the rest of the day together enjoying

the amenities of the beach and amusement park. Jim and Mary are surrounded by strangers consuming ice cream and soda, screaming, partaking in the various rides and attractions; but they are no longer lonely, because they have each other's company.

A fire breaks out while Jim and Mary are on a rollercoaster, and they become separated in the rush of the crowd. They search for each other frantically, but without success. Unfortunately, they had not exchanged names or addresses, and they fear that they have lost each other forever. In desperation, each returns home. Jim lives in a boardinghouse, and once there he plays on his phonograph the record of a song to which he and Mary had danced earlier. Mary, who by coincidence lives in the next room, hears the music, cries, and pounds on the wall in an effort to silence the sounds that remind her of her tragedy. When Jim knocks on the door, to find out the cause of the noise, he and his beloved are reunited, presumably to live happily ever after.

Lonesome features sound effects: the noises that surround Jim and Mary are heard as are voices on several occasions. The difference in quality between many of the last silents and early talkies is profound: the former are stunningly beautiful in their silence, while the latter are awkward, even vulgar. "Sound" was added to *Lonesome* after it was completed, and its noises are heard for no reason other than the technical breakthrough of, and demand for, sound. Unfortunately, the result is a break in the mood that Fejos had carefully labored to create. *Lonesome* is thus a victim of the point in which it was made.

Nevertheless, the film remains a realistic, perceptive depiction of alienation in the metropolis, of human beings lost in the big city, solitary even when surrounded by hundreds of people. The corny and unbelievable ending is a plot device of questionable quality, but Fejos subtly, sensitively, and even humorously examines people's feelings, needs, and desires with great flair. He effectively utilizes a hand-held camera, resulting in a *cinéma vérité* effect. *Lonesome* is filled with double exposures and dissolves, all of which are visually pleasing.

The film even may be compared favorably with another feature that is far more celebrated: King Vidor's classic *The Crowd* (1928). Although the specifics of the plot are different, the characters are named simply John (which is close to Jim) and Mary, the setting is New York and Coney Island, and the theme—a man and woman struggling to survive in a large, impersonal metropolis—is similar. *Lonesome* may be flawed, while *The Crowd* is near perfect, but the former still holds up well and is highly regarded among French film historians. It is deserving of far more notoriety among American critics than it has received to date.

Glenn Tryon and Barbara Kent are excellent as Jim and Mary. Tryon, who also directed, produced, and wrote scripts, began his film career in 1924. He received top billing in many silents and early talkies, but never was a ranking star performer. In the 1930's, he became more involved in "B"-grade work. If Tryon is only dimly recalled, however, his co-star here is completely forgotten. Kent appeared in silents and talkies, appearing most notably as Harold Lloyd's co-star in *Welcome Danger* (1929) and *Feet First* (1929). Her name appeared prominently on credit lists only into the early 1930's.

Lonesome, which was supervised by Carl Laemmle, Jr., the twenty-year-old son of the president of Universal, received generally favorable reviews. Fejos made only a few more films in the United States: *Broadway* (1929); *The Last Performance* (1929); and, more memorably, the French and German versions of George Hill's groundbreaking prison drama, *The Big House* (1930). He then returned to Europe and continued making his features and documentaries until the end of the decade.

Rob Edelman

THE LOST WORLD

Released: 1925
Production: Associated First National
Direction: Harry O. Hoyt
Screenplay: Marion Fairfax; based on the novel of the same name by Sir Arthur Conan Doyle
Cinematography: Arthur Edeson
Chief technician: Fred W. Jackman
Technical director: Willis O'Brien
Special effects: Willis O'Brien, Fred W. Jackman, Ralph Hammeras, and Marcel Delgado
Length: 10 reels/9,700 feet

Principal characters:
Edward Malone	Lloyd Hughes
Paula White	Bessie Love
Professor Challenger	Wallace Beery
Sir John Roxton	Lewis Stone
Professor Summerlee	Arthur Hoyt
Ape-man	Bull Montana
Gladys Hungerford	Alma Bennett

The technique of stop-motion animation, used to impart cinematically the illusion of motion to inanimate objects, has been in use almost since the cinema began. One of the most basic of all special effects, it simply involves the exposure of one frame of film at a time, with a slight shifting of the objects being photographed between each exposure. During the cinema's early years, this technique was used primarily by the makers of novelty or "trick" films—not for dramatic purposes, but for the "magical" effect (sometimes called pixilation) of making objects such as fountain pens or teacups appear to dance around under their own power. Not until the production of *The Lost World* (1925) was stop-motion animation employed extensively for a feature-length film.

The Lost World was also the first major work of special-effects pioneer Willis O'Brien, best known for the classic *King Kong* (1933). O'Brien, born in 1886, had tried his hand at a number of occupations before becoming a filmmaker. He gained some expertise at sculpture while working as a stone-cutter, and his interest in boxing led him to sculpt clay figures of fighters. It was apparently while he and a co-worker were posing the figures to simulate boxing matches that it occurred to O'Brien that such models might be animated by the stop-motion method. Another of his interests was prehistoric animals, and he decided to make them the subject of his first experiment. Fashioning models of a dinosaur and a caveman using clay formed around jointed wooden skeletons, he enlisted the aid of a newsreel cameraman and filmed a brief test reel, barely a minute in length. Although the results were crude, the film was interesting enough to persuade a San Francisco producer-exhibitor named Herman Wobber to advance O'Brien five thousand dollars to produce a more sophisticated version. O'Brien spent two months on the five-minute production, entitled *The Dinosaur and the Missing Link* (1915); it was eventually purchased by the Edison Company, which also hired O'Brien to make a series of similar films. From late 1916 to 1917, he made approximately ten half-reel films for Edison. Several of these had prehistoric themes, and a few also involved miniature human figures; for a short-lived series called *Mickey's Naughty Nightmares*, he even combined stop-motion miniatures with live actors, through the use of split screen and double exposure methods. After leaving the Edison Company, O'Brien was hired by New Jersey producer Herbert M. Dawley to produce a two-reel film called *The Ghost of Slumber Mountain* (1919). O'Brien's animation for this film—a sequence in which a man dreams he is looking through a "magic telescope" at a prehistoric world—was relatively brief, but both his models themselves and their movement on the screen evidenced a growing sophistication.

During this period, O'Brien had been working constantly to refine his methods. His most important step was the abandonment of the too-pliant clay-and-wood models with which he had begun. Recognizing the need for figures that could be more precisely adjusted and could stand up under the intense heat of studio lights, he began using rubber for the skin and muscles of his miniature creatures, forming them around metal skeletons with screws in the joints to hold them rigid while filming. Accounts differ as to exactly when O'Brien made these improvements, but by 1920, he had reached a point where he felt ready for a truly ambitious project.

Following *The Ghost of Slumber Mountain*, O'Brien went to work on a series of "novelty" shorts for producer Watterson R. Rothacker. It is unclear whether or not any of these films were actually produced, for soon after the two got together, Rothacker secured the screen rights to Sir Arthur Conan Doyle's 1912 novel *The Lost World*. The novel, which dealt with the discovery of a remote Amazon plateau where prehistoric creatures still thrived, was a natural for O'Brien, and it sparked his enthusiasm. He made extensive sketches and shot test footage, ultimately convincing Rothacker that it would be feasible to film Doyle's adventure. Although such a large-scale special-effects undertaking was completely unprecedented, Rothacker agreed to commit one million dollars to the project, and arrangements were made for preliminary work to be done at the Associated First National Studios in Burbank, California. Two men were present at Associated First National who were to be of enormous help to O'Brien in the years ahead: Fred W. Jackman, head of the studio's special-effects department, and Ralph Hammeras, one of the most accomplished practitioners of the "glass shot" (a technique whereby a prohibitively elaborate background could be simulated by shooting a scene through a pane of glass on part of which the "background" was painted). The third important member of the technical crew was Marcel Delgado, a nineteen-year-old Mexican art student whom O'Brien had met at the Otis Art Institute in Los Angeles. Delgado, a talented sculptor despite his relative youth, was hired to design and construct the more than fifty dinosaur models that would be needed.

Preliminary work on *The Lost World* consumed two years. Very careful preplanning was necessary, for more complex and convincing results would be demanded than O'Brien had ever achieved before. The project was kept in strict secrecy as the small crew began working out technical details, designing and building sets and models, and shooting extensive tests. The first fruits of their labors were revealed, appropriately enough, by Doyle himself, who astonished a meeting of the Society of American Magicians in June, 1922 by presenting a sample of the test footage. He intimated vaguely that the film was authentic, but refused to answer any questions or to in any way allay the general confusion he had caused. Doyle withheld any comment until the next day, when he explained the film's origin in a note to the Society's president, magician Harry Houdini.

The New York Times carried accounts of the brouhaha, which had an unforeseen result: it brought the project to the attention of Herbert M. Dawley, who filed a $100,000 lawsuit against Rothacker, claiming patent violation. Dawley had rather unscrupulously taken most of the credit for *The Ghost of Slumber Mountain*, but he had also had the foresight to take out patents on O'Brien's processes, on which his lawsuit was quite firmly based. The considerable evidence in support of O'Brien's prior claim to stop-motion, however, coupled with Rothacker's promise of a stiff legal battle, persuaded Dawley to settle out of court. The net result of the affair was to delay the start of production on *The Lost World* until early 1923, by which time the script had been written and the building of the sets and models was largely completed.

The miniature sets were an average of six feet long and three or four feet deep, standing about three feet above the floor. Every piece was carefully secured; such things as leaves and grass were either cut from tin or heavily lacquered to prevent them from moving between exposures. The sets were designed to allow O'Brien easy access to any portion, and to provide the greatest possible freedom and comfort, to facilitate the difficult animation work. Delgado's models were sixteen to twenty inches long and were based on the famous Charles R. Knight dinosaur paintings in the American Museum of Natural History. The creatures' steel skeletons were fleshed out with sponge, and their skin consisted of sheets of rubber dental dam. Many of the models were internally equipped with football bladders, which could be inflated or deflated slightly to produce the illusion of breathing.

The special-effects portion of the production took a total of fourteen months. Remarkably, the complicated and laborious stop-motion work (with the exception of one scene—the dinosaur stampede) was done solely by O'Brien, working behind partitions to prevent interruption—since any break in his concentration might have prevented him from remembering each of the tiny adjustments necessary to bring his creatures to life on the screen. Every move of the dinosaurs had to be determined precisely in advance, so that holes could be drilled into the sets and the models fastened securely into place (often off-balance) for each exposure. The lighting, in order to prevent a flickering effect in the final film, had to remain absolutely constant from exposure to exposure; this was accomplished by hanging several banks of steady Cooper Hewitt lights about five feet above the sets, which created intense heat. For many scenes, portions of the camera lens were masked off, so that O'Brien's film could later be combined with live-action footage by means of matte shots, a double-exposure method requiring great precision. Under these difficult conditions, O'Brien considered a ten-hour work day successful if it resulted in 480 frames (thirty-five feet) of finished film—a little more than thirty seconds' worth. Following the completion of the technical work and its combination with the concurrent work of Harry O. Hoyt, director of the live-action sequences, *The Lost World* was released in February, 1925.

The story begins in London, in the offices of the *Record-Journal*, where brash young reporter Edward Malone (Lloyd Hughes) is asking his editor for an "exciting" assignment, to impress his fiancée. He is sent to Zoological Hall to cover a speech by Professor Challenger (Wallace Beery), an eccentric scientist who claims to have evidence that prehistoric beasts still live on a volcanic plateau in the back country of the Amazon. Malone soon finds himself part of an expedition which is formed to verify Challenger's disputed claims. In addition to Challenger and Malone, the expedition includes: Professor Summerlee (Arthur Hoyt), one of Challenger's most vocal rivals; Sir John Roxton (Lewis Stone), noted sportsman and adventurer; and Paula White (Bessie Love), with whom Roxton, although much older, is romantically interested. Paula is the daughter of explorer Maple White, who discovered the plateau and then vanished, and whose diary is the primary evidence of its existence.

Deep in the Amazon jungle, they camp at the base of the plateau, which appears inaccessible. They manage to scale an adjacent pinnacle, however, and cross to the plateau on a felled tree. Soon thereafter, they encounter a brontosaurus, which destroys their bridge, stranding them. The group makes camp, and while Challenger and Summerlee pursue their scientific interests, Malone and Paula begin to develop a romantic relationship. The group observes, and is threatened by, a variety of prehistoric creatures, including a man-like ape (Bull Montana) who watches and harasses them throughout their stay.

There are many dinosaurs, chief among them an allosaurus, which engages in battles with several other beasts, including a triceratops and a brontosaurus. Eventually, Roxton discovers a possible escape route: a cave leading to an opening on the side of the plateau. (The cave also contains the remains of Maple White.) While the servants left in the camp below assemble a long rope ladder, Roxton returns to tell the others; he witnesses Malone and Paula (the former having renounced his fiancée under the circumstances) declare their love for each other and realizes that his own desire for Paula must remain unfulfilled.

In the meantime, Challenger and Summerlee are stalking a brontosaurus to observe its habits; they witness a fight between the allosaurus and the brontosaurus, which results in the latter being forced over the edge of the plateau and becoming mired in a swamp below. Suddenly, the long-dormant volcano erupts, turning the plateau into a blazing inferno and stampeding the dinosaurs. The explorers manage to escape down the rope ladder just in time, despite the last-minute interference of the ape-man. They make arrangements to return to London with the captured brontosaurus.

Back in London, as Challenger is preparing to address the Zoological Society, word is received that the brontosaurus has escaped while being unloaded from the ship. Rampaging through the streets of the city, it creates a panic and causes much damage before falling through a bridge into the Thames and swimming out to sea. Challenger, devastated at the loss, sits dejectedly on the bridge; Malone and Paula go off together in a taxi, while the resigned Roxton watches.

Prints of *The Lost World* generally available today are approximately one-half the length of the original release version (five reels as opposed to ten). The above synopsis is based on such a print, which is probably descended from the 16mm Kodascope Library edition issued for home use in the 1930's. Obviously, this alteration has radically affected the film's pacing and dramatic structure; the action rushes along at an almost breakneck pace, occasionally at the expense of continuity. Documentation is inadequate to determine specific cuts, although most of the dinosaur footage was probably retained (except for a few details of the Brontosaurus' final rampage).

The subplot of Edward Malone's engagement to one Gladys Hungerford (who is mentioned only in passing, but still listed in the credits as played by Alma Bennett) is the only obvious excision, but the latter portion of the group's adventure on the plateau, including the discovery of the caves and the volcanic explosion, is choppy and confusing, indicating the elimination of considerable connecting material.

The most important aspect of the film, however, can still be fairly assessed—the work of O'Brien. Intensely involved with his physical materials in a way that today's filmmakers cannot match, O'Brien is unquestionably the *auteur* of *The Lost World*. The sophistication of modern special effects makes it somewhat difficult to be impressed by O'Brien's comparatively simple achievements in *The Lost World*, but placed in perspective, his work is far more significant than the zooming spaceships and nightmarishly grotesque monsters of the current cinema.

Given the essentially primitive conditions under which he worked, the smoothness of motion achieved in many sequences is nothing less than astonishing. The realistic choreography of the dinosaurs' fight scenes makes it easy to forget that one is watching a pair of animated models. Particularly clever was O'Brien's decision to give his creatures personality as well as movement—they sneer, twitch, hesitate, look quizzical, and generally exhibit a catalogue of "human" characteristics. Their detailed actions—including breathing, eye-rolling, and the like—are all the more impressive when one takes into account the fact that they were accomplished not by a small army of technicians aided by computers, but by one man and a handful of assistants.

As good as they look today, in 1925—if contemporary accounts can be trusted—the effects were nothing short of a sensation. While O'Brien's earlier short films may have made an impression on a few viewers, the general filmgoing public could hardly have been prepared for *The Lost World*, any more than D. W. Griffith's gradual (and highly visible) development of narrative technique had prepared audiences of a decade before for the stunning impact of *The Birth of a Nation*.

Although the film follows the general contours of Doyle's novel, the differences between the two are revealing with regard to the process of adapting a novel to the silent cinema, and as a presaging of O'Brien's crowning achievement, *King Kong*. The major alterations in the transition from book to film were: first, the addition of the character of Paula White; second, the addition of two spectacular scenes (the eruption of the volcano and the London rampage of the brontosaurus); and third, the greater emphasis on the dinosaurs as the primary feature of the lost plateau (in the novel's later stages, the dinosaurs take a back seat to the party's capture by and subsequent escape from a tribe of ape-men).

The Paula White character's most obvious function, that of "love interest," was no doubt deemed necessary to make the film more than an exclusively masculine quest for scientific adventure, and as such, the device works well enough. The romantic situation thus created is a standard triangle, but the charm of the individual players gives it a weight worthy of any "straight" dramatic film of the period. Lewis Stone's playing of Roxton—especially his realization of the emptiness of his celebrity without Paula—is particularly fine. The other function of Paula, however—the "damsel-in-distress" angle—points to the character's inconsistent conception. As the daughter and chief assistant of Maple White, intrepid discoverer of the lost world, she might be expected to be a bit more self-sufficient during the expedition's difficulties; once upon the plateau, however, most of her time seems to be spent cowering in fear. Every sequence in which the group is threatened (usually by a dinosaur) invariably includes one or more close-ups of Bessie Love staring in horror at the offcamera proceedings; the frequency of such inserts quickly renders them tiresome and ludicrous. Paula White is clearly a forerunner of Ann Redman (Fay Wray) in *King Kong*, but the crucial element of personal involvement is missing. *King Kong* achieved great poignance because of Kong's obvious affection for Ann; in *The Lost World*, the beasts are just beasts, and Paula is simply a frightened woman.

The eruption of the volcano and the brontosaurus on the loose in London were added purely for spectacular effect, with the latter in particular looking forward to Kong's rampage through the streets of New York City. In the novel, although the plateau's volcanic origin is noted, there is no eruption and no dinosaur stampede; the creature brought back to London as living proof of the expedition's success is not a brontosaurus, but a pterodactyl— which is agitated by the scientific assemblage (foreshadowing *King Kong* again), escapes, and flies about causing a general commotion before vanishing through an open window. The ape-man concept, obviously of great interest to Doyle, barely survives in the film, in the person of the single ape-man, who hovers around the expedition like a primitive omen of some sort, but is more of an annoyance than a real threat. The makeup for actor Bull Montana is effective, but the "character" serves no real purpose, except as a cheap way to mystify the audience; no motive for his curious actions is ever provided. *The Lost World*'s additions to the novel's action, as well as the shift in emphasis from the ape-men to the dinosaurs, were natural enough, however, and the effects by O'Brien certainly justified themselves.

Overall, the changes made in the adaptation constitute a significant shift in point of view. The film is a spectacle, an adventure; Doyle's novel is certainly that, but for all its pulp-fiction elements, it is also seriously concerned with the follies and foibles of scientific inquiry. This is not to belittle the film, but merely to provide a reminder that the silent cinema was a less than ideal medium for the communication of anything more than the simplest concepts. It should also be noted that the 1960 remake of *The Lost World*, despite the advantages of dialogue and an additional thirty-five years of film technology, made no more of the book's intellectual qualities and was markedly inferior to the original film even as a straight adventure story.

The success of *The Lost World* was twofold. Most immediate, it was a box-office success, and more than justified Rothacker's faith in O'Brien. More importantly, however, it brought together O'Brien and Delgado and proved that their techniques were applicable to a feature-length film. Their next completed film was *King Kong*, one of the best-loved horror films of all time. O'Brien's career as a special-effects wizard continued sporadically for nearly forty more years, but was marked by a number of unrealized projects and much inferior work—primarily because of budgetary restrictions. Among his later works were the *King Kong* follow-ups *Son of Kong* (1933) and *Mighty Joe Young* (1949), and the destruction of Pompeii for *The Last Days of Pompeii* (1935). At the age of seventy-three, O'Brien was engaged as "technical adviser" on the remake of *The Lost World*, but soon discovered that he had been hired solely for his name and was to have virtually no part in the actual production. He was particularly disappointed by producer Irwin Allen's decision to use live reptiles with artificial fins to represent the dinosaurs.

Shortly before O'Brien's death in 1962, he was to endure one final disappointment—a proposed film, *King Kong vs. Frankenstein*, was abandoned for various reasons. The concept for another King Kong film, however, was appropriated by the producer, who decided to make the film in Japan, without O'Brien. Ironically, the giant ape was ultimately played by a man in a costume—another repudiation of the stop-motion techniques which O'Brien had so painstakingly developed, and which are his continuing legacy to the modern cinema.

Howard H. Prouty

MABEL AT THE WHEEL

Released: 1914
Production: Mack Sennett for Keystone Comedies
Direction: Mack Sennett and Mabel Normand
Screenplay: no listing
Cinematography: no listing
Length: 2 reels/2,004 feet

Principal characters:
Mabel .... Mabel Normand
Villain .... Charles Chaplin
Boyfriend .... Harry McCoy
Father .... Chester Conklin
Rube .... Mack Sennett
Henchmen .... Al St. John
William Seiter

When Charlie Chaplin was hired by Mack Sennett early in 1914 to appea∴ in Keystone comedies, he was not completely unknown: he had clowned in music halls, acted with William Gillette, and toured with Fred Karno's Pantomime Troupe. The Little Tramp character was not yet invented, however, and Chaplin was still developing as a comedian. At Keystone, he was merely another employee. His slapstick had no distinguishing characteristics, and he was without any great creative control or freedom to experiment while the cameras rolled.

Sennett was in charge, as was to a great extent Mabel Normand. Sennett, the king of slapstick, began his career as a boilermaker. He first worked in films for D. W. Griffith, directing most of the Biograph comedies. Griffith thought his brand of humor—which included throwing pies in the faces of policemen—was undignified and disrespectful, so Sennett went out on his own and soon perfected the art of cinematic slapstick in his Keystone comedies. Normand, sweet and pretty, was one of his greatest stars, appearing in hundreds of his shorts. She, too, had also worked for Griffith, but she reached superstardom under the guidance of Sennett. She became so popular that she even appeared in films with her name in the title.

Normand is the star and co-director, with Sennett, of *Mabel at the Wheel* (1914, also known as *His Daredevil Queen* and *Hot Finish*), a two-reeler. Chaplin, too, was in the cast, but Normand was the star. Chaplin's name in the title would have been inappropriate, for his role was simply the "villain," a shady saboteur who does all within his power to prevent Mabel and her boyfriend (Harry McCoy) from winning a race.

The film is a typically silly, amusing Keystone comedy. It is also fascinating to see Chaplin so out of character: he may be funny, but as the Villain, he is unendearing and even obnoxious. In *Mabel at the Wheel*, he wears a black frock coat and high hat, with a mustache and two tufts of hair on his chin. At first, he rides a motorcycle and tries to compete with the Boyfriend, his rival for Mabel's affections, who drives a chic racing car. The Villain offers Mabel a ride on the pillion, but instead drops her in a mud puddle. Mabel is angry, and as a result, the Villain has lost any chance of winning her.

The Villain is in turn peeved at Mabel and seeks revenge. With a couple of shady characters (Al St. John and William Seiter, who later became a prolific director with credits spanning more than thirty years) he kidnaps and binds the Boyfriend just as the race for the Vanderbilt cup is set to begin. The Boyfriend is locked in a shed and will be unable to compete, so Mabel takes his place. The Villain does all he can to sabotage Mabel, even slicking down the track with water to cause her to lose control of the car as she rounds a curve. The vehicle skids in several directions and overturns, but Mabel escapes. The car is still in working order, so Mabel resumes the race and wins. Sennett also appears in the film as the Rube, a naïve press representative who organizes a photo session at the race's finale. If he looks ill at ease, it was because his forte was behind, not in front of, the camera.

Mabel at the Wheel, released to coincide with the actual Vanderbilt cup competition, was Chaplin's tenth film, his first two-reeler, and his second with Normand. The spunky Normand is the hero of the piece; despite her sex, she has no inhibitions about racing a car—a rather unfeminine act for 1914. She triumphs in spite of the Villain's wetting the track.

Normand began the direction, but she and Chaplin quarreled when he wanted to alter the scenario. Chaplin was eager to write and direct and doubted Normand's ability as director; she was, after all, only twenty years old. Normand ordered him to water down the track with a hose, but he suggested that he step on the hose, stop the water, and then let the liquid squirt in his face when he looks down the nozzle. He thought he was adding to the film's mirth, but Normand, perhaps threatened by Chaplin, felt the gag was old hat and would slow down the film's pace. Besides, she was working on a strict production schedule, with no time available for improvisation.

Chaplin allegedly threatened to quit Keystone and even leave films, but Sennett resolved the conflict by taking over the direction and promising Chaplin a chance to make films on his own. Chaplin and Normand quickly proved popular with audiences, however, and they became a team. They had previously appeared in *Mabel's Strange Predicament* (1914, a one-reeler and Chaplin's third film); and, after *Mabel at the Wheel*, they co-starred in *Caught in a Cabaret*, *The Fatal Mallet*, *Her Friend the Bandit*, *Mabel's Busy Day*, and *Mabel's Married Life*, all released during the first half of 1914; and *Gentlemen of Nerve*, *His Trysting Place*, and *Getting Acquainted*, released between October and December of the same year. Some were even co-directed by Chaplin and Normand. Also in 1914, Sennett directed them and Marie Dressler in the first-ever feature-length comedy, *Tillie's Punctured Romance*.

While Chaplin's creative influence on *Mabel at the Wheel* is nil, he was within months co-directing and even signing his name to two-reelers by himself. At Keystone, he was able to observe and learn from Normand and Sennett, Ford Sterling and Fatty Arbuckle. Although in no way as memorable as his later short films, Chaplin's earliest works were critical and commercial successes, earning more money than any other Keystones.

Sennett, however, created his films on an assembly line, with little time and opportunity for experimentation and development of specific comedy characters and styles. He preferred working with malleable funnymen such as Sterling and Chester Conklin, who could alter themselves and easily play heroes or villains and could throw pies as well as be on their receiving end.

Chaplin thus could not thrive with Sennett. In early 1915, after only a year with Keystone, he moved to the Essanay Film Company at ten times his Keystone salary. Here, he could play down the slapstick and develop his own style. A year after that, he went on to Mutual, where he produced his classic shorts: *The Vagabond* (1916), *One A.M.* (1916), *The Pawnshop* (1916), *The Rink* (1916), *Easy Street* (1917), *The Immigrant* (1917), and others. From 1917 on, he produced films independently. By this time, his Little Tramp character had been born, and Chaplin attained immortality.

When he completed his year at Essanay, after only two years as a motion-picture performer, Charlie Chaplin was undoubtedly the top performer in the motion-picture industry. Films like *Mabel at the Wheel* are fine examples of Sennett-Normand Keystone two-reelers, as well as intriguing footnotes in the Chaplin filmography.

Rob Edelman

MADAME SANS-GENE

Released: 1925
Production: Adolph Zukor and Jesse L. Lasky for Famous Players-Lasky; released by Paramount
Direction: Léonce Perret
Assistant director: Jean Durand
Screenplay: Forrest Halsey; based on the play of the same name by Victorien Sardou and Émile Moreau
Cinematography: George Webber
Set decoration: Herry Menestier
Costume design: René Hubert
Music: Hugo Reisenfeld
Length: 10 reels/9,994 feet

Principal characters:

Catherine Hubscher	Gloria Swanson
Napoleon	Emile Drain
Lefebre	Charles De Roche
Count de Neipperg	Warwick Ward
Caroline, Queen of Naples	Arlette Marchal
Elizabeth, Princess of Bacciochi	Renee Heribelle
Empress Marie Louise	Suzanne Branchetti
La Roussotte	Madeline Guitti
Fouche	Henry Favieres
Madame De Bulow	Denise Lorys
Salvary, Minister of Police	Jacques Marney

The play *Madame Sans-Gene* was written by Victorien Sardou and Émile Moreau expressly for the great French comedienne Réjane (1857-1920), who first appeared in it on October 27, 1893. It becomes a popular vehicle for stage actresses during the early part of this century and one of its most notable incarnations was Ellen Terry's 1901 London production.

The play has also been the source of two operas under the title *The Duchess of Danzig*: a 1903 version by Henry Hamilton and Ivan Caryll and a more popular interpretation in 1915 by V. Giordano and R. Simoni which was a successful production at the New York Metropolitan Opera starring the exceptionally talented Geraldine Farrar and Giovanni Martinelli.

On film there was a six-reel 1923 version, a 1945 Argentinian version starring Nini Marshall, and a 1963 version starring Sophia Loren entitled simply *Madame*. The 1925 version starring Gloria Swanson remains the definitive film treatment of this work but unfortunately it numbers among the "lost films."

This Paramount project came about when Swanson was about to sail to England where she planned to meet with playwright Sir James M. Barrie to discuss the possibility of her starring in a film version of *Peter Pan*. Paramount screenwriter Forrest Halsey suggested that while she was abroad she should also look into the possibility of purchasing the screen rights to the Sardou/ Moreau play.

As Swanson familiarized herself with the play and the starring role of the saucy laundress who rises to the French court during the First Empire, it became apparent to her and Halsey that the film should be made in France with the cooperation of the French government, with a French director, and with as many of the real locations as they might be permitted to use.

The inimitable and forceful Swanson, then at the peak of her popularity, was able to convince all parties involved of the viability of the project with the result that the film was made in France with her being the only American in the cast. Two versions were shot, one for French consumption and one for the United States.

Chosen to direct was Léonce Perret, a Frenchman who had studied American filmmaking technique in New York and returned to Paris where he had directed French propaganda films during World War I. For costumes, Perret selected young René Hubert who stunningly re-created French period styles and provided Swanson with some of her "chicest" (a popular new phrase in 1924-1925) screen clothes, not the least of which was a dramatic black and white vertically striped dress with matching parasol which appears in numerous photographs from this lost film.

The publicity hoopla which surrounded Swanson's arrival in France and the subsequent shooting of the film in and around Paris was abundant. Immediately upon her arrival, she paid a respectful tribute to Réjane by visiting her gravesite where she said, "I come very humbly to endeavor to place upon the screen the play which you immortalized upon the stage." To further add to the whirl of publicity she fell in love with and married the handsome young man Perret had hired as her official interpreter and liaison, the Marquis de la Falaise de la Coudraye, making her the first American actress to marry a titled man.

In *Madame Sans-Gene*, Swanson played Catherine Hubscher, a sassy young laundress known for her sharp, witty tongue. She is known as Madame Devil-May-Care and Madame Free-and-Easy, and one of her customers is a shabbily dressed lieutenant named Napoleon Bonaparte (Emile Drain). He is too poor to pay his laundry bill but Catherine fancies him and flirts with him. He is so caught in his own soaring ambitions that he pays little attention to her and does not respond to her flirtations. Yet undauntedly, she mends his laundry and even steals new hosiery for him from her rich clients.

At the outset of the French Revolution she takes up the cause of her workers and meets a handsome young sergeant named Lefebre (Charles De Roche) and likewise openly flirts with him, but this time her advances are accepted. Count de Neipperg (Warwick Ward), who is an Austrian officer in the service of Queen Marie Antoinette, seeks refuge in Catherine's laundry and Catherine hides him in her bedroom. This concealment is discovered by a jealous Lefebre, but when Neipperg gallantly pleads his loyalty to the Queen, Lefebre is so impressed that he lets him go. To assuage any further jealousy Catherine declares her love for Lefebre, and they are married.

Lefebre rises in the military ranks and Catherine follows him into battle, cheering him on and nursing the wounded soldiers. Napoleon is crowned Emperor and Lefebre is promoted to a Marshal of France and named Duke of Danzig. This new turn of events changes Catherine the former washer-woman into the Duchess of Danzig. While attempts are made at acquiring manners and deportment befitting her new station in life, Catherine remains an incorrigibly good-natured diamond-in-the-rough. She is gauche, has a spit-fire temper, is contemptuous of the pretensions and trappings of society, and is oblivious to the sneerings of her own servants.

Neipperg returns to Paris on a mission for the Austrian Empire, renews his acquaintance with Catherine and her husband, and also catches the eye of Napoleon's wife, Marie Louise (Suzanne Branchetti).

In the meantime Catherine has become the laughing stock of Napoleon's court. She wears the appropriate clothes but with no decorum. In one scene, as she enters her carriage, she loses her petticoat. In another, she proclaims that her shoes pinch her feet and that she cannot wait to kick them off. Her impertinent behavior results in a warning to Lefebre from Napoleon that unless she mends her crude ways, it will be necessary for him to divorce her.

Catherine is the particular brunt of jokes and taunts of the court ladies, especially Caroline, Queen of Naples (Arlette Marchal), and Elizabeth, Prin-cess of Bacciochi (Renee Heribelle). These two conspire to ruin Catherine and induce Napoleon to throw a grand reception for Catherine at Compiegne which will once and for all reveal her crudities and finally disgrace her.

At the reception Catherine puts on a wonderful act of ladylike behavior but eventually she no longer is willing to repress her anger at their taunts, and she turns on her tormentors and denounces them, reminding them that they are Revolutionary-made nobodies, no better than she.

This display of outrageousness results in a summons from Napoleon, and when she arrives for her audience with him, Catherine brings along the unpaid laundry bills and waves them in his face. She reminds him that she was once in love with him but that he spurned her attentions, then she flirts with him anew. Napoleon reaches into his pockets to pay her for the long overdue bills, but discovers that as Emperor, he has no money on his person.

While Catherine is with Napoleon, word comes that Neipperg has been seen in the Empress' bedroom. Catherine restrains the Emperor from per-sonally killing Neipperg at that moment, but he orders Neipperg to be shot. Catherine declares the Empress innocent and arranges for a letter to fall into Napoleon's hands which contains a message from the Empress to her father,

Emperor of Austria, begging him to recall Neipperg, declaring her undying love for Napoleon. The letter of course is a fraudulent one composed by Catherine herself in an effort to spare Neipperg's life.

Napoleon believes the ruse and rewards Catherine by permitting her to remain married to Lefebre. Back at her own home with her husband, Catherine exclaims, "Let's go to bed; I feel as though I've done a hard day's wash."

The film boasts numerous on-location sets, from the Salle Henri II at Fontainbleau for Catherine's presentation to Napoleon, to Louis XV's game room, and to Napoleon's library a Compiegne with his personally bound books and quill pen.

The film was well received by critics with a few remarking that Swanson slightly overacted in her attempt at gauchery, and one writer remarked that "her linen frocks (were) cut so low one would think that saucy Catherine was impervious to colds."

The film opened in New York at the Rivoli Theater on April 17, 1925, with an original score written and conducted by Hugo Reisenfeld. Swanson attended with her Marquis and was greeted by literally thousands of fans blocking the streets. It broke house attendance records, and the scene was repeated when she attended the Hollywood premiere at Grauman's Chinese Theater. For its general release in the United States, Paramount cut out thirty minutes of the historical scenes to the dismay of both Swanson and the French government. The reason they gave for the cuts was to enable five complete showings a day instead of only four. The French officials made Paramount promise that in France the complete ten-reel version be shown and Paramount complied.

Ronald Bowers

MADAME X

Released: 1920
Production: Goldwyn Pictures Corporation
Direction: Frank Lloyd
Screenplay: J. E. Nash and Frank Lloyd; based on the play of the same name
  by Alexandre Bisson
Cinematography: Dev Jennings
Art direction: Cedric Gibbons
Length: 7 reels

Principal characters:
Jacqueline Floriot	Pauline Frederick
Louis Floriot	William Courtleigh
Raymond Floriot	Casson Ferguson
Dr. Chesnel	Hardee Kirkland
Cesaire Noel	Albert Roscoe
M. Robert Parissard	Lionel Belmore
M. Merival	Willard Louis
Victor	Cesare Gravina
Marie	Maude George

From 1915 to 1919, Pauline Frederick had an illustrious career at Parmount
as a dramatic actress. When her option came up, studio head Adolph Zukor
wanted her to sign again with him. Frederick, however, had taken as her third
husband Willard Mack, who was in charge of the scenario department at
Goldwyn Pictures, and he persuaded her to leave Zukor and sign with Samuel
Goldwyn, where she would have her own company, the Frederick Feature
Film Company. Frederick, very much in love with Mack, did as he advised,
and thereupon made ten feature films for Goldwyn release, all of them
mediocre except for the next to the last, *Madame X*. Her performance as
Jacqueline Floriot, the much-abused heroine whose life climaxes in a stirring
courtroom drama, was the finest she ever gave, and, therefore, Goldwyn can
be forgiven for consistently misusing her great talents as an actress.

Madame X is a perfect example of the well-made play, best done by the
French, in which every scene follows another in perfect pattern. This type of
French play is built upon one attention-riveting situation, and the central
character is usually a misunderstood woman who runs the gamut of emotions.
Madame X was a great success in France and then was neglected until a very
good actress/writer, Dorothy Donnelly, rediscovered it. She made her own
translation and played the title role herself; it became a hit with American
audiences. She also made a successful film of the play for Pathé Exchange
(1916), with a very young and handsome John Bowers playing Raymond, the
son. French stage star Sarah Bernhardt had also included it in her American

tour repertory, with Lou Tellegen playing her son. Frederick filmed it in 1920, and this film is far better than any subsequent talking version, of which there have been several. She had made a worldwide tour with the play, and audiences in Australia and England loved her performance; it almost had a presold audience by the time talkies came in. Ruth Chatterton made the first talking version in 1929, but it was mannered and not believable. A better screen version was offered in 1937, with Gladys George giving a superb interpretation, and in 1965, Ross Hunter produced a very popular version with Lana Turner giving a surprisingly effective performance. It is the Goldwyn production, however, starring Frederick that remains the definitive version, for Frederick was always a charismatic star, and even in the film's most melodramatic moments, she held the audience firmly in her power. She knew every trick of the theater, and she also knew how to translate emotion to the screen so that it was always believable.

In the film, Jacqueline Floriot (Pauline Frederick) is a much-envied woman in Parisian society. She has a husband named Louis (William Courtleigh) who jealously adores her, and she has a little son whom she adores. Her husband is a very busy and very proper man, and Jacqueline frequently finds herself alone and bored. She unfortunately becomes attracted to a young man of the world, and when her husband finds that she is having an affair, he cruelly determines to cut her out of his life. Her personal possessions are packed, and she is given the assurance that a certain sum will be regularly banked in her name, but she must leave her husband's home, and never return to Paris. Finally, she is told that she must make no attempt ever to see her little boy, who, in time, will be told that his mother is dead.

Trapped and despondent, Jacqueline is forced into a solitary existence. She begins to seek romance in other countries, and unfortunately she finds it with a man who is no good. Driven to further depths of lonely despair, she seeks solace in absinthe and dreams, abandoning her old lover and going to a new country and a new love. Eventually, she meets an operator who remains with her because he suspects that something in her past will mean money to him. He engages detectives and eventually finds that her name is Jacqueline Floriot, that her husband is still alive in Paris, and that she is the mother of a son, Raymond (Casson Ferguson), now grown and on the threshold of what is a promising legal career.

They return to France, and Jacqueline is disturbed at first, because she left her native country twenty years earlier and was paid never to return. Very soon she finds that she has just cause to have qualms about being in Paris, because she learns that her detestable lover intends to blackmail her husband. She is frantic, and, driven to put a stop to his plans, she takes the pistol she carries, planning to use it on herself some day, and shoots him dead.

Jacqueline makes no resistance when the police come to arrest her. She will not give her name, nor will she in any way defend herself. She is known only as Madame X. She is assigned a lawyer who will defend her, and her attorney is Raymond Floriot, her son. He finds her curiously sympathetic, but she is apathetic about him, not knowing who he is, just as he does not know who she is.

The case of Madame X is opened, and Raymond's defense of the woman who has been driven to murder is brilliant, but suddenly Jacqueline recognizes William Floriot in the courtroom, and when she realizes that it is her own son who has so eloquently defended her, she breaks down and in utter collapse, protests. A doctor is called, but she is dying. When she pleads with her eyes for her husband to maintain his silence about her, he, stunned, can only do so. Madame X kisses the son whom she cannot acknowledge and dies in his arms.

Jacqueline Floriot is the kind of role that any actress might covet. Frederick underplays it beautifully, and her performance is a credit to her skill as a fine actress, one of the best the screen has ever known. Frederick came to films in 1915, starring for Zukor first in Hall Caine's *The Eternal City*, with many of the exteriors shot in Rome. *Madame X*, however, remained her finest screen achievement. She alternated films with stage appearances, because all audiences adored her. She returned to films on occasion: for Ernst Lubitsch in *Three Women* and for Clarence Brown in *Smouldering Fires*, both in 1924. Her first talking film, *On Trial*, was made in 1928, and her last, *Thank You Mr. Moto*, in 1937. In 1938, at the age of fifty-five, she died in Los Angeles, falling a victim to asthma, a disease which had plagued her for many years.

DeWitt Bodeen

MALE AND FEMALE

Released: 1919
Production: Cecil B. De Mille for Famous Players-Lasky/Paramount
Direction: Cecil B. De Mille
Screenplay: Jeanie Macpherson; based on the play *The Admirable Crichton*
   by James M. Barrie
Cinematography: Alvin Wyckoff
Editing: Anne Bauchens
Art direction: Wilfred Buckland
Length: 9 reels

Principal characters:
Lady Mary Lasenby	Gloria Swanson
William Crichton, the butler	Thomas Meighan
Tweeney	Lila Lee
Lord Loam	Theodore Roberts
Honorable Ernest Wooley	Raymond Hatton
Lady Agatha Lasenby	Mildred Reardon
The King's Favorite	Bebe Daniels

In his excellent book, *The Rise of the American Film* (1939), Lewis Jacobs pointed out that the post-World War I year of 1919 saw the release of two motion pictures which heralded a new hard-edged materialism and which "openly acknowledged sex." The two films were *The Miracle Man*, a Paramount production directed by George Loane Tucker, and *Male and Female*, the Cecil B. De Mille/Paramount production of Sir James M. Barrie's successful play, *The Admirable Crichton*. Quite by accident both films starred Thomas Meighan.

The Miracle Man, which was based on a play by George M. Cohan from a story by Frank L. Packard, cast Meighan as a petty thief who cons a blind faith healer and exploits both the healer and the faithful public for money. Despite its regenerative ending, the film presents a new world of racketeers in which principles are forsaken for material ends. Barrie's play presents the English caste system and its sexual morality, neither of which reflects or allows human equality, except possibly in moments of emergency. As Jacobs explained, the cynical philosophies presented by both of these films and the new freedom they proselytized would drastically change filmmaking, and they did.

Most film historians regard De Mille with disdain, depicting him as a showman, self-promoter, and producer of Biblical spectaculars which emphasize sex and sadism over authenticity. These allegations are well-founded when one looks at De Mille's overall output, but closer evaluation, particularly of his presound films, reveals that he was also a creative and inventive director who was able to spot trends in advance and anticipate the desires of the motion-picture public.

The writings of Scottish playwright James M. Barrie (1869-1937) have provided theater and film audiences with many happy hours of entertainment. Among his chief works are *The Little Minister, Quality Street, What Every Woman Knows, Dear Brutus*, and the timeless classic *Peter Pan. The Admirable Crichton* was the iconoclastic Barrie's satiric criticism of the unbearably stuffy English social caste system and proved a popular stage vehicle for many years, including a 1903 Broadway production starring the eminent William Gillette.

De Mille was always searching for popular works to film and requested that his partner Jesse Lasky negotiate with Barrie for the screen rights to this play. Lasky succeeded, but in the ensuing correspondence between Lasky in New York and De Mille in California, the title of the play invariably ended up being "The Admiral Crichton" with everyone mispronouncing "Crichton." The "take charge" De Mille modestly took it upon himself to change the title to *Male and Female*. Barrie's approval was, however, necessary, and when they cabled him for permission, Barrie's reply was, "Capital. Why didn't I think of it myself?"

The film tells of Lord Loam (Theodore Roberts) who holds monthly teas at his fashionable turn-of-the-century Marfair mansion, based on the democratic principle. At these teas, according to a Victorian custom, the servants are served by the Loam family, much to the embarrassment of all concerned. William Crichton (Thomas Meighan), the butler, is a conservative figure who believes that class distinction should be maintained and that only with a return to the primitive state would society possibly be able to determine who would be master and who would be servant.

Lord Loam and some of his friends, including Lady Mary Lasenby (Gloria Swanson), embark on a yachting expedition to the South Seas, where they are shipwrecked. Their very survival depends on the strategy of those who are accustomed to work, and it becomes evident that Crichton is the natural one to assume command of the situation. Not only his ability to cook but also his facility for organization make it clear that he will be the group's leader, and in doing so, he wins the love of Lady Mary. To this tale, De Mille also inserted an elaborate scene in Babylonia in which Crichton is King and Lady Mary plays a young Christian slave who must accept the King's advances or be thrown to the lions. (Bebe Daniels plays the part of the King's Favorite in this segment.)

Once the shipwrecked party is rescued and returned to England, the social structure of their relationships reverts to it original form: Lady Mary will marry one of her own class, and Crichton marries Tweeney (Lila Lee), the scullery maid.

De Mille had planned to cast Elliott Dexter, an actor he had used in his films many times before, as Crichton, but when Dexter became seriously ill, De Mille, who had been impressed with Meighan's work in *The Miracle Man*, hired him instead. Meighan proved an excellent choice.

The shipwreck scene was filmed on Santa Cruz Island. Here, the ship's steering wheel becomes a chandelier, shells are used for dishes, and animal skins are used as carpets. In one scene, Crichton kills a leopard with a bow and arrow and brings it back to camp for food. De Mille did not like the look of a stuffed leopard so he used a real one which he had chloroformed. During the scene, there were numerous delays and finally a nervous, cursing Meighan pleaded with De Mille to complete the scene as the leopard was coming back to life.

In the Babylonia scene, Gloria Swanson appears in a tableau entitled "The Lion's Bride" and here also a real animal was used. Swanson is bedecked in headdress, pearls, and little else; the scene shows the lion's paw on the bare shoulder of the prostrate actress. This, along with the famous bathtub scene, again with Swanson apparently nude, are two of the most famous in the De Mille filmography.

One of the most striking aspects of *Male and Female* is the costuming. For the Babylonian flashback (a sequence entitled "When I Was a King of Babylon and You Were a Christian Slave), De Mille hired an inexperienced designer named Mitchell Leisen to execute the gowns. His natural flamboyance made up for what he lacked in experience, and his costumes were exceptional. Leisen went on to do costumes and art direction for De Mille in *The King of Kings* (1927), *Madam Satan* (1930), and *The Sign of the Cross* (1931). He later became a successful director himself with *Midnight* (1939), *Hold Back the Dawn* (1941), and *To Each His Own* (1946). When asked once what it was like working for De Mille, Leisen said he adored it, and that one simply had to think in capital letters like De Mille did himself: "Everything was in neon lights, six feet tall: LUST, REVENGE, SEX."

Male and Female was an opulent, witty, daring, and hugely successful film. It cost $170,000 to make and earned $1,250,000. It was the premiere attraction of the newly built Sid Grauman's Million Dollar Theater in Los Angeles.

Swanson exuded a new kind of womanly sex appeal more subtle and feminine than the vamping of Theda Bara, and De Mille would capitalize on this new-fashioned ingredient in a succession of popular "domestic" comedies. De Mille was always on the lookout for what the motion-picture public wanted, and when his screenwriter, Jeanie Macpherson, promulgated the universality of *feminine* and independent sex appeal, De Mille accepted and developed the idea.

A number of reviewers criticized *Male and Female* for being more De Mille than Barrie, and this would be a criticism constantly hurled at De Mille throughout his career, as he freely changed stories as he saw fit. The best assessment of the film was written for *Photoplay* (December, 1919) by Julian

Johnson who called it "A truly gorgeous panorama. . . . It is a typical DeMille production—audacious, glittering, intriguing, superlatively elegant, and quite without heart."

Ronald Bowers

MAN WITH A MOVIE CAMERA
(CHELOVIEKS KINOPARATOM)

Released: 1929
Production: VUFKU (Ukraine)
Direction: Dziga Vertov
Screenplay: semi-documentary
Cinematography: Mikhail Kaufman
Editing: Dziga Vertov and Yelizaveta Svilova
Length: 7 reels/6,004 feet

As though to prove that "art" is universal and that the Soviet cinema, for all its revolutionary political aspirations, could not escape this fact, Western film societies and devotees of "art" cinema have, since the early 1930's, latched onto certain masterpieces of the Russian silent cinema, most notably Sergei Eisenstein's *Potemkin* (1925) and Alexander Dovzhenko's *Earth* (1930). Because the films of Dziga Vertov (1896-1954) resolutely refuse to accord with this notion of a universal cinema, they have never, on the other hand, been a mainstay of art cinema programs and tend to be seen, at best, as interesting but limited experiments in documentary—a genre which Western cinema has relegated to the status of program filler or worse.

During the short period of formal and political revolution in film, particularly European film, in the late 1960's and early 1970's, Vertov's name became a banner. To stress his own position in the debate, French director Jean-Luc Godard for a time submerged his identity into the ideologically purer "Dziga-Vertov Group": his aim was to follow the lead given by the Russian pioneer and to move cinema in a more truly revolutionary direction. He failed as Vertov, under different circumstances, had failed. *Man with a Movie Camera* survives, however, as a fascinating indication of what the history of the Soviet cinema might have been and as a film of major importance in its own right.

Vertov, whose real name was Denis Kaufman, was born in Poland. During the Russian Civil War, he was in charge of the new science of photography and, in 1918, became Head of the Cinema Department of the All-Russia Central Executive. It was a key position for a twenty-two-year-old, since Lenin had declared that the cinema was the most important of all the arts, being the one most capable of educating the working people of Russia. Vertov devoted ten years of his life to this task, before falling afoul of the Stalinist line on socialist realism. The way in which he believed the task was to be fulfilled was through a certain kind of documentary—a documentary which would show people their own lives and the truths contained therein.

Vertov was a staunch opponent of what he called the "cine-nicotine" of the Western film industry (then making serious inroads into Russian taste) and believed that for his Kino-Glas (Cinema-Eye) movement, the obligation was to make use of "All cinematographic means. All cinematographic images.

All processes capable of revealing and showing the truth." Western narrative cinema was, he argued, founded on the idea of enchantment, of putting the audience in a position where all they could do was admire the behavior of larger-than-life figures and become involved in the artificial problems of these figures' love lives. What was needed, he wrote in 1924, was a kind of cinema that would enable people to look at their own lives, not those of others. Only then could the cinema be useful, only then would it help the people to make crucial choices. "The conscious alone can fight against magical suggestions of every kind," he felt. Far from being conceived as propaganda, Vertov's Kino-Glas and his subsequent series of Kino-Pravda (Cinema-Truth) documentaries were designed to counteract the insidious propaganda of entertainment cinema.

Man with a Movie Camera had its premiere in Kiev on January 8, 1929, and was shown shortly afterward to great effect in the nation's capital; it is one of very few Vertov films to have survived (or at any rate to be readily available in the West) and certainly the only feature-length one. At first sight, it has similarities with two other well-known documentaries of the period, Alberto Cavalcanti's *Rien que des heures* (1926) and Walter Ruttman's *Berlin, Symphonie of a Great City* (1927), both of which observe, as does Vertov's film, the changing faces and rhythms of a city between dawn and darkness. Both Cavalcanti's and Ruttman's films, however, use their material to create art films for which the two cities—Paris and Berlin—do little more than provide the excuse. Vertov does more: he records; he shows "what the eye does not see;" and he manages, through his selection and his rhythmic editing, to engage the audience in some of the meanings of life in the city (probably Odessa, although it is not formally identified). He also makes his audience reflect on the way in which the images have been recorded, to reflect on cinema itself.

Man with a Movie Camera obliges viewers to keep in mind throughout, that this film is not only a series of pictures of a city, but is also a *film*, shot by the cinematographer of the title, processed and edited by a technician, and projected in a motion-picture theater. Shots of the filmmaking process alternate with shots which are the product of that process. The film opens with images of a theater being readied for a show: the projector is loaded, the people come in, and the orchestra tunes up. Then, the "film" begins: the city wakes. Business and industry start working, a man asleep on a park bench stirs, and the cinematographer goes out to work. He films an express train but, rather disconcertingly, these shots are intercut with images of a young woman waking, dressing, and washing. Various images of work follow: a garment factory, a heavy industrial plant, and a shop opening.

As the film continues, shots of the cinematographer moving his equipment around, setting it up, filming scenes of everyday life, and shots of the editress assembling his material alternate with shots of "life": a childbirth, a street accident, and the faces of ordinary people. As the workday ends, the camera moves on to sport and leisure activities; and then, as night falls, to restaurants, cafés, beer halls, and even to a tramp's unmistakable feet moving across the bottom half of a cinema screen. As the film draws to a close, the rhythm becomes more frenzied and the possibilities of cinema as an autonomous art—not merely the servant of literature and theater—are explored: superimpositions turn the life of the city into a kaleidoscope of movement and tilted buildings, and a gigantic cinematographer appears behind his tripod towering above the homecoming crowds. Finally, the "film within the film" is over. The cinema drapes close, the camera takes a solo bow on its tripod, and, in a last superimposition, a lens aperture and a human eye blink several times and finally close.

Man with a Movie Camera is an impossible film to summarize, since its impact depends so heavily on the framings of the cinematographer (Vertov's brother Mikhail Kaufman) and, above all, on the rhythms and juxtapositions of the editing done by Vertov himself and Yelizaveta Svilova. The film foregrounds its own methods, never allowing viewers (as traditional filmmaking does) to forget that these are selected images—not the only images possible—and that they have been chosen to say something. The shots of film stock, of an editing table, and a splicing deck make sure the audience does not lose sight of this fact, as does the repeated use of such devices as stop frames, slow motion, and pixilation. The images that are chosen, however, do more than merely record life, they invite viewers to think about its meaning, whether it be on the relatively simple level of movement (the camera observes an elevator go up, then itself goes up in the elevator, contrasting different movements within the same action) or form (the investigation of such visually similar but functionally different line patterns as those of a tramway and those of shadows in a doorway); or whether it be in connection with other, more profound similarities of behavior that social convention often makes one overlook. The intercutting between the young woman getting up and the express train rushing toward the camera has an undoubted erotic charge that is only suggested by the film but must be thought through by the viewer. The cutaways from a fashionable lady putting on makeup and a woman on the beach daubing herself with mud require a similar mental contribution on the part of the spectator. *Man with a Movie Camera* calls, above all, for a different relationship between viewer and screen, one that is not simply passive, but requires a conscious engagement with the images. It is a difficult film in the sense that one has to do more than simply watch it, but it repays that effort and hints at—although perhaps in the end it does not really achieve—a new kind of cinema.

Nick Roddick

MAN, WOMAN, AND SIN

Released: 1927
Production: Metro-Goldwyn-Mayer
Direction: Monta Bell
Screenplay: Alice D. G. Miller; based on an original screen story by Monta
  Bell
Titles: John Colton
Cinematography: Percy Hilburn
Length: 7 reels/6,280 feet

> *Principal characters:*
> Albert Whitcomb .... John Gilbert
> Vera Worth .... Jeanne Eagels
> Mrs. Whitcomb .... Gladys Brockwell
> Bancroft .... Marc MacDermott
> Albert Whitcomb, as a child .... Philip Anderson
> The Star reporter .... Hayden Stevenson
> The city editor .... Charles K. French

Like James Dean, Jeanne Eagels was another talented but self-destructive star whose screen appearances were few. She acted in only three films of any consequence before dying of a heroin overdose in 1929 at age thirty-five.

Eagels did appear in several films a decade before her greatest cinematic fame, including *The World and the Woman* (1916), *Fires of Youth* (1917), and *Under False Colors* (1917), but after making these films, she decided to concentrate solely on a career in the theater. Her greatest success was as Sadie Thompson in *Rain* based on W. Somerset Maugham's novel, a role she first played in 1922. Eagels returned to the screen in the seductively entitled *Man, Woman, and Sin* in 1927. Her co-star was John Gilbert, fresh from his successes opposite Greta Garbo in *Flesh and the Devil* and *Love*, both released earlier that year; in fact, the New York opening of *Man, Woman, and Sin* at the Capitol Theater was postponed because of the premiere of *Love*.

Man, Woman, and Sin is set in Washington. In the film, Albert Whitcomb (John Gilbert), a young man who grew up in the slums, has worked since he was a little boy to help support his mother (Gladys Brockwell), who ekes out a living by sewing ironing pads. He begins a career in journalism by folding newspapers, and later works in the pressroom of an important daily. Eventually, with the help of a friendly editor, Al is promoted to cub reporter. For one assignment, Al is asked to accompany Vera Worth (Jeanne Eagels), the paper's haughty society editor, to an embassy ball. He rents a dress suit and silk hat for the occasion, and afterwards, he writes about his experiences, describing Vera as the most beautiful woman at the party.

Al and Vera begin dating, and the reporter falls in love with his colleague.

Vera, a vamp, enjoys gifts of jewelry, so Al raids the cookie jar and spends his mother's modest savings on a bracelet which he presents to the proud society editor. She seems to care for Al, but she has neglected to tell him that she is the mistress of the paper's owner, Bancroft (Marc MacDermott). He could not escort her to the ball as, after all, he is a husband and father.

When Bancroft surprises Al and Vera in the lavish apartment he maintains for her, Vera realizes that she is unwilling to break off with the publisher—and give up her luxurious life-style. Al becomes angered when Vera calls him a fool. He argues with Bancroft, and they have a brief fight during which the publisher is killed when Al accidentally strikes him with a bronze statuette. The bewildered Al is arrested and tried for Bancroft's murder. Vera lies on the witness stand about the events leading up to the tragedy, deciding to perjure herself to maintain her reputation. As a result, Al is condemned to death.

Before Al's execution, however, Vera's love for him finally causes her to recant her testimony and tell the truth. Al is freed and is reunited with his mother outside the prison. Both are dazed by the events and converse as if Bancroft's death, the trial, and its outcome are all a bad dream. Meanwhile, Vera watches the pair from the back seat of her limousine.

Man, Woman, and Sin is a newspaper story more in line with *The Front Page* (filmed with this title in 1931 and 1974, and as *His Girl Friday* in 1940) and the dozens of other Hollywood mysteries and melodramas with big city dailies as settings and intrepid reporters as heroes than with *All the President's Men* (1976) and *Absence of Malice* (1981), which address the issue of the power and responsibility of journalists. Also, a cub reporter would never be assigned to accompany a society editor to an embassy ball, let alone attend the festivities in any official capacity. Actual newspaper work is incidental to the story. The ambience of a newspaper office, however, with its constant deadlines, paper-littered floors, and copy boys scampering about with proofs, is authentic and convincing. While Al Whitcomb's fate is as unbelievable as *Superman*'s Jimmy Olson winning a Pulitzer Prize, *Man, Woman, and Sin* is still effectively dramatic and above-average entertainment.

The film received conflicting reviews. Some critics hailed it, others abhorred it, and some took a middle ground. Most, though, were on the positive side; if the melodramatic aspects of the plot were criticized, the performances, direction, and particularly the atmosphere were praised. Although a bit old to be cast as an eighteen-year-old cub reporter, John Gilbert—age thirty-two when the film was released—gives an impressively restrained performance. *Man, Woman, and Sin* was made at the height of his career, and some reviewers thought that his acting was the best he had done.

Gilbert is today perhaps best remembered for his onscreen and offscreen relationships with Greta Garbo—they appeared together in *Flesh and the Devil, Love, A Woman of Affairs* (1928), and *Queen Christina* (1933)—and his starring performance in King Vidor's World War I spectacle, *The Big Parade* (1925). One of the great romantic stars of the 1920's—after Rudolph Valentino died in 1926, he went virtually unchallenged as the top screen lover—Gilbert was a versatile actor who also appeared in a large number of other Metro-Goldwyn-Mayer features, among them *He Who Gets Slapped* (1924), *The Merry Widow* (1925), *La Bohème* (1926), *Bardelys the Magnificent* (1926), and *The Cossacks* (1928). His role in *Man, Woman, and Sin* is unlike any he had previously undertaken. Contrary to the legend that his high-pitched voice prevented the actor from successfully crossing into talkies, Gilbert did appear in ten sound films. His career decline was attributable more to the fact that the "lover" roles for which he was most noted were out of vogue. Gilbert virtually drank himself to death, dying in 1936 as the result of a heart attack.

Man, Woman and Sin's director, Monta Bell, was also involved with Garbo, but only on a professional level: he directed her in her Hollywood debut, *The Torrent* (1926). Appropriately, he began his career as a newspaperman, eventually becoming an editor at the *Washington Herald*. His knowledge of journalism and the Washington social scene aided him immeasurably in his story for and staging of *Man, Woman, and Sin*, especially since part of the film was shot on location. Bell had previously acted in Charles Chaplin's *The Pilgrim* (1922) and edited *A Woman of Paris* (1923) for him. In 1929, he was named head of production at Paramount's Astoria Studios, New York, where he occasionally directed but mostly produced and wrote screenplays.

Most critics lauded Eagel's natural, unaffected performance in *Man, Woman, and Sin*, which was erroneously billed as her screen debut; a few, however, felt that she was merely a pretty face, with little screen presence and much to learn as a film actress. She appeared in only two more films: *Jealousy* (1929), directed by Jean de Limur; and a version of *The Letter* (1929), also made by Limur, and supervised by Bell; for *The Letter*, she received a Best Actress Academy Award nomination. This was her last performance. Twenty-eight years after her death, however, she was portrayed by Kim Novak in an undistinguished Hollywood biography.

Rob Edelman

MANHANDLED

Released: 1924
Production: Allan Dwan for Famous Players-Lasky/Paramount
Direction: Allan Dwan
Screenplay: Frank Tuttle; based on the story of the same name by Arthur Stringer
Cinematography: Harold Rosson
Editing: William LeBaron and Julian Johnson
Length: 7 reels/6,998 feet

Principal characters:
Tessie McGuire	Gloria Swanson
Jimmy Hogan	Tom Moore
Pinkie Moran	Lilyan Tashman
Robert Brandt	Ian Keith
Chip Thorndyke	Arthur Housman
Paul Garretson	Paul McAllister
Arno Riccardi	Frank Morgan
Bippo	M. Collose

When *Manhandled* was reviewed in 1924, critics all complimented Gloria Swanson on her remarkable comedic performance and one critic stated that this film pushed Swanson to the top of the small group of expert screen comediennes—small, he said, because there were only two others—and he diplomatically refrained from mentioning any names.

Swanson's portrayal of Tessie McGuire, the Cinderella shopgirl in *Manhandled*, surprised many who had simply regarded her as a glamour queen, for in this lively little romp, charmingly reminiscent of an O. Henry short story with its real-life characters and situations and its natural, unfilmlike pathos, Swanson emerged a delightful comedienne, displaying abilities at both light-hearted slapstick and mimicry.

Manhandled was the third of eight films Swanson made with director Allan Dwan and all were made in New York at Paramount's Astoria Studios on Long Island: *Zaza* (1923), *A Society Scandal* (1924), *Her Love Story* (1924), *Wages of Virtue* (1925), *The Coast of Folly* (1925), *Stage Struck* (1925), and *What a Widow!* (1930).

The original idea for *Manhandled* came from Sidney R. Kent, general sales manager of Famous Players-Lasky/Paramount, who had Arthur Stringer write the story which appeared in the *Saturday Evening Post* before Frank Tuttle adapted the screenplay. As with all Dwan's films, the script was but a basis from which he worked, for he always allowed his actors to improvise material which accounted for a great deal of the naturalism in his pictures.

Dwan opens the film with an impressive 360-degree shot of the panoramic

New York City skyline which sets the scene for his Cinderella tale of feisty little Tessie McGuire (Gloria Swanson).

Tessie is an inveterate gum chewer who lives in a boardinghouse in Brooklyn and works as a salesgirl in the bargain basement of Thorndyke's department store. Tessie's boyfriend is Jimmy Hogan (Tom Moore), a taxicab driver-mechanic who has an automobile invention up his sleeve, and who lives in the same boardinghouse as Tessie.

Dwan shows the social milieu of working-class New Yorkers with great humor and lack of pretense. The two most famous scenes are funny and appealing and just the kind of scenes that could be rehearsed only so far, then had to rely on the spontaneity of the cast. One scene shows Tessie behind her counter at Thorndyke's on the day of a bargain sale. In her frantic efforts to attend to each customer, Tessie finds herself literally backed against the wall and fighting for her life as the heaving crowd of women shoppers grows larger and more demanding.

The second scene is one of the finest in film comedy. Viewers watch Tessie, who stands almost five feet tall, struggle to get through the subway turnstile, then into the crowded train car in the middle of rush hour. Tessie, with her unfashionable working-girl clothes and a felt hat with a cluster of grapes over the left ear, struggles to find an empty space in the car; she finds herself pushed, shoved, elbowed; she drops her handbag, cannot keep her hat on her head, and almost hangs herself when she finds her chin in battle with the arm of a tall strap-hanger.

For these scenes, Dwan had Swanson do the real thing before shooting them. He arranged for her to work in Gimbels disguised in a blond wig and took her into the subway, pushed her into the crowd and left her to fend for herself. Swanson recalls that it was the first and last time she ever rode a subway.

Tessie has aspirations for a better life, and one evening when Johnny is too busy with his invention to take her to the cinema—a shopgirl's world of fantasy—she gets angry and goes off to a party with fellow salesgirl Pinkie Moran (Lilyan Tashman). At the party, Tessie embarrasses herself by tripping over a rug, gets up looking disheveled, and trying to make it all look like an act, she grabs a bowler and a cane and does an impersonation of Charlie Chaplin's Little Tramp. The party-goers applaud her antics, and she goes on to impersonate Beatrice Lillie impersonating a Russian countess. She ends up being the life of the party and the center of attention of all the men, especially Chip Thorndyke (Arthur Housman), the novelist son of the store owner; Robert Brandt (Ian Keith), a sculptor; and Arno Riccardi (Frank Morgan), the owner of a Fifth Avenue dress salon.

Tessie inspires the novelist, but he wants to compromise her; then she quits her job and goes to work as a model for the sculptor, who also want to compromise her. She dons a turban which makes her look like Nazimova and adds her Beatrice Lillie Russian-countess accent and goes to work in the dress shop, where she encounters yet another compromising situation. Tessie's new way of life makes Johnny jealous, and at one point, he burns his finger with a match and warns her that those who play with fire get burned.

Finally, Tessie tires of the specious party crowd and returns home to find that Johnny is sorry for being jealous of her trying to better herself and they reconcile, after which he tells her he has sold his invention and is now a millionaire. Cinderella comes full circle.

Swanson's clever mimicry of Chaplin and Lillie was another example of Dwan letting his actors "go." At the party scene, Dwan told his actors to whoop it up as if they were at a real party, and Swanson says she simply grabbed a hat and cane and did her impersonation of the Little Tramp. Dwan liked it so much he kept it in. Twenty-six years later she would successfully repeat the imitation in the stunning *Sunset Boulevard* (1950).

Manhandled opened at the Rivoli Theater in New York City on July 28, 1924, and grossed $29,771 during its first week. Critics praised Swanson's newfound comedic abilities and her versatility, and they lauded Dwan for his flair for the natural. He was able to contrast the New York tenement life with that of high society with verve and flair. The picture's "message" was not lost amidst all this frivolity. Critics said the film was daring in its realistic presentation of what dirty dogs men are in a big city and what a tough time a girl has in trying to get along without "paying, paying, paying."

Simultaneously with the premiere of *Manhandled*, the New York *Bulletin* ran the story in a cartoon series format, with the story by Stringer and caricatures of the stars by John Decker. It was entitled: *Manhandled: A Movie Serial Featuring Gloria Swanson*.

This film was a popular and pivotal one in Swanson's career for it offered her public a new image, something she insisted upon during this phase of her career and something she was powerful enough to demand. She had debuted at Essanay in 1915 in Chicago and gone on to appear in Mack Sennett's slapstick comedies. Then with her six pictures in association with Cecil B. De Mille beginning in 1919, she became world famous as a sophisticated glamour queen. She knew the importance of change, and her comedies with Dwan were a calculated risk which paid off. She did not stop changing but went on to fine dramatic performances such as *Sadie Thompson* (1928).

The reasons for her self-imposed "retirement" in 1934 are not quite clear, although Dwan maintained it was partly because she allowed herself to be surrounded by sycophants. She made the comeback of all comebacks by portraying the deluded Norma Desmond in *Sunset Boulevard* and today her name remains synonymous with that of the Hollywood Film Star.

Ronald Bowers

MANSLAUGHTER

Released: 1922
Production: Cecil B. De Mille for Famous Players-Lasky; released by Paramount
Direction: Cecil B. De Mille
Screenplay: Jeanie Macpherson; based on the novel by Alice Duer Miller
Cinematography: Alvin Wyckoff and L. Guy Wilky
Editing: Anne Bauchens
Set decoration: Paul Iribe
Length: 10 reels/9,061 feet

> *Principal characters:*
> Daniel O'Bannon .... Thomas Meighan
> Lydia Thorne .... Leatrice Joy
> Evans, her maid ....Lois Wilson
> Governor Stephen Albee .... John Miltern
> Judge Homans .... George Fawcett
> Mrs. Drummond ....Julia Faye

Among the themes which Cecil B. De Mille's silent films encompassed was the idea of there being one set of laws for the rich and another for the poor. He had explored this theme brilliantly in *Male and Female* (1919), the film version of Sir James M. Barrie's play *The Admirable Crichton*, which expressed the view that the caste system in English society was permanently established and unbreakable except in times of extreme emergency, and then would automatically and absolutely revert to its former guise after the emergency.

Male and Female dealt with the world of master and servant, and De Mille pursued that theme once again in *Saturday Night* (1922). In that film, a debutante is engaged to a young man of her own social position but falls in love with her chauffeur and marries him. Concurrently, her fiancé falls for the daughter of his family's laundress and marries her. Both marriages fail, end in divorce, and in the last reel, the four young people are rematched with the partners from their own social backgrounds, thus showing that the rules of life are established and cannot be transgressed.

It is a cynical point of view but one over which revolutions have been fought, and De Mille, whom many called an absolute cynic, knew this theme was one to which the filmgoing public would respond. It was his ability to discover the lowest common denominator of public taste, and if his detractors made fun of his lack of artistic merit, De Mille simply went ahead and made his pictures "for the people."

In his book, *The Parade's Gone By*, Kevin Brownlow quotes veteran journalist/screenwriter Adela Rogers St. Johns as describing De Mille as "one hundred per cent cynical. . . . There wasn't a moment when he wasn't acting. He was so good a ham he could sell anything." This combination of ham, cynic, and showman had earned De Mille his reputation as a director who was sure-fire at the box office. His remarkable directorial talents as displayed in *The Cheat* (1915) and *Male and Female* among others, additionally made him a force with which to be reckoned. As the 1920's progressed, however, and the overall result of his films continued to present his notorious combination of sex, sadism, and moralizing, he began to decline as a viable director.

Manslaughter, neither as good as some think nor as deplorable as his detractors would have one believe, was the film which best marks the end of the innovative period in De Mille's career. It reveals some of his best and worst traits as a filmmaker and presages his decline into simply a circus showman, king of the spectaculars.

The film is based on a novel by Alice Duer Miller which appeared in the *Saturday Evening Post*. De Mille read it and asked Jesse L. Lasky to buy it for him. It is the story of Lydia Thorne (Leatrice Joy), a rich society girl who is one of the jazz crazy, thrill-seeking pretty young things of the post-World War I era. While recklessly driving her roadster convertible a motorcycle cop tries to arrest her; she speeds up and races him only to have his cycle hit her automobile. The policeman's body flies into the air and lands across the hood of her car, killing him. The policeman had just been honored for saving the lives of some children, and when his wife arrives at the scene of the accident, she places the chevrons which he had just earned on his sleeve and salutes him. Lydia sobs in remorse at this touching scene which is the result of her carelessness.

Arrested and brought to trial, Lydia is prosecuted by Daniel O'Bannon (Thomas Meighan), the young district attorney to whom she is engaged. The upstanding O'Bannon adamantly preaches that there is too often one set of laws for the rich and another for the poor, and he believes that the only way for Lydia to find salvation is to serve a just sentence in prison.

In one scene, O'Bannon compares the reckless ways of today's youth with that of the kind of behavior which caused the fall of Rome and here, in typically excessive De Mille style, appears an all-out Roman orgy. With elaborate sets, near naked dancing girls, and gladiators, De Mille pulls out all the stops in giving his escape-seeking audience a taste of the pleasure-seeking ways of hedonism. In this flashback, Joy appears as the Roman empress who hosts the orgy and Meighan plays the chief of the Barbarians who sack Rome.

Continuing the story, once Lydia is convicted and sent to prison, the weight of his decision in having her convicted rests heavily on O'Bannon's mind, breaks his spirit, and drives him to drink.

In prison, Lydia discovers a side of life, a harshness and cruelty, she never knew existed. At first, in her typical spoiled manner, she is bitter, but finally she sees the errors of her ways and vows to reform. She discovers that another of her inmates is her former maid, Evans (Lois Wilson), who has been arrested and jailed for stealing Lydia's jewelry. Lydia has by now so changed from the rich, spoiled brat that she was, that she is able honestly and democratically to become friends with Evans. Lydia becomes a model prisoner and even accepts the degradation of having to scrub floors. When she is finally released from jail after serving a one-year sentence, Lydia and Evans open a soup kitchen, rehabilitate O'Bannon, and help him run for governor. True love overcomes even political ambitions, however, and O'Bannon abandons politics and marries Lydia

In preparation for the film, screenwriter Jeanie Macpherson decided she should experience prison life at first hand in order to create a sense of realism in those scenes. She arranged to go to Detroit where she knew that the Detroit House of Detention incarcerated petty criminals with killers. She arranged to be arrested for stealing a furpiece (from a friend) and, as planned, was caught and jailed along with hardened criminals. After three days of lice, horrible food, and watching female prisoners fight and/or have sex with each other, she arranged her release, and upon arriving back in California, tearfully fell into the arms of De Mille, saying she had never experienced anything so horrible. When the film was released, the prison scenes were praised for exactly the sense of reality for which Macpherson had striven. Both the acting of Leatrice Joy and Lois Wilson in these scenes, as well as the prison sets, which had been designed by Paul Iribe, earned words of tribute.

The film was billed as "A Drama of the Mad Age! Is the Modern World Racing to Ruin on a Wave of Jazz and Cocktails?"; and De Mille was in a way preaching against the fast-living habits of an immoral society. Some feel, however, that he was just cynical enough to add the preachment so he might have the artistic freedom, and the poetic license, to film his elaborate Roman orgy.

It is curious that 1922, the year after the film was released, was also the year that Will H. Hays became president of the Motion Picture Producers and Distributors Association of America and vowed to crack down on the immoral aspects of the motion-picture industry both on and off the screen. This followed the sensationalism of the notorious Fatty Arbuckle trial over the accused/rape murder of starlet Virginia Rappe. Certainly, De Mille regarded this act as an intrusion into the filmmaker's freedom of expression, so he, by necessity, had to envelope his sex, sadism, and titillation in the polite framework of morality, thus giving the cynic the last word.

Joy had appeared in the lesser De Mille opus, *Saturday Night*, and was now the star of *Manslaughter*. Beautiful and talented, she was then the wife of John Gilbert and had come to De Mille's attention through her Goldwyn films. He envisioned her as a replacement for Gloria Swanson in his films, for Swanson, with his consent, had gone on to better things. Joy appeared in two more De Mille vehicles: she was the young girl in the modern sequence of *The Ten Commandments* (1923) and an opera star in *Triumph* (1924).

While criticized for the spectacle excesses of the Roman orgy sequence, *Manslaughter* earned praise for its modern story and for the acting of both Joy and Wilson. The film cost $380,000 to make and, proving De Mille right once again, earned $1,200,000. *Manslaughter* was remade twice: once in 1930 with Fredric March and Claudette Colbert and again in 1936 under the title *And Sudden Death* starring Randolph Scott and Frances Drake.

Ronald Bowers

MANTRAP

Released: 1926
Production: Adolph Zukor for Famous Players-Lasky; released by Paramount
Direction: Victor Fleming
Screenplay: Adelaide Heilbron and Ethel Doherty; based on the novel of the same name by Sinclair Lewis
Titles: George Marion, Jr.
Cinematography: James Wong Howe
Length: 7 reels/6,077 feet

Principal characters:
Alverna	Clara Bow
Joe Easter	Ernest Torrence
Ralph Prescott	Percy Marmont
E. Wesson Woodbury	Eugene Pallette
Curly Evans	Tom Kennedy
Mrs. McGavity	Josephine Crowell
Mr. McGavity	William Orlamond
Lawrence Jackfish (Indian Guide)	Charles Stevens
Mrs. Barker	Miss DuPont
Stenographer	Charlot Bird

Victor Fleming was one of the most popular directors in Hollywood during the 1930's. Even before his legendary M-G-M films of 1939, *Gone with the Wind* and *The Wizard of Oz*, had permanently captivated the hearts of the world, Fleming had made several significant films including *Mantrap*, *The Virginian* (1929), *Red Dust* (1932), *Bombshell* (1933), *Treasure Island* (1934), *Reckless* (1935), and *Captains Courageous* (1937). Noted for his spectacular action sequences and highly charged atmospheres, Fleming went on to direct the 1941 version of *Dr. Jekyll and Mr. Hyde*, *A Guy Named Joe* (1943), and *Joan of Arc* (1948).

Based on the Sinclair Lewis novel of the same name, *Mantrap* is a clever romantic comedy full of illicit innuendo. Satirizing the "great open spaces" and the love triangle, the film offers an atypical husband, who looks philosophically upon his wife's amatory inclinations; a magnetic, maneuvering, meandering, manicurist-wife; and a misogynic male. *Mantrap* enjoys the reputation of being one of the "high class" vamp films of the 1920's, and it dates better than the more famous *It* of 1927, which also stars Clara Bow and in which the sixty-year-old Elinor Glyn appears to explain what "it" is to a sexually insecure public.

In real life, Clara Gordon Bow grew up in extreme poverty and tragic circumstances. At fourteen, she won a beauty contest sponsored by a film magazine, and after playing small parts in cheaply made pictures for several years, was given a contract by B. P. Schulberg of Preferred Pictures when he was still head of that makeshift company. When he became head of Paramount, he cast Bow in *Dancing Mothers* (1926) and *Mantrap* in an all-out effort to rival Colleen Moore's popularity. These films made Bow an overnight sensation. Her driving ambition to escape her childhood memories became part of her public mythology, and she became an international star who represented, quintessentially, the get-rich-quick American dream.

The "It" girl, Bow is at her irrepressible best here. *Mantrap* was one of the few films in which she found a role worthy of her talents. Glyn once stated that Bow's natural talents could have made her one of the greatest dramatic actresses in film, but Paramount exploited her drawing power, turning out mediocre pictures at a frantic pace. Her serious roles, such as those in *Wings* (1927) and *Ladies of the Mob* (1928), were few. She symbolized the new post-War personal freedom that was being enjoyed by the American youth who were in open rebellion against their puritan heritage and Victorianism. Vampishly naughty, Bow burned the candle at both ends as she hedonistically pursued the fast life. Like Marilyn Monroe, Bow could project vulnerability and sex appeal at the same time. She was a sympathetic heroine who simply wanted too much too soon. Reckless and a bit naïve, she usually learns her lesson just in the nick of time.

In *Mantrap*, Bow plays a slang-slinging, Minneapolis manicurist named Alverna who meets and marries Joe Easter (Ernest Torrence), a trader from the Canadian backwoods. The pairing of these two is delightful. Bow is perfect as the bobbed-haired, painted, rolled-stockings manicurist, and Easter is equally good as the oafish backwoodsman.

The film begins as Joe, sitting in his trading store, melancholy and alone, fondly remembers his last big thrill—a glance he gave to a lady's ankle twenty years ago. This induces him to take off for the city, where he meets Alverna and becomes smitten with the feisty ways of the big-city vamp. Impetuously, the flapper takes off for the Canadian wilderness with Joe who is big, lumbering, and primitive.

Joe whisks Alverna back to the trading post where she proceeds to vamp anything remotely resembling a man. When a suave, misogynistic lawyer from New York named Ralph Prescott (Percy Marmont) appears on the scene, she instantly reeks good-natured debauchery from every pore. Ralph is a bachelor who is seeking refuge from the women who comprise his wealthy, grasping, lecherous divorce clients, and who have flimsy excuses, tearful stories, and propositions. He embarks on a camping trip with E. Wesson Woodbury (Eugene Pallette), an office colleague. When they arrive at Mantrap Landing, Mr. Woodbury soon tires of Ralph's constant complaints about the absence of city luxuries, and Joe arrives on the scene just in time to separate the feuding pair. Joe takes Ralph to the trading post and introduces him to Alverna under the altruistic misconception that Ralph will be good company for his new wife. When Alverna gets her first glimpse of Ralph, she makes it clear that "open season" has arrived. Ralph recoils as she begins to flirt with him outrageously. He battles her wiles as long as possible, finally coming to the conclusion that he will rejoin his camping companion. She pleads with him to take her back to civilization, and even follows him against his wishes. She finally wheedles Ralph into promising that he will ask Joe to divorce her. Joe, the worried husband who is feeling just as sorry for Ralph as for himself, overtakes the errant couple and, seeing the humor of the situation as Ralph admits his acquiescence to Alverna's plotting, joins Ralph in a discussion about what is best for Alverna. This infuriates her and she, in a huff, takes Joe's boat leaving both the men stranded.

The final shots depict the lawyer back in civilization with a brassy, blond client waiting for him in his private office, while Joe is peeling potatoes with some well-meaning neighbors telling him that he should be glad to be rid of the hussy. As Joe begins to defend Alverna, she arrives. Framed by the doorway, in all her radiant, flapper glory, she applauds her stalwart husband. Back in Minneapolis, she had begun to see her husband in a different light and began to yearn to come home. She promises to be faithful, but Joe knows she will always be a bit of a coquette. While still in Joe's arms, she looks over his shoulder and sees a handsome Royal Mounted Policeman, but as she starts giving him the eye, she realizes that she is faltering, and she hides her batting eyelashes behind her husband's broad shoulder.

Humorous and charming, *Mantrap* treats its audience to excellent casting and acting, witty subtitles, and Bow at her best. The film is also notable for the lovely outdoor photography of young cinematographer James Wong Howe who went on to become one of the best-known cameramen in film history.

Tanita C. Kelly

MARE NOSTRUM

Released: 1926
Production: Rex Ingram for Metro-Goldwyn-Mayer
Direction: Rex Ingram
Screenplay: Willis Goldbeck; based on the novel of the same name by Vicente Blasco Ibáñez
Cinematography: John F. Seitz
Editing: Grant Whytock
Length: 10 reels/9,894 feet

Principal characters:
Freya Talberg .... Alice Terry
Ulysses Ferragut .... Antonio Moreno
Esteban, his son .... Michael Brantford
Doña Cinta, his wife .... Mlle. Kithnou
The Triton .... Uni Apollon
Caragol .... Hughie Mack
Dr. Feldmann .... Madame Paquerette
Submarine Commander .... Andre von Engelmann

There is a great deal of symbolism to be found in Rex Ingram's *Mare Nostrum*. The Latin title means "Our Sea," a term still in common usage among Mediterranean peoples. It is a story of naval warfare, taking place largely during World War I and centering in the Mediterranean. The author, Vicente Blasco Ibáñez, was Spanish, and Spain was a neutral country during that war, abounding in espionage and intrigue. Ingram shot his entire picture abroad in natural settings, and there are many scenes shot in Barcelona, Marseilles, Pompeii, Paestum, and Naples, providing undeniably beautiful backgrounds as well as authenticity.

Ingram has always said that *Mare Nostrum* was his favorite film. He took his time making it, and the film seems saturated with the atmosphere of the sea and seaports. He gave his wife, Alice Terry, her best film role in this picture, and she made her portrait of Freya, the Austrian spy who leads her lover astray, both exciting and glamorous. She had always wanted to play a *femme fatale*, once even begging her husband to cast her in the role played by Barbara La Marr in *Trifling Women* (1922). It was worth waiting for the role of Freya Talberg, however, and Terry reveled in impersonating the woman. Similarly, Ingram had always wanted to work with Antonio Moreno. As far back as preproduction on *The Four Horsemen of the Apocalypse* (1921), he was pushing to use Moreno as Julio, and only settled on June Mathis' choice, Rudolph Valentino, because Mathis agreed not to stand in the way of Terry's being cast as the heroine. This time Ingram got Moreno, and again it was worth the long wait; for Moreno, always romantically handsome, was perfectly cast as a Spanish sea captain who loves but is destroyed by an adventuress, symbolizing the sea.

From the beginning, young Ulysses Ferragut (Antonio Moreno) knows that the sea is his destiny. He does not have much of a home life because the male Ferraguts have been seamen for centuries, and they are only home between voyages. He has married Doña Cinta (Mlle. Kithnou), a girl of his father's choice, but he does not feel anything for her, and loves only the sea and his son, Esteban (Michael Brantford). Esteban is growing up and is a cadet in the naval academy, where all the Ferragut men have gone and graduated with honors.

Ulysses is the owner-captain of a fast-freight steamer which he has called *Mare Nostrum*. He is faced, however, with having to give up the ship because of heavy losses he has had in trade prior to the outbreak of World War I. With the war, however, the profits he realizes from each cargo he carries brings him fabulous rewards. It is almost as if the goddess of the sea, Amphitrite, were displaying signs of her gratitude for his loyalty. There has always been an old portrait of an artist's conception of Amphitrite hanging in the Ferragut home, and Ulysses is well aware of the physical attributes of the sea goddess. He sees Amphitrite's exact likeness in a girl he meets in the ruins of Pompeii, and with whom he immediately falls in love. She is Freya Talberg (Alice Terry), an Austrian of Scandinavian background. She responds to him, because she is under orders. He does not know, at first, that she is a secret agent for Germany, and by the time he finds out, he does not care.

They meet secretly once in the maritime museum in Naples outside a tank where an octopus stretches its tentacles towards them behind the glass, and they whisper of their love. Ulysses is so deeply infatuated that he neglects his business affairs, and by the time he learns that she is a secret agent, he, to show his love for her, pilots a boat to a rendezvous at sea where fuel and supplies are transferred to a German submarine.

What he does not consider is how tragically her changing allegiance will affect his own life. His son Esteban has come to Naples to meet him, but Esteban cannot find him because Ulysses has become Freya's slave. Disappointed, Esteban starts back home on a neutral ship, but it is torpedoed by the Germans, and he is among those lost.

At the same time, Freya has begun to despise her work and what she is being forced to do. Her superiors realize that she is of no further use to them, and they arrange to send her to France on a mission that will lead to her capture. Ulysses, sorrowing for his son, goes to the south of France to see her, but his infatuation is finished, and he breaks off his relationship with her. At the same time, he turns over his ship as expiation to the French.

Freya is trapped, put in prison as a spy, and sentenced to face a firing squad. In the early morning, dressed in full furs and wearing her jewelry and a feathered hat, she is led out by the French to her death. Ulysses is captain of a troop ship that is torpedoed by a submarine. He is caught on the deck as his ship sinks, but manages to crawl to the uptilted bow, where he fires upon the submarine that had sunk his ship, and destroys it. He then sinks with his ship and is swallowed by the sea. As his body drops down into the depths, the spirit of Amphitrite rises to take him in her arms and to carry him to the comfort of death. Thus, in death, Ulysses, Amphitrite, and Freya, a divine triumvirate, become one.

Terry has said, "I feel that *Mare Nostrum* was the only film I ever did really." She was much praised by everybody, including the critics and Blasco Ibáñez himself, who wrote Ingram a letter of gratitude:

> I personally thank you for the wonderful way in which you have interpreted my novel.
> Of all the stories I have written, *Mare Nostrum* is my favorite. For that reason, only to
> a great artist like yourself could I trust it to be put in motion pictures.

Ingram stayed on in Europe after *Mare Nostrum* and made four other features: W. Somerset Maugham's Gothic tale *The Magician* (1926), with Terry, Paul Wegener, and Ivan Petrovitch; Robert Smythe Hichens' *The Garden of Allah* (1927), with Terry and Petrovitch; Cosmo Hamilton's *The Three Passions* (1929), with Terry and Petrovitch again; and *Baroud* (1932), which was his only sound film. Terry did not act in *Baroud*, but she assisted Ingram in directing it, for, as a switch, he played the lead. Terry returned to Hollywood in 1934, and two years later Ingram joined her, and they made their home in adjacent bungalows.

Ingram was one of the greatest of all film directors, and from 1916 to 1932, his contributions to the motion-picture medium as director, writer, and actor are much valued. With D. W. Griffith and Erich Von Stroheim, he belongs to a small circle of silent-film directors who possessed real taste, talent, and a continuing sense of beauty. His work will always reflect the best that was in the silent film.

DeWitt Bodeen

THE MARK OF ZORRO

Released: 1920
Production: Douglas Fairbanks for United Artists
Direction: Fred Niblo
Screenplay: Elton Thomas (Douglas Fairbanks); based on the story "The Curse of Capistrano" by Johnston McCulley
Cinematography: William C. McGann and Harry Thorpe
Length: 7 reels

Principal characters:

Zorro/Don Diego Vega	Douglas Fairbanks
Lolita	Marguerite De La Motte
Captain Juan Ramon	Robert McKim
Sergeant Pedro Garcia	Noah Beery
Don Carlos Pulido	Charles Hill Mailes
Doña Catalina	Claire McDowell
Governor Alvarado	George Periolat
Fra Felipe	Walt Whitman
Don Alejandro Pulido	Sidney de Grey
Bernardo	Tote du Crow

The Mark of Zorro was a landmark in the career of Douglas Fairbanks and a milestone in motion-picture history. With it, Fairbanks inaugurated the swashbuckling film and established the prototype for swashbuckling heroes ever since. He also changed the direction of his career. Although Fairbanks is best remembered for his legendary roles in the 1920's as the screen's first super-swashbuckler, his first twenty-nine films had been contemporary comedies or comedy-adventure stories; none of them was more than five reels long.

The source of *The Mark of Zorro* is a forgettable story by Johnston McCulley, "The Curse of Capistrano," published in the August 9, 1919, issue of *All-Story Weekly*, a pulp magazine. Various accounts give credit to Fairbanks' brother Robert, to Mary Pickford, and to an agent named Ruth Allen for bringing the story to Fairbanks' attention, persuading him to break with the formula he had followed for the past five years and to undertake his first period costume picture.

The film takes place in early nineteenth century California. As it begins, young Don Diego Vega (Douglas Fairbanks) returns from school in Spain to his family estate, where he finds his father and the other hidalgos deposed and replaced by the tyranny of Governor Alvarado (George Periolat) and his villainous henchmen. Locally, Capistrano is terrorized by the evil Captain Juan Ramon (Robert McKim) and his subordinate, Sergeant Pedro Garcia (Noah Beery), who does most of the dirty work. Sizing up the situation, Don

Diego immediately establishes the *persona* of an effeminate fop, a languid dilettante given to squeamish revulsion from any sort of crudity, let alone violence. He uses this masquerade as a cover to conceal his activities as Zorro the Fox, a masked rebel who acts as a sort of Californian Robin Hood, rescuing the oppressed and stealing the governor's exorbitant taxes to return them to the poor peasants. As the supposed fop, Diego carries a parasol, minces about with a lace handkerchief, yawns with ennui, and tries to amuse the aristocracy with card tricks and bits of amateur magic. As Zorro, he wears a thin mustache that enhances his daredevilish grin, leaps about like an acrobat, duels like a demon, and slashes Z's all over the woodwork, walls, and occasionally the bodies of his opponents. Every time he crosses swords with them, he makes fools out of Sergeant Garcia and Captain Ramon.

Their families try to arrange a marriage between Diego and the lady Lolita (Marguerite De La Motte), a lovely aristocrat who despises the ruling tyrants and scorns Don Diego as a cowardly popinjay. Diego's father shares this scorn and complains with contempt of the disappointment his son has become to him.

There are a number of spectacular swordfights and a marvelous chase sequence in which Zorro outwits and outmaneuvers his pursuers with amusingly improbable acrobatics. Revealed at last as Zorro ("My son—Zorro," says his immensely gratified father), Diego in his own person fences circles around Garcia until the latter throws down his sword with a laugh and embraces Diego as a comrade. The wicked governor is overthrown, justice triumphs, and Lolita is ecstatic to find that the dashing hero of whom she is enamored is the man she is to marry after all.

Fred Niblo directed the film with considerable flair and went on to direct such costume adventures as Fairbanks' *The Three Musketeers* (1921), Ramon Novarro's *Ben-Hur* (1925), and Ronald Colman's *Two Lovers* (1928). Fairbanks was supported by a memorable cast. Marguerite De La Motte was one of his favorite leading ladies and starred with him in *Arizona* (1918), *The Nut* (1921), *The Three Musketeers* (1921), and *The Iron Mask* (1929). Noah Beery became a leading villain in silent films, perhaps most memorably as Sergeant Lejaune in *Beau Geste* (1926). Robert McKim was an accomplished villain from the old Thomas H. Ince studio.

Not all critics were happy with Fairbanks' change of pace. The anonymous reviewer for *The New York Times* found the film tamer than those of the earlier Fairbanks, even a bit tedious at times, and complained that the "fun and thrills" were "intermittent" but conceded that "there are moments . . . which must delight anyone, no matter how preposterous they are . . . spirited races and pursuits, sudden appearances, quick changes, and flashes of tempestuous love-making that are typically, and entertainingly, Fairbanksian."

Confronted by such critical reservations and uncertain of the public reception of his new film, Fairbanks proceeded to follow it with another contemporary comedy called *The Nut*. It was his first commercial failure, whereas *The Mark of Zorro* turned out to be his most popular film to date. Accordingly, Fairbanks committed himself to swashbucklers and made nothing else for the next ten years, during which time he produced and starred in his best-known classics, including *The Three Musketeers*, *Robin Hood* (1922), *The Thief of Bagdad* (1924), *The Black Pirate* (1926), *The Gaucho* (1928), and *The Iron Mask*. In 1925, he made *Don Q, Son of Zorro*, in which he played both the original Don Diego thirty years older and his son, Don Cesar de Vega, who becomes involved in daring adventures during a trip to Spain.

In some ways *The Mark of Zorro* is Fairbanks' best swashbuckler, perhaps because it is the most light-hearted and least pretentious. His subsequent films became more elaborate productions, with immense sets and more of an epic scope, but despite their elaborate action sequences, they lack the breathless pace of *The Mark of Zorro*. Nevertheless, all his subsequent films are indebted to *The Mark of Zorro*, in which Fairbanks not only first developed his image as a dashing swashbuckler but also set the model for most swashbucklers to follow. In previous films, Fairbanks had always been clean-shaven, and he is still so as Don Diego; but as Zorro, he wears the thin, dashing mustache that was later taken up by John Barrymore, Ronald Colman, Errol Flynn, Tyrone Power, and Douglas Fairbanks, Jr. Fairbanks' archetypal swashbuckler has a cheerful nonchalance, a devil-may-care grin, an acrobatic agility, an engaging impudence, and dashes through his adventures with a contagious enthusiasm. Numerous subsequent swashbucklers, such as *The Scarlet Pimpernel* (1935), *The Son of Monte Cristo* (1940), and remakes of *The Mark of Zorro* have the dashing hero masquerade in the dual roles of a simpering fop and a masked or disguised defender of the oppressed.

There had been some earlier attempts to film classic swashbuckling novels, such as *Ivanhoe*, *The Count of Monte Cristo*, *Lorna Doone*, and *The Three Musketeers*, but these primitive early silents were all short, stiff, dignified, and static. What Fairbanks did was combine the swashbuckler with the fast pacing and high good humor of silent comedy and thus make costume pictures that moved. Although Fairbanks was not a particularly good fencer by comparison to Barrymore, Flynn, Basil Rathbone, or Cornel Wilde, he was an immensely acrobatic one; and it was the spirited and comic extravagance of the dueling in *The Mark of Zorro* that made it "distinctly original" and set the style for much subsequent screen swordplay.

In the 1930's, Republic downgraded Zorro for two serials, *Zorro Rides Again* (1937) and *Zorro's Fighting Legion* (1939), low-budget programmers that are mere formula Westerns with Zorro not as an elegant swordsman but merely as a masked man closer to the Lone Ranger than to D'Artagnan. In 1940, however, Twentieth Century-Fox resurrected *The Mark of Zorro* as a major production, directed by Rouben Mamoulian and starring the studio's chief matinee idol, Tyrone Power. This version, although it retains the humor of Don Diego's foppishness, takes the adventure more seriously, without slapstick. Power's Zorro is more realistic, within the framework of romantic adventure, but has as much panache as Fairbanks', and the swordplay between him and Rathbone is among the best ever filmed. Thereafter, Zorro declined again into two more Republic serials. Walt Disney had a popular television series about Zorro (played by Guy Williams) in the 1950's, and during the 1960's and 1970's, there were numerous low-budget foreign films featuring Zorro. An American television version in 1974, with Frank Langella in the lead, practically duplicated the Mamoulian version, even using the same musical score by Alfred Newman.

In the 1970's and early 1980's, films ceased to take period adventure seriously and produced parodies of Westerns, detective films, Dracula and Frankenstein pictures, and classic swashbucklers, such as Peter Sellers' misbegotten *Prisoner of Zenda* (1980). In this vein, George Hamilton starred in *Zorro, The Gay Blade* (1981), a burlesque in which the original Zorro has two sons, one a dashing carbon copy of his father, the other a simpering homosexual. The former swashes, the latter swishes, as if the dual roles of Zorro were embodied in two distinctly different persons. As the swashbuckling brother, Hamilton gave an admirable imitation of Fairbanks' exaggerated heroics and extravagant style; critics much preferred this part of the film and wished that the rest had been as good a tribute to the spirit of the legendary film *The Mark of Zorro*.

Robert E. Morsberger

THE MARRIAGE CIRCLE

Released: 1924
Production: Warner Bros.
Direction: Ernst Lubitsch
Assistant direction: James Flood and Henry Blanke
Screenplay: Paul Bern; based on the play *Nur ein Traum* (*Only a Dream*) by
   Lothar Schmidt
Cinematography: Charles Van Enger
Length: 8 reels /8,200 feet

Principal characters:
Charlotte Braun	Florence Vidor
Dr. Franz Braun	Monte Blue
Mizzi Stock	Marie Prevost
Dr. Gustav Mueller	Creighton Hale
Professor Josef Stock	Adolphe Menjou
Detective	Harry Myers
Neurotic patient	Dale Fuller
Miss Hofer	Esther Ralston

The cinema of Ernst Lubitsch is special and unique. He directed almost thirty films in America, most of which could never have been made by a native because he infused them with European wit, manners, and sophistication as only a continental could. Born in Berlin in 1892, Lubitsch directed shorts and features in Germany between 1915 and 1923 before coming to the United States. His second film in his new country, and his most famous silent, is *The Marriage Circle* (1924).

The film is set in Vienna in the first years of the twentieth century. Professor Josef Stock (Adolphe Menjou) and his wife Mizzi (Marie Prevost) have recently moved to the city. They are unhappily married, and the film opens with a scene showing them squabbling. The Professor tries to put on a sock, but his big toe protrudes from a large hole, and he has no more in his drawer. Mizzi's drawer, however, is crammed with stockings, all neatly arranged. Later, when he attaches a small mirror to a window in order to shave, she selfishly pushes him aside.

Mizzi receives a letter from her best friend, Charlotte Braun (Florence Vidor), chastizing her for not visiting since arriving in Vienna. When Mizzi enters a taxi on the way to see her friend, by coincidence it has already been engaged by Charlotte's new husband, Dr. Franz Braun (Monte Blue), a fashionable physician whom Mizzi has never met. The strangers agree to share the cab, and Josef observes them drive away together as he shaves. He smiles as he sees them, thinking that this might potentially develop into an excuse for a divorce.

The racy, temperamental Mizzi is attracted to the doctor and tries to capture his attention. As the taxi turns, she almost falls into his lap, and she inches closer to him to look in a mirror on his side of the cab. Franz, who is deeply in love with his wife, is bothered by Mizzi's actions, so he asks the driver to stop, and he leaves. Mizzi arrives at her destination and is chatting with Charlotte when Franz arrives home. Both are startled.

When Mizzi returns home, she fakes an illness so that Franz may be summoned. Charlotte unknowingly talks her wary husband into visiting Mizzi, while in the meantime, Mizzi powders her face and rearranges a chair so that the doctor will be forced to sit near her. Franz takes Mizzi's pulse, and she responds by holding his wrist. Josef enters and notices the contact.

The home lives of the Stocks annd Brauns are now contrasted: the former sit at opposite ends of the table when eating breakfast, while the latter embrace. The unperturbed Mizzi next visits Franz's office, again attempting to seduce him. Franz's partner, Dr. Gustav Mueller (Creighton Hale), arrives and observes the doctor's back and a woman's arm around his neck. He assumes it is Charlotte and is then surprised to find her outside in the waiting room. Gustav is secretly delighted, because he himself is in love with Charlotte.

The Brauns hold a dinner party, and Franz rearranges the place cards so that he will not be seated next to Mizzi. Charlotte, at Mizzi's urging, thinks her husband has a crush on an attractive blond, Miss Hofer (Esther Ralston), and has changed the seating arrangements to sit near her; thus, she switches the cards back to their original places with her husband next to her friend. Charlotte confides to Mizzi her fears about Franz's feelings for Miss Hofer and requests that her friend keep the doctor preoccupied. Mizzi then switches the place cards a third time, and Charlotte is angered at the final seating arrangement. She glares at her husband and purposely flirts with Gustav.

Mizzi dances with Franz, while Charlotte does the same with Gustav, then Mizzi maneuvers her partner outside, into a garden. When they are seated on a bench, she wraps her arm around his leg, puckers her lips expectantly, and tosses away her scarf. Charlotte and Gustav enter the garden and see Franz's foot dragging the scarf. Charlotte knows it is Mizzi's, who by now has been abandoned by Franz, who in turn is now on the terrace, innocently conversing with Miss Hofer.

Mizzi passes a note to Franz, explaining that she will wait for him in a taxi after the party. He tears it up but meets her anyway after the angry Charlotte throws him out of the house. Charlotte is sorry, however, so she closes her eyes to kiss her husband, but mistakenly kisses Gustav instead. When she realizes her error, she orders Gustav to leave. Meanwhile, Mizzi again fails to seduce Franz.

Josef, by this time, has enough evidence against his wife and orders her to leave their house; then he confronts Franz, who denies his part in the affair.

Charlotte visits Mizzi at her hotel in an effort to console her friend, who meanwhile has requested that Franz also come to see her. Franz and Charlotte accidentally meet in Mizzi's room, and Charlotte realizes her husband is the "guilty party." As he declares his innocence, Charlotte admits her flirtation with Gustav, so both are equally to blame, and they can be reconciled. Gustav then passes Mizzi, who is riding in a cab. She waves to him, and as the film closes, he sets out to join her.

The Marriage Circle is the first of Lubitsch's sly, urbane, nonchalant social comedy-satires. The director claimed that Charles Chaplin's *A Woman of Paris* (1923, and also featuring Adolphe Menjou, as the "richest bachelor in Paris") as his source of inspiration, and *The Marriage Circle* seems at times to satirize the Chaplin film. *A Woman of Paris* was a moralistic tale of a country girl (Edna Purviance) who thinks that she has been jilted by her art student boyfriend, travels to Paris, becomes the mistress of the frivolous Menjou character, but eventually leaves him and Paris to return to the country. Lubitsch imbues his film with an air of cynicism in that he depicts the state of marriage as a never-ending cycle of love obliterated by time, of love inexorably destroyed and replaced by antagonism and hatred.

On the surface, the two relationships in *The Marriage Circle* are completely opposite. The marriages are best personified by the shots of the couples at their respective breakfast tables. The Stocks tolerate each other at best; their involvement with each other is based on self-indulgence, lies, and manipulation. This is apparent from the opening sequence onward. Conversely, the Brauns are naïvely in love. Charlotte consoles her best friend, who is heartlessly scheming to steal her husband; Franz gallantly deflects Mizzi's passes, but in the end cannot avoid being "found out" by his wife. The Stocks have been married longer than the Brauns; obviously, they cared for each other early in their relationship, perhaps as much as do Charlotte and Franz, but something has come between them—maybe, only time—and they now despise each other. Charlotte and Franz' problems are caused by their constant overreaction to situations; in particular, Charlotte allows herself to become jealous of Miss Hofer and then flirts with Gustav to get even. At the finale, their misunderstanding is resolved, but one wonders how many misunderstandings will occur before their relationship again deteriorates. As the title indicates, Lubitsch sees marriage as cyclical, and thus, it is predictable that Charlotte and Franz will end as Mizzi and Josef. According to Lubitsch, marriage is not necessarily the happy-ever-after state presented and taken for granted in so many other motion pictures.

The Marriage Circle is expertly cast. Menjou is at his best in a role tailor-made for his talents. Florence Vidor, Monte Blue, and Marie Prevost, all popular silent stars, and Creighton Hale, who played sophisticated first and second leads during the 1920's, are all superior. The actresses in particular are at the zenith of their respective careers. The film received stunning reviews, and if it no longer seems original, it is because the formula has been repeated so often with varying degrees of success by Lubitsch and other filmmakers in the last sixty years.

The film was one of the all-time favorites of George Jean Nathan, Akira Kurosawa, and Chaplin (who wrote of Lubitsch in his autobiography, "He could do more to show the grace and humor and sex in a nonlustful way than any other director I've ever heard of"). It was also Alfred Hitchcock's favorite Lubitsch work and was named to *The New York Times* ten best films of the year list. Both *The Marriage Circle* and *A Woman of Paris* immediately inspired a series of mediocre domestic comedies made by such directors as Harry d'Abbabie d'Arrast (Chaplin's assistant on *A Woman of Paris*), Richard Rosson, Monta Bell, Malcolm St. Clair, and Roy Del Ruth. Lubitsch himself went on to make other films similar to *The Marriage Circle*, such as *Three Women* (1924), *Forbidden Paradise* (1924), *Kiss Me Again* (1925), *Lady Windermere's Fan* (1925), and *So This Is Paris* (1926), often using the same cast. He remade *The Marriage Circle* with sound in 1932 as *One Hour with You*, but in that film he focused solely on the "good couple" (Maurice Chevalier and Jeanette MacDonald), whose relationship is upset by the arrival of coquettish Mitzi Olivier (Genevieve Tobin). In *One Hour with You*, the characters also talk directly to the camera, and the film is certainly more fun than *The Marriage Circle*, but it also seems more trivial and is not the cornerstone that is the original.

Rob Edelman

THE MASKED RIDER

Released: 1916
Production: Metro
Direction: Fred J. Balshofer
Screenplay: Fred J. Balshofer; based on his original screen story
Cinematography: Ray Smallwood
Length: 5 reels

> *Principal characters:*
> Bruce Edmunds .... Harold Lockwood
> Jill Jamison .... May Allison
> Squid Archer .... Lester Cuneo
> Grant Carr .... H. W. Willis
> Patrick Hart .... Harry Berkhart
> Mrs. Hart .... Clarissa Selwynne
> George Edmunds .... Harry Linkey
> Tom Monjar .... John MacDonald
> Jimmy Jamison .... Howard Truesdell

In 1916, Owen Moore, who was still married to Mary Pickford, told director Fred J. Balshofer about the films that Harold Lockwood was making with May Allison in Santa Barbara, California, at the American Flying "A" Studios. Moore spoke in such glowing terms about the couple that Balshofer went to Santa Barbara, was impressed by Lockwood and Allison in person, and relayed a proposition to them about a series of pictures which he would produce and direct. They signed contracts with him, and on that same day, he left for New York to see about the series being released by Metro. He was in luck, for he, and his partners Dick Rowland and Joe Engel, formed a company which they called Yorke Film Corporation, and their principal product at the time was a series of romantic action films, shot in some of the most interesting and photogenic parts of the United States. Lockwood and Allison, who had been a popular team at American, made eight co-starring features for Yorke that were released by Metro. They were so well liked by the public that Metro naturally decided to split the team and star each player with his or her name above the title.

Although Lockwood and Allison were young, their services had been very much in demand. Lockwood had played in about one hundred features from 1911 on, including a long term at Selig with Kathlyn Williams, and he had been a leading man to both Mary Pickford and Marguerite Clark at Famous Players-Lasky before he and Allison joined forces at American. Lockwood was tall, blond, and handsome, while Allison was golden-haired, intelligent, and beautiful. It is not often that two blonds are so attractive together, but they were an instant favorite as a team, and by the time Balshofer took over their careers, their fame was international. During the period of 1916 to 1917, they were the best liked couple in films.

Their second release was *The Masked Rider*, written and directed by Balshofer, which was shot around Bat Cave in the very heart of the Blue Ridge Mountains in North Carolina. Lockwood played Bruce Edmunds, who joins the revenue service to help rout the moonshiners in the hills of North Carolina. His real purpose in becoming a revenue officer, however, is to find and bring to justice the man who had killed his brother George (Harry Linkey), a painter whose landscapes have been enjoying great popularity throughout the country. George Edmunds had become infatuated with Jill Jamison (May Allison), a mountain girl and daughter of Jimmy Jamison (Howard Truesdell), the owner of the Bat Cave Hotel. The three delight in one another's company, but their relationship arouses the enmity of Squid Archer (Lester Cuneo), boss of the moonshine gang. Archer deliberately antagonizes George, quarreling with him over Jill's favors, and later George's body is found with a bullet in the head.

Bruce Edmunds comes to Bat Cave disguised as a parson and seeking his brother's killer. He immediately tangles with Squid Archer, who resents Bruce's instant popularity with Jill. Only the fact that Bruce is a minister keeps Archer from going after him. From his acquaintance with Jill, Bruce learns a great deal about his dead brother. Jill also tells Bruce about the superstitions of the mountain people, so Bruce decides to masquerade as a masked rider, who dresses in white buckskin and rides the country at night on a white horse. The moonshiners are frightened by the apparition, and Archer fires at the mysterious rider, but Bruce eludes him, and the mountaineers are convinced that he is a ghost. Archer is secretly terrified because he thinks that the masked rider may be the ghost of George Edmunds, his own victim.

Jill is out riding near a stream one day when she is surprised by the masked rider, who is watering his horse. He covers her with a gun, but then, realizing her identity, apologizes. She is pleased to find that the masked rider is so gallant a man, and Bruce, smiling behind his mask, touches one of her golden curls and tells her that she may have her freedom if she will give him a curl. She lets him cut off a curl, and the next day, while cleaning his room at the hotel, she finds the curl hidden behind a picture of his mother, and so she knows that Bruce is the masked rider.

That night, Bruce leads a group of government agents to round up the illicit distillers. The moonshiners take refuge underground but are driven into the open when Bruce blows up their catacomb. They are captured, but Archer escapes and hurries to the Bat Cave Hotel, where he tries to force Jill to accompany him. Bruce arrives, and there is a fierce battle between the two men. Bruce rolls downstairs, losing his revolver, then Archer shoots at Bruce, wounding him in the shoulder. Archer is about to fire a fatal shot into Bruce, who is lying unconscious on the floor, when Jill crashes a chair down on his head. The government agents tie up Archer, making him their prisoner. Bruce is brought around to consciousness. Jill embraces him, and he grins, saying that the two of them must soon be seeking out a real parson.

Balshofer revealed that he had difficulty convincing the suspicious moonshiners that the filmmakers were not in reality revenue officers out to get them. Thanks to the owner of the inn where the company was staying, who explained the situation to the moonshiners, they relented and allowed the company to use authentic liquor stills and even took part in playing themselves in order to make the picture more realistic.

All the films that Lockwood and Allison made together are noted for their accurate realism. Their first release, *The Comeback* (1916), had been shot in the logging country, in the timberlands of northern Maine. *River of Romance* (1916) was shot among the Thousand Islands in the St. Lawrence River; *Mister 44* (1916), at Lake Tahoe; *Big Tremaine* (1916), in Imperial Valley, California; *Pidgin Island* (1917), in Monterey and Big Sur; and *The Promise* (1917) in Oregon logging camps. Their last picture, *The Hidden Children* (1917) set in pre-Revolutionary War times, was shot in real Eastern Indian wilderness country.

When they were parted, Lockwood worked successfully as a star on his own; but in 1918, while he was aiding the government in liberty Bond sales, he contracted the Spanish influenza and died shortly thereafter. When Allison resumed her career as a Metro star, her vehicles were well liked, putting her in the same class as Nazimova and Viola Dana at Metro. She thought her films inferior, however, and did not renew her contract with Metro when her option was up. She went on a round-the-world cruise, and when she came back to New York, she married James R. Quirk, editor of *Photoplay* magazine. She continued acting as an important supporting actress, but after Paramount's *The Telephone Girl* (1927) she retired from the screen to assist Quirk who was in failing health. She never made a talking feature, but she remained active, and after Quirk's death, she married three more times.

DeWitt Bodeen

MEMORY LANE

Released: 1926
Production: John M. Stahl Productions; released by Associated First National
Direction: John M. Stahl
Screenplay: John M. Stahl and Benjamin Glazer
Cinematography: Percy Hilburn
Editing: Margaret Booth
Art direction: Cedric Gibbons and Arnold Gillespie
Length: 8 reels/6,825 feet

Principal characters:
Mary .... Eleanor Boardman
Jimmy Holt .... Conrad Nagel
Joe Field .... William Haines
Mary's father .... John Steppling
Mary's mother .... Eugenie Ford

Even after fifty-five years, *Memory Lane* remains a memorable film experience. Released in 1926, with Louis B. Mayer presenting it through Associated First National, it had the "classy" look which made most M-G-M features glow. The people who made it were all borrowed from M-G-M, where Mayer was shortly to go as head of production. The studio facilities were already being opened wide to him even before his name would go in the company's logo.

It is a simple story of life and love as they were in a small town in the mid-1920's. It is about a girl named Mary (Eleanor Boardman) who has two sweethearts: Jimmy Holt (Conrad Nagel) and Joe Field (William Haines). She is going to marry Jimmy, but on the night of her marriage, she finds herself reluctant to say good-bye to Joe, who had left town to make his fortune and has returned on Mary's wedding night. Joe pleads with her not to marry Jimmy, but to give him a chance, instead, even if he has no money. Mary kisses Joe, says "No!" firmly, and hurries into her parent's house to get ready for the wedding. It begins to rain, and Joe, who has not even been invited to the wedding, lingers outside, looking longingly through a window at the ceremony that is taking the girl he loves away from him.

The bride and groom try to get away, but they are deluged by the customary rice and old shoes, and they take refuge in the tonneau of a limousine, for which Joe, the brim of his hat pulled down, is officiating as chauffeur. He drives off, and Jimmy does not realize who the driver is until several blocks later. Jimmy forces Joe to stop the car, gets out, and starts giving Joe a piece of his mind, whereupon Joe simply steps on the gas and leaves Jimmy behind, yelling protests in the pouring rain.

Hours later, Mary and Joe are stranded on a country road, their car having run out of gas, and it is not until daylight that they are rescued, and Mary is returned to her husband. He never even questions her and takes her back as his lawful bride. He considers the whole experience a misadventure, something that was supposed to be funny, and was dreamed up by Joe who now has disappeared again and is still presumably seeking his fortune.

Two years pass, which are happy for Mary and Jimmy. They have become parents of a son, Jimmy's business prospers, and they live in a charming house. Only occasionally does Mary remember Joe. When he had returned the night of her wedding, a choral group had been singing "Memory Lane," and every time Mary hears the song, she thinks of Joe. She wonders, however briefly, where he is, what he is doing, and if he has found another girl to love as he had once loved her.

Then Joe returns again unannounced, and Jimmy calls Mary to say that he is bringing Joe home to dinner that night. Mary's heart is fluttering, and she wonders how life has treated Joe, even if she did do the right thing in relinquishing him in favor of Jimmy.

Joe appears, loud in his voice and manners, a bragging show-off. He is overdressed, shallow, and vulgar. It is shocking and sad when Mary sees how he has deteriorated. She wonders if he was always like this and if she was too blind to see his real nature. Dinner is an ordeal, because Joe's conduct only grows worse. Mary realizes how lucky she is to have chosen Jimmy over a racetrack tout such as Joe. Finally, Joe says goodnight, and with several unfunny wisecracks, departs.

Jimmy goes after him to drive him to the station and finds him leaning against a treetrunk, his fist clenched to his mouth as he weeps. It was all an act on Joe's part, an act designed by him so that Mary would forget him forever. Jimmy says that he guessed it was an act, but is confident that Mary was completely fooled. Joe wishes Jimmy luck, and says he will get to the station on his own. Jimmy watches him leave, and then goes back inside the house, where Mary takes him in her arms and tells him that she is glad that she made the right choice in husbands.

Director John M. Stahl wisely chose to play the bittersweet romance straight and for comedy whenever he could. The popular song, an old standard now, "Memory Lane," becomes a fitting title. All three principals were never better. It remains one of the best films that William Haines ever did, and he makes his role utterly believable, putting on precisely enough vulgar show to convince Mary as well as the audience that he is real. When the two men are together at the end, and the audience realizes that it was all an act on Joe's part, and that he is really very nice, it is a tearful moment. The audience wonders if Mary may have done better had she married Joe, and whether she could have made him a successful man and loving husband.

Haines had an extraordinary career. Both Eleanor Boardman and he were brought to Hollywood by Samuel Goldwyn as "new faces" and contest winners. They learned fast how to be stars at M-G-M when they were promoted there, and Haines especially proved in the romantic comedies he did what a gift for laughter he really had. He did not like talkies and never really projected fun and good humor in them. He was the star of *Alias Jimmy Valentine* (1928), to which a final reel of dialogue was attached, making it the first M-G-M part-talkie. He was a silent-film star, and the days of the silents were over by that time. He immediately began to plan his life differently. Because of his excellent taste and great knowledge of interior decorating, when his acting career was over, he became a professional decorator. Joan Crawford and George Cukor were two of his first clients, and one of his better-known assignments was the interior of the American Embassy in London. He died in 1973, at age seventy-three.

Boardman did well in talking features, but she married Harry d'Abbadie d'Arrast, a prominent director, went abroad with him, and eventually retired. She now lives in Montecito, California. Conrad Nagel quickly proved that he was one of the best leading men in talkies, went back to the theater, later played in television, and did an occasional supporting role in films such as *All That Heaven Allows* (1955). He died in 1970, at age seventy-two.

DeWitt Bodeen

THE MERRY WIDOW

Released: 1925
Production: Irving Thalberg for Metro-Goldwyn-Mayer
Direction: Erich Von Stroheim
Screenplay: Erich Von Stroheim and Benjamin Glazer; based on Henry W.
Savages's stage adaption of the musical by Victor Leon (Victor Hirschfeld)
and Leo Stein (Leo Rosenstein) and the operetta by Franz Lehár
Cinematography: William Daniels and Oliver T. Marsh
Editing: Frank E. Hull and Margaret Booth
Art direction: Richard Day and Cedric Gibbons
Length: 10 reels/10,027 feet

Principal characters:
Prince Danilo	John Gilbert
Sally O'Hara	Mae Murray
Crown Prince Mirko	Roy D'Arcy
Baron Sixtus Sadoja	Tully Marshall
King Nikita I	George Fawcett
Queen Milena	Josephine Crowell
Doorkeeper	George Nichols

Franz Lehár's operetta *The Merry Widow* had its debut in Vienna in 1905 to immediate popular acclaim. It remains in the repertoire of major opera companies throughout the world, and it is not surprising that Metro-Goldwyn-Mayer has filmed three verison of this enduring and appealing musical play. Erich Von Stroheim filmed the silent version in 1925, Ernst Lubitsch directed the first sound production in 1934, and Curtis Bernhardt's adaption in 1952 was the first in color, although Von Stroheim had included a color sequence at the end of his film. The three films are dissimilar even though all three retain the basic plot device, that a prince must marry the widow of the wealthiest man in the kingdom in order to keep her money in the country and thus insure the solvency of the throne. None of the films is otherwise faithful to the original. As a musical comedy, Lubitsch's version is perhaps most satisfying because he is a skillful comic director, the stars (Jeanette MacDonald and Maurice Chevalier) can sing, and the audience can enjoy some of the delightful Lehár melodies, although several songs were deleted from Lehár's score with new ones added by Richard Rodgers and Lorenz Hart. As a film, Von Stroheim's version is the most successful because he is the least constrained by the admittedly superficial libretto of the original, and he brings the greatest creativity to the production.

Von Stroheim's film begins on a Sunday with the royal family of Monteblanco exiting the cathedral after the service. Titles introduce King Nikita I (George Fawcett) and Queen Milena (Josephine Crowell). They are accompanied by the crippled, ancient Baron Sixtus Sadoja (Tully Marshall), the wealthiest man in the kingdon and the real ruler of Monteblanco. The scene shifts to a mountain village in the principality where the Army is seeking billets for the night having completed maneuvers in the region. Crown Prince Mirko (Roy D'Arcy) is the first to arrive, politely but grudgingly acknowledged by his troops. His cousin, Prince Danilo (John Gilbert), drives in and is greeted with genuine enthusiasm by the soldiers, the innkeeper, and the women of the village.

Mirko commandeers the best room in the inn for himself. He is abusive to the maids and his valet, in contrast to Danilo who jokes with his valet and flirts with the maids. An American vaudeville troupe arrives and asks for rooms in the inn. There are no available rooms, but Danilo, attracted to Sally O'Hara (Mae Murray), the leading actress of the company, arranges for the soldiers to share rooms in order that the women may be accommodated. Danilo conceals his title from Sally and orders the soldiers not to call him Prince in her presence. Mirko is also attracted to Sally, so the royal cousins discreetly vie for her attentions. Mirko warns Sally of Danilo's reputation as a cold-hearted seducer, but Sally is drawn to him in spite of Mirko's advice. Danilo dances with Sally, but the waltz is interrupted as the scene ends.

Back in the capital city, the Manhattan Follies performs for Monteblanco society. In the royal boxes, Danilo focuses on Sally's face, Mirko looks at her body, and Baron Sadoja watches only her feet. When her act is finished, Sally refuses dinner invitations from both the Baron and the Crown Prince. She finds Danilo in her dressing room and at first refuses his invitation as well, but she is finally persuaded to dine with him. Danilo maintains an apartment in an exclusive bordello, and it is there that he takes Sally for dinner. Rejected by Sally, Mirko also arrives at the *maison de rendezvous* and is cruelly abusive to the crippled doorkeeper (George Nichols). Danilo has maneuvered Sally to the bed chamber when Mirko and his orgiastic friends invade the apartment. Mirko mockingly apologizes for the intrusion, but Danilo defends Sally by announcing his intention to marry her. Once the intruders have left, Sally and Danilo realize that they love each other and do indeed want to marry.

Mirko informs Danilo's father of the Prince's intentions, and the King refuses to permit the marriage. Queen Milena comforts Danilo by telling him that she too had to choose duty before love. Danilo gives his mother a letter for Sally, but the Queen destroys it instead. Mirko gleefully tells Sally that Danilo will not marry her and implies that it is because Danilo does not love her. Jilted in her wedding dress, Sally is very susceptible to Baron Sadoja's proposal of marriage. As his wife, she will control the kingdom. Sally accepts the offer, but on their wedding night the anticipation is too much for the Baron's aged heart. He dies before he can consummate the marriage, leaving Sally the wealthiest woman in Monteblanco.

After a period of mourning, Sally leaves Monteblanco for Paris taking with her the millions needed to run the country. Mirko announces to his mother and cousin that he intends to go to Paris to marry her, thereby saving the national treasury. Danilo follows him to Paris and sees Sally again at a party in the Monteblanco legation. Sally asks Danilo to finish their interrupted waltz, and as they whirl about the floor their love for each other is apparent to everyone but themselves. In order to punish Danilo for his desertion, Sally now pretends to be attracted to Mirko. The rivalry between the cousins intensifies to such a point that Mirko challenges Danilo to a duel after a drunken encounter in the Bois de Boulogne. The night before the duel, Sally goes to Maxims' where she tries to persuade Danilo to call off the duel. Thinking she is pleading for Mirko's life, he refuses, but during the duel Danilo does not fire upon Mirko and is seriously wounded by his cousin. Seeing him hurt, Sally cannot hide her love any longer and rushes to Danilo's side. She takes him back to Monteblanco where she nurses him back to health.

In the meantime, King Nikita dies. During the funeral procession, Mirko is shot by the doorkeeper from the bordello, the man Mirko had cruelly mistreated. Danilo is now king, and in a double ceremony, he and Sally are married and then crowned King and Queen of Monteblanco.

If Von Stroheim's *The Merry Widow* does not resemble Lehár's operetta, it does have many similarities with his other films. The constant theme in his productions is the destruction of innocence. Whether through money, as in *Greed* (1925), or through the insidious influence of decadent Europeans (*Blind Husbands*, 1919; *Foolish Wives*, 1922; *The Merry-Go-Round*, 1923; *The Wedding March*, 1928; and *Queen Kelly*, unfinished), innocence, usually personified by Americans, is seduced and painfully changed, although rarely improved. Van Stroheim is fascinated by the almost irredeemable corruption of the Central European nobility. Crown Prince Mirko is a relatively benign figure in comparison to some of the princes, dukes, and officers in Von Stroheim's other films. Baron Sadoja, a quintessential Von Stroheim invention, is visibly corrupt, his crippled body a mirror to his twisted soul. His death under humorous circumstances, and Mirko's murder by a revengeful servant are viewed by Von Stroheim as justifiable resolutions to lives misspent in indulgence and exploitation. Ironically, even a positive character such as Prince Danilo is also doomed as World War I will destroy the crown he assumes at the end of the film. An institution is ended, a life-style that glittered and charmed but that also was marked by moral decay.

Because of Von Stroheim's contributions, *The Merry Widow* transcends the conventional operetta plot. Even without music, the waltz scene is lilting and erotic, a musical moment conveyed in visual terms. While primarily Von Stroheim's achievement, credit must also be extended to the performances of his actors. Neither John Gilbert nor Mae Murray were Von Stroheim's first choices for the lead roles, but Gilbert soon proved himself to Von Stroheim, and their collaboration was successful. Murray, however, was married to

Robert Leonard, another director on the M-G-M lot, and was accustomed to deferential treatment from everyone. Von Stroheim deferred to no one, resulting in epic battles between the director and his leading lady. In spite of, or perhaps because of, this friction, Murray was to give the best performance of her career as the merry widow.

Of equal importance to the artistic success of the film were the cameramen, William Daniels and Oliver T. Marsh, and the set designers, Richard Day and Cedric Gibbons. The cinematography is consistently effective and, in several scenes, beautiful as well. When Sally is jilted, the camera watches her through a rain-streaked hotel window. The mist surrounding her image markedly enhances the poignancy of her predicament, increasing the viewer's understanding of her decision to marry the Baron. Equally, the sets are always authentic, creating a specific time and place on the backlot of M-G-M. The *maison de rendezevous* and the palace sets create milieus for the characters that comment visually on their personalities.

Like all of his films, *The Merry Widow* is clearly a Von Stroheim production. Without the contributions of Von Stroheim, the film would probably have been a lifeless copy of the Lehár operetta. With Von Stroheim's screenplay and direction, *The Merry Widow* was selected as one of the ten best films of the year by Mordaunt Hall, film critic for *The New York Times*. Von Stroheim insured that the widow would continue to enchant even without Lehár's melodies. Soley through the magic of the visual medium, Von Stroheim created life that retains the ability to charm. As long as film exists, Sally and Danilo will waltz their way into the hearts of audiences.

Don K Thompson

MERRY-GO-ROUND

Released: 1923
Production: Universal
Direction: Erich Von Stroheim (uncredited) and Rupert Julian
Screenplay: Erich Von Stroheim
Titles: Mary O'Hara
Cinematography: Charles Kaufman and William Daniels
Editing: Maurice Pivar
Costume design: Erich Von Stroheim
Length: 10 reels/9,178 feet

> *Principal characters:*
> Count Franz Maxmillian
> von Hohenegg .... Norman Kerry
> Agnes Urban .... Mary Philbin
> Sylvester Urban .... Cesare Gravina
> Countess Gisella von Steinbrueck ... Dorothy Wallace
> Bartholomew Gruber .... George Hackathorne
> Shani Huber .... George Siegmann

Erich Von Stroheim was quite possibly the most colorful character ever to become a director. His extravagant expenditures, minute attention to detail, and preoccupation with bizarre fetishes have become Hollywood legends. His career seems to consist of one film after another being taken away from him, and studio after studio getting fed up with his methods. *Merry-Go-Round* provides the perfect example of his genius at war with film executives.

Von Stroheim's directorial reputation was at its peak after the fabulous artistic success of *Foolish Wives* in 1922, so Universal subsequently wanted him to create another one of his sophisticated continental dramas. He took a brief vacation in the mountains and came back with a script which everyone, including boy-wonder producer Irving Thalberg, who, at that time, had not yet left Universal for M-G-M, thought was his best yet. With his script approved, he began designing the sets and costumes which would be needed for his lavish production. Palaces were built, elaborate uniforms bought, and a vast copy of Vienna's amusement park, The Prater, constructed over several acres.

Von Stroheim had been directing the filming for five weeks when he had his climactic clash with Thalberg. He was shooting night scenes on the outdoor Prater set until long after midnight, while Thalberg watched him from a distance. Von Stroheim had an important scene ready to be shot and before he called "Action!" he reached into his coat, pulled out a flask, and took a swig. Immediately, the puritanical Thalberg sent word that he was fired, and the production was terminated, but not before some of the cast quit and the

Universal employees threatened a strike. A new director was put in charge and finished the picture. Von Stroheim's name was totally removed from the film, but his stamp is unmistakable.

Merry-Go-Round opens in Vienna at the palatial residence of Count Franz Maxmillian von Hohenegg (Norman Kerry), the Captain of the Imperial Guards for Emperor Franz Josef, and also the Emperor's favorite. It is not a happy morning for the Count, because it has been decreed by the Emperor that he must marry the Countess Gisella von Steinbrueck (Dorothy Wallace), a woman that he definitely does not love. The Count is a handsome fellow in his gleaming uniform when his valet is through dressing him.

In another part of Vienna, at the Countess Gisella's house, she is coming into the stables from her morning ride where her groom helps her to dismount. Then, with a commanding look in her eyes, she pulls him down in the hay and seduces him. When she is through, she goes inside to her boudoir, lights a cigar, and puts out a boot for her maid to pull off. She then has some fun with the girl by kicking her backward each time the maid attempts to take hold of the boot.

That night, the Count's officer friends throw him a bachelor party. In the midst of the food-laden table is a huge champagne bowl with a naked girl laughing in the bubbles. After the party, they decide to go slumming at The Prater. They go in their civilian clothes and stroll through the crowds visiting all of the shows and games. At the big merry-go-round they stop for a rest. The Count watches the carousel, and then through the carved horses he spies a beautiful girl turning the crank of the calliope. He jumps aboard and makes his way to the center of the merry-go-round. Stepping down, he introduces himself to the girl as Franz, a necktie salesman. She is Agnes Urban (Mary Philbin), the daughter of a puppeteer.

Franz soon begins seeing Agnes, and on their first date he takes her to a café with private rooms, where he plans to seduce her. All goes according to his plan, but he restrains himself when he realizes that he has fallen in love with the girl, but cannot marry her.

Agnes' life is brightened now that she has Franz to love. Her life at the amusement park has not been happy, for her boss, Shani Huber (George Siegmann) is an extremely cruel man who has made many vicious attempts to rape her. He also hates her father (Cesare Gravina), because he thinks the puppet show takes business from his carousel.

Agnes has a champion in her struggle with Huber; he is Bartholomew Gruber (George Hackathorne), a young hunchbacked boy, who takes care of the orangutan's cage. He has been badly beaten more than once by Huber and holds an intense hatred for the man.

Huber drops a flowerpot on the puppeteer's head one day, and smiles from the balcony as the poor old man lies bleeding. Bartholomew watches from the steps of the orangutan's wagon and wishes for the strength to kill Huber.

Later, Huber strolls by, as the hunchback feeds the orangutan, and pokes the creature with his cane. The animal hates Huber, and this gives Bartholomew an idea. That night, he leaves the cage door open and watches as the ape leaves and steals into Huber's open window.

In the morning, Huber's body is discovered with his neck broken. Not even the police can guess who has done it, because after murdering Huber, the animal has quietly reentered its cage, and Bartholomew has locked the door.

Count Franz is married to Countess Gisella at the court, but their honeymoon is mercifully cut short by the outbreak of World War I. The Prater, of course, closes during the War. Agnes is totally destroyed when she learns of the marriage and the true identity of her lover. Bartholomew, however, cares for her, and she promises to marry him.

At the war's end, Count Franz returns, a ruined man. The monarchy is fallen, and he is penniless. The Countess, however, has died, leaving him free. He comes to The Prater, as the workers there are getting the place ready to open. Franz finds Agnes at the merry-go-round, dusting off the horses. He asks her to marry him but she tells him that she is going to marry Bartholomew. The hunchback overhears Agnes tell Franz that she does love him, but is obligated to Bartholomew. The little hunchback then sneaks off to commit suicide, thus leaving Agnes free to marry Franz.

Norman Kerry was really the perfect Von Stroheim hero, although in the beginning the director had wanted to play the role himself and only relinquished it after the studio's refusal. Kerry was born Norman Kaiser, but changed his surname during World War I. He is best remembered for his romantic leads in two Lon Chaney films, *The Hunchback of Notre Dame* (1923) and *The Phantom of the Opera* (1925).

Mary Philbin became a Universal star as a result of this picture, and D. W. Griffith even borrowed her later to play his heroine in *Drums of Love* (1928). She lives in Los Angeles today, a religious recluse, and does not wish to talk about her film career.

George Hackathorne received some very kind words from the critics, and, along with Gareth Hughes, was one of the most popular juvenile actors in the early 1920's.

Larry Lee Holland

METROPOLIS

Released: 1927
Production: Ufa; released in the United States by Paramount
Direction: Fritz Lang
Screenplay: Thea von Harbou; based on her novel of the same name
Cinematography: Karl Freund and Günther Rittau
Length: 11 reels/10,400 feet

Principal characters:
Maria .... Brigitte Helm
Joh Fredersen .... Alfred Abel
Freder .... Gustav Fröhlich
Rotwang .... Rudolf Klein-Rogge
Grot .... Heinrich George
Slim .... Fritz Rasp
Josaphat .... Theodor Loos
Georg, No. 11811 .... Erwin Biswanger

Of the many memorable films produced in Germany during the 1920's, perhaps none is as fascinating as Fritz Lang's *Metropolis*, the most spectacular example of the cinematic style known as "German Expressionism." Expressionism was an early twentieth century movement that influenced a broad spectrum of artistic pursuits. Rejecting the simple reproduction of reality, it employed nonnaturalistic forms in an abstract, symbolic approach to thematic material. In post-World War I Germany, the conventions of silent cinema were absorbed into a hybrid style which was heavily influenced by the theater of Max Reinhardt, which used light and shadow effects in a similar fashion. Economic conditions of the period favored production in the studio, which allowed for the total control of the visual elements and encouraged the stylization which came to be loosely called "expressionistic." This was particularly true in Great Britain and the United States, where German films were receiving much attention for their "artistic" qualities. The style that evolved was highly artificial: stylized and distorted sets and decor, unnatural lighting that created deep shadows and sharp contrasts, visual compositions that emphasized the grotesque, and an exaggerated acting style, meant to externalize the characters' psychological torment. There is a danger in generalizing, however, in that the imprecise application of the label "German Expressionism" has resulted in the indiscriminate lumping together of a diverse group of films. It also implies a conscious and unified artistic movement (rather than an extremely generalized set of conventions) and obscures the fact that, out of the two or three hundred feature films turned out annually by the German film industry during this productive period, only a handful of films were truly expressionist. There is no denying, however, that the style was pervasive, for few of the important films of this "Golden Age" of German cinema were entirely devoid of expressionist influences.

Despite a few scattered antecedents, *The Cabinet of Dr. Caligari* (1920), written by Carl Mayer and Hans Janowitz, and directed by Robert Wiene, is generally acknowledged as the beginning of the expressionist trend and has come to symbolize the style as well. In a postwar cinema dominated by the United States, the film helped to bring international attention to the German filmmakers. Among these were Fritz Lang, a native Austrian who had begun writing for motion pictures in 1916, while recovering from a war injury. Lang became a director in 1919 and was originally hired to direct *The Cabinet of Dr. Caligari* by its producer, Erich Pommer. Lang was forced to withdraw because of other commitments, but historians often credit him with devising the film's narrative device, which reveals the narrator as an inmate in an insane asylum. This missed opportunity did not prove a serious setback to Lang's career; two years later, following a string of popular melodramas and potboilers, he made his first major artistic success, *Der Müde Tod* (1921). The title translates as "The Weary Death," although the film is usually known as *Destiny*, its British release title. Douglas Fairbanks drew heavily on *Der Müde Tod* for his 1924 production *The Thief of Bagdad*, even purchasing the American rights and holding up release until after his film had debuted. Lang's film opened in July, 1924, in New York as *Between Worlds*. Lang further enhanced his growing reputation with his next film, *Dr. Mabuse Der Spieler* (1922), a two-part thriller about an omnipotent master criminal. That same year, the departure for Hollywood of fellow director Ernst Lubitsch, whose specialty had been the historical costume drama that constituted another major trend of the German cinema, left Lang as Germany's leading director. His epic rendition of the famous German heroic legend *Die Niebelungen* (1924), again in two parts, was his most notable achievement up to that time.

Lubitsch was among the first in a long line of German film artists who would eventually find their way to the United States—at first in response to Hollywood's technological and economic lure, and later in search of a haven from the repressive political climate of the Third Reich. The latter reason would eventually impel Lang into this tide of film emigrants, but in 1924, following the release of *Die Niebelungen*, his reputation in Germany was at its peak; when he visited the United States in October of that year, it was only to observe American methods of production. The trip also netted him an unexpected bonus; while his ship was docked on the West Side of Manhattan, he later recalled, "I looked into the streets—the glaring lights and the tall buildings—and there I conceived *Metropolis*." He discussed the idea with his wife and frequent writing collaborator, Thea von Harbou, and together they devised a scenario. *Die Niebelungen* had been an expensive film for Ufa (Germany's largest film production company), but it had been successful enough to enable Lang to mount another sizable project. His visit abroad was brief, and upon his return to Germany preparations for *Metropolis* were begun. Production commenced on May 22, 1925, and ended nearly a year and a half later, on October 30, 1926.

The film is set in the city of Metropolis, in the year 2000, where society has been divided into two distinct classes. The ruling class, the "Masters of Metropolis," indulge themselves in hedonistic pleasures, while the workers, segregated in their own city far beneath the surface, perform the backbreaking and dehumanizing work in the machine rooms that provide power to Metropolis. Freder (Gustav Fröhlich), the only son of Joh Fredersen (Alfred Abel), the ruler of Metropolis, becomes fascinated with Maria (Brigitte Helm), a worker's daughter. Maria, held in great reverence by the workers, quells their rebellious spirit by preaching a gospel founded on the belief that "between the brain that plans and the hands that build, there must be a mediator . . . the heart." Freder descends into the machine rooms, where he experiences at firsthand the terrible lives of the workers. He is rebuffed when he tries to communicate their anguish to his father, but he continues to become more involved in their affairs, spurred on by his interest in Maria.

Fredersen, meanwhile, becomes increasingly worried by mysterious plans which are being conveyed to him by Grot (Heinrich George), a foreman of the machine rooms and Fredersen's spy among the workers. Fredersen appeals to the scientist/inventor Rotwang (Rudolph Klein-Rogge) to help him determine the meaning of the plans. Eventually, Rotwang leads him into the ancient catacombs deep beneath the city, where they eavesdrop on one of Maria's sermons. Rotwang has invented a robot, which Fredersen now instructs him to make in the image of Maria, intending to send it down among the workers to discredit the real Maria. Imprisoning Maria, Rotwang carries out Fredersen's instructions. The robot, a perfect likeness of the real Maria, exhorts the workers to rise up in revolt and destroy the hated machines. Whipped into a frenzy, they do so without realizing that they are also flooding their own city, thus endangering the lives of their children. Maria, however, manages to escape from Rotwang and, with the help of Freder, rescues the children. The workers, alerted by Grot to the near tragedy (but still unaware that they have been duped by a robot), storm into the upper city in search of "Maria." They find the robot and burn her at the stake, at which point they discover the ruse. Rotwang, meanwhile, has gone insane and pursues Maria to the top of a great cathedral. Freder goes to her aid, and after a struggle, Rotwang falls to his death from the parapet. Fredersen, meanwhile, fearing for his son's life, has gone among the mob and with them has watched the fight between Freder and Rotwang—an experience which turns his hair completely white. On the steps of the cathedral at the film's conclusion, Freder convinces his father to shake hands with Grot, now acting as the leader of the workers. Thus, Freder fulfills the role of mediator, according to Maria's teachings.

Metropolis had its premiere in Berlin on January 10, 1927, and had its American debut two months later at New York's Rialto Theater. The critical orthodoxy on the film was established at that time by observers on both sides of the Atlantic and has not changed substantially in nearly sixty years. There always has been almost universal agreement that the film's simplistic social content, muddled philosophy, and faulty dramatic construction are all overwhelmed by its astonishing degree of technical accomplishment and its dynamic visual style. This is not an unfair assessment, for the film's central thesis—that the heart (emotion) must act as the agent of mediation between the hands (labor) and the brain (capital)—was naïvely sentimental, even for 1927. In evaluating the film's narrative structure, however, one must take into account that no prints of the film in its original German version appear to have survived, thus the judgments of present-day critics are based on the version prepared for exhibition in the United States.

The "adaptation," ostensibly performed to tailor the film for American sensibilities, involved much more than the changing of character names (Joh Fredersen became John Masterman; Freder became Eric)—the film was reduced in length by about one-fourth. This cutting was accomplished by a team of editors consisting of playwright Channing Pollock, *Photoplay* magazine editor Julian Johnson, and Edward Adams; Pollock also did the English-language titles, which have been variously altered in later prints. This reediting may not have been as drastic as some writers have claimed. One states that seven reels were cut from an original seventeen, but the length usually given for the German version is 4,189 meters (13,730 feet), or closer to fourteen reels; the initial American version was 10,400 feet, and existing prints are somewhat shorter, probably due to additional trimming for general release, or by state and local censorship boards. Nevertheless, coupled with the alteration of the titles to cover the excised material, the editing had a profound effect on the film and on perceptions of it today.

Fortunately, there is some basis for speculation about the nature of the material removed by this drastic cutting: Thea von Harbou's novel *Metropolis*, first published in English translation in 1927 and reissued in paperback in 1963. The film is usually credited as being "based" on the novel, but this was not strictly true, for the book was not an independent, preexisting work. Only a few months elapsed between Lang's American trip and the start of production, which would seem to indicate that the novel and the scenario were created concurrently; although it has even been suggested by one writer that the novel may have been written later. Whatever the exact circumstances of creation, the two have a much closer affinity than in a usual case of adaptation; while there may be a danger in regarding the novel as an exact prose equivalent of the complete scenario, it is nevertheless the best available foundation for a sort of ersatz "reconstruction" of the original film. The events shared by the book and the extant versions of the film occur in the same sequence, and it is possible to plug some of the film's gaping lapses of continuity by referring to the von Harbou novel.

An exhaustive catalog of the excised elements is not possible here (and in any case should be regarded as problematic), but the profound effects stemming from the removal of one particular establishing character should be noted. This is a woman named Hel, whose elimination—because of the name's connotations for American audiences—is corroborated by an account of the editing published in *The New York Times*. Hel, once the beloved of Rotwang, was stolen away by Fredersen, whom she then married. She died while giving birth to Freder, although the novel attributes her death primarily to Fredersen's oppressively strong love. These events transpire long before the opening of the story, and Hel evidently appeared in the film only as a statue in Rotwang's home. Her prior existence, however, establishes the psychological basis for the unusual relationship between Fredersen and Rotwang, and to a lesser degree between Fredersen and his son. The loss of all mention of this character strips these relationships of all but their surface dimensions, in particular eliminating the irony of the strange interdependence of Fredersen and Rotwang.

Narrative repercussions also exist because of Hel's deletion, throwing the latter part of the film seriously off balance by rendering certain of Rotwang's actions almost inexplicable. Part of the problem is that, following the "debut" of the robot Maria, Rotwang virtually vanishes from the film—almost as though the editors felt that he had fulfilled his primary function and was no longer of significant interest. He is next seen telling Maria, whom he is holding prisoner, about Fredersen's plot (although this information, conveyed by titles, does not jibe fully with his actions); after this brief scene, Rotwang does not appear again until the film's climactic sequence. Maria has "managed to escape" by this time (the details remain unexplained), and Rotwang has apparently gone insane—he staggers out of his house toward the camera, arms outstretched in a ludicrously stylized representation of derangement. He discovers Maria hiding on the steps of the cathedral, and as they observe the rioting workers burning the robot at the stake, he tells her (irrationally) that "if the mob sees you, they will kill me for having tricked them"; there ensues the final chase described above. The motivation for Rotwang's abrupt shifts of sympathy and sanity, as well as the simple narrative continuity that is so sorely lacking at this point, can be found in the novel. His change of heart toward Maria is much easier to understand in the light of the Hel connection; von Harbou attributes it to his desire to defy the will of Fredersen, whom he claims has "made me evil." In addition, in a segment missing from this scene, he offers to help Maria warn the workers and expose the robot; at this point, he is assaulted by Fredersen, who has been hiding nearby. Maria is able to make her escape while Rotwang lies unconscious. When he awakens, he believes that he has died and so goes in search of his lost love Hel. This casts quite a different light on his subsequent actions—he pursues Maria not out of malevolence, but because in his delusion he has quite plausibly mistaken her for Hel. The clarification of these psychological and narrative points leaves one with a considerably more coherent sequence of events than does the reedited version of the film.

Symptomatic of the narrative chaos created by the reediting is the awkwardness with which the various secondary characters are presented. Fredersen's secretary Josaphat (Joseph in the English-language titles, Theodor Loos) is an excellent example. He appears fairly early in the film, when he is dismissed by Fredersen and subsequently prevented from committing suicide by Freder. Freder solicits his aid (to exactly what purpose is unclear), but Josaphat then vanishes, not reappearing until the final reels, when he accompanies Freder on his search for Maria and participates in the rescue of the workers' children. No explanation of his intervening activities is provided. The character of Slim (Fritz Rasp), a tall, dark-clad figure who hovers around Fredersen for much of the film, is underdeveloped almost to the point of invisibility; apparently a servant, Slim actually seems to function as a sort of conscience to Fredersen. The character is given the spotlight for the briefest of moments: when Fredersen frantically inquires of him "Where is my son?" Slim, taking on an almost demonic appearance, raises his hand and dramatically states: "Tomorrow thousands will ask in anguish—'Where is my son?'" This is a visually striking scene that only serves to highlight the vagueness surrounding the character.

Shortchanged in a different manner is the character of Georg, No. 11811 (Erwin Biswanger), with whom Freder exchanges places at one of the control machines; donning Freder's clothing, Georg is given some sort of instructions, dashes away purposefully—and is never seen again. Perhaps most curious thematically is the depiction of the foreman, Grot. His change of heart in warning the workers about the danger to their children is understandable, but given his history as an informer, his final presentation as the workers' representative seems an inappropriately cynical touch to an otherwise idealistic conclusion. Interestingly, the final handshake scene does not appear in the novel, which instead concentrates on Fredersen's spiritual rebirth—with future social harmony remaining implicit.

Not all the weaknesses of *Metropolis* can be so clearly attributed to the reediting. The exact purpose of Fredersen's plot to replace the real Maria with the robot (around which the latter part of the film revolves) is a case in point. He instructs the robot to "undo Maria's teaching; stir the workers up to criminal acts"—but Maria's advocacy of patience and nonviolence would seem to be to Fredersen's advantage. Rotwang tells Maria that Fredersen "is looking for an excuse to use violence against the workers," but there is no indication that Fredersen is poised to take such an action. Perhaps he anticipates the consequences of the uprising, namely the destruction of the machinery (which he abets by ordering Grot to admit the mob into the control room) and the flooding of the workers' city; but surely he would also foresee the adverse impact this would have on the operations of Metropolis, and thus on the luxurious life-style of his peers. Essentially, all the reasons provided in the film (at least the extant versions) are inadequate. The novel, in this case, is of little help. The motivational uncertainty surrounding this crucial issue plagues the latter section of the film, blunting its impact considerably. The tidiness of the film's ending cannot conceal the underlying confusion, which has its effect on modern audiences; as critic Arthur Lennig astutely observed, "to enjoy the film the viewer must observe but never think."

Thematically, *Metropolis* as it is known today is equally confused. Lang once stated that the film was originally intended to depict symbolically "a battle between modern science and occultism," but that "we cut out all the magic." The raw material of this opposition survives as a dense but fragmented mixture of visual elements and in the contrast between Fredersen and Rotwang. Fredersen, the "Master of Metropolis," with the city's technology at his behest, is characterized as a corporate head. Rotwang, identified as a "scientist" or "inventor," is clearly more in the nature of an alchemist. The reediting has simplified both characters, Fredersen becoming more of a ruthless Dr. Mabuse-like figure, while Rotwang is forced into a stereotypical "mad scientist" mold. Fredersen's ultimate capitulation to the pull of sentiment is unconvincing largely because his more sympathetic side, especially his love for Freder, has been given short shrift; the tragic aspects of the Rotwang character have been eliminated along with Hel. Still, it is apparent that the Fredersen-Rotwang relationship is hardly as simple as that of employer and employee; "as always," remarks Fredersen, "I turn to you for advice when my experts fail me." Despite the absence of the necessary connective tissue, the fine performances of Alfred Abel and Rudolf Klein-Rogge manage to evoke some of the psychological complexity of the relationship. It is worth noting in this context that Klein-Rogge had been married to Thea von Harbou before her marriage to Lang, at least a partial correlation to the Fredersen-Hel-Rotwang triangle, and perhaps the experiential basis for Klein-Rogge's performance.

The Fredersen-Rotwang contrast, Maria and her robot double, and the divisive social structure of Metropolis all variously illustrate the duality of human nature, a common theme of the German silent cinema that was always to fascinate Lang. In fact, the entire film is a virtual catalog of Lang's favorite themes: the opposition of social and moral forces; the illusory nature of free will in a world governed by fate; an innocent hero in a hostile, enclosed environment; the redemptive power of a pure love; an omnipotent mastermind; and healthy doses of insanity, mob violence, and sexual enticement. In most aspects, *Metropolis* is entirely typical of Lang's work, differentiated primarily by its enormous scale and chaotic scenario.

Unfortunately, considering the film's thematic potential, the most clearly developed motif (perhaps partly attributable to emphasis by the American editors) is a rather heavy-handed Christian allegory. This is embodied in the characters—the virgin/whore Maria (Mary), the God-like figure of Joh (Jehovah) Fredersen, and his son/savior Freder—and reinforced by the film's explicit and abundant religious imagery. Naturally, there are Biblical references: Freder "crucified" on the control dial of a machine, crying out to his father; the "Tower of Babel" parable used by Maria in her teachings; the flood; Rotwang's "fall from grace" from atop the cathedral; and others. Curiously, however, even though the action is set in an ultramodern city of the future, much of the iconography is distinctly medieval: Maria's tabernacle; the cathedral and the "seven deadly sins," especially the figure of Death which appears in Freder's hallucinations; the burning at the stake of the false Maria; Rotwang's ancient house in the midst of the city, with the symbol of the pentagram prominently displayed; and Rotwang himself, with the long flowing robes and unmistakable mien of a sorcerer right out of the Middle Ages. This plethora of evocative imagery, unfortunately, is not crystallized into a coherent thematic pattern.

On balance, the case of *Metropolis* does not appear to be that of a complex masterpiece "mutilated" by its American editors. If the novel is indicative of the content and structure of the original film, then *Metropolis* may have been misshapen at any length. While some of the narrative and thematic weaknesses can be attributed to the reediting, many of the problems seem to have been inherent rather than imposed. Neither Lang's spectacular visual conceptions nor von Harbou's overwrought prose can overcome their basically unsatisfactory treatment of a difficult theme. The film preaches that the emotions should act as the foundation for social harmony, at the same time depicting the workers as mindlessly passionate, and thus exceptionally vulnerable to Fredersen's manipulations. *Metropolis* seems to say that the emotions are both indispensable and dangerous, a source of both strength and weakness. This is not an impossible premise, but given Lang's predilection for melodramatic oversimplification and visual bombast, it is hardly surprising that he failed to transform the jumble of allegorical and symbolic materials into an aesthetically satisfying whole.

Whatever the film's weaknesses, it remains a stunning visual experience, perhaps the most purely impressive product of the German "Golden Age." Lang eschewed the "expressionist" label, but this speaks more of the pervasiveness of the style during this period and of the fact that it has been largely perceived and defined by critics rather than filmmakers (comparisons with the *film noir* are appropriate in this regard). Whether or not Lang was consciously making an expressionist film is a moot point, for the evidence is on the screen; *Metropolis*, in terms of both its visual and thematic preoccupations, is firmly within the mainstream of the style. Lang's entire career reveals his expressionist tendencies, but it was in *Metropolis* that he achieved the most spectacular fusion of his early training as an architect and his considerable skills as a filmmaker. In *Metropolis*, architecture becomes drama; the film's meanings are inseparable from its visual design, and the most fascinating "character" is of the city itself. Those critics who unfairly condemn Lang's cinema as cold and manipulative may be thinking first of *Metropolis*, and Lang himself later expressed his dislike for the film "because it was a picture in which human beings were nothing but part of a machine."

Ultimately, however, much of the enduring strength of *Metropolis* lies in just those qualities and in its orchestration of light, shadow, decor, and movement on a grand scale. The opening of the film establishes its essentially geometric harmonies and oppositions: the title itself is formed by a series of diagonal lines crisscrossing the screen, then dissolves into a rhythmic montage of the components of the great machines that run the city. This abstract presentation of the city's mechanical "heart" gives way to the image of its human cogs: the workers, an undifferentiated mass of black-clad figures, trudging mechanistically across the screen in rigid formation, heads down, arms at their sides, shoulders slumped, their bodies and spirits weighed down by the symbolic burden of oppression. This is the changing of the shift in the machine rooms: as one column files six abreast into the vast elevators to descend to the workers' city far below, another column files out. The workers' city itself is a bleak and soulless place, identical buildings grouped around a central square that is barren but for a gigantic gong—no doubt used to summon them once again to their work.

Effectively establishing the anonymous, thankless drudgery of the workers' existence, this opening sequence is then contrasted with the carefree life-style of the young men of privilege. "The sons of the Masters of Metropolis," including Freder, are first seen engaged in a footrace in the city's vast athletic stadium, then romping in the Eternal Gardens, an opulent club that is sort of a rich boy's playground. The stadium scene and the first part of the club sequence have survived, but are often missing from prints in general circulation.

Having thus established the basic dichotomy between capital and labor (couched largely in architectural terms), the film proceeds to concentrate on Freder's social awakening. His fascination with Maria lures him into the underground, where he experiences a sort of mystical, hallucinatory revelation. In the machine rooms, he watches in horror as the workers lose control of the gigantic "Pater Noster" machine (so named in the novel), which explodes causing general pandemonium and considerable carnage; in Freder's vision, the machine is transformed into "Moloch" (a Babylonian deity to which children were sacrificed by their own parents) and is literally consuming the workers. "The machines of Metropolis roared," wrote Harbou, "they wanted to be fed." This experience leads Freder into a futile attempt to convince his father of the suffering of the masses; his rejection impels Freder to become an active participant in the workers' lives, rather than merely an observer. Returning to the machine room, Freder changes places with one of the workers, thus experiencing personally the dehumanizing agony of the ten-hour shift.

Because of the film's futuristic setting and the importance of its special effects (of which the "Moloch" sequence is the first sustained example), *Metropolis* is generally considered to be the first great science-fiction film, although its generic aspects constitute only a portion of its value. Particularly influential in this respect was the scene depicting the creation of the false Maria in Rotwang's Frankensteinian workshop, a fantastic conglomeration of technological apparatus. The technique most predominantly used in *Metropolis* was the "Schüfftan process," named after its inventor Eugene Schüfftan. This was a photographic system that allowed people and miniature sets to be combined in a single shot, through the use of mirrors rather than laboratory work. Modern technology has long since rendered the techniques of *Metropolis* obsolete, but they are still remarkably effective. The heritage of *Metropolis* is to be seen not only in subsequent science-fiction films, but in virtually the entire spectrum of American filmmaking from the 1920's through the 1950's. The conventions of expressionism crossed the Atlantic with the emigrant German filmmakers and were in turn absorbed into the Hollywood style—most strikingly in the horror film and the *film noir*.

This discussion may give the impression that Lang's accomplishments in *Metropolis* were primarily a matter of set design, special effects, and simple geometric groupings, but this view ignores his uniquely cinematic virtuosity. His use of the camera is consistently inventive and occasionally brilliant. There are isolated instances throughout the film, such as the sequence in which Rotwang pursues Maria through the caverns, illuminating her with the beam from his flashlight, and the simulation of the impact of an explosion by mounting the camera on a swing. A more sustained example of Lang's mastery of composition and editing is the depiction of the "debut" of the robot Maria. "Now we shall see whether people believe the robot is a creature of flesh and blood," declares Rotwang, just prior to its seminude performance of a seductive dance for an exclusively male audience (presumably the elite of Metropolis's society). The pace of the montage quickens as the dance becomes progressively more suggestive, and the faces of the men contort with lust; a parallel thread is introduced as Freder is seen in bed, where he is recovering from the extreme shock of having discovered "Maria" in the arms of his father. The faces of the men soon dissolve into a surrealistic collage of staring eyes, which in turn becomes part of Freder's hallucination. In his feverish vision, he sees the figure of Death, backed by the "seven deadly sins," lurching toward him, swinging its scythe. Having begun with the robot, the sequence ends with Freder lapsing once again into unconsciousness. Even in its apparently truncated form (the robot's highly suggestive dance shows evidence of trimming), this sequence is an excellent illustration of Lang's command of the film medium. The subsequent events are, if anything, even more impressive. The latter part of the film is a relentless gush of action, with Lang's feeling for movement and spectacle at its peak. However confused the narrative may have become by this point, Lang's orchestration of the hordes of people sweeping across the screen in an orgy of destruction is still rousing.

Metropolis came at a crucial juncture for the German film industry, and its repercussions were far-reaching. By far the most expensive German production to date, it stretched the financial resources of Ufa to the limit. During the extended period of its production, the troubled company was forced to increase its dependence on several major German banks, as well as on foreign capital (which came primarily in the form of a four-million-dollar loan from two American companies, Paramount and Metro-Goldwyn). The huge cost and relatively small return of *Metropolis* helped to facilitate the passage of control of Ufa into the hands of the industrialist and newspaper publisher Alfred Hugenberg. Hugenberg, whose nationalist views were similar to those of Adolf Hitler (and who would, in fact, briefly occupy a government post in the Third Reich), bought out the American interests and gained control of the company's board of directors in April, 1927. Within a few years, its films (particularly the newsreels) exhibited a marked nationalist outlook. This increasingly politicized creative climate accelerated the emigration of the country's major film talent to Hollywood, and by the early 1930's, the so-called "Golden Age" had effectively come to an end. *Metropolis* can hardly be held completely accountable for the downfall of Ufa, for the company had been financially unstable almost from its inception; Lang's film, rather, represented a very large straw on the back of a very frail camel.

It seems likely that Lang's dislike for *Metropolis*, noted above, was influenced somewhat by its commercial failure as well as by his desire to dissociate himself from its "mutilated surrogate" (as he referred to the truncated American version). Yet, he had an even better reason to shudder at the memory of the film: *Metropolis*, it seems, had, in 1927, made a lasting impression on Hitler. (One need only look at the spectacle of the Nuremburg rally, or consider the concept of a "master race," to understand the appeal the film had for Hitler.) When the Nazi Party rose to power in 1933, Lang was approached by Propaganda Minister Joseph Goebbels, who offered him the leadership of the "new" German film industry. Fearing the possible discovery that his mother was Jewish, Lang fled the country immediately. His wife, Thea von Harbou, an ardent member of the Nazi Party, remained behind. Lang went first to Paris, where he made one film, before arriving in Hollywood in 1934. His subsequent American career, which has only recently emerged from beneath the shadow of critical neglect, included such classics as *Fury* (1936), *Scarlet Street* (1945), and *The Big Heat* (1953), but *Metropolis* in many ways is his most enduring film. It continues to overwhelm new generations with its sheer majesty and has lodged itself firmly in the consciousness of all who have beheld its wonders.

Howard H. Prouty

MICKEY

Released: 1918
Production: Mack Sennett for Mabel Normand Feature Films Company; released by Western Import Company
Direction: F. Richard Jones
Screenplay: Based on a story by J. G. Hawks
Cinematography: Hans F. Koenekamp
Length: 7 reels

Principal characters:
Mickey .... Mabel Normand
Joe Meadows .... George Nichols
Herbert Thornhill .... Wheeler Oakman
Elsie Drake .... Minta Durfee
Mrs. Geoffrey Drake .... Laura LaVarnie
Reggie Drake .... Lew Cody
Tom Rawlings .... Tom Kennedy
Bookie .... Edgar Kennedy
Minnie .... Minnie Ha Ha

Mickey arrived in theaters by accident. Sometime in 1918, a Long Island, New York, theater owner lost his Sunday feature and asked the exchange for a substitute. By mistake, *Mickey*, begun in 1916, finished in 1917 and languishing on the shelf since then, was dispatched.

Its history goes back to a promise Mack Sennett had made to his star, Mabel Normand, that he would showcase her talents in a more dignified feature-length comedy, rather than the slapstick for which she was famous. To realize his promise, Sennett borrowed heavily. He gave Normand everyone she wanted: F. Richard Jones, who had guided her through countless shorts with "Fatty" Arbuckle, to direct; Lew Cody, whom she later married, as the villain; and Wheeler Oakman as her hero. "Mickey," the theme song was also created, which is still heard occasionally.

When the film was finished, *The Moving Picture World* stated: "Mabel Norman [*sic*] in 'Mickey' Bids Farewell to Squash Pie Comedy to Do Something More Genteel." Exhibitors apparently thought this was the kiss of death, for Sennett was unable to interest them in booking the film until filmgoers saw it through that fortuitous mishap and word of mouth built *Mickey* into a success.

"Madcap" Mabel appears in diluted form in *Mickey*. The Sennet shorts which had made her famous showed Normand hurtling through each film, kicking, shoving, tripping, and falling. *Mickey* is akin to the more sedate pictures Mary Pickford was making for Famous Players at the time than to the plotless insanity of the Keystone comedies. Despite a plot that keeps her enclosed inside a gloomy Long Island mansion for too long, the irrepressible Normand manages to slide down a hill on her derriere, leap about on over-stuffed furniture, and clean a banister in the mansion by sliding down it.

At the (aptly named) Tomboy mine in California, Mickey's father, Joe Meadows (George Nichols), worried that he is about to die, writes to the Drakes, relatives in the East, asking them to take care of his daughter, Mickey (Mabel Normand). At the same time, Herbert Thornhill (Wheeler Oakman), a friend of the Drake family and a representative of the mine's owners, arrives to look over the property. Although Herbert is engaged to Elsie Drake (Minta Durfee), he and Mickey fall in love. While he is away, a letter from the Drakes invites Mickey East, and Joe accompanies Mickey to the Drake home where both are awed by the oppulent surroundings. Herbert returns to the mine and is disappointed to find Mickey gone. Mrs. Drake (Laura LaVarnie) accepted Mickey only because she believed the mine was flourishing, and when she finds that it is not, she turns Mickey into the household drudge. Mickey thwarts her aim, sweeping dirt under the rug and turning up at Elsie's reception for Herbert in Elsie's dress.

Mickey has been banished to California and is en route when a telegram arrives from Joe saying that the mine is worth millions. Mrs. Drake then hurries after Mickey and drags her back to the house where she is once again treated as an honored guest. Elsie's brother, Reggie (Lew Cody), learning of her financial desirability, woos her forcefully, but she rejects him. Mickey unwillingly consents to go horseback riding with Reggie and bolts when he makes a pass. Reggie then chases her into his house where she races upstairs and out onto a balcony. Reggie drags her back in, and while they are wrestling, Herbert arrives to rescue her. As Mickey and Herbert leave for California on their honeymoon, Tom Rawlings (Tom Kennedy), Herbert's lawyer, tells them that he sent the telegram about the mine being a disaster to get Herbert out of his engagement to Elsie.

Mickey is nothing more than the old Country Cousin story, but Normand is adorable, tiny, saucer-eyed, and energetic. There is not enough for her to do, however, since the film keeps her windmilling furiously through its various houses, but she is not going anywhere. The titles indict the East as a "heartless society" and it is clear that everyone's sympathies lie in the West. The East is artificial, decadent, and stultifying, while the West is open, healthy, and free. It is as simple as that, a point the film makes by showing Mickey playing with her cat, cavorting through a dry-goods store with her dog, then whisking into Herbert's hotel room to hide under his bed from the irate proprietor.

Nevertheless, the two scenes which best illustrate Normand's talents take place in that citadel of sin, the Eastern mansion. The first shows Normand as Mickey, transformed into a saucy Cinderella, cleaning the enormous foyer by whisking the dirt from one place to another. She is cheerful, impudent, and mugs unrestrainedly as she makes fun of her stodgy aunt. In the second scene, Mickey swipes brandy-soaked cherries from a cake made for Herbert's homecoming party. She reels around the kitchen bugging her eyes and clutching her tummy, then pops another cherry into her mouth.

Normand is an inventive performer, and she gives her all to *Mickey*, making the girl an engaging, sympathetic individual. More than that, she is Douglas Fairbanks' equal in taking risks for the sake of a stunt. She is not as athletic as Fairbanks, but she is every bit as daring, climbing around a roof and dangling from the eaves. *Mickey* is a character, courageous and selfless to be sure, but she is not allowed to grow, except to fall in love. She is nothing more than a plot device, a plot with which Sennett became uncomfortable. More than halfway through the film, the story, such as it is, is discarded and *Mickey* becomes a series of unrelated, action-filled events, strung together on the slightest of pretexts. Mickey upsets a scheme to fix a race by riding in it herself and knocking the crooked jockey off his horse. She dashes around the villain's house trying to escape his clutches, and winds up hanging from the eaves. Director Jones does everything he can to keep that chase going. It is not enough to have Mickey escape onto a balcony, she has to be hauled back, go a few rounds with Reggie, then flee again to the roof where Herbert will, once and for all, deliver her from Reggie's grasp.

The conclusion of *Mickey* leaves one wondering what would have happened if Sennett had fulfilled his promise to Normand and given her a vehicle worthy of her comedic gifts. On the evidence of *Mickey*'s most successful scenes, she could have risen to any occasion and realized the promise that she showed throughout her aborted, unsatisfactory career.

Unfortunately, Normand's association with the principals of three Hollywood scandals, during the early 1920's, put an early end to her career. She co-starred with Arbuckle, who was tried in the Virginia Rappe rape/murder case, in many Sennett shorts; she was said to be one of the lovers of director William Desmond Taylor whose murder was never solved; and finally, her chauffeur was found leaning over the dead body of millionaire Cortland S. Dines—the gun in his hand was supposedly Normand's. In *The Parade's Gone By*, Kevin Brownlow offers another suggestion, referring to "a charming, apparently inoffensive actor on the Sennett lot," who may have led to her decline. He quotes director Eddie Sutherland as saying,

Everyone who took drugs in the industry was started by this man. He was one of the quietest, nicest actors I've ever known. He put Mabel Normand on the junk, Wallie Reid, Alma Rubens. All three died as a direct result. Somebody would have a hangover, and he'd say, "I'll fix it for you," and that was that.

Judith M. Kass

MIGHTY LIKE A MOOSE

Released: 1926
Production: Hal Roach for Roach/Pathé
Direction: Leo McCarey
Screenplay: no listing
Cinematography: no listing
Length: 2 reels

> *Principal characters:*
> The husband .... Charley Chase
> The wife .... Vivien Oakland

Despite his career lasting from the early years of the silent cinema well into the talkie era, Charley Chase is not one of the better-known comedians. His films continue to entertain audiences thanks to television and the film collectors' market, and, because his shorts were some of the few available to television stations in the early 1950's, Chase has managed to remain in the public eye. Yet, despite the constant exposure, Chase does not have a name— or even a face—which brings instant recognition. One problem is that he was basically a star of short subjects. He did make a number of sound features, but they were not particularly good and did little for his image. So, while Charles Chaplin has *The Gold Rush* (1925) and other features, Harry Langdon has *The Strong Man* (1926), Harold Lloyd has *Safety Last* (1923), and Buster Keaton has *The General* (1926), Chase has no one feature-length comedy with which to prove his worth. Also, other comedians had gimmicks or trademarks. There was the Chaplin walk, the baggy pants, mustache, and cane; Keaton had a porkpie hat; Lloyd had his glasses; and Langdon had a baby face. The best that Chase has to offer is a straw boater, and that is not always part of his screen image.

Lloyd's screen *persona* probably comes closest to that of Chase. Both are amiable bumblers, for whom one feels instant sympathy and experiences empathy. Chase's problems were usually domestic in nature and were of the variety that many husbands have had to face, although usually with not such entertaining and amusing results.

Born in 1893, Chase had worked in vaudeville and burlesque before entering films in the early teens. He first came to prominence in Mack Sennett's company, appearing in a number of early Chaplin shorts. Chase soon began to direct as well as play supporting roles in comedies and moved from Sennett to the William Fox studios. In 1921, Chase joined the Hal Roach studios, initially as a director, and—as Laurel and Hardy were to do later—it was at Roach where Chase matured as a comedian, polishing his screen character with the guidance of director Leo McCarey.

Leo McCarey (1898-1969) is highly respected as the director of features such as *Duck Soup* (1933), *Ruggles of Red Gap* (1935), *Make Way for Tomorrow* (1937), *The Awful Truth* (1937), *Going My Way* (1944), and *The Bells of St. Mary's* (1945), and many people forget that he first came to prominence as a gag writer and director with Hal Roach. McCarey became Chase's director in 1924 and has said of the comedian,

> My association with Charley Chase was one of the most pleasant memories I have in motion pictures. He was a great man, had a keen sense of comedy values, and we were together in fifty pictures at Hal Roach studio. I received credit as director but it was really Chase who did most of the directing. Whatever success I have had or may have, I owe to his help because he taught me all I know.

During this period, the Hal Roach studio, where the supervising director was the brilliant F. Richard Jones, was turning out comedy shorts featuring such notables as Mabel Normand, Our Gang, Chase, and Glenn Tryon, with Jimmy Finlayson and Max Davidson in very active supporting roles. At the same time, Fox was producing shorts featuring Earle Foxe; Universal had the Arthur Lake comedies; Educational offered shorts with Al St. John, Johnny Arthur, Billy Dooley, and Bobby Vernon; while Mack Sennett, Roach's major rival who also released through Pathé, was producing comedy shorts featuring Alice Day, Ben Turpin, Billy Bevan, Vernon Dent, and Andy Clyde.

Between 1924 and 1929, Chase starred in more than eighty silent-comedy shorts for Roach; they had titles such as *Why Husbands Go Mad* (1924), *Should Husbands Be Watched* (1925), *Long Flib the King* (1926), *The Lighter That Failed* (1927), and *The Way of All Pants* (1927). Of all these productions, film historians are unanimous in selecting as the finest Chase silent comedy, *Mighty Like a Moose*, initially released on July 18, 1926.

Mighty Like a Moose has Chase as a husband with an ugly set of buck teeth and Vivien Oakland as his wife with an embarrassingly hawklike nose. Without revealing their plans to each other, the husband has his teeth straightened while the wife undergoes a nose job. After their respective changes, the two meet, fail to recognize each other and agree to go out for a night on the town. A party which they attend is raided, and when their pictures appear in the morning newspaper, the two must face the consequences of having been unfaithful.

As Peter Milne commented in *The Moving Picture World* (July 17, 1926), "The laughs are thickest when, after a party, the husband discovers the identity of his partner and then, to test her, poses alternately as the husband, using a false set of buck teeth, and then as the lover." Roach studios advertised *Mighty Like a Moose* as "just about the greatest two reel comedy ever made," and there are many who would agree, including film historian Leonard Maltin, who has commented, "It's a superb comedy, which deftly blends sophistication and sight gags and depends as much on *acting* and *personality* to bring it off as any other element. This is where Chase stood out from the crowd of second-echelon comics."

Chase remained with Roach through the coming of sound, starring in more than fifty shorts for the producer, many of which he also directed under the name of Charles Parrott. Chase also made two features for Roach, *Sons of the Desert* (1933, a Laurel and Hardy vehicle) and *Kelly the Second* (1936), a disastrous production co-starring Patsy Kelly. In 1936, Chase left Roach and moved to Columbia, where he was featured in a number of shorts through 1940. He died, while still a relatively young man, on June 30, 1940. Chase, who at all times displayed ingenuity and a flair for the unexpected in his films and did so in an era of frenetic slapstick, had a pleasantly sobering influence on the industry.

Lennox Sanderson, Jr.

THE MIRACLE MAN

Released: 1919
Production: Mayflower; released by Artcraft/Paramount
Direction: George Loane Tucker
Screenplay: George Loane Tucker; based on the play of the same name by
George M. Cohan and a short story by Frank L. Packard
Cinematography: Philip Rosen and Ernest Palmer
Length: 7 reels

Principal characters:
Tom Burke .... Thomas Meighan
Rose .... Betty Compson
The Frog .... Lon Chaney
The Dope .... J. M. Dumont
The Patriarch .... Joseph J. Dowling
Richard King .... W. Lawson Butt
Claire King .... Elinor Fair

In the film biography of Lon Chaney, *The Man of a Thousand Faces* (1957), James Cagney beautifully and accurately re-creates Chaney's big moment in *The Miracle Man*. Cagney (as Chaney) portrays a half-paralyzed cripple on a pilgrimage to see a famous faith healer. Propelled by his hands, he drags his twisted legs through the small town to the tall commanding figure of the healer. With hurt in his eyes, he looks up at the religious man, and then with convulsions, his body slowly straightens until he is at last standing. The effect on film audiences inevitably brings spontaneous applause, just as it did in the original picture.

In the actual film version of *The Miracle Man*, Chaney is a con man known as "The Frog." His con consists of twisting his limbs and taking them out of their sockets to give the impression that he is crippled. He is a beggar, but he is also involved in other shams with a gang. His best friend in the gang is a seedy-looking embezzler known as "The Dope" (J. M. Dumont), who spends his money on syringes of cocaine. The leader of the gang is a good-looking fellow named Tom Burke (Thomas Meighan). His girl friend is Rose (Betty Compson), a beautiful, young but hardened member of the little gang.

The night the story begins finds the four gathered about the table of their Chinatown den, about to divide the shares of their latest heist. Tom Burke suddenly stops dividing the money and announces that he has a plan which will change their little pile into a fortune. Although they do not appear interested, he pulls out a newspaper clipping and reads it to them. The story tells about a deaf and dumb man rapidly going blind, who is revered as a faith healer in the small village where he lives alone. The villagers fondly call him their "Patriarch" (Joseph J. Dowling).

The Frog and the Dope say that they do not believe in that stuff, and ask where the money is in Tom's scheme. Tom explains that he will go to the town, get into the old man's confidence, and then have the Frog come and pretend that the old man has cured his paralysis. "We'll advertise it big and get all the suckers in the country flocking to us," Tom concludes. Tom asks them if they agree to his scheme, and then unflinchingly stares at them until they each uneasily agree. His last instructions are for each of them to stay out of trouble and be ready to come when he sends for them.

A few weeks later, Rose receives a letter from Tom, telling of his progress. He has managed to get close to the Patriarch by faking heart pains. He tells Rose that he has slipped a bit of paper into the old man's Bible with Rose's name and address and the words "my grand-niece" written upon it. He tells her to be ready, for as soon as one of the villagers sees it, they will certainly send for her.

Not long afterward, Rose arrives by train in the small village. Tom is disappointed to see her sexy outfit and reminds her that she must appear virginal if the scheme is to work. She moves in to care for her old "uncle," who is fond of her, and she also becomes popular with the villagers. As soon as Rose has fitted into the village life, Tom announces that they are ready for the next stage, and he wires for the Frog.

When the Frog's train pulls in, Tom is surprised to see that it has a swarm of reporters aboard and a private railroad car attached. Tom sees the Dope in the crowd and motions him over. "That is Richard King's car—the asbestos tycoon," the Dope informs Tom. "His sister is a cripple."

Just then, the Frog flounders down the steps of the car and painfully makes his way through the crowd. As he drags himself down the main street, the reporters follow. Behind them all, Richard King (W. Lawson Butt) slowly pushes his sister Claire (Elinor Fair) in her wheelchair.

When Rose sees the approaching crowd, she leads the Patriarch out into the front yard. He stands there, neither seeing nor hearing, as the crowd gathers outside the picket fence, and the Frog crawls up the garden path to his feet. Looking for a sign after none comes, the Frog spies Tom in the crowd and with a sign from him begins the convulsions of "the miracle."

The spectators are amazed when the Frog finally stands erect, and Tom smiles contentedly to himself. He is frightened, however, when he sees Richard King push his sister Claire up to the old man because he thinks that everything will certainly be ruined.

Then a real miracle amazes Tom as Claire rises from her wheelchair. Tom is so flabbergasted that he almost forgets his next move. In a daze, he moves toward the old man, writes a check, and puts it in the Patriarch's pocket. Richard King does likewise, and the crowd accordingly gives lesser amounts.

Tom amasses a vast sum of money and is a little surprised to see that his cohorts are not anxious to get their share. The Dope has fallen in love with a village girl and has given up drugs. The Frog, meanwhile, has become devoted to the Patriarch and waits on him full time. Rose spends long refined hours with Richard King, who is in love with her. Tom is jealous and thinks that Rose only wants to land a millionaire. It is only when Rose turns down Richard King's proposal of marriage that Tom begins to see that her love for him is more important than money.

On the night that the Patriarch dies, the four numbly sit around the body. They vow to use his money for good works, for, as Tom says, "A good thought can't die, and that's what he was—a good thought."

The director of *The Miracle Man*, George Loane Tucker, made no more films, for he died shortly afterward. His other famous film was *A Traffic in Souls* (1913), a sensationally popular exposé of the white-slave traffic in New York.

The Miracle Man made stars of Chaney, Thomas Meighan, and Betty Compson. Along with *Broken Blossoms*, it was the most highly praised and successful picture of 1919.

Larry Lee Holland

THE MIRACLE OF THE WOLVES

Released: 1924
Production: Raymond Bernard for La Société des Romans Historiques Filmés
Direction: Raymond Bernard
Screenplay: A. Paul Antoine; based on the novel by Henry Dupuis-Mazuel
Cinematography: Forster, Bujard, and Batton
Art direction: M. R. Mallet-Stevens
Costume design: Job
Length: 13 reels

Principal characters:
Louis XI	Charles Dullin
Charles, Duke of Burgundy	Vanni-Marcoux
Robert Cottereau	Romuald Joube
Jeanne Fouguet	Yvonne Sergyl
Philippe the Good	Mailly
Tristan the Hermit	Philippe Hériat
Count du Lau	Gaston Modot
Bische	Armand Bernard
Fouquet	Maujain

The major French silent-film production *The Miracle of the Wolves* was little known outside of its native land until fairly recent times. To be sure, Georges Sadoul mentions it in his 1953 volume, *French Film*, commenting, "The finished film, authentic, polished and stately, with the right degree of pomp and splendour, was a great success in France and abroad." The Cinémathèque Française screened the film on an irregular basis, and it was from the Cinémathèque that historian/film programmer William K. Everson obtained a 16mm print in the early 1970's. Everson heralded the feature as "a staggering and often lyrical film." *The Miracle of the Wolves* was eventually screened at the 1978 New York Film Festival, and, at last, recognized as a major work in the history of the silent motion picture.

The film was directed by Raymond Bernard (1891-1977), whose first connection with both the stage and the screen was in playing Sarah Bernhardt's son in *Jeanne Doré*, a vehicle written for Bernhardt by Raymond's father, Tristan Bernard. Raymond Bernard later became an assistant to Jacques Feyder at Gaumont and made his directorial debut in 1917 with *Le Ravins sans fond*. Bernard's work on *The Miracle of the Wolves* has been well documented by Elliott Stein in an article in the September-October, 1978, issue of *Film Comment*. It was Henri Dupuis-Mazuel, author of the novel on which the film was based, who selected Bernard as director. Shooting began at the Joinville studios, on the outskirts of Paris, in December, 1923, and was not completed until August of the following year.

A historical drama set during the reign of King Louis XI, the film version of *The Miracle of the Wolves* was sponsored by the French government. Wherever possible authentic locations were used, but because the city of Beauvais no longer retained its medieval battlements, scenes set there were actually shot at the walled city of Carcasonne in the South of France. Extras came from the French armed forces.

The film takes place during the fifteenth century in France, and Louis XI (Charles Dullin) is battling for control of his Kingdom with Charles, the Duke of Burgundy (Vanni-Marcoux). Robert Cottereau (Romuald Joube), a loyal knight in the service of the Duke of Burgundy, is infatuated with Jeanne Fouquette (Yvonne Sergyl), who later became known as Jeanne Hachette, because of her use of a battle axe to defend the town of Beauvais. The title of the film derives from the episode in which Jeanne must race across a snowy and frozen countryside to save the life of her King, pursued by the Duke of Burgundy's men. Just as Jeanne is about to be seized, a pack of wolves surrounds the praying girl. Then, the wolves attack her pursuers in a surprisingly realistic and vicious sequence. Thanks to Jeanne's efforts, Louis XI is safe and able to create a unified France rather than allow the various factions to split the country into small feudal states.

The film is at times complex and perhaps relies too heavily on its viewers' knowledge of French medieval history. The battle scenes, particularly the attack on Beauvais, are both dramatic and authentic, at times putting to shame the historical epics of Cecil B. De Mille and the like.

Charles Dullin as Louis XI is not required to participate in the action sequences but is generally seen sitting behind a chess board, which dissolves into a map of France. Dullin was a major theatrical figure in France, but, unfortunately, he closely resembles Western star William S. Hart, and American critics were not very impressed by his performance.

Upon completion, *The Miracle of the Wolves* received its world premiere at the Paris Opera, in November, 1924, before an invited audience which included the French president, members of the government, and all the prominent figures in the world of French arts and letters. A specially composed score was conducted by Henri Rabaud and played by a full symphony orchestra. *The Miracle of the Wolves* was the first film to be screened at the Opera. The film was presented in the United States under the auspices of a committee, which included William Wrigley, Jr., Cornelius Vanderbilt, and General Coleman duPont, and began a special engagement at New York's Criterion Theater on February 23, 1925. At that time, the film ran 113 minutes, but it was subsequently cut to seventy-five minutes for a more appropriate arthouse screening at the Fifth Avenue Playhouse on July 27, 1926.

Despite the number of prestigious names backing the film on its initial American presentation, reaction from the critics was generally poor. *Variety*

(February 25, 1925) was particularly scathing, with its critic, "Fred," commenting,

> There was nothing to grow enthusiastic about. The big scene from which the production derives its name resolves itself into seven police dogs, well trained in protection and the fight they put up with the men was to all appearances a real one . . . the picture itself after all is another costume affair and that about sums it up. . . . In the cast of French players there is no one that offers anything in particular any American producer would want with the possible exception of the leading lady.

Taking a second look at the production, on July 30, 1926, *Variety* noted,

> This film supposedly got the raves from such fellows like Baron Rothschild, Sascha Guitry and other intellectuals but for the exhibitors to take such exploitation for value is to discredit the entertainment seeking angle of the customers.

Photoplay (May, 1925) commented, "More than half of this picture should have been cut out, the rest of it edited in good American fashion and then made over."

Only Mordaunt Hall in *The New York Times* (February 24, 1925) was sympathetic toward the production, but even he had some criticism for the poorly written English subtitles, the confusing plot line, the prolonged fadeouts, and the lethargic romance. Hall did, however, proclaim *The Miracle of the Wolves* as "a wonderful picture in many respects."

Viewed today, one can agree with much of the criticism. It is a complex historical drama which seems to make up in authenticity for what it lacks in dramatic impact. The scenes with the wolves, however, still contain considerable power. The shots of the animals surrounding the praying Jeanne are emotionally stirring, and there is a viciousness to the wolves' attack on her pursuers which is horrifying even by the standards of the 1980's.

André Hunebelle remade *The Miracle of the Wolves* in the mid-1950's as a widescreen color epic, featuring Jean Marais and Jean-Louis Barrault, but it most assuredly did not have the impact of its silent predecessor.

Lennox Sanderson, Jr.

MISS LULU BETT

Released: 1921
Production: Adolph Zukor for Famous Players-Lasky/Paramount
Direction: William C. deMille
Screenplay: Clara Beranger; based on the novel and the play of the same name by Zona Gale
Cinematography: L. Guy Wilky
Length: 7 reels/5,904 feet

Principal characters:
Lulu Bett	Lois Wilson
Neil Cornish	Milton Sills
Dwight Deacon	Theodore Roberts
Diana Deacon	Helen Ferguson
Mrs. Dwight Deacon	Mabel Van Buren
Monona Deacon	May Giraci
Ninian Deacon	Clarence Burton
Grandma Bett	Ethel Wales
Bobby Larkin	Taylor Graves
Station Agent	Charles Ogle

"The highest function of motion-picture art is to express the people to themselves," wrote William C. deMille in his 1939 autobiography, *Hollywood Saga.* "The voice of the screen is the voice of common humanity trying to put into living words its thoughts and emotions, its ideals and its dreams." Through the body of films that deMille (1878-1955) directed between 1916 and 1934, he tried to carry out that belief. Unlike his more famous brother, Cecil, William seemed preoccupied with the film as an art form; his films generally were not conceived as box-office attractions. He was a man of the theater, who came to films when he and others (such as D. W. Griffith) had come to believe that the medium could be the twentieth century art form. With pro-ductions such as *Conrad in Quest of His Youth* (1920), *What Every Woman Knows* (1921), and *His Double Life* (1934), William C. deMille demonstrated a remarkable and finely tuned directorial ability, but there can be little ques-tion that his supreme triumph, his single greatest achievement, was the 1921 production of *Miss Lulu Bett.*

Miss Lulu Bett by Zona Gale had been both a novel and a play; in fact, it was the Pulitzer Prize-winning play of 1920-1921, with Carroll McComas in the title role. Famous Players-Lasky purchased the screen rights for fifteen thousand dollars and produced the entire film for the surprisingly low sum of sixty-six thousand dollars. William C. deMille had already achieved one successful transition from stage to screen with his production of *What Every Woman Knows*, and so it was perhaps natural that he and his leading lady from that feature, Lois Wilson, should be assigned to the new film. Clara Beranger, in real life Mrs. William deMille, adapted the play for the screen.

The film was very much concerned with deMille's "common humanity" in the shape of Lulu Bett, "the family beast of burden, whose timid soul has failed to break the bonds of family servitude." As portrayed by Wilson, Lulu Bett has a plain face, not ugly but hardened beyond its years by lack of love and affection. Her hair is pulled tightly back, and she is the cruel stereotype of the doomed spinster. Wilson (born in 1896) gives an extraordinary performance, perhaps the greatest of her long career. *Miss Lulu Bett* was the film in which Wilson proved herself an actress; unlike her later insipid-heroine parts in *The Covered Wagon* (1923), *The Vanishing American* (1925), and *The Great Gatsby* (1926), here the actress was required to become the character of Lulu Bett, a curious mixture of servitude and strength, a character who takes life as it comes but can still overcome despair when necessary.

Miss Lulu Bett opens with two titles which set the mood for the production: "The greatest tragedy in the world, because it is the most frequent, is that of a human soul caught in the toils of the commonplace," and "This happens in many a home where family ties, which should be bonds of love, have become iron fetters of dependence." Lulu Bett (Lois Wilson) is the spinster sister-in-law of Dwight Deacon (Theodore Roberts), a small-town justice of the peace and dentist. She takes the place of a servant in the Deacon household, cooking and cleaning for her sister, brother-in-law, mother, and her brother-in-law's two daughters. Lulu Bett is the family Cinderella, but there is no deliberate animosity toward her in the Deacon family; it is simply that everyone has become used to her being an unpaid servant. Of course, she is also the only "normal" member of the family, with Mr. Deacon being well-meaning if totally lacking in sympathy and understanding, while Grandma Bett (Ethel Wales) considers that the only way to get what she wants is by throwing tantrums. When chided by her son-in-law for being late to dinner, she refuses to eat at his table and sulks in the kitchen, where she surreptitiously feeds herself. Particular mention should be made of Ethel Wales, a character actress who generally portrayed elderly ladies in countless silent films and early talkies, and who here gives one of the best performances of her long career.

Ninian Deacon (Clarence Burton), the black-sheep brother of Dwight, pays a surprise visit, and, feeling some sympathy toward Lulu Bett, suggests a supper party in her honor. During the dinner, Ninian, for fun, takes Lulu Bett's hand and announces that he is taking her for his wedded wife. Also in fun, Lulu Bett responds. Suddenly, Dwight realizes that such a declaration in front of a justice of the peace—himself—is binding, and Ninian and Lulu Bett are indeed husband and wife. Ninian accepts the situation as does Lulu Bett, realizing that here lies an escape from the drudgery of her life. The two leave on their honeymoon, and only later does Ninian casually recall that he is already married, although deserted by his wife.

Lulu Bett feels no animosity toward Ninian, but decides that rather than risk committing bigamy, she must return to Dwight Deacon and his family. They, naturally, are pleased to see their unpaid servant return, although unwilling to let Lulu Bett know of their satisfaction. DeMille indicates to the audience what Lulu Bett's absence has meant to the family by presenting a shot of bugs darting around the kitchen sink.

Lulu Bett's unhappiness with her lot becomes apparent to the local school-teacher, Neil Cornish (Milton Sills). An affection develops between the two, and when confirmation of the existence of Ninian's first wife arrives, Neil and Lulu Bett are married.

Miss Lulu Bett is not a film that boasts of any outstanding cinematographic technique. It is a production which relies on human emotions for its success, on refined acting, on minor touches, and a warmth that envelops the spectator. It is simple, and it is in its simplicity that it pleases.

The reviewers all expressed admiration for the production, coupled with great regard for Wilson's acting. *Photoplay* (March, 1922) commented, "Mr. deMille has shown rare skill and intelligence in his handling of the story. What is more he receives stalwart assistance from Lois Wilson." In *Filmplay* (February, 1922), Arthur Denison commented,

William deMille has done a fine thing in his screen adaptation of *Miss Lulu Bett*. From the novel, and from Zona Gale's dramatization of her book, he has made a photoplay which holds up an accurate mirror to an interesting slice of American life. We suppose many producers imagine they are doing the same thing; but for the most part they have indulged in those curved and awry looking glasses of the nickelodeon which distort everything they are called on to reflect. Mr. deMille has made a heartening discovery: that it is sometimes advisable and even feasible to be faithful to the novel or play which one is picturizing. He has followed Miss Gale's original with fidelity and the result is one of the most genuine and truthful, and at the same time interesting, transcriptions of life to the screen which we have met with in several years of picture going.

In the issue of February 25, 1921, the critic for *The New York Times* wrote,

It takes rank as an entertaining and significant screen work. Undoubtedly the greater share of credit for this should go to Mr. deMille, for he, surely, was chiefly responsible for the expressive settings, the independent pantomime and the illuminating sideshots which enrich the photoplay. He was aided, presumably, by Miss Clara Beranger and others of his staff, but it was his own work as the director in charge that counted for most in the production of the picture, one imagines, and therefore *Miss Lulu Bett* is put down as one of the best things he has ever done.

Unlike the films of his brother Cecil B. De Mille, the productions of William C. deMille are seldom seen, but when viewed they prove to be far superior efforts from an artistic point of view, standing out as the works of an intelligent and sensitive director rather than a mere showman. *Miss Lulu Bett* is one of a small group of deMille films known to exist, and it is preserved at the Museum of Modern Art in New York.

Anthony Slide

MR. ROBINSON CRUSOE

Released: 1932
Production: The Elton Corp.; released by United Artists
Direction: Edward Sutherland
Screenplay: Tom Geraghty; based on a story by Elton Thomas (Douglas Fairbanks)
Cinematography: Max Dupont
Editing: Robert Kern
Music: Alfred Newman
Length: 8 reels

> *Principal characters:*
> Steve Drexel .... Douglas Fairbanks
> William Belmont .... William Farnum
> Professor Carmichale .... Earle Browne
> Saturday .... Maria Alba

Charles Chaplin's *City Lights* and Robert Flaherty's *Tabu* (both 1931 releases) are often referred to as the only silent films made in the early 1930's. Overlooked and usually slighted by historians when it is mentioned is a third 1930's silent, *Mr. Robinson Crusoe*, a zesty adventure tale with Douglas Fairbanks which was filmed in Tahiti. When it was released in the summer of 1932, few filmgoers and fewer critics found it to their liking, and it quickly disappeared, only rarely appearing at revival theaters and on television decades later.

Profit was not Fairbanks' motivation for making the film, even though his three previous films, all of them talkies, had been disasters at the box office. *The Taming of the Shrew* (1929), *Reaching for the Moon* (1930), and the documentary of his world tour, *Around the World in 80 Minutes* (1931) were all commercial failures. Sound and Fairbanks simply did not mix, and audiences turned away from their favorite swashbuckler of the 1920's in droves.

The reason Fairbanks made *Mr. Robinson Crusoe* was strictly a personal one: he wanted to get away from his wife, Mary Pickford, and her open involvement with actor Charles "Buddy" Rogers. There seemed no better way to distract himself than by traveling to an exotic island and there film one of his favorite adventure stories as a modern vehicle for himself. It was to be a silent in the sense that Chaplin's *City Lights* and his later *Modern Times* (1936) are silent, that is with a musical score and sound effects but no dialogue *per se*. The closest that *Mr. Robinson Crusoe* comes to dialogue is a scene in which a song is played on a radio. Other than that, there is blissful silence playfully underscored by Alfred Newman's music.

Fairbanks plays a wealthy sportsman named Steve Drexel, who is cruising on his yacht in the South Seas with two companions when one of them,

William Belmont (William Farnum), playfully wagers that Drexel could not exist for three months on a desert island. Belmont goes further to bet a thousand dollars that not only can Drexel not survive, but that he will also end up being roasted over a slow fire by savage natives. Being an eager sport, Drexel agrees to the wager and jumps ship with only his clothes and his dog, heading for a nearby island.

Over the next ninety days, Drexel not only survives on his desert island but also transforms it almost overnight into a jungle suburb, complete with grass hut, street signs, an overhead trolley line, and a radio. Inspiring this burst of technological showmanship is an island girl he meets and whom he dubs Saturday (Maria Alba, who was discovered by Fairbanks and apparently made only one film). Drexel, an inveterate showoff, goes out of his way to impress Saturday (and by extension the audience), building elaborate gadgets for her and generally turning a tropical no man's land into a mechanized Utopia.

Meanwhile, Belmont and Professor Carmichale (Earle Browne), Drexel's other sailing buddy, are afraid that their athletic friend might succeed, so they hedge the bet by paying a native tribe to capture Drexel the day the wager is supposed to end, hoping to catch him being roasted by those natives over a slow fire. Drexel is simply too bright and energetic for the natives, however, and with Saturday's help, he beats them and his buddies at their own game. The film ends with Drexel, Belmont, and Carmichale taking in a Broadway revue where the hottest attraction is a hip-swaying Saturday.

Mr. Robinson Crusoe is a virtual one-man show designed as a showcase for Fairbanks' athletic prowess. It is directed with such exuberance by Edward Sutherland and performed with such panache by Fairbanks that the lack of a substantial plot never becomes bothersome, although one does wonder quite often where on the island he is literally digging up all the metals he is using. It is not a great film, but it is a good, solid, jolly romp, a throwback to the preswashbuckling Fairbanks and the, later, costumed one as well. After three consecutive failed talkies, Fairbanks is at ease and in his element conquering nature to show what can be done with pluck, initiative, and a miracle supply of raw materials for building a small private city.

Some critics have found upsetting the implication that through "American initiative" the hero can build a radio from the resources of a desert island. One wonders, though, what is wrong with the building of a radio as the highlight of a jaunty light comedy that deals with survival? The very fact that Fairbanks can scrounge and meld the raw parts and has the mechanical knowledge to make a wireless is an amusing conceit, although to some it may be disturbing to think that he is tampering with an unspoiled natural environment in order to prove himself. Fairbanks, however, was not out to make a masterpiece of comic social commentary. He was out to make a bouncy feature home film for his own amusement, hoping in turn that audiences would also be amused and awed once more by the flamboyant prowess that had made him a world superstar for nearly fifteen years. Even if the joke of a dashing American turning nothing into a sprawling metropolis is a slight one, it in no way detracts from seventy-two minutes of breezy, escapist fun.

The reviewer for the *Motion Picture Herald* in 1932 had the right idea when he wrote

> Fairbanks has chosen for his theme here an idea bizarre in conception, diverting, occasionally amusing and sprightly. The star, as always, creates an atmosphere of surging good health, of a youthful ardor which refuses to be dimmed and should communicate itself to the audience in a manner to assure a hearty reception, however lacking in red meat the finished product may seem.

After *Mr. Robinson Crusoe*, Fairbanks made only one more film, the sluggish, stolid, English-made *The Private Life of Don Juan* (1934), in which he plays the legendary lover at age fifty, which is how old Fairbanks was when filming began. This was Fairbanks' fourth and final talkie and the biggest commercial flop of all. Thereafter, he concerned himself professionally with developing projects for Douglas Fairbanks, Jr., envisioning two of them as father-son vehicles: the stories of Lord Byron in Venice and of Alexander the Great and his father, Philip of Macedon. The only project that came close to realization was a biography of Marco Polo and that one bottomed out when Samuel Goldwyn, the producer, chose to star Gary Cooper in the title role instead of the younger Fairbanks. What all these projects had in common was that they were historical subjects about men of action.

Of the five films, then, that Fairbanks made after the coming of sound, *Mr. Robinson Crusoe* is the most important, both dramatically and historically because it gave filmgoers a final, fleeting glimpse of the Fairbanks who was. It is not as good an adventure saga as *The Mark of Zorro* (1920) or *The Black Pirate* (1926) or any of the other swashbucklers by which he is best known today, but it, rather than *The Private Life of Don Juan*, makes a fitting swan song for a debonair film star.

Sam Frank

MODERN TIMES

Released: 1936
Production: Charles Chaplin for United Artists
Direction: Charles Chaplin
Screenplay: Charles Chaplin
Cinematography: Rollie Totheroh and Ira Morgan
Editing: Charles Chaplin
Set decoration: Charles D. Hall
Musical direction: Alfred Newman
Music: Charles Chaplin, with assistance from David Raksin
Length: 10 reels

> *Principal characters:*
> A Tramp .... Charles Chaplin
> A Gamine .... Paulette Goddard
> Café Proprietor .... Henry Bergman
> Mechanic .... Chester Conklin
> Burglars .... Stanley Sandford
> Louis Natheux
> Hank Mann
> President of a Steel
> Corporation .... Allen Garcia

Modern Times is one of Charles Chaplin's most significant landmark films. In it, Chaplin's beloved "little fellow," Charlie the tramp, appears for the last time. It is also Chaplin's final stand against the synchronized sound film, and, as a product of its time, it reflects the tensions of America during the Depression years of the mid-1930's. The film opens with a title proclaiming: "Modern Times is a story of industry, of individual enterprise—humanity crusading in the pursuit of happiness," after which there is an overhead shot of sheep rushing through a shute, followed by an overhead shot of workers pushing into and out of a subway station at rush hour. This associative editing makes the metaphor clear—modern men are like sheep. The next shot cuts to an assembly line where we first meet the tramp (Charles Chaplin), a worker whose job is to tighten bolts on gadgets passing in front of his work station on an endless conveyor belt. With wrenches aloft, he swoops down to perform the task. A sneeze or an itch, however, disrupts his clockwork movements and, in turn, the tasks of his fellow workers so that only the most frantic catch-up efforts can restore order to the assembly line.

Later, Charlie is selected as a guinea pig for a demonstration of a new feeding machine designed to reduce the time needed for lunch breaks; its ultimate purpose is to improve the factory's production capacity. The machine, however, runs amuk: soup is dumped down his front, a spinning corncob threatens menacingly, metal bolts are shoved into his mouth instead of meat, and, finally, a shortcake is forced into his face. Trapped inside the feeding device, a tempting meal becomes a mechanized nightmare. After the disastrous lunch, Charlie and his cohorts return to the line. The boss has ordered an increase in production, so the conveyor belt becomes a virtual blur. After heroic efforts to keep apace, Charlie succumbs, collapses onto the conveyor belt, and is swallowed up by the machine. When he finally emerges, he is in a trancelike state, dancing around the factory with his arms aflutter, his two wrenches tightening everything in sight, including the buttons on the bodice of a woman's dress. Having gone "nuts" twisting nuts, he is taken away to a mental hospital.

Once cured and released from the hospital, Charlie's next problem is unemployment. After finally finding a job which he works at for several hours, a strike is called. The police prohibit workers from gathering together, and Charlie, the little tramp, is picked on by an overzealous policeman. His escape from the authorities is made only after he backs onto a board which releases a brick that hits the policeman on the head. Soon, however, he is walking down a street with a red danger flag that has just fallen off the end of a truck. A moment later, a large and noisy crowd of Communist demonstrators rounds the corner just in back of Charlie. In the meantime, Charlie frantically waves the red flag in a vain attempt to catch the truck driver's attention. The police, mistaking him for the leader of a Communist demonstration, haul him off to jail.

In prison, Charlie inadvertently mistakes what a title describes as "joy powder" for salt—another inmate has stashed his cocaine in a salt shaker in the mess hall. Then, with fearless abandon and muscle-man strength, Charlie quells an attempted jailbreak and as a reward is given a private cell with all the comforts of home. Just as he is settling in to his new life of leisure, however, he is abruptly pardoned.

Back on the street again, Charlie first sees the gamine (Paulette Goddard), a young orphan who has stolen bread and bananas for her younger sisters. Juvenile officers, however, break up the family and take the gamine's younger sisters to the "proper" authorities. In the meantime, thanks to an enthusiastic letter of recommendation from a prison official impressed with his heroics during the jailbreak, Charlie gets a job at a shipyard. His misadventures there are climaxed in an incident in which he accidently "launches" and sinks a half-finished ship. Fired once again, he longs for the comfort and security of his life at the jail.

Then he meets the gamine again. Sympathizing with her sad story and seeing a way to get back to jail, he attempts to take the blame when she is arrested, but the ploy does not work. Unsuccessful at this attempt, he tries another strategy: he enters a restaurant, orders practically everything on the menu, enjoys the feast, and finally announces that he is unable to pay. The scheme works, and he is soon heading back to jail. On the way, he meets the gamine inside the same paddy wagon that is taking him to jail. The two escape from the police when a fortuitous accident occurs with the paddy wagon.

As their tender relationship evolves, there is a lovely dream sequence which contrasts the rough reality of their situation to an idealized vision of bourgeois bliss. As they sit on a curb in a comfortable residential community, a film dissolve takes them, and the audience, into a bright, cheery home with grapes and oranges just beyond the kitchen door, a cow available for the freshest milk possible, and a steak sizzling on the stove. Their collective dream, however, is brought to a sudden halt when a cop moves them on their way. As they wander, they eventually find a deserted, ramshackle cabin on the waterfront. Although harboring a number of pitfalls (a beam falls on Charlie's head and a table collapses as he leans on it), the cabin, suffused with their warm feelings for each other, is dubbed "Paradise." Charlie, always the gentleman, sleeps outside in the doghouse. In the morning, a dive into brackish waters, which he sees as his "swimming pool," turns out to be a shallow puddle only inches deep.

Later, Charlie gets a job as a night watchman in a department store into which he brings the shivering gamine and drapes her in a fur coat borrowed from a mannequin. For her amusement, he performs a deft skating routine while blindfolded, and suspense is built as he skates dangerously close to the edge of a balcony without a railing. Then, with the gamine tucked safely in one of the store's largest beds, Charlie stumbles upon a trio of burglars (Stanley Sandford, Hank Mann, and Louis Natheux), out-of-work friends from the factory. His sympathies aroused, Charlie and the "gang" dig into the delicacies of the grocery department; and for his troubles, Charlie finds himself in jail once again.

During his confinement, the gamine gets a job as a dancer in a cabaret, and upon Charlie's release, she finds a job for him there as a waiter. Charlie, in his new job, attempts to serve a roast duck to a customer across the crowded dance floor. Buffeted by the multitude, the duck is delayed, and eventually becomes a football as a frenzied game spontaneously develops.

Later, Charlie is pressed into service as a singer. Since he is nervous about not knowing the lyrics, the gamine scribbles them on his cuff. When he enters with a fanfare and extends his arm, the cuff flies off. Forced to improvise, Charlie sings a mishmash of doubletalk and foreign-sounding phrases. The scene represents the first and last time the tramp was ever to utter a sound on film. Charlie's bold bravura is a hit but the triumph is brief: juvenile officers have entered the club in pursuit of the gamine. Charlie and the gamine make their getaway, however, and in the last shot optimistically saunter down the road and into the horizon. A departure from Chaplin's usual endings where the tramp departs alone, this conclusion closed the little tramp's film life on a note of hope: he finally gets his girl.

The story line of *Modern Times* was a rather thin thread designed mainly to string Chaplin's brilliant comedic episodes together. In later films using the full resources of dialogue, Chaplin would have to plot his stories with much greater care and detail. As his last essentially "silent" film, Chaplin relied heavily on sound effects, inserted titles, and a musical score created by Chaplin and composer-arranger David Raksin. Aside from his performance as the singing waiter, Chaplin used the spoken word sparingly. In the factory sequences, there are several effective shots of the boss barking commands through a television system similar to that used by George Orwell for Big Brother in *Nineteen Eighty-Four*. Of the sound effects, one of the most memorable is the stream of gaseous bubblings emanating from the nervous stomach of the parson's wife.

Among the visual effects, the elaborate machine of cogs, cams, rollers, and gears is the most striking. As Charlie and the mechanic (Chester Conklin) work on it, the machine gobbles up the mechanic, and Charlie's efforts to find the right lever to free him are interrupted by the lunch whistle. The machinery temporarily shuts down and Charlie feeds the protruding mechanic from his lunch pail. When the power is turned back on, Charlie finds the right control and the contorted mechanic eventually is freed.

The "message" of *Modern Times* has been debated at length by critics, some seeing it as a satiric jab at the industrial system, others regarding it mainly as comic entertainment. Although both views are at least partially correct, Chaplin himself has said: "There are those who attach social significance to my work. It has none. I leave such subjects for the lecture platform. To entertain is my first consideration." Regardless of how it is categorized, *Modern Times* remains one of Chaplin's most loved and popular films. It is, perhaps, Chaplin's adroitly ambiguous blend of comic invention, emotional pathos, social commentary, and the heroic embodiment of the common man in the figure of the tramp, that ultimately accounts for his ability to involve us so deeply and at so many levels.

Charles M. Berg

MONSIEUR BEAUCAIRE

Released: 1924
Production: Famous Players-Lasky/Paramount
Direction: Sidney Olcott
Screenplay: Forrest Halsey; based on Booth Tarkington's and Evelyn Green-leaf Sutherland's dramatization of the novella of the same name by Booth Tarkington
Cinematography: Harry Fischbeck
Editing: Patricia Rooney
Art direction: Natacha Rambova
Costume design: Natacha Rambova
Length: 10 reels/9,932 feet

Principal characters:
Duc de Chartres
(Monsieur Beaucaire) .... Rudolph Valentino
Princess Henriette .... Bebe Daniels
King Louis XV of France .... Lowell Sherman
Queen Marie of France .... Lois Wilson
Lady Mary .... Doris Kenyon
Madame Pompadour .... Paulette Duval
Richelieu .... John Davidson

The most legendary of all male stars, Rudolph Valentino, was off the screen from November, 1922, until mid-August, 1924. The quarrel that kept him away, abetted by his wife, Natacha Rambova, was one for not only more power and control over his pictures but also for more money. The settlement, as agreed upon eventually, required him to make two more features for Jesse L. Lasky at Paramount at seventy-five hundred dollars a week, and he was to "have influence over stories, co-stars, and directors," while his wife was to be in absolute control on production design. The film that brought him back to his public was based on Booth Tarkington's novella *Monsieur Beaucaire*, a fanciful comedy romance set in the late eighteenth century at the court of Louis XV in France and in and around London court circles at the same time.

It was probably the most eagerly anticipated film of the 1920's, and, quite naturally because of that, one of the most disappointing. Valentino left the screen with *The Sheik* (1921) and the *Blood and Sand* (1922) image; he came back as his wife saw him, a beautiful beau who languished and wore two beauty marks upon his cheek, who let courtiers and women insult him and was not in the least the swashbuckling hero of the day. As Rambova saw the eighteenth century, the men were fops, and that image did not really suit Valentino. He was graceful but not effete; he could be mannered, but there was a twinkle in his eyes. He was always good in comedy, and it is unfortunate that he got to play so little of it. A viewing of a routine comedy, *All Night*, that he did with Carmel Myers at Universal in 1918 reveals what a pleasant comedian he could be when given the opportunity. He became a star because of his heroic presence in serious action films such as *The Four Horsemen of the Apocalypse* (1921) and serious romantic films such as *The Sheik*, which gave him no time for fun and laughter. Rambova molded him into something that he was not, which was not becoming and did not enhance his mystique.

The story of *Monsieur Beaucaire* concerns the Duc de Chartres (Rudolph Valentino), who is the pride of the royal French Court and the favorite of King Louis XV (Lowell Sherman). The young Duc, however, is filled with self-love: he preens before his mirror, admiring his very photogenic physique and permits his servants to revel in their adulation, as they pluck his eyebrows and renew his lipstick. The Princess Henriette (Bebe Daniels) taunts him for his foppish ways, turns caustic looks in his direction, and utters scathing asides because of his unmanly vanities.

The Duc, however, is finally forced into defense. Even though fencing is against the law among French courtiers, he skillfully takes on several opponents who attack him. The King appears on the scene angrily, and the Duc realizes that he has gone beyond polite forgiveness for his deeds and faces at least temporary banishment. With an excellent flourish of bravado, he bids the King and his court farewell and disappears, not without exciting the admiration of the Princess Henriette, however, who smiles approvingly at his gallantries and calls "Bravo! Au revoir!" to him as he leaves.

The young Duc goes to London, where he installs himself as "Monsieur Beaucaire," the French Ambassador's barber. He attracts an approving and very elegant clientele, but on certain afternoons he goes over to Vauxhall and mingles with society, dressed in elegant Parisian fashion. He sees the beautiful but haughty Lady Mary (Doris Kenyon) and manages an introduction to her. She is fascinated because he is a Frenchman with a droll wit and beautiful manners. They dance together with grace and charm, and Lady Mary lets it be known that she likes him more than a little. For the first time since the Princess Henriette, he is drawn to a woman.

Then, just as Lady Mary gets serious, Monsieur Beaucaire is exposed as a French barber, and Lady Mary scorns him, regretting that she ever was kind to him, cutting him to ribbons verbally, as only a snobbish woman can. The men of Vauxhall move in with their rapiers to avenge the insult done to one of their first ladies, and now, never telling anybody that he is really the Duc de Chartres and has a reputation and title of far more worth than any of the lords at court, he defends himself brilliantly, knocking his attackers aside and vanquishing them in a truly elegant show of swordsmanship.

The French ambassador cautions, when "Beaucaire" seeks shelter at the embassy, that he leave England at once, because the English also have laws against dueling, and it would be a coup for any one of them to hold "Beaucaire" at sword's point. Besides, Louis XV has let it be known that the sudden departure of the prize of his court has left him a very bored monarch, and so the Duc goes back to his native country, hoping to regain his King's favor and the Princess Henriette's love. He is received at Versailles with delight, and the Princess welcomes him back as her true lover.

Throughout the film, slowing the action down, there are many tableaux of court courtesies, as directed by Sidney Olcott. The final scene, however, is almost a courtly parade of the principal characters taking a cast bow; it is similar to a curtain call against the steps, the balconies, and walks of Versailles, before the Duc and the Princess embrace at the final fade-out.

The picture was shot entirely in Long Island at Paramount's Astoria Studios. It opened at the Strand during the blazing weeks of an August heat wave in Manhattan. Nevertheless, the audiences packed the house to capacity at every screening, and Valentino was enthusiastically applauded when he made his first well-set-up appearance on the screen. It was a sumptuous production, and the wardrobe and sets designed by Rambova were breathtakingly beautiful.

Bebe Daniels, Lowell Sherman, and Lois Wilson (as the Queen of France) were the principal players of the French court. Every scene glittered with true elegance, all in the best of taste. The scenes in London sparkled too, and Valentino's performance, once past his Parisian ennui, opened up into some scenes of sly wit. Doris Kenyon, as Lady Mary, the cold-hearted English lady, provided precisely the right show of vulgarity when she realized that she had let herself be wooed by a common man, or so she thought.

Valentino and Rambova rushed their final production for Lasky, *A Sainted Devil* (1924), so that they would be free to work as producers on their own. It certainly was a more spirited production than *Monsieur Beaucaire*, set, as it was, in South America, bringing Valentino back more closely into the colorful devil-may-care antics that had made him a star. Rambova had trouble with the one star she had really wanted in her cast: Jetta Goudal. Originally cast as the siren, Dona Florencia, Goudal was dismissed by Rambova because she criticized, and tried to change, her dresses. Also, Rambova let it be known that Goudal was becoming too familiar with Valentino, and that was not permitted.

Once on his own, Valentino only made three more features: a modern sex melodrama, *Cobra* (1925); a beautiful period romance, *The Eagle* (1925), based on the Alexander Pushkin novel *Dubrovsky*, in which the leading lady was Vilma Banky; and a desperate attempt to recapture some of the glamour that he had shown originally, *The Son of the Sheik* (1926), also with Banky. In New York for that film's premiere, Valentino fell ill; his situation turned worse, and he died on August 23, 1926. He was mourned internationally, and there were two funerals for him, the first in New York and then one in

Hollywood, where he is buried. Rambova had little to do with *Cobra*, and Joseph Schenck saw to it that she had nothing to do with the production of Valentino's last two films. Rambova and Valentino parted. When he saw her off at the train station, they pretended it was only a temporary parting, and although they both knew it was to be permanent, neither guessed that Valentino would be dead so soon. With him went the last of the great silent-film idols.

DeWitt Bodeen

MOTHER

Released: 1926
Production: Mezhrabpom-Rus
Direction: Vsevolod Pudovkin
Screenplay: Nathan Zarkhi; based on the novel of the same name by Maxim Gorky
Cinematography: Anatoli Golovnya
Art direction: Sergei Kozlovsky
Length: 6 reels/5,900 feet

Principal characters:
The mother	Vera Baranovskaya
Vlasov, her husband	A. Tchistyakov
Pavel (Pashka)	Nikolai Batalov
Anna	Anna Zemtsova
Misha	N. Vidonov

In a very few years in the mid-1920's, the film industry in the Soviet Union rose from the disintegration and disarray that followed the war and revolution. In 1921, few films were made in the country, but by 1925, the Soviet Union was one of the leaders in the art of cinema. Three main reasons account for this dramatic emergence. First, film and equipment began to become available after years of being almost unobtainable. Second, the Soviet government decided to give filmmakers free reign stylistically (although the content of their films had to adhere to the government's position). The most important reason, however, is probably the fact that three brilliantly talented men began to make major films. These men were Vsevolod Pudovkin, Sergei Eisenstein, and Alexander Petrovich Dovzhenko. Eisenstein produced *Potemkin* in 1925, and by the end of the decade, each of the three had made two or three undeniable film classics.

Although they are often classed together as members of the Russian school of filmmakers, the three did not have the same aesthetic values or use the same techniques. The greatest difference between Eisenstein and Pudovkin is that Eisenstein stressed groups rather than the individual and his editing style was one of *shocks* between separate shots. Pudovkin, on the other hand, often focused on the individual and his or her personal emotions (although these usually were emblematic of the feelings or conditions of groups of people), and his editing style stressed a relatively smooth *linkage* of shots. Critics sometimes overstate the difference by saying that Eisenstein appeals to the intellect and Pudovkin appeals to the emotions.

Mother is a perfect example of the style and technique of Pudovkin as well as of his differences from Eisenstein. The plot, which is loosely derived from the novel by Maxim Gorky, concerns events of the unsuccessful revolutionary activity in 1905 that was a precursor of the successful revolution of 1917. Eisenstein's *Potemkin* (which was made one year before *Mother*) also takes its subject from the 1905 events, but it stresses the actions of groups of people and has no individual heroes or heroines. *Mother*, however, features two characters—a mother and her son—and shows the feelings and actions of the masses through two individual examples.

The film begins almost as a domestic melodrama, with a drunken father Vlasov (A. Tchistyakov) and his abused, long-suffering wife (Vera Baranovskaya). Soon, however, the father and their son Pavel (Nikolai Batalov) become engaged on opposite sides of the developing resistance to the governmental authorities. Although his parents do not know it, Pavel belongs to an organized group of students and workers that is planning revolutionary activities. Vlasov, on the other hand, is bribed by drink to assist the Black Hundred, a reactionary anti-Semitic society that opposes the revolutionaries.

Father and son confront each other in a factory where Pavel and his comrades have come to organize a strike, and Vlasov and members of the Black Hundred have gathered to fight them. Pavel's group has to retreat, and most of them are barely able to escape from the factory grounds. As Pavel tries to climb over a wall to get out, Vlasov seizes his leg to stop him. Finally, Pavel kicks his father and escapes. He and two others, Anna (Anna Zemtsova) and Misha (N. Vidonov), race through the town pursued by the other group. They try to find safety in a tavern by barring the door behind them, but the pursuers force their way inside. In the ensuing struggle Vlasov is killed by an accidental shot from Misha's gun, and Misha is killed by the mob.

The scene then shifts to the mother in the family's one-room dwelling. As she prays, she remembers that the previous evening she had seen Pavel hide something under a loose floorboard. The audience saw him receive this package from Anna the night before and saw his mother watch him hide it although she was half asleep; now the action is repeated in a flashback. The mother finds that the package contains revolvers and ammunition. She quickly replaces it under the floorboard just as a group arrives with the body of her husband. Later, when Pavel comes home and asks who killed his father, she responds, "Your lot killed him," and urges her son to abandon his association with this group that she sees only as a danger to her family. She believes that Pavel, too, will be killed if he does not abandon his radical activities.

It is at this point that the basic subject of the film shifts to the mother's growing understanding of the cause of the revolutionaries. Her first lesson is a strong and painful one. Soldiers come to question Pavel and to search the room, but they find nothing and Pavel admits nothing. Then they decide to arrest him anyway. When the mother hears them say that all will be forgiven if he confesses, she becomes feverish in her misguided effort to save her son. She gets the hidden package and gives it to the soldiers. Pavel, of course, is not forgiven but is instead thrown into prison.

Within a few days, the mother is visiting Anna's room, helping to care for a worker injured in a struggle with factory guards and smuggling radical leaflets into the factory. When Pavel's case reaches trial, he is quickly convicted and sentenced to unlimited hard labor. His mother cries out, "Where is justice?" and to her son she says, "Forgive me." The climactic action of the film then begins after the mother passes a note to her son in prison telling him that there will be a demonstration outside the prison wall the next day to create a diversion so that he can escape. The next day, however, the escape does not work as planned. Finally, Pavel does get outside the walls, but he is mortally injured. He reaches the front ranks of the demonstration, rushes into his mother's arms, and dies. Then the dragoons attack the demonstrators, and after the attack, two bodies are seen—the mother and her son.

The political or patriotic content of the film is obvious, especially since Russian audiences of the time would realize that the ending was not a total defeat, since the revolutionaries would ultimately succeed—over a decade later. Thus, through the poignant story of one family, Pudovkin conveys the story of a whole movement, although the ideas of the radicals are slighted to emphasize the impact of the ideas on individuals.

Three strengths of *Mother* are not evident in the description of the plot. The first is the evocative performances given by all the major actors and actresses. The second is Pudovkin's ability to compose a shot so that the important elements stand out and there are no superfluous ones to distract the viewer. Aided by his cinematographer, Anatoli Golovnya, and his art director, Sergei Kozlovsky, he produced powerful images that linger in the mind (and are also powerful when seen as stills in a book). The third is Pudovkin's use of what he called plastic synthesis in editing. The best example occurs when Pavel reads the note that promises his freedom the next day. Rather than merely show his joyful face, Pudovkin intercuts shots that are evocative of joy: a brook, sunlight on water, and a laughing child. "By the junction of these components," Pudovkin has written, "our expression of 'prisoner's joy' takes shape." *Mother* is truly a masterpiece of the silent cinema.

Timothy W. Johnson

MY BEST GIRL

Released: 1927
Production: Mary Pickford for United Artists
Direction: Sam Taylor
Screenplay: Hope Loring, Allen McNeil, and Tim Whelan; based on the novel
  of the same name by Kathleen Norris
Cinematography: Charles Rosher
Length: 9 reels/7,460 feet

> *Principal characters:*
> Maggie Johnson .... Mary Pickford
> Joe Grant .... Charles "Buddy" Rogers
> Ma Johnson .... Sunshine Hart
> Pa Johnson .... Lucien Littlefield
> Mr. Merrill .... Hobart Bosworth
> Liz Johnson .... Carmelita Geraghty
> The judge .... Mack Swain
> The butler .... Frank Finch Smiles
> The beggar .... Max Davidson

It is perhaps appropriate that Mary Pickford's last silent film should be not only one of her best efforts but also the film in which she appeared with Buddy Rogers, who, a few years later, was to become the actress' third and final husband. The two interact so well together on the screen that it is not difficult to accept the statement that they fell in love while making *My Best Girl* and, equally, to understand why Pickford's husband at the time, Douglas Fairbanks, was far from happy at their filmed lovemaking. One of the titles in the film has Pickford prophetically saying to Rogers, "I may take you in hand and try and make something out of you."

My Best Girl was directed by Sam Taylor, an expert craftsman with light comedy (as evidenced by his films for Harold Lloyd and Beatrice Lillie), who was to direct Pickford two years later in *The Taming of the Shrew*, which, coincidentally, was the only film in which the actress appeared with Fairbanks, her second husband. It is interesting to compare the fiery fury of the love-making in the latter film with the gentle affection and charm of the love scenes in *My Best Girl*; here seems to be a case where art and life were imitating each other. *My Best Girl* also marked the end of Pickford's working association with cameraman Charles Rosher, who had photographed all of the star's films during the 1920's and to whom must go the credit for the superb visual quality of the Pickford features.

Unlike most of Pickford's films, *My Best Girl* has a working class contemporary setting, with the actress playing Maggie Johnson, a stockroom girl in a five-and-ten-cent store. (Pickford is first introduced at her comedic best, dealing with sales day at the store, when the chief sale item appears to be a granite stew pan.) She falls in love with a new clerk named Joe Grant (Buddy Rogers), not realizing that, in reality, he is the son of the store's owner. In one of the many endearing moments in *My Best Girl*, Joe and Maggie share a lunch of a sandwich and a pint of milk sitting inside a packing case in the stock room. Joe gives up his society girl friend, and takes Maggie to his home for a far more elegant meal, much to the displeasure of his absent parent's servants. Maggie reciprocates by taking Joe to her home for an encounter with her unusual and very visible relatives.

The Johnson family consists of Ma Johnson (Sunshine Hart), a grossly overweight lady whose hobby is attending funerals and who (despite the actress' name) seldom smiles and generally cries; Pa Johnson (Lucien Littlefield), who is as bony as his wife is plump and is the most put-upon member of the household; and Liz (Carmelita Geraghty), a second daughter who is generally mixed up with the wrong type of people. When Joe arrives, he discovers a screaming match in progress with a policeman investigating Liz's boyfriend. An embarrassed Maggie pretends it is all a rehearsal for a play, exclaiming to the policeman, "What a lovely costume! You look exactly like a policeman—he's a swell actor; his uncle knows Lon Chaney."

The Pickford character is the self-sacrificing member of the family and the one to whom everyone cries out in trouble. At one point, for example, when she returns home from an enchanting walk in the rain with Joe, she is rapidly brought down to earth when she learns that her sister has been arrested. She must go down to the night court and resolve the matter, a resolution which includes a verbal attack on the judge (played by Mack Sennett veteran Mack Swain) and the creation of a courtroom brawl. This element of self-sacrifice (an element present in many of Pickford's features) is carried still further in the final scenes, where Joe's father (Hobart Bosworth) visits Maggie and offers her a substantial sum of money if she will give up his son. Fully believing that a marriage will indeed ruin Joe's career, Maggie pretends that she was only a gold digger interested in his money; tearfully, she smears her face with lipstick and gyrates violently to a jazz record. She does not fool anyone, not the audience and more assuredly not the father, who realizes the genuine love the young couple have for each other and consents to the wedding. After a frantic packing session and car ride, the couple set sail on their honeymoon to happiness.

There is indeed a wondrous happiness surrounding the scenes between Pickford and Rogers. The two have an inner warmth which glows out from the screen. Certainly, Rogers never accomplished acting of this calibre again, and even Pickford seldom seemed as genuine as she is here. One sequence that stands out is when the young couple are walking home in the rain, stopping to admire and fantasize in front of a department store window, while under the gentle gaze of an old Jewish beggar (Max Davidson). Although it is raining, Maggie and Joe are oblivious to the storm around them; they walk on through cars, trucks, and pedestrians, their eyes on each other with the love light shining forth. The intellectual film magazine *Close Up* remarked on this scene in its March, 1929, issue, comparing *My Best Girl* favorably to *Sunrise* (1927), which it considered an artificial endeavor. Of *My Best Girl*, the *Close Up* critic wrote, "In that film, if one took away what Pickford stands for . . . one got, suddenly, a common couple, very happy, walking through the rain, slashing across everyone's little bothers with their love. And, of course, all that Pickford stands for takes itself away."

As was the norm with all Pickford features, *My Best Girl* was well received by the critics. *The National Board of Review Magazine* (November, 1927) praised the direction for "giving the sense of fidelity to this homely tale." *Variety* (November 9, 1927) praised Rogers for overcoming "his good looks with a display of naturalistic humanness." One sour note was sounded by Mordaunt Hall in *The New York Times* (November 7, 1927), who commented, "It is a subject that causes one to reflect that Miss Pickford would do better to employ her talent in a more intelligent type of picture."

In recent years, *My Best Girl* has come to be screened more than any other Pickford feature largely because it does co-star the gentleman who usually is on hand to introduce it, Rogers. He was inordinately fond of noting, at least until his remarriage after Pickford's death, that Pickford was indeed his best girl. Although perhaps screened today not entirely for the right reasons, *My Best Girl* does show Pickford at her best and at her most palatable from a modern viewpoint. Audiences can still relate to Pickford's Maggie Johnson while they might find it difficult to sympathize with some of her other characterizations such as Little Lord Fauntleroy, Stella Maris, Rebecca of Sunnybrook Farm, Little Annie Rooney, or Suds.

Anthony Slide

THE MYSTERIOUS LADY

Released: 1928
Production: Metro-Goldwyn-Mayer
Direction: Fred Niblo
Screenplay: Bess Meredyth; based on the novel *War in the Dark* by Ludwig Wolff
Titles: Marian Ainslee
Cinematography: William Daniels
Editing: Margaret Booth
Length: 9 reels/7,652 feet

Principal characters:
Tania .... Greta Garbo
Karl von Heinersdorff .... Conrad Nagel
General Alexandroff .... Gustav von Seyffertitz
Colonel von Raden .... Edward J. Connelly
General's aide .... Richard Alexander

It was inevitable that an actress with the screen mystique of Greta Garbo should be cast in an espionage drama. Actually, it was a gross bit of miscasting since, historically, most female spies have been dumpy, not a bit alluring, and resemble math professors, if one may judge from their photographs in the Sunday supplement stories when they have been captured or have grown old and decided to tell all. Mystery, however, was a major part of the Garbo allure, and M-G-M had registered the title *The Mysterious Lady* as one they wished to use for her. Lady spies were in vogue in the late 1920's, and they continued on into the talkies of the next decade, when Garbo portrayed the most notorious of all female spies, Mata Hari. Her role as Tania, a Russian spy, in *The Mysterious Lady*, although a silent film, was actually more believable than her characterization of Mata Hari, and the picture had class, as well as a memorable sequence occurring after she has killed her mentor, General Alexandroff, played by Gustav von Seyffertitz. It is a handsome production guided by Fred Niblo, who was riding the crest of the high wave of success after directing *Ben-Hur* (1925).

Tania (Greta Garbo) goes to almost every big ball given in Vienna, and there are several each week that are graced by her glamorous attendance. At one of them, she grants her favors to a handsome blond officer named Karl von Heinersdorff (Conrad Nagel, whose forthright bearing, provided an effective contrast to the seductive charms that Garbo exuded). What Tania is really after, however, are some military plans. She gets them and then openly quarrels with Karl to cover up her escape. Later, when the theft is discovered, Karl is publicly stripped of his rank and drummed out of his company in disgrace.

He is determined, however, to find Tania again and get even. The Austrian secret service quietly extracts him from the prison to which he has been assigned and gives him information, so that he can trail Tania to Warsaw, where she has taken refuge. Earlier, there had been several sequences where Tania, an opera enthusiast, entertained by singing an aria or two. (Since Garbo was not known for her singing ability, she may have been miming "Frere Jacques" while dress extras obligingly looked on.) Karl, thus, poses as a pianist, in the hope that his musical prowess will bring him in contact with Tania. It eventually does, and he and Tania meet secretly at a party so that she can return the military plans that she had taken from him in Vienna. She admits that she has now restolen them from her mentor, General Alexandroff (Gustav von Seyffertitz).

She agrees to meet Karl later, and the two of them will escape to Vienna. Karl quietly disappears into the garden to await Tania, but she is soon closeted with Alexandroff, who quite rightly suspects her of having taken the plans with which she had entrusted him. He accuses her of having been the thief and is about to summon his aide when she shoots and kills him.

The next scene allows Garbo to show her skill as an actress. A knock comes to the door, and she, realizing that it might be the general's aide, seats herself on the dead man's lap, with one arm around his neck. She calls out to the aide to enter, and he stands on the threshold, embarrassed that he may have interrupted an intimate scene. Tania has poured herself a glass of champagne and is laughing. She turns to see the aide and pantomimes that he should leave her alone with the general. The aide bows politely and backs out.

The minute that the door is closed, Tania slides out of the general's embrace, snatches up a wrap, and slips out the secret door leading to the garden, where she meets Karl, and they are off to the border. They barely make it ahead of the pursuing Polish guard who can only watch helplessly as they drive on to Vienna and to safety.

Garbo was the most remarkable of all actresses to appear on the American screen. All of her Hollywood features were released by M-G-M over a fifteen year period from 1926 to 1941. In all, there were ten silent and fifteen talking features. Of the silents, one feature film, *The Divine Woman*, is now "lost." It was released in 1928, directed by a countryman, Victor Seastrom, casting another Swede, Lars Hanson, as her leading man. Now, the negative has apparently disintegrated and all of the prints are lost. The best of her silent films were Clarence Brown's *Flesh and the Devil* (1926); Sidney Franklin's *Wild Orchids* (1929); and the last one, Jacques Feyder's *The Kiss* (also 1929). Her talking features were mostly flawed except for Edmund Goulding's *Grand Hotel* (1932), George Cukor's *Camille* (1937), and Ernst Lubitsch's *Ninotchka* (1939). Every one of them is worth seeing, however, because of her talent. Because of the efforts, primarily, of Swedish director Mauritz Stiller, who had discovered her and brought her with him to the United States, she learned to master the camera, which seemed to love her. She had a glorious face with eyes that betrayed every emotion that she felt, every thought that crossed her mind. When Rouben Mamoulian shot the memorable final scene in *Queen Christina* (1933), he suggested that she simply stand at the ship's rail and empty her mind of every thought. That is almost too much to ask of anybody, even an actress, but Garbo gave him a close-up that was free of thought, free of emotion, completely free.

It was never easy to cast men with her, because she had a way of unconsciously emasculating them on the screen. There are only four actors who played scenes with her who were not merely feeding her her cues. They were Lewis Stone in every film that he did with her, and, in particular *Wild Orchids*; Charles Bickford in *Anna Christie* (1930); John Barrymore in *Grand Hotel*; and Charles Boyer as Napoleon in *Conquest* (1937).

Today, she still remains an enigma. She was a hardworker, who, when she was making a picture, was dedicated to its being right. She was more than a perfectionist; she never even thought of a scene as being less than perfect. M-G-M was lucky to have her under contract, although they did not always give her good stories with which to work. Yet, with her performances, every scene came out looking as if it were a masterpiece.

DeWitt Bodeen

NANA

Released: 1926
Production: Jean Renoir for Films-Renoir
Direction: Jean Renoir
Screenplay: Pierre Lestringuez; based on the novel of the same name by Émile Zola
Titles: Jean Renoir and Denise Leblond-Zola
Cinematography: Jean Bachelet, Edmund Corwin, M. Asselin, and others
Art direction: Claude Autant-Lara
Length: 9 reels/8,858 feet

Principal characters:

Nana	Catherine Hessling
Count Muffat	Werner Krauss
Count de Vandeuvres	Jean Angelo
Georges Hugon	Raymond Guerin-Catelain
Zoe, Nana's maid	Valeska Gert
Bordenave	Pierre Philippe (Pierre Lestringuez)
Fauchery	Claude Moore (Claude Autant-Lara)

Jean Renoir's name belongs on virtually everyone's list of pantheon film-makers. *Grand Illusion* (1937) and *The Rules of the Game* (1939) are his most revered works and among the greatest films ever made. Like so many other directors remembered for their films of the 1930's, 1940's, and 1950's—John Ford and Alfred Hitchcock among others—Renoir's career did not commence with the advent of sound. From 1924 on, he made a number of silents. *Nana*, based on the Émile Zola novel and released in 1926, is his best.

Zola's book chronicles the rise and fall of Nana, a famous courtesan, whose uninhibited sexuality enslaves the male members of the upper levels of Parisian society during the Second Empire. Renoir's film centers on Nana's involvement with the theater, and her relationship to three men: Count Muffat (Werner Krauss), a stiff, humorless chamberlain to the emperor; Count de Vandeuvres (Jean Angelo), who is handsome, poised, and masculine; and Georges Hugon (Raymond Guerin-Catelain), the latter's timid young nephew. Nana devilishly victimizes and devours these aristrocrats, proving that they are, after all, simply mere mortals.

Renoir's Nana (acted by Catherine Hessling, the director's first wife, with exaggerated gestures, like a little girl aping the movements of a woman) is sometimes generous and good-natured, but she is mostly heartless, arrogant, and vulgar. An aspiring actress, Nana appears triumphantly as Venus at Bordenave's theater. Her sex appeal, not her skill as an actress, is the reason for her success. After the performance, Bordenave (played by Pierre Lestringuez, who adapted the scenario but is billed as Pierre Philippe) brings Count Muffat to Nana's dressing room. The half-naked Nana flirts with the count, who is practically hypnotized but is still able to respond when she asks for her comb.

Nana craves the leading part in Bordenave's new production, *La Petite Duchesse*. Her fellow performers jeer when she announces her desire for the role, but she persuades Muffat to buy her the assignment. Opening night is an abysmal failure, and Nana is angry. She is having a tantrum when Muffat brings Count de Vandeuvres and Georges Hugon backstage; the latter falls immediately in love with her despite her ravings.

Nana then abandons the stage to exploit her only real talent—sex. Muffat installs her in an opulent townhouse, while Hugon follows her about like a faithful dog. Nana squanders Muffat's fortune, and Vandeuvres criticizes her for corrupting his nephew—but he, too, is now taken by her charms and becomes an aspiring lover. Vandeuvres plans to fix a horse race to earn the fortune he feels will be necessary to win Nana, but his plot is exposed, and he is ruined. Nana scorns him. He warns Muffat that the chamberlain's relationship with Nana will also end in catastrophe, but Muffat turns his back.

Muffat, garbed in his official uniform, enters Nana's bedroom, where she forces him to act like a dog: he barks, sits up, rolls over, plays dead, with her smirking servants observing the humiliation. Hugon, who until now has been ignored by Nana, has witnessed the treatment of Muffat and his uncle. He commits suicide by stabbing himself with a pair of scissors and falls to the floor of Nana's wardrobe. His uncle also follows him in death: Vandeuvres locks himself in with his horses, drinks poison, and sets fire to the stable.

Nana is shocked by these actions, and her companions from the theater talk merrily in an attempt to console her; they persuade her to join them at the Bal Mabille. The ever-faithful Muffat arrives to comfort the "grieving" Nana but, instead, finds her servants celebrating. They laugh at the chamberlain, informing him that Nana has gone to a dance hall. At the Bal Mabille, Nana gets drunk and joins the show on stage in a frenzied cancan (which could easily be a sequence from Renoir's *French Cancan*, made in 1955), Muffat enters, observes this, and chides her on her actions. She drives him away and then goes into convulsions.

At this point, Nana becomes gravely ill. As Muffat rests dejectedly on a bench outside her house, her servants steal whatever they can carry and abandon their mistress. A doctor diagnoses Nana's ailment as smallpox, and she dies in Muffat's arms, hallucinating visions of Hugon and Vandeuvres.

In *Nana*, Renoir attempts to analyze upper-class French customs and gestures in a realistic, naturalistic manner, with its heroine's downfall personifying the decadence not simply in France at this point but in any society, in any era—a favorite Renoir theme. The character of Nana, a destructive little girl playing at womanhood, was also the first of a dozen similar characterizations in the director's later works. Renoir was inspired here by the paintings of his father, Auguste Renoir, one of the founding fathers of Impressionism, and other contemporary artists, as well as by Erich Von Stroheim's *Foolish Wives* (1922). Zola had also been his father's friend, and the author's daughter, Denise Leblond-Zola, assisted Renoir in composing the film's titles.

As the novel is crammed with dozens of characters and intertwining incidents, much of it had to be simplified or eliminated, for example, Nana's relationship to most of her lovers and her career as a courtesan were excised. Still, Renoir captures the essence of Zola and the spirit of the original. The Second Empire period was thoroughly researched and re-created, with Claude Autant-Lara's palatial settings effectively evoking the vulgarity of the time. Renoir also experimented with cinematic technique, building a dolly out of the chassis of a Ford and deflated tires which he utilized for his long tracking shots.

Nana, Renoir's third film (after *Une Vie sans Joie* and *La Fille de l'Eau*, both 1924), was budgeted at more than one-million francs. It was the first German-French coproduction, as financing and talent came from both countries. Interiors were filmed at Berlin's Grunewald Studios and Paris' Gaumont Studios, with exteriors shot in Paris and Montigny. The bulk of the budget came from the director's personal fortune, and most of the paintings bequeathed him by his father went to pay creditors.

The film opened to a mixed reaction: French intellectuals ignored it because of its stress on the scenario's dramatic elements rather than on any attempt to create a new cinematic vocabulary. It had a respectable run in Paris, but not lengthy enough to earn back its cost. While it received critical support in Germany, it was still a commercial failure with Renoir making no money and losing most of his investment. A shortened version was released later, but to no commercial avail. Yet, *Nana* was the only silent film with which Renoir was pleased. He believed all his other efforts before sound were pedestrian, made strictly for fun or profit. It is, in fact, his only serious silent.

Nana has been filmed many times: in Denmark in 1912; in the United States in 1934, by Dorothy Arzner, starring Anna Sten, whom Samuel Goldwyn was unsuccessfully trying to make into the new Greta Garbo; in Mexico in 1943, by Celestino Cerostiza, starring Lupe Velez; in France in 1955, by Christian-Jaque with Martine Carol; and in 1970, in a Swedish-French production directed by Mac Ahlberg. The last is perhaps the most pompous and pretentious; Renoir's version, although far from the best film of his career, was a great thematic advance for the director and his key silent effort.

Rob Edelman

NANOOK OF THE NORTH

Released: 1922
Production: Robert J. Flaherty for Revillon Frères; released by Pathé Exchange
Direction: Robert J. Flaherty
Screenplay: documentary
Titles: Robert J. Flaherty and Carl Stearns Clancy
Cinematography: Robert J. Flaherty
Editing: Robert J. Flaherty and Charles Gelb
Length: 6 reels/5,036 feet

Robert J. Flaherty's *Nanook of the North*, a landmark in the history of nonfiction or documentary film, was the product of twenty years' work. Beginning with four expeditions to determine the extent of mineral resources in the Hudson Bay area of Canada, Flaherty had immersed himself in the lifeways of the native inhabitants of the Arctic Circle. In 1913, Sir William Mackenzie, the Canadian railroad magnate who was sponsoring Flaherty's expeditions, suggested that the explorer take along a Bell & Howell movie camera to film his observations of Eskimo life. For the next two years, Flaherty shot many hours of film and was in the process of editing his footage into a finished product when an accident with a cigarette caused all thirty thousand feet of his highly flammable silver nitrate negatives to burst into flames. Despite this disastrous fire, Flaherty was enthusiastic about the potential of film for recording the actualities of human existence in the Arctic wastes. During World War I, he exhibited the one surviving print of his Eskimo film in order to raise funds for another trip to Hudson Bay, where he hoped to film another view of Eskimo life, which would be less a travelogue than his previous effort and would concentrate on a single Eskimo family. It was not until 1920, though, that the fur company Revillon Frères offered funding for a sixteen-month trip to the North. The material recorded during the expedition became *Nanook of the North*.

The story of Nanook, a celebrated hunter of the Itivimuit tribe of Eskimos who lived along Hopewell Sound of Hudson Bay, develops by means of vignettes of native life: Nanook and his family emerging from a small kayak in seemingly endless numbers; Nanook killing a polar bear with only a harpoon; the family bartering at a trading post; Nanook listening to a gramophone and trying to bite the record; Nanook fishing for salmon; a child taking a dose of castor oil with obvious relish; a walrus hunt involving several hunter-filled kayaks; Nanook stalking a fox; Nanook building an igloo and fashioning a window for it from ice; Nanook instructing his son in the use of bow and arrow; the domestic pursuits of Nyla, Nanook's wife; Nanook spearing a seal through the ice; and the family snug in an igloo while a blizzard rages outside. All these scenes contribute to the unifying theme which Flaherty imposed on the reality of Nanook's life—the portrayal of a family group struggling to eke out an existence in an intensely harsh environment. Flaherty develops the theme through his selection of images to include in the film and through his technique of recording them. Usually, the struggling Eskimos are dwarfed by the vast, empty spaces of ice and sea which comprise the panoramas which Flaherty shot for the film. In fact, this framing of minute figures by vast stretches of icescape parallels common practice in Eskimo art.

The use of a theme to unify the vignettes made *Nanook of the North* a historically significant film. Previous nonfiction films, including Flaherty's own first attempt at recording Eskimo life, consisted of series of scenes and images with no cohesive design. Flaherty's major contribution in *Nanook of the North* was to bring approaches from fiction filmmaking, such as the concentration on a single theme and subject matter, to nonfiction filmmaking. Although traces of nonfiction filmmaking survive in *Nanook of the North*—for example, the occasional grins at the camera from the Eskimos—Flaherty's design for the film is essentially that of a work of fiction as he infuses almost every scene in the film with his thematic construct.

Flaherty's emphasis on a design for the film explains, and perhaps justifies, the staging of incidents, which critics who are primarily concerned with *Nanook of the North*'s value as an anthropological document have deplored. Throughout the process of shooting the film, Flaherty and the Eskimos, who became almost as committed as he to producing an effective "aggie" (the term they used for "film"), carefully contrived ways to communicate the excitement and perils of Eskimo life. For example, the walrus hunt which involves several kayaks filled with hunters sailing through choppy seas in search of prey was suggested by Nanook himself. When Flaherty filmed the actual killing of the walrus, he allowed the lives of the hunters to be endangered by a struggle with the beast which he could have easily ended with a shot from his rifle. The result, however, is one of the film's most exciting scenes. Even in the details of daily Eskimo life, some contrivances occurred. The actual clothing which Nanook and his family wore were garments obtained from white traders, so Flaherty had to scrounge traditional clothing for them to wear in the film.

Flaherty's interest was in Eskimo life before the European contact, and the only signs of white presence in the film are the semicomic scenes at the trading post. Another instance of artificiality in *Nanook of the North* is the igloo built for the family. A traditional igloo would have been too small for the film-maker's purposes, thus the one constructed for the film was almost twice the normal size. When it came time to film interior shots in the building, it was necessary to remove a portion of a wall so that enough light would be available. Consequently, when Nanook and his family go to bed in apparent coziness, they are actually exposed to the harsh climate filtering through the gaps in the igloo's walls.

It is clear, then, that *Nanook of the North* cannot stand as a totally accurate depiction of Eskimo life, but it does represent a perception of that life from a filmmaker who had lived for years among the Eskimo, who understood their ways, and who elicited their cooperation and input while making the film. It is this close familiarity with the culture that makes *Nanook of the North* a valid, although somewhat fictionalized, portrayal of Eskimo reality. It is interesting to note, though, that it is common practice for modern ethnographic filmmakers to follow Flaherty's lead in involving their subjects as intensely in the filmmaking process as possible.

When Flaherty had completed editing the film in 1922, he offered it first to Paramount for distribution, but the company perceived the film as having little commercial potential. Four other distribution companies refused the film before Pathé contracted to market it. *Nanook of the North* was an immediate success among critics, who were enthusiastic about its accurate evocation of primitivism, and also among the general public. The film's impact was felt throughout popular culture. For example, in 1922, the year of the film's release, composers John Milton Hagen and Herb Crooker produced the song "Nanook." Moreover, a line of ice cream products bearing Nanook's visage on the wrapper enjoyed some success.

Another major result of the film's success was the development of Flaherty's career as a professional filmmaker. Paramount, who reconsidered their earlier hesitation about *Nanook of the North*, offered Flaherty a contract to film the lifeways of South Sea Islanders (a project which led to *Moana*, released in 1926). For the next twenty years, Flaherty produced a steady output of non-fiction films: *The Pottery-Maker* (1925), *Industrial Britain* (1933), *Man of Aran* (1934), *Elephant Boy* (1937), *The Land* (1942), and *Louisiana Story* (1948). For none of these films, however, did Flaherty have the experience and empathy with his subjects that was so vital to the production of *Nanook of the North*. Perhaps only *Man of Aran* can stand up to a comparison with Flaherty's first film.

Nanook of the North was rereleased in 1947 in a sound version with narration written by Ralph Schoolman and spoken by Berry Kroger. The visual images of the film, though, did not need any reinforcement from the spoken word to convey the impact of Flaherty's vision of Eskimo life. The silent version seems superior even today.

Frances M. Malpezzi
William M. Clements

NAPOLEON

Released: 1927
Production: W. Wengoroff and Hugo Stinnes for Westi
Direction: Abel Gance
Screenplay: Abel Gance
Cinematography: Jules Kruger
Editing: Abel Gance
Music: Arthur Honegger
Length: 20 reels/19,600 feet

Principal characters:
Napoleon Bonaparte .... Albert Dieudonne
Napoleon (younger) .... Vladimir Roudenko
Josephine de Beauharnais .... Gina Manes
Danton .... Alexandre Koubitzky
Marat .... Antonin Artaud
Robespierre .... Edmond Van Daele
Rouget de Lisle .... Harry Krimer
Saint-Just .... Abel Gance
General Hoche .... Pierre Batcheff

Without question, the cinematic event of 1981 was the reappearance of Abel Gance's masterpiece, *Napoleon*. Although first released in 1927, *Napoleon* had been lost to the world in its original form for fifty-four years. A variety of reedited, severely truncated versions had received showings over the years, but the chance of viewing anything resembling Gance's own vision of the film seemed remote indeed. Yet, those who had consigned *Napoleon* to the ranks of the permanently lost classics had not reckoned with the persistence and dedication of film historian Kevin Brownlow.

Brownlow had long been fascinated by Gance and his work; and *Napoleon*, with its tantalizing history of missing footage and ground-breaking special effects, had been of particular interest to him. Over a period of several years, he contacted film archives throughout the world, viewed countless reels in varying stages of disrepair, and, finally, painstakingly reconstructed *Napoleon* in a form remarkably close to Gance's original. Only a few scenes remain missing, including additional three-screen projections like those employed during the film's dazzling closing sequences, but these omissions do not prevent Brownlow's lovingly assembled version from restoring the film's power and breathtaking imagery.

At this point, Francis Ford Coppola, a filmmaker long noted for the power and scope of his own cinematic vision, entered the project. Coppola's interest in films has never been limited to his own work, and his support and financial backing have aided a variety of filmmakers and their projects. It was Coppola who provided the necessary funds for the presentation of *Napoleon*, enabling the film to open in New York's Radio City Music Hall with a sixty-piece orchestra accompanying it. To compose and conduct the film's monumental score, he enlisted the talents of his father, composer Carmine Coppola, and the result is a blend of music and film so precise and so stirring that it adds immeasurably to the film's impact.

Yet, *Napoleon* remains the creation of its director, Abel Gance. Gance was born in Paris in 1889, and, following a brief career as a stage actor, he entered the motion-picture industry as a writer. The dramatic and technical possibilities of motion pictures intrigued him, however, and it was not long before he tried his hand at directing. In such films as *J'Accuse!* (1919), a powerful antiwar statement, and *La Roue* (1921), Gance experimented with camera movement, editing styles, and superimposition, using each technique to enhance the film's story. These films served as a testing ground for Gance's greatest achievement, and it was in *Napoleon* that he put to use his technical expertise and imagination in a manner that stretched the boundaries of filmmaking.

Gance's original plans for *Napoleon* had been to portray Bonaparte's life in a series of films, but lack of money cut short his scheme. Consequently, this *Napoleon*, the only one of the series that he was able to complete, covers Napoleon's life only up to the beginning of his march on Italy. Yet, its ability to convey both the sweep of history and the details of human individuality is so great that one cannot help but feel the loss of the added perspective that Gance could have given to Napoleon in decline had the later films been made.

The film is divided into three segments: "The Youth of Napoleon," "Napoleon and the French Revolution," and "The Italian Campaign." The first segment opens with a high-spirited snowball fight among the schoolboys of the Brienne military academy. A young Napoleon (Vladimir Roudenko) is leading the defense of his team, aided by the friendly warnings of the school's scullion, who spots the opposing team putting rocks in their snowballs. Using tactics that he will later employ on real battlefields, Napoleon directs the action as the screen becomes a flurry of flying snow and frantic activity. Gance uses rapid-fire editing to convey the fury of the snow battle, with Napoleon's face filling the screen every fourth frame. Only when the day is won does the young boy allow his serious expression to soften into a slight smile.

Later that day, when the boys are in class for a geography lesson, another side of Napoleon's personality is revealed. A disdainful description of his birthplace, the island of Corsica, leaves him angry and defensive, an outsider among the other boys. That night, two of the boys whom he had defeated in the snowball fight open the door of the cage that holds Napoleon's pet eagle, and the bird escapes. Discovering the empty cage, Napoleon rushes into the dormitory and demands to know who has freed the bird. When no one confesses, he challenges them all and a pillow fight ensues. This scene, which served as the model for the famous pillow fight in Jean Vigo's *Zero for Conduct* (1932), is another remarkable example of Gance's innovative film techniques. As the fight escalates and feathers begin to fly, he divides the screen into nine squares, each containing a different view of the overall scene. The effect is dazzling, and the multiple imagery conveys a far headier sense of the youthful free-for-all than would have been possible with a more conventional shot.

When the fight is halted by the schoolmasters, it is Napoleon who is singled out for punishment and sent off to spend the night alone. Once again, he is set apart from his schoolmates, isolated and different, and he goes in his unhappiness to the place where he had kept his pet eagle. Curling up to sleep on a large cannon near one of the windows, the lonely little boy looks up to see his eagle returning. It swoops in through the window and perches majestically on the cannon, a fierce guardian spirit and a symbol of defiance for the youth who will become France's greatest hero.

Gance uses the film's opening segment to foreshadow the course of Napoleon's later life. The young boy's skill as a military strategist, his pride, his determination, and his sense of isolation are all traits that will appear in Napoleon the man. The eagle, too, will reappear throughout the film, serving both as a manifestation of Napoleon's own proud spirit and as a symbol of the unification of his personal dream with the dreams and hopes of his beloved France. It is clear from the outset that the path to greatness which the Fates have chosen for Napoleon will also lead him to great loneliness and pain.

The film's second segment, "Napoleon and the French Revolution," begins with one of the film's most stirring sequences. It is Paris in 1789, and the government of France is in turmoil as the spirit of the Revolution grows. Anxious crowds gather as the men who will shape the course of French history, Danton (Alexandre Koubitzky), Marat (Antonin Artaud), Robespierre (Edmond Van Daele), and Saint-Just (Abel Gance) argue over political strategies. When a young soldier, Rouget de Lisle (Harry Krimer) appears with a song that he has written, copies are distributed to the crowd. Tentatively at first, then with growing strength, the assembled throng sings "La Marseillaise." Its words capture perfectly the revolutionary fervor that grips the country, and a young army officer tells Lisle that his song will help lead the French people to freedom. The officer is Napoleon Bonaparte (Albert Dieudonne).

Napoleon returns home to Corsica, where he is greeted affectionately by his family. The joy of their reunion is short-lived, however, when he learns that Corsican officials are attempting to turn the island away from France and unite it with England. Napoleon takes them on in a losing political battle and is soon forced to flee from the enemies he has made. Seizing the French flag, which he feels the island no longer deserves to fly, he escapes on horseback to the sea, where taking refuge in a small rowboat, he uses the flag as a sail and evades his pursuers.

A storm overtakes the tiny boat, and the huge waves threaten to capsize it while at the same moment in Paris, the convention is in a state of upheaval as political factions battle one another for control of the government. Gance intercuts the two scenes with startling dramatic results. As Napoleon's boat pitches and rocks on the sea, Gance makes use of subjective camera techniques, swaying and weaving the camera to create the effect of the audience itself being pummeled by the waves. He then continues the effect as he cuts to the convention, sweeping the camera back and forth over the shouting crowd to draw a striking visual parallel between the storm-tossed boat and the feverish emotional pitch of the French political situation. The fate of Napoleon seems to become the fate of France, and when he is rescued by his brothers and the entire family sets sail for France, the eagle appears, perching on the masthead as the ship carries Napoleon toward the mainland.

Several years pass and Napoleon is now a captain in the army on his way to Toulon where the British are staging an invasion. Faced with an incompetent general, Napoleon draws up plans of his own to regain the site, and when a new general replaces the old, Napoleon's courage and skill are finally noticed, and he is given command of the artillery. He stages a vicious attack during a pouring rainstorm, urging his men on through the sheer force of his own personality. Continuing against the General's wishes, he emerges victorious and falls into an exhausted sleep as the eagle once again appears in the sky above him. Upon his return to Paris, however, Napoleon is swept up in the Reign of Terror and is accused of disloyalty by his enemies when he refuses to fight his fellow Frenchmen. He is assigned to a lowly post in the office of Topography where he fills his empty days drawing plans for the military defeat of Italy.

In Paris, Josephine de Beauharnais (Gina Manes), one of the great beauties of the day, is arrested and sent to prison. She narrowly escapes the guillotine when her estranged husband takes her place. As Royalist sympathizers threaten a counter-revolution, Napoleon is called back to Paris and given command of the Parisian forces. He defeats the Royalists in their attempt to regain control of the government, and order is finally restored to France. The Reign of Terror ends, and the remaining prisoners are released, among them Josephine and her lover, General Hoche (Pierre Batcheff). At the gala Bal de Victimes, she and Napoleon, now a well-known figure in Paris, meet and are immediately drawn to each other. Josephine is fascinated by the Corsican's aloofness in the midst of the drunken celebration taking place around them, and her interest is clearly returned. Indeed, when she coyly asks him which weapon he most fears, he responds, "The fan, Madame."

The tone of the film now shifts as Napoleon is seen caught surprisingly off guard by his growing love for Josephine. The forceful, authoritative soldier becomes a shy suitor, ill at ease with the object of his affections. In a series of lighthearted, often comical scenes, Napoleon courts Josephine in a style reminiscent of Charles Chaplin's Little Tramp, made physically awkward by the sight of a pretty girl. He stands nervously beside her, finding himself tongue-tied in her presence, plays blind-man's buff with her children as she spirits another lover out of the house, and finally arrives two hours late for their wedding, after forgetting the time as he worked on his plans for the invasion of Italy. Following a hurried ceremony, the two retire to the bed-chamber, where veil after veil falls across the camera lens, obscuring the couple's passion in a hazy mist.

Now happily married to Josephine, Napoleon turns his attention to the conquest of Italy, and soon departs to join his troops. Stopping at the Convention Hall on his way, he stands alone in the now-empty chamber and is visited by the ghosts of the great leaders of the Revolution. They urge him to carry the spirit of the Revolution to the rest of the world, and Napoleon swears that he will carry out their wishes.

Upon his arrival at the Italian border, Napoleon addresses the assembled troops and promises to lead them to greatness. As his own zeal infects them, the film enters its final, and most spectacular phase. It is here that Gance makes use of his remarkable Triptych three-screen process, a technique that predates Cinerama by some thirty years. An additional screen appears suddenly on either side of the one already in use, and the film's action is projected across all three. The vastness of the French army and the scope of Napoleon's plans seem to burst forth from the screen as Napoleon, in one breathtaking moment, gallops his horse toward the camera and flashes almost three-dimensionally across the screens. It is a grandstand gesture on both his and Gance's parts, and it captivates the viewer just as thoroughly as it does the French troops.

The army now begins its march on Italy and Gance divides the action among the three screens, sometimes displaying different shots on each screen, sometimes counterpointing the action on the two outer screens. Napoleon's face fills the central screen as the marching troops stream across on either side of him. A revolving globe appears, with Josephine's face super-imposed on its surface. The succession of images is exhilarating, combining moments from throughout the film until, at last, each screen takes on one color of the French tricolor flag, and Napoleon and his armies become part of the very fabric of the emblem of France. In the film's final image, the majestic eagle appears, its wings spreading across all three screens as it soars toward the camera carrying the spirit of France within it.

The most striking narrative point in *Napoleon* is the theme of personal destiny that runs throughout the film. The use of the eagle, the recurring intimations of greatness in Napoleon's future, indeed, the sometimes Christ-like effect of his personal magnetism over a hostile crowd, all serve to convey the feeling that Napoleon's course has been charted for him from birth. Again and again, coincidence and fate play a part in Napoleon's life: the friendly scullion at the military academy turns up as the innkeeper in Toulon; Napoleon sees Josephine by chance when she is on her way to consult a fortune-teller, who predicts that one day she will be a queen. The most improbable, and vastly amusing, coincidence occurs as Napoleon and his family sail for France. Their ship is spotted by a young British naval officer who requests permission to sink the small vessel. The officer is Horatio Nelson, and his request is, of course, denied. Gance's use of such fantastic tricks of fate, as well as the considerable artistic license he takes with history, might have proved damaging in the hands of a less talented filmmaker. In Gance's case, however, his fiery vision of Napoleon translates so compellingly to the screen that the viewer finds himself swept along by the director's passion. The notion of Bonaparte as a man somehow irrevocably chosen for the role he must play in history delights viewers with its power and romanticism, and any perception one may have of the flaws of such an idea seems unimportant by comparison. If Gance plays havoc with details, it is because it better enables him to capture the essence of Napoleon and what he has meant to France.

For Gance, the revival of *Napoleon* after fifty-four years proved to be the final vindication of a lifetime spent struggling to see his dreams transferred to the screen. Too ill to attend the New York opening of the film in January, 1981, he heard the thunderous applause which greeted its conclusion by way of a telephone call made from the wings of the theater. The film's enthusiastic reception brought the career of its director to a triumphant close; Gance died ten months later in Paris.

Janet E. Lorenz

THE NARROW TRAIL

Released: 1917
Production: William S. Hart Productions for the Thomas H. Ince/Artcraft
  Company; released by Paramount
Direction: Lambert Hillyer
Screenplay: Harvey Thew; based on an original story by William S. Hart
Cinematography: Joseph H. August
Length: 5 reels

Principal characters:
Ice Harding	William S. Hart
Betty Werdin	Sylvia Breamer
"Admiral" Bates	Milton Ross
"Moose" Holloran	Robert Kortman

The Narrow Trail is regarded by many critics as William S. Hart's best picture, but if so, it is best by only a small margin, for he had many fine films to his credit. Two factors play an important part in this film's success: the script and the budget. The script was Hart's own idea for a Western play. He developed the original story, which was then written into a screenplay by Harvey Thew. Also, *The Narrow Trail* was Hart's first film for Paramount, and his new budget was ten times what he had previously spent at Triangle. Hart had been spending approximately $15,000 on each feature for Triangle, but his new contract allowed $150,000 for each film.

Unfortunately, not all of Paramount's money found its way into Hart's films, for Thomas H. Ince, his mentor and executive producer, added production expenses from other films onto Hart's books. This dishonest but rather common practice upset Hart, and was the beginning of the disintegration of his friendship with Ince. Hart had been brought to Paramount by Ince when the latter moved from Triangle in late 1917. They shared equally thirty-five percent of the profits made by Paramount's films, although Ince's involvement was nominal. Ince had so little to do with Hart's films that he did not even view footage until the whole picture was assembled.

When Ince first saw *The Narrow Trail*, he told Hart to stop using Fritz, Hart's pinto pony. He thought that Hart's six-foot-two-inch frame looked ridiculous riding the little spotted horse. Hart was furious, for next to his sister, the bachelor loved that horse more than anything on earth. Fritz has a very prominent role in *The Narrow Trail* and is even preferred by the hero over the heroine near the finish. Ince may not have liked Fritz, but Hart's fans certainly did. In advertisements for the film, Hart announced that this was the last film in which Fritz would appear, for he did not want Ince ever again to profit from the animal.

Basically, *The Narrow Trail* was a synthesis of all the things Hart's previous films had expressed: a love for his horse, action, dusty realism, sentiment, reformation, and a portrayal of an outlaw with Puritan morals. Hart plays Ice Harding, the leader of a gang of highwaymen living in California in the 1880's. Ice observes a pack of wild horses one day and is strangely attracted to the leader, a pinto pony. He is determined that he, the outlaw leader, must have the pack leader, and after long hours of pursuit, Ice ropes the swift horse. With much work and love, Ice finally breaks the pony and names him "the King."

King becomes a great asset to Ice and his gang in holding up stagecoaches. The sheriff's attempts at catching Ice are hopeless as long as the bandit rides King. One day Ice and his gang spot a stagecoach twisting its way up a dusty mountain road, and Ice tells his men to watch him rob the stage alone. He rides swiftly to a bend in the road and waits for the lumbering vehicle. As it rounds the bend, Ice springs forward with a black mask over his face and two guns in his hands. The driver stops and jumps down with his hands over his head, while Ice commands the passengers out. First down is "Admiral" Bates (Milton Ross), a San Francisco vice king on his way to Saddle City to look over a new saloon he has purchased. Next, he helps a pretty girl step down. She is Betty Werden (Sylvia Breamer), known as the Admiral's niece.

Ice, stunned by her beauty, tells her to keep her jewels and her money, but he is not so generous to the other passengers. He then mounts his pinto and rides away. When the driver reports the hold-up to the sheriff, a posse is formed. Ice and his gang easily elude them, but the gang is worried. Ice's men feel that he should get a new horse because the peculiar markings of King make him very identifiable. Ice refuses, pulls a gun on his men, and tells them to "beat it."

Alone, Ice and King make their way to Saddle City in search of the beautiful Betty Werdin. Before entering the town, Ice leaves the well-known King with a trusted farmer and enters Saddle City on a new steed. He soon meets Betty outside her hotel, but she, of course, does not recognize the bandit. The Admiral comes by as they converse and, thinking Ice is a rich farmer, pushes the two together. Betty refuses to fleece Ice, as the Admiral requests, because she likes his chivalrous ways. Upon parting, Ice asks for her San Francisco address, and she gives him a false number.

One month later, Ice stands before the door of a Nob Hill residence, asking for Betty, and is stunned to learn that no such person has ever lived there. Dejected, he walks along the waterfront, where he is spotted by two gorillas looking for someone to shanghai. They introduce themselves to the lonely Ice and ask him to come and have a drink. They lead him to a seedy Barbary Coast dive and ply him with liquor. After many drinks, he sees Betty dressed in a low-cut gown strolling among the customers. He is outraged and denounces her in strong language. He leaves her sobbing, and then she rises from the floor and announces that she is going back to the mountains, where life is clean. The two shanghaiers follow their pigeon, and a fierce fight ensues, with Ice the bloodied victor.

After months of riding with King alone, Ice is tempted to return to Saddle City, where a horse race with a thousand-dollar purse is to be held. On the day of the race, Ice enters the town on King, sees Betty, obviously a person changed for the better, and tells her to be ready to meet him after the race.

The Sheriff knows that Ice will be in the race and has planned to arrest him at the finish line. Ice, of course, wins the race, and as he accepts the prize money, knocks over the Sheriff, jumps off the judges' stand onto King's back, scoops up Betty, and races off. Their exit is blocked by a fence, but King, even with the double load, clears it. After the escape, Ice and Betty vow to go straight and ride down the narrow trail together.

Larry Lee Holland

THE NAVIGATOR

Released: 1924
Production: Joseph M. Schenck for Buster Keaton Productions
Direction: Buster Keaton and Donald Crisp
Screenplay: Clyde Bruckman, Joseph A. Mitchell, and Jean C. Havez
Cinematography: Elgin Lessley and Bryon Houck
Editing: Buster Keaton (uncredited)
Length: 6 reels/5,600 feet

> *Principal characters:*
> Rollo Treadway .... Buster Keaton
> The girl .... Kathryn McGuire
> The girl's father .... Frederick Vroom

Several times in his film career, Buster Keaton played a bumbling, inept, usually spoiled, young man who becomes skillful and successful when he faces a sufficient challenge. This character change gave the audience a chance to laugh at his ineptness and then marvel at his accomplishments. It also gave Keaton a chance to indulge in two of his favorite and most effective comic devices: acrobatics and complicated mechanical contrivances. Sometimes the bumbling phase of his character's development required considerable physical dexterity, and the character's skillful phase usually involved impressive physical feats. Beginning as a young child, Keaton had performed with his father and mother in a vaudeville act that required much acrobatic proficiency. Therefore, virtually all his film stunts were performed by Keaton himself and few cinematic tricks were used. In fact, there is only one known instance in which another man doubled for Keaton, a pole-vaulting stunt in *College* (1927). In addition, Keaton liked to work with mechanical items, both onscreen and offscreen. As a result his characters frequently construct intricate contraptions to accomplish small tasks.

In *The Navigator*, Keaton plays Rollo Treadway, a young man whose ineptness does not show at first because he is rich and has a staff of servants to do everything for him. His character is quickly revealed, however, when, in one of the first scenes, he has his chauffeur drive him even though his destination is only across the street. Before the film ends, however, Rollo proves to be courageous, resourceful, and ingenious.

The film begins by informing the audience in a long explanatory title that the story will show that by "one of those queer tricks that fate sometimes plays" an American girl and boy will have their lives changed by a war between two faraway small countries. Spies from both countries are in a Pacific seaport, "each trying to prevent the other getting ships and supplies." Then, the audience is introduced to the characters. First seen is a group of spies who are planning to set adrift a ship called *The Navigator* because the rival country is buying it. Then a wealthy shipowner (Frederick Vroom) and his daughter (Kathryn McGuire) are shown. The shipowner is the man who is selling *The Navigator*. Then Rollo Treadway, "heir to the Treadway fortune—a living proof that every family tree must have its sap," is shown. He is in a large, ornate bedroom and is just finishing the breakfast served him by a servant. When Rollo looks out his window and sees a happy newlywed couple, he announces to his butler, "I think I'll get married." Then, after a momentary pause, he says, "Today." He instructs the butler to buy two tickets to Honolulu for the honeymoon, but viewers soon find that he has not yet consulted the girl. She is the shipowner's daughter and lives directly across the street from Rollo.

This necessitates the chauffeur-driven trip across the street (in an open touring car that simply makes a U-turn) mentioned above. The girl then ruins his plans by answering his proposal with a curt "certainly not," and Rollo barely pauses a moment before turning and retracing his path back to his own house. This time, however, he announces to his servant that a long walk will do him good, and he walks back across the street.

Except for the small part about the spies, the opening of this film could stand alone as an amusing and artfully executed short film. Indeed, at this point Rollo seems an unlikely candidate as the hero of a full-length film. Viewers soon find, however, that the opening has merely begun to set up the basic situation of *The Navigator*—Rollo and the girl alone on an ocean liner drifting on the sea. This circumstance comes about when Rollo, having decided to sail to Honolulu alone, boards the wrong ship because the number of the pier is partially obscured; so he goes to pier twelve instead of pier two. The same evening, the shipowner and his daughter (who is never given a name in the film) visit the pier to complete the sale of the ship. The spies seize the father and set *The Navigator* adrift while the girl is on it. It is, of course, also *The Navigator* that Rollo has inadvertently boarded.

The next morning, therefore, finds the two on a ship that has drifted out to sea, although neither yet knows that the other is aboard. When Rollo discards a still-burning cigarette and the girl finds it and yells, however, a madcap scene begins in which each searches for the other. The three deck levels and several stairways connecting them are visible to the audience, but the characters can see only a small part of the ship at a time; therefore, the comic possibilities are great as the film shows all the ways the two can *miss* seeing each other. Whether they walk or run, whether they stay on the same level or change levels, they never meet each other. Finally, Rollo falls down an air shaft and lands on a bench on which the girl is sitting. As soon as he sees who she is, he asks her again to marry him, but she again replies "certainly not."

She is interested in food instead, so the two go to the ship's galley and attempt to prepare breakfast. They are thwarted by two circumstances, however, their own ignorance and the fact that all the equipment in the galley is designed for preparing meals for hundreds of people, rather than two. For example, Rollo tries to light a large lump of coal with a match, and the girl tries to make coffee with unground coffee beans and seawater. Their disastrous attempts at cooking are interrupted by the sight of another ship. Hoping to be rescued, they raise a signal flag, but their inexperience betrays them again when they accidentally use a quarantine flag because the girl likes its color. When the other ship sees that, it turns away.

"Try and catch them!" the girl cries. What follows is a series of misadventures that includes Rollo trying to tow *The Navigator* with a small, leaking rowboat, the girl's novice attempts to rescue Rollo from the water, Rollo's having to rescue her, and a final, unsuccessful bout with a folding deck chair. When night comes, the two have a new set of problems. Their efforts to find peaceful sleep are thwarted by such items as a picture that seems to be a man looking into the porthole of Rollo's cabin, fireworks that are mistaken for candles, and rain.

A title informs viewers that weeks have passed, and it is soon seen that the couple has learned to cope with the situation. In fact, they have adapted quite well. They now sleep in adjoining boilers with bunks in them. With a Rube Goldberg-like collection of ropes, pulleys, and weights they prepare breakfast quickly and efficiently. Nearly all the unsuccessful actions of their earlier, failed attempt at preparing a meal are seen again, but this time they are not only successful but also ingeniously mechanized.

Before they can eat their meal, however, they spot land, but soon discover it is an island populated by cannibals to which they are drifting; then their ship hits a sandbar and begins to sink. Rollo is persuaded to don a diver's suit to go underwater to make the needed repairs. While he does so, he also uses one swordfish as a foil with which to fight off another swordfish. Meanwhile, however, the cannibals overrun the boat, cut Rollo's airhose, and take the girl back to the island, but Rollo scares the natives away by walking out of the ocean and onto the island in his outlandish diving suit. The two then return to *The Navigator* in a unique way: Rollo lies down in his air-filled suit and becomes a raft that the girl paddles through the water. When they reach the ship and Rollo removes his helmet, his suit fills with water so that he can barely move. He solves this problem in a startling but humorous fashion—he uses a knife to slash open the stomach of his suit (hari-kari style), and the water gushes out.

A fierce battle between the couple and the attacking cannibals then follows, with both sides displaying remarkable resourcefulness. Finally, the overwhelming numbers of the cannibals force the two into the water and they begin to sink, only to be rescued at the very last moment by a submarine. Inside the submarine the girl gives Rollo a very tentative kiss, which is the first kiss in the film. Rollo's reaction is so abrupt that he accidentally hits a control lever and causes the submarine to spin dizzily. The crew then corrects the problem and the film ends with Rollo and the girl sitting together on the floor of the submarine.

Keaton stated that the inspiration for the story of *The Navigator* was simply the fact that he could buy an ocean liner for only twenty-five thousand dollars. He was so captivated by the idea of this huge "prop" that he had his writers devise a story to fit it. They succeeded remarkably well, producing an integrated story that had opportunities for many large and small gags as well as a balance between the ineffectual and the ingenious aspects of the protagonist. Keaton is, of course, the principal reason for the success of the film, since he contributed to the script, did most of the direction (although Donald Crisp gets credit as codirector), and is the principal actor. He is well supported by Kathryn McGuire as the girl. The combination was obviously successful with the public, for *The Navigator* was, according to most accounts, Keaton's most financially successful film.

Marilynn Wilson

NEVER THE TWAIN SHALL MEET

Released: 1925
Production: Cosmopolitan; released by Metro-Goldwyn-Mayer
Direction: Maurice Tourneur
Screenplay: Eugene Mullin; based on the novel of the same name by Peter Bernard Kyne
Titles: Peter B. Kyne
Cinematography: Ira Morgan and J. B. Shackleford
Editing: Donn Hayes
Art direction: Joseph Urban
Costume design: Dhetl Urban
Length: 8 reels/8,143 feet

Principal characters:
Tamea .... Anita Stewart
Dan Pritchard .... Bert Lytell
Mark Mellenger .... Huntley Gordon
Maisie Morrison .... Justine Johnstone
James Muggridge .... George Siegmann
Gaston Larrieau .... Lionel Belmore
Mrs. Pippy .... Emily Fitzroy
Julia .... Florence Turner

The first year of M-G-M-Loew's Inc. was one of its biggest. So many important big productions were released that year, 1925, including *Ben-Hur*, *The Big Parade*, *The Unholy Three*, and *The Merry Widow*, that one of the studio's most memorable films frequently is overlooked: Maurice Tourneur's production of the beautiful and very moving novel by Peter B. Kyne, *Never the Twain Shall Meet*, starring Anita Stewart.

The company went on location to Tahiti and other parts of the South Pacific, and production was under the best auspices. It had been set up as a Cosmopolitan production, but it was at the time of the amalgamation of the three companies comprising M-G-M, and its star ironically soon found herself fated to be in a picture on which her *bête noire* assumed producership. Stewart had been Louis B. Mayer's first star; he stole her from Vitagraph, where she had been that company's most important player. Now in a feature which had what she always characterized as her favorite role, she found herself in a position where she could be dominated by Mayer. No one could ever persuade Stewart that Mayer had come to resent her, yet it was obvious that he did. She was fortunate in that *Never the Twain Shall Meet* was preeminently a William Randolph Hearst/Cosmopolitan production, which gave it a very special standing. The fact that Stewart was its star also had influence with Hearst, for she was one of his and Marion Davies' best friends.

Her performance as the heroine Tamea, the half-breed South Sea Island girl, a princess on her own island, the daughter of its queen, was not only her own personal favorite of all the many roles she had played, but it also had the advantage of Tourneur's sensitive direction, and she was better and more endearing than she had ever been. Yet, praised as she certainly was, Mayer stubbornly resisted casting her in any other M-G-M release, and although she made many other pictures, she never again had a chance to make one of the quality of *Never the Twain Shall Meet*.

The story begins in the South Seas as Gaston Larrieau (Lionel Belmore), a French sea captain, is about to sail for San Francisco. Larrieau had come to this little island in the South Seas and had married the native queen, who had borne him his only daughter, Tamea (Anita Stewart). Larrieau's wife has been dead for a long time, and the pagan priest prophecies that Larrieau will never return from San Francisco. In order to insure his return, he takes along the beautiful Tamea.

Before the ship enters San Francisco Bay, Larrieau learns that he is a leper. He leaves the carefree Tamea in the care of his young employer, Dan Pritchard (Bert Lytell), and then quietly ends his life by jumping overboard into the Bay. Tamea is grief-stricken, but she is forced to admire her father more than she ever had in life for possessing the courage to quit it with such finality. Tamea is soon enraptured with San Francisco, and Dan is fascinated by her and her delight in the city. Everything about the ways of modern civilization pleases her: the call bells in the hotel; the switchboard that lights up; and especially the elevators, which are a never-ending source of wondrous delight. Dan is supposedly engaged to Maisie Morrison (Justine Johnstone), and he has entrusted Tamea's training in the ways of civilization to Maisie and his own best friend, Mark Mellenger (Huntley Gordon).

Maisie realizes that Dan and Tamea are falling in love. When Tamea learns that Dan's business is failing because of bad speculative investments, she wants to give Dan as much money as he needs, for she is very rich in her own right. Dan, however, refuses her generosity, and she misunderstands his attitude. Very quietly, she leaves San Francisco, hurt, and sails back to her island. Dan commandeers a fast boat and follows her, arriving just in time to save her from being attacked by James Muggridge (George Siegmann), a dangerous island renegade.

Tamea realizes that Dan must indeed care for her, and Dan, enraptured with her, recklessly asks her to marry him, and she consents happily. Their marriage ceremony, the big production of the film, with native customs, is a very colorful highlight, involving hundreds of natives participating in the event, dancing, singing, and feasting.

Their marital happiness, however, is of short duration, for Dan, consumed by boredom, starts drinking, as has many a white man who has stayed too long on a tropical island. Tamea's heart is broken by his show of weakness, and tearfully she writes Maisie a letter, saying that Dan and she were not meant for each other; they are from different worlds, and the idleness of life on her island is killing her husband's love of her.

At this point, Mark Mellenger arrives on the island, and as soon as Dan learns what Tamea has written to Maisie, he assents to its truth, and so says good-bye to his wife and returns to San Francisco and Maisie, leaving Mellenger, who has always loved Tamea, to take over his place in her life. He does so, and a more mature happiness and contentment come to rule Tamea's destiny.

It was, in its way, a kind of modern *Madame Butterfly* story, without a tragic, melodramatic ending, although some audiences admitted that they would have liked the picture better had it ended immediately after its large production number—the wedding of Tamea and Dan. There is moving beauty in the two worlds which director Tourneur shows—the civilized loveliness of America's most photogenic city and the extraordinary beauty of the island wildness of the South Pacific.

It is small wonder that Stewart should have expressed so much fondness for the role of Tamea, for she plays it as if she understood every facet of the little island princess who quickly learns that the ways of civilization are not for her. Bert Lytell as Dan was a handsome hero, while Huntley Gordon, as the more mature Mellenger, was equally good.

It was a very popular film, and it was remade by M-G-M as a talking film in 1932, with Conchita Montenegro and Leslie Howard as the lovers who find that they are mismatched and can only destroy each other.

Good as Stewart was as Tamea, *Never the Twain Shall Meet* remains her last important release, although she worked right up to 1928, and one Tiffany release of the prize-winning novel *Wild Geese* attracted good notices for her. She never made a talking film; nobody asked her to do so, although she had made vaudeville tours, and her speaking and singing voice was much admired. She died in 1961, at age sixty-six according to some sources.

Peter B. Kyne, author of the novel, *Never the Twain Shall Meet*, liked Stewart's performance of Tamea so much that in 1929, he sent her the galleys of his new novel, *Tide of Empire*, a story of old California. She loved that heroine's role, which Kyne had told her he had written with her in mind. She took the galleys to M-G-M and turned them over to Louis B. Mayer, and he supposedly read them, or had them synopsized by a reader. He called Stewart and told her that he was not interested in the story; but that same day he opened negotiations to purchase the property. In 1929, it was made as one of the last silents at M-G-M, starring Renée Adorée, a big Western with synchronized sound. It was out of date before it could complete its initial screening dates, overwhelmed by the tide of talking film.

DeWitt Bodeen

DIE NIEBELUNGEN
Part One: SIEGFRIEDS TOD (SIEGFRIED'S DEATH)
Part Two: KRIEMHILDS RACHE (KRIEMHILD'S REVENGE)

Released: 1924
Production: Erich Pommer for Decla-Bioscop-Ufa
Direction: Fritz Lang
Screenplay: Thea von Harbou; based on *The Nibelungenlied* and the Norse sagas
Cinematography: Carl Hoffmann, Günther Rittau, and Walter Ruttmann (Dream of the Falcons sequence)
Art direction: Otto Hunte, Karl Vollbrecht, and Erich Kettelhut
Makeup: Otto Genath
Costume design: Paul Gerd Gudesian and Anne Willkomm
Length: Part One: 12 reels/10,551 feet; Part Two: 13 reels/11,732 feet

> *Principal characters:*
> **Siegfrieds Tod**
> Siegfried .... Paul Richter
> Kriemhild .... Margarete Schön
> Gunther .... Theodor Loos
> Brunhild .... Hanna Ralph
> Hagen Tronje .... Hans Adalbert von Schlettow
> Volker von Alzey .... Bernhard Goetzke
> Alberich .... Georg John
> **Kriemhilds Rache**
> Kriemhild .... Margarete Schön
> Gunther .... Theodor Loos
> Etzel, King of the Huns .... Rudolf Klein-Rogge
> Hagen Tronje .... Hans Adalbert von Schlettow
> Hildebrand .... Georg August Koch
> Volker von Alzey .... Bernhard Goetzke

Fritz Lang is best remembered as a maker of classic crime dramas and thrillers, from *Dr. Mabuse, Der Spieler* (1922), *Spies* (1928), and *M* (1931), his first sound film, up through *The Big Heat* (1953). He also dealt in epic fantasy, however, most memorably in *Metropolis* (1927), detailing the struggles between labor and management in a futuristic city, and *Die Niebelungen* (1924), a poetic, two-part film chronicling the legend of the Nibelungen.

The original source for the film is *Die Nibelungenlied*, an epic saga of the death of Siegfried and the revenge of his wife Kriemhild, probably written about 1200 by an anonymous Austrian poet. The story itself was based on traditional folk songs and stories, and the Nibelungen is central to the mythology of the German nation. The project was in fact assigned to Lang by the

Ufa studio to create a national monument to the greatness of Germany.

The first part of *Die Niebelungen* is called *Siegfrieds Tod*, or *Siegfried's Death*. It opens with Volker von Alzey (Bernhard Goetzke), a minstrel, recalling the accomplishments of the handsome, blond hero Siegfried (Paul Richter), apprenticed by his father, King Siegmund, to Mime, a blacksmith. Presented in flashback are the highlights of Siegfried's life up to the time when he arrives at the court of Gunther, King of the Burgundians (Theodor Loos), where he comes to court the King's sister, Kriemhild (Margarete Schön). In the flashback, Siegfried is seen slaying a dragon and destroying Alberich (Georg John), the dwarf king. He captures the Nibelungen's treasure, including a magic cloak that enables him to alter his appearance. He bathes in the dragon's blood, but a falling leaf sticks to his shoulder, making him vulnerable to death in that spot alone.

Siegfried is opposed by the jealous, suspicious Hagen Tronje (Hans Adalbert von Schlettow), half-brother of Gunther. Siegfried's death is revealed to Kriemhild in a symbolic dream, in which a white dove is attacked by a pair of black hawks. Siegfried assists Gunther in his attempt to marry the warrior maiden Brunhild, Queen of Iceland (Hanna Ralph), who has pledged that the man she will wed must have the power and agility to defeat her in athletic games. Siegfried dons the cloak, which allows him to take Gunther's form, and bests Brunhild. At the court of the Burgundians, Gunther marries Brunhild—while Siegfried takes Kriemhild for a wife.

Brunhild learns from Kriemhild of Siegfried's deceit, however, and insists that he be killed. On Gunther's order, Hagen Tronje dupes Kriemhild into revealing Siegfried's vulnerability spot and spears him in the shoulder as he drinks from a pool in the forest. Siegfried dies and Brunhild, who has secretly loved the hero, poisons herself and commits suicide. Kriemhild learns of Hagen Tronje's deed, and her brother's role in her husband's death. At first, she is depicted as a nice, lovely young woman, but now, she becomes consumed by bitterness and anger, her face contorted in rage. The major character transformation in the story occurs as Kriemhild changes from that white dove to a black hawk. She deserts the Burgundians and plans revenge.

Part Two is appropriately entitled *Kriemhilds Rache* or *Kriemhild's Revenge*. Kriemhild first marries Etzel, King of the Huns (Rudolf Klein-Rogge). At the birth of her son, she invites Gunther, Hagen Tronje, and other Burgundian leaders to a feast at Etzel's court to celebrate the summer solstice. As Hagen Tronje holds Kriemhild and Etzel's baby, news arrives that Burgundians have been slaughtered by Huns—presented in a lengthy sequence. Hagen Tronje responds by killing the boy, and the celebrants quickly take up arms. Kriemhild kills Hagen Tronje with the same sword he had taken from Siegfried. She is slain by Hildebrand (Georg August Koch), one of her vassals, but is happy to die, for now she will be released from her anguish.

After Lang and his wife-collaborator, Thea von Harbou, completed *Dr.*

Mabuse, Der Spieler, they began preparing *Die Niebelungen*, the director's most ambitious film to date. The scenario is based less on Richard Wagner's opera (Mordaunt Hall wrote his *New York Times* review as if it had been) than on the original source of the Nibelungen legend, *The Nibelungenlied*, and other stories and folk songs. Harbou possibly may have been influenced as well by Friedrich Hebbel's drama, *Die Nibelungen*, written in 1862, because she had appeared in a stage production of the play before World War I.

The action and performances in the film are secondary to its expressionistic scenery and special effects. *Die Niebelungen* was made between 1922 and 1924, on a scale unparalleled in German film history. The forest of the Nibelungen was constructed on a large outdoor stage with an earth floor. The side walls were up to one hundred feet high, and at the rear was a panoramic, two-hundred-foot-long backdrop. Fog could be made available on demand. Immense, larger-than-life trees, casting impressive shadows, were built out of plaster and concrete. "Bird shapes" shot especially by Walter Ruttmann with subtle lighting and distortion were used in the dream sequence, not a real dove or hawks.

The major technical achievement, however, is the dragon. Constructed by Karl Vollbrecht, it was seventy feet long, with skin made of plaster coated with vulcanized hard rubber and jaws and teeth drenched with fluid to suggest drooling. Seventeen technicians operated controls inside the dragon, taking directions from small windows in the animal's forward spine; they had to be trained in their duties for several months. Additionally, seven technicians worked in a pit, receiving their instructions by telephone. The result enabled the dragon to move in the forest, drink water from a pool, and give off smoke and fire, produced by bellows. Another device pumped out "blood" when Siegfried's sword pierced the dragon's skin.

There is spectacle in *Die Niebelungen*: four-hundred Russian horsemen were used in the staging of the Huns attack on the Burgundians (the sequence was shot at Rebergen, in the outskirts of Berlin). There is also subtlety, though: near the beginning of *Siegfrieds Tod*, Kriemhild is shown praying in a cathedral bathed in sunlight, and at the end, when she visits Siegfried's body lying in state in the church, the same location is harshly lit. In this film, it is the picture, the visual images—not necessarily the screenplay—that tells the story.

Siegfrieds Tod was released in February, 1924, with *Kriemhilds Rache* opening in April. Nine years later, Ufa reopened *Siegfrieds Tod*, edited down from 10,500 to 7,400 feet and retitled *Siegfried*, with spoken dialogue and a Wagnerian sound track. A print of both films edited together opened in the United States in 1925; versions now in existence are shorter. The reviews were all laudatory, commenting admirably on the production values and visual beauty.

Rob Edelman

NOSFERATU

Released: 1922
Production: Prana-Film
Direction: F. W. Murnau
Screenplay: Henrik Galeen; based on the novel *Dracula* by Bram Stoker
Cinematography: Fritz Arno Wagner
Art direction: Albin Grau
Length: 7 reels/6,500 feet

Principal characters:
Count Dracula	Max Schreck
Jonathan Harker	Gustav von Wangenheim
Nina Harker	Greta Schroder
Renfield	Alexander Granach
Captain	Max Nemetz
First mate	Wolfgang Heinz
Professor	John Gottowt

The reputation of director F. W. Murnau rests primarily upon three films: *Nosferatu* (1922), *The Last Laugh* (1925), and *Sunrise* (1927). Less than four years after the release of *Sunrise*, his career and his life were ended tragically by an automobile accident in California, but even though he was not able to create a large body of films, he did—according to nearly every film historian—create a few masterpieces of such high quality that he is still regarded as one of the greatest film directors of all time.

Although he was later to go to Hollywood and make *Sunrise* on vast expensive sets, Murnau made *Nosferatu* in his native Germany on actual locations, and did very little photographing on sets. This was especially noteworthy in view of the fact that expressionism was the dominant style of the German film industry of the time. This style—which was epitomized in Robert Wiene's *The Cabinet of Dr. Caligari* (1920)—stressed distorted sets and artificial lighting. Murnau, however, used other methods to emphasize the grotesque in his film.

Nosferatu is based upon Bram Stoker's 1897 novel, *Dracula*. Murnau reportedly used *Nosferatu* rather than the original title both for its evocative sound and to avoid copyright problems because he had not secured the rights to the book. At any rate, he presents the story of the count who was also a vampire, and he presents it in a way that remains fresh today despite numerous treatments of the subject on the stage, screen, and television in the intervening years.

The film begins in Bremen in 1838. Viewers first see that Jonathan Harker (Gustav von Wangenheim) and his wife Nina (Greta Schroder) are extremely happy together. Soon, however, Jonathan's employer, Renfield (Alexander

Granach), sends Jonathan to an isolated area in the Carpathians to negotiate the sale of a building to Count Dracula (Max Schreck). As he travels, the audience begins to get stronger and stronger hints of the terrifying events that are to come. First, there is a glimpse of a hyena; then, when Jonathan mentions in an inn that he is going to the castle of Count Dracula, all of the people in the room stop what they are doing. From then on, he is warned to go no farther. In addition, he finds a book on vampires which he begins to read. He does not take the warnings seriously, however, and does not connect this reading about vampires with his mission to see Count Dracula. Even when his coachman stops and refuses to go any closer to Dracula's castle, Jonathan is not afraid.

Jonathan is then picked up by a "phantom coach" sent by Dracula. In order to show that Jonathan has entered a different world, Murnau photographed the phantom coach in fast motion and used negative film for part of the landscape so that the trees are white against a black sky. The negative section is effective, but today the fast motion appears more humorous than eerie. Then Jonathan has a strange meeting with Dracula during which many indications of the Count's true nature are seen, although Jonathan does not notice them. Vampires are awake only at night, and Dracula remarks that he has all day to sleep. Also, when Jonathan accidentally cuts his finger while cutting a loaf of bread, Dracula suddenly starts and exclaims, "Blood! Your precious blood!"

The next morning Jonathan awakes and notices two bites on his neck, but he does not know what they mean. In this film, the victim does not die immediately but may yield his blood to the vampire's fangs several times. Soon, however, Jonathan begins to learn more of his danger. He reads in the book on vampires about the mark of the fangs, and that evening he is warned by his wife Nina. Although still back in Bremen, she senses her husband's danger in a somnambulistic dream, and viewers are informed in a title that Jonathan hears her warning. After he searches during the day through the castle and finds the Count sleeping in a coffin, he escapes from the castle and returns to Bremen.

Jonathan, however, is not the only one traveling to Bremen. Before he realized the nature of Dracula, he concluded his business, which was to sell the Count a building in Bremen, directly across from the one in which he and Nina live. Dracula has seen a picture of Nina and has expressed his interest in being a "neighbor" of Jonathan and his wife. Therefore, Dracula, too, makes his way to Bremen. He does so aboard the ship *Demeter*, in a coffin. He must, the audience discovers, always sleep in the same unhallowed ground in which he was buried, so he travels with dirt-filled coffins. Aboard the *Demeter*, the crew succumbs to the plague until only the Captain (Max Nemetz) and the first mate (Wolfgang Heinz) are left.

When the first mate goes to investigate the hold, he finds rats coming out of the coffins, and then Dracula suddenly rises from one of them. Although in many treatments of this story the vampire looks outwardly ordinary or even charming, in Murnau's version he is supremely threatening and ugly, with a bald skull-like misshapen head and long claw-like fingers. The first mate immediately jumps overboard, and the Captain dies at the wheel. The *Demeter* then sails into the port of Bremen without a single living soul aboard.

Shortly thereafter Dracula is seen carrying his coffin into his new residence in Bremen; then a plague hits the city, striking down mostly young, strong people. It is when Nina reads the book on vampires that she finds what she must do to overcome the vampire and save the city. The book says that a vampire can be conquered only by a woman who is pure in heart who will offer her blood freely to the creature and keep him by her side until the cock crows. That night she sends Jonathan out on an errand and, with her arms outstretched, welcomes the Count, who has been watching her frequently from his window. The vampire notices only her neck and not the time. The cock crows, the sun rises, and Dracula vanishes in a puff of smoke. At that moment the sick cease to die, and the final title states, "the menacing shadow of the vampire disappeared with the rays of the morning sun."

The atmosphere of *Nosferatu* is certainly as important as its plot. Two of the obvious devices that Murnau used have been mentioned, but far more effective are many more subtle ones. The location shooting gives a background of the commonplace against which the extraordinary events stand out, and that background also serves to highlight the theme of Jonathan, the young protagonist, being unable to imagine or comprehend the evil with which he is faced. Murnau artfully complements this theme by causing the appearance of the vampire to become somewhat more grotesque as the film continues.

The director also uses shadows effectively to convey menace, while they exaggerate the misshapen figure of the creature, especially in the sequence in which Nina lures him to his doom. Indeed, for many viewers the strongest image in the film is not of the hideous vampire itself but of its shadow. Murnau also introduces other "atmospheric" effects. There are several shots of rats running out of coffins, and the audience also sees a strange professor (John Gottowt) demonstrating vampirism in the plant world by showing his students a plant devouring a fly. The film is, however, not without certain touches of humor. When Dracula sees a picture of Jonathan's wife he says, "Is this your wife? What a lovely throat."

The character names which appear in most currently available prints of *Nosferatu* have been used here, although, because of the copyright problems, the first prints used different names for most characters—Count Orlock instead of Count Dracula, for example. The film was reissued in Germany in a sound version in 1930.

When *Nosferatu* was first released, it was a great success in both Germany and France but was less favorably received in England and the United States.

Time, however, has now established its reputation with film critics and historians. The aptness of its full German title—*Nosferatu: A Symphony of Terror*—has been proven.

Timothy W. Johnson

OCTOBER
(TEN DAYS THAT SHOOK THE WORLD)

Released: 1927
Production: Sovkino
Direction: Sergei M. Eisenstein
Screenplay: Sergei M. Eisenstein and G. Alexandrov; based on the book *Ten Days That Shook the World* by John Reed
Cinematography: Eduard Tisse
Length: 9 reels/8,600 feet

> *Principal characters:*
> Lenin .... Nikandrov
> Kerensky .... N. Popov

Sergei M. Eisenstein's *October* (also called *Ten Days That Shook the World*) was commissioned by the Special Cinematographic Committee as one of several films to be made in commemoration of the tenth anniversary of the Bolshevik revolution. These films were to be entered in a film festival as part of the 1927 October Jubilee which was viewed by critics and popular audiences alike as a unique opportunity to compare the relative prowess of the Soviet Union's two most innovative filmmakers, Eisenstein and Vsevolod Pudovkin. Both had been students of the radical genius Lev Kuleshov and both were treating the same subject (the revolution) with unlimited resources and a generous production schedule. Eisenstein even received control of the Winter Palace in Leningrad for the amount of time needed to film his scenes there.

Yet, Eisenstein also saw the festival as an opportunity to effect his own revolution in the techniques of filmmaking. Although he conceded the need, as emphasized by the Cinematographic Committee, to re-create actual historical occurrences, he decided to apply his own particular artistic interpretation in the presentation of them. Undeterred either by the import of the anniversary or by the public's expectations for his project (a result of the wide popularity of his earlier film *Potemkin*, (1925), the director proposed to adhere fully to his theories of intellectual montage.

In his normal usage of it, Eisenstein conceived of montage as a means of eliciting an emotional response from his audience through an embellished grouping of individual shots which are juxtaposed to create a conflict between each pair of adjoining images; the result is intended to be a new unit with a new meaning completely independent of the two entities that brought it into being. Intellectual montage was essentially the same except that its emphasis was on the visual expression of abstract ideas. In *October*, for example, the concept is brilliantly expressed in the opening scenes which feature shots of workers clambering up a huge cast iron statue of the czar and attaching long ropes to it to pull it down. The toppling of the czarist government is symbolized through the slow-motion portrayal of various parts of the statue falling off and finally through the granite remains of the czar teetering and collapsing to the ground. With the subsequent establishment of the Kerensky government, however, the statue resurrects itself and floats back to its pedestal followed by the detached parts, which quickly resume their former places. The meaning that comes through to the audience is one that indicates a resumption of the status quo with new figures serving in the czar's stead.

October is based on the book by John Reed, an American who lived in St. Petersburg during the critical days leading to Kerensky's downfall. Reed's experiences were portrayed in a more subjective fashion in Warren Beatty's 1981 film *Reds*. Eisenstein, however, was not interested in anything even resembling individual subjectivity, other than his own. He was concerned primarily with the crowd, not with the individual. In casting his film he demanded that types be emphasized rather than specific characters or actors. He used no professionals and instead took people from the streets and factories to appear in the film. Of historical significance is the fact that many of the members of his cast came from the ranks of the people who had played roles in the actual October revolution. The director also made heavy use of the mass re-creation of the attack on the Winter Palace that was staged annually by the people of Leningrad.

The Winter Palace and, in fact, the entire city of Leningrad, was placed at Eisenstein's disposal. He, further, had access to almost eleven thousand people to re-create scenes such as the aforementioned assault on the Winter Palace. To facilitate the shooting, the Soviet Army outfitted all of the extras with uniforms and rerouted all of the city's electricity (during a power shortage) so that all available voltage went into lighting Eisenstein's night scenes while the rest of the city remained in darkness.

Pudovkin was filming his festival entry, *The End of St. Petersburg* (1927) in Leningrad at the same time, and although ostensibly being granted the same resources as his rival, he was, in actuality, forced to defer to Eisenstein's shooting schedule much of the time. They did, however, occasionally have to shoot similar scenes on the same sets at the same time. As Pudovkin described one occurrence later, the situation consisted of his bombarding the Winter Palace from the cruiser *Aurora* while Eisenstein shelled it from the Fortress of Saints Peter and Paul. "One night I knocked away part of the balustrading of the roof, and was scared I might get into trouble, but, luckily enough, that same night Sergei Mikhailovich broke 200 windows in private bedrooms." Eisenstein was subsequently admonished by an elderly porter delegated to clean up the glass, who told him that the actual revolution had wreaked less damage to the building than had the two competing filmmakers.

October and *The End of St. Petersburg* treat the same subject, the days of the Bolshevik revolution and the ultimate victory, in vividly contrasting ways. Pudovkin centered the convulsion of the uprising around the peasant face of one individual swept up in its chain of events. The peasant comes to St. Petersburg and eventually blunders, betraying his fellow workers. Furious at his own stupidity, he becomes caught up in the revolutionary struggle. The organization of the film around these events in his life provides a unity that governs the scenes of fighting for the possession of the city.

October has no such central focus. It is constructed out of a progressive sequence of what some scholars have termed "imaginary newsreels." It flits about the country, charges through time, and skips entirely over a number of historical events to concentrate its focus on a battle cruiser coming up the Neva river, on peasant women ransacking the wine cellars of the czar, and on Kerensky (N. Popov) solemnly shaking hands with the palace servants. Other images include gigantic drawbridges rising into the air, sailors running up marble staircases with bayonets on the ends of their rifles, Lenin (Nikandrov) gesticulating while addressing the crowds, and Russian and German soldiers fraternizing at the front while breadlines and mobs haunt the foggy streets of Petrograd.

Kerensky's assumption of the reins of government is dramatized, or more accurately satirized, in a montage of successive shots of him ascending the steps of the Winter Palace at a steady pace while, injected between the shots, are subtitles indicating each progressively more powerful rank that he has meanwhile assumed. A certain incongruity thus arises through the juxtaposition of the prestigious ranks with the essential monotony of Kerensky's plodding steps.

In other instances, Eisenstein attempted a dynamization of static events to convey an emotional effect. One of these was an intensification of the striking of a clock. As the director later indicated in his book *The Film Sense*, while filming in the Winter Palace, he came upon an unusual clock which, in addition to its main dial, featured a wreath of smaller dials arranged around the rim of the large one. Each of the dials carried the name of a city: Paris, New York, London, Shanghai, and a number of others. Each dial was set to the actual time of a particular city in contrast to the time reflected on the main dial. When, in the film, Eisenstein wanted to drive home forcefully the historic moment of victory and the establishment of the Soviet power, he utilized this clock as a montage. "We repeated the hour of the fall of the Provisional Government, depicted on the main dial in Petrograd time, throughout the whole series of subsidiary dials recording the time in London, Paris, New York, and Shanghai." Accordingly, the effect was created that the hour was totally unique in history through all the myriad local readings of time. This device created a unity fusing people everywhere together in a perception of the moment of victory.

A similar montage with a more intellectual and inflammatory bent is a scene in which the director attempts to depict the nature of the "God" for whom the counterrevolutionaries are battling. He represents the concept of

God through a beautiful baroque statue of Christ. He then reduces it by crosscutting shots of other types of statues and idols until the image concludes with a vision of a dull oblong mask of Vzume, the goddess of mirth.

As these examples indicate, *October*'s effect was to eliminate film as a dramatic vehicle and reconstitute it as an interplay between what is depicted as objective reality and the director's personality. The importance of the human character and of the actor who played him was significantly reduced and in many cases removed entirely in favor of expressing abstract ideas. In comparison to Pudovkin's use of people in *The End of St. Petersburg*, some critics have termed Eisenstein's characters as newsreel faces and have said that Pudovkin's people possess visages of "old master" quality. The latter director also lingered on the characters longer and created moods and pacing through his composition of each frame. In *October*, because of its director's theory of montage, each photographic image disappeared before the audience could turn its subject from an intellectual concept into a recognizably human character.

October was a failure at the October Jubilee. Not only was Eisenstein's effort less coherently structured than Pudovkin's in the minds of the audience, but also most viewers could not understand *October*'s abstract intellectual montage; furthermore, political forces also acted to influence detrimentally the released version of the film. Eisenstein, while producing an overtly political film, was unfortunately oblivious to the changing political currents that were sweeping the country during the filming. The edited, final version of the film ran approximately thirteen thousand feet—almost four hours of running time. As such, it featured a number of shots of Leon Trotsky and other officials who had played important roles in the Revolution and Civil War. During the production of Eisenstein's film, Trotsky fell from power and was forced into exile by Joseph Stalin, who then compelled the director to cut *October* by more than four thousand feet to remove all references to his political opponent. Additionally, according to Yon Barna in his book *Eisenstein*, Stalin dropped in unexpectedly at the director's studios late one night when he was editing the film. He was shown several sequences, including a speech by Lenin. He reacted strongly, stating that "Lenin's liberalism is no longer valid today" and ordered another nine hundred meters cut from the film. As if that were not enough, the version released under the title *Ten Days That Shook the World*, mainly to Britain and the United States, was further abridged by the elimination of key montage sequences. Thus, it is understandable that the film was poorly received when it was released. It was new and innovative but was never allowed to stand on its own merits until 1967 when it was reconstructed in its entirety and shown at the fiftieth anniversary of the Revolution.

A viewing of *October* on its own terms does not support the charges of its critics that it undermined revolutionary dogma, nor is it, as some have charged, excessively formalistic. Some American viewers noted in 1928, however, that although individual shots and scenes are beautiful, they seem to exist only as still photographs rather than as part of a motion picture. Today, audiences realize that pure intellectual montage will not work without some sort of objective reference points of the kind that Pudovkin provided in *The End of St. Petersburg*. When intellectual montage exists as pure symbolism free of narrative confinement, meaning cannot also exist since there are no longer any concrete means of interpreting it. A chaos of nonreferential metaphors and symbols thus exist only as pure abstractions and the film becomes nothing more than an intellectual experiment that ultimately fails for lack of a practical application. *October* is a fascinating exercise and a major influence on modern filmmaking, but it is ultimately less of a masterpiece than Eisenstein's earlier film *Potemkin*.

Stephen L. Hanson

OLD IRONSIDES

Released: 1926
Production: Adolph Zukor and Jesse L. Lasky for Paramount
Direction: James Cruze
Screenplay: Dorothy Arzner, Walter Woods, and Harry Carr; based on a
  story by Laurence Stallings
Titles: Rupert Hughes
Cinematography: Alfred Gilks and Charles Boyle
Special effects: Roy Pomeroy
Music: Hugo Riesenfeld
Length: 12 reels/7,910 feet

Principal characters:
Esther	Esther Ralston
Bos'n	Wallace Beery
Gunner	George Bancroft
The Commodore	Charles Farrell
Lieutenant Stephen Decatur	Johnny Walker
Captain Preble	Charles Hill Mailes
The cook	George Godfrey

James Cruze's *Old Ironsides* glorifies the American Navy at the beginning
of its career and details the exploits of the frigate *U.S.S. Constitution*, "Old
Ironsides," against the pirates of Tripoli. It is much more, however, than a
dramatic reconstruction of an important period in American naval history;
it is, without question, one of the greatest sea adventures ever filmed.

Fifteen frigates were used in the production, along with more than two
thousand extras, not to mention a specially built dock stretching more than
two hundred feet into the ocean at Catalina. Catalina Island, off the coast
of Southern California, was used as the chief location for the film, and on it
was built the makeshift "Camp Cruze"—named in honor of the film's
director—from which twelve speed boats, two airplanes, and a steamer made
daily runs to the Los Angeles Harbor, transporting the cast and supplies.
Twenty-two cameramen were utilized to film the battle sequences between
the *Constitution* and the Tripolitan pirates, and Cruze directed these and
other scenes using a shortwave radio to issue instructions to his assistant
directors, the first time such a device was utilized. One reason for the film's
continued appeal is that so many of the props appear real; there are no model
boats and no obvious studio sets in the film, only realism and patriotic fervor.

Much of the credit for the film's success must obviously go to its director,
Cruze, here making his last major contribution not only to the silent cinema
but also to the industry in general. Aside from *The Great Gabbo* (1929),
which has some wonderful moments, Cruze did not direct another memorable

film (except perhaps *I Cover the Waterfront*, 1933) during the rest of his career, a sad and curious end for the man responsible for such classics as *The Covered Wagon* (1923), *Beggar on Horseback* (1925), and *Pony Express* (1925). Aside from Cruze, one should also single out Laurence Stallings for praise. It was Stallings who contributed the original story, from which director-to-be Dorothy Arzner created the screenplay. Stallings also wrote *The Big Parade* (1925) and coauthored *What Price Glory?* (1926), and the same blending of comedy and romantic drama which made those two films so successful is very apparent here also. Reviewing the film in its issue of December 8, 1926, *Variety* was quick to note, "*Old Ironsides*, as a picture, has everything that one could ask for. There is a love story that stands out tremendously, there is a comedy element . . . there is the patriotic element."

Old Ironsides received its premiere on December 6, 1926, at New York's Rivoli Theater, before an audience which included the entire Naval upper echelon from Secretary of the Navy Curtis D. Wilbur down. He and others in the audience were treated to something that more recent viewers of *Old Ironsides* are not; using a process called Magnascope, a special lens attached to the projector, the screen size was expanded for the end of the first half of the film so that the frigate filled the entire theater proscenium. The audience cheered as the music, arranged by Hugo Riesenfeld, swelled to "Ship of State." This same widescreen system was also apparently used for the climactic naval battle.

Mordaunt Hall, in *The New York Times* (December 7, 1926), provides a good contemporary description of the device: "Some conception of the magnificent effect of this enlarged screen can be gained from its dimensions, which are 30 by 40 feet, whereas the usual screen in the Rivoli is about 12 by 18. Following the intermission most of the scenes of *Old Ironsides* were depicted by this apparatus, a device discovered by Glenn Allvine of the Famous Players-Lasky Corporation. Mr. Allvine said that he called the idea or invention a magnascope. It is a magnifying lens attached to the ordinary projection machine."

The first scene that the audience saw was of Thomas Jefferson delivering his famous "Millions for defense but not a cent for tribute" speech to the Congress in Philadelphia. The setting then changes to New England, where the Commodore (Charles Farrell) is leaving his farm and dreaming of perhaps joining the crew of the *U.S.S. Constitution*. Upon reaching Salem, however, the Commodore falls in with Bos'n (Wallace Beery) and is shanghaied by him as a crewman for the *Esther*, named by the ship's captain after his daughter (Esther Ralston). Also on board the *Esther* is Gunner (George Bancroft), also shanghaied by Bos'n. Gunner and Bos'n soon teach the Commodore how to be a good sailor, while he finds time to fall in love with Esther.

When the *Esther* reaches the Mediterranean, it is attacked by pirates. The men are taken for slaves while the girl is seized as a gift for the sultan. The

Commodore, Gunner, Bos'n, and the black cook (George Godfrey) escape after being chained together and are picked up by the *Constitution*. Gunner had been a master gunner on the ship, before being shanghaied by Bos'n, and for desertion he is sentenced to two hundred lashes on his bare back. After the first lash, Lieutenant Stephen Decatur (Johnny Walker) counts one hundred and after the second, two hundred.

Decatur suggests to Captain Preble (Charles Hill Mailes) of the *Constitution* that he take a small boat and blow up the *U.S.S. Philadelphia*, which has been captured by the Tripolitan pirates. This is done, and then the *Constitution* attacks the pirate fort and saves Esther in surely what is the most thrilling naval battle ever transferred to film.

The acting of the principals is particularly fine, not so much in the case of Esther Ralston, who really does not have that much to do, but in the playing of Wallace Beery, George Bancroft, and Charles Farrell. Just as the character he is portraying grows in body and spirit, so does Farrell seem to expand on the screen. He starts the film a slim, sallow youth and is last seen as a rugged, handsome hero. It is a remarkable performance.

As might be expected, praise was lavish for *Old Ironsides*. Laurence Reid wrote in *Motion Picture News* (December 18, 1926), "Only the richest superlatives can do justice to *Old Ironsides*, which takes rank with the biggest achievements of the screen." *Photoplay* (February, 1927), commented, "The greatness of the film lies in Cruze's sure grasp of the principle involved and in his uncanny ability in recreating the very spirit of the times. He makes you see America as a young and vital nation." *Old Ironsides* cost an estimated $2,400,000 to produce. It is one example of money well spent.

Anthony Slide

THE OLD SWIMMIN' HOLE

Released: 1921
Production: Charles Ray Productions; released by Associated First National
Direction: Joseph De Grasse
Screenplay: Bernard McConville; based on the poem of the same name and the collection *The Old Swimmin' Hole and 'Leven More Poems* by James Whitcomb Riley
Cinematography: George Rizard
Editing: Harry L. Decker
Length: 5 reels

Principal characters:
Ezra	Charles Ray
His Pa	James Gordon
His Ma	Blanche Rose
Myrtle	Laura La Plante
Esther	Marjorie Prevost
Skinny	Lincoln Stedman
Schoolmaster	Lon Poff

Charles Ray was a star during the years surrounding World War I, when America was still innocent. He played simple, unspoiled small-town boys and country heroes who became good, overgrown Huck Finns in open-neck shirts and straw hats whose favorite possessions were their fishing rods. He was too much of a nice guy to be considered a rube, yet was not aggressive enough to prevent others from bullying him—until the final reel, when he would fight back at the villain and win the girl, all to the delight of the audience.

"These country boys are the very spine of the nation. . . ," Ray told Katherine Ann Porter in 1920. "They come to town full of hopes and plans, and they grab at life like a pup grabbing at a thistle, and they don't let go when it stings. They just grab harder." The titles of some of the actor's films are indicative of the "nice" characters he played and the pastoral settings in which they took place: *An Old Fashioned Boy* (1920); *Peaceful Valley* (1920); *A Village Sleuth* (1920); and, best of all, *The Old Swimmin' Hole.*

When the rural hero became passé during the first years of the 1920's, Ray was unwilling to adapt his style to the public's new taste. Flappers and sex and bathtub gin were in; sweet, naïve country lads were now corny, too Victorian for the Jazz Age. Because he would not alter his screen character, Ray's career foundered. He then spent more than $600,000 to produce and star in *The Courtship of Miles Standish* (1923), during a brief period when costume epics were momentarily popular. The result, however, was boring. It was poorly produced—Ray has naked Indians galavanting about during the icy Massachusetts winter—and a major box-office disappointment. His decision to attempt change was sadly belated.

The Courtship of Miles Standish was based on the poem by Henry Wadsworth Longfellow. Another Ray vehicle released two years earlier, also based on a poem, is far more representative of its star: *The Old Swimmin' Hole*, from James Whitcomb Riley's *The Old Swimmin' Hole and 'Leven More Poems*. The Indiana-born Riley was known as "the Hoosier poet" and is often referred to as the Robert Burns of America; he is to American poetry what Mark Twain is to American prose. He published "The Old Swimmin' Hole" and the other "'leven" poems in 1883, in a small paperback that was sold over newspaper counters throughout the country.

Ray stars in the film as Ezra, a healthy, wholesome fourteen-year-old country boy. (Perhaps Ray is a bit too mature for the part, but this is a quibble.) He mischievously steals apples and smokes his father's pipe and becomes ill. Throughout the scenario, made up of a series of incidents in Ezra's life, he and his friends are shown playing pranks at school, acting as pirates, chasing after girls at a picnic, fighting, and, of course, swimming.

Ezra adores the conceited Myrtle (Laura La Plante), a dimpled, frizzy-haired coquette who cares only for herself. He tries to be the center of attention whenever Myrtle is present: he risks the displeasure of the old schoolmaster (Lon Poff), who believes in "spoiling the rod rather than the child," by passing her notes and sugar hearts in class. He pleases the girl by inviting her to go rowing while on a picnic, but his rival, a fat boy called "Skinny" (Lincoln Stedman), throws rocks at the boat. Our hero disembarks and prepares to fight for his honor, only to fall into the creek and the fickle Myrtle goes off with Skinny.

Ezra is disgusted, and he writes in his diary, "I'm through with wimmin." Just then, however, Esther (Marjorie Prevost) appears. Esther is a plain little girl, previously scorned by Ezra; in fact, he had even given Myrtle an apple that Esther had presented to him. Esther has been silently, longingly admiring Ezra. She is loyal and true, and generously shares her lunch with Ezra. The film ends with the boy removing the final page from his diary. He has changed his mind about "wimmin." There is a moral: Love is where you find it; you can't control other people or their feelings, no matter how hard you try.

The Old Swimmin' Hole, told in a compact five reels, is a simple, charming tale of rustic America unraveled without a single subtitle and very little plot. Executives at Associated First National, the studio that produced the film, begged Ray to insert quotations from Riley's poem at appropriate points, but he refused. The only written hints to the action are the few words Ezra scrawls in his diary. A film without subtitles was then an innovation: *The Old Swimmin' Hole* is, truly, a silent film as Ray's remarkably agile face interprets the incidents in the scenario. It is one of the best examples of film as pure pantomime, of telling a story without the use of title cards. The film is also a homage to rural America, hardly more than a dozen interior scenes may be found in the story: the major locations are beneath trees, on dusty roads, and at the "old swimmin' hole" itself, where a sign warns, "No Swimmin' Without Clothes." Together with *The Girl I Loved* (1923), also based on a Riley poem, the simple tale of an Indiana farm boy's first romances and disappointments, *The Old Swimmin' Hole* is the finest and most representative of all of Ray's films.

Ray is supported by Laura La Plante, who is lovely and mischievously charming as the flirtatious Myrtle. This was her first major role in a film—she had previously worked mostly as an extra. La Plante took advantage of her opportunity and was soon signed by Universal. During the 1920's, she was the studio's top star. Marjorie Prevost, younger sister of Marie, is adequate as Esther, the "nice girl," a far less meaty role. The film is ably directed by Joseph De Grasse, elder brother of actor Sam, one of the oiliest villains of the silent screen, and uncle of cinematographer Robert, who filmed a number of Hollywood classics from *Alice Adams* (1935) to *The Window* (1949). Joseph began his career as a journalist, acted in early silents during the mid-1920's, and also directed Ray in *The Girl I Loved*.

The Old Swimmin' Hole received fine reviews and earned money for its makers, but Ray's career was now past its zenith although in two years he would star in the superior *The Girl I Loved*. Unfortunately, he followed it up with *The Courtship of Miles Standish*, which left him penniless. Like the "innocent" silent comedian Harry Langdon, he could not see himself and his career objectively. He was no longer Thomas Ince's "Boy Wonder."

By 1925, Ray was working in programmers on poverty row, and later ludicrously and unsuccessfully played slick men-about-town in such films as *Vanity* (1927) and *The Garden of Eden* (1928). He had small roles and bits in several films during the 1930's and early 1940's. In *Hollywood Boulevard* (1936), a drama about a vain silent star who writes his memoirs for a "Confidential"-type magazine, he appears briefly but noticeably as an assistant to director Frances X. Bushman. Maurice Costello, Betty Compson, Mae Marsh, and other silent stars were also in the cast. The film resuscitated no one's career.

In 1940, Ray wrote a play entitled "The Old Swimming Hole," which he supposedly toured. A year later, he had his last significant part, a business executive in *A Yank in the R.A.F.* In 1942, he declared bankruptcy—he had been forced to do the same after the fiasco of *The Courtship of Miles Standish* and a year later he died from an infection caused by a decayed tooth.

Rob Edelman

OLIVER TWIST

Released: 1916
Production: James Young for Jesse L. Lasky Feature Play Company; released by Paramount
Direction: James Young
Screenplay: Based on the novel of the same name by Charles Dickens
Cinematography: Harold Rosson
Length: 5 reels

Principal characters:
Oliver .... Marie Doro
Bill Sikes .... Hobart Bosworth
The Artful Dodger/
Jack Dawkins .... Raymond Hatton
Mr. Brownlow .... James Neill
Mrs. Brownlow .... Edythe Chapman
Fagin .... Tully Marshall
Mr. Bumble .... Harry L. Rattenbury
Nancy .... Elsie Jane Wilson
Monks .... Carl Stockdale

Until late 1916, when Jesse L. Lasky's Feature Play Company merged with Adolf Zukor's Famous Players to form the Paramount Picture Corporation, Cecil B. De Mille retained the title "Director General" of all Zukor's productions even when another director actually would direct a particular film under De Mille's supervision. This was the case with the Feature Play Company production of *Oliver Twist*, which, in fact, was directed by James Young, although it is often accredited to De Mille.

In preparation for the film, the Lasky Company did exhaustive research on the milieu and feeling of the period in order to create precisely the right atmosphere for the adaptation of Charles Dickens' famous novel to the screen. The descriptive scenes of the masterpiece were reproduced with remarkable fidelity using the drawings of George Cruickshank, who had illustrated Dickens' works. The period and locale was evoked with as much accuracy as possible by the Lasky group, which also used the costumes worn in the original stage production of *Oliver Twist*.

Marie Doro appears in the title role as Oliver Twist. Doro made her theatrical debut in musical comedy and reached the peak of her legitimate theater fame under the direction of Charles Frohman who became an avid supporter of filmed theater through Zukor's Famous Players enterprise. Doro appeared before King George V at Windsor Castle in the theatrical production of *Diplomacy* by royal invitation, the only American actress to be so honored up to that time. Other notable roles were Peggy in *The Butterfly*, Adelina in

The Climax, and Oliver, the pathetic child protagonist in the stage production of *Oliver Twist* before it was filmed for the Lasky Company. Promoted as an "international ingenue," Doro was actually from a small town in the Middle West. She learned to speak French fluently and became an accomplished pianist. A Frohman star for many years, her elfin charm and Continental innuendos prompted the reviewer for the March, 1919, issue of *Motion Picture Classic* magazine to exclaim, "Marie Doro is to the American stage what the Renaissance was to Rome." Her marriage to the handsome leading man Elliott Dexter, also with Lasky's Famous Players, assured the couple a prominent place in all of the fan magazines and created a popular romantic aura around both stars.

Doro, as Oliver Twist, the workhouse waif, headed an all-star cast of favorites in Lasky's version of Dickens' sentimental novel. The large assemblage of stars in a single production was a Lasky maneuver which proved highly successful in the promotion of, and reaction to, *Oliver Twist*. Hobart Bosworth who plays Bill Sikes, one of the worst of the denizens of London's horrible slums of the time, and Tully Marshall who plays Fagin, the old miser and thief-trainer, both give brilliant performances. Others carefully selected to give convincing portrayals were Raymond Hatton, James Neill, and Elsie Jane Wilson.

Dickens' deep concern for the underprivileged of his day inspired him to write *Oliver Twist*. The only complaint against the 1916 filmed version of Dickens' story was that it was too short. A great amount of material was deleted in order to fit into only five reels. The film adaptation remained faithful to the novel as far as chronology and evocation of style, but much of the original story had, of necessity, to be edited.

In the film, as in the novel, Oliver Twist was born in a workhouse north of London. His mother, discovered unconscious by the roadside, dies, leaving only a locket and ring as tokens of her son's identity and her own. These items are quickly stolen by old Sally the pauper. A bullying workhouse official by the name of Bumble (Harry L. Rattenbury) names Oliver "Twist" because he has arrived after Swubble and before Uawin on Bumble's list. Apprenticed to Mr. Sowerberry, a casket maker, Oliver (Marie Doro) is heckled unmercifully by another employee, Noah Claypole. Finally, Oliver attacks the troublemaker and is locked in the cellar. Upon his release, Oliver packs his meager belongings and starts out for London. Jack Dawkins (Raymond Hatton), a sharp-witted delinquent known as The Artful Dodger, discovers Oliver who is weak from hunger and wandering the streets. He offers Oliver lodging, and the young boy soon discovers himself among a gang of thieves led by the old miser Fagin (Tully Marshall) who quickly trains Oliver as a pickpocket.

On his first mission, Oliver is caught and taken to the police station where he is rescued by Mr. Brownlow (James Neill), the kindly man whose pocket the boy has picked. Mrs. Bedwin, the old housekeeper for Mr. Brownlow, marvels at the resemblance of the young boy to a portrait of a young lady in Mr. Brownlow's possession. Oliver stays with Mr. Brownlow and recuperates until one day when Oliver is sent to deliver some books and money to a bookseller. On the way, Fagin and his gang intercept Oliver and put him, once again, at their mercy. The brutal young coleader of the gang, Bill Sikes (Hobart Bosworth), is sent with Oliver to rob a house. When they are discovered, the boys flee, but Oliver is wounded by gunshot. Fagin becomes more interested in Oliver after Nancy (Elsie Jane Wilson), Bill Sikes's loyal girl friend, tells him of a conversation she has overheard concerning Oliver's parentage. Meanwhile, Oliver has crawled into the house he had tried to rob and is taken in by the owner, Mrs. Maylie, and her adopted daughter, Rose.

During this time, Mr. Bumble has married the widow Corney who is found to be very domineering. Mrs. Bumble, it turns out, has redeemed a locket and a wedding ring with a pawn ticket she recovered from old Sally. Monks (Carl Stockdale), who is Oliver's half-brother, buys the trinkets and throws them into the river, telling Fagin that he has disposed of Oliver's parentage. Eventually, Rose and Oliver call on Mr. Brownlow who forgives Oliver and all enjoy a reunion. Rose tells Mr. Brownlow Nancy's story (which she had secretly told Rose before returning to Bill Sikes who would later kill her when he discovers that she had betrayed him).

Monks is finally apprehended and confesses his plot against Oliver to Mr. Brownlow. He tells everyone that Oliver's father, Edward Leeford, had married a woman older than himself and their son, Edward Leeford, Jr., was now called Monks. Edward Leeford had left his wife and later met a seventeen-year-old girl with whom he fell in love. She had a sister who was aged three when Leeford contracted to marry the young woman, but before they could marry, Leeford was sent to Rome. On the way, he stopped at Mr. Brownlow's house and left a portrait of his betrothed. He fell sick in Rome and died, and his former wife seized his papers. Leeford's wife-to-be was pregnant, and she ran away to hide her condition when she heard of Leeford's death. Her father died and her younger sister was adopted by Mrs. Maylie and named Rose (Oliver's aunt), Monks had lived a prodigal life, and when his mother died he went to the West Indies. He returned to make sure that Oliver did not receive part of his father's settlement.

Fagin is eventually hanged publicly after revealing the papers concerning the boy's heritage, and Harry Maylie, who has become a minister, marries Rose Maylie. Mr. Brownlow adopts Oliver and buys a home near the church of Reverend Harry Maylie. Mr. and Mrs. Bumble lose their positions and become inmates of the workhouse, and Monks, who is allowed to keep his share of his father's property, goes to America and dies in prison. Oliver lives happily ever after.

Perhaps it was Doro's statement after completing the film that led people to believe that De Mille had directed *Oliver Twist*. In the February, 1916, issue of *Photoplay*, she said, "I am very partial to the De Mille constructive and artistic methods of production."

Oliver Twist was remade in 1922 by Frank Lloyd with child star Jackie Coogan in the lead. It was a very popular production, even though it was released less than a year after another version of the story entitled *Oliver Twist, Jr.* This 1921 film, starring Harold Goodwin, was a modernized version which took place in New York, but which had essentially the same plot as the Dickens story. The novel has been popular on film, as have many other Dickens novels. Perhaps the most critically acclaimed version was the 1948 David Lean British production which starred Alec Guinness as Fagin and Robert Newton as Bill Sikes. This film was much less romanticized than the silent versions with emphasis more on the adults in the film than Oliver. The most recent production of the story, *Oliver!* (1968), was a British musical version directed by Sir Carol Reed. Although in retrospect this sentimental, overly sweet film does not hold up very well in comparison with the others, it is enjoyable to watch and hear, and it won an Oscar for Best Picture of the year.

Tanita C. Kelly

OLIVER TWIST

Released: 1922
Production: Sol Lesser for Jackie Coogan Productions; released by Associated First National
Direction: Frank Lloyd
Screenplay: Frank Hay and Harry Weil; based on the novel of the same name by Charles Dickens
Titles: Walter Anthony
Cinematography: Glen MacWilliams and Robert Martin
Editing: Irene Morra
Length: 8 reels/7,761 feet

Principal characters:

Oliver Twist	Jackie Coogan
Nancy Sikes	Gladys Brockwell
Fagin	Lon Chaney
Mr. Brownlow	Lionel Belmore
Monks	Carl Stockdale
Bill Sikes	George Siegmann
The Artful Dodger	Edouard Treboal
Noah Claypole	Lewis Sargent
Mr. Bumble	James Marcus

The second adaptation for the screen of Charles Dickens' classic novel *Oliver Twist* was the creation of producer Sol Lesser, who saw the project as a perfect vehicle for child star Jackie Coogan, with whom he had worked in *Peck's Bad Boy* (1921). Lesser was one of the few silent producers who understood that a child star's career was always brief, so it was important to extract as much money from the moppets as possible while they were still children. Lesser was something of a child prodigy himself, having bought his own motion-picture theater in San Francisco by the age of fifteen. In Coogan, he saw a veritable gold mine and proceeded to make several films with him for both Jackie Coogan Productions and Associated First National. *Oliver Twist* seemed tailor-made for Coogan; after the popularity of *The Kid* (1921), Coogan's film with Charlie Chaplin, the child actor's face was familiar around the world. Lesser's sense of showmanship, however, did not stop at employing child stars. In a master stroke of casting, he chose Lon Chaney, the so-called "Man of a Thousand Faces," to play the malevolent head of the pickpocket gang of children, Fagin. This would insure the two stars many scenes together and give Chaney a chance to devise yet another superb makeup concept.

Frank Lloyd directed and was quite selective about which parts of the Dickens' story he filmed. Although closely following the book as far as it goes, the film concentrates on the situations that allow Oliver to triumph and ends before Oliver starts to grow up. The picture is melodramatic in the extreme, wringing a tear from Coogan whenever possible, but it is also strangely affecting, with an atmosphere that accurately reproduced Dickens' London.

The film starts when Oliver Twist (Jackie Coogan) is orphaned and sent to the establishment of Mr. Bumble (James Marcus), which is essentially a workhouse orphanage for destitute boys. Even at an early age, Oliver shows his pluck by rebelling against the rules and, on one occasion, demanding more food. He is a fighter, but can do little to escape his situation. When Oliver reaches early adolescence, he is apprenticed to an undertaker and there suffers ill treatment at the hands of Noah Claypole (Lewis Sargent), the undertaker's assistant. All of this is familiar to the readers of the Dickens novel, but the film starts to come alive when Oliver leaves the funeral establishment and meets "The Artful Dodger" (Edouard Treboal), a street urchin adept at the ways of the world. Dodger introduces Oliver to Fagin (Lon Chaney), a rather scurrilous old Jewish man who heads a gang of young boys that roam the streets of London and pick the pockets of "the swells." Oliver becomes part of Fagin's motley group, and, in a strange way, also finds a home and companions. The scenes between Oliver and Fagin are interesting, for Chaney portrays the old man as a person full of cunning, rather unsavory, and not particularly frightening.

Oliver also meets Monks (Carl Stockdale) and Bill Sikes (George Siegmann), both underworld denizens who continually seek to exploit the boy. When Oliver is caught stealing, he is rescued by the kind Mr. Brownlow (Lionel Belmore), who takes him home and provides for him the only stable and secure environment that Oliver has ever known. His joy is short-lived, however, for Oliver is kidnaped by Monks and Sikes, and the rest of the film deals with the tension and melodrama that occurs until Mr. Brownlow gets Oliver back for good. Before this happens, a great deal of violence occurs, which leaves Nancy Sikes (Gladys Brockwell) and Bill Sikes dead, and Fagin's pickpocketing game over.

The film was well received when it was released in November, 1922. Although Coogan and Chaney got the best reviews, the supporting cast was remarkable, with Brockwell a tough but touching Nancy and Treboal a roguish Artful Dodger. It has often been remarked that there is something patently false about Dickens' character of Oliver Twist; that is, how can he remain so aristocratic in bearing and so seemingly innocent compared to the other children in the workhouse, when, in fact, his life has been one of hardship, ignorance, and poverty. It is almost as if his genes have won out over his environment. The recent 1968 version of *Oliver*, which won an Oscar as Best Picture of the Year, is certainly a case in point, with a hero who speaks perfect Oxford English, and who looks more like a product of Eton than the orphanage. In Lesser's version of *Oliver Twist*, this complaint is somewhat undercut because of Coogan, who comes off as more of a scamp than a swell. Coogan's character in *The Kid* was tough but vulnerable and audiences were prepared to accept him again as a child of ill fortune. In this film, he is altogether convincing as someone who has suffered adversity all his life, yet has not lost his essential innocence. Innocence does not mean mealymouthed, however, and this Oliver uses his wits, and he fits in very well with Fagin's gang of rascals.

Oliver Twist may seem dated for audiences today because of the melodramatic style of acting so often employed in silent films, but it is certainly Dickensian and remains one of the finest adaptations of a well-known novel produced during the silent era.

Joan L. Cohen

ONE WEEK

Released: 1920
Production: Joseph M. Schenck for Buster Keaton Productions; released by
  Metro
Direction: Buster Keaton and Eddie Cline
Screenplay: Buster Keaton and Eddie Cline
Cinematography: Elgin Lessley
Editing: Buster Keaton (uncredited)
Length: 2 reels

> *Principal characters:*
> Man .... Buster Keaton
> His Wife .... Sybil Sealy

In the early days of cinema, all films were short, usually less than ten
minutes long. Feature-length films then began appearing in the middle of the
second decade of the century, becoming the dominant form by 1920. Short
films continued to be made for several decades, although they had been
relegated to the status of being simply an "added attraction" to the showing
of a feature film. For a time, however, they had a valuable function as a
showcase and training ground for film comedy. Just as D. W. Griffith had
developed his art in hundreds of short films before he made *The Birth of a
Nation* (1915), all of the major figures of silent-film comedy—Buster Keaton,
Charlie Chaplin, and Harold Lloyd, as well as others—served an apprenticeship in short films before advancing to make the feature films for which
they are best known. Seen today, these shorts are often comic gems in themselves as well as interesting studies of an artist as he develops.

When Keaton first appeared as the star of *One Week*, it was by no means
the beginning of his performing career or film career. He had first appeared
before an audience in 1898 at the age of three as part of his family's medicine
show performance. This family act continued, soon moved into vaudeville,
and Keaton became its star as an acrobatic comedian. Then, after nineteen
years on the stage, Keaton began learning about film in a series of shorts that
featured Roscoe "Fatty" Arbuckle. In 1920, Keaton ended this apprenticeship
and began making his own shorts. He not only starred in them but was also
largely responsible for the scripts and direction. Keaton also starred in *The
Saphead* in 1920, a feature that is outside the mainstream of his career.

One Week is truly a masterwork of comic cinema as well as a clear ante-
cedent of the features that were to come. It has a definite plot that holds
together the myriad comic sequences and gags that develop throughout the
fast-paced twenty minutes of the film. It is the story of the first week of
marriage of a young couple (Buster Keaton and Sybil Sealey), and the progression from one day to the next is indicated by a shot of a calendar. As a

wedding present, the couple is given a new house and lot. The only problem is that they must build the house; it is delivered in a group of numbered boxes with instructions telling how to assemble it. The man bravely starts the task of building the house, but Handy Hank, who was introduced to viewers after the wedding as "the fellow she turned down," changes the numbers on the boxes out of spite. The result is that when the house is finished on Wednesday, it is a crooked construction in which each separate part seems to be leaning in a different direction, and crazy angles abound.

This, however, is only the beginning of their troubles and the viewers' amusement. On Friday (the 13th), during the housewarming, with the house full of guests, rain begins to fall and the wind begins to blow. The ceiling leaks so badly that umbrellas are required inside, and finally, the wind causes the whole structure to rotate as if it were a berserk merry-go-round. After the last guest has left (or escaped), the couple is left somberly sitting together on a box in the rain in front of their nightmare of a house.

The week, however, is not yet over. On Saturday, they are informed that they built the house on the wrong lot. It must be moved to another lot on the other side of the railroad tracks. This is, of course, no small task. They move the house only as far as the middle of the tracks and can get it no further when they see a train speeding toward them. Failing in one last try to budge the building, they stand aside and await the inevitable collision. Instead, the train speeds by on another track. Before they can breathe a sigh of relief, however, an unnoticed train from the opposite direction demolishes their house. The man merely erects a "For Sale" sign by the wreckage, attaches the building instructions to the sign, and the couple walks away as the film ends.

Not only is the overall outline of the film humorous, but it also is filled with astonishing comic invention. This is seen in small bits as well as in longer sequences. For example, when the happy couple emerges from the church after their wedding, the man looks at the old shoes that have been thrown, sees that one pair is his size, and picks up that pair and takes it with them. Later, when he is nailing down the carpet in one room of the newly completed house, he inadvertently leaves his jacket under the carpet. His solution is simple; he cuts a rectangle out of the carpet and picks up his jacket. He covers up the resulting hole in the carpet with a small rug and then uses the rectangle he had cut out as a welcome mat.

One of the most impressive effects is one that Keaton was to use again in one of his best feature films, *Steamboat Bill, Jr.* (1928). One of the walls of his house falls on top of him, but he is not injured because he happens to be standing exactly where the window opening lands. This surprising event is treated almost matter-of-factly by the character. Another device used in *One Week* that Keaton was to use later is the changing of numbers; the house is built on the wrong lot because a sign denoting lot 66 is upside down, and

Handy Hank changes the numbers on the boxes in which the house comes. Comedy thrives on confusion, and Keaton was fond of using wrong numbers to induce some of that confusion.

Keaton was also an early experimenter with the self-reflexive film, that is, a film that reminds the audience that it is watching a film. In one scene, the wife is taking a bath, but because of the camera angle all but her head and shoulders are concealed by the side of the bathtub. When she drops the bar of soap, however, and must reach out of the tub to retrieve it, a hand comes into the frame and covers the camera lens to preserve her modesty. More than forty years later, a similar shot in *Tom Jones* (1963) provoked much comment.

The filmic talent of Keaton was noticed as soon as it appeared. When *One Week* was released, *Motion Picture World* called it "the comedy sensation of the year" and predicted more superb films from its creator. Now that Keaton is recognized by virtually every critic as one of the two or three great silent-film comedians, *One Week* can be seen not only as an artistic and funny film in itself but also as a stage in the development of Keaton's genius. The film is, as drama critic Walter Kerr wrote in *The Silent Clowns*, "a garden at the moment of blooming."

Timothy W. Johnson

ORPHANS OF THE STORM

Released: 1922
Production: D. W. Griffith, Inc.; released by United Artists
Direction: D. W. Griffith
Screenplay: Gaston de Tolignac (D. W. Griffith); based on the play *The Two Orphans* by Adolphe Dennery and Eugène Cormon
Cinematography: Hendrik Sartov, Paul Allen, and G. W. Bitzer
Editing: James Smith and Rose Smith
Art direction: Charles M. Kirk
Length: 13 reels/12,000 feet

Principal characters:
Henriette Girard	Lillian Gish
Louise Girard	Dorothy Gish
Chevalier de Vaudrey	Joseph Schildkraut
Count de Linières	Frank Losee
Countess de Linières	Catherine Emmett
Marquis de Praille	Morgan Wallace
Pierre Frochard	Frank Puglia
His mother	Lucille La Verne
Jacques Frochard	Sheldon Lewis
Danton	Monte Blue
Robespierre	Sidney Herbert
Picard	Creighton Hale

Orphans of the Storm has often been pointed out by film historians as the pivotal film in the "decline" of pioneering American film director D. W. Griffith. One reason for this attention is the fact that it followed *Dream Street* (1921), an unusual film which was not financially successful, that had directly followed his highly successful *Way Down East* (1920). Because of the great success of *Way Down East* and the great failure of *Dream Street*, Griffith decided to undertake a project of epic proportions, hoping to recapture some of the success of earlier ventures such as *Intolerance* (1916) or *Way Down East*.

Orphans of the Storm was well received by the critics and did relatively well at the box office, but it was not the tremendous success that Griffith needed. From that point on, his films never attained the financial plane which was reached by his earlier films. In Hollywood (or virtually any other film center), financial success and freedom of artistic movement are almost synonymous. Thus, when Griffith's films declined in profits, his options became less varied. Forced to make films to fulfill contractual obligations, or to keep financially afloat, he made fewer films, and they were less well received. As a consequence, many film historians have expressed the opinion that the late films of Griffith are much inferior to the early, pre-*Orphans of the Storm* films.

The merits of this argument are certainly questionable when one carefully views some of Griffith's later films, even his last, *The Struggle* (1931), one of only two talkies he made. Yet, the popular conception (or misconception) of Griffith in the middle and late 1920's is that of a once great, yet now pitifully behind the times old man (although he was only fifty-five in 1930). Those who consider Griffith's decline in the 1920's as a foregone conclusion point to the out-of-date nature of parts of *Orphans of the Storm* as further evidence of his fall.

Although it is an excellent and enjoyable film, full of spectacle, fine performances, and moments of great poignancy, *Orphans of the Storm* does have elements of melodrama which seem more akin to the teens than the 1920's. The core of the story, the relationship of the two girls to each other and to the evil forces surrounding them, is typical Griffith of the teens. The Victorian morality of *The Birth of a Nation* (1915) or *True Heart Susie* (1919) are equally visible in *Orphans of the Storm*.

The story, which is as complicated as a Charles Dickens novel, and is reminiscent of *A Tale of Two Cities* in part, begins after a brief introductory section in which a woman (Catherine Emmett) has abandoned her baby on the steps of Notre Dame Cathedral in Paris. Because her family is angry that she has married beneath her, the woman must leave her child. With the child, however, she leaves a great deal of money hidden in her blankets and a note saying "Her name is Louise. Save her." Just at this time, a man has come to the Cathedral to leave his baby because he and his wife are too poor to care for her. The man's heart softens when he sees little Louise, however, and he goes home with both little girls.

The audience learns that the man and his wife were able to use the money left with little Louise to move to the country and rear both girls. The girls, Louise (Dorothy Gish) and Henriette (Lillian Gish) were very happy, until a plague kills both of their parents and leaves Louise blind. The main action of the film begins as the girls go to Paris to find a doctor who can cure Louise.

The real melodrama of the story begins in Paris. The girls are separated when Henriette is kidnaped by the henchmen of the Marquis de Praille (Morgan Wallace) because the Marquis has designs on Henriette. Louise, still blind, almost falls into the river Seine when Pierre Frochard (Frank Puglia) saves her, but Pierre's mother (Lucille La Verne) is cruel and traps Louise so that she will sing and beg for them. Pierre, however, is kind to her and protects her from his mother and his brother, Jacques (Sheldon Lewis).

While Louise is held captive by the Frochard family, Henriette is taken to the Marquis' home where a handsome young man, the Chevalier de Vaudrey (Joseph Schildkraut) takes an interest in her. In a coincidence which rarely happens outside of melodrama, Vaudrey is the nephew of the Countess de Linières, the woman who had abandoned Louise as a baby. Her husband (Frank Losee), the Prefect of the Paris police, does not know about his wife's past. When Vaudrey comes to Henriette's aid and defends her honor by wounding Praille with his sword, the Count de Linières refuses to help him search for Louise, but the kind-hearted Countess offers to help. When the Countess visits Henriette in her rooms, Henriette hears a girl singing outside and recognizes Louise's voice as she begs in compliance with the wishes of the Frochards. Before Henriette can go to Louise, however, she is arrested by men from the Prefect of Police and sent to La Salpêtrière.

Soon after Henriette is arrested, she is set free by the citizens when the Bastille is stormed and the French Revolution begins. In one of the more famous scenes of the film, and one which is frequently seen clipped into film histories, Henriette wades her way through the reveling crowds to the place where Louise lives. When she arrives at the Frochard house, however, she is told that Louise has died.

Because of the violence of the Reign of Terror, Henriette must shield the aristocrat Vaudrey, and they are both arrested for being members of the old regime. While they are on trial, Pierre, who has recently helped Louise to escape, is there with her in the courtroom. Both Henriette and Vaudrey are sentenced to the guillotine and are taken away, but not before Henriette silently recognizes her adopted sister. Just after they leave, Danton (Monte Blue), who had earlier befriended Henriette, makes an impassioned speech asking for the reprieve of the young lovers and a return to sanity. The court agrees, but, as Henriette and Vaudrey are already on the way to be executed, Danton must rush through the streets of Paris to save them. He arrives in time because the now strong and impulsive Pierre has delayed Henriette's execution by stabbing the executioner in the back.

The denouement of the film reveals that Henriette and Vaudrey will be married, Louise has regained her sight through the efforts of a kindly doctor, and Countess de Linières has told her husband the truth about Louise. Her husband does not condemn her and allows her to take care of Louise and also young Pierre who had helped her.

Although *Orphans of the Storm* did not have an actual shooting script (Griffith never worked with one), Lillian Gish recalled that the cast all read Thomas Carlyle's *History of the French Revolution* for inspiration. *Orphans of the Storm* is based on a famous play and had been filmed previously in 1907, 1911, and 1915, so the basic story was set, but the scene-by-scene construction of the film remained spontaneous. Yet, the spontaneity occasionally led to inconsistencies of characterizations or repetition of detail. As film historian Edward Wagenknecht has pointed out in *The Films of D. W. Griffith*, "*Orphans of the Storm* remains a practically perfect film."

On the positive side, the sweep of the story, the staging, and the acting are impeccable. Lillian Gish, although she had equally moving performances in such films as *Broken Blossoms* (1919) and *Way Down East* (1920), would never have a greater one. Dorothy Gish, although a completely different type of actress from her sister, was also excellent. The Gish sisters made many films together early in their careers, but later appeared together only once in a great while. This was their last film together, and, in fact, was their last film for Griffith, either separately or together.

On the negative side, the film has a lot of moralizing about extremism and revolution which are taken rather badly today. Griffith made a deliberate attempt to make the French Revolution appear parallel to the recent Russian Revolution and put words into the mouths of Danton and Robespierre (Sidney Herbert) which were historically anachronistic. Additionally, there is some comic relief by Creighton Hale as a character named Picard which seems out of place. The inappropriateness of the comic scenes may have been the result of a later reediting of the film by Griffith himself, who never felt that his films were complete.

Griffith died in Hollywood in 1948 after nearly seventeen years since the completion of *The Struggle*. In the interim, he had worked on only one film, *One Million B.C.* (1940), made by Hal Roach Studios. Griffith reportedly directed a few segments of the film and generally assisted on its production, but he received no screen credit. Griffith's idle years remain an enigma. There are those who blame Hollywood and "the system" for refusing to give a genius more opportunities to practice his art, and there are those who feel that he simply could not adapt. Whatever the reasons, it is grossly unfair to point at this film, or any other individual film of the later years and say "this is when Griffith declined." *Orphans of the Storm* should instead be remembered for what it is, an exceptionally good film.

Roberta LeFeuvre

OUR DANCING DAUGHTERS

Released: 1928
Production: Cosmopolitan for Metro-Goldwyn-Mayer
Direction: Harry Beaumont
Screenplay: Josephine Lovett
Titles: Marion Ainslee and Ruth Cummings
Cinematography: George Barnes
Editing: William Hamilton
Art direction: Cedric Gibbons
Length: 9 reels/7,652 feet

Principal characters:

Diana Medford	Joan Crawford
Ben Black	Johnny Mack Brown
Beatrice	Dorothy Sebastian
Anne	Anita Page
Norman	Nils Asther
Anne's mother	Dorothy Cumming
Diana's father	Huntley Gordon
Freddie's mother	Evelyn Hall
Freddie's father	Sam De Grasse
Freddie	Edward Nugent

Most screen heroines during the motion pictures' age of innocence were categorized as being either virtuous, such as Mary Pickford and Lillian Gish, or as the Vamp, such as Theda Bara. As films matured and audiences grew larger, themes in screenplays encompassed a truer reflection of the changing mores in American society, such as the many Cecil B. De Mille marital films in which marital infidelities and sexual improprieties are witnessed. A natural extension of this trend was an emphasis on youth and particularly on the "flaming youth" of the American Jazz Era. This trend also gave birth to the screen "flapper," a sobriquet describing one who flaps or slaps and calls attention, which well describes the wild young girls of the 1920's who were given to exaggerated styles and sophisticated conduct.

Countless actresses have depicted jazz babies on the screen, including Gloria Swanson, Louise Brooks, and Marion Davies. The extremely popular and adorable Colleen Moore gave her version of these young "hot mamas" in such films as *Flaming Youth* (1923), *The Perfect Flapper* (1924), and *Flirting with Love* (1924), but Moore's innate wholesomeness prevented her from being the definitive or typical flapper.

On the other hand, Clara Bow is remembered historically as the red-haired sensation who became the symbol of that era of change, the essence of the jazz-age flapper who flaunted convention. She threw herself into a life of hedonism and was immortalized by F. Scott Fitzgerald and John Held. In such films as *Dancing Mothers* (1926), *Mantrap* (1926), *Red Head* (1928), and Elinor Glyn's notorious *It* (1927), Bow exhibited the reckless insouciance which epitomized post-World War I youth.

Of all the films depicting the flapper, however, *Our Dancing Daughters* ranks among the very best, not only because of its technical finesse, but also, and more importantly, because of Joan Crawford's portrayal of Diana Medford, a flapper whose uninhibited façade is but a mask to protect her virtue rather than indiscreetly relinquish it. This façade of self-protection was an important ingredient in showing the humanity of the flapper.

Crawford was not the first flapper on the motion-picture screen, but she was an indelible one. On screen and off at that time in her life, she was the archetypal flapper, so much so that Fitzgerald, more enamored of her vivaciousness than her talent, was inspired to write:

> Joan Crawford is doubtless the best example of the flapper, the girl you see at smart clubs, gowned to the apex of sophistication, toying iced glasses, with a remorseful, faintly bitter expression, dancing deliciously, laughing a great deal, with wide, hurt eyes. Young things with a talent for living.

Fitzgerald's succinct description was based as much upon the real Crawford as it was on her screen *persona*. In films, she was a young starlet who, while struggling to find her "on screen image," off screen was girl-about-town who danced the hours away to the Charleston and the Black Bottom and collected prize-winning cups for her efforts.

After three years as an ingenue with Metro-Goldwyn-Mayer, the ambitious twenty-four-year-old Crawford discovered Josephine Lovett's story running as a serial in the Hearst newspapers. She had already learned that she must look out for herself, so she brazenly stole a copy of the script M-G-M had already prepared and took it to producer Hunt Stromberg. She begged him for the part, and he wisely cast her in it. Years later, she would say, "I think it was the first time the script department was told to write directly for Crawford," and the story did seem to be personally tailored to her blossoming talents.

Our Dancing Daughters is regarded by many as the best of the jazz-age films, accurate enough in its depiction of wild young women to be almost a documentary of one aspect of that colorful era. As Crawford said,

> . . . it was a way of life I knew. As Diana, I was the *flapper*, wild on the surface, a girl who shakes her windblown bob (mine started a craze) and dances herself into a frenzy while the saxes shriek and the trombones wail, a girl drunk on her own youth and vitality.

This "dangerous" Diana is in fact a rather dignified young socialite whose brazen façade as a flapper is a ruse both to compete with and to admonish

her partying parents. She embraces this noisy life-style with complete abandon, joining her new girl friends in flirtatious schemes to attract the opposite
sex. As one of the film's titles quotes her, Diana's credo is, "I want to hold
out my hand and catch it [life] like the sunlight." Much of the script shows
Diana the center of attention at endless parties highlighted by frenzied dances,
carefree and careless drinking, flirting, and men, men, men. In one famous
and shocking sequence, Diana sheds her dress and dances in her white satin
step-ins.

Diana's friend Anne (Anita Page) is a baby-faced innocent on the outside,
but driven by her mercenary mother (Dorothy Cumming), she is really a
selfish and promiscuous gold digger. The third girl in the trio—in this film,
the plot is little more than a variation on *Sally, Irene and Mary* (1925), which
starred Constance Bennett, Sally O'Neil, and Crawford—is Beatrice (Dorothy Sebastian), a likable socialite whose aplomb is shattered by the guilt of
a past sexual indiscretion.

Anne deceptively competes with Diana for the affections of Ben Black
(Johnny Mack Brown). Ben is the level-headed son of a multimillionaire who
is deceived by Anne's sweetness and dismayed by Diana's apparent indifference. Anne and Ben marry but are soon unhappily aware that Diana and Ben
really do love each other.

At a drunken party, Anne, in an alcoholic stupor, accuses Diana and Ben
of carrying on an affair behind her back, despite the fact that the bitchy Anne
has more than once been unfaithful to Ben. In the typical "things are not
always what they seem" manner in film storytelling, the wild but idealistic
Diana realizes that the reason she had lost Ben in the first place was her own
frivolous image. She has not been true to herself. When the intoxicated Anne
falls down a flight of stairs and dies, Diana and Ben are cruelly awakened to
the fact that they are really in love and that they must change their way of
life.

As simple and ordinary as this story was to both serial readers and filmgoers,
it was timely and effective. When the film opened at the Capitol Theater in
New York City in October, 1928, it grossed a spectacular forty thousand
dollars its first weekend, and the attendance was so heavy and the lines so
long, according to *Variety*, it was all the ushers could do to keep the aisles
clear.

One of the many reasons for *Our Dancing Daughters* being acclaimed the
best film depiction of jazz babies was its lush M-G-M production values. The
film was shot in Carmel, California, which added to the authenticity of its
Bohemian look, and technically it boasted the M-G-M expertise. The absolutely gorgeous sets were by the masterful Cedric Gibbons and were an
excellent example of Art Deco, a direct result of Gibbons having attended
the 1925 Exposition des Arts Decoratifs in Paris. The able direction was by
Harry Beaumont, who, the same year, was nominated as Best Director for

Broadway Melody, the pioneering and innovative "musical-with-sound" which won the 1928-1929 Best Picture Award, the second film to do so.

It is important to note that while *Our Dancing Daughters* was a silent film, the imminence of sound was so great that M-G-M added sound effects to the film which reproduced a combination of music—to enliven the romantic and dancing sequences—and in the words of *The New York Times*, "stentorian cheering and, at the end, a chorus of shrieks." While *The New York Times* critic failed to appreciate the intrusion of this sound track, especially the shrieks, the audiences were audible in their enthusiasm over this still unfamiliar innovation. Only four months after the release of *Our Dancing Daughters*, Beaumont's "musical-with-sound," *Broadway Melody*, would be considered revolutionary.

Our Dancing Daughters was, however, really quite a small, clichéd motion picture, and the proficiency of M-G-M's technical staff and even the addition of a sound background were not responsible for its success and its place in film history. That was the result of "personality," a quintessential ingredient in the acceptance by the public of this kind of film. Here, the personality was Crawford.

Crawford had begun her career in motion pictures in 1925 at M-G-M, and *Our Dancing Daughters*, her nineteenth picture, was finally the film which crystallized those characteristics which would dominate the early part of her career. From the moment audiences first see her dancing in front of a three-way mirror, Crawford's energy and vivacity completely rivet their attention. From that moment onward, she is always in a state of constant motion. The audience responded to that energy and vitality—that personality—not to any remarkable acting ability, for Crawford had yet to polish the skills evident in her later films.

Our Dancing Daughters was such a success that M-G-M's Louis B. Mayer doubled her $250 a week salary and instructed his producers to concentrate on this new talent. The roles that followed were, predictably, variations on Crawford's Diana: *Our Modern Maidens* (1929); *Hollywood Revue of 1929*, her talky debut; *Our Blushing Brides* (1930), again under Beaumont's direction; and even *Dance, Fools, Dance* (1931), her first with Clark Gable; and *Laughing Sinners* (1931), again with Gable.

In fact, Crawford did not discard the flapper image entirely until well into the 1940's with *Mildred Pierce* (1945); and then, despite the enormous impact this new dramatic period had on the Crawford screen personality, there are many admirers who, rightly so, feel that when Crawford left behind the Diana in her screen performances, part of her vitality, freshness, and accessibility went with it. *Our Dancing Daughters* and many of Crawford's 1930's comedies deserve attention by those who think of this actress only in terms of *Mildred Pierce*.

Ronald Bowers

OUR HOSPITALITY

Released: 1923
Production: Joseph M. Schenck for Buster Keaton Productions; released by Metro
Direction: Buster Keaton and Jack C. Blystone
Screenplay: Clyde Bruckman, Jean C. Havez, and Joseph A. Mitchell
Cinematography: Elgin Lessley and Dev Jennings
Editing: Buster Keaton (uncredited)
Length: 7 reels/6,220 feet

Principal characters:
Willie McKay	Buster Keaton
Canfield girl	Natalie Talmadge
Canfield father	Joe Roberts
Canfield brothers	Ralph Bushman
	Craig Ward
Train engineer	Joe Keaton
Minister	Monte Collins

Buster Keaton is now recognized by virtually every film critic and historian as one of the top ten or fifteen filmmakers of all time. He excelled as a performer, as a director, as an editor, and as a creator of scenarios—although he seldom took screen credit for his work behind the camera. His film career divides easily into four sections. First, he served a sort of apprenticeship in a number of Fatty Arbuckle films; second, he made a series of short films and one feature (*The Three Ages*, 1923, that was admittedly three shorts put together); third, he made a series of nine feature films for his own production company; and fourth, he lost his independence as a filmmaker and worked as a studio employee. His progress through these stages was quite rapid. The first began in 1917, the second in 1920, the third in 1923, and the fourth in 1928. *Our Hospitality* was the first film in the amazingly productive third period of his career, during which he made two films a year—all of which are today recognized as classics of silent film and indeed among the best films of any type ever made. Keaton had learned the art and craft of filmmaking so well in the preceding five or six years that *Our Hospitality*, although his first true full-length film, is a fully realized, mature work. It combines romance, melodrama, and exciting action into a skillfully developed comic narrative.

The premise of the film is a Romeo-and-Juliet-like romance in which two young people who are members of feuding families fall in love. *Our Hospitality* is, however, set in the American South in the 1830's and focuses on the conflict between one family's Southern hospitality and its murderous feud with another family. (The families are called Canfield and McKay in an obvious reference to the famous Hatfield-McCoy feud.) The conflict between hospitality and feud comes about when a Canfield girl (Natalie Talmadge, Keaton's wife) invites Willie McKay (Buster Keaton) to dinner when neither knows the other's identity. Once the girl's brothers (Ralph Bushman and Craig Ward) discover Willie in their house, they want to kill him, but their father (Joe Roberts) reminds them that according to the Southern code they cannot harm anyone who is a guest in their house.

Willie's visit then becomes a comic game with a deadly edge as he tries to stay as long as he can, and the brothers anxiously wait for him to leave. At one point the piano sheet music the girl is playing blows out the door, and she asks Willie to retrieve it, but he knows that one of her brothers is waiting outside with a gun. His solution to the problem is both funny and ingenious; he takes the single-shot pistol from the surprised brother and fires it; then he hands it back and retrieves the music before the brother can reload the gun. The sequence ends with Willie leaving the house disguised in women's clothes. At the last moment, however, when the Canfields see his trousers under the dress, they pursue him, and the "game" becomes a full-scale chase.

Before the chase and even before the dinner and the "hospitality," the film has two sections that set up the entire situation. In the first, a Canfield and a McKay kill each other in a gun battle when Willie is only a very small child. (He is played by Keaton's own fifteen-month-old son in this scene.) Then the second section begins twenty years later in New York, when Willie receives word that he has inherited his father's estate. He envisions a grand house and immediately sets off to claim it even though he is warned of the feud and the danger of the Canfields.

The journey to the South is a substantial part of the film and is important and enjoyable for three reasons: the train itself, Willie's meeting of the girl, and the establishing of Willie's character. Keaton researched the early trains in this country and found that in the first part of the 1830's, there was one called the Stephenson Rocket that was quite funny-looking. He had an exact replica built and used it for the shots of the train trip. The engine has an oversized smokestack at the front, front wheels much larger than the rear ones, and no covering at all for the engineer. The cars resemble stagecoaches more than they do later railroad cars. The whole appearance of the train is that of a toy or a fantasy rather than of a serious means of travel, but it does make the trip, even though it does not always stay on the track. Incidentally, Keaton's father, Joe, plays the engineer of the train.

Just as this strange train is about to leave New York, another passenger boards and sits by Willie. It is the Canfield girl. They make each other's acquaintance on the trip, but they do not exchange last names. Thus is established the incipient romance as well as the reason for the dangerous dinner invitation.

The third important element of the trip is that it establishes the character of Willie. He is a characteristic Keaton hero in that he is rather diffident and ineffectual in the first part of the film and only becomes truly heroic in the last part. Critic Daniel Moews overstates the case only slightly when he writes, "He is a Woody Allen hero who is also a Clint Eastwood hero, an Ashley Wilkes who is simultaneously a Rhett Butler." In the train, the Woody Allen side is primarily seen; Willie has difficulty with his tall hat in the small coach and is very hesitant with the girl.

It is after the railroad trip and after the tense time in the Canfield house that the opposite side of Willie's character emerges. He is chased by the brothers and barely escapes, but then he finds himself on a log rushing down a river toward a huge waterfall. Just as he saves himself, he sees that the girl—who had followed him—is about to plunge over the falls. In a breathtaking acrobatic feat he swings out on a rope, catches her, and brings her back to safety. As usual, Keaton did his own stunts, at no little risk to himself.

The end of the film brings together all the threads of the plot. The Canfields return to their house after dark, planning to resume their hunt for Willie at daybreak. Then they find Willie and the girl in her room embracing, but as they open the door further they see the minister (Monte Collins) and learn that the two have just been married. The father decides that the time has come to end the feud, so he congratulates the two, and he and his sons place their guns on the table. Willie then reveals that he is carrying some half a dozen guns. He lays them on the table beside the others; then he remembers something and takes one more out of his boot. The film then ends with Willie and the girl kissing.

It is not surprising that *Our Hospitality* was a great hit at the box office in 1923, since it demonstrates Keaton's mastery of both comic and dramatic direction and performance. It is also not surprising that Keaton made eight more classic films in the next four years. What is surprising is the fact that Keaton's reputation suffered a tremendous decline during the 1930's and 1940's. Then in the 1950's, his artistry began to be recognized again. The recognition during his lifetime was climaxed by a personal appearance at the Venice Film Festival in 1965, where he received an overwhelming, enthusiastic response. He died only a few months later, but his films live on and continue to be appreciated whenever they are shown.

Timothy W. Johnson

PANDORA'S BOX
(DIE BÜCHSE DER PANDORA)

Released: 1929
Production: George C. Horsetzky for Nero Film A. G.
Direction: G. W. Pabst
Screenplay: Ladislaus Vajda; based on the plays *Erdgeist* and *Die Büchse der Pandora* by Franz Wedekind
Cinematography: Günther Krampf
Editing: Joseph R. Fliesler
Length: 8 reels/10,675 feet

Principal characters:
Lulu	Louise Brooks
Dr. Peter Schön	Fritz Kortner
Alwa Schön	Franz Lederer
Schigolch	Carl Götz
Countess Anna Geschwitz	Alice Roberts
Rodrigo Quast	Krafft Raschig
Marquis Casti-Piani	Michael von Newlinsky
Man/Jack the Ripper	Gustav Diessl

Franz Wedekind's turn-of-the-century plays *Erdgeist* (*Earth Spirit*) and *Die Büchse der Pandora* (*Pandora's Box*) provide the basis for two masterpieces of twentieth century art. Alban Berg's *Lulu* is a towering achievement in the operatic repertory, and G. W. Pabst's film *Pandora's Box* is one of the monuments of German cinema and deserves consideration in any discussion of the history of world cinema. The plays had been filmed in the early 1920's in productions starring the great Danish actress Asta Neilsen. The Neilsen versions were influenced by the Expressionistic Theater movement, and Pabst wished to emphasize a more realistic, intimate approach focusing on the innocent eroticism of Lulu, rather than viewing her as a monster of evil as Wedekind had portrayed her in his plays. Pabst therefore eliminated or condensed many of the elements in the two plays much as Berg was to do in his opera libretto. The result is an endlessly fascinating, irresistible dissection of an amoral enchantress, a film that is as compelling as its heroine; for Lulu is finally heroic in her willful self-indulgence, and her downfall, while inevitable, is tragic.

The structure of the film is divided loosely into five scenes with two shorter scenes providing variations to the main themes. The film opens with Lulu (Louise Brooks) in her apartment where she flirts with the meter man, when a shabbily dressed, elderly man arrives to her evident delight. As the newcomer, Schigolch (Carl Götz), inspects her apartment and freely samples her liquor, Lulu demonstrates her dancing skills and her carefree, sensual personality for her friend. Their reunion, however, is interrupted by the arrival of Dr. Peter Schön (Fritz Kortner), who is a newspaper editor and Lulu's benefactor. She hides her visitor on the balcony accompanied by a bottle and her little dog. Dr. Schön is very nervous yet manages to tell Lulu that he is engaged and about to be married. Lulu is both relieved and amused at this revelation and his discomfort. Yet her joy is short-lived as her little dog awakens, barks at Schigolch and reveals the presence of the disreputable old man to Schön. Schön angrily ignores Lulu's insistence that Schigolch is her father and leaves the apartment. Schigolch is pleased, though, since he can now invite his friend Rodrigo up to meet Lulu. Rodrigo (Krafft Raschig) is a circus strong man who hopes to entice Lulu to join his act. Once she feels Rodrigo's muscles, she eagerly agrees to his proposition.

The scene shifts to the Schön residence where Alwa (Franz Lederer), Dr. Schön's handsome young son, is finishing the compositions for a musical revue. Countess Anna Geschwitz (Alice Roberts) arrives bringing her costume designs for Alwa's approval. Lulu also arrives and excitedly tells her friends of her new trapeze act with Rodrigo. It is obvious that Alwa and the Countess are both in love with her. Lulu ignores the woman, but teases the young man, enjoying her power over him although unaware of the torment that this power causes. Dr. Schön enters and is angry that Lulu is in his house. In retaliation, Lulu flirts more openly with Alwa and promises to see him soon. Lulu then leaves, and Alwa gloomily asks his father why he does not marry Lulu. Dr. Schön replies that one does not marry that kind of girl, it would be suicide. Yet, Schön learns of the trapeze act and tells Alwa to put Lulu in his revue but warns Alwa to beware of the girl.

The opening night of Alwa's revue is a huge success. Director Pabst follows the stage manager as he skillfully but frantically maneuvers the actors, sets, and props into place amidst the backstage chaos. Alwa and Geschwitz watch from the wings as Lulu triumphantly wins the audience. Suddenly, Dr. Schön arrives with his fiancée, a prim, respectable girl. Schön and his fiancée are quickly separated by moving sets and hustling stagehands and Schön meets Lulu backstage. She is delighted to see him at first, but becomes furious when he attempts to leave her to search for his fiancée. She then refuses to go on stage and rips off her costume and beats her makeup man. Schön tries to calm her, but she is inconsolable so they go into the prop room for more privacy. Once there Schön's physical desire for her overcomes his sense of duty and responsibilty. His fiancée finds him in the arms of the nearly nude actress and leaves the theater in tears. Savoring her victory, Lulu returns exultantly to the stage, while Schön accepts his fate with foreboding.

At the wedding reception in Schön's house, he entertains his guests while Lulu, in radiant white, insures that Schigolch and Rodrigo have an adequate supply of food and drink in the kitchen. Lulu then returns to the reception, where she leads the Countess in a dance that is both pleasure and agony for the love-stricken woman. Schön attempts to introduce his bride to the other guests, but Lulu wants to take her new husband to bed. She, thus, slips off to the bedroom, while Schön bids farewell to departing guests. Schigolch and Rodrigo, however, have invaded the bedroom in order to strew flowers on the bed, but are now too drunk to leave. Lulu vainly tries to help Rodrigo up, but his bulk is too much for her. Schön enters, sees his wife in Rodrigo's embrace, and leaves, only to return with a pistol. He chases the two drunks through the reception area, to the astonishment of the other guests. Returning to the bedroom, he finds Alwa kneeling in front of Lulu with his head in her lap telling her of his love for her. Schön leads his son from the bedroom and turns back to his bride. He grabs her and attempts to force her to kill herself, muttering "it is the only way to save us." In the struggle the gun goes off, but Schön is shot, not Lulu. Alwa breaks in to find his father dying and Lulu with the gun in her hand. Schön tries to speak, perhaps to warn his son, as he dies.

Lulu is placed on trial for the death of her husband. She is convicted of manslaughter but the Countess and Rodrigo engineer her escape by creating a panic in the courtroom. Lulu returns to the Schön residence, where she calmly takes a bath. Alwa discovers her there, but his horror of her complicity in his father's death is overcome by his desire for her, and she easily persuades him to escape with her. On the train to France, Lulu is recognized by the Marquis Casti-Piani (Michael von Newlinsky) who blackmails Alwa in exchange for not turning her into the Frontier Guards. He then suggests that they accompany him as they will not be safe in Paris. Having no choice, Alwa agrees.

On Casti-Piani's gambling ship, Alwa and Lulu sink further into degradation and despair. Alwa looses all their money at the gambling tables. Schigolch, Rodrigo, and Geschwitz have followed the couple to the ship and contribute further to their misery. Rodrigo demands money from Lulu, threatening to turn her over to the police, and Casti-Piani schemes to sell Lulu to an Egyptian brothel owner. Schigolch gives Alwa a deck of cards in order to help him cheat at the tables and plots with Lulu to use Geschwitz to distract Rodrigo. Geschwitz and Rodrigo fall for the ruse. Rodrigo believes that she has money and is attracted to him, and the Countess is willing to use her body to save her beloved Lulu. Alwa, however, is caught cheating. Geschwitz, overcome with disgust, kills Rodrigo; and in the ensuing police raid, Lulu, Alwa, and Schigolch are able to escape.

The final scene opens on a foggy London street at Christmas. The camera follows a man (Gustav Diessel) wandering aimlessly through the streets peering in windows at families enjoying the holiday feast. He comes upon a Salvation Army band dispensing tea to passersby. A pretty young soldier offers him tea and asks how she can help. In terror and despair, the man replies "nobody can help me. I cannot be helped." She gives him a candle and some mistletoe, which he puts in his pocket and wanders off. Then, Lulu is seen in a heatless attic, shabbily dressed, and with only a crust of bread to eat. She offers some to Alwa who only stares at it. Schigolch comes in and watches as Lulu combs her hair and applies makeup. He has a bottle which they all share before Lulu leaves. Alwa stirs from his stupor and follows her out. Schigolch prevents him from following her, but Alwa begins pacing in front of the tenement.

Lulu meets the mysterious man and invites him back to her room. He is very frightened and says that he has no money, but Lulu shrugs and says that she likes him anyway. The man is clearly enticed, and the audience sees him remove a knife from his pocket and drop it down the stairwell. Now at ease, he readily accompanies Lulu to the garret. As they relax, she discovers the candle and the mistletoe. She lights the candle and stands to be kissed by the man. Yet he has spotted the breadknife in the candleglow; he struggles with an inner turmoil and then yields to the impulse to pick up the knife. As Lulu looks up to be kissed, the knife flashes, and Lulu's hand falls limply away from his shoulder. The man descends the stairs, passing the waiting Alwa, and disappears in the fog. The Salvation Army band marches into view, and Alwa follows as it too fades from view in the fog.

Despite the inexorable destruction that follows Lulu in her wake, the viewer can not resist feeling sympathy for the pathetic woman. As embodied brilliantly by Louise Brooks, Lulu is so charming and so unaware of the misery that she causes that it is impossible not to be fascinated by this beautiful child-woman. She is truly an innocent in her amorality. Society's rules place no bounds on her. Although Wedekind's first play *Earth Spirit* describes in more detail the forces that have brought Lulu to the point where the film begins, Pabst correctly understands that the results, and not the causes, of this behavior is the factor that is so compelling for the audience. It is enough that Lulu exists for everyone to admire and to be astonished by her will to live unfettered and unrestrained. In her final moments, when even stale bread is precious, she is still celebrating life and still affirming it as she embraces death.

Lotte Eisner, eminent critic of German film, has referred to the "miracle of Louise Brooks." Brooks, an American, is truly miraculous in the role, but she would not have had the opportunity to play Lulu if Pabst had not recognized in her the qualities he was seeking for his heroine. Pabst had interviewed hundreds of actresses for the part before spotting Brooks in Howard Hawks' *A Girl in Every Port* (1928). Under contract to Paramount, Brooks was unavailable to Pabst, and he had virtually decided on the young Marlene Dietrich for the role, when Paramount suddenly fired Brooks who had not been successful in American films. She rushed to Germany, where she was plunged into a world of jealous intrigue concocted by the other actors in the film. Pabst was extremely dictatorial, interfering in her private life, refusing her the right to choose her own costumes, and giving her virtually no direction on the set. Yet, as miserable as she was, Pabst knew how to elicit the effect he desired from her, and her performance is continually exciting and one of the most memorable ever recorded on celluloid.

Pabst himself, however, is the reason why *Pandora's Box* can still thrill the audience. His genius as a filmmaker enlivens every frame. Brooks is admittedly a joy to watch, but even when she is not on screen, the film is consistently enthralling. The depiction of a theater backstage on opening night is rivaled on film only by Rouben Mamoulian's *Applause* (1929). The tension, the humor, the excitement, and the energy involved in entertaining an audience is depicted with economy and wit while also moving the narrative toward the denouement of the scene. The scene on the gambling ship is appropriately hellish, claustrophobic, and grasping as everyone converges on Lulu for needs that she cannot fulfill. Again, Pabst imbues the scene with movement and telling vignettes. In two or three shots, a cabin boy is introduced who is obviously infatuated with Lulu; and viewers are not surprised, therefore, when he helps her escape. The ability of the audience to grasp this crucial bit of information without dialogue, and in a shot or two, attests to Pabst's understanding of the visual impact of film and his trust in the intelligence of his audience.

The final scene in London should be studied by anyone who loves cinema, for here is filmmaking at its most brilliant. The atmosphere, the sets, the actors' movements, and the camera placement in the shots are exact and convey only the information necessary for the scene. This simplicity makes the tragedy all the more shocking. The horror of Lulu's death at the hand of a man who turns out to be Jack the Ripper is more palpable because so little of it is seen. The look in his eyes, the flash of the knife, and the sudden relaxation of Lulu's hand on his shoulder tells all that one needs to know.

Pandora's Box is not a perfect film, and Pabst made other equally important films, such as *Diary of a Lost Girl* (1929, also starring Brooks), *Westfront 1918* (1930), and *Kamradschaft* (1931). *Pandora's Box*, however, remains that happy conjunction of actress, director, and story that results in a sublime work of art. One of the purposes of art is to move and to effect change in the audience. The viewer of *Pandora's Box* must respond to the film, thereby attesting to the artistic accomplishment of Pabst and insuring a place in the history of cinema for *Pandora's Box*.

Don K Thompson

PANTHEA

Released: 1917
Production: Lewis J. Selznick
Direction: Allan Dwan
Screenplay: Mildred Considine; based on the play of the same name by Monckton Hoffe
Cinematography: Roy F. Overbaugh
Length: 5 reels

Principal characters:
Panthea Romoff .... Norma Talmadge
Gerald Mordaunt .... Earle Foxe
Baron de Duisitor .... L. Rogers Lytton
Prefect of Police .... George Fawcett
Secret Agent .... Murdock MacQuarrie

During the shooting of *Panthea* for Lewis J. Selznick, Norma Talmadge married producer Joseph Schenck. It was perhaps the wisest move she ever made, for Schenck was deeply in love with her, and, under his sponsorship, she became the top dramatic actress in Hollywood, as well as one of the richest. She purchased some of the choicest property in Los Angeles, including a large apartment house still in existence on Wilshire Blvd. called the Talmadge; and, with her sister Constance, she also owned her own studio in West Hollywood. Furthermore, any story property that she wanted to produce for herself, Schenck usually bought.

Talmadge, Schenck, and Allan Dwan joined forces to produce *Panthea*, and after she completed her Selznick contract, Talmadge formed the Norma Talmadge Production Company, with Schenck supervising the films that she made. *Panthea*, a 1913 play by Monckton Hoffe, showed in London and then on Broadway, with Mme. Olga Petrova as its star.

In the film, Talmadge plays a Russian pianist named Panthea Romoff, a graduate of the Moscow conservatory, who is suspected of revolutionary sympathies. While attending one of Panthea's concerts, the Baron de Duisitor (L. Rogers Lytton) conspires with the Moscow Prefect of Police (George Fawcett) to have her home raided, after which she was to be brought up before him on charges of nihilism and advocating the overthrow of social institutions. The Baron would then secure her release and thus make her indebted to him. Circumstances, however, conspire against them. Panthea's brother actually is a nihilist and is holding a meeting in the house when the police come to arrest Panthea. The brother manages to escape, but a soldier is killed in the process. The Baron curses fate, especially when Panthea escapes her prison and sails for England. Her ship is wrecked off the English coast, and Panthea, unconscious, is rescued and brought to the nearby Mordaunt estate to recover. Young Gerald Mordaunt (Earle Foxe), heir to the estate, immediately falls in love with her. Their mutual love of music is a special bond, and Gerald confesses that he lives to have one of his original operas produced. They marry and move to Paris, where they live in happiness for a year. Panthea herself takes her husband's opera around to producers, but she cannot generate any interest in his work.

Then she again encounters Baron de Duisitor, and he agrees to produce her husband's opera, provided that she becomes his mistress. The opera is a great success, and the Baron arranges to have her arrested as soon as he seduces her. The Baron, however, has a heart attack and dies when the international police, headed by the Moscow prefect, come to arrest her. Panthea must go back to Russia, possibly to be condemned to Siberia, but Gerald insists that he will go with her. At the end of the story, he has already started the diplomatic corps working on evidence that will free her entirely so that they can both eventually return to London.

If Talmadge's career had begun to blossom with a promising start at Vitagraph, where she is said to have made over a hundred short features, and later with a short term at Triangle, it finally burst into full bloom with *Panthea*, her first film for Selznick. She gained a real following with subsequent vehicles such as *Poppy* (1917), released six months after *Panthea*; *The Forbidden City* (1918), in which she played a dual role; and *The Safety Curtain* (1918), in which she was a much-abused waif. She changed releasing companies to Associated First National in 1920, and the ensuing decade marked the bulk of her great successes. Eugene O'Brien had been her leading man in ten of the features that she made in the 1917-1918 period, and since it was openly acknowledged that O'Brien was a homosexual, Schenck did not mind how torrid their love scenes were. He was, in fact, very happy when O'Brien could give up his short-lived starring career and return to being leading man again for his wife in a second series that included *Secrets* (1924) and *Graustark* (1925).

The Schencks nevertheless drifted apart, although he still managed her career and brought her to United Artists in 1927 with *The Dove*. When she played Marguerite Gauthier in 1927 in a beautiful modern production of *Camille*, based as much on the novel as it was on the play, she chose Gilbert Roland to be her Armand. They were a handsome couple, and Lionel Barrymore even coached Roland for the role in a Los Angeles stage production of *Camille* starring Jane Cowl. By this time, Roland and Talmadge were lovers, and it was, oddly enough, for the time, well known and fully accepted in the Hollywood community. She was a well-liked, generous woman and even gave Roland so many marvelous close-ups in *Camille* that at least one local critic remarked that perhaps the title of the piece should be *Armand*. Roland was her leading man four times, in *Camille*, *The Dove* (1928), *The Woman Disputed* (1928), and her first talking film, *New York Nights* (1929), a gangster melodrama.

Realizing that sound pictures were going to change the industry forever, Talmadge feared for her career since she had no stage training which was a liability in the early sound period, and both she and her sister Constance had very identifiable Brooklyn accents. Leslie Carter was hired to coach her in *Dubarry, Woman of Passion* (1930). Carter had created that role for David Belasco on stage, but she could do nothing for Talmadge, who thereupon retired, divorced Schenck, and soon afterward, married George Jessel. They did a vaudeville act together, for which Jessel coached her. They did not last long as a team, and when they divorced, Talmadge married San Francisco physician, Dr. Carvel James. They lived most of the time in San Francisco, or in Florida, where she also owned a home. She was a very rich woman when she died in 1957.

The films she made, starting with *Panthea*, were wonderfully romantic, and this type of drama was clearly her forte. She suffered gloriously on the screen, and most of her vehicles were styled around at least one tearful scene. *Panthea* was perfect for her; it even included a scene in which she was to "give all" in order to let her husband live in a dream world. Among her most memorable films are *Smilin' Through* (1922), *Within the Law* (1923), and *The Lady* (1925); and it is because of her that these films remain unforgettable today.

The reviewer in *Photoplay* magazine wrote of her performance in *Panthea* that she played it

> with a verve, abandon and surety which denominates her queen of our younger silver-sheet emotionalists. There is no woman on the depthless stage who can flash from woe to laughter and back again with the certainty of this particular Talmadge.

DeWitt Bodeen

PASSION
(MADAME DUBARRY)

Released: 1919
Production: Ernst Lubitsch for Union-Ufa; released by Associated First National
Direction: Ernst Lubitsch
Screenplay: Hans Kraly and Fred Orbing
Cinematography: Theodor Sparkuhl
Art direction: Karl Machus and Kurt Richter
Costume design: Ali Hubert
Length: 9 reels

Principal characters:
Jeanne Bécu/Madame DuBarry .... Pola Negri
Louis XV .... Emil Jannings
Armand de Foix .... Harry Liedtke
Jean DuBarry .... Eduard von Winterstein
Duc de Choiseul .... Reinhold Schünzel
Duchesse de Grammont .... Elsa Berna
Duc de Richelieu .... Frederick Immler
Duc d'Aiguillon .... Gustave Czimeg
Guillaume DuBarry .... Carl Platen

With the outbreak of World War I, the motion-picture industries of the major European countries were shattered, many virtually coming to a standstill for the duration of the war. The German film industry, which in 1911 numbered one dozen companies, became a tool of the German government, specializing in propaganda films to inspire their military troops. Following the war, the government sponsored the merger of several larger companies to create the Universum Film, A. G., known as Ufa, and by 1922, the German film companies numbered 360 with Ufa the foremost among them.

During World War I, there was a ban on the importation of German films into the United States, and during that time, the prolific Hollywood industry took the forefront as the dominating production center in the world, a reputation it arguably still holds today. In 1919, immediately after the war, the German film industry saw two revolutionary films released: Robert Weine's *The Cabinet of Dr. Caligari* (produced by Erich Pommer) and, perhaps more significantly for the industry, Ernst Lubitsch's *Madame DuBarry*, the film which ended the American importation ban, and opened at New York City's Capitol Theater on December 15, 1920, under the more provocative title *Passion*.

The chief reason that *Passion* was the first European production to be released in the United States following the war was its star, Pola Negri, who had gained a reputation in several previous Lubitsch productions as the fore-most actress in Europe. She represented an earthy and exotic kind of sex appeal, unique among screen heroines of the day.

Despite Negri, however, Ufa found it difficult to find a United States company that had the courage to purchase the American distribution rights to the film until they were approached by John D. Williams, one of the founders of First National Exhibitors Circuit. He paid $130,000 to distribute the film in the United States, an investment which earned that company more than one million dollars. Ironically, *The Cabinet of Dr. Caligari*, which is not only regarded by most critics as the greatest German silent film, but also as one of the all-time great films, would not be released in the United States until 1921, after *Passion* had paved the way.

These two greatly different films, however, do represent the quintessence of German cinema at its finest. *The Cabinet of Dr. Caligari* represented the epitome of what would become known as the expressionistic and psychological genre of German cinema. It was a film conceived by three painters, Robert Weine, Walther Reimann, and Hermann Warm, and an architect, Walter Rohrig, who were more interested in the "form" of cinema than in "movies." While it was the most talked about European production of its day, it remained largely unseen by the masses. They preferred the more accessible historical dramas of Lubitsch, which comprised the second most important German film genre of the day. These two films were landmarks in what became known as the Golden Period of German Cinema, a period which lasted until 1926, following the general release of E. A. Dupont's *Vaudeville*.

The Berlin-born Lubitsch began his career as an actor of Jewish comedy and, from 1911 to 1918, was a member of the famed Max Reinhardt's theater company. He first acted in films in 1912 and made his directorial debut in 1914 with a one-reeler entitled *Fraulein Seifenschaum*, in which he also starred.

His first feature film, *Die Augen der Mumie Ma* (*The Eyes of the Mummy Ma*, 1918) was significant for bringing Lubitsch together with Negri (it was also her first feature) and the noted German actor Emil Jannings. Lubitsch followed that with *Carmen* (1918) starring Negri and released in the United States in 1921 as *Gypsy Blood*. *Carmen* secured prosperity and top billings for both Lubitsch and Negri, and they followed that success with *Madame DuBarry*, with Jannings portraying Louis XV.

With *Madame DuBarry*, Lubitsch gained a reputation as the "humanizer of history," a reputation which essentially rested on the fact that despite frequent historical discrepancies, his historical dramas relied upon depicting boudoir politics in a subtle, witty, and satiric manner while often debunking historical fact. They were highly successful because the public seldom came to the theaters for facts.

Jeanne Bécu (1743-1793), the last mistress of the dissolute King Louis XV of France, was a beautiful woman of illegitimate birth and vulgar background.

The philosopher Voltaire, upon first witnessing her extraordinary loveliness, commented, "The original must have been made for the gods." The Lubitsch version of her life concentrates on three main characters as the victims of political and social fate: Jeanne Bécu/Madame DuBarry (Pola Negri), the toy of erratic destiny; Louis XV (Emil Jannings), the mad king; and Armand de Foix (Harry Liedtke), DuBarry's humble first love. Lubitsch uncannily symbolizes these three by three lighted candles on a candelabra to the left of the screen, beautifully filmed in Prisma colored sequences with each candle extinguishing as each of the three characters meets their fate.

The film begins with a ballroom scene showing an aristocratic gathering dancing the minuet when the room is stormed by a surging crowd of revolutionaries singing the "Marseillaise." This clash of social forces, the contrast of opulent court life with the poverty-stricken squalor, the wealthy ruling class with the extreme deprivation of the commoners, was a device which Lubitsch used masterfully throughout the film. He was especially adept at juxtaposing crowd scenes of considerable dramatic force with intimate love scenes.

Jeanne Bécu is shown as a vulgar young milliner's apprentice who falls in love with young Armand, then comes to the attention of Jean DuBarry (Eduard von Winterstein) and becomes his mistress. When Louis XV shows an interest in the beauty, Jean DuBarry obliges the King by turning his mistress over to him in order to advance his own personal career; and the King arranges for her to marry Jean DuBarry's brother, Guillaume (Carl Platen), so that she might acquire a title and be properly presented at court.

Even after acquiring her new status, Jeanne remains a common and vulgar personality—upon first meeting Louis, she gives him a kiss. Louis dotes on her by giving her manicures—when he cuts her finger, she slaps him—and one marvelously decadent scene shows him kissing her bare foot. While her position as mistress to the King did involve political intrigue, she was a generous woman, not really interested in politics and ambition as had been her predecessor Madame de Pompadour.

When Armand learns of the real identity of Madame DuBarry, he is so angered that he joins the revolution, and when she is arrested and tried by the Revolutionary Tribunal, he presides over the court which condemns her. In remorse he disguises himself as a monk in order to help her escape prison but is shot in the attempt, so she goes to the guillotine as planned.

Lubitsch directed the film with bold strokes of dramatic intensity with the best scenes being the crowd scenes which depict the uprising of the populace, the storming of the Bastille, and the beheading of Madame DuBarry. The film originally ran for two hours and fifteen minutes and opened at the Ufa-Palast Am Zoo Theater in Berlin on September 19, 1919. When finally released in the United States with a musical score by David Mendoza and William Axt, the film ran eighty-five minutes. One famous scene which was deleted portrays the Parisian crowd playing ball with the severed head of the mad king's mistress.

The film received universally outstanding reviews and set box-office records in both Germany and the United States. It also was responsible for the eventual emigration to the United States of its three creators, Lubitsch, Negri, and Jannings. Lubitsch and Negri stayed in Germany for several years after *Passion*'s release, during which time they made four more films together including: *Sumurun* (1920), released in the United States in 1921 as *One Arabian Night*; and *Anna Boleyn* (1920), released in the United States in 1921 as *Deception* and with Jannings as Henry VIII.

Lubitsch arrived in the United States in 1922 where his first American picture was *Rosita* (1923), starring Mary Pickford. Negri arrived a year later and it is often said that with the arrival of these two artists, a new sophistication was brought to the American screen. Lubitsch brought his famous "touch" with satire; and Negri brought her honest, earthy sex appeal and considerable acting talent, which today finds her recalled as an early Anna Magnani. Jannings did not arrive in the United States until several years later to make his American debut in *The Way of All Flesh* (1927), and by that time he was being hailed as the world's greatest living actor.

Passion is a pivotal film in motion-picture history. As for the character of Madame DuBarry, she has appeared on the screen in many transformations over the years, including Theda Bara in *Madame DuBarry* (1918), Norma Talmadge in *DuBarry, Woman of Passion* (1928), Dolores Del Rio in *Madame DuBarry* (1934), Gitta Alpar in *I Give My Heart* (1936), Gladys George in *Marie Antoinette* (1938), and even a musical comedy version in 1943 called *DuBarry Was a Lady* starring Lucille Ball.

Ronald Bowers

THE PASSION OF JOAN OF ARC
(LA PASSION DE JEANNE D'ARC)

Released: 1928
Production: Carl Theodor Dreyer for Société Générale de Film Paris
Direction: Carl Theodor Dreyer
Screenplay: Carl Theodor Dreyer; based on the novel by Joseph Delteil
Cinematography: Rudolph Maté
Editing: Carl Theodor Dreyer
Art direction: Hermann Warm and Jean Hugo
Length: 7 reels/6,720 feet

Principal characters:

Joan	Maria Falconetti
Pierre Cauchon	Eugène Silvain
Jean d'Estivet	André Berley
Nicolas Loiseleur	Maurice Schutz
Jean Massieu	Antonin Artaud
Jean Lemaître	Michel Simon
Guillaume Erard	Jean d'Yd
Jean Beaupère	Ravet

Since her martyrdom in 1431, Joan of Arc, the peasant girl whose visions inspired her to become the spiritual leader of the French forces wishing to establish Charles VII as king of France, has been a frequent subject in literature and film. Outstanding among the treatment of her story are George Bernard Shaw's play *Saint Joan*, Ingrid Bergman's portrayal of the maid in the film *Joan of Arc* (1948), and Carl Theodor Dreyer's 1928 film *The Passion of Joan of Arc*. The last, which many cinema critics and historians rank among the best films ever made, focuses on the last day in Joan's life.

That life began in the countryside of Donremy where Joan, born in 1412, began receiving visitations from St. Michael, St. Catherine, and St. Margaret at the age of twelve. As a result, four years later, the young girl offered her services to the Dauphin, later Charles VII, in his quest for the French throne, a quest that was opposed by the Burgundians and their British allies. Joan's major military accomplishment occurred when she led the Dauphin's army in breaking a seige of the city of Orleans in 1429. After several other military triumphs, though, she was captured and turned over to the Burgundian clergy, who, in the name of the Church and with British encouragement, tried her for heresy. She was convicted and burned at the stake.

As the title of Dryer's films suggests, its concern is with the agony of Joan's trial before the ecclesiastical court. Working from the actual trial records as well as a book by Joseph Delteil, Dreyer condensed the twenty-nine examinations which Joan underwent into one day. Such condensation reflects

Dreyer's use of the unities of classical drama. Not only does the action occur within a circumscribed time period (unity of time), but it also is situated in a single locale (unity of place)—although the latter reflects a departure from historical accuracy. These ties to classical dramatic technique highlight the film's thematic resemblance to several classical plays. For example, like Sophocles' Antigone, Joan finds herself, a helpless girl, in conflict with the power structure because she obeys a law higher than that of worldly authority. Moreover, both Joan and Antigone, although physically destroyed by the power structure, are vindicated when their sacrifices are recognized as inspired by religious devotion.

After Joan's execution at the stake, the British soldiers who have superintended the affair find her heart unscathed by the flames and realize that they have been involved with someone special. The heart serves as an emblem of the integrity of Joan's vision. Another dimension of Joan's ultimate triumph lies outside the film itself. The film's audience, like that for a classical Greek drama such as *Antigone*, is familiar with the legend behind the dramatic events. In Joan's case, the audience knows that the verdict against Joan was annulled in 1456, and that she was canonized in 1920, only a few years before Dreyer's film was released.

Perhaps even more striking than the film's parallels with classical drama are its allusions to the most important of Christian dramas, the Passion of Christ. The film's title prepares the viewer for similarities with the trial and execution of Christ, and Joan's sufferings are made to resemble those of Christ, from her humiliation at the hands of the British soldiers through her death. Like Christ, she is tried by an ecclesiastical court which demands she deny that her mission is from God; like Christ, she is made to wear a mock crown, one that she herself has fashioned from the straw of her prison cell; and like Christ, she goes through a Gethsamene of doubt in which she feels forsaken by everyone.

Dreyer's Joan emerges as a much more human figure than the characters from classical drama, the New Testament, or even many of the pious handlings of Joan's own story. Throughout the film, Maria Falconetti, in her only screen performance, creates a Joan who has sincere religious devotion, but who also experiences the doubts and fears one would expect of an unlettered peasant girl confronted by the learned doctors of the Church. Time after time in the course of the trial, Joan is on the verge of being ensnared by the sophistry of her accusers, only to see through their loaded questions and respond with divinely inspired simplicity. Her uncertainties culminate when she signs the confession stating that her visions are not from God, but she soon recognizes her error and recants the confession. She perceives that her signing was motivated by fear for her life and realizes that the reward that awaits her after martyrdom will compensate for any earthly loss.

Her fears and doubts make her credible as a human being and the film credible as a depiction of human conflicts. Dreyer approaches these conflicts in a way that differs from many of his predecessors and contemporaries. A director such as Sergei Eisenstein, for example, portrayed human conflict on a massive scale, with crowds of people surging against other crowds. For Dreyer, however, conflict is a much more individual matter, a concept he emphasizes by the film's most important technical feature, its reliance on the facial close-up for dramatic development. The images of individual faces dominate the film: Joan at various stages in her passion; her chief accuser Pierre Cauchon (Eugène Silvain); the sympathetic Jean Massieu (Antonin Artaud); and Warwick, the *eminence grise* of the whole proceeding. Even in the scenes in court where Joan stands before an array of judges (André Berley, Maurice Schutz, Michel Simon, Jean d'Yd, and Ravet) and in the crowd scenes during the public aspects of her passion, Dreyer picks out individual faces and allows them to reflect the more general conflict. Camera angles, adroitly maneuvered by Rudolph Maté, who worked with Dreyer on his first sound film *Vampyr* (1931), usually show Joan from above and her accusers from below, thus enhancing the relationships among the adversaries in the conflict. The stark stage design by Jean Hugo and Hermann Warm (who had earlier designed the effective settings for *The Cabinet of Dr. Caligari*, 1920) forces the viewer's unadulterated attention onto the faces of the actors.

Those actors demonstrate the potential which silent film had. Some such as Falconetti and Eugène Silvain came to Dreyer from the *Comédie-Française* and were making rare screen appearances in *The Passion of Joan of Arc*. Some such as Antonin Artaud (who became a leading surrealistic writer) brought artistic backgrounds other than acting to the film. Some such as the anonymous café proprietor who portrayed Warwick were nonprofessionals chosen by Dreyer for their physiognomies. The quality of these players' performances makes dialogue unnecessary. In fact, the use of titles in the film becomes more an intrusion into the drama than a device of clarification.

The Passion of Joan of Arc was Dreyer's ninth feature film and represents a maturation of the themes which he had been developing in his earlier work. The conflict of the individual with society and society's fear of the nonconforming individual, so central to *The Passion of Joan of Arc*, pervade the Danish director's earlier films such as *Blade af Satans Bog* (*Leaves from Satan's Book*, 1919) and *Elsker Hverandre* (*Love One Another*, 1921). As the best of his silent films, though, *The Passion of Joan of Arc* represents the flowering of these themes.

The film, despite its critical success, was a financial failure, and Dreyer did not make another film until *Vampyr* in 1931.

The most interesting contemporary response to *The Passion of Joan of Arc* was its censorship by British authorities, whose patriotic sensibilities were offended by the assignment of blame for Joan's trial and execution to the influence of their man Warwick, and by Dreyer's dressing the brutal British soldiers who torment Joan in uniforms reminiscent of those worn by the British army in World War I. Such a reaction seems particularly dated. Because of its thematic significance, its technical flourishes, and the high quality of its acting, *The Passion of Joan of Arc* transcends any topical or political references to deserve its reputation as a masterpiece.

Frances M. Malpezzi
William M. Clements

THE PENALTY

Released: 1920
Production: Samuel Goldwyn Productions
Direction: Wallace Worsley
Screenplay: Charles Kenyon; based on the novel of the same name by Gouverneur Morris
Cinematography: Donovan D. Short
Editing: Frank E. Hull
Art direction: Gilbert White
Length: 7 reels/6,730 feet

Principal characters:
Blizzard	Lon Chaney
Wilmot	Kenneth Harlan
Rose	Ethel Grey Terry
Dr. Ferris	Charles Clary
Barbara	Claire Adams
Frisco Pete	James Mason
Lichtenstein	Milton Ross

It is not entirely accurate to call Lon Chaney "the man of a thousand faces." As critic Richard Schickel has pointed out, he was really "the man with no face at all," so completely did he eradicate all traces of his own visage through skillful applications of makeup. He was a man of many bodies, however, all of them deformed, all contributing to, or the cause of, his malignant screen personalities.

In *The Penalty*, a child lies sick in bed, attended by the young, inexperienced Dr. Ferris (Charles Clary). Calling in an older colleague, he explains the child's malady as a "contusion at the base of the skull." Then, in what appears to be an accident of the titles, he says that he has amputated the child's legs. The senior doctor says this was the wrong remedy.

Twenty-seven-years later, the boy, now an archcriminal named Blizzard (Lon Chaney), is the underworld czar of San Francisco. The Federal Secret Service plants an agent, Rose (Ethel Grey Terry), with Blizzard, and she quickly becomes a trusted assistant, to the extent of supplanting the girl who works the pedals the crippled Blizzard cannot reach when he plays the piano.

Dr. Ferris' daughter, Barbara (Claire Adams), a sculptress, vows to marry her intended, another doctor, only when she has done something magnificent and plans to sculpt "Satan—After the Fall." Blizzard, seeking a means of access to Dr. Ferris' household, makes sure that he is the only applicant for the job. Blizzard insinuates himself into Barbara's emotional and artistic life, dazzling her with his erudition. Leaving the atelier after a sitting, he runs into her fiancé and makes a chillingly prophetic remark: "What an admirable pair of legs."

Meanwhile, Rose has scouted the house and finds a completely equipped operating room. Her report to her chief is intercepted by one of Blizzard's men, who shows it to his boss. Blizzard plans to loot the city and bring it to its knees by distracting the law with a series of explosions in the suburbs which will draw the police away from the action. Full-scale warfare will be conducted to subjugate San Francisco to Blizzard's army of "disgruntled foreign laborers."

Blizzard sends a message to Ferris saying that he has kidnaped Barbara. When Ferris and Barbara's fiancé arrive at Blizzard's den, he informs them of his master plan: Barbara's life for the younger man's legs. Ferris remembers the boy he crippled twenty-seven-years before and operates on Blizzard's head, not his legs, thus liberating the good soul that was always struggling to get out of the evil mastermind. The only sign that Blizzard gave, over the years, of being a decent human being was his yearning, soulful piano-playing which temporarily freed his tortured spirit. Rose and Blizzard are united, but his junkie henchman, fearing that the reformed criminal will squeal on his former cohorts, shoots Blizzard, who dies in Rose's arms. As he expires, Blizzard tells Rose that his death is the penalty for his previous life.

The most interesting aspect of *The Penalty* is the way in which Blizzard makes everyone his accomplice: from Rose, the agent sent to spy on him; to Barbara, who hires his evil face for her Satan sculpture; to the two doctors who loathe him, but save his life. Blizzard draws everyone into his hotbed of crime through sheer willpower. They are not, however, merely fascinated by his physically repellent body. Chaney's acting makes it clear that it is Blizzard's personality which lures them, and beyond that, variety. Rose, for example, oversees the hat factory; cases the layout looking for clues to Blizzard's criminal plans; and as Blizzard's piano-pedaler, becomes the love of his life. She also seems to have some unexplained managerial duties which allow her free rein, at least in the upper precincts of what is obviously a huge enterprise.

With *The Penalty*, "piano-pedaling" assumes the proportions of a screen perversion on a par with murdering people in showers, such as in Alfred Hitchcock's *Psycho* (1960). Rose's chief attraction has nothing to do with her sexual charms; she is simply a better "pedaler" than her blond predecessor.

Early in the film, the script makes a point of a large group of girls tucked secretly into a back room making thousands of hats, and periodically viewers see Rose overseeing the girls. In Blizzard's vision of a San Francisco overrun by his thousands of laborers, those hats are the only uniform the men have, the badge that says they work for Blizzard. This is not, however, enough to justify the amount of time the film spends showing them and making the audience wonder what the hats are for. The idea simply tails off into nothingness.

Chaney's face is more than sufficiently mobile to express the full range of Blizzard's emotional torment. He does not need the catalog of silent-screen mannerisms that he trots out to show Blizzard's bestial scheming. Chaney's great gift was to make cruelty and degeneracy seem normal, or at least to delineate them in a manner with which they can be sympathized. For Chaney, low-life was real life and in film after film, such as *The Black Bird* (1926), *West of Zanzibar* (1928), and others, he demonstrates the spiritual suffering the tortured men he plays must endure to reach either redemption or punishment.

Blizzard's motive for all the havoc he wreaks in *The Penalty* is revenge for the deformation of his body at the hands of an incompetent doctor, but the reprisal is aimed at society at large. The scope of his activities makes him a fiend for the fun of it, not for the understandable one of vengeance. Of course, his devilishness is explained away by the device of that "contusion at the base of his skull," and the doctor goes so far as to say that Blizzard will become as great a force for good as he was for evil. A man who can inspire such faith in his sworn enemies is a man of great strength of character and charisma.

Dope users were not common in films, even those made before the Production Code pulled the studios up by their moral bootstraps. As late as *Three on a Match*, released in 1932, Humphrey Bogart has to explain Ann Dvorak's drug addiction by miming wiping his nose, a reference to a junkie's habitually runny nose. So it comes as something of a surprise that one of the most visible aides-de-camp in *The Penalty* is obviously a drug user and always in need of a fix. Just as surprising is the naked model in the scene which introduces Barbara to the audience. The film underlines the girl's nudity by having the doctor open the door, close it hastily, and gasp in embarrassment, addressing his remarks to Barbara around the half-open door.

The film makes a point of demonstrating the lengths to which Chaney would go to achieve verisimilitude in a part. He hauls himself hand over hand up a series of pegs in his office wall to watch his girls make the hats and descends into the secret chamber on a pair of chains. It is not hard to see that Chaney bent his body at the knees and strapped his lower legs to his back. The extra width at the back of his coat gives his stratagem away. In most of his films, Chaney bound himself up in ways that were confining and painful. If he was not harnessed in leather or twisted around a pair of crutches, he weighed himself down under tons of makeup, none more constricting than that devised for his masterpiece, *The Hunchback of Notre Dame* (1923). Chaney's death was a grotesque parody of his professional life: artificial snow made of cornflakes stuck in his throat while shooting a film caused an infection which eventually led to the fatal congestion of his bronchial tubes.

One of the most striking aspects of Chaney's screen *persona* was that, in addition to making his audiences root for the criminal at the expense of the law, he was clearly superior to those around him. Here, only Rose is his match, and he quite rightly spares her life in spite of her duplicity. Barbara comments that Blizzard understands art better than the author of a noted text on the subject, and both the doctors, when Blizzard is unconscious and at their mercy, operate to save him rather than turning him over to the law. His power over people is almost superhuman and the reason for this mastery is a subtext of most of Chaney's films.

Chaney's films are not concerned with such superficial matters as crime and punishment: they are about aspiration and ambition. Blizzard is what modern writers would call an overachiever. The audience can see, through the complicated web of spies, henchmen, and workers, that Blizzard presides over a vast network of criminals, not only those in his lair but also an army of laborers controlled by his minions. His threat of conquering San Francisco is no idle boast. It is clear that he is more than capable of realizing this aim. It is interesting to speculate on just what species of malign delight Blizzard would have wrought for himself if he had been allowed to achieve his goals.

Judith M. Kass

PETER PAN

Released: 1924
Production: Adolph Zukor and Jesse L. Lasky for Paramount
Direction: Herbert Brenon
Screenplay: Willis Goldbeck; based on the play of the same name by James M. Barrie
Cinematography: James Wong Howe
Special effects: Roy Pomeroy
Length: 10 reels/9,593 feet

Principal characters:
Peter Pan .... Betty Bronson
Captain Hook .... Ernest Torrence
Mr. Darling .... Cyril Chadwick
Mrs. Darling .... Esther Ralston
Tinker Bell .... Virginia Browne Faire
Wendy .... Mary Brian
Tiger Lily .... Anna May Wong
Michael .... Philippe De Lacey
John .... Jack Murphy
Nana .... George Ali

Unlike many of its contemporary silent features, which are both intellectually and artistically superior, *Peter Pan* has stood the test of time well, chiefly because it is a piece of timeless whimsy that can still charm and entertain, much like the Fred Astaire-Ginger Rogers musicals of the mid-1930's. Ignoring the Freudian, sexual undertones, the story of *Peter Pan* is one that requires no great intelligence to appreciate, demanding little of its audience except that it sit back and enjoy the presentation. James M. Barrie's old-fashioned, moralizing entertainment is still revived on the stage, almost eighty years since its first performance on December 27, 1904. It has been filmed in animated form by Walt Disney in 1953, has been a Broadway musical vehicle first for Jean Arthur, later for Mary Martin, and more recently Sandy Duncan, and has reappeared twice as a network television special for Martin. As a straight production, for years *Peter Pan* was revived almost annually in England. The best-known American actresses to have played the title role are Maude Adams and Marilyn Miller.

The story is so well-known that it requires only a brief retelling: Peter Pan (Betty Bronson) is the boy who never grew up. Soon after he was born and heard his parents discussing his future, he ran away from home to live in Never Never Land with the lost boys, babies who fell out of their cradles when they were little. He has lost his shadow in the nursery of the Darling children and, when he returns to reclaim it, persuades Wendy Darling (Mary

Brian) and her two brothers, John (Jack Murphy) and Michael (Philippe De Lacey), to fly away with him. Peter's personal fairy, Tinker Bell (Virginia Browne Faire), is jealous of Wendy and tries to poison her, but Wendy is adopted by the boys as their mother, and they build for her a Wendy House. Captain Hook (Ernest Torrence), the villainous pirate, after a fight with the children's friends, the Indians, captures the boys and Wendy and takes them to his ship. Peter goes after the children and, using subterfuge, seizes the pirate band and forces Captain Hook to walk the plank. The lost boys decide to return to the Darling household with Wendy, but Peter Pan refuses to join them, although it is agreed that from time to time Wendy will return to Never Never Land to take care of Peter.

The film remains fairly close to the stage production, accepting the tradition of Peter Pan being portrayed by a girl, a tradition which obviously stems from British pantomime where the principal boy is always a girl. Likewise, Nana the dog, who takes care of the Darling children, is always played by an actor in a dog's suit; in the film George Ali, who played Nana on the stage, essays the role. One major break from tradition is that in the 1924 film version, Mr. Darling is played by one actor, Cyril Chadwick, and Captain Hook by another, Ernest Torrence, while on the stage the same actor always played both roles— casting which continues to delight amateur and professional psychologists. Finally, the film has a definite American slant, with American jargon in the titles (many of which are taken directly from the playscript) and the children swearing allegiance to the American flag.

When Famous Players-Lasky first announced plans to film *Peter Pan*, there was much discussion as to who should play the title role. Many established screen stars, including Mary Pickford, were suggested for the coveted role. The part finally went, with the approval of Barrie, to Betty Bronson, an actress with only a few minor roles to her credit. Bronson seems a perfect choice for the part, exhibiting a pleasing mixture of mannish behavior and coquetry. "At times," wrote *Variety* (December 31, 1924), "she reminds one of Marguerite Clark of the earlier days of screen history. She has that same dash of youthful verve; then in another moment will come the gentle hint that she is as Mary Pickford was."

Exceptional Photoplays (January, 1925) wrote that Bronson "has youth, which is an asset in this part, but she also has a charming conception of the character—roguish, daring and with that air of utter freedom that this play boy of fairyland should have." Unfortunately, *Peter Pan* effectively typecast Bronson, and she was never really able to achieve the same success or appeal in later silent films, with the exception of *A Kiss for Cinderella*, another Barrie adaptation by Famous Players-Lasky, directed in 1926 by Herbert Brenon.

Two actresses who were helped immeasurably by their appearances in *Peter Pan* were Esther Ralston, who played Mrs. Darling, and Mary Brian, who portrayed Wendy. Both became competent, established Paramount contract stars, whose careers continued not only for the rest of the decade but also well into the 1930's. Virginia Browne Faire, as Tinker Bell, has little to do except look either pretty or irritated, but she does it well. Torrence is generally given to overacting, but here, as Captain Hook, he needs to turn on the melodramatics and so gives a superbly rich and colorful performance.

Brenon, whose directing career stretches back to the early teens and includes such important films as *Neptune's Daughter* (1914), *A Daughter of the Gods* (1916), *The Passing of the Third Floor Back* (1918), *Beau Geste* (1926), *The Great Gatsby* (1926), and *Laugh, Clown, Laugh* (1928), demstrates a remarkable ability for appreciating and capturing precisely on film the whimsy without which *Peter Pan* cannot succeed. He understood the need for an appeal to the audience to clap their hands if they believed in fairies in order to save Tinker Bell's life after she had drunk the poison intended for Wendy; a device which Disney, for example, ignored in his animated version. Brenon's lightness of touch is apparent throughout the film, but particularly in the early scenes in the Darling nursery, where Nana is giving the children their medicine and later when Peter Pan is teaching them to fly. One can even manage to forget that the wires, unfortunately, are all too visible in some of the shots. The one fault with the film, and it is not a fault that necessarily should be blamed on Brenon, is that it is far too long and seems rather drawn out in the central part.

Aside from Brenon's direction, James Wong Howe's photography should also be mentioned. His lighting is admirable, and to him should go the credit for creating the light that serves for Tinker Bell in the long shots, which actually is nothing more than an ordinary light bulb.

With enormous good sense, Paramount released the film during the Christmas season, and for a few weeks had a box-office success on their hands. In like manner, the critical response was excellent. Mordaunt Hall in *The New York Times* (December 28, 1924) wrote, "It is not a movie but a pictorial masterpiece." *Exceptional Photoplays* (January, 1925) commented, "The picture has about it the veritable air of fairy fantasy and ranks as a noteworthy pioneer in the penetration, by motion pictures, of still another realm of thought expression." *Photoplay* (March, 1925) summed it all up: "A perfect picture of a perfect story, with a perfect cast." Unfortunately, once the Christmas season was over, the film lost some of its appeal and was not quite the success that its producers hoped it might have been. Films such as *Peter Pan*, however, can never entirely lose their audiences or their appeal, and the production continues to be a perennial favorite not only with film buffs but also with general audiences of all ages.

Anthony Slide

PETTIGREW'S GIRL

Released: 1919
Production: Famous Players-Lasky; released by Paramount
Direction: George Melford
Screenplay: Will H. Ritchey; based on the short story of the same name by Dana Burnett
Cinematography: Paul Perry
Length: 5 reels

Principal characters:
Daisy Heath .... Ethel Clayton
Private William Pettigrew .... Monte Blue
Hugh Varick .... Charles Gerard
Piggy .... Clara Whipple
Private Jiggers Botley .... James Mason

Ethel Clayton was a golden-haired beauty who had an aura of quality on the screen. In real life, she was considered a lady by all who knew her, and her private life was spent mostly in quiet evenings at home, much to the frustration of fan magazine writers who could not think of anything sensational to write about her. Her features for Paramount were all good, solid money-makers, but she never had a great success. This may explain why such a well-liked film star is almost totally forgotten today.

Pettigrew's Girl was without doubt her most popular picture, and it was remade as a film twice. In 1928, Nancy Carroll and Gary Cooper played in it as *The Shopworn Angel*, and in 1939, Margaret Sullavan and Jimmy Stewart also had wonderful success with an altered version of the story, also called *The Shopworn Angel*.

In *Pettigrew's Girl*, Clayton plays a chorus girl named Daisy Heath, who has attracted the attentions of a young millionaire named Hugh Varick (Charles Gerard). She is the envy of all the other chorus girls, for he is considered the best catch in New York. Hugh has asked Daisy to marry him, but she is determined to hold out for a second proposal, since her mother always told her never to say "Yes" the first time.

Outside New York City, in an army training camp, there is a lonely young soldier, Private William Pettigrew (Monte Blue). No letters ever arrive for him, although his fellow soldiers get all sorts of mail, including packages and photographs of their sweethearts. One fellow private seems determined to be his enemy, and he jokes about Pettigrew's apparent lack of friends or sweethearts. Pettigrew tells him in front of others that that is not true, for he has a sweetheart, and a beautiful one as well.

When Pettigrew finally gets a leave of absence, he goes into New York. He takes in the sights alone, and as he passes a photographer's shop, he sees a picture in the window of the stage beauty Daisy Heath. He buys the picture intending to show it to his fellow privates, but after the purchase he realizes that it has no inscription and asks the photographer who she is. He directs the soldier to the theater, and Pettigrew buys a front-row seat.

Daisy is very nervous about that night's performance, for Hugh is bringing his father to see the show. Pettigrew is instantly smitten at Daisy's first appearance, and his ill-timed applause causes laughter and makes her miss a step.

At the end of the show, Pettigrew hurries around to the stage door to await Daisy. A few hours later, she steps out and instantly recognizes him as the boob who almost spoiled her performance. When he rushes to her with the photograph, she is perturbed and decides to rebuff him quickly. When he shyly asks her to enscribe the picture "To the Soldier I Love," she demands an explanation first. His lonely station in life softens her heart so much that she writes what he asks and even agrees to go have a "sody water" with him.

On his return to camp, he shows her picture to everybody, and, of course, his old foe accuses him of lying. Furthermore, a newspaper is produced that has a gossip column item telling of Daisy's engagement to Hugh Varick.

Unknown to Pettigrew, however, he has started a flame in Daisy's heart. She is not sure she loves Hugh and wonders if perhaps there is something she could do for the war effort, so she decides to entertain at the nearby training camp. Her performance is loved by all the soldiers. Pettigrew gets in a fight with a soldier who says something derogatory about Daisy. He gets kitchen duty for punishment and is peeling potatoes when Daisy comes upon him in the company of the camp commander. Ashamed, he refuses to tell her why he is being punished, but she finds out anyway and is deeply moved. She tells Hugh that she cannot marry him. Pettigrew is shipped abroad, and she writes letters and waits anxiously, as do millions of other girls for the men they love.

Upon his company's return to the United States, Pettigrew marches in a ticker-tape parade down Fifth Avenue. Daisy runs to join him and marches with him, arm in arm.

Ethel Clayton was born in Chicago in 1884. She did extra work in the theater while in school and shocked her family by announcing that she would train to become an actress. She had her earliest success in Minneapolis. In the summer of 1912, while working with Lew Cody's stock company, she received an offer of $175 a week from Lubin Pictures of Philadelphia. Her first film for that concern was *For the Love of a Girl*, a one-reel picture. In 1914, she married one of Lubin's best directors, Joseph Kaufman, and they began turning out a steady stream of critically acclaimed and popular domestic dramas. They gave the Lubin Company a few more years to live before it collapsed, along with all the other members of the patents company, Vitagraph excepted. Their films were features, and among their successes were *Daughters of Men* (1915), *The Blessed Miracle* (1915), and *Dollars and the Women* (1916).

Her biggest success for Lubin was the Western perennial *The Great Divide* (1916) with House Peters.

The Kaufmans went to World Pictures next and made about a dozen features. As a team, they were at the height of their career, and Paramount offered them a five-year contract at five thousand dollars a week, which they accepted. They were in the East finishing one of their films for World Pictures in 1919 when Kaufman suddenly died of influenza, and Clayton collapsed.

Paramount still wanted her to come to California, however, and they promised her good directors. Jesse L. Lasky was one of her greatest admirers and did what he could to see that she got interesting story properties and the pick of contract directors. In 1922, she was thirty-eight and Paramount felt that she was too old for them to renew her contract. She went over to FBO (Film Booking Offices of America) and did a popular romance with Warner Baxter, *If I Were Queen* (1922). She worked on through the 1920's; later, she married an actor, Ian Keith, and did stage work with him. She died in 1966.

Monte Blue, who gave a fine performance as Private Pettigrew, was a popular leading man in the silents. He was of American Indian ancestry, handsome, and very tall. He was Mary Pickford's leading man in *Johanna Enlists* (1917), and Cecil B. De Mille used him in *The Squaw Man* (1918), *Something to Think About* (1920), and *The Affairs of Anatol* (1921). One of his best roles was in D. W. Griffith's *Orphans of the Storm* (1922), when he played Danton and saved the character played by Lillian Gish from the guillotine. Ernst Lubitsch liked him best, however, and gave him his favorite role in *The Marriage Circle* (1924). Lubitsch gave him two more fine roles in *Kiss Me Again* (1925) and *So This Is Paris* (1926). He appeared in character parts for decades, with his last film being *Apache* in 1954. He died at age seventy-four in 1964.

Larry Lee Holland

THE PHANTOM OF THE OPERA

Released: 1925
Production: Universal-Jewel
Direction: Rupert Julian
Screenplay: Elliott Clawson; based on the novel of the same name by Gaston Leraux
Cinematography: Charles Van Enger, Milton Bridenbecker, and Virgil Miller
Length: 10 reels/8,464 feet

> *Principal characters:*
> Erik (the Phantom) .... Lon Chaney
> Christine Daae .... Mary Philbin
> Raoul de Chagny .... Norman Kerry
> Florine Papillon .... Snitz Edwards
> The Persian .... Arthur Edmund Carewe

The Phantom of the Opera, made in 1925, has in succeeding years become one of the best-remembered films of the silent screen and one of the most influential horror films of all time. Although it has been remade several times in the sound era with little success (the most prominent versions were in 1943 and 1962 as well as 1974's popular *Phantom of the Paradise* featuring the music of Paul Williams), its most immediate influence was realized in the famous Universal series of horror films in the 1930's. French director Jean Cocteau's 1946 *Beauty and the Beast* also came under its influence and made extremely effective use of symbolic values derived from it, such as the horse and the mirror images.

The Phantom of the Opera was produced under a shroud of secrecy that inevitably gave rise to numerous rumors about "behind the scenes" mysteries, clashes of temperament, and technical problems. The story receiving the widest publication was one concerning Lon Chaney's makeup, which was popularly deemed to be so terrifying that the standard advance publicity photos could not be released for fear of startling the public. To some degree, this audience guessing game preceded every Chaney film and was adroitly managed by Universal, which realized the dollar value of keeping Chaney a mystery by varying his roles and by not giving viewers too much of the same type of character. Thus, each new film appearance by the actor was both eagerly anticipated by his fans and preceded by guessing games as to the kind of costume and makeup that Chaney would be wearing. Studio publicity normally fanned the flames of this curiosity by keeping the fans in doubt as to the exact nature of the role and by releasing selected still photographs of the actor in costume. As Chaney scholar Robert G. Anderson points out, "even in the films in which he played straight roles there was always the possibility that he might appear in a minor character role, unbilled." In fact, his ability with makeup and costume was so widely respected that he became the subject of a reverential joke attributed to director Marshall Neilan, "Don't step on it, it may be Lon Chaney."

Although there was the usual publicity preceding *The Phantom of the Opera*, there were, as mentioned earlier, no advance photographs. This fact actually enhanced the dramatic impact of the film itself since the Phantom's face was not revealed until midway through the film. In one of the most dramatic and horrifying scenes in any Chaney film, the heroine pulls a mask from his face revealing the Phantom's grotesque visage.

This striking visual appearance was achieved through masterful application of makeup, which was further enhanced by lighting conditions created to accentuate the effects of the greasepaint. The guiding idea in the creation of Erik, the Phantom's facial features, was to simulate the look of a death's head. A high forehead was created through the application of a built-up head piece and some wisps of hair. The face was further elongated by taping back Chaney's ears. His cheekbones were emphasized by the use of putty and the cheeks were darkened to accentuate further the gaunt face. The nose was tilted back and up toward the scalp through the use of a strip of fishskin pulled up and attached to the bridge. The nostrils were widened with wires inserted inside and dark paint was applied to the outside of the nose to heighten the effect. To top off the skeletal image, the eye sockets were deepened by darkening the eye area, and the upper portion of the lower eyelid was highlighted to give emphasis to the eyeballs. Jagged teeth and a snug, dark suit completed the image of the death's head.

Chaney clashed with director Rupert Julian over the interpretation of the character of the Phantom. Apparently Julian, who had earlier stepped in to replace Erich Von Stroheim as director of *Merry-Go-Round* (1923), had adopted some of that director's practices, causing him to be stubborn in his dealings with Chaney. The result was that Julian was replaced in his directorial duties midway through the film by Edward Sedgwick, who allowed the actor to set up and direct many of his own scenes. Chaney's characterization of Erik the Phantom maintains a delicate balance between terror and sympathy. Although the audience can sense that in his insane way, Erik has a passion for his female captive, Chaney imbues the interpretation with enough elements of horror that viewers never lose sight of the fact that Erik is a fundamental part of the bizzare subterranean domain. Thus, the viewer's sympathy for him never becomes admiration.

The film opens with the murder of a stagehand at the Paris Opera which has just been sold to two new owners, who were not deterred by stories circulating among the members of the opera company concerning a mysterious phantom haunting the cellars beneath the theater. Such is the fear of the performers toward a creature that has apparent access to all corners of the building, that a private box is always reserved for him.

The Phantom (Lon Chaney) has, in fact, taken a particular interest in a beautiful singer, Christine Daae (Mary Philbin). Although only a member of the chorus, she is secretly coached by an unseen voice that she refers to only as "The Spirit of Music." The voice promises to make her a diva and tells her to "Think only of your art and your master," and, in return for her success, "Soon this spirit will take form and demand your love."

Christine soon gets her hoped-for opportunity—a chance to substitute for the prima donna. Although she is revealed as possessing great talent and potential as a singer, she is replaced by the new management with a singer of greater reputation. The Phantom, however, places warnings on stage suggesting tragedy if Christine is not allowed to sing. The new singer goes on stage anyway, and, during her performance, a terrifying voice whispers sharply to the panicky directors, "She sings to bring down the chandelier!" The huge light, mysteriously freed from its fasteners plunges down upon the audience. As panic spreads throughout the theater, the voice of the "Spirit of Music" is heard by Christine backstage in her dressing room. The voice lures her into a new world as a masked figure materializes from behind her mirror to lead her through an underground maze of tunnels and stairways to what appears to be a subterranean lake. When they reach the Phantom's apartments, she finds herself in a strange perverse replica of a bridal suite far below the opera house. It is there that she belatedly realizes that her "Spirit of Music" and the Phantom of the Opera are one and that she is a prisoner.

The Phantom plays his composition for her, and while he is at the keyboard of a huge organ, Christine sneaks behind him and rips off his mask. In one of the most powerful scenes in film, the head of Erik the Phantom is revealed to be a death's head—a skull that breathes. The girl shrinks away in terror. Although angered by her curiosity, the creature tells her of his past and of his opera "Don Juan Triumphant." Finally, he allows her to return to the world if she promises not to tell anyone about what she has seen and heard.

Christine, however, cannot keep her promise. During a masquerade ball, held annually at the opera house, Christine takes her lover, Raoul de Chagny (Norman Kerry) up on the roof where she tells him of her experiences with Erik, the Phantom of the Opera. Unknown to the lovers, though, they are overheard by Erik himself who has come to the ball disguised as the "Red Death." Once again he kidnaps Christine; and Raoul accompanied by "The Persian" (Arthur Edmund Carewe), who is in reality a member of the French police force, descends into the underground world to rescue her. After a furious chase, the girl is freed and Erik returns to the surface where he is pursued through the streets by a mob of Parisians. He is finally cornered at the edge of the river Seine. After a final act of defiance in which he deludes the mob into thinking that he has a grenade in his hand, he slowly opens it to reveal nothing. As he laughs hideously, the mob closes in once more and forces him into the Seine, where he drowns.

Although modern audiences tend to be disappointed when they view *The Phantom of the Opera* today, it is still a powerful document if only for its showcasing of Chaney's pantomimic art. As a film, it is somewhat old-fashioned, with roots in the theater and its dramatic continuity heavily influenced by the old serials (not necessarily a drawback after the huge success of *Raiders of the Lost Ark*, 1981, which utilizes a similar structure) and places less emphasis on horror and more on melodrama.

The first half of the film primarily concerns itself with the task of creating a situation that will lead the audience to guess at the motives of the mysterious creature that inhabits the opera. His appearances during this part of the picture are fleeting and create an air of suspense that is heightened by the fact that his face is covered by a mask that reveals just enough of his chin and mouth to hint that there is something more hideous that lies hidden beneath it. The actual unmasking is constructed in such a manner as to provide a double shock to the audience. Both characters, Christine and the Phantom are facing the audience. Thus, she is behind him when she tears the mask from his face and cannot see how hideous it really is. The film's viewers, however, are jolted right out of their seats. Then the creature turns to face the girl and the camera switches to a subjective point of view. He is then seen from Christine's point of view as he advances toward the audience, looking hideous and out of focus. It is one of the great moments of terror on the screen. Chaney's careful interpretation of the character also enhances the terror of the unmasking. The Phantom's actions are complex in their motivations, a curious blend of lust, revenge, even paternal love. Thus, viewers are divided in their feelings of identification. They sympathize with Erik but are pulling for Christine to be rescued from her perilous situation.

The rest of the film reflects the choppy look of too many directors and too many differences of opinion regarding its overall direction. Yet, it was a major success at the box office in 1925, and Chaney's performance has influenced those of every major horror-film actor since. The success of Claude Rains's difficult performance in *The Invisible Man* (1933), for example, is due in no small part to his study of Chaney's gestures, mannerisms, and hand and head movements in *The Phantom of the Opera*. Chaney, himself, went on to make one talking film, a 1930 remake of *The Unholy Three* (1925) which gave promise of great things in a new medium. He died of cancer, however, in August of the same year. A 1957 film, *The Man of a Thousand Faces*, was made as Chaney's screen biography and starred James Cagney as Chaney. As remarkable as it was, however, it could only hint at the artistry of a man considered by many to be the greatest screen actor of all time.

Linda Edgington

POLLY OF THE CIRCUS

Released: 1917
Production: Goldwyn Pictures
Direction: Charles Horan and Edwin L. Hollywood
Screenplay: Adrian Gil Speare and Emmett Campbell Hall; based on the play
of the same name by Margaret Mayo
Cinematography: no listing
Length: 8 reels

Principal characters:

Polly	Mae Marsh
The Minister	Vernon Steele
Deacon Strong	Charles Riegel
Jim	Wellington Playter
Toby	Charles Eldridge
Circus Owner	George Trimble
The Minister's Black Servants	Lucille La Verne
	Dick Lee

Polly of the Circus is an innocuous, eight-reel romance that was not a box-office success. It was not applauded by the critics, either; most acknowledged it as a modest work only enlivened by the appearance of an entire circus troupe. Somewhat kinder than most, *The New York Times* called the film "a careful and painstaking piece of work" and cited acceptable performances by Mae Marsh and Vernon Steele. Considering Marsh's exceptional career as one of the era's great performers, however, *Polly of the Circus* is but a footnote alongside legendary titles such as *The Birth of a Nation* (1915), *Intolerance* (1916), and other D. W. Griffith projects (including the lesser-known *The White Rose*, 1923, in which Marsh gives a mesmerizing performance as a heroine jilted by her lover).

Polly of the Circus is an important work, however; its significance is derived from behind-the-scenes business dealings, rather than the images on the screen. For *Polly of the Circus* is the film that initiated Samuel Goldwyn's forty-year career as one of Hollywood's legendary (and certainly most colorful) producers.

Prior to forming Goldwyn Pictures, which was launched with *Polly of the Circus* in 1917, Goldwyn (then known by his real name, Samuel Goldfish) and his brother-in-law Jesse L. Lasky co-founded Lasky Feature Plays. The teaming resulted in *The Squaw Man* (1914), directed by Cecil B. De Mille, who was then also a partner. In 1916, the company was merged with Adolph Zukor's Famous Players and became Famous Players-Lasky. Goldwyn then decided to establish Goldwyn Motion Picture Company. His partners were Archie and Edgar Selwyn, Margaret Mayo, and Arthur Hopkins. (*Polly of the Circus* was written by Mayo—author of the original stage play—who was married to Hopkins.) Goldwyn became an independent producer in 1925, three years after breaking away from the Selwyns and having his company acquired by the Metro and Mayer concerns which thus created Metro-Goldwyn-Mayer.

As a producer, Goldwyn had a penchant for looking to performers, rather than properties, as the key to his studio's success, especially during his earliest years, when he embarked on a much-publicized campaign to lure leading names of stage and screen to his company. Among the first performers under the aegis of Goldwyn Pictures were Mae Marsh and Blanche Sweet (both Griffith players), comedienne Mabel Normand, stage star Madge Kennedy, and opera divas Mary Garden and Geraldine Farrar. Of these performers, Marsh was the original "Goldwyn Girl"—a designation Goldwyn bestowed upon his cluster of female players.

Launched without modesty, (a *Saturday Evening Post* advertisement for the Goldwyn studio read "Brains write them. Brains direct them. Brains are responsible for their wonderful performances"), Goldwyn's career as a producer had a shaky start, though he did release several now-revered works including Germany's *The Cabinet of Dr. Caligari* originally made in 1920, and although some performers did excel in his projects such as Lon Chaney who did especially notable work before moving on to other studios, and scarier efforts, it took Goldwyn some time to decipher that a good script was as integral a part of a successful film as its star. By the mid-1920's, however, he was on his way—with teary melodramas such as *Stella Dallas* (1925). During the 1930's, his production prowess peaked with timeless romances that were exceedingly well acted, such as *The Dark Angel* (1935), starring Fredric March, Merle Oberon, and Herbert Marshall as a love triangle, and *Wuthering Heights* (1939) showcasing Oberon's delicate beauty and the legendary Laurence Olivier. Although he was a producer who delivered spirited entertainment such as the Eddie Cantor musicals and message films for the masses as in *They Shall Have Music* (1939) which brought classical violinist Jascha Heifetz to the screen in a story of slum kids reformed by music lessons, Goldwyn probably achieved most honor with *The Best Years of Our Lives* (1946), William Wyler's classic film about war veterans readjusting to civilian life. Goldwyn climbed to these heights following his shaky start, which included *Polly of the Circus*.

The premise of this early film is simply that adversity comes between two lovers. Lending the film a mark of distinction is its circus background, as well as the presence of Marsh who is delightful as Polly, the circus rider who falls in love with a handsome young minister (Vernon Steele). Injured in a fall from her horse during a show in a small town, Polly is taken to the Minister's home for medical attention. The two fall in love despite the strong objections of Deacon Strong (Charles Riegel), who heartily disapproves of the circus girl. (At the time of the film's release, the circus was not a haven for "respectable" people.) The Deacon's harsh feelings escalate when Polly competes against him in a race sponsored by a county fair. Polly has entered out of loyalty to her "family"—the circus people, for one of them, Toby the clown (Charles Eldridge) is ill and in need of money. After winning the race, Polly's triumph turns to sorrow when she learns that Toby has already died. Moreover, the Deacon cruelly threatens to fire Polly's beloved minister, unless she agrees to leave town. Polly sadly complies, leaving a heart-broken and curious minister. A year later, however, when the circus returns to town, their story has a happy ending; the Minister has learned of the Deacon's threats and has chosen to ignore them. He and Polly are reunited in love.

For decades, *Polly of the Circus* was a "lost" film; the title was known mostly because of the 1934 remake, directed by Alred Santell, that stars Marion Davies and Clark Gable. In 1978, however, this film enjoyed renewed life when what was believed to be the last surviving print of the film was located beneath the Arctic tundra, in the heart of Yukon territory. *Polly of the Circus* was among more than five hundred reels of vintage film that were discovered when workmen prepared the site for a Dawson City, Canada, recreation center. Dawson City was the last stop on a silent-film distribution route.

When the film cache was discovered, its survival was credited to the area's often freezing temperatures which helped in "storing" the film, and its most publicized title was this first feature of Goldwyn. Yet *Polly of the Circus* was also applauded as a rare work by Marsh, one of the most gifted performers of the silent screen.

She was discovered by Griffith when she was nineteen years old and was on the lot watching the filming of a Mack Sennett comedy. Marsh captivated the famous director with her "frail, wispy look," which proved the perfect accompaniment for her captivating performance as Flora Cameron in *The Birth of a Nation*. For the role, she was initially paid thirty dollars a week; later that sum was raised to thirty-five dollars. She will also be forever enshrined as "The Dear One" of *Intolerance*.

Of her work in the unsuccessful *Polly of the Circus*, Goldwyn contended that she "seemed incapable of any notable achievement when removed from the galvanizing influence of Griffith." This statement seems a bitter excuse, however, and one which fails to acknowledge a lackluster property, for Marsh's work remains a hallmark of the silent era. It is an achievement that has been occasionally recognized: in 1957, she was honored with the George Eastman Award, naming her as one of the five leading actresses of silent film (joining Mary Pickford, Gloria Swanson, Norma Talmadge, and Lillian Gish). In fact, Marsh's work is sometimes overlooked, to the ire of many historians, who point to her tremendous range (she could evoke childlike wonder one minute and despair the next), and her ability to portray young girls as well as mature women. Many of her contemporaries, including Pickford, could not convincingly play older characters.

Marsh's career as a silent heroine ended in 1921 when she decided to commit herself full-time to her husband, press agent Louis Lee Arms. In 1931, however, she returned to the screen, for a speaking role in *Over the Hill*. It signified the start of a new career for Marsh, who went on to appear as a supporting player in more than forty films—nine of them directed by John Ford. Her last appearance was as a crazed Indian captive in Ford's 1961 film *Two Rode Together*. When Marsh decided to leave the screen a second (and final) time, it was to concentrate on family life. As she told one reporter, "Personally, I wouldn't trade six weeks of Mom and Grandmom happiness for six years of Hollywood glamour."

A performer who successfully balanced professional and personal happiness, the actress, who died of a heart attack in 1968, at the age of seventy-two, used to note, "Acting is a paradox. You try to make the unreal seem real on the screen, and off the screen it takes self-discipline to keep from slipping from the real into the unreal."

Pat H. Broeske

POOR LITTLE RICH GIRL

Released: 1917
Production: Artcraft Films for Paramount
Direction: Maurice Tourneur
Screenplay: Frances Marion; based on the play and novel of the same name by Eleanor Gates
Cinematography: Lucien Andriot and John van den Broek
Art Direction: Ben Carré
Length: 6 reels

Principal characters:

Gwendolyn	Mary Pickford
Her mother	Madeline Traverse
Her father	Charles Wellesley
Jane, the nurse	Gladys Fairbanks
The plumber	Frank McGlynn
Miss Royle, the governess	Marcia Harris
The doctor	Herbert Prior
Maxine Hicks	Susie May Squaggs
The organ grinder	Emile La Croix

From beginning to end, *Poor Little Rich Girl* is a delight. For the first time in her already lengthy career, Mary Pickford plays a child, and she is entirely convincing. The narrative is not as trite as a bald reading of it might sound, for the events are seen from the perspective of the girl, and Pickford was such a superb actress that viewers understand her hopes and fears instinctively, having doubtlessly experienced some of the same feelings themselves. What is hard to comprehend is the film's premise that such an overprotected, privileged upbringing could result in a girl so normal, life-loving, and emotionally stable.

In her parents' mansion, Gwendolyn (Mary Pickford) endures a life of loneliness and luxury, surrounded by servants of every description who cannot fathom why she is not happy. From her window she sees other children playing, skating, and doing all the things she wants to do. When another rich child named Maxine Hicks (Susie May Squaggs) is brought in to play with her, she is everything Gwen is not: spoiled, arrogant, and stuck-up. Gwen quickly has her revenge for the girl's taunts by sticking a plate of food under Maxine's derriere when she sits, and then throwing her entire wardrobe out the window rather than lend the child a dress to substitute for the ruined one.

Gwen's father (Charles Wellesley) loses almost everything he has in the stock market just as the nurse, Jane (Gladys Fairbanks), and the footman drug Gwen so they can spend a night at the "theayter." Downstairs, the adults celebrate Gwen's eleventh birthday without her. The gifts she has received are wholly inappropriate for a girl of her age and underscore the fact that her parents have no idea who she is. Gwen gets out of bed, falls down the stairs, and at the bottom is rescued by the plumber (Frank McGlynn).

As a result of the fall, she hallucinates a series of events that take place in the Garden of Lonely Children, while she tries to reach The Land of Happy Children. Her mirages are based on things she has heard grown-ups say, and reiterate the idea that she has no idea of everyday speech since she takes what she hears literally. Her governess, Miss Royle (Marcia Harris), has been called a "snake in the grass," so Gwen imagines the woman's head on a long snake twisting through the roots of a tree. Her father works on Wall Street with the "bulls and bears," so she pictures him devoured by the animals in the middle of the street. The nurse is "two-faced," and the footman has "sharp ears," so she sees them that way. In the dream, the plumber and an organ grinder (Emile La Croix), whom she once invited into the house only to have him rudely expelled by the servants, are her only protectors in the garden. A woman offers her "eternal sleep" as relief from these imagined horrors, an offer she almost accepts. Soon she sees a nymph dancing in the sunlight, and she recovers. The doctor (Herbert Prior) who brings her around writes out a prescription for "gingham dresses, iodine for scratches," gathering flowers, riding a fat pony, and going barefoot. Her father rejects a chance to recover his financial position in the market, saying that, despite his losses, "There is enough for the life we are going to lead." As her parents lean over her bed, the doctor's last bit of advice reaches her ears: "Make mud pies," and Gwen squeals happily, "Oh! I love mud."

The idea of a life so bereft of happiness that an eleven-year-old can regard death with equanimity rather than face a loveless existence in the so-called real world is a terrifying one, and Pickford makes little Gwen's choice seem quite believable. Her house is the typical mansion of the period, with its dark wainscoting, heavy drapes and furniture, and disapproving servants. Her mother (Madeline Traverse) is a social butterfly and her father a workaholic, and the girl is an only child whose life is pictorially linked early in the film with that of her only pet, a bird in a cage.

The house exists in two worlds, apparently an unintentional oversight. The first view shows it on an imposing estate surrounded by land, the second as being on a street where the organ grinder plays for the local children. The other children pity Gwen and make comments about her not being so bad for a rich kid. When they enter her garden to look for a missing ball, however, she turns the hose on them and starts a mud fight. When the gardener wrestles the hose away from her, she pelts him with mud.

The mud sequence is an illustration of film stardom power in action. French director Maurice Tourneur was on the threshold of his most important American work, but Pickford did not think he was ideally suited to the material in *Poor Little Rich Girl*. He protested that French children would not throw mud, and thus, he did not want to shoot the sequence. Pickford replied that she was American, and she thought it would work. She was also extremely loyal to her good friend and scenarist, Frances Marion, who had written several of her most successful films. The mud scene does work: it's shorter than the quarrel over it would indicate and is an important instance of youthful high spirits finding a needed escape valve.

Pickford was twenty-four when *Poor Little Rich Girl* was released, and if she does not look eleven, she at least creates her idea of an eleven-year-old with such conviction that it is impossible not to accept it. She is not like a real child, but she is not like an adult either. She is her own creation, and insofar as the audience sees almost no other representations of children in the film, she must be taken at face value. She certainly is "America's sweetheart," with long ringlets, bee-stung lips, and wide eyes. It is hard to understand, though, where she got the reputation of being a saccharine, naïve, fairyland princess. In her films, she was none of these things; they usually represented a contemporary view of a young girl *in extremis*: such as the portraits in *Ramona* (1910), *Suds* (1920), and *Sparrows* (1926). Yet, it seems that even Pickford saw herself this way. Since she controlled almost all of the rights to her pictures, she could do what she wanted with them, and when she realized that her sort of films were fading from popularity, she toyed with the idea of destroying them. Her friend Lillian Gish fortunately talked her out of it.

Pickford hardly seems to merit the comment of one of her most talented contemporaries, Mabel Normand. "Say anything you like," Normand remarked when asked what her hobby was, "but don't say I like to work. That sounds too much like Mary Pickford, that prissy bitch." She did enjoy her work; she was a consummate businesswoman who amassed fifty million dollars between the ages of five and her retirement at forty. Samuel Goldwyn once said that "It took longer to make one of Mary's contracts than it did to make one of Mary's pictures," but when the pictures were made, they were worth all efforts. They looked beautiful, with the sort of careful lighting, enhanced by printing on nitrate stock, and attention to detail, such as the oversized sets for *Poor Little Rich Girl*, that have all but vanished from present-day films.

Tourneur may not have been the best choice to direct this film, but he did it with taste and, in the garden sequence, imagination. The sets are impressionistic, like those of a grammar school play with a big budget, and there are a number of mattes, superimpositions, and complicated dissolves that enhance one's perception of Gwen's hallucinogenic experience.

Pickford herself, in the course of making the film, invented the "baby spot," to get a special effect she wanted for her face. As the cameraman for many of her pictures Charles Rosher (Lucien Andriot and John van den Broek performed the marvels for this film) said, "She knew everything there was to know about making a movie; she could do everything—she was a walking motion picture company." She also knew what many stars never learned: when to quit. When she retired she commented, "I left the screen because I didn't want what happened to Charlie Chaplin to happen to me. When he discarded the Little Tramp, the Little Tramp turned around and killed him. The Little Girl made me—I wasn't waiting for the Little Girl to kill me, too."

This film depicts the quintessential "little girl," in a world she did not make and does not like. She does the best she can with it and then goes on with life. She is obedient, spunky, and loving. It is not surprising that Pickford was no youngster when she received her first screen kiss, her audience did not want to see her mature; and in *Poor Little Rich Girl*, it is easy to see why her viewers wanted to maintain the status quo.

Judith M. Kass

POTEMKIN

Released: 1925
Production: First Studio of Goskino
Direction: Sergei M. Eisenstein
Screenplay: Sergei M. Eisenstein; based on a scenario by Sergei M. Eisenstein
　and Nina Agadzhanova Shutko
Cinematography: Eduard Tisse
Editing: Sergei M. Eisenstein
Length: 5 reels/5,708 feet

Principal characters:
　　Vakulinchuk .... Alexander Antonov
　　The Captain .... Vladimir Barsky

　　The films of Russian director Sergei M. Eisenstein had a great impact upon the world of cinema when they were first seen, and today he is regarded as one of the major artists and innovators in the history of film. In the first years of the 1920's, after years of revolution and war, Russia's film industry was almost nonexistent, but in the theater there was a great deal of activity, with new artistic and intellectual ideas being introduced. There, Eisenstein worked as a set designer and a director, trying such experiments as staging a play in an actual gas factory and developing many ideas that he would later use in his films. Based upon his work in the theater and only a bit of experience in film, he was assigned in 1924 to direct an episode of a planned eight-part film that would explore the events that led to the 1917 revolution.

　　The resulting film was *Strike* (1925), which was released as an individual film because the plans for the eight-part epic were never realized. *Strike* is a quite accomplished film for a first-time director and in many ways can be seen as a rough draft for Eisenstein's first masterpiece—*Potemkin*. The latter film was also planned as part of a longer work. The Russian leaders, having recognized the power and potential of film as a persuasive and patriotic medium, wanted a film to mark the twentieth anniversary of the uprisings of 1905 that were precursors to the revolution of 1917. Eisenstein and Nina Agadzhanova Shutko prepared a script in which the mutiny on the battleship *Potemkin* was only a small part. When filming began, however, Eisenstein decided to concentrate on the mutiny and the events connected with it as "the emotional embodiment of the whole epic of 1905."

　　The finished film presents the story of the *Potemkin* in five parts. In the first, "Men and Maggots," viewers see the mistreatment of the sailors by the officers, focusing upon the fact that the meat for the midday meal is covered with maggots. The ship's doctor examines the obviously infested meat and pronounces it edible, further provoking the men. In the second part, "Drama on the Quarterdeck," the Captain (Vladimir Barsky) threatens to shoot any sailor who will not eat the meal. Some relent and some continue to refuse. The mutineers are then covered with a tarpaulin and a firing squad is ordered to execute them. Vakulinchuk (Alexander Antonov) pleads with the men not to shoot, and after a long suspenseful sequence that alternates between the condemned men and the firing squad, the squad refuses to fire. In the ensuing confusion, the doctor is thrown overboard and Vakulinchuk is killed. In the third section, "Appeal from the Dead," the townspeople of Odessa visit the body of the dead sailor lying in state at the harbor.

The fourth section, "The Odessa Steps," is the highlight of *Potemkin* and one of the most famous sequences in the history of the cinema, arguably the most famous. It has been studied, dissected, and analyzed for more than half a century, and it nevertheless retains its artistry and power. The section begins with some of the townspeople taking food to the sailors while others wave to them in support. Suddenly, some of the citizens begin scurrying down a long series of outdoor steps. The reason for this action becomes clear when viewers see a shot of a line of Cossack soldiers with their guns at the ready. The action continues as the Cossacks march down the steps, occasionally firing, as the citizens flee before them. Close-ups of injured people, hands being stepped on, and horrified faces convey the terror. Once there is a change in the relentless movement downward, as a mother picks up her badly injured child, who is probably already dead, and walks up the steps, appealing to the soldiers not to shoot. They do not listen; they shoot her and continue the downward march. Another mother is holding onto a baby carriage with her child in it. When she is shot and slowly falls, the time elongated by the editing, the carriage begins rolling down the steps uncontrolled. Intercut with the shots of the runaway carriage are shots of the horrified face of a young man wearing glasses.

In the last section, "Meeting the Squadron," the *Potemkin* has to sail out of the harbor past a squadron of other ships. There are tense moments as sailors prepare to do battle, but when they signal to the other ships "Comrades, join us," the battleship *Potemkin* is allowed to sail out unmolested.

The film *Potemkin* is based upon an actual incident in 1905, but certain liberties were taken with the facts to make the film a more powerful patriotic and visual statement. For example, many citizens of Odessa were killed by the Cossacks, but it was only when Eisenstein saw the steps that he thought of staging the massacre at that location. Also Eisenstein deliberately avoided the use of an individual protagonist in the film because he wanted to stress the group working together rather than being led by a hero. In fact, to stress the appearance of realism he used nonprofessionals rather than actors in many of the roles. Since he did not put any significant emphasis upon character development, the look of the characters was much more important to him than acting ability.

The editing style of Eisenstein is one of the primary virtues of *Potemkin*.

The editing made the film noteworthy and powerful when it was first released, and the editing techniques and theories of Eisenstein and other Russian directors, particularly Vsevolod Pudovkin, have been studied and discussed ever since. Indeed, they remain an influence, conscious or unconscious, on filmmakers today. Eisenstein stated that his theory of editing was based upon collision. Instead of trying to make a series of shots link smoothly together as most filmmakers did, he wanted to produce a "shock" when one shot changed to another. He was particularly concerned with the rhythm established by this series of "shocks," so that the length of individual shots was often determined by the underlying rhythm of the sequence rather than by the requirements of the narrative.

One aspect of *Potemkin* and several of Eisenstein's other films that frequently caused him trouble both inside and outside the Soviet Union was their patriotic or propagandistic content. He frequently had to revise a film because Communist Party dogma had changed between the beginnning and end of a project, and in the United States and other Western countries he was greatly admired as an artist by some people and despised as a Communist by others.

Today, however, Eisenstein's reputation is secure. In a 1958 survey of film historians, *Potemkin* was chosen as the best film of all time; and in international surveys of film directors and of film critics through the years, it has continued to rank in the top six of the greatest films ever made.

Timothy W. Johnson